International Criminal Law

This book offers a comprehensive analysis of the major areas of international criminal law (ICL). It approaches its subject matter from both a criminal law and an international law perspective, analysing the various topics exhaustively but in an accessible manner. While looking at the jurisprudence of the international tribunals, it is not confined to this approach, instead analysing all the fields in which ICL is employed. Thus it covers the theory of ICL, including the concepts of individual responsibility, the sources of ICL, State criminality, legality and legitimacy; the subjective (*mens rea*) and objective (*actus reus*) elements of international crimes and the particular position of the International Criminal Court Statute; the various modes of liability and participation in international crimes; the doctrine of command responsibility; defences and grounds for excluding liability; immunities; an extensive analysis of all war crimes; crimes against humanity; genocide; the crime of aggression; international criminal law of the sea, including piracy, armed robbery at sea, pollution-related offences, fisheries-related offences, maritime terrorism, injury to cables and pipelines, illegal broadcasting and enforcement against such offences; transnational crimes, including organised crime, corruption, money laundering, illicit trafficking of drugs and postal offences; particular international offences against the person, especially slavery and related practices, apartheid, enforced disappearances and torture; the legal contours of the crime of terrorism; an analysis of the historical development of ICL and of the legal processes relating to the Nuremberg Tribunal; an analysis of the UN tribunals for Yugoslavia and Rwanda; an examination of the International Criminal Court; an analysis of hybrid internationalised tribunals, such as those of Iraq, Sierra Leone, Cambodia, East Timor, Kosovo, Lebanon and Lockerbie, as well as an examination of truth commissions and amnesties; the various strands of criminal jurisdiction; and the different modes of inter-State cooperation in criminal matters, including cooperation with international tribunals, extradition, illegal rendition and mutual legal assistance.

International Criminal Law

Ilias Bantekas

·H A R T·
PUBLISHING

OXFORD AND PORTLAND, OREGON
2010

Published in the United Kingdom by Hart Publishing Ltd
16C Worcester Place, Oxford, OX1 2JW
Telephone: +44 (0)1865 517530
Fax: +44 (0)1865 510710
E-mail: mail@hartpub.co.uk
Website: http://www.hartpub.co.uk

Published in North America (US and Canada) by
Hart Publishing
c/o International Specialized Book Services
920 NE 58th Avenue, Suite 300
Portland, OR 97213–3786
USA
Tel: +1 503 287 3093 or toll-free: (1) 800 944 6190
Fax: +1 503 280 8832
E-mail: orders@isbs.com
Website: http://www.isbs.com

British Library Cataloguing in Publication Data

Data Available

ISBN: 978-1-84946-045-3

Typeset by Columns Design Ltd, Reading
Printed and bound in Great Britain by
TJ International Ltd, Padstow, Cornwall

Preface

This book is significantly different from the three previous editions published with Routledge under the same title. For one thing, I am now the sole author. Secondly and most importantly more than half of the material contained in it is new. Moreover, some chapters have been removed altogether and new ones have taken their place. Those readers who have followed the past editions will not fail to notice that this is in fact a new and indeed very different book and not simply a revision of previous editions. When I started back in 1999 to author a treatise on international criminal law the legal landscape was not what it is today. The discipline was largely dominated by public international lawyers and the jurisprudence of the ad hoc tribunals for Yugoslavia and Rwanda was not totally averse to this approach. During that time, however, the discipline has largely been taken over by criminal lawyers, which in my opinion represents the final step in the culmination of an international criminal process akin to that encountered in domestic criminal justice systems. This is a natural and welcome progression because it means that international criminal law has become less esoteric, having evolved in specificity and elaboration, thus satisfying the demands of justice and legitimacy. In respect of legal scholarship this develop-ment necessarily means that international criminal law has become a complex enterprise requiring knowledge of at least international law and criminal law – or criminal laws to be exact – in addition to human rights and EU law, the latter for those working within this jurisdictional remit. Despite professing to belong to the camp of public international lawyers I purposely set out to balance the content and focus of this book to reflect current scholarship and direction. I have tried to strike a fair balance between international law and criminal law in the belief that interna-tional criminal law does not start or end with the core international crimes or the work and jurisprudence of international criminal courts and tribunals. I have attempted for example to show that the various maritime belts encompass an abundance of criminal activity, as is true with transnational crime, which generally goes unnoticed and which I believe the new blood of our discipline should be familiar with. Equally, because the vast majority of offences are prosecuted by national courts, an exploration of their jurisdictional powers is warranted. I am also cognisant of the growing role of victims in domestic and international criminal trials, apart from their status as such and the protection due to them under international law and this reality is duly reflected in a specifically devoted chapter. One of the dangers when writing a treatise that is undergoing a global process of formation and transformation is achieving an equilibrium between a sufficiently high level of scholarship and a textual accessibility that would not only satisfy the demands of a largely postgraduate student audience, but would moreover entice it into our discipline. I have made strenuous efforts to explain every concept more elaborately and avoid unnecessarily complex assertions that are not conducive to lunch time reading. My hope therefore is that the book is not only authoritative and scholarly, but also accessible and enjoyable.

I have been very fortunate to share the views and acumen of a few trusted colleagues during the final stages of this project and would like to thank them individually for their patience and time, namely Olympia Bekou (Nottingham), Efthimios Papastavridis (Thrace) and Ricardo Abello (Rosario).

Foremost, I would like to thank Caroline Buisman, a Ph.D. candidate and practitioner with extensive experience before the ICTY, ICTR, SLSC and ICC, currently working on the *Katanga* case at the ICC, who has in addition to other friendly advice authored the chapter on evidence before international criminal tribunals. This is a very significant contribution to this book, which practitioners in particular should find appealing.

I would also like to express my gratitude to Professor Susan Nash for her contribution to the previous manifestations of this work. Finally, I would like to thank my wife Dimitra for putting up with me in the course of last year when the work seemed endless and my colleagues at Mourgelas & Associates Law Firm in Athens for giving me time to pursue my research in the midst of a very busy schedule.

The law stated in this book is accurate as of 1 April (no, really!!) 2010. I would like to take this opportunity to invite readers to send me any comments or suggestions through which future editions of this book can be improved.

Ilias Bantekas
Lefkas and London
April 2010

Contents

Table of Cases

NATIONAL CASES

UNITED KINGDOM

UNITED STATES OF AMERICA

INTERNATIONAL COURTS AND TRIBUNALS

AFRICAN COURT AND COMMISSION OF HUMAN RIGHTS

CAMBODIAN EXTRAORDINARY CHAMBERS (ECCC)

COMMITTEE AGAINST TORTURE

EAST TIMOR SPECIAL PANELS

EUROPEAN COURT AND COMMISSION OF HUMAN RIGHTS

EUROPEAN COURT OF JUSTICE

HUMAN RIGHTS COMMITTEE

INTER-AMERICAN COURT OF HUMAN RIGHTS

INTERNATIONAL ARBITRAL AWARDS

INTERNATIONAL CRIMINAL TRIBUNAL FOR RWANDA

INTERNATIONAL CRIMINAL TRIBUNAL FOR YUGOSLAVIA

INTERNATIONAL TRIBUNAL FOR THE LAW OF THE SEA

IRAQI SPECIAL TRIBUNAL

LEBANON SPECIAL TRIBUNAL

LEIPZIG TRIALS

PERMANENT COURT OF INTERNATIONAL JUSTICE

SIERRA LEONE SPECIAL COURT

WORLD WAR II TRIALS

Table of Treaties

Table Of National Legislation

UNITED STATES OF AMERICA

Part I

Fundamental Principles of International Crimes and Criminal Justice

1

Fundamentals of International Criminal Law

1.1 Introduction

International criminal law (ICL) constitutes the fusion of two legal disciplines: public international law and domestic criminal law. While it is true that one may discern certain criminal law elements in the science of international law, it is certainly not the totality of these elements that make up the discipline of ICL. Its existence is dependent on the sources and processes of international law, as it is these sources and processes that initially create it and ultimately shape and define it. This can be illustrated by examining any one of the acknowledged international offences. Piracy *jure gentium*, for example, exists simultaneously as a crime under customary international law, as well as under treaty law, specifically the 1982 United Nations Convention on the Law of the Sea (UNCLOS).[1] In examining its status and nature, whether as a treaty or customary rule, recourse is to be made not only to the relevant sources and norms of international law, but also to the non-piracy clauses of UNCLOS itself. The concept of piracy cannot be fully realised unless other concepts are first explored, such as the freedom to navigate on the high seas, delimitation of maritime zones, Flag State jurisdiction and many others. Similarly, one cannot examine an international offence, such as piracy, without recourse to those rules which delineate the legal standing of natural persons in the international legal system and their capacity to enjoy rights directly from this system, as well as to suffer lawful consequences for any violations (international legal personality). Undoubtedly, it does not suffice simply to discern and extrapolate mechanically all those criminal elements that are abundant in general international law and then combine them to establish a new discipline, as this does not help explain the binding nature of rules, nor their role in any given normative system.

The criminal laws of nations, expressed both through legislative action and the common law, constitute a vital component of ICL. International rules are generally imperfect and imprecise, not least because of the political difficulties in their drafting and in reaching agreement among competing national interests. With few exceptions, and in correlation to the preceding argument, international treaties rely on signatory States to further implement their provisions with precision at the domestic level, not necessarily in identical manner, but with a certain degree of consistency and

---

[1] (1982) 21 ILM 1261.

uniformity based on the object and purpose of each particular treaty.[2] In the case of piracy *jure gen-tium*, for example, the national legislation implementing the piracy provisions of UNCLOS into domestic criminal law will have to address the question of the material and mental attributes of the offence. UNCLOS is largely silent on the *mens rea* of piracy and so a myriad of mental components has to be prescribed at the domestic level, including whether or not the offence is one of strict liability or whether it requires a special intent (*dolus specialis*) and if it may be excused or mitigated by reference to any defences. Some States may posit that according to general principles of their own criminal law an accused is relieved from criminal culpability if the criminal conduct was based on political or other ideological motivation (the so-called political offence exception), especially where the relevant convention was silent as to the applicability of such a defence.[3] Similarly, the imposition of penalties at the discretion of parliament or the national judiciary, as well as the judicial determination of the extent of the various maritime zones, serve to indicate that certain elements of even a very old and reasonably well established international offence, such as piracy, may vary from country to country. But, this is an unavoidable occurrence, since criminal law is above all a practical discipline, and so ICL cannot operate in a theoretical vacuum, but in strict accordance with its objectives: that is to prevent the commission of offences, to prosecute and ultimately to punish offenders. In the absence of an all-embracing international criminal authority, these functions have been bestowed to national authorities, whose conformity to international law generally passes through domestic channels, such as national law and the dictates of the executive. As will be demonstrated below, however, the discretion of States to define international offences in their domestic law is not unlimited, but circumscribed by general international law and certain ICL principles.

1.2   Sources of International Law and Individual Legal Personality

Article 38(1) of the 1945 Statute of the International Court of Justice recognises two types of sources: primary and secondary. The primary sources of international law are treaties, international customs and general principles of law, all being independent and capable of producing binding rules. The secondary sources of international law, namely the writings of renowned publicists and the decisions of international courts, simply serve to ascertain and perhaps interpret the primary sources. Treaties are agreements between sovereign nations that are governed by international law and which are generally binding only upon their respective parties. Evidence as to the existence of customary law may be ascertained by reference to two elements: an

---

[2]   This type of implementation relies on member States' existing legal forms, particularly as regards modes of participation, mental standards (*mens rea*), liability of legal persons, defences and others. Member States are however obliged to adopt the new offence as prescribed in the treaty and, or, to refuse particular defences (eg political offence exception) or the applicability of statutory limitations.

[3]   This defence is now largely obsolete in relation to terrorist-related offences, following the adoption of SC Res 1373 (28 Sep 2001) and other subsequent developments.

objective and a subjective.[4] The objective element is made up of the uniform and continuous practice of States with regard to a specific issue and, depending on its adherents, this may take the form of a universal or a local custom. The subjective element involves a State's conviction that its practice in a particular field emanates not from comity but from a legal obligation which it feels bound to respect. It has been reasonably argued that the objective element is not always required in the formation of a customary rule. This is predicated on the notion that although every sovereign State has an interest in the development of international norms not all States have the capacity to demonstrate some kind of material action. For example, the utilisation of outer space has been achieved by only a limited number of developed nations, as has the exploration of the natural resources lying beneath the seabed of the high seas. This incapacity to undertake physical practice in particular fields should not prevent less developed States from having a voice in the regulation of these areas. It is for this reason that General Assembly resolutions, which are not otherwise binding, may be declaratory of customary law where they evince universal consensus through the unanimity of participating States.[5] This is not to say, of course, that materially able States will necessarily be constrained by the normative effects of less able nations, as is the case with nuclear weapons and non-proliferation. In this manner, a State may express its approval or disapproval of an emerging norm (and thus shape a customary rule) without actually having undertaken any material action. But, even where State practice may be deemed to be required, material action is not necessarily the best determinant. In the field of international humanitarian law, for example, it would be impracticable to ascertain State practice with regard to the behaviour of troops on the battlefield, not least because such practice may be antithetical to the orders received. As a result, it is argued that recourse should be made to military manuals and decrees, ratification of relevant instruments and other similar official pronouncements indicating a legal commitment.[6] What this means is that even if the agents of States commit serious and widespread crimes, despite their national laws and statements to the contrary, they cannot point to their material action to avoid liability by arguing that their customary obligations stem from that material practice. National courts have on numerous occasions upheld the customary nature of particular crimes.[7]

International customary rules bind all States, except for those that have consistently and openly objected to the formation of a rule from its inception.[8] This general

---

[4] *North Sea Continental Shelf cases (FDR v Denmark; FDR v The Netherlands)* (Merits), (1969) ICJ Reports 3, paras 73–81; see generally M Akehurst, 'Custom as a Source of International Law' (1974–75) 47 *British Yearbook of International Law* 1.

[5] R Sloan, 'General Assembly Resolutions Revisited (Forty Years After)' (1987) 58 *British Yearbook of International Law* 39.

[6] *ICTY Prosecutor v Tadić*, Appeals Chamber Decision on the Defence Motion for Interlocutory Appeal on Jurisdiction (2 Oct 1995), para 99; see T Meron, 'The Continuing Role of Custom in the Formation of International Humanitarian Law' (1996) 90 *American Journal of International Law* 238, 239–40, who states that due to the scarcity of supporting practice in both human rights and humanitarian law evidence of *opinio juris* is compensated through official statements.

[7] *Re Piracy Jure Gentium* [1934] AC 856, regarding piracy; *R v Jones (Margaret)* [2007] 1 AC 136, regarding aggression, and; *USA v Arjona* (1887) 20 US 479, regarding counterfeiting of foreign currency.

[8] J Charney, 'The Persistent Objector Rule and the Development of Customary International Law' (1985) 56 *British Yearbook of International Law* 1.

framework is subject to a single exception; peremptory norms of international law (*jus cogens* rules). These are norms from which no derogation whatsoever is possible because of their fundamental importance in the community of nations.[9] *Jus cogens* comprise the fundamental human rights and rules of international humanitarian law, as well as the prohibition of the use of unlawful armed force. Similarly, treaty provisions reflecting peremptory norms of international law are binding upon third parties to such treaties by virtue of their peremptory nature, despite the fact that third States are not ordinarily bound by treaties to which they are not parties. Customary law is particularly important in ICL because it is used to fill in gaps in situations where treaty law is silent. The ad hoc tribunals for Yugoslavia and Rwanda have in fact relied heavily on custom to demonstrate, *inter alia*, that war crimes perpetrated in internal armed conflicts are regulated under international law or that particular modes of liability, such as joint criminal enterprise, are applicable.

General principles of law can be found both in international law itself, as well as in the domestic legal systems of States.[10] General principles of international law, such as *pacta sunt servanda*, constitute *a priori* principles that underlie both customary and treaty law. On the other hand, general principles of domestic law are practices or principles common to a substantial number of nations.[11] It has been accepted by post-Second World War military tribunals,[12] as well as by contemporary international judicial bodies such as the European Court of Justice (ECJ),[13] that for a domestic principle to be regarded as generally accepted it must be recognised by most legal systems, not all. Under customary international law, reliance upon principles deriving from national legal systems is justified either when rules make explicit reference to national laws,[14] or when such reference is 'necessarily implied by the very content and nature of the concept'.[15] This suggests that the practice of international tribunals has been to explore all the means available at the international level before turning to national law. It is instructive to note that the 1998 International Criminal Court (ICC) Statute places general principles of law derived from legal systems of the world in a position of last resort and only then to be utilised if they are consistent with

---

[9] 1969 Vienna Convention on the Law of Treaties, 1155 UNTS 331, Art 53.

[10] B Cheng, *General Principles of Law as Applied by International Courts and Tribunals* (Cambridge, Cambridge University Press, 1987); AD McNair, 'The General Principles of Law Recognised by Civilised Nations' (1957) 33 *British Yearbook of International Law* 1.

[11] *AMCO v Republic of Indonesia*, ICSID Decision (1990) 89 ILR 366, 461.

[12] The tribunal in the *Hostages* case (below) noted that, if a principle is found to have been accepted generally as a fundamental rule of justice by most nations in their municipal law, its declaration as a rule of international law would seem to be fully justified. *USA v List* (*Hostages* case, 8 Law Reports of Trials of War Criminals (LRTWC) 34, at 49.

[13] In the words of Advocate General Lagrange in Case 14/61, *Hoogovens v High Authority* [1962] ECR 253, 283–84: 'The Court is not content to draw on more or less arithmetical common denominators between different national solutions, but chooses from each of the Member States those solutions which, having regard to the objects of the Treaty, appear to be the best or . . . the most progressive'.

[14] As does, for example, the International Criminal Tribunal for the Former Yugoslavia (ICTY) Statute, Art 24(1) of which states that, in determining the terms of imprisonment, the Trial Chambers shall have recourse to the general practice regarding prison sentences in the courts of the former Yugoslavia.

[15] *Advisory Opinion Concerning Exchange of Greek and Turkish Populations* (1925) Permanent Court of International Justice (PCIJ) Reports, Ser B, No 10, 19–20, cited by Judges McDonald and Vohrah in *ICTY Prosecutor v Erdemović*, Appeals Chamber Judgment (7 Oct 1997).

international law.[16] To a very large degree, these propositions reflect the fact that the vast majority of fundamental general principles of national laws, such as the principle of legality and the prohibition of retroactive laws, have matured into customary and treaty norms. The fundamental problem with general principles, however, concerns their identification and use by international criminal tribunals without having set forth in advance a clear and consistent methodology. In practice, judges at the International Criminal Tribunal for the former Yugoslavia (ICTY) and International Criminal Tribunal for Rwanda (ICTR) have referred to principles encountered in legal systems with which they, or their legal assistants, were familiar with, but: (a) omitted significant references to legal systems that would better represent a global consensus, such as that of Muslim,[17] former communist or African States, and; (b) did not provide the legal context in which a particular concept is framed, thus failing to clearly demonstrate whether a particular concept is identical only in name or essence in two or more nations.

The sources of ICL do not adequately explain the status of natural persons in relation to international crimes. Can they be held criminally liable under international law or solely under the relevant rules of domestic law? The answer to this may seem obvious today, but it has not always been so. States have been the traditional subjects of international law, the entities primarily endowed with international legal personality, that is, the ability to enjoy and enforce rights and duties directly under international law.[18] From the latter part of the nineteenth century a certain amount of international legal competence was granted to intergovernmental organisations. It has been advocated that natural persons became subjects, and not merely objects, of the international legal system at the end of the Second World War, at which time they assumed personal liability under the 1945 London Agreement for the Prosecution and Punishment of the Major War Criminals of the European Axis.[19] This is not true, as a substantial number of international and transnational offences were recognised by the international community prior to the dawn of the twentieth century, such as piracy *jure gentium*, war crimes, injury to submarine cables, postal offences and others. This personality, however, was limited strictly to these instruments and relevant customary law and the prosecution of the accused took place at

---

[16] This formulation was consistent with the Report of the Preparatory Committee on the International Criminal Court at the Diplomatic Conference held in Rome (15 Jun–17 Jul 1998), UN Doc A/CONF 183/2/Add 1 (14 Apr 1998), at 46–47.

[17] In the course of this book references to classic Islamic criminal law doctrine will be made, particularly as regards modes of participation, mental element standards and defences. It should of course be acknowledged that Islamic law is not viewed as constituting a legal system in its own right on account of its latent indeterminacy (ie it does not speak with a single voice, is not always foreseeable and is scattered). As a result, courts around the world in practice apply the laws of particular Muslim States, rather than 'Islamic law'. See *Beximco Pharmaceuticals v Shamil Bank of Bahrain EC* [2004] 1 WLR 1784, which involved a choice of law clause referring to the *Sharia*. The situation is further exacerbated by the fact that increasingly Western courts find that certain Muslim laws and practices are discriminatory or otherwise unacceptable, see *EM (Lebanon) v Secretary of State for the Home Department* [2008] UKHL 64. The reality is, however, that with some exceptions the legislation of many Muslim nations make *renvoi* references back to 'Islamic law' (the Qur'an, the *sunna* and other secondary sources) and it is thus within this body of law (subject to its four main schools) that general principles should be sought; not the secular law of Muslim nations.

[18] See generally R Higgins, *Problems and Process: International Law and How We Use It* (Oxford, Oxford University Press, 1994) 48–55.

[19] 59 Stat 1544.

the domestic level on the basis of local criminal law. At present, natural persons are endowed with legal personality in a plethora of international fields, such as human rights and humanitarian law, international investment and commercial transactions, European Community law and others.[20] For the purposes of ICL, the fundamental question is whether the conferral of legal personality to natural persons by means of a treaty crime necessarily entails, as a direct correlation, the attribution of individual criminal liability under international law. To put it simply, where the United Nations Convention on the Law of the Sea (UNCLOS) defines piracy as an act that may be perpetrated only by natural persons, does it establish an offence under international law or an offence under domestic law, and what is the difference between the two in practical terms? This question will be discussed by reference to the international criminalisation process elaborated in the following section.

1.3   The International Criminalisation Process

An international offence is any act entailing the criminal liability of the perpetrator and emanating from treaty or custom. The heinous nature of an act, such as the extermination of an identified group, is not the sole determinant for elevating its underlying conduct to the status of an international offence, although this may serve as a good incentive to do so. Rather, as Dinstein correctly points out, 'the practice of States is the conclusive determinant in the creation of international law (including international criminal law), and not the desirability of stamping out obnoxious patterns of human behaviour'.[21] Simply put, the establishment of international offences is the direct result of inter-State consensus, all other considerations bearing a distinct subordinate character.

The legal basis for considering an offence as being of international import is predicated on whether existing treaties or custom consider the conduct in question as being an international crime.[22] Since every international offence is now codified in multilateral agreements we shall continue our analysis on the basis of treaty law. Although international treaties define or prescribe offences by employing inconsistent terminology it is possible to discern two broad typologies of criminalisation. The first category includes treaties such as the 1948 Convention on the Prevention and Punishment of the Crime of Genocide,[23] which contain a categorical provision that the forbidden conduct constitutes a crime under international law (usually termed 'universal' or international crimes). A second category of treaties may or may not

---

[20] See I Bantekas, 'The Private Dimension of the International Customary Nature of Commercial Arbitration' (2008) 25 *Journal of International Arbitration* 449, where it is argued that natural persons in fact create international rules in particular commercial or industrial fields that are subsequently accepted by States as binding under the principle of *lex mercatoria*.

[21] Y Dinstein, 'International Criminal Law' (1985) 20 *Israel Law Review* 206, at 221.

[22] This author has not found an international offence emanating independently from general principles of international law or the criminal laws of nations. If this were so it may even offend the principle of legality where the crime in question was found to lack foreseeability. For a contrary view, see CM Bassiouni (ed), *International Criminal Law* (Ardsley, Transnational Publishers, 1986) 2.

[23] 78 UNTS 277.

describe the forbidden conduct as a crime, but clearly imposes a duty on contracting parties to prosecute or extradite the alleged offender, or simply render the said conduct an offence under their national law. The different variants of this latter category have attracted wide application in the international criminalisation process and have been the major vehicle for anti-terrorist treaties and transnational crimes such as corruption and organised crime. The fact that a treaty defines certain conduct simply as an offence, or imposes a duty on States to take action at the domestic criminal level without, however, describing the conduct as an international crime, in no way detracts from the international nature of the offence prescribed by the treaty, although there is a difference of quality between the two types of criminalisation as will be shortly explained.

A distinction is quite rightly made in the literature between international criminal law *stricto sensu* and transnational criminal law. The former refers to core international crimes, namely war crimes, genocide, crimes against humanity and crimes against peace, whereas the latter concerns so-called treaty crimes, such as drug-trafficking, organised crime, corruption, terrorism and others. This distinction is said to be functional because, unlike international crimes, their transnational counterparts produce only transboundary harm. This contention is, however, untrue because terrorists, organised criminal groups and drug-traffickers operate globally. The distinction between the two should be sought on a different basis; a doctrinal one. Whereas the objective (*actus reus*) and subjective (*mens rea*) elements of international crimes apply universally and uniformly between States, in respect of transnational crimes these elements are prescribed by the penal provisions of domestic laws. The same is true of the defences applicable to international crimes and the modes of participation therein.[24] Thus, the criminalisation and prosecution of transnational crimes necessitates the existence of developed criminal justice systems. Moreover, core international crimes provide for international criminal liability that persists irrespective of whether any criminal liability is prescribed under domestic laws. As such, they are directly enforceable and increasingly States apply them on the basis of their customary origin alone. Transnational crimes, on the other hand, are not autonomous from the treaties in which they are contained and which require participating States to criminalise on the basis of their existing principles of criminal law.[25]

When examining the general effect of treaties and their passing into the realm of customary law, one automatically looks at the status of ratifications. This does not necessarily paint a true picture. Treaties that encompass a wide variety of topics and, at the same time, expressly exclude reservations, or where certain reservations would be deemed to conflict with the object and purpose of a treaty will in most cases attract few parties. This sparse participation is not because dissenting States fundamentally disagree with the entire convention, but only certain portion(s) of it. A good example is the 1949 Convention for the Suppression of the Traffic in Persons and of the Exploitation of the Prostitution of Others.[26] This instrument, which penalises the procurement and enticement to prostitution as well as the maintenance of brothels,

---

[24] N Boister, 'Transnational Criminal Law?' (2003) 14 *European Journal of International Law* 953, 957–59.
[25] Ibid, pp 962–63.
[26] 96 UNTS 271.

has received a marginal number of ratifications, simply because a large number of States possess legislation legalising voluntary prostitution. From a number of sources, such as the *travaux préparatoires* of the Convention, in addition to the global uniformity ascertained in national legislations, as well as from official pronouncements in international fora and other relevant treaties, it is beyond doubt that the enticement to and maintenance of all forms of involuntary prostitution constitute international offences under customary law. Thus, even though the Convention is not widely ratified, one of the conducts it criminalises is clearly an offence under customary law. In respect of treaties dealing with a single subject matter, such as those prohibiting statutory limitations to international offences, sparse participation demonstrates opposition to the proposed rule; as a result, the rule in question is unsusceptible to customary formation.

Where international custom criminalises certain conduct, the incumbent court must also satisfy itself that the particular offence is 'defined with sufficient clarity under customary international law for its general nature, its criminal character and its approximate gravity to have been sufficiently foreseeable and accessible'.[27] In the *Vasiljević* judgment, the Prosecution charged the accused, *inter alia*, with the offence of violence to life and person. The Trial Chamber was faced with the decision whether the definition of the offence was of sufficient clarity in order to satisfy the requirements of the principle *nullum crimen sine lege*. Despite the existence of the offence in the ICTY Statute, the Trial Chamber very boldly stated that in the absence of any clear indication in the practice of States as to what the definition of the offence of violence to life and person may be under customary law, it was not satisfied that such an offence giving rise to individual criminal responsibility existed under that body of law.[28]

Every offence prescribed in treaties or custom must ultimately be implemented into national law through an act of legislation. This process is followed not only where the offence is not precisely defined in the treaty, but also where it is set out in detail in its constitutive instrument. The national legislator may wish to further elaborate the substantive or procedural elements of the offence and/or adapt it to domestic exigencies, albeit he should be guided in this respect by the framework established in the relevant treaty. In practice, contemporary ICL treaties dealing with transnational offences leave their implementation, such as the modes of liability (eg perpetration, co-perpetration, conspiracy, corporate criminality etc), domestic investigations and others to be adapted in accordance with their member State's domestic legislation, in conformity to the 'functional equivalence' doctrine. For example, the 1997 OECD Bribery Convention simply provides that States parties must adopt 'effective, proportionate and dissuasive sanctions' against legal persons, recognising that legal persons do not incur criminal liability in all States. Thus, functional equivalence is a result-based method, rather than a form-based method, but should not be considered generally applicable in respect of definitions of crimes found in ICL treaties. A State violating its treaty obligations by either failing to incorporate a treaty into its domestic legal system, or by omitting fundamental aspects of the treaty from its

---

[27]   *ICTY Prosecutor v Vasiljević*, Trial Chamber Judgment (29 Nov 2002), para 201.
[28]   Ibid, para 203.

implementing statute, will generally be held liable vis-a-vis other contracting parties. In the field of ICL there may be great divergence in the views of States during the negotiation of a treaty. Where the treaty is finally adopted through a compromise the divergence remains and in the absence of a contrary provision there is no reason why a State party cannot adopt implementing legislation that helps to supplement or fortify the provisions of a weak treaty. A State may decide, for example, that the 1977 Protocol II Additional to the 1949 Geneva Conventions and Relating to the Protection of Victims of Non-International Armed Conflicts[29] does not cover enough offences, nor does it establish a high enough gravity, nor sufficient jurisdictional bases. Such fortifications to ICL treaties should be accepted with extreme caution however, as long as they: (a) are not expressly or tacitly prohibited; (b) do not conflict with the object or purpose or other obligations under that or prior treaties to which the State in question is a party, and; (c) they, moreover, do not violate the rights of the accused.

The practical difference between offences clearly specified under international law and those whose further elaboration is left to the discretion of contracting States relates primarily to the removal of perplexities associated with the negotiation and drafting of definitions at preparatory conferences. This is generally the case with transnational crimes. Past practice demonstrates a preference for 'weaker' conventions with the aim of getting as many States on board, rather than rigid treaties that would leave little or no room for manoeuvring. As a result, the drafters thought it wise, although unfortunate, to sacrifice specificity, depth and a range of binding modes of cooperation. Thankfully, this position has now been eliminated in international treaty making in the field of ICL and quality is preferred over quantity of participants. This is true for example in respect of the ICC Statute where major players, such as the USA and China, were left out in order to create a strong and independent institution.

ICL is not strictly concerned with 'international' crimes. Besides the high seas, the international seabed and outer space there exists no other international territory. As a result, criminal conduct would only acquire an international dimension where it was transnational, such as war crimes committed in the context of an inter-State conflict. Most modern conflicts, however, do not transcend international frontiers and yet current developments in international law view them through the prism of internationalisation. There are several reasons associated with this approach. Whereas during the Cold War the non-interference principle permitted horrendous crimes by authoritarian regimes in order to avoid the scourge of inter-State conflict, the post-Cold War era gives greater weight to the individual and the protection of his or her rights. In this light, human rights can best be served where they are placed in an international context because they are better scrutinised, rather than in a domestic setting where the risk of abuse is high. This artificial internationalisation, whether by treaty, custom or Security Council prescription has had a marked impact on the range of offences subject to international law, which has in turn elevated the status of human rights globally. This development is clearly demonstrated by the elevation of breaches of humanitarian law applicable in non-international armed conflicts to the

---

[29] 1125 UNTS 609.

status of international offences entailing the individual responsibility of the offend-ers.[30] Non-international armed conflict violations do not by their nature possess international or transnational elements and are confined to a single territory, unless other States decide to intervene. This development, and the process of internationali-sation generally, demonstrate the erosion of the principle of non-interference and of the exclusivity of domestic jurisdiction..

In conclusion, the prohibition of certain conduct by treaty or custom always entails criminal liability under international law, irrespective of whether the prohib-ited conduct is defined as a universal crime or an offence to be further elaborated through domestic law. This represents the first step in the criminalisation process. In the dawn of the twenty-first century one should dismiss the notion espoused in 1950 by Schwarzenberger that ICL is 'merely a loose and misleading label for topics which comprise anything but international criminal law'. This great international lawyer had further argued during that formative state of ICL that whatever the content of these rules there is no evidence that they are endowed with a prohibitive character and specific penal sanctions.[31] Schwarzenberger grounded his argument on the fact that, and in the absence of international enforcement mechanisms, the concept of offences against the law of nations was redundant, unless regulated and enforced before a domestic setting, believing that ICL could not function outside each individual State. This led him to believe that ICL was, in fact, domestic criminal law. He also argued that sovereign States could not and would not agree to being held liable for State crimes, a notion that now seems to be settled within the ranks of the International Law Commission and general *opinio juris*.[32] Next, we will examine the final step of the international criminal process, which comprises the enforcement of substantive ICL.

1.4   Enforcement of International Criminal Law

States create their law on the basis of a vertical system of authority. Parliament legislates or delegates minor legislative authority to entities below it (eg ministries or public utilities), all of which is binding on every other entity or person down the chain of authority. In the relations between States the principle of juridical equality is paramount in the sense that no single State can unilaterally impose an obligation upon another. It is, therefore, a horizontal system of law-making. Since the interna-tional community does not possess a legislative body, a law enforcement agency, or a compulsory judicial jurisdiction, its primary subjects must necessarily premise their

---

[30]   *Tadić* Appeals Jurisdiction Decision, para 134.
[31]   G Schwarzenberger, 'The Problem of an International Criminal Law' (1950) 3 *Current Legal Problems* 263, at 274.
[32]   The much contested draft Art 19 of the ILC's Draft Articles on State Responsibility, which made reference to international offences giving rising to State responsibility, was removed from the ILC's finalised Articles. See UN Doc A/CN4/L600 (21 Aug 2000).

relations on a framework of mutual interdependence. International enforcement action against natural persons for violations of ICL takes two general forms: direct and indirect.

Direct enforcement implies prosecutorial and judicial action against persons suspected of having committed an international offence. Although in the past a substantial number of quasi-judicial commissions were set up to investigate breaches of the laws of war alleged to have taken place in various armed conflicts it was not until the establishment of the Nuremberg and Tokyo tribunals at the close of the Second World War that enforcement took place before an international forum and on the basis of international law. Two later conventions, specifically Article VI of the 1948 Genocide Convention and Article V of the 1973 Convention on the Prevention and Suppression of Apartheid,[33] called for the creation of an international penal tribunal with authority to adjudicate violations of these agreements. Similarly, on the basis of Article 25 of the UN Charter, which renders Security Council resolutions binding on UN Member States, the ad hoc tribunals for Yugoslavia[34] and Rwanda[35] were established under the process of Article 41 of the Charter (that is, measures authorised by the UN Security Council not involving the use of armed force). Criminal jurisdiction was also conferred on a more permanent judicial institution, the International Criminal Court (ICC), whose Statute was adopted by means of a treaty.[36] Unlike the ad hoc tribunals the ICC is not endowed with primary or compulsory jurisdiction; rather, its jurisdiction is residual to that of national courts. In the course of this book the reader will have a chance to study other hybrid international tribunals, particularly those established in Sierra Leone, East Timor, Kosovo, Iraq, Lebanon and Cambodia.[37]

It is not only international tribunals that possess the capacity to take direct enforcement action, but also domestic criminal courts. When domestic courts exercise wide-ranging extraterritorial jurisdiction, especially universal jurisdiction over piracy *jure gentium*, war crimes and crimes against humanity, they, too, are acting as international tribunals since they are directly enforcing international law. The prosecution of cases subject to universal jurisdiction in particular, in situations where the forum State does not have any connection to the elements of the offence, necessarily implies that domestic courts assume much more than a mere judicial character; to some degree they may be viewed as discharging that State's obligation to the whole of the international community, in protecting and enforcing fundamental human rights (*erga omnes* obligations). As the International Court of Justice (ICJ) pointed out in the *Barcelona Traction* case all States have a legal interest in the protection of fundamental rights worldwide.[38] This would render the exercise of extraterritorial jurisdiction, particularly of the universal nature, not only a right but an obligation.

Indirect enforcement of ICL takes place at the procedural level, but always with a view to prosecution. In the absence of international tribunals and general reluctance

---

[33] 1015 UNTS 243.
[34] SC Res 827 (25 May 1993).
[35] SC Res 955 (8 Nov 1994).
[36] (1989) 37 ILM 999.
[37] See chapter 20.
[38] *Barcelona Traction Light and Power House Co Ltd (Belgium v Spain)*, Second Phase Judgment (1970) ICJ Reports 3, at 32.

in the exercise of universal jurisdiction, States have found themselves compelled to reach minimum agreement on international cooperation in criminal matters. The various facets of this cooperation extend not only to purely domestic offences, but are more importantly concerned with international crimes with a view to preventing impunity. Most prominent among these measures is the insertion of a provision in ICL treaties obligating parties either to prosecute or extradite (*aut dedere aut judicare*). This clause, whose origin can be traced in the work of Hugo de Groot (Grotius), does not constitute an independent basis for extradition but requires an additional agreement between the requesting and requested States. It does nonetheless serve as a deterrent to establishing safe havens for alleged criminals and forces parties to a convention to take responsible enforcement action. The mechanism of extradition itself also supplements indirect enforcement processes by enabling a more willing and better-equipped (in terms of evidence and proximity to the facts of the case) jurisdiction to investigate a particular case. Another complementary safeguard is the inclusion of broad jurisdictional competence in most international criminal treaties, thereby enabling national prosecutorial authorities to assume direct action. Similarly, contemporary treaties have allowed few or no reservations[39] and have refused contracting States the ability to characterise offences within the framework of a convention as politically or ideologically motivated.[40] This has deprived States of the ability to otherwise refuse extradition and has created a large degree of uniformity. Finally, through bilateral and multilateral mutual legal assistance agreements it has become possible to communicate evidence and other documentation in order to facilitate criminal prosecution between two or more States.

The threefold objective of ICL, that is, to prevent, prosecute and punish offenders, must ultimately be beneficial to all people. If international criminal justice does not serve this purpose, it will have failed. At the same time other international processes will work towards post-conflict reconciliation and development. Ideally, the two processes (ie criminal justice and post-conflict development) will coincide and complement each other. What happens, however, if they are antithetical and one negates the other? For example, if the only way that a ravaging civil war could stop, or for an authoritarian regime to be deposed, was to offer amnesties to those accused of serious international crimes, should this alternative be preferred over the imposition of criminal justice? The tension between the two cannot be easily resolved.[41] As the reader will observe in a following section of this chapter dealing with the justificatory objectives of international criminal justice, the international community

---

[39] 1993 Convention on the Prohibition of the Development, Production, Stockpiling and Use of Chemical Weapons and on Their Destruction, Art 22, (1993) 32 ILM 804; 1997 Convention on the Prohibition of the Use, Stockpiling, Production and Transfer of Anti-Personnel Mines and on their Destruction, Art 19, (1997) 320 *International Review of the Red Cross* 563; ICC Statute, Art 120.

[40] See, eg 1970 Convention for the Suppression of Unlawful Seizure of Aircraft, Art 8, 860 UNTS 105; 1971 Convention for the Suppression of Unlawful Acts against the Safety of Civil Aviation, Art 8, 974 UNTS 177; 1998 UN Convention for the Suppression of Terrorist Bombings, Arts 5 and 9, (1998) 37 ILM 249.

[41] The negotiations leading to the adoption of the Statute of the 2002 Sierra Leone Special Court, after agreement between the UN and the Government of Sierra Leone, vigorously reflected the position of the UN Secretary-General that the granting of amnesties would not bar prosecutions. Report of the Secretary General on the Establishment of a Special Court for Sierra Leone, UN Doc S/2000/915 (4 Oct 2000), para 22. See chapter 20.2.1.

is not prepared to sacrifice prosecution over reconciliation. This is natural, given that there is no guarantee that war will not break out again or that the culprits will not return to power and resume their criminal activity. As will be demonstrated, prosecution signifies that the law exists and that no one can hope to escape from its claws. In practice, post-conflict and criminal justice mechanisms work alongside each other, albeit their relationships are not always devoid of tension. As will become evident in other chapters the UN is opposed to blanket immunities and not to truth commissions in general.

Moreover, the aforementioned threefold objective of ICL is served not only through State action, but also through the efforts of private organisations. These efforts relate solely to preventive action, since prosecution and punishment constitute exclusively public functions. Private organisations such as the International Committee of the Red Cross (ICRC), the Piracy Reporting Centre,[42] established by the International Chamber of Commerce, and the International Cable Protection Committee, established by corporations active in that industry, undertake a range of preventive measures to minimise the risk of offences associated with their field of interest. This is welcome and unavoidable to a large extent, as in the case of piracy, for example, most developing States do not have the resources to patrol their coastlines, let alone the adjacent high seas. Moreover, these organisations have, in the past, been the protagonist instigators for the evolution of international norms in certain fields, such as the development of international humanitarian law through the efforts of the ICRC. Soft law is also a major component of ICL processes and in some cases States have agreed to implement particular instances of soft law, as is the case with the Financial Action Task Force's (FATF) Forty Recommendations on Money Laundering and Terrorist Financing. Thus, although the primary function of soft law is related to standard-setting, it is also employed to address the gaps of hard law.

The process of ICL enforcement, however, may also involve State entities as perpetrators or as transgressors of their international obligation to cooperate with other States in the suppression of international and transnational offences. A State that breaches any of its international obligations commits an internationally wrongful act and bears responsibility vis-a-vis injured States. Some wrongful acts, however, especially those relating to gross violations of human rights against a country's own nationals do not produce harm to other countries. They do nonetheless breach obligations owed to the international community as a whole and, as such, every country possesses a legal interest in their termination and satisfaction of the victims. In both aforementioned cases (that is, direct injury and obligations *erga omnes*) recourse is available to the ICJ or other inter-State judicial bodies, although no case has so far been entertained by the ICJ on account of a non-injured party alleging breach of a *jus cogens* norm.[43] Increasingly, natural persons have been granted legal standing before international judicial bodies endowed with compulsory jurisdiction

---

[42] This entity operates a Live Piracy Report, thereby giving advance warning to the shipping industry.

[43] The European Court and Commission of Human Rights has had a chance to examine inter-State complaints alleging human rights violations taking place solely on the territory, and against the nationals, of a single State. See *Denmark, Norway, Sweden and The Netherlands v Greece* (*Greek* case) (1969) 12 *European Court of Human Rights Yearbook* 134.

and capable of rendering binding judgments, such as the European Court of Human Rights. Judgments and non-binding rulings emanating from other quasi-judicial bodies, such as the UN Human Rights Committee, have in recent years been respected and complied with by a large number of States. This does not always mean that all States are compliant,[44] yet these mechanisms give rise to a fermentation process through which the normative potency of rights is enhanced.

One should not underestimate the authority and willingness of the Security Council in the pursuit of international criminal justice.[45] Security Council resolutions are binding upon all States, thus rendering any recalcitrant State subject to possible Council countermeasures on account of its refusal to comply. The Security Council may even authorise the use of armed force in accordance with Article 42 of the UN Charter, where it is convinced, and its members are capable of deciding, that such action would best counter a particular breach or threat to the peace or an act of aggression. This was amply exemplified in the case of Iraqi aggression against Kuwait in 1990 in respect of which the Council authorised a coalition of allied States to use force in order to restore not only Kuwaiti independence but also international peace and security in the region.[46] Sanctions can also be imposed by regional organisations and this is usually decided and executed in cooperation, or in execution of, relevant Security Council resolutions.[47]

1.5   State Criminality

The notion of 'criminality' essentially refers to liability of a criminal nature. Liability itself is based on the attribution of particular conduct and an appropriate mental element to a physical person. Criminal liability in both national and international law is generally attributed to natural persons and, exceptionally, also to other legal entities, as was the case with several Nazi-related organisations after the Second World War. Even so, it was not the legal person that was deemed to be liable; rather, it was individual membership that constituted the particular criminal offence.[48] It is, therefore, evident that any discussion of liability that does not involve any natural persons as perpetrators – or in some specific instances of private legal persons – is devoid of a criminal nature, but not necessarily a civil one.

Equally, it has become common for private sector associations to self-regulate themselves in order to avoid the intrusion of criminal legislation. This is particularly common with regard to the banking and financial services industry in relation to

---

[44]   D McGoldrick, *The Human Rights Committee* (Oxford, Oxford University Press, 1994) 202–04.

[45]   JD Fry, 'The UN Security Council and the Law of Armed Conflict: Amity or Enmity?' (2006) 38 *George Washington International Law Review* 333.

[46]   SC Res 678 (29 Nov 1990).

[47]   EU implementation of petroleum embargo, 1999 OJ L 108/1; Freezing of Yugoslav funds abroad and bar of future investment in Serbia, Council Regulation 1294/1999, 1999 OJ L153/63 and Council Decision 1999/424/CFSP, 1999 OJ L163/86, 26 Jun 1999. See also HP Gasser, 'Collective Economic Sanctions and International Humanitarian Law' (1996) 57 *Zeitschrift für ausländisches öffentliches Recht und Völkerrecht* 876.

[48]   See chapters 17.2.1 and 3.11.

money laundering and terrorist financing and not simply financial crime that causes economic loss to such institutions. The European Banking Federation (EFB), for example, tabled seven recommendations aiming to improve the implementation of the EU anti-terrorist financing sanctions regime.[49] The EFB Recommendations clearly suggest that its member institutions are only bound to adhere to EU legislation. Hence, EFB members support the application only of that portion of international law that has been transposed into EU law and not of all relevant Security Council resolutions. Additionally, on 30 October 2000, eleven of the world's largest banks, later followed by two others, established anti-money laundering guidelines applicable to private international banks. The Group adopted a set of principles guiding its members on how to better conduct their business and avoid the circulation of illegitimate funds. On this basis the members unanimously adopted the so-called Wolfsberg Principles.[50] As a result of the 11 September 2001 events, the group met again in January 2002 to discuss terrorist financing, and updated its Principles to make reference to the role of financial institutions. Additional measures were adopted by the Basel Committee, which was established by the central-bank governors of the Group of Ten (G10) Countries in 1974. It is composed of about 30 technical working groups and task forces and its conclusions or recommendations do not have the force of law but are intended to formulate broad supervisory standards and guidelines. At the same time the Basel Committee is mandated with recommending statements of best practice in the expectation that individual authorities will implement them based on their own particular needs.

All crimes are committed by natural persons and it seems self-evident that personal culpability should somehow follow. The translation of personal attribution into criminal liability is a complex exercise in the international legal system. The majority of international offences are committed by individuals acting under the guise of, or on behalf of, State orchestrated policies, whether overtly or clandestinely. The policy of apartheid in South Africa, the genocides against Jews, Armenians and the Tutsi, as well as cases of State-sponsored terrorism (for example, Libyan involvement in the Lockerbie case)[51] are just some instances where an international offence originates from the highest echelons of a State apparatus and is subsequently executed by its subordinate organs or agents. Leaving aside the issue of personal immunity for acts perpetrated by or on behalf of the State,[52] is there any room for the State itself to be viewed as having committed a criminal act, and if so, is this a worthwhile exercise? Until August 2000 this notion, even though progressive, was entertained although not wholly accepted by the international community. Then draft Article 19 of the International Law Commission's (ILC) Draft Articles on State Responsibility distinguished between international crimes and delicts. In accordance with the now deleted Article 19(2), an international crime resulted 'from the breach by a State of an international obligation so essential for the protection of fundamental interests of the international community that its breach is recognised as a crime by that community

---

[49] EFB Recommendations for Drafting, Interpreting and Implementing Financial Sanctions Regulations (21 Dec 2001).
[50] Available at <http://www.wolfsberg-principles.com>.
[51] See chapter 12.4.
[52] See chapter 6.

as a whole'. Any other breach falling below this standard was classified as an international delict. The formulation found in draft Article 19, however, was not universally acceptable and was possibly unnecessary. Nonetheless, the idea that there do exist obligations owed to the international community as a whole and that serious breaches should attract special consequences was never doubted.[53]

In August 2000 the ILC, prompted also by its then new rapporteur, James Crawford, decided to delete draft Article 19, as well as any reference to the word 'crime', from the text. The Articles no longer differentiate between criminal and delictual responsibility, viewing instead a State's internationally wrongful acts as forming a single category of violations. While, as explained, the problematic notion of 'international State crime' was deleted it was recognised that a State may be liable for acts breaching peremptory norms (*jus cogens*), as well as obligations owed to the international community as a whole.[54]

State responsibility in no way precludes individual responsibility, but if the ILC Articles are to have any real significance it is imperative that additional consequences flow from the serious breach of community obligations. In its last reading the Commission favoured the idea of proportionate damages in accordance with the gravity of the offence. Such damages would be sought by the victim State, or in the absence of such a State, by any other State acting on behalf of, and in the interests of, the individual victims of the breach.[55] Moreover, the Commission's draft endorses, under strict circumstances, the possibility of countermeasures. Article 54 constitutes a compromise balance between the reservations about collective countermeasures and the revulsion against turning a blind eye to gross breaches, especially human rights breaches. This provision limits such countermeasures to those which are taken in response to serious and manifest breaches of obligations to the international community and obliges participating States to cooperate in order to ensure that the principle of proportionality is observed.[56]

Although the debate on the international criminality of States seems to have ended as far as the ILC is concerned, many still argue that the rationale contained in former draft Article 19 answers an indisputable need, pointing out, however, that it was the legal regimes of the envisaged crimes that were debatable.[57] The new regime contained in the adopted Articles strikes a right balance between the need to formulate a

---

[53] J Crawford, 'Revising the Draft Articles on State Responsibility' (1999) 10 *European Journal of International Law* 435.

[54] In the criminological literature the concept of State crime is defined as 'State organisational deviance involving the violation of human rights'. The degrees of such deviance vary from acts typically associated with the State apparatus, such as corruption, to crimes committed chiefly by States, such as genocide and torture. A third variation encompasses situations in which the State is not the principal perpetrator and in respect of which there is no intention as to the criminal consequence. State crime of this nature may arise in cases of natural disasters which culminate in massive death tolls on account of poor construction, lack of adequate infrastructure and others. Where these deficiencies are the direct result of clientelistic governance they foster corruption and authoritarianism which perpetuate the likelihood of similar disasters and other human rights violations against dissenters. See P Green, T Ward, *State Crime: Governments, Violence and Corruption* (London, Pluto Press, 2004).

[55] J Crawford, P Bodeau, J Peel, 'The ILC's Draft Articles on State Responsibility: Toward Completion of a Second Reading' (2000) 94 *American Journal of International Law* 660, 673.

[56] Crawford *et al*, The ILC's Draft Articles, at 674.

[57] A Pellet, 'Can a State Commit a Crime? Definitely, Yes!' (1999) 10 *European Journal of International Law* 425.

realistic framework for enforcement of *jus cogens* and *erga omnes* obligations, while at the same time rendering the text more accessible to States that would otherwise have objections to the definitional uncertainty and scope of draft Article 19.

1.6   International Criminal Law and Human Rights

Bassiouni convincingly argued that the last stage in the development of a rights regime is the criminalisation stage.[58] It is there that the shared values contained in the violated right are further protected and enhanced by the promulgation of penal proscriptions. This is true of all rights. The entire rationale of human rights was premised on the notion that the State is the violator, despite the fact that non-State actors frequently resort to depredations equivalent to those of States. Obligations contained in human rights treaties have a twofold objective. On the one hand, they impose negative burdens on their addressees, in the sense that in respect of some rights the State should refrain from interfering (eg right to life, freedom of expression). On the other hand, some rights require the positive conduct of States in order to be realised. Some are self-evident (eg the right to education), whereas others involve both a negative and a positive obligation (eg the right to life requires the State to both abstain from killing its citizens, but also to protect them from other threats). On this basis, it may reasonably be argued that the promulgation of an entitlement at the international level entails a positive obligation to criminalise at the domestic level. For example, the right to be free from involuntary servitude[59] would be meaningless unless implementing legislation, among other measures, effctively penalised and suppressed all forms of slavery – although slavery is explicitly criminalised by a plethora of international conventions.

Many offences that were traditionally attributable to State agents, such as crimes against humanity and war crimes, are at present also attributable to non-State entities, in particular paramilitary organisations.[60] Although private individuals bear criminal liability for committing international offences they cannot assume international responsibility for violating international human rights *per se*, as the obligations arising from this legal regime are addressed exclusively to States. Despite this observation a number of States have been supporting the idea that non-State entities are responsible for the 'destruction' of human rights, especially where acts of terrorism are attributed to national liberation or other guerilla movements.[61] Such a discourse can only have adverse effects on the human rights movement since it helps

---

[58]   CM Bassiouni, 'International Criminal Law and Human Rights' (1982) 9 *Yale Journal of World Public Order* 193.

[59]   International Covenant on Civil and Political Rights, Art 8(1) and (2), 999 UNTS 171.

[60]   ILC Report, Draft Code of Crimes Against the Peace and Security of Mankind, UN Doc A/51/10 (1996) Supp No 10, p 94; in *ICTR Prosecutor v Kayishema and Ruzindana*, Judgment (21 May 1999), para 125, the ICTR convicted the accused Ruzindana, a local businessman, of crimes against humanity because he partook in the overall Hutu extremist policy to exterminate the minority Tutsi; see also *ICTY Prosecutor v Karadžić and Mladić*, r 61 Decision (11 Jul 1996), paras 60–64.

[61]   GA Res 48/122 (20 Dec 1993); GA Res 49/185 (23 Dec 1994); GA Res 50/186 (22 Dec 1995); GA Res 51/210 (17 Dec 1996); GA Res 52/133 (27 Feb 1997).

certain States that frequently violate human rights to shift global attention from their obligations. As a result, if this contention is sustained it legitimates States to deny the enjoyment of rights, especially the right to self-determination.[62]

Selectivity in international criminal law is undeniable. The great powers of our times praise or remain silent in respect of atrocious regimes that suffocate and exterminate their people, simply because it suits their geopolitical agenda. On the other hand, they are willing to go to great lengths to invade a nation, willingly accept the loss of many thousand civilian lives – most of which inflicted directly by the acts of the occupying power – when their interests are no longer entertained by the incumbent regime they had helped install in the first place.[63] The same great powers openly abuse fundamental human rights and have no hesitation to abduct and torture persons over whom they may only have a suspicion of criminal conduct, or secretly transfer them to undemocratic regimes that routinely torture their political opponents. Moreover, under the pretext of sanctions the aim of which is to topple a 'brutal' regime the great powers accept that many innocent civilians will go unnourished and that thousands will die due to lack of medicines. When a government does the same to its people by denying it food and medicines it is branded as authoritarian and brutal. I am not for one minute advocating that those denying their people of fundamental rights should not be brought to justice. Rather, I am simply highlighting the fact that there exist others, particularly those heading the great powers, that are responsible for the deaths and hardship of hundreds of thousands of civilians. They proclaim themselves as liberators and few dare discuss their criminal liability which is a disgrace for the modern world.

Finally, as will be evident throughout this book, the rights of the accused in the context of criminal trials should prevail above all other considerations. Fundamental procedural and judicial guarantees, such as the right to a fair trial within a reasonable time, the prohibition of retroactive legislation, the observation of the doctrine *ne bis in idem* and others, have matured as general principles of law, or generally accepted custom and have found their way into the statutes of all contemporary international criminal tribunals. The same set of principles should also guide domestic criminal proceedings on the basis at least of their customary force, which are not to be dismissed lightly under the guise of emergency measures, as occurs all too often with terrorist-related offences. In many countries, so-called domestic terrorism constitutes a pretext for suspending democracy and civil liberties and is a solid excuse for engaging in widespread curtailment and violation of fundamental freedoms. On the basis of the aforementioned the reader will come to realise that the international criminal process is inextricably linked with the development and application of human rights.

---

[62] See chapter 12.5
[63] The former leader of the Bosnian Serbs, Radovan Karadžić, has challenged the jurisdiction of the ICTY on the basis that a US negotiator had promised him immunity for ending the then civil war and for disappearing from political life. See chapter 18.2.

1.7   The Principle of Legality

The principle of legality is otherwise reflected in the Latin maxim *nullum crimen nulla poena sine lege scripta*. Although its original formulation was intended to postulate the notion against the application of retroactive criminal legislation, its contemporary meaning encompasses three other customary principles, which relate to: a) the specificity of criminal rules; b) the ban on analogy, and; c) interpretation of criminal rules in favour of the accused. Its focus is on the rights of the accused against the excesses of power by those who wield it, within the limitations imposed by the dictates of international criminal justice.[64] The principle of legality and all its particular manifestations apply *mutatis mutandis* in respect of penalties.

1.7.1   Specificity

The rule of specificity requires that criminal rules are as detailed as possible in the sense that they clearly articulate to their addressees what type of conduct is expected of them. Whereas the grave breaches provisions of the 1949 Geneva Conventions were very weak in this respect, given that they failed to accurately spell out both the relevant *mens rea* or *actus reus* of the underlying criminal conduct, the ICC Statute has gone many steps further in satisfying the specificity principle. The ICC Statute has not only provided detailed definitions as to applicable mental element standards, defences and forms of liability, it has also been endowed with a mini criminal code in the form of the Elements of Crimes where the objective and subjective requirement for each offence is clearly spelled out. Nonetheless, the ICC Statute does not have binding force outside its particular context and other criminal tribunals, international as well as domestic, do not generally have access to such detailed definitions. Moreover, it is common in the practice of the vast majority of courts to expand the ambit of criminal attribution in cases where a particular conduct is obviously immoral, harmful or deviant and in respect of which the legal system in whose jurisdiction it falls has no specific criminal rule to counter it. Where the courts arbitrarily expand criminal liability in this manner they may indeed appease general public sentiment, but they also violate a most fundamental rule of law. Unfortunate as the moral tension may be in a particular case it is up to the national legislature to enact precise criminal rules in advance and not rely on judicial innovations. As a result, the public enactment of criminal laws satisfies to a large degree the rule of

---

[64] A Cassese, *International Criminal Law* (Oxford, Oxford University Press, 2008) 36–41, identifies two phases in the development of this principle. The first encompassed the principle of *substantive justice*, according to which any behaviour perceived as socially harmful was punished even if it was not criminalised at the time it was undertaken. With the advent of human rights this State-centred approach gave way to the current person-centred phase, which is premised on *strict legality*. This corresponds to the *nullum crimen* principle explored in this section; see S Gallant, *The Principle of Legality in International and Comparative Law* (Cambridge, Cambridge University Press, 2008).

specificity,[65] but does not precisely tell us how clearly an offence must be defined in a statute. The European Court of Human Rights stated that:

> This condition is satisfied where the individual can know from the wording of the relevant provision and, if need be, with the assistance of the court's interpretation of it, what acts and omissions will make him liable.[66]

This does not mean, however, that all criminal laws must explain in minute detail what conduct is expected. Legislative drafting of this nature would render criminal laws rigid and inflexible and unsusceptible to future social, economic and other developments. Moreover, if such rigid rules were construed restrictively, according to their letter alone, many forms of criminal conduct would escape liability because they would not exactly fit into the relevant definitions. On the other extreme, if the criminal law was excessively vague[67] with a view to countering the problems of rigidity just explained it would allow great latitude to judges and would ultimately offend the rule against the employment of analogies. Thus, a balance between the two extremes is necessary and within the parameters of legitimacy.[68] Offences established on the basis of multilateral treaties, particularly those adopted prior to the ad hoc tribunals, are rather general in their formulation because it is asking too much of negotiating States to specify the underlying conduct and mental elements in detail. The objective of these treaties is to criminalise particular behaviour in general terms and to set out the modalities for inter-State cooperation and as a result it is expected that further specificity will come about through the mode of transformation into domestic law. It is therefore permissible to rely on international crimes – drafted in general terms[69] – for the prosecution of natural persons, especially where such crimes have been analysed and defined extensively by national and international tribunals, or otherwise incorporated in domestic statutes.[70]

---

[65] *Sunday Times v UK* (1979) 2 EHRR 245, para 49, where the Court remarked that public enactment must entail adequate accessibility and must allow a person to 'foresee, to a degree that is reasonable in the circumstances, the consequences which a given action may entail'.

[66] *Kokkinakis v Greece* (1994) 17 EHRR 397, para 52.

[67] In *Hashman and Harrup v UK* (2000) 30 EHRR 241, the applicants were activists that had disturbed a fox hunt and were subsequently handed with binding over orders to keep the peace. The law upon which this penalty was imposed purported to criminalise behaviour that is 'wrong rather than right in the judgment of the majority of contemporary citizens'. In accepting that the applicants' freedom of expression had been violated the Court also ruled that this provision did not satisfy the standards set out by the rule of specificity.

[68] *Kokkinakis* judgment, para 40; in *US v McNab et al*, 324 F 3d 1266 (2003) the court was considering the legality of the Lacey Act which purported to criminalise all illegal wildlife imports in the USA contrary to foreign and international laws. The court noted that given the changing understanding of wildlife and of protected species, not to mention the constant perpetual law and treaty-making in these fields, that: 'Congress would be hard-pressed to set forth a definition that would adequately encompass all of them'.

[69] In *R v Jones (Margaret)* [2007] 1 AC 136, para 19, Lord Bingham was of the unanimous view that the crime of aggression did not lack definitional certainty simply because it was not incorporated in any multilateral treaty since its first inclusion in Art 6(a) of the Nuremberg Tribunal Charter.

[70] In *Ruling on Compatibility of the ICC Statute with the Colombian Constitution*, Judgment No C-578/2002, the Colombian Constitutional Court held that despite the fact that the principle of legality in internal law requires precision, international criminal law requires a lesser degree of precision and this state of affairs is acceptable under the 'different treatment' principle. According to this, because domestic and international crimes and domestic law and treaties are different in nature, a different methodological and juristic approach is permissible.

1.7.2 Non-Retroactivity

We have already made reference to the impulse of courts to expand the ambit of liability in cases where particular interests are harmed and for which the law is silent. This phenomenon is more acute in situations where criminal law is not the product of parliamentary legislation but is instead derived from judicial processes, as is the case with the common law.[71] The prohibition against the application of retroactive criminal rules is simple enough. It posits that no one shall be guilty of an act or omission that did not constitute a criminal offence at the time when it was committed.[72] It naturally follows that no one may be deprived of defences or other exculpatory or mitigating elements that were available to him or her at the time when the contested conduct was committed.[73] The arbitrary discretion to introduce new criminal rules is by no means a feature of the past practice of common law courts, but was, and still is, pertinent to any discussion of international criminal tribunals. The Nuremberg Tribunal would ordinarily have been unable to attribute international criminal liability on the basis of the crimes encompassed in its Charter, because the infractions described therein did not possess an international criminal nature prior to its establishment. They were typically viewed as violations that were certainly prohibited, but were not criminal under international law. Criminal liability was only possible under domestic law and moreover the country of which the accused was a national incurred State responsibility. Almost fifty years later the ICTY was faced with an analogous legality question when asked to determine whether or not war crimes committed in domestic armed conflicts gave rise to international criminal liability. Both tribunals (ie the ICTY and Nuremberg) adopted more or less the same approach. Their first argument in support of extending international criminal liability over the conduct charged was legal in nature. It was contended in both cases that the processes of customary international law had in the meantime transformed these conduct rules into criminal offences. The second justification offered by the Nuremberg Tribunal was moral in nature. It asserted that crimes are committed by men and not abstract State entities, whereas the ICTY alleged that the crimes under its jurisdiction were also enacted in the laws of the warring States and as a result their actors were well versed as to their criminal and repugnant character. The Nuremberg argument was framed under the same terms as the so-called 'thin ice' principle, which has been held to postulate that anyone engaging in conduct that is known to him or her to be on the border of illegality assumes a risk of it being labelled as such.[74]

This 'thin ice' principle is, however, a dangerous rule than cannot seriously be sustained in contemporary international law. The ICTY argument is more convincing because it does not purport to suddenly criminalise otherwise permitted conduct –

---

[71] See for example *Shaw v DPP* [1962] AC 220 and *Knuppler v DPP* [1973] AC 435, both of which concerned the formulation of public decency and morals offences by the courts on the alleged ground that they were long recognised as common law offences.

[72] Art 7(1) European Convention on Human Rights (ECHR); Art 22(1) ICC Statute.

[73] As a result, the decision in *R v Howe* [1987] AC 417, by which the accused was denied the defence of duress to a charge of murder, when it had been applied consistently prior to that case, was a blatant violation of Art 7 of the ECHR.

[74] This was expressed in *Knuppler* by Lord Morris. See A Ashworth, *Principles of Criminal Law* (Oxford, Oxford University Press, 2006) 73–74.

even if morally reprehensible – but to import criminality from the domestic to the international sphere. The true test in any event is whether the accused would have been able to mount a reasonable mistake of law defence. Where the 'new' offence could not have *reasonably been foreseen* by the accused it violates the principle against retroactive legislation. The European Commission on Human Rights commented that although it is permissible for an offence to undergo a process of refinement and clarification:[75]

> ... its constituent elements ... may not however be essentially changed to the detriment of an accused and any progressive development by way of interpretation must be reasonably foreseeable to him with the assistance of appropriate legal counsel or advice.[76]

Some crimes, both domestic and international, are not always clear to members of the international community and the same applies to certain modes of participation in crime, their equivalent defences and the jurisdiction of the international tribunal itself.[77] The ICTY and ICTR have at times imported novel modes of participation and challenged the traditional interpretation of the *mens rea* and *actus reus* of international crimes. Their express mandate to apply customary law, although sustained in order to alleviate any concerns that they may be applying retroactive rules, may in fact cause the opposite effect, particularly where a customary norm has not been incorporated in the legislation of concerned States. The importation of customary law in criminal proceedings may sometimes concern a rule that is in practice unknown to some domestic jurisdictions. A point in case is the articulation of the joint criminal enterprise (JCE) doctrine, which is unknown in civil law systems and is sparingly, if any, used in common law jurisdictions, at least under the terms elaborated by the ICTY.[78] Equally, the satisfaction of genocidal intent where the accused perceived his victim as belonging to a distinct racial group, when in fact this perception was wrong,[79] does not conform to the relevant elements in the definition of genocide. The rule to be followed under such circumstances is that the importation

---

[75] In *ICTY Prosecutor v Aleksovski*, Appeals Chamber Judgment (24 Mar 2000), paras 126–27, the accused argued that a subsequent chamber could not overrule a prior judgment by reason of the operation of precedent and that if precedent was overturned the principle against retroactivity would be violated. The Appeals Chamber rejected this contention, stating that the *nullum crimen* rule does not prevent courts from further clarifying and interpreting the elements of particular crimes or of repealing prior judgments.

[76] *CR v UK*, Report of the Eur Comm HR (27 Jun 1994), para 49. Reference to the Commission arose as a result of the famous case of *R v R* [1992] 1 AC 599, in which a husband was accused of raping his wife, even though a long line of authority had previously resisted the legal propriety of this eventuality, particularly in the absence of common law and statutory provisions to this effect.

[77] Some authors have asserted that the jurisdiction of the ad hoc tribunals violated the fair notice principle. See L May, *Crimes Against Humanity: A Normative Account* (Cambridge, Cambridge University Press, 2005) 109.

[78] See chapter 3.2.

[79] *ICTR Prosecutor v Rutaganda*, Trial Chamber Judgment (6 Dec 1999), para 58; but see chapter 9.4 for a discussion of group membership for the purposes of genocide.

of progressive interpretations, customary crimes, defences and modes of participation is permissible if they are deemed to be *foreseeable* to the accused.[80]

The stance of the European Court of Human Rights on foreseeability in respect of international crimes is expansive. It has, for example, accepted the German Federal Constitutional Court's argument that genocidal intent does not require biological or physical destruction – a fact that does not conform to treaty law – on the basis of scholarly opinion. The Court was content that this wide interpretation was reasonable and foreseeable to the accused.[81] In *Kolk and Kislyiy v Estonia*, in a poorly argued judgment, it held that conduct lawful under USSR law at the time could half a century later be criminalised by the introduction of a new domestic law on the ground that said conduct was a crime under international law at the time committed.[82]

Finally, besides statutory enactments a crime may exist in domestic criminal justice systems by means of its incorporation through a customary rule, albeit not in statute. The problem in this case is that the operation of such a customary rule will not be contemporaneous with the conduct charged, at least *ratione loci*. There is also the additional challenge that one cannot expect each person to know what customary rules his country of nationality or the territorial State has subscribed to, without some written confirmation. As a result, legal certainly may be in doubt where it is unclear whether the offence was foreseeable. In principle, national courts refuse to assess the liability of a person solely on the basis of a newly-incorporated customary rule, in the absence of a statute to the same effect, although some countries are willing to accept quite the opposite.[83] The expansive view of the European Court of Human Rights and of the countries that rely on posterior codification in respect of past crimes suggests an emerging trend whereby the requirement of written law is no

---

[80] This was the rationale of the decision in *ICTY Prosecutor v Hadžihasanović and Others*, Appeals Chamber Decision on Interlocutory Appeal Challenging Jurisdiction in Relation to Command Responsibility (16 Jul 2003), paras 10–36. The Chamber, despite overwhelming evidence that command responsibility liability was not recognised in respect of non-international conflicts at the time when the accused were charged, employed a construction of the doctrine that in its opinion should logically be applied beyond international armed conflicts.

[81] *Jorgić v Germany*, Eur Ct HR Judgment (12 Jul 2007), paras 109–13. To its credit the Court argued that in certain circumstances a particular interpretation may offend the requirement of foreseeability, para 109.

[82] *Kolk and Kislyiy v Estonia* Admissibility Decision (17 Jan 2006); in *Kononov v Latvia*, Judgment (24 Jul 2008), which is similar to *Kolk*, the accused had killed a number of civilians who it was alleged were Nazi collaborators. The Court assimilated the victims to combatants and thus held that a subsequent statute which purported to criminalise those acts as war crimes violated the principle of legality.

[83] Exceptionally, in *R v Jones (Margaret)*, [2007] 1 AC 136, paras 27–30, the issue was whether aggression, deemed to be a crime under customary law, was as a result a crime under English law in the absence of a statutory provision. Lord Bingham accepted as a general rule that international crimes may be assimilated into English law, but that this did not follow automatically. He stated that a customary crime 'may, but need not, become part of the domestic law of England without the need for any domestic statute or judicial decision'. This incorporation of customary crimes was subject to two limitations: a) the *Knuller* rule, whereby the courts cannot introduce new crimes, and; b) that Parliament typically enacts statutes in respect of treaty and customary crimes and that if it refuses to do so with regard to a particular offence this is the end of the matter. In the present instance, the International Criminal Court Act 2001 intentionally excluded aggression from its ambit, thus leading to the conclusion that it should not be treated as a domestic crime in England. See R O'Keefe, 'Customary International Crimes in English Courts' (2002) 72 *British Yearbook of International Law* 293.

longer sacred if the existence of any international crime may be derived from customary processes. Readers should approach this trend with caution.

1.7.3 Prohibition of Analogy

Article 22(2) of the ICC Statute states that 'the definition of a crime shall be strictly construed and shall not be extended by analogy'. This provision introduces two principles, namely the prohibition against analogies in the criminal law and the principle of strict construction. Neither is straightforward. If particular conduct is not regulated by a substantive criminal rule no other substantive rule can be employed by reason of analogy to cover the situation. The use of analogies in this manner is an extension of the retroactivity prohibition.[84] This ban on analogies applies strictly in respect of substantive rules (ie those relating to the existence of crimes) but does not operate as a ban on construction by means of general principles, or by reference to the *travaux* of a treaty or other secondary sources of interpretation. For example, if a new weapon were to be used in an armed conflict, such that caused paralysis to its victims, it could not be argued that its users could escape liability because no multilateral treaty regulated its employment. Rather, the general rule encompassed in Article 35(2) of Protocol I of 1977 will find application whether by operation of custom or as a general principle of international criminal law.[85] Equally, in respect of a generally-defined treaty or customary crime whose mental element is not adequately circumscribed, no criminal tribunal, whether domestic or international, can refuse to recognise some *mens rea* standard, given that the offence already exists. It may be that in such circumstances the court will choose the mental standard that is more favourable to the accused, but it cannot refuse the existence of said offence. Quite obviously, a tribunal cannot, for example, deduce by analogy that a particular crime should be endowed with a special intent (*dolus specialis*) on the grounds that the definition of another crime of equal gravity encompasses a special intent of this nature.

As a corollary to the analogy ban most legal systems naturally aim to curb judicial arbitrariness by imposing a strict construction of criminal statutes. This entails a duty to interpret statutes narrowly, which should after all be relatively straightforward given that if national legislatures have followed the specificity rule their criminal statutes would be self-explanatory. In practice, the courts in judicially active jurisdictions have not followed this rule.[86] Equally, such an imposition would have been far too onerous on the ad hoc tribunals for Yugoslavia and Rwanda, given that their Statutes provided little or no clues as to the material and mental elements of the

---

[84] *Kokkinakis* judgment, para 52.

[85] According to this, 'it is prohibited to employ weapons, projectiles and material and methods of warfare of a nature to cause superfluous injury or unnecessary suffering'.

[86] See Ashworth, *Principles*, 79–82.

applicable crimes and moreover they were mandated to apply customary international law. A strict construction has also proved very difficult in the early jurisprudence of the ICC, where despite the clear and unambiguous wording of Article 30 of its Statute on the general *mens rea* standard (ie intent and knowledge), a decision by a Trial Chamber on the Confirmation of Charges in the *Lubanga* case argued that *dolus eventualis* is also applicable.[87]

1.7.4 The *Favor Rei* Rule

The second sentence of Article 22(2) of the ICC Statute reads that: 'in case of ambiguity, the definition [of a crime] shall be interpreted in favour of the person being investigated, prosecuted or convicted'. This principle is also known under another Latin maxim, as *in dubio pro reo*. It applies to all findings required for conviction, including all the elements that make up an offence.[88] In this sense when the evidence is doubtful the accused can challenge a particular element of the *mens rea*, such as his knowledge of the existence of an armed conflict,[89] or conflicting witness statements as to the *actus reus*. The *favour rei* principle is also consistent with the presumption of innocence and the burden of proof beyond a reasonable doubt rule, of which they are a necessary extension. Moreover, it is a direct corollary of the analogy ban, albeit the dividing line between the two is marginal. In practice, judges do not go out of their way to construe criminal rules in a way that favours the accused; this is rather exceptional.[90] Instead, the practice of the ad hoc tribunals suggests that only rarely will judges support a measure in favour of the accused (in the presence of two conflicting rules) and then only either at the appellate level, or where they have exhausted all other means in their arsenal. I need only refer once again to the introduction of the JCE principle, the extension of command responsibility to non-international armed conflicts, the legalisation of abductions[91] and others.

In the *Furundzija* case, the ICTY was faced with the task of ascertaining the status of forced oral penetration in international law; that is, whether it should be classified as rape and therefore carry a heavier sentence, or as mere sexual abuse. The chamber correctly went through the relevant primary sources, finding that neither treaty nor customary international law had dealt with this matter until then. In its investigation of the treatment of the offence in the criminal justice legislation of a good number of

---

[87] *ICC Prosecutor v Lubanga*, Trial Chamber Decision on Confirmation of Indictment (29 Jan 2007), para 352. See chapter 2.4.

[88] *ICTY Prosecutor v Limaj, Bala and Musliu*, Appeals Chamber Judgment (27 Sep 2007), para 21.

[89] *ICTY Prosecutor v Naletilić and Martinović*, Appeals Chamber Judgment (3 May 2006), para 120.

[90] In *ICTR Prosecutor v Akayesu*, Trial Chamber Judgment (2 Sep 1998), paras 500–01 the term 'killing' was construed to encompass only intentional, as opposed to unintentional, homicides; equally, in *ICTY Prosecutor v Krstić*, Trial Chamber Judgment (2 Aug 2001), para 502, the offence of extermination was interpreted as embracing the destruction of a numerically significant part of the population concerned, rather than merely a part of the population.

[91] *ICTR Prosecutor v Barayagwiza*, Appeals Chamber Decision on Request for Review or Reconsideration (31 Mar 2000).

States it came to the realisation of an equal split between the various legal systems under scrutiny. As a result, no general principle of criminal law could be found to exist.[92] Instead of classifying the conduct of the accused as sexual abuse, which would have been more favourable to him, it continued its search further and discovered what it called general principles of international criminal law. From there it was not a long leap to argue that since this conduct violated human dignity, which was the raison d'etre of these principles, it should be classified as rape.[93] One should contrast this judicial reasoning with the clear injunction in Article 24(2) of the ICC Statute, which reads that:

> In the event of a change in the law applicable to a given case prior to a final judgment, the law more favourable to the person being investigated, prosecuted or convicted shall apply.

The *favor rei* rule is not meant to favour the accused under any circumstances. Thus, where D has sex with children in a country where this conduct is not criminal or in respect of which persons are not prosecuted, but is otherwise prohibited under his home State, the courts will not generally enforce the more favourable rule, because it offends fundamental notions of justice. It is clear in such cases that the accused is forum shopping for the most favourable criminal law but knows all too well that his or her conduct is prohibited. Thus, once more, the foreseeability rule will come into operation.

1.8   Statutes of Limitation for International Crimes

Statutes of limitations are rules that prescribe limits to the time for which conduct can be prosecuted. These rules therefore set out an expiration period, during which the authorities must prosecute the accused, failing which the liability of the accused is extinguished.[94] The effect of statutes of limitation is similar to amnesties, albeit the justificatory reasons behind each of these is distinct; whereas the aim of amnesties is to bring about national reconciliation, limitation statutes are typically concerned with the avoidance of perpetual persecutions and are thus only indirectly related to the primary objective of amnesties. Perpetual prosecutions involve significant financial resources, increased personnel allocation and in the passage of time they may turn out to be socially or politically inexpedient in respect of particular types of conduct or perpetrators. It is no wonder therefore that no customary rule exists which would serve to render statutory limitations impermissible. This is so, firstly, because the two agreements on the matter, the 1968 UN Convention on the Non-Applicability of Statutory Limitations to War Crimes and Crimes Against Humanity and the 1974 Council of Europe's Statutory Limitations Convention under more or less the same terms have been sparsely ratified. Secondly, it is true that the statutes of international criminal courts either explicitly refute the validity of statutory limitations, such as Article 29 of the ICC Statute, or implicitly, as is the case with the ad hoc tribunals.

---

[92] *ICTY Prosecutor v Furundžija*, Trial Chamber Judgment (10 Dec 1998), para 182.
[93] Ibid, para 183.
[94] RA Kok, *Statutory Limitations in International Criminal Law* (The Hague, TMC Asser Press, 2007).

The practice in domestic jurisdictions does not suggest that States are willing to accept a general rule that prevents them from setting firm expiration dates, although the inconsistency in State practice is mostly attributable to historical, social and political realities.[95] International tribunals, on the other hand, acting within their sphere of judicial activism generally support the view that statutory limitations to serious international crimes are impermissible.[96]

Just like amnesties, it is fair to say that statutory limitations to international crimes are impermissible under international law and by implication within international institutions, but there is no general rule that prohibits States from applying them at the domestic level.[97]

1.9   Justificatory Bases for International Trials and the Quest for Legitimacy

The justification of punishment is inherent in the operation of criminal law, but it is not a purpose within itself; that is, whereas punishment is legalised through the processes of criminal law its legitimacy is derived from the proven veracity of the rationale for which it is imposed. The typical justifications for punishment in domestic legal systems include general and special deterrence, incapacitation, rehabilitation and retribution. With respect to the most serious of international offences, such as war crimes and crimes against humanity, these justifications carry little value. For example, the deterrence of mid-level executioners is hardly warranted given that it is unlikely that they will ever find themselves in a situation of mass criminality or of an armed conflict; the same rationale is obviously true in respect of incapacitation. This is not to say that such measures are unlikely to have any impact in the international sphere at all. It is certainly prudent to go after the planners and instigators of genocide and other mass crimes because of the likelihood that they may once more turn against their perceived opponents given their rein of power.

In addition to the aforementioned justifications, however, the protagonists of international criminal law have asserted other objectives that to a large degree reflect the magnitude of the crimes concerned. These include: national reconciliation, the writing of a historical record and providing victims with a voice.[98] Laudable as these objectives may be, they certainly cannot function as the sole rationales for international criminal justice, because their purposes may just as well be served by truth commissions, amnesties and the pouring of international financial aid to devastated

---

[95]   Thus in the *Barbie* case, Judgment (26 Jan 1984), 78 ILR 132, the French Court of Cassation held that crimes against humanity were not subject to a statute of limitations under customary law. In a subsequent decision issued on 20 December 1985, 78 ILR 136, it accepted that war crimes alone were subject to a statutory limitation; other States are quite happy to ban all statutory limitations in respect of all serious international crimes, such as s 5 of the 2002 German Code of Crimes against International Law.

[96]   *Furundžija* Trial Judgment, para 157, in respect of torture; *Chumbipuma Aguirre and Others v Peru* (Barrios Altos case), IACHR Judgment (14 Mar 2001), para 41, (2002) 41 ILM 93.

[97]   Certain recent treaties, such as Art 29 of the UN Convention against Corruption request State parties to affix longer than usual statutes of limitation, or 'to provide for the suspension of the statute where the alleged offender has evaded the administration of justice'.

[98]   See L Douglas, *The Memory of Judgment: Making Law and History in the Trials of the Holocaust* (New Haven, Yale University Press, 2001).

communities. These objectives, if viewed as exclusive or primary, raise additional questions of legitimacy because by their very nature they are not meant to determine whether a person is liable for a crime, but only the impact of the crime on the victims, thus taking liability for granted. On the contrary, it is wholly legitimate to construct a record of events following the conclusion of fair criminal proceedings on the basis of the evidence collected. The danger otherwise is that certain events are presumed *a priori* to have taken place by particular individuals and thus the record is not written in accordance with the accumulation of undoubted evidence. Equally, when the primary goal of a trial is to provide a voice to the victims the guilt of certain persons is presumed and this is dangerous for the impartiality and independence of any criminal tribunal. In the *Plavšić* case, the accused was co-President of the Serbian Republic of Bosnia and Herzegovina between February and May 1992, occupying thereafter other significant posts within the Bosnian Serb leadership. Having been informed of an indictment against her she surrendered to the ICTY and entered a guilty plea with regard to a wide range of crimes against humanity. A number of mitigating factors were set out by Plavšić, among which was that her unequivocal guilty plea, surrender and acceptance of responsibility contributed to the establishment of truth and was a significant effort towards the advancement of reconciliation. The Trial Chamber went to great pains to demonstrate that the process of reconciliation was one of its primary aims, besides retribution, and that the accused's full disclosure and acceptance of responsibility facilitated the purpose and processes of reconciliation, thus indeed constituting a mitigating factor.[99]

Whatever the merit of these additional objectives (ie truth, historical record and reconciliation), which I find significant and convincing as part of the overall process, their attainment has only been pursued through the vehicle of trials, not punishment.[100] Thus, the Allies rejected the idea of assassinating the Nazi high command, even though hinted by Churchill, because it was felt that a mere execution would serve to cover truth and would not bring about the full gamut of Nazi crimes. Equally, the ICTY's non-binding injunction to peace-enforcement missions in Bosnia was to apprehend the accused under secret indictments and bring them back alive to stand on trial. It certainly did not prefer them dead. This is because international trials are able to fulfil two fundamental functions. The first concerns the justifications already pointed out. The second is legal in nature. Trials express and project the validity of international norms in a way that punishment alone cannot. They help to de-politicise acts of barbarity by turning them into legally enforceable criminal violations, making it clear that they do not belong outside the realm of law.[101]

That international tribunals are established by a legal process, ie Security Council resolutions or multilateral treaties, does not necessarily make them legitimate. Whereas legality refers to a determinate value in the law, in the sense that a proposition is either legal or illegal, legitimacy refers to a proposition that may or

[99] *ICTY Prosecutor v Plavšić*, Sentencing Judgment (27 Feb 2003), paras 79–81.

[100] D Luban, 'Fairness to Rightness: Jurisdiction, Legality and the Legitimacy of International Criminal Law' Georgetown Public Law Research Paper No 1154117 (Jul 2008) 7–9.

[101] RA Duff, *Trials and Punishments* (Cambridge, Cambridge University Press, 1986) 235ff, for an account of expressive theories of punishment in the domestic setting; Luban, 'Fairness to Rightness', 10.

may not be legal, albeit it is perceived as fair, appropriate or desirable within the system of norms, values and beliefs in which it is set.[102] Legitimacy therefore involves the pursuit of external moral approval and is not a concept that falls within the ambit of law; it is extra-legal. For obvious reasons, the objective of legitimacy (ie external approval) is rarely ever universal given the diverse interests of those stakeholders making up the international community, from States to NGOs. By way of example, the assumption of universal jurisdiction by some States over wholly extraterritorial offences, although premised on parliamentary statute and thus legal, has been attacked as an emanation of neo-colonialism, particularly where it concerns the prosecution of officials of one's former colonies. Most international efforts to prosecute persons for serious international crimes have been accused as suffering from a legitimacy deficit, as opposed to a legality deficit. The most common accusation is that of 'victors' justice'. Another concerns the fact that few weak States are able to oppose the expansive interpretation of treaty bodies and their assumption of powers, which it is alleged leads to the creation of institutions and norms which are forced upon them.[103] It is for this reason that hybrid tribunals have been set up on the basis of a process that is locally-owned and a particular manifestation of which is the parallel use of domestic criminal law and local judges, albeit in an otherwise international tribunal. These forms of international criminal justice have generally served to alleviate legitimacy concerns and remedy any democratic deficit. In turn, the process of establishing tribunals, truth commissions and the application of international penal rules will be judged for its procedural legitimacy[104] because its legality is not denied. The legitimacy of these institutions will generally be perceived as lacking where double standards are employed, the rules used are imprecise and the powers of the relevant actors (ie judges, prosecutors and creators) are ill-defined or unnecessarily vague.[105]

[102] For example, the abduction of Eichmann by Israeli agents was illegal under international law because it violated Argentine sovereignty; yet, because of the repugnant crimes committed by the accused it was universally perceived as legitimate.

[103] M Kumm, 'The Legitimacy of International Law: A Constitutionalist Framework of Analysis' (2004) 15 *European Journal of International Law* 907.

[104] See generally, TM Franck, *Fairness in International Law and Institutions* (Oxford, Oxford University Press, 1998) 25–46, where he focuses on the procedural legitimacy of international rules by reference to four distinct properties of the rule. These are its coherence, determinacy, symbolic validation through ritual and pedigree and its adherence to a normative hierarchy. Franck's idea of procedural legitimacy, through the interaction of these properties, concerns the degree to which the rule will be obeyed by States and not if it is necessarily perceived as fair by individual stakeholders.

[105] Art 53(1)(c) of the ICC Statute allows the Prosecutor to discontinue an investigation, after 'taking into account the gravity of the crime and the interests of victims ... [he finds that] there are nonetheless substantial reasons to believe that an investigation would not serve the interests of justice'. This 'interests of justice' discretion is unnecessarily vague given its tremendous significance; for the Prosecutor may in theory determine that a particular investigation may cause widespread civil unrest or that an inter-State conflict may erupt if it were to accept a Security Council deferral. See D Robinson, 'Serving the Interests of Justice: Amnesties, Truth Commissions and the International Criminal Court' (2003) 14 *European Journal of International Law* 481.

1.10   Lawfare: International Law as a Weapon for the 'Weak'

The concept of 'lawfare' is typically employed in the legal and political literature to denote the communication of international law by non-State actors to the international community about the abusive behaviour of particular States. The contemporary use of the term[106] is linked to former US Air Force Colonel Charles Dunlap who argued that international law was actually impeding US military operations because his country's opponents were using international law through statements or lawsuits to demonstrate that the US was waging wars that were in violation of the letter or spirit of international law.[107] Lawfare is essentially a continuation of war through legal means and usages, along the lines, albeit reversed, of Carl von Clausewitz's famous pronouncement that war is a continuation of politics by other means.[108] It is obvious that for Clausewitz lawfare was an impediment to powerful nations, but a tool for weak nations and other entities. The vilification of this type of lawfare has now become an entrenched political position of the two main target States, ie the USA and Israel. The 2005 US National Defence Strategy claimed that 'the USA will continue to be challenged by those who employ a strategy of the weak using international fora, judicial processes and terrorism', albeit the term lawfare was not used.[109] Israel's frustration is directed at the employment of international humanitarian law by human rights NGOs and pro-Palestinian groups and their sympathisers in order to allegedly discredit Israel's defence of its homeland. Thus many of its senior political and military figures have been accused as war criminals and applications have been lodged before domestic and international tribunals in respect of both criminal and civil cases.[110] Equally, a sizeable campaign by a number of NGOs has taken place since 2002 to indict former US Secretary of Defence Donald Rumsfeld for torture inflicted against persons in the custody of the USA, following the revelation of the so-called torture memos in which he seems to have authorised illegal interrogation techniques. This campaign has been seeking Rumsfeld's criminal liability on the basis of universal jurisdiction through the courts of Germany, France,

---

[106] Its origins, in fact, seem to lie in J Carlson, N Yeomans, 'Whither Goeth the Law: Humanity or Barbarity' in M Smith, D Crossley (eds), *The Way Out: Radical Alternatives in Australia* (London, Landsdowne Press, 1975).

[107] CJ Dunlap, 'Law and Military Interventions; Preserving Humanitarian Values in 21st Century Conflicts' available at: <http://www.duke.edu/~pfeaver/dunlap.pdf>.

[108] See C von Clausewitz, *On War* (1832), trans. A Rapoport (London, Penguin, 1968). Clausewitz defines war 'as an act of violence intended to compel our opposition to fulfil our will'. He then famously goes on to say that 'self-imposed restrictions, almost imperceptible and hardly worth mentioning, termed usages of international law, accompany it without essentially impairing its character', 101.

[109] Department of the Defence, 'The National Defence Strategy of the USA (2005)', available at: <http://www.defenselink.mil/news/Mar2005/d20050318nds1.pdf>, at 5.

[110] See A Herzberg, *NGO "Lawfare": Exploitation of Courts in the Arab-Israeli Conflict* (NGO Monitor Monograph Series, 2008). The author argues, *inter alia*, that this type of lawfare against Israel is evident in attempts to indict former Prime Minister Ariel Sharon in Belgium and Doron Almog for war crimes and crimes against humanity. Equally, this is also true in respect of civil actions in *Matar v Dichter*, 500 F Supp 2d 284 (SDNY, 2007) and *Belhas v Ya'alon*, 466 F Supp 2d 127 (DDC 2006), both of which were dismissed by the courts on account of the defendants' immunities, as well as with a string of cases seeking to block trade with Israel, particularly *Corrie v Caterpillar*, 403 F Supp 2d 1019 (WD Wash, 2005) and *Saleh Hasan v Secretary of State and Industry*, [2007] EWHC 2630. The application for an advisory opinion to the ICJ on the Legality of the Construction of a Wall is also cited as a form of lawfare against Israel.

Spain and the USA.[111] Moreover, NGOs routinely petition governments to abide by their international obligations in order to promote and enforce compliance of international law by other States, thus bringing international law to the forefront of confrontation.[112] That international criminal law is employed in this manner is hardly lamentable. On the contrary, it demonstrates in any particular nation that the rule of law is supreme and that civil society is healthy. It is absurd to argue that the courts would entertain a far-fetched notion or violate domestic law as a result of lobbying or other pressure. International law cannot be viewed as having positive and negative applications or consequences.

Governments, in addition to non-State actors, actively engage in lawfare themselves and when they do so they refrain from employing political or other language but instead employ international law rhetoric. The USA, for example, during the Bush Administration, routinely argued that the detained Al-Qaeda captives were specifically trained to manipulate the US legal system and that the assignment of independent counsel for the accused exacerbated this situation.[113] As a result, it is easier for the US government to justify to its people the impediment of the accused's counsel.[114] In this manner it is claimed that international law is a tool used by the enemy, which must be restricted; or to put it crudely, the argument is that the benefits of international law must only accrue to self-professed democratic peoples and nations, given that everybody else only wants to manipulate it! Israel has taken its lawfare campaign a step further from the USA, by not simply defending its policies and discrediting the 'enemy', but by actively employing international law to promote and legitimise its practices. Daniel Reisner, a former international law advisor to the Israeli Army, stated that his job consisted of finding '*untapped potential in international law* that would allow military actions in the grey zone: International law develops through its violation . . . an act that is forbidden today becomes permissible if executed by enough countries [. . .] If the same process occurred in private law, the legal speed limit would be 115 kilometres an hour and we would pay income tax of 4 percent'.[115] Reisner offered as an example the tactic of targeted killings introduced by Israel and which allegedly had subsequently been accepted by the majority of States.[116] To a large degree, these attempts aim to demonstrate that the existing rules

---

[111] K Gallagher, 'Universal Jurisdiction in Practice: Efforts to Hold Donald Rumsfeld and Other High-Level United States Officials Accountable for Torture' (2009) 7 *Journal of International Criminal Justice* 1087.

[112] *Al-Haq v Secretary of State for Foreign Affairs et al*, which is currently ongoing and concerns the failure of the UK Government to act to promote compliance with humanitarian law under Arts 1 and 146 of Geneva Convention IV (1949) in respect of Operation Cast Lead in December 2008 that left 1300 civilians dead in the Israeli offensive against Gaza.

[113] T Yin, 'Boumediene and Lawfare' (2009) 43 *University of Richmond Law Review* 865, 879ff.

[114] See D Luban, 'Lawfare and Legal Ethics in Guantanamo' (2008) 60 *Stanford Law Review* 1981.

[115] See E Weizman, 'Lawfare in Gaza: Legislative Attack' (1 Mar 2009), available at: <http://www.opendemocracy.net/article/legislative-attack>.

[116] See N Melzer, *Targeted Killings in International Law* (Oxford, Oxford University Press, 2008), who argues that the lawfulness of targeted killings can under extreme circumstances be justified in respect of suicide bombers and some hostage-taking operations and that no new rule is required because the existing legal framework is more than sufficient.

of international law on a particular matter cannot meet the exigencies of contemporary security situations, or that an exception to an otherwise sufficient rule is warranted for humanitarian purposes, as was the case with the NATO Kosovo campaign in 1999.

2

The Subjective and Objective Elements of International Crimes

2.1 General Principles of the Objective Element

International, as well as domestic, crimes are composed of two elements: a) *conduct*, which consists of an act or omission which is prohibited by a positive rule, or which rule otherwise imposes a particular behaviour (*actus reus*), and; b) *an element of volition* to bring about the prohibited conduct, which as a result renders the act blameworthy (*mens rea*).[1] One of the fundamental principles of criminal law is that relating to respect for individual autonomy, in which it is assumed that an individual is free to engage in any conduct or behaviour. It follows that individual autonomy also carries with it the doer's responsibility for the consequences of such conduct.[2] Both elements, objective (the conduct) and subjective (the mental element), are necessary for the satisfaction of a criminal offence, although domestic criminal justice systems regularly recognise crimes for which no mental element is required. These are so-called *strict liability* offences for which the mental state of the accused is irrelevant, as long as it is demonstrated that he or she simply engaged in the prohibited conduct (eg drink driving offences that lead to the death of a third person).[3] Strict liability offences constitute an exception to the fundamental rule that crimes should be constructed on the basis of objective as well as subjective criteria; as a result they are reserved for offences involving lower levels of gravity. Given the serious nature of international crimes, strict liability is not generally accepted.

The relevant processes of criminalisation tend to distinguish between crimes of *conduct* and crimes of *result*. A crime of conduct materialises irrespective of its consequence for the victim, so long as the perpetrator committed the prohibited act with the requisite mental element. For example, in cases where D uses a prohibited weapon or refuses to offer physical protection to a POW under his authority, albeit

---

[1] In classic Islamic legal theory the *mens rea* element of crimes under the Qur'an consists of three components: a) the perpetrator must have had the power to commit or not to commit the prohibited conduct (*qudra*); b) he or she must have known the act was an offence (*ilm*), and; c) the perpetrator must have acted with intent (*qasd*). Criminal intent in Islamic law will be examined more fully later in this chapter. See R Peters, *Crime and Punishment in Islamic Law* (Cambridge, Cambridge University Press, 2005) 20.

[2] A Ashworth, *Principles of Criminal Law* (Oxford, Oxford University Press, 2008) 122–23.

[3] In *Sweet v Parsley* [1970] AC 132 it was held that where a criminal statute is silent on *mens rea*, the courts must presume a culpable mental state into that provision. This presumption was later rebutted in *Gammon v AG Hong Kong* [1985] AC 1 in those cases where public safety was threatened.

none of his victims die as a result, he is nonetheless liable for violating the relevant conduct rule.[4] In both of these cases the conduct is in itself prohibited, regardless of the possible outcome. Conduct crimes are also known as inchoate offences, albeit a very slight theoretical distinction may be discerned between those conduct crimes that are criminal in and of themselves (eg using a prohibited weapon) from those that are not *prima facie* criminal (eg incitement or conspiracy which are rendered criminal on account of the illegality of their purpose) and which are *continuous* in nature, in the sense that the effects of an incitement to commit genocide may provoke and sustain genocide well after the actual incitement or conspiracy.

In situations, however, where the rule in question requires a specific result, the accused is liable only where that result has actually come about. The crime of murder requires the death of the victim, which means that even if the victim is beaten badly but does not die, even if D wished to bring about the victim's death, D will not be liable for murder, but at best for attempted murder or a non-lethal offence against the person. It is evident therefore that in respect of result crimes the *consequence* of D's act is of paramount importance, since the conduct which brought it about may not always be prohibited by a positive rule (or may otherwise amount to a different conduct crime). For example, engaging POWs to dig trenches for the captor is not prohibited, but where a prisoner dies as a result of excessive work and harsh conditions the conduct that brought this result about is culpable. Moreover, the consequence arising from a particular conduct tells us that said conduct caused the consequence, as long as an external intervening act did not break the chain of causation. D is criminally liable for the murder of V where he shot him at close range and where it was D's bullet that caused V to die (assuming of course he intended to kill V). However, where D badly injures V and abandons him to die and as V lays in this condition is shot to the head by A, it is A that would have caused the death of the victim and thus the offence of murder.[5] D will be charged with other offences, particularly attempted murder.

Both crimes of conduct and of result can materialise by means of action as well as omission.[6] Nonetheless, crimes of omission require a pre-existing legal duty between the accused and the victim, stipulated either in specific terms (familial, doctor-patient or other) or generally (commander of occupied territory vis-a-vis the occupied civilian population).

An additional factor pertinent to the objective elements of some crimes is that of *circumstances*. The definitions of certain offences require the satisfaction of *quantitative* and *qualitative* conditions in order for the crime in question to materialise. Certain of these pertain to the *actus reus* of the offence, whereas in respect of others they do not form part of either the objective or the subjective element of the offence. For example, the intentional killing of V constitutes murder in peace time, whereas if perpetrated in an armed conflict it is elevated to a war crime of murder. Moreover, if

---

[4]   Art 13, Geneva Convention III.

[5]   It should be noted that international criminal law does not always require causation, as is the case with the jurisprudence of the ICTY and ICTR which rejects the element of causation in the definition of command responsibility. See chapter 4.1.

[6]   *ICTY Prosecutor v Krstić*, Appeals Chamber Judgment (19 Apr 2004), para 188; *ICC Prosecutor v Lubanga*, Trial Chamber Decision on Confirmation of Indictment (29 Jan 2007), paras 351–55.

committed in the context of a widespread or systematic attack against a civilian population the same conduct amounts to a crime against humanity. Equally, war crimes and grave breaches can only be committed against those protected persons designated as such by the 1949 Geneva Conventions. In all of the above examples, the circumstances relating to the existence of an armed conflict or that of protected persons concern objective conditions of a qualitative nature. On the other hand, crimes or forms of liability requiring a multiplicity of victims or perpetrators encompass quantitative conditions in their relevant definition (eg the requirement of a widespread attack in the context of a crime against humanity). An additional distinction should be made. Circumstances, such as those already described are objective in nature, whereas others are purely subjective, such as the knowledge of the accused as to the protected status of his victim, or of the widespread and systematic character of an attack, or that his conduct risked bringing about a consequence. A significant question arises from the incorporation of *circumstances* in the definition of domestic and international crimes, particularly whether their satisfaction should be encompassed within the objective or subjective element of the crime in question. In some cases the distinction is obvious, whereas in others a *circumstance* may be an element of either the *actus reus* or the *mens rea*, none of the two, or a combination thereof. For example, the circumstance of a widespread or systematic attack in the definition of crimes against humanity forms part of the *mens rea* of the offence, but is also required in the conduct of certain of its authors. The fact of armed conflict, on the other hand, although a circumstance in the definition of war crimes and grave breaches, is not required in the determination of either the objective or the subjective elements of these crimes. In this latter case D's knowledge of the armed conflict is irrelevant to his liability and only impacts on whether his particular conduct will be classified as a murder or a grave breach. Any international or domestic criminal tribunal would take these circumstances into consideration even in the theoretical scenario that the parties chose not to raise them.

That which pertains to the objective element of a crime can only be negated by reference to the objective elements of that crime. What this means in practice is that if D's conduct, although prohibited, is not voluntary that conduct will not be considered blameworthy. For example, where D kills V while in a state of automatism, his blameworthiness will be negated, but not because he is deemed to lack the requisite *mens rea* (ie on account that he never formed an intention to violate the prohibited act). Rather, D is not liable under such circumstances because he cannot be considered as the moral agent of the act, given that his conduct lacks voluntariness. As a result, D's conduct (in relation to the offence) is not the result of him doing something, but of something happening to him.[7] These considerations are crucial for determining the exact place of excuses and justifications in the definition of an international crime.

Finally, although the objective element of most international offences is derived from their counterparts in domestic law, several factors serve to distinguish these from the latter through the passage of time. Firstly, the statutes of international tribunals are drafted in accordance with their contextual underpinnings and as a

---

[7] Ashworth, *Principles*, at 98.

result one can readily discern divergences in the definitions of crimes even among themselves. Secondly, even where a domestic offence is transplanted into an international setting, such as murder or rape, the pertinent *circumstances* incorporated into the international definition, such as the armed conflict, the element of gravity, the vulnerability of victims, the involvement of State officials or paramilitary groups and others, serve to ultimately distort the original definition. Thirdly, when a crime enters the realm of international law it is thereafter construed in accordance with the relevant sources of international law. Finally, the subjective and objective elements of crimes are not identical between the common and civil law traditions and as such any compromise solution will not wholly reflect the law in any of these two traditions or of any particular State.

2.2   General Principles of the Subjective Element

Where D desires to kill V but does not go on to implement this desire he possesses a criminal volition no doubt, but is nonetheless free from liability because he has not satisfied the conduct element of murder. Let us consider, however, the following acts by which D caused the killing of V: a) shooting him in the head at close range; b) shooting him on the foot and consciously leaving him live, although a few days later V meets his final demise, and; c) failing to feed V for a week while under his custody because he was called elsewhere and believed that V would suffer but would survive a week without food. In all three of these situations what the accused desired and what he believed as the outcome of his conduct are different. In the first case his desire and belief as to V's death are unquestioned. In the second and third cases it is not clear that D desires to cause V's death, albeit in both situations D must possess some awareness as to the risk of V dying – assuming of course that D does not already intend V's death through his conduct. If criminal law is to criminalise D's desire or volition in all of these cases it must accordingly construct several degrees of *mens rea*. These largely correspond to *intent*, *recklessness* and *negligence*.

To each crime corresponds a mental element. Yet, simply designating a single mental element in respect of a particular criminal conduct may prove problematic where the definition of an offence must necessarily include additional *circumstances* and *consequences*. This is particularly poignant where international crimes are concerned, because their definitions are complex and are composed of multiple circumstances and consequences. It is for this reason that certain national and international law-makers choose to endow each objective element of such complex offences with its own distinct *mens rea*. Thus, an offence could encompass multiple mental elements within a single definition. This represents the so-called 'element analysis' approach, which inspired the drafters of Article 30 of the ICC Statute.[8] This provision requires a culpable state of mind for each prescribed conduct, consequence and circumstance. This multiple layering of mental elements obviously makes life

---

[8]   PH Robinson, JA Grall, 'Element Analysis in Defining Criminal Liability: The Model Penal Code and Beyond' (1983) 35 *Stanford Law Review* 681.

hard for prosecuting authorities. Its opposing counterpart is the 'offence analysis' approach where the mental element of crimes is defined in general terms and not in respect of each particular material element contained in its definition. This approach was implicitly adopted in the context of the ICTY and ICTR Statutes (ie intent crimes, reckless crimes or a combination of the two).

Some scholars argue that the definitions of certain crimes in the ICC Statute give rise to three quasi-material (otherwise known as contextual) elements that are different from the material elements of *conduct, consequence* and *circumstance*. The first relates to 'legal character' and covers situations such as the protected status of the victim. The second refers to 'value judgments', such as the determination of 'serious injury to body' in Article 7(1)(k) of the ICC Statute. The third concerns 'circumstantial elements', such as the existence of an armed conflict.[9] If the law ascribed a distinct mental state to these quasi-elements there would be a risk that D's subjective opinion would ultimately determine whether a crime had been constituted. As a result, the prevailing opinion is that these quasi-elements are not subject to the general mental qualification of Article 30 of the ICC Statute.[10] What this means is that there is no need to prove D's awareness or volition as to these quasi-material elements.

Finally, it must be strongly emphasised that contemporary criminal law, both domestic and international, recognises two components to all mental elements; a *volitional* (by which D intends, wills or desires to varying degrees) and a *cognitive* (knowledge as to the outcome of one's conduct, or the risk of said conduct).[11] D may certainly intend to kill V, but he is not at all certain that firing a pistol against him from a distance of over a mile can actually bring about that result. D's knowledge as to the harm of killing V is different where he suffocates him and waits until he is no longer conscious. The volitional and cognitive components encompassing the *mens rea* of an offence must meet at the level required, otherwise a lower mental element will be found to exist, which may turn out to be insufficient to satisfy the definition of the offence in question. Thus, if D strongly desires to kill V but is wholly uncertain if his particular method of slow poisoning will bring that result about, D's desire and knowledge fail to meet at the same threshold for murder.

One should distinguish between the cognitive dimension inherent in the *mens rea* formulation of a criminal offence from cognition as a circumstance in the context of an international rule that allows State actors to undertake enforcement action against criminal activities. For example, Article 111(1) of the UN Convention on the Law of the Sea (UNCLOS) allows non-flag States to commence hot pursuit against a foreign vessel on the high seas if they have 'good reason to believe' that said vessel has

---

[9] M Badar, 'The Mental Element in the Rome Statute of the International Criminal Court: A Commentary from a Comparative Criminal Law Perspective' (2008) 19 *Criminal Law Forum* 473, 477–78.

[10] Ibid, at 478. This was also confirmed in *ICC Prosecutor v Bemba*, Trial Chamber Decision on Confirmation of Charges (15 Jun 2009), para 194.

[11] *ICTY Prosecutor v Blaškić*, Appeals Chamber Judgment (29 Jul 2004), para 41; for a detailed analysis of *mens rea* theory, see J Hall, *General Principles of Criminal Law*, 2nd edn (New Jersey, LawBook Exchange, 2005) 180ff; G Williams, *The Mental Element in Crime* (Jerusalem, Magnes Press, 1965) 20. This distinction is slowly trickling down in the text of recent treaties dealing with transnational crime, as is the case with Art 28 of the UN Convention against Corruption which recognises that the offences within its ambit require *intent, knowledge* and *purpose*. This is certainly a crude breakdown of the *mens rea*, but it is representative of a trend whereby international crimes are better defined by their drafters.

committed a violation in the coastal State's maritime belts. This has been interpreted as requiring either actual knowledge or reasonable suspicion on the part of the pursuing authorities, as opposed to a mere suspicion of criminal activity.[12] It is clear therefore that the cognitive requirement in Article 111(1) UNCLOS is unrelated to the subjective element of a crime, but is a mere circumstance in the entitlement of hot pursuit.

Let us now examine the various degrees of *mens rea*, as these are found in the jurisprudence of the ad hoc tribunals and the Statute of the ICC. In particular, the analysis will focus on *dolus*/intent (of the first and second degree), recklessness, negligence and special intent (or *dolus eventualis*).

2.3 Intent or *Dolus*

Despite the complexities associated with the legal definition of *intent* its lay counterpart is not far removed from its common meaning. In general terms it means acting with a desire to bring about a particular result. In the civil law tradition this desire (ie intent) is not an autonomous form of *mens rea*; rather, it is simply an element that is part of the broader mental state of *dolus* (dol, Vorsatz).[13] This broader mental element, the *dolus*, consists of a very high degree of awareness as to the necessary features of the *actus reus*, in addition to the desire to bring it about.[14] Depending on the intensity of one's will and his awareness of all relevant factors lower degrees of *dolus* may be established (such as *dolus eventualis*). In the common law tradition awareness is more or less implicit in situations where D desires to bring about a particular consequence and commits a criminal act in pursuance of that desire. This desire alone (coupled with the implicit awareness that is taken for granted in such circumstances) suffices to satisfy the mental state of *direct intent* (or *dolus directus* of the first degree). The requirement of *knowledge* or *awareness* in the common law tradition becomes explicit in all the mental elements that are lower than direct intent because in respect of these it is not always obvious that knowledge and desire coincide. The alternative variation of intent (other than direct) in English criminal law is so-called *oblique intent*, which is distinguished from direct intent by reason of D's knowledge – although it is best to call it *perception* – as to the consequence of his conduct. Thus, where D locks V in a remote and sealed house and sets fire to it with the desire to kill him, he is said to be acting with direct intent to kill V. Both his desire and knowledge as to the consequence coincide and his knowledge of all relevant factors is taken for granted because of the undoubted nature of his conduct.

---

[12] *Saint Vincent and the Grenadines v Guinea* (The *M/V Saiga*) *(No 2)*, Judgment (1 Jul 1999), Judgment on Merits, (1999) 38 ILM 1323, para 147. See chapter 14.8.

[13] M Bohlander, *Principles of German Criminal Law* (Oxford, Hart Publishing, 2009) 60–63.

[14] J Pradel, *Droit Pénal Général*, 16th edn (Paris, Cujas, 2006) 244.

As a result, the two legal traditions are not all that distinct given the equivalency between direct intent and *dolus directus* of the first degree.[15] However, their proximity is better demonstrated by reference to *oblique intent*. Where D desires to kill V who is travelling in an aircraft carrying twenty other passengers by blowing up the aircraft in mid-flight, but without having any motive or desire to kill or injure the other passengers, it would be absurd to exculpate him for the other twenty deaths simply because he did not possess a desire (intent) to kill them. It is at this juncture that the incorporation of the element of awareness of outcome is crucial to the conduct of D. In English law where D, as per the above example involving the destruction of the aircraft in flight, is virtually certain that his conduct will bring about a certain result, even though he may not desire it, he is presumed to be acting with intent to bring that result about (oblique intent).[16] His lack of desire to kill the twenty passengers is wholly irrelevant. This largely corresponds to the civil law notion of *dolus directus* of the second degree.[17] The preceding analysis was not undertaken with a view to simply outlining a comparative criminal perspective of intent, although this was indeed one of my principal purposes. Rather, as a result of this convergence the ad hoc tribunals have been able to apply a consistent theory of *mens rea* into their proceedings.

Intention or *dolus* was never defined in international law. All the post-WWII treaties, particularly the 1949 Geneva Conventions, the 1977 Protocols thereto, as well as specific treaties dealing with torture, apartheid, slavery and others never envisaged the creation of international tribunals. As a result, the understanding was that as long as the material and jurisdictional elements of the offence, or the regulation of conduct, was sufficiently described, any subsequent infractions would be prosecuted under implementing criminal legislation before domestic courts where the subjective elements of crimes would be premised on long-standing and well defined *mens rea* standards. This does not mean that the aforementioned treaties make no reference to mental standards whatsoever. Rather, it is not clear what they

---

[15] In Islamic criminal law the concept of criminal intent is quite complex and only tangentially corresponds to the *dolus directus* doctrine of the European legal systems. Generally, it is held that in respect of injury crimes the perpetrator is strictly liable, regardless of any intent, but the exact nature of his liability depends on what he wished to achieve through his conduct. This is obviously incongruous and represents an intention-based strict liability test! Muslim scholars, particularly those adherent to the Hanafi school, distinguish between: a) intentional (*amd*) homicide; b) accidental (*khata*) homicide, and; c) quasi-intentional homicide (*amd al-khata*), which is not, however, accepted by the Maliki school. While *amd* obviously corresponds to *dolus directus* of the first degree, the third type, *amd al-khata*, is described as striking knowingly but without an intention to kill. This is tantamount to *dolus directus* of the second degree and this is particularly so because of the requirement of *amd* in its definition. In respect of all three categories of intent the perpetrator is equally liable, albeit jurists realised the consequence of ascribing any of these mental elements with regard to *hadd* (corporal punishment) offences and used them sparingly. Three factors are generally required for the purpose of substantiating the existence of *amd*: a) the type of action; b) the instrument or weapon used and the normal expected use of such weapon; c) the physical and social context of the conduct. See P R Powers, *Intent in Islamic Law: Motive and Meaning in Medieval Sunni Fiqh* (Leiden, Brill, 2005) 173–76. It should be noted that there does not exist a single Islamic criminal law and moreover within Muslim-majority States the prevalence of Islamic law varies significantly. I Bantekas, 'The Disunity of Islamic Criminal Law and the Modern Role of Ijtihad' (2009) 9 *International Criminal Law Review* 651.

[16] *R v Nedrick* (1996) 83 Cr App R 267, and particularly as later clarified in *R v Woolin* [1999] AC 82.

[17] See Badar, *The Mental Element*, at 486, who cites the judgment of the German Federal Supreme Court of Justice (*Bundesgerichtshof-BGH*), *BGHSt* 21, 283 (vol 2, at 283), wherein it was held that a perpetrator who foresees a consequence of his conduct as certain is deemed to be acting willfully with regard to this consequence, even if he regrets its occurrence.

mean by the use of the terms 'wilful' or 'wilfully', particularly as these are employed to describe the mental state required for the perpetration of grave breaches in the context of international armed conflicts.[18] The ICRC Commentary to Article 85 of the 1977 Protocol I although identifying *wilfulness* as synonymous to *intent*, goes on to encompass also under the same terminology the conduct of a person who 'without being certain of a particular result, accepts the possibility of it happening'.[19] This suggests, if correct and not simply the product of confusion or misunderstanding, that in respect of grave breaches not only intent (of the first and second degree) but also *recklessness* or *dolus eventualis* suffice for the attribution of liability to the accused. This is certainly the understanding of the ad hoc tribunals that have interpreted the term *wilfully*, as this emanates from the relevant grave breaches provisions.[20] The same result must equally be presumed in relation to treaties, such as the 1984 UN Torture Convention, Article 1(1) of which requires the element of *intent* in the definition of torture.

The situation of intent of the first and second degree in the context of the ICC Statute is certainly a lot clearer because the drafters of the Statute paid attention to the need to clarify the various mental states so as to leave no room for arbitrary analogies or judicial innovations. Article 30 of the ICC Statute is adamant from the outset that the general rule applicable to all its crimes and forms of liability will be *intent* and *knowledge*. As a result, all lower mental standards (ie recklessness, *dolus eventualis*, negligence) are excluded from its ambit, in contradistinction to the unambiguous jurisprudence of the ad hoc tribunals. This general rule is subject to a notable exception however. 'Unless otherwise provided' by the terms of a specific crime or form of liability, in which case the mental element designated therein will apply, the general rule of intent and knowledge will be applicable. Given that some crimes and liability forms are indeed endowed with their own distinct mental element, such as Article 28 dealing with command responsibility, mental standards lower than intent of the first and second degree are thus only exceptionally admitted into the ICC Statute.[21]

The meaning of *intent* in Article 30 of the ICC Statute is further qualified, depending on whether the material element of the offence relates to conduct or consequence. D possesses intent in relation to particular conduct where he 'means to engage in the conduct',[22] whereas he is said to possess intention in relation to a consequence if he 'means to cause that consequence' or 'is aware that it will occur in the ordinary course of events'.[23] As to intent relating to conduct it must be shown that D voluntarily desired to engage in particular conduct with knowledge of those facts that would make his conduct illegal. Intent as to consequence is clearly

---

[18] These terms are employed especially in Art 130 Geneva Convention III and Art 85(3), Protocol I (1977).

[19] C Pilloud, J De Preux *et al*, *Commentary on the Additional Protocols of 8 June 1977 Additional to the 1949 Geneva Convention* (Geneva, Martinus Nijhoff, 1987) 994–95.

[20] *Krstić* Trial Judgment, para 511; *ICTY Prosecutor v Delalić and Others* [*Čelebići* case], Trial Chamber Judgment, (16 Nov 1998), paras, 433, 511; *Blaškić* Trial judgment (3 Mar 2000), para 152.

[21] See G Werle, F Jessberger, 'Unless Otherwise Provided: Article 30 of the ICC Statute and the Mental Element of Crimes under International Criminal Law' (2005) 3 *Journal of International Criminal Justice* 35.

[22] Art 30(2)(a) ICC Statute.

[23] Art 30(2)(b) ICC Statute.

composed of two separate mental states. Meaning to cause a consequence requires a conscious and purposeful desire, irrespective of the outcome of one's conduct. This first alternative therefore is tantamount to *direct intent* or *dolus directus* (*Absicht*), or *dolus directus of the first degree*. In fact, the *Lubanga* decision on the Confirmation of Charges made it clear that where D undertakes particular conduct with the concrete intention to actuate the material element of a crime in the knowledge that this will come about possesses *dolus directus* of the first degree.[24] The second alternative of intent as to consequences suggests a mental state akin to the notion of oblique intent, in those cases where D although perhaps not willing to activate the *actus reus* of a particular crime is fully aware of what "will occur" and that this is a necessary outcome of his conduct.[25]

Let us now examine the status of other lower mental standards in the workings of international criminal tribunals and whether any of these may be validly imported in the general rule contained in Article 30 of the ICC Statute, despite the clear injunction against such an eventuality.

2.4 Recklessness and *Dolus Eventualis*

It should be stated from the outset that I find no substantive differences between these two mental states, albeit one may truly discern terminological, cultural or other distinctions depending on the theoretical approaches employed in the various jurisdictions. Nonetheless, these have no impact on the essence of their subject matter. Acting with recklessness is generally defined in the common law as undertaking an unjustifiable and significant risk. This gives rise to a significant problem. If D is a military commander who desires to neutralise enemy artillery that is situated in the middle of a densely inhabited village by bombarding that part of the village he risks causing civilian casualties. True enough, in this scenario D is assuming an unjustifiable risk. But is this fact alone sufficient to ground a conviction for wilfully targeting civilians? What if the enemy's artillery battery was not visible to D who in the midst and urgency of combat was only handed the coordinates of the battery and nothing more? It would be unfair to hold D liable for the underlying offence simply because he took an unjustifiable risk, especially when he was not aware of all relevant circumstances and thus of the risk itself. Thus, recklessness requires the taking of a risk in the knowledge, or with foresight, that it is unjustifiable, despite the fact that D did not wish that risk to materialise. As a result, D's order to target the enemy battery in the knowledge, or foresight, that given the close proximity of civilians there was a probability that some would be injured or even killed gives rise to culpability on the basis of recklessness. It is obvious therefore that recklessness requires not only an element of volition, but also a degree of knowledge. The problem identified in this equation goes as follows: risks by their very nature relate to uncertain and unstable

---

[24] *Lubanga* Trial Decision on Confirmation of Charges, para 351.
[25] This mental state was classified by the *Lubanga* Decision, ibid, para 352, as *dolus directus* of the second degree.

future events in respect of which knowledge, in the sense of *dolus directus*, is impossible. Therefore, to demand of D knowledge of uncertain events would in most cases negate any *mens rea* because D could argue that he does not possess prophetic powers. Hence, it is not *knowledge* in the broad sense that is required in recklessness but *appreciation* of the possibility of the risk and a conscious volition that it may in fact come about. As a result, any assessment of a reckless mental state is premised on the subjective appreciation of the accused.

In the manner described above recklessness does not seem to differ from the concept of *dolus eventualis* as this has developed in civil law jurisdictions.[26] Despite the theoretical disagreements between criminal law scholars, this mental state requires both a volitional element and a foresight of concrete possibility in such a way that D reconciles himself with the prohibited conduct. This is markedly different from the 'virtual certainty' required in the case of *dolus directus* of the second degree. The jurisprudence of the ad hoc tribunals has rightly conflated *dolus eventualis* and recklessness, taking them to convey the same legal meaning, encompassing 'an awareness of a higher likelihood of risk' and a conscious desire to take it nonetheless.[27]

Recklessness, as indeed *dolus eventualis*, is confined solely to those risks in respect of which D possesses advertence, that is, not only foresight but also a mental consideration of those risks. Therefore, where D does not make the mental effort to see the consequence of his conduct or to consider the possible risks involved (essentially he has no appreciation of the risk) he is said to be negligent, not reckless. This position has only recently concretised in English criminal law (inadvertent recklessness which now qualifies as negligence),[28] despite its long-standing tradition in civil law jurisdictions.

Given the express rejection of lower mental standards (other than the two strands of *dolus directus*) from the general rule in Article 30 of the ICC Statute, it came as a great surprise when the *Lubanga* Confirmation Decision ruled that *dolus eventualis* could in fact be read in this provision.[29] The Lubanga Decision essentially distinguished between advertent and inadvertent recklessness, holding that only the former qualifies as *dolus eventualis*.[30] The admission of *dolus eventualis* was justified in respect of Article 30 of the ICC Statute by the fact that co-perpetration requires an awareness of the substantial likelihood that implementing the common plan would result in the realisation of the *actus reus* of the offence.[31] This is similar to the foresight of probability required for recklessness and *dolus eventualis*. A wholly antithetical position was, however, adopted by a subsequent Trial Chamber in the *Bemba* Confirmation Decision. There it was held that not only was *dolus eventualis* excluded by its drafters from the ambit of Article 30 of the Statute, but the words 'will occur' – referring to the criminal consequence – read together with the phrase 'in

---

[26] Bohlander, *Principles*, at 63, makes the point that German law possesses no category of *mens rea* that fully equals the concept of recklessness as found in English law.

[27] *Blaškić* Appeal Judgment, para 41; *ICTY Prosecutor v Stakić*, Trial Chamber Judgment (31 Jul 2003), para 587.

[28] *R v G* [2004] 1 AC 1034; see generally, Ashworth, *Principles*, at 181–86.

[29] *Lubanga* Confirmation of Charges Decision, para 352.

[30] Ibid, paras 353–55.

[31] Ibid, paras 361–65.

the ordinary course of events' clearly suggests a mental standard in which foresight of a criminal consequence must be virtually certain.[32] The rationale of this judgment is a clear suggestion in favour of the English notion of recklessness. If this is the final word of the ICC chambers, it waits to be seen, although this is the solution that best conforms to the letter of Article 30. It should be stated, however, that the relevant scholarship militates either in favour of the future incorporation of *dolus eventualis* in the ICC Statute because of its general acceptance in international law,[33] or its implicit recognition therein by reason of the fact that there exist more cognitive concepts of *dolus eventualis* requiring awareness or certainly as to a consequence.[34] In any event, irrespective of its admission in the ICC Statute, it is a *mens rea* standard acceptable in international law generally and the jurisprudence of the ad hoc tribunals in particular.

2.5 Negligence

Negligence-based liability is exceptional in domestic criminal justice systems and is typically reserved for those types of conduct that result in the most minimum of harm. Given the severity of international crimes generally this mental state is unlikely to find any serious application therein. There is yet another reason against the wholesale importation of negligence from the domestic sphere; where it is sustained it may serve to not only mitigate punishment but to alter the offence. In the case of murder, D's negligent mental state turns the offence into manslaughter, a practice that is unknown in the law of international criminal tribunals. Overall, negligence does not require knowledge or appreciation of a risk, particularly where the risk is not very significant; yet, the law demands of everyone to think about the consequences of our actions and to exercise a certain degree of diligence. Where D is entrusted with guarding a POW that unknown to him is diabetic, D is acting negligently if he leaves him in a cell without insulin for a number of days and V dies. The law expects from D to make some enquiry about the health of each POW, even if only to ask that person about the state of his or her health. Domestic laws also expect from certain classes of professionals or persons entrusted with the welfare of others to maintain a standard of care that is inherent in their particular function. For example, in the case of *Adomako* the accused was an anaesthesiologist charged with gross negligence manslaughter because during an operation one of the tubes supplying the patient with oxygen became disconnected, which he failed to notice and the patient died as a result. It was held that for this type of manslaughter to arise D must have breached a duty of care towards V; that said breach caused V's death, and; that the breach amounted to gross negligence.[35]

---

[32] *Bemba* Confirmation of Charges Decision, para 362.
[33] M Badar, 'Dolus Eventualis and the Rome Statute Without It' (2009) 12 *New Criminal Law Review* 433.
[34] K Ambos, 'Critical Issues in the Bemba Confirmation Decision' (2009) 22 *Leiden Journal of International Law* 715.
[35] *R v Adomako* [1995] 1 AC 171.

Given our discussion so far in this chapter it is evident that some space for the employment of negligence in international criminal proceedings may eventually exist. No doubt, although negligence cannot support the mental element of international crimes, it may prove useful with respect to certain contextual (or quasi-material) elements of crimes, where this is warranted by their definition. Equally, it may be pertinent in situations involving a duty of care, as in the case of command responsibility. In the former case, an ICC Trial Chamber in the *Lubanga* Confirmation Decision, while assessing the liability of the accused in relation to charges of conscription and enlistment of children below the age of 15 under Articles 8(2)(b)(xxvi) and 8(2)(e)(vii) of the ICC Statute, queried as to the appropriate mental standard pertinent to D's awareness of the children's age. If the general rule of Article 30 was found to be applicable, D's awareness of child enlistment would have to be judged on the basis of intent and knowledge, a standard difficult to satisfy. The Trial Chamber correctly noted that this specific element of the offence requires that the 'perpetrator knew or should have known that such person or persons were under the age of 15 years'. This 'should have known' requirement was found to be an exception to the general *mens rea* rule and in fact imposed a standard of negligence.[36] According to the Trial Chamber, the correct test is that of negligence because it is met when the accused did not know that the victims were under age when enlisting or conscripting them and he 'lacked such knowledge because he or she did not act with due diligence in the relevant circumstances . . . (failing in his or her duty to act with due diligence'.[37]

Equally, in the case of command responsibility superiors are under a duty to prevent or punish subordinate criminality when they are put on notice of such criminality under the 'had reason to know standard'.[38] Failure to act upon such notice amounts to gross negligence because of a superior's duty to assess and act upon such notice when it becomes available to him or her on the basis of the superior's overarching duty to act.

In the context of the secondary legislation of the European Communities the ECJ was asked to determine whether criminal liability based on 'serious negligence' for ship source pollution arising from an EU Framework Decision[39] was compatible with the relevant provisions of the multilateral conventions from which it was inspired, particularly UNCLOS and MARPOL.[40] In finding that 'serious negligence' was not unnecessarily vague and thus consonant with the principle of legality, the ECJ attempted to define it as a matter of general principle. It held that:

[It] must be understood as entailing an unintentional act or omission by which the person responsible commits a patent breach of the duty of care which he should have and could have complied with in view of his attributes, knowledge, abilities and individual situation.[41]

---

[36] *Lubanga* Confirmation of Charges Decision, paras 357–58.

[37] Ibid, para 358.

[38] See chapter 4.4.

[39] Council Framework Decision 2005/667/JHA of 12 July 2005 to Strengthen the Criminal-Law Framework for the Enforcement of the Law against Ship-source Pollution, OJ L 255 (30 Sep 2005), Art 4(6) and (7). This Framework Decision was soon after repealed on procedural grounds.

[40] For a fuller discussion of the issues relative to ship-source pollution, see chapter 14.6.

[41] *International Association of Independent Tanker Owners (Intertanko) and Others v Secretary of State for Transport, Case* C-308/06, ECJ Judgment (3 Jun 2008), para 77.

Clearly, this 'serious negligence' standard is no different from the gross negligence tests employed in the vast majority of legal systems and which presuppose a duty of care. It is important to note of course that unlike my general comment in the beginning of this section, the harm resulting as a result of ship-source pollution is hardly minimal. No wonder, this *mens rea* standard was vociferously resisted by the shipping industry and the big shipping powers.

2.6 Special Intent

Certain international crimes are composed of both a generic and an additional special intent (*dolus specialis*). Thus, for example, in the case of genocide the generic intent relates to the commission of any conduct that leads to the killing of members of the group, prevention of births and others. The special intent in genocide consists of committing these crimes with the intent of destroying the group in whole or in part.[42] This special (or specific) intent must be satisfied together with the mental elements of all the pertinent crimes in the definition of genocide.[43] There are two justifications underlying the special intent inherent in the crime of genocide. The first serves to distinguish it from other similar crimes, such as crimes against humanity or its underlying offences (ie torture, murder and others). If it were not for the intention to destroy the group in whole or in part, murders committed against members of the group would be viewed as an attack against a civilian population and hence as a crime against humanity, if widespread or systematic. Failing that they could alternatively be classified as war crimes if committed in armed conflict, or otherwise as a series of murders punishable under domestic law.[44] The second rationale in the construction of *dolus specialis* is to provide a psychological platform to particular conduct in such a manner that it maybe used to characterise the crime and distinguish it from ordinary crimes. Genocide would not be the king of crimes had it not been for its special intent. The *Akayesu* Trial Chamber defined *dolus specialis* as 'the specific intention, required as a constitutive element of the crime, which demands that the perpetrator clearly seeks to produce the act charged'.[45] The reader should be reminded that in addition to demonstrating the overall specific intent for genocide, the prosecution must furnish proof that all of the underlying crimes charged were committed with their pertinent intent under Article 30 of the ICC Statute (ie in respect of killing members of the group it must be shown that the perpetrators acted with intent).[46]

The major practical, albeit also crucially legal, problem associated with the specific intent of a mass scale crime such as genocide is the mental state of mid-level and lower executioners. While some may indeed share the *dolus specialis* of genocide in

---

[42] 1948 Convention on the Prevention and Punishment of the Crime of Genocide, Art II.

[43] Although in the case of genocide the consummation of the special intent (ie the destruction of the group) need not be achieved for liability to arise. *Krstić* Trial Judgment, para 571.

[44] *ICTY Prosecutor v Jelisić*, Trial Chamber Judgment (14 Dec 1999), para 66.

[45] *ICTR Prosecutor v Akayesu*, Trial Chamber Judgment (2 Sep 1998), para 498.

[46] ICC Elements of Crimes, Art 6 (introduction), ICC Doc PCNICC/2000/1/Add.2 (2 Nov 2000).

equal measure with the planners and organisers, others will not concern themselves with formulating such a mental state – nor can this be easily proven – but will certainly be aware as to the existence of the genocidal plan and be prepared, for whatever other reason, to contribute to its execution. Should those that have not formed the *dolus specialis* for genocide, but are nonetheless aware of the genocide and the specific intent of the principals, be liable for genocide themselves? The school of thought in support of the so-called 'knowledge-based' doctrine argues that mid-level and lower-ranking executioners that are merely aware of the ultimate object of a genocidal campaign should be deemed liable as principals to genocide.[47] This approach is convenient for prosecutors and it is certainly reasonable to assume that he who is clearly aware of a genocidal plan and consents to partake in its execution should in some measure be deemed to accept the planner's specific intent as his own. As attractive as this theory may be, a crime of the magnitude of genocide – and the stigma it carries – does not readily lend itself to assumptions as to the perpetrators' mental state; it is not as though genocide is the only charge that can be levelled against mid-level and lowly executioners on the basis of their criminal conduct. This latter view conforms to the early, at least, jurisprudence of the ICC, which is supported by a literal interpretation of its Statute and Elements of Crimes. As will be explained in the chapters dealing with genocide and liability (particularly the section on aiding and abetting) the ad hoc tribunals distinguish between key planners and executioners (principals) and persons that associate themselves with the execution of the genocide (accomplices). Whereas principals must possess the specific intent for genocide, aiders and abettors need only know of their assistance and be aware of the principal's genocidal intent (it is true of all specific intent crimes that aiders and abetters thereto need not possess the specific intent required for that crime).[48] The *Krstić* Appeals Chamber, however, went on to hold that complicity to genocide was broader than mere aiding and abetting the same offence, finding moreover that in respect of complicity to genocide mere knowledge was insufficient. The Appeals Chamber argued, *obiter dictum*, that the *travaux* to the Genocide Convention clearly demonstrated the requirement of the specific intent of genocide in those cases of complicity other than aiding and abetting.[49]

Genocide is not the only international crime whose definition encompasses a special intent. This is also admitted in persecution as a crime against humanity, which in addition to an intention to commit particular offences against the victims, a discriminatory intent is required, the aim of which is to cause serious suffering or damage on political, racial or religious grounds.[50] Equally, the crime of apartheid requires a special intent to sustain an institutionalised system of racial domination[51] and the definition of torture necessitates the existence of an additional prohibited purpose, consisting of obtaining a confession, punishment, coercion, intimidation or

---

[47] AKA Greenawalt, 'Rethinking Genocidal Intent: The Case for a Knowledge-Based Interpretation' (1999) 99 *Columbia Law Review* 2259, at 2265ff; C Kress, 'The Darfur Report and Genocidal Intent' (2005) 3 *Journal of International Criminal Justice* 562, at 565ff.

[48] *Krstić* Appeals Judgment (19 Apr 2004), paras 140–41; *ICC Prosecutor v Al-Bashir*, Decision on the Prosecution's Application for a Warrant of Arrest against Omar Al-Bashir (4 Mar 2009), para 139.

[49] *Krstić*, ibid, para 142. See chapter 9.3.

[50] *Blaškić* Appeal Judgment, para 164.

[51] Art 7(2)(h) ICC Statute.

discrimination against the victim.[52] A similar *dolus specialis* is also encountered in the implicit definition of terrorism under international law (ie the intention to spread terror to civilian populations or to coerce governments), although this is only expressly stated in the 1998 Terrorist Bombings Convention[53] but not its predecessors. This special intent has also recently been iterated and concretised by the Security Council in resolution 1566, as encompassing:

> Criminal acts, including against civilians, committed with the intent to cause death or serious bodily injury, or taking of hostages, with the purpose to provoke a state of terror in the general public or in a group of persons or particular persons, intimidate a population or compel a government or an international organisation to do or to abstain from doing any act.[54]

It is evident that in respect of international crimes encompassing an element of *dolus specialis* that this mental element involves such volition and knowledge on the part of the perpetrator that amounts to *dolus directus* of the first or second degree. Hence, it is absurd to claim that D is liable for genocide where he intentionally murdered ten people, but was reckless as to whether they belonged to a particular racial group. In such case he is liable for other crimes, such as multiple murders or a crime against humanity. This conclusion is true even where the generic mental element of a crime is satisfied with a reckless mental state because the special intent must always be explicitly willed by the perpetrator.

2.7   The Principle of Transferred Fault and of Mistaken Object

International criminal courts have not been presented with a chance to deal with the principles of transferred fault (or transferred malice) and mistaken object, yet their occurrence is common before domestic courts. Where D intends to kill A, who is standing in a crowd of people but misses and kills B instead, the pertinent offence (ie murder) may be said to have been committed despite the mistaken object. If D, however throws a dart at A with the intention of causing a very minor injury but misses and hits B in the eye and kills him it cannot be said that D is blameworthy for the murder of B because he neither desired his death nor could he have foreseen this development. Thus, where the target of D's criminal conduct is different from its intended addressee, the *mens rea* for the latter (the mistaken object) offence is deemed to have been satisfied if it falls within the same legal category as the offence

---

[52]   Art 1(1), 1984 UN Torture Convention; for the *dolus specialis* of torture see *Čelebići* Trial Judgment (16 Nov 1998), para 494.

[53]   Art 2(1), UN Convention for the Suppression of Terrorist Bombings. A similar special intent is also written into Art 2(1) of the 2005 UN Convention on the Suppression of Acts of Nuclear Terrorism. See chapter 12.3.3. Specific intent is also required in Art 2(a) of CATOC, in which a person is liable for membership to an organised criminal group if he moreover intended to commit a serious crime in order to obtain a benefit. See chapter 11.2.

[54]   SC Res 1566 (8 Oct 2004).

committed against the unintended target.[55] In the second of the two scenarios described above D's conduct not only results against a mistaken object but is also antithetical to his volition in terms of its intended consequence. D quite clearly did not desire to kill V and he could not have foreseen such an eventuality. The law therefore accepts that D transfers his mental state to both the mistaken object as well as to the unintended consequence. What this means is that since D was acting negligently he is not liable for the killing of V because the appropriate *mens rea* for murder is intent and recklessness. As in the case of mistaken object, D's fault may only be transferred within the same offence and all defences ordinarily available to D in respect of the intended offence are equally transferred.

It is logical to transplant this theoretical construction into the sphere of international criminal law, subject to two notable exceptions. Where D is a party to a joint criminal enterprise (JCE) whose aim is to expel a civilian population – but without resorting to killings – and several members of the JCE murder some civilians without consulting D or soliciting his consent, D is nonetheless liable for these murders in accordance with the third strand of the JCE doctrine. This holds that an unintended and excessive criminal consequence of a JCE is attributable to all its members if the risk was foreseeable and D appreciated and reconciled himself with its likelihood.[56] This result defeats the rationale of the transferred malice doctrine because D is presumed to have intended to commit the most severe crime (ie murder) although this does not fall in the same legal category as the crime of forcibly removing a civilian population (without an intention to kill).

The second exception relates to the mental state of the accused in respect of complicity. In the common law, where D provides assistance to A with the aim of killing X, but A later changes his mind and kills Y – in respect of which D would never have agreed to provide assistance – D will not be considered liable for aiding and abetting A's murder of Y.[57] The rationale is that D's conduct is not wholly voluntary, since if he was aware of the eventual victim he may well have refused to aid and abet the direct perpetrator. There is no reason why this rule cannot be admitted in international criminal jurisprudence. Its application will, however, prove problematic in those situations where the victims are multiple and in respect of which the accomplice identifies them by a particular class. It would make little sense to accept D's argument that in aiding and abetting the murder of twenty enemy civilians from village X he was not at fault because he was told by the principal that he would kill twenty civilians from nearby village Y. Thus, in cases where although D was mistaken as to the particular identity of the victim, but not as to the victim's status or class characteristics he is presumed to have formed the *mens rea* for the pertinent offence.

---

[55] AM Dillof, 'Transferred Intent: An Inquiry into the Nature of Criminal Culpability' (1998) 1 *Buffalo Criminal Law Review* 501. The same approach is accepted in civil law jurisdictions. See Bohlander, *Principles*, 72–73, for the position in German criminal law.

[56] *ICTY Prosecutor v Tadić*, Appeals Chamber Judgment (15 Jul 1999), para 204. See chapter 3.2.

[57] Ashworth, *Principles*, 199.

3

Modes of Liability and Criminal Participation

3.1 The Legal Nature of Perpetration and Participation

A person incurs individual criminal responsibility when liability for a particular crime can be ascribed or attributed to that person. Attribution is premised on the satisfaction of the conduct elements that constitute the *actus reus* of the offence and provided that the accused possessed the required volition and knowledge or foresight. In assessing whether the accused has satisfied the constitutive elements of the *actus reus* of the offence under consideration we must distinguish between what the accused actually did (perpetration), or omitted to do as the case may be, from his overall participation in the offence. A person generally perpetrates a crime by directly and solely committing that crime, by committing it jointly with others, or by committing it through another person. The Appeals Chamber of the ad hoc tribunals has made attempts to widen the scope of 'committing' beyond the range of physical acts that result in the prescribed harm. As a result, it has been argued that in the case of genocide commission encompasses not only acts of killing but in addition includes approval of genocidal crimes as one's own and the exercise of influence over the perpetrators – particularly where the accused is a leading figure.[1] Under such circumstances the conduct of the accused is more akin to commission rather than aiding and abetting because it is not limited to giving practical assistance, encouragement and support to the physical perpetrator. Moreover, the accused does not merely act in the knowledge that he is assisting the principal, but rather he possesses the requisite *mens rea* for the offence.[2]

The notion of 'committing' is moreover generally perceived as encompassing omissions.[3] Thus, a person may 'commit' a crime by failing to do a positive act that was incumbent upon him; liability for omissions is, however, exceptional. For

---

[1] *ICTR Prosecutor v Seromba*, Appeal Chamber Judgment (12 Mar 2008), para 171.

[2] Ibid, paras 173–74. This widening of the scope of 'commission' is not without its fair share of criticism. See Dissenting Opinion of Judge Liu to the *Seromba* Appeal Judgment. This is particularly so since it does not seem that the application of this principle is confined solely to genocide. In *ICTR Prosecutor v Ndindabahizi*, Appeal Chamber Judgment (16 Jan 2007), para 123, it was accepted that the distribution of weapons, the transport of attackers and the utterance of words of encouragement suffices for the commission of extermination.

[3] Although first and foremost it means physical perpetration. See *ICTY Prosecutor v Tadić*, Appeals Chamber Judgment (15 Jul 1999), para 188. That the concept of perpetration or commission encompasses also culpable omissions, see *ICTY Prosecutor v Krstić*, Appeals Chamber Judgment (19 Apr 2004), para 188; *ICC Prosecutor v Lubanga*, Trial Chamber Decision on Confirmation of Indictment (29 Jan 2007), paras 351–55.

example, commanders are liable for their failure to prevent or punish the crimes of their direct subordinates when they knew or had reason to know that they were about to commit crimes. This particular type of criminal omission is known as command responsibility and will be explored in the following chapter. Inciting others to commit genocide and attempting to commit a crime constitute expansions of perpetration and thus amount to expansions of liability. This is duly reflected in Article 25(3)(a)(d)(e) and (f) of the ICC Statute, whereas the concept of joint criminal enterprise (JCE) is not expressly encountered in the ICC Statute but only in the jurisprudence of the ICTY and ICTR as a matter of customary international law.[4] Numerous commentators, however, argue that Article 25(3)(d) of the ICC Statute is a form of JCE.

Once it has been determined that the accused committed the offence, one must then establish the mode of his or her participation. In most cases, particularly in respect of one-to-one offences, this is a simple enough exercise. However, in the context of serious international crimes, such as genocide and crimes against humanity, where a multiplicity of persons partake in numerous planned or widespread acts the participation of each person in the overall offence (ie the genocide or the crime against humanity itself) is not readily obvious. Some persons will have planned and set in motion the genocide, others will have been aware of the genocidal plan and will have played a part in its execution and yet others will have carried out particular functions without knowledge of the overall plan. In all of the above cases the mode of participation does not only highlight the existence of mitigating or aggravating factors with regard to sentencing (as it would, for instance, in relation to a robbery involving three persons, all of which assume different roles), it more importantly determines whether the accused in fact committed the overall crime charged. In order thereafter to assess whether the accused is liable for the criminal consequences of the overall crime it is necessary to determine that he or she satisfied the conduct and cognitive elements of the relevant rule that criminalises participation in the plan, the common design, the conspiracy, or other. It may in fact turn out that the cognitive element required in respect of a particular form of participation differs from the general rule, according to which a person incurs liability where a prohibited conduct was undertaken willingly and with knowledge or foresight that it will come about.

The most obvious form of participation in crime is through direct commission. Irrespective of the participation and liability of other persons in the context of a criminal offence there must always exist at least one principal;[5] ie the person through the direct actions of which the harm or criminal consequence was caused. The other forms explored in this chapter constitute variations to the general rule. To a certain degree some of these necessarily overlap given that only minor differences exist

---

[4]   See generally, W Schabas, 'General Principles of Criminal Law' (1998) 6 *European Journal of Crime, Criminal Law & Criminal Justice* 400.

[5]   The various forms of participation analysed in this chapter give rise to multiple principals either because the mere agreement to participate in a criminal plan is unlawful by and of itself (conspiracy), or because participation in a criminal design with knowledge and intent renders each participant a principal. There are, however, instances where two or more persons embark on the commission of an offence against the same victim and independently of each other, in which case they constitute multiple independent principals (Nebentäterschaft). This concept should be distinguished from co-perpetration, as will be explained.

between a good number of them, or, in any event more than one forms of participation may be charged in the alternative on the same set of facts against the same person. Equally, the instruments of certain tribunals, or their jurisprudence, recognise some, but not all, of the principles of liability and modes of participation that have arisen through the years. In such cases the application of the said principles is context-specific and not universal.

3.2 Joint Criminal Enterprise

The need for joint criminal enterprise (JCE) liability in the criminal law arose from the need to attribute liability to a plethora of persons involved in a criminal scheme involving a multitude of offences. Whereas the leaders and organisers of such common purpose may be charged by reason of the orders they transmitted down the chain of command or on account of their failure to prevent or punish subordinate criminality (command responsibility), it is not clear what type of liability, if at all, may be attributed to those who participate in more minor roles in the implementation of such criminal schemes. Thus, a plan to effectuate mass population transfers as a matter of ethnic cleansing may involve terrorising civilian populations, murders, widespread looting and the running of unlawful detention facilities, among others. The persons that transport the prisoners and those who guard them have not committed an obvious crime and would generally go unpunished unless a particular form of liability is established whereby volitional participation in the overall criminal scheme is duly criminalised. Equally, even if the acts of some participants are of a criminal nature, such as a single act of forceful removal, they are of little significance when viewed individually. However, when one assesses all relevant crimes and other non-criminal behaviour in light of the overall common design a different picture is painted and the puzzle of genocide or crimes against humanity is pieced together. The JCE doctrine is the tool that serves this purpose and as a result is a manifestation of collective criminality and resembles the Nuremberg concepts of conspiracy and membership of illegal organisations.

The ICTY Appeals Chamber in the *Tadić* case was the first ever post-WWII judicial institution to pronounce the existence and applicability of joint criminal enterprise liability. The Appeals Chamber further claimed that JCE had long existed under customary international law,[6] rendering each and every member of a common design equally liable regardless of the gravity of the crime or the contribution of each participant.[7] According to the Appeals Chamber, a joint criminal enterprise consists of a common plan, design or purpose, the participation of a plurality of persons therein, all of which are acting with the aim of committing one or more international crimes.[8]

---

[6] *Tadić* Appeal Judgment, paras 194ff. JCE liability was subsequently adopted unquestionably before other ICTY Chambers. See, for example, *ICTY Prosecutor v Vasiljević*, Trial Chamber Judgment (29 Nov 2002), para 63ff; *ICTY Prosecutor v Furundžija*, Appeals Chamber Judgment (21 Jul 2000), para 119.
[7] *Vasiljević* Trial Judgment, para 67.
[8] *Tadić* Appeal Judgment, para 188.

The ICTY chambers espoused the view that participation in a joint criminal enterprise is a form of 'commission' within the meaning of Article 7(1) of the ICTY Statute, just like other forms of physical perpetration.[9] It was further claimed that there is no need for the plan to be organised under a formal guise or structure; nor is there a requirement for the plan to be conceived before the crime is committed, thus rendering JCE formulation and participation therein a spontaneous event.[10] This would then render JCE liability in relation to genocide and crimes against humanity problematic if charged as 'spontaneous designs', since both require substantial planning and preparation. Unlike common complicity where the accomplice shares the liability of the principal only when he or she significantly contributes to the execution of the objective elements of the offence, this is not a requirement for participants to a JCE. Instead, causation as to execution is irrelevant for the purposes of attributing liability.[11]

The Appeals Chamber distinguished between three JCE categories. The first (JCE I), and more general, consists of cases where a group of persons possesses a shared intent to commit a crime and a common design is accordingly formulated. Participants in the common design will inevitably assume differing roles and levels of responsibility and depending on the magnitude of the eventual crime some participants will contribute to its planning and intermediate stages of implementation while others will play a significant role in its execution. JCE liability arises even for those participants that do not directly contribute to the execution of the crime, as long as they are found to enjoy a significant contribution in the formulation and perpetration of the common design. Contributions of this nature may vary, but can include all types of assistance at any stage of the design. A significant difficulty with JCE liability concerns the construction of an appropriate *mens rea* for those participants that did not take part in the execution of the crime. The *Tadić* Appeals Chamber was of the view that the participant must willingly contribute to at least one element of the common design and intend the result of the ultimate crime(s) undertaken by his co-perpetrators.[12] In this manner liability does not arise simply by virtue of one's membership in the common design but by reference to sufficient knowledge and intent in respect of particular offences. It is evident that JCE I is a form of participation predicated on the concept of co-perpetration, in which participants to a common plan are liable as principals where they have been assigned essential tasks and share joint control. In this manner JCE I is the only strand of the JCE doctrine that can safely be classified as 'commission' under Article 7(1) of the ICTY Statute and as 'co-perpetration' under Article 25(3)(a) of the ICC Statute.[13]

The second category (JCE II) is more specific, derived by the *Tadić* Appeals Judgment from JCE cases involving concentration camps. After further refinement this category is now known as 'systemic', covering all cases 'relating to an organised system with a common criminal purpose perpetrated against the detainees'.[14] These

---

[9] *ICTY Prosecutor v Krnojelac*, Appeal Chamber Judgment (17 Sep 2003), para 73.
[10] *Tadić* Appeal Judgment, para 227.
[11] Ibid, para 199.
[12] Ibid, para 196.
[13] V Haan, 'The Development of the Concept of Joint Criminal Enterprise at the ICTY' (2005) 5 *International Criminal Law Review* 167, at 201.
[14] *ICTY Prosecutor v Kvočka*, Appeal Chamber Judgment (28 Feb 2005), para 182.

consist of a common design in which multiple persons participate in a 'system of ill-treatment' of detainees in camps. The participants enjoy positions of authority in the camp and have either established or are aware of the system and contribute to its furtherance in whatever capacity each is called upon. Thus, tasks undertaken within such a system of ill-treatment will vary significantly. The participants must be aware of the system and intend to contribute to it.[15] Camps of this type will certainly be staffed with multiple persons and in the absence of an agreement to ill-treat detainees the prosecution will have to infer the participation of each staff member in the common design.[16] The *Kvočka* Appeals Judgment agreed with the conclusions of its Trial Chamber in that the holding of an:

> . . . executive, administrative or protective role in a camp constitutes general participation in the crimes committed therein. An intent to further the efforts of the JCE so as to rise to the level of co-perpetration may also be inferred from knowledge of the crimes being perpetrated in the camp and [from] continued participation which enables the camp's functioning.[17]

According to the *Kvočka* Appeals Judgment, inference of *mens rea* may be taken from the position of the accused in the camp, the amount of time spent there, his function, movement throughout the camp and any contact he had with detainees, staff personnel, or outsiders visiting the camp, as well as through ordinary senses.[18] It is obvious that not every person staffing an abuse camp is necessarily a participant in the common design. This is especially true for those in the lower echelons who are not aware of the crimes, or who although aware of them take no part and have no capacity to prevent them. Persons who do commit crimes in camp-related common designs, but do so unwillingly as a result of duress or superior orders, cannot logically be deemed to share the intent of the other co-perpetrators. In this case, however, for the purposes of doctrinal consistency it may be best to say that they share the required direct intent but their culpability is negated by the defences they invoke, or that they otherwise simply aid and abet an underlying crime but are unaware of the JCE itself.

The third category (JCE III) refers to common plans or designs in which the actions of one or more participants exceed the aim of the original design and as such the excessive action no longer coincides with the intention of them all (so-called 'extended JCE'). Should all participants be equally liable for the unintended action, or only for that which they had originally intended? It is unlikely that an exception could plausibly be made for a standard lower than direct/oblique intent (*dolus directus* of the first and second degree) for such serious offences, but the *Tadić* Appeals Chamber was of a different opinion, although its choice of terms was in the circumstances unsatisfactory and confusing. It first noted that liability for the

---

[15]   *Tadić* Appeal Judgment, paras 202–03.

[16]   The fact that abuses do take place in a camp does not necessarily mean that a systemic JCE has been established. In *ICTY Prosecutor v Limaj*, Trial Chamber Judgment (30 Nov 2005), para 669, the Chamber held that no evidence of a common design could be inferred in the absence of proof demonstrating that a group of individuals whose identities could be established at least by reference to their category as a group had furthered a common plan.

[17]   *Kvočka* Appeal Judgment, paras 103, 184.

[18]   Ibid, paras 201–202.

unintended deaths would arise where 'the risk of death was a predictable consequence ... and the accused was either reckless or indifferent to that risk'.[19] Predictability certainly suggests a degree of foresight that lacks virtual certainty and as a result introduces recklessness into the equation. This conclusion is further endorsed by the fact that the Chamber then went on to say that liability arises if 'it was foreseeable that such a crime might be perpetrated by one or other members of the group and the accused willingly took that risk'.[20] The particular choice of words is rather unfortunate because it is unclear if they are meant to impose the higher standard of oblique intent, rather than its lower counterpart of recklessness. Just when one thought the standard was clear and that some consistency had come about, the Appeals Chamber noted that:

> What is required is a state of mind in which a person, although he did not intend to bring about a certain result, was aware that the actions of the group were most likely to lead to that result but nevertheless willingly took that risk. In other words, the so-called *dolus eventualis* is required (also called 'advertent recklessness' in some national legal systems).[21]

I have taken the view in the chapter dealing with the mental element of crimes that recklessness is substantially the same as *dolus eventualis*. This passage, despite once again its choice of words, clearly posits a recklessness standard in the *mens rea* definition of the third JCE type.[22] This later culminated in some confusion that was duly acknowledged by the various ICTY chambers, which eventually led to the adoption of a more coherent and acceptable *mens rea* formulation that fully encapsulates the essence of recklessness within, however, the particular context of JCE III. Rather than a 'probability' standard, a 'possibility' one has been broadly accepted to require foreseeability that a crime may be perpetrated even as a 'possible consequence' of the execution of the common purpose.[23] This standard requires that the possibility of a crime being committed must be sufficiently substantial as to be foreseeable to an accused.[24] For what it is worth, if the risk is sufficiently substantial so that it becomes foreseeable to the accused its realisation is best determined as 'probable' rather than merely 'possible'.

It has now been accepted in the ICTY Appeals Chamber that the third type of JCE liability and the crime of genocide are compatible.[25] This is a dangerous precedent for

---

[19]   *Tadić* Appeal Judgment, para 204.

[20]   Ibid, para 228.

[21]   Ibid, para 220.

[22]   In English criminal law, indifference as to the consequence (couldn't care less attitude) was until 2004 encompassed within the domain of recklessness, as an inadvertent species thereof, introduced by the House of Lords in *Caldwell* [1982] AC 341. Such inadvertent recklessness was rightly criticised because it lacked the element of awareness, even if that was down to the irresponsible character of the accused and was applied by the courts in cases of criminal damage. It was finally repealed in *G* [2004] 1 AC 1034. As a result of these observations its application in the third JCE type is highly problematic from a comparative point of view.

[23]   *ICTY Prosecutor v Brđanin*, Appeals Chamber Judgment (3 Apr 2007), para 411; *Vasiljević* Appeal Judgment, para 101; *ICTY Prosecutor v Stakić*, Appeals Chamber Judgment (22 Mar 2006), para 65; *ICTY Prosecutor v Blaškić*, Appeals Chamber Judgment (29 Jul 2004), para 33; *ICTY Prosecutor v Martić*, Appeals Chamber Judgment (8 Oct 2008), para 168.

[24]   *ICTY Prosecutor v Karadžić*, Appeals Chamber Decision on Prosecution's Motion Appealing Trial Chamber's Decision on JCE III Foreseeability (25 Jun 2009), para 18.

[25]   *ICTY Prosecutor v Brđanin*, Appeals Chamber Decision on Interlocutory Appeal (19 Mar 2004), paras 9–10; *Stakić* Appeal Judgment, para 38.

a specific intent crime such as genocide, since if only the excessive and unintended crimes were to amount to genocide the Court would not require the normal JCE participants to demonstrate the *dolus specialis* for genocide, but a *dolus eventualis* for genocide instead. This would work well for the vast majority of offences but would defeat the *raison d'etre* of the *mens rea* for genocide.[26]

The status of JCE II and III within the general framework of international criminal law is *sui generis*. Clearly, given the *Kvočka* Appeal judgment that JCE II does not require a substantial contribution to the enterprise save for membership thereto and foreseeability,[27] it resembles the legal nature of JCE III and thus does not amount to co-perpetration. Equally, JCE II and III are not susceptible to classification as aiding and abetting a criminal enterprise not only because they are not encompassed in their substantive terms as such under the relevant provisions of the ICTY and ICC Statutes, but more importantly because they lack the requisite *mens rea* under these instruments; that is, intent and knowledge. As a result, the only comparable form of participation is Article 25(3)(d) of the ICC Statute, which reads:

> [A person incurs liability where he] contributes to the commission or attempted commission of a crime by a group of persons acting with a common purpose. Such contribution shall be intentional and shall either:
>
> (i)   be made with the aim of furthering the criminal activity or criminal purpose of the group, where such activity or purpose involves the commission of a crime within the jurisdiction of the Court; or
>
> (ii) be made in the knowledge of the intention of the group to commit the crime.

Ambos correctly points out that JCE II and III are not encompassed within this provision on account of two reasons. Firstly, subparagraph (d)(ii) requires knowledge as to the common intent of the enterprise, rather than the foreseeability required by JCE II and III.[28] Secondly, JCE resembles to some degree liability by reason of conspiracy, which was explicitly rejected by the drafters of the ICC Statute.[29] Some of these limitations are accepted even by those who support the notion that JCE may implicitly be inferred from Article 25(3) of the ICC Statute.[30]

The boundaries between JCE and aiding and abetting are imprecise at best. Let us assume that D contributes to a crime perpetrated by A, who is a participant to a criminal scheme, and whose crime was undertaken in pursuance of the scheme. Would D's contribution amount to actual commission under the JCE, aiding or abetting as to the particular crime, or aiding and abetting as to the JCE? The Appeals Chamber in the *Kvočka* case argued that where the accused knows that he is aiding

---

[26] See chapter 9.3.

[27] *Kvočka* Appeal Judgment, para 97.

[28] Unless of course the ICC chambers ultimately accept that recklessness is a mental standard applicable in Article 30 of the ICC Statute, which they seem to have done on the basis of the *Lubanga* Confirmation of Charges Decision (29 Jan 2007), para 352, which accepted the compatibility of *dolus eventualis* with Art 30 of the ICC Statute. See chapter 2.3 and 2.4.

[29] K Ambos, 'Joint Criminal Enterprise and Command Responsibility' (2007) 5 *Journal of International Criminal Justice* 159, 172–73.

[30] See A Cassese, *International Criminal Law* (Oxford, Oxford University Press, 2008) 212, who argues, however, that because Art 30 of the ICC Statute requires intent or knowledge, even if JCE were to be adopted within the ambit of the Statute the third JCE category which is described in the course of this section will be inapplicable.

and abetting a single crime he is liable only for that crime, even if the principal perpetrator commits it in pursuance of a JCE. On the other hand, where the accused provides assistance in the knowledge that he is helping the JCE and moreover shares the group's intent he is liable as a co-perpetrator of that JCE.[31] As a result, it is not possible as a matter of juridical reasoning to aid and abet a JCE under any circumstances.[32] Ambos rightly points out that while this restrictive view may be justified on the basis of Article 7(1) of the ICTY Statute it is not necessary from a doctrinal perspective and as a result different forms of participation in a JCE are in fact possible.[33]

Some criticism is rightly due to the formulation of the JCE doctrine by the *Tadić* Appeals Chamber. For one thing, it is unacceptable for a criminal tribunal to come up *de novo* with a legal construction that is unfavourable to the accused, especially when it is not explicitly provided in its Statute. This criticism is particularly poignant given that other long-established forms of liability were more appropriate in the circumstances, especially co-perpetration, discussed more fully in a subsequent section. Secondly, it is equally unacceptable for the tribunal to claim the validity of this legal construction on conspicuously declared customary law[34] that itself is based on scattered post-World War II case law. Finally, as already explained it is by no means clear that the criminal liability grounded in Article 25(3) of the ICC Statute reflects the ICTY's JCE construction. Of course, this is no reason to dismiss the JCE doctrine wholesale, given that the ICC Statute is context-specific and does not necessarily reflect customary international law in all of its provisions, even if one assumed that the JCE doctrine had become a creature of customary law. Nonetheless, despite the JCE precedent within the context of the ICTY and ICTR chambers and its elevation therein to a customary principle, it should not be lightly assumed that this statement is also applicable outside the ICTY framework, since in my opinion there is insufficient State practice in this regard.[35] This in no way means that it is not a valuable and legitimate doctrine for the prosecution of otherwise culpable persons that would normally fall outside the ambit of the criminal law, especially where it is explicitly incorporated in criminal legislation prior to its judicial application.[36]

---

[31]   *Kvočka* Appeal Judgment, para 90.
[32]   Ibid, para 91.
[33]   Ambos, 'Joint Criminal Enterprise', at 170.
[34]   In *ICTY Prosecutor v M Milutinović et al*, Appeals Chamber Decision on Ojdanic's Motion Challenging Jurisdiction: Indirect Co-Perpetration (22 Mar 2006), para. 21, the Appeals Chamber declared the existence of JCE liability in customary international law as early as 1992.
[35]   Some, but understandably, limited criticism of JCE liability has come even from within the ICTY. In the *Stakić* Trial Judgment (31 Jul 2003), paras 438, 441, the Trial Chamber expressed its reservations about the doctrine, indicating that a 'more direct reference to commission in its traditional sense should be given priority before considering JCE liability'. As a result, it applied *de novo* (for the purposes of the ICTY) a form of liability it termed 'co-perpetratorship'. At the Appeals stage, the Appeals Judgment in *Stakić* (22 Mar 2006), paras 58ff, dismissed co-perpetratorship, deeming it inconsistent with ICTY jurisprudence and outside the ambit of customary law. It thus reapplied the evidence on the basis of the JCE doctrine. It should be noted that co-perpetration is recognised in German criminal law as Mittäreschaft, in which participants pursue a common goal through co-ordinated action and joint control over the criminal conduct, albeit for liability to arise each must make an essential contribution to the commission of the crime. This notion will be explored more fully in a subsequent section.
[36]   It should also be noted that JCE liability did not make it into the Lebanon Special Tribunal Statute either, Art 3(1)(b) of which entertains common purpose liability, but not JCE. A species of JCE exists in classic Islamic law through the Hanafi doctrine of *qasama*, which concerns collective punishment. It is

3.3 Commission through Another Person or Indirect Perpetration

This form of participation in crime is entertained in Article 25(3)(a) of the ICC Statute, but not expressly in Article 7 of the ICTY Statute.[37] In fact, it has never been utilised by the ad hoc tribunals. It entails the employment or use of another person (the direct perpetrator) to commit a crime for which the 'behind the scenes' indirect perpetrator commits no physical acts as to its execution. The commission of a crime through another person must be distinguished from situations where a superior directs an order to his subordinate, although this is also a particular form of commission through another person. The difference between the two is that whereas ordering requires *a priori* a superior-subordinate relationship (a vertical relationship), committing through another does not, given that this form of liability presupposes the existence of a horizontal relationship. It should be noted that ordering is also treated as a form of complicity in some domestic legal systems.[38] One of the rationales for indirect perpetration was premised on the notion of *Organisationsherrschaft*, meaning control over an organisation, encompassing the idea that the orders and plans of political and military leaders will automatically be carried out by their populace.[39] Nonetheless, this is not the sole justificatory reason or function of indirect perpetration, as already explained, but it is certainly one where the boundaries of vertical and horizontal relationships are blurred.

Perpetration through another generally suggests that the physical perpetrator is an 'innocent agent' or has available to him, or her, the defence of mental incapacity or that of infancy. It is unclear whether this mode of perpetration is applicable to situations where the physical perpetrator possesses the requisite intent and knowledge to commit the crime for which he is rendered a tool. Judge Schomberg in an ICTY separate opinion, as well as subsequent ICC jurisprudence, have answered this query in the affirmative[40] and some national jurisprudence certainly points towards this direction, as long as the indirect perpetrator is sufficiently able to dominate the direct (physical) perpetrator in order to justify attributing to him his conduct;[41] otherwise, alternative forms of liability will be more appropriate. I share this view that where the physical perpetrator is criminally liable the perpetrator behind the perpetrator can

---

accepted that the inhabitants of a people or village can be held collectively liable for the financial consequences of a homicide of which the perpetrator is unknown and which is committed in the house or village. Thus, one need not prove the particular liability of each village or house dweller. R Peters, *Crime and Punishment in Islamic Law* (Cambridge, Cambridge University Press, 2005) 20.

[37] Although ordering another to commit a prohibited act is a particular species of commission through another person, which is indeed recognised by the ad hoc tribunals.

[38] *ICTR Prosecutor v Akayesu*, Trial Chamber Judgment (2 Sep 1998), para 483.

[39] HG van der Wilt, 'The Continuous Quest for Proper Modes of Criminal Responsibility' (2009) 7 *Journal of International Criminal Justice* 307, at 309.

[40] *ICTR Prosecutor v Gacumbitsi*, Appeals Chamber Judgment (7 Jul 2006), Separate Opinion of Judge Schomberg, paras 18–21; *ICC Prosecutor v Lubanga*, Trial Chamber Decision on the Confirmation of Charges (29 Jan 2007), para 339.

[41] O Triffterer, *Commentary on the Rome Statute of the ICC* (Oxford, Hart Publishing, 2008) [Triffterer Commentary] 752–53.

also be held liable. This issue, at the time of writing, is evolving and more authoritative pronouncements are forthcoming from both the ICC and the ad hoc tribunals.

Despite the existence of this form of liability in the ICC Statute, scholarly opinion strongly suggests that it is not a principle that is widely employed in domestic criminal justice systems. Its origins are traced in German legal theory,[42] albeit even there scholars disagree about its precise ambit. What is acutely problematic about indirect perpetration is the required quantity of control over the will of the physical perpetrator. If said control is absolute, then clearly the physical perpetrator possesses no volition of his own and the criminal conduct can be attributed to the indirect perpetrator if he so willed this conduct or its consequences. If, however, the control exercised by the indirect perpetrator is not absolute, given the horizontal nature of the relationship between the two actors, it would be unsafe – and contrary to the safeguards afforded to accused persons – to assume that the degree of domination is such that justifies attribution to the indirect perpetrator for the acts of the physical perpetrator. As a result, it seems that two appropriate, and non-mutually exclusive, options are available: a) that the indirect perpetrator exercised full and absolute control over the will of the direct perpetrator, or; b) that the indirect perpetrator exercised effective control over the direct perpetrator, in a manner similar to the superior-subordinate relationship found in command responsibility.[43] Any control that is lower than these standards is fraught with unsustainable assumptions and should be excluded, since a large number of persons can be singled out as indirect perpetrators.

As will be demonstrated at the close of the next section the ICC pre-Trial chambers have so far merged the two notions of co-perpetration and indirect perpetration to formulate the so-called indirect co-perpetration liability.

3.4 Co-Perpetration

This form of participation in crime arises in those circumstances where more than one perpetrator execute a criminal offence not simply jointly but in such a manner that the actions of each one make a significant contribution to the commission of the crime on the basis of a functional cooperation.[44] Any other contribution that does not have such a potent effect on the conclusion of the crime will render said participant merely an accomplice but not a perpetrator. Thus, where D intends to inflict bodily harm upon a POW and in fact does so and all the while A serves as a lookout for possible witnesses, D is the direct perpetrator and A is liable for aiding and abetting. Were A, however, to beat the victim alongside D with intent to cause

---

[42] For example, s 25(1) German Criminal Code. This form of perpetration is termed principal by proxy (*Mittelbare Täterschaft*).

[43] This rationale seems to have been adopted by Defence counsel in their submission in *ICC Prosecutor v Katanga and Chui*, Corrigendum to Defence for Katanga's Pre-Trial Brief on the Interpretation of Article 25(3) of the ICC Statute (30 Oct 2009) [*Katanga* Corrigendum to Article 25(3)], para 33.

[44] M Bohlander, *Principles of German Criminal Law* (Oxford, Hart Publishing, 2009) 161–67.

him serious bodily harm he will be counted as a co-perpetrator together with D. In the two scenarios it is not very difficult to differentiate between the various forms of attribution. Now consider an incident where ten soldiers known for their brutality and proclivity to crime enter an enemy village with the aim of terrorising its inhabitants and in the generalised scuffle that follows between the villagers and the soldiers a villager falls dead. In this case it is impossible to demonstrate which of the ten soldiers threw the fatal punch (given that more than one culprit punched the victim), which would as a result render that person the principal and everybody else an accomplice. Thus, instead of aimlessly trying to single out a sole direct perpetrator under such circumstances it makes sense to attribute liability for the offence to all equally as joint perpetrators where it can be shown that each of them would have committed the offence had she or he been given the physical opportunity to do so.[45] Much like the JCE doctrine, the rationale behind the various strands of co-perpetration is to set out an appropriate mode by which to counter instances of mass criminality, in which although a criminal conduct or consequence comes about as a result of the actions of one person, it could just as well have been perpetrated by any other member of the group that was with him. As a result, the presumption that any one of the ten soldiers could have thrown the fatal punch is not irrebuttable. If one demonstrates that he did not share the will or the proclivity of his comrades and that he was at the scene of the crime unwillingly he will certainly not be counted as a co-perpetrator. This form of attribution is well recognised in domestic criminal justice systems and is incorporated in Article 25(3)(a) of the ICC Statute as committing a crime 'jointly with another'.

Before we go about determining the rationale behind the liability of all co-perpetrators it is worth examining the available legal tests for distinguishing between principals and accomplices. The objective test focuses on the quantum and level of contribution made by the accused, which if substantial gives rise to liability as a matter of direct perpetration. The subjective test, on the other hand, is concerned exclusively with the mental state of the accused; thus, proof of intent to commit the underlying crime suffices for attribution as a direct perpetrator. A third test posits that the control of the accused over the crime should have the effect of rendering that person a direct perpetrator. Certainly, the effect of this test is to limit co-perpetratorship to leading figures. The initial jurisprudence of the ICC clearly suggests that its chambers are intent on employing the 'control over the crime' test.[46] This test requires concerted action in which:

---

[45]   See A Ashworth, *Principles of Criminal Law* (Oxford, Oxford University Press, 2006) 411–13. In *R v Rahman and Others* [2007] 3 All ER 396 the accused was joined by a group of friends that became involved in a violent altercation with a person unknown to them and who eventually died from a knife wound. Although it could not be determined which member of the group committed the killing, those members of the group that shared the joint intent to kill were held liable as co-perpetrators.

[46]   *ICC Prosecutor v Lubanga*, Trial Chamber Decision on the Confirmation of Charges (29 Jan 2007), paras 331, 338. This test (*Tatherrschaft*) clearly attests that co-perpetration is borrowed from the civil law notion of Mittäreschaft, whose statutory form is enshrined in s 25(2) of the German Criminal Code. See Bohlander, *Principles*, at 162. See, however, T Weigend, 'Intent, Mistake of Law and Co-Perpetration in the Lubanga Decision on Confirmation of Charges' (2008) 6 *Journal of International Criminal Justice* 471, 479–80, who notes that the courts of some nations, such as Germany, do not necessarily rely on the

although none of the participants has overall control over the offence because they all depend on one another for its commission, they all share control because each of them could frustrate the commission of the crime by not carrying out his or her task.[47]

Co-perpetration liability requires proof of objective and subjective elements. The objective element necessitates the existence of a mutually co-ordinated agreement or common plan between two or more persons, thus excluding opportunistic collaborations.[48] Not every member of a common plan can be charged as a principal, but only those persons to whom essential tasks have been assigned and who can at any time frustrate the offence. What this means is that co-perpetratorship requires an essential – as opposed to merely a substantial – contribution to the execution of the common plan. The co-perpetrators must have agreed to achieve a criminal goal, even if this arises at a later stage and as long as the culprits are aware of the risks from the implementation of the common plan and ultimately accept its criminal outcome.[49]

The subjective elements of co-perpetratorship require: a) each co-perpetrator's intent and knowledge as to the crime committed, and; b) mutual awareness and acceptance that implementation of the common plan may result in the realisation of the objective elements of the crime.[50] While these two conditions are largely uncontroversial and pinpoint to intent as the appropriate mental standard, some ICC Trial Chambers have additionally required, without offering any serious legal justification, that the accused possessed awareness as to the factual circumstances enabling him to jointly control the crime.[51] It has rightly been suggested that this last element (ie awareness of the factual circumstances of the joint control) demands far too much from co-perpetrators on account of their mutual horizontal relationship which precludes them at all times from asserting full control and knowledge over their respective activities, unlike the case of indirect perpetration where the relationship between the direct and indirect perpetrator is vertical in nature and thus susceptible to control and knowledge by the indirect perpetrator.[52]

What is somewhat foreign to both domestic criminal justice systems and the statutes of international criminal courts and tribunals is the fusion of co-perpetration and indirect perpetration (so-called indirect co-perpetration).[53] According to this although D who has no control over A, through whom the crime was committed, cannot be liable for the conduct of A, D may nonetheless be liable for the crime of A

---

concept of control to distinguish between co-perpetrators and accessories. Rather, making a contribution that promotes the offence, in conjunction with an interest in the success of the common enterprise suffices for liability as a co-perpetrator.

[47] *Lubanga* Confirmation Decision, ibid, para 342.

[48] This is certainly the case in the related English criminal law concept of joint ventures where a spontaneous coming together will generally be deemed insufficient. *Petters and Parfitt* [1995] Crim LR 501.

[49] *Lubanga* Confirmation Decision, paras 343–47.

[50] Ibid, paras 349–64. See G Werle, 'Individual Responsibility in Article 25 ICC Statute' (2007) 5 *Journal of International Criminal Justice* 953, at 963.

[51] Ibid, *Lubanga* Confirmation Decision, paras 365–67; *ICC Prosecutor v Bemba*, Pre-Trial Chamber Decision on the Confirmation of Charges (15 Jun 2009), para 351.

[52] K Ambos, 'Critical Issues in the Bemba Confirmation Decision' (2009) 22 *Leiden Journal of International Law* 715, 719–20; the Trial Chamber in *ICC Prosecutor v Katanga and Chui*, Decision on Confirmation of Charges (30 Sep 2008), paras 534–35, disagrees with the third requirement espoused in the *Bemba* and *Lubanga* confirmation decisions.

[53] Identified initially in *Katanga* Confirmation of Charges Decision, paras 492–93.

if he acts jointly with another person, X, who in fact controls A. Notwithstanding that this type of liability is not absolutely clear in the ICC Statute, it is by no means unreasonable. If it were not applicable D would otherwise be considered an accessory, despite acting in concert with X, who is counted as a principal. The Defence before the ICC pre-Trial chambers has strenuously argued that this type of liability does not conform to customary law and general principles of law and by early 2010 the ICC Trial Chamber in the *Katanga* case had asked the parties to submit their views on the legal nature and viability of indirect co-perpetratorship. Although a determinative conclusion is still pending we have already demonstrated that the *Katanga/Chui* Confirmation Decision validated indirect co-perpetratorship through a purposive construction of Article 25(3)(a) of the ICC Statute, holding that the disjunctive 'or' between co-perpetration and indirect perpetration possesses an inclusive meaning in that it allows 'either one or the other and possibly [a combination of] both'.[54] In the case at hand, Katanga and Ngudjolo were charged with crimes allegedly committed by each other's subordinates, with both of the accused being co-perpetrators. The result is that if Katanga were to be found guilty for crimes committed by subordinates of Ngudjolo, this would be on the basis of direct perpetrators whom he has never before seen or conversed with. In any event, indirect co-perpetratorship must be solidly placated on the same level of control required in liability pertinent to indirect perpetration. The matter, however, is a sensitive one and a more coherent theoretical grounding is required because its application may well lead to vicarious liability.

3.5 Conspiracy

References to conspiracies in international criminal law textbooks are most commonly included in the section concerning inchoate offences (ie crimes that incur liability without the perpetration of any principal offence). We should, however, distinguish the double life of the concept as it appears in domestic criminal laws from its namesake counterpart in international law. The concept is better known in common law jurisdictions and in general terms it consists of an agreement between two or more persons with the intention of carrying out a crime and playing a part in that course of conduct.[55] Significantly, this common law conspiracy need not be consummated and anyone found to have been a party to such agreement, although absent during perpetration of the principal crime, is liable. Liability is incurred with

---

[54] Ibid, para 491. This type of liability was also confirmed in *ICC Prosecutor v Abu Garda*, Pre-Trial Chamber Decision on the Confirmation of Charges (8 Feb 2010), paras 158–62.

[55] AP Simester, GR Sullivan, *Criminal Law: Theory and Doctrine* (Oxford, Hart Publishing, 2004) 271–95; I Dennis, 'The Rationale of Criminal Conspiracy' (1997) 93 *Law Quarterly Review* 39. It should be emphasised that the current position of conspiracies in English criminal law is contradictory and hence unsatisfactory. On the one hand, it has been held by the House of Lords in *Anderson* [1986] AC 27, that a person is liable even without intending to carry out the agreement, as long as he intended to play some part in the agreed course of conduct. Some years later the Privy Council in *Yip Chiu-Cheung* [1995] 1 AC 111 required that liability could only arise where each conspirator in fact intended the agreement to be carried out.

regard to the conspiracy itself, rendering it therefore a distinct offence.[56] Its justificatory existence is apparently of a preventive nature, but it also serves to bring within the ambit of the criminal law those who plan and yet do not take part in an offence (the so-called godfathers).[57] The concept of conspiracy in international law, however, rests on different premises. Its inclusion in Article 6(a) of the Nuremberg Charter clearly was aimed at formulating a particular form by which a person could perpetrate the crime of aggression. It is, therefore, not a crime at all.

Although the wording of Article 6(a) suggests that a crime against peace may be perpetrated through a conspiracy to commit (extensive) war crimes and crimes against humanity, the Nuremberg Tribunal declined to entertain that notion and instead confined conspiracy to crimes against peace. The Nuremberg and subsequent World War II tribunals required three criteria for the existence of this hybrid international law conspiracy: a) the existence of a concrete plan involving the participation of at least two persons; b) clear outlining of the criminal purpose of the plan; c) the plan be not too far removed from the time of decision and action.[58] *Mens rea* consisted of knowledge of the conspiracy and direct intention to play a part in its execution, irrespective if this was not eventually carried out.[59] Certainly, a good part of the elements of conspiracy were borrowed, as a matter of general principles, from common law legal systems. Nonetheless, it is equally undeniable that the armed conflict context of Nuremberg and subsequent tribunals, as well as the fact that in international practice it was employed as a form of participation rather than as an inchoate crime, suffice to render international law conspiracy a distinct legal creature. The Nuremberg Tribunal required a very high threshold of participation and knowledge of the plan and limited the charge of conspiracy only against those that participated in preparatory acts materialising into actual acts of aggression.[60]

The conspiracy legacy of the Nuremberg Charter and Tribunal did not survive the Cold War, at least in most respects. Article III(b) of the Genocide Convention, which criminalises conspiracy as a particular inchoate crime pertinent to genocide – as is also the case with incitement and attempts – was hotly debated during the conference that preceded its adoption. It was agreed that genocide could not be charged for mere preparatory acts without some form of attempt or completion.[61] Similarly, Article 2(3)(e) of the ILC's 1996 Draft Code of Crimes required the implementation of the criminal plan in relation to conspiracy. Nonetheless, the inclusion of conspiracy in

---

[56] In *Hamdan v Rumsfeld* (2006) 548 U.S 557, Judge Stephens pointed out that conspiracy is not recognised as a war crime in the laws of the USA.

[57] The 2000 Convention against Transnational Organised Crime reflects this definition in Article 5(1)(a)(i), which criminalises merely the agreement to 'commit a serious crime for a purpose relating directly or indirectly to the obtaining of a financial or other material benefit'. Member States are free to require that liability arises only where a concrete overt act is also perpetrated subsequent to the agreement. This type of conspiracy is also encountered in those treaties that encompass an element of organised crime, as is the case with Art 36(2)(a)(ii) of the 1961 Single Convention on Narcotic Drugs and Art 22(2)(a)(ii) of the 1971 Convention on Psychotropic Substances.

[58] See *Krupp* case, 10 Law Reports of Trials of War Criminals (LRTWC) 69, 110, 113.

[59] *I.G. Farben* case, 10 LRTWC 1, at 31, 40; Official Transcript of the Judgment of the IMTFE (*Tokyo* Trial) 1142–43. Although conspiracy was charged and ultimately found in the context of the Tokyo Trials, it did not sit well with some judges on the panel.

[60] I Bantekas, *Principles of Direct and Superior Responsibility in International Humanitarian Law* (Manchester, Manchester University Press, 2002) 47.

[61] Ibid, p 48.

Article III of the Genocide Convention, together with the actual perpetration of genocide, is evidence enough that it was intended as an inchoate offence.

This position was subsequently overturned in the context of the ad hoc tribunals. In fact, the ICTR Trial Chamber in the *Musema* case after defining genocidal conspiracy as 'an agreement between two or more persons to commit the crime of genocide' argued that since it is the agreement which is punishable, it is irrelevant whether or not it results in the actual commission of genocide.[62] It is obvious, moreover, that in this manner genocidal conspiracy is treated as an inchoate crime, rather than as a form of liability. Given that what is required is the existence of a mere agreement, the mental standard applicable to conspiracies can only be that of intent (*dolus directus* of the first and second degree). As to the existence of a conspiratorial agreement, the *Nahimana* Trial Judgment considered that this may be inferred

> ... from coordinated actions by individuals who have a common purpose and are acting within a unified framework. A coalition, even an informal coalition, can constitute such a framework so long as those acting within the coalition are aware of its existence, their participation in it, and its role in furtherance of their common purpose. [A] conspiracy can be comprised of individuals acting in an institutional capacity as well as or even independently of their personal links with each other. Institutional coordination can form the basis of a conspiracy among those individuals who control the institutions that are engaged in coordinated action.[63]

The ICTR is, nonetheless, divided as to whether upon consummation of genocide the accused should be convicted for both genocide and conspiracy on the basis of the same set of facts. The *Musema* Trial judgment took a negative approach to this question,[64] while in the *Niyitegeka* case the Trial Chamber was inclined to punish the accused for both.[65] The issue at heart is whether cumulative charging is permissible and under what circumstances. The *Čelebići* Appeals judgment affirmed that cumulative charging was permissible only if each statutory provision has a materially distinct element not contained in the other. An element is materially distinct from another if it requires proof of a fact that is not required by the other.[66] Although the *Musema* Appeals judgment did not address the permissibility of charging the accused with both genocide and conspiracy, it did approve separate convictions for genocide and extermination as a crime against humanity on the same set of facts.[67] On the basis of this test it is logical to assume that multiple convictions are permissible because whereas genocide does not require an agreement or plan, but merely a specific intent, conspiracy requires such an agreement.

During the preparatory conferences on the ICC Statute it was suggested that the Nuremberg-type conspiracy be included because of its legacy. In this regard two

---

[62] *ICTR Prosecutor v Musema*, Trial Chamber Judgment (27 Jan 2000), paras 189, 193; *ICTR Prosecutor v Kajelijeli*, Trial Chamber Judgment (1 Dec 2003), paras 787–88. The latter argued that the agreement must be shown to have been reached and that the showing of a mere negotiation in progress will not suffice.

[63] *ICTR Prosecutor v Nahimana*, Trial Chamber Judgment (3 Dec 2003), paras 1047–48.

[64] *Musema* Trial Judgment, para 197.

[65] *ICTR Prosecutor v Niyitegeka*, Trial Chamber Judgment (16 May 2003), paras 429, 480, 502.

[66] *Čelebići* Appeal Judgment, paras 412–13.

[67] *Musema* Appeal Judgment (16 Nov 2001), paras 358–70.

proposals were submitted; one where the conspirators simply plan but do not carry out the conspiracy themselves and another where it is the conspirators that perpetrate the overt act.[68] The compromise solution, as has already been stated, is now Article 25(3)(d) of the ICC Statute, which is akin to the Nuremberg concept of common plan (Article 6(a) thereof) since it requires attempt or completion, which was not the case with conspiracy as an inchoate crime, nor with the recent ICTR deliberations. Even if some sort of conspiracy is recognised, thus, in the ICC Statute, this is not an inchoate crime but a form of participation in crime and liability thereof. It seems to constitute a subsidiary form of liability to aiding and abetting. Whereas aiding and abetting requires knowledge that one's assistance contributes to the commission of a crime, participation in a common purpose under the meaning of subparagraph (d) of the ICC Statute necessitates the existence of said common purpose, an intentional contribution of the participant and an additional aim of furthering the criminal activity or criminal purpose of the group. Alternatively, the participant must act in the knowledge of the intention of the group, thus requiring that he is aware of the specific crime of the group and accepts the foreseeable outcome.

3.6   Attempts

In domestic legal systems attempts are treated invariably either as inchoate crimes or as a form of criminal participation. The general rule, accepted also in Article 25(3)(f) of the ICC Statute, is that a person that has taken action which commences the execution of a crime by means of a substantial step (attempt) is nonetheless liable for the ensuing crime irrespective if such a crime does not eventually occur because of circumstances independent of that person's intentions. This result is typically exemplified in cases where the accused inflicts an injury upon a victim with an intention to kill, but the victim does not ultimately die, or where the same action of the accused is thwarted or prevented by acts of nature or by the intervention of third persons. In all these cases the accused will incur liability for the attempted commission of the underlying crime because of his intention to bring about the particular result from start to end.[69] Because the accused must have intended to commit the underlying crime, if he was not reasonably aware of factual circumstances giving rise thereto, he will not be considered as having attempted that crime. This is true, for example, in respect of those offences whose mental element requires that the accused possessed the consent of the victim, as is the case with rape. If the accused reasonably believed that such consent had been provided and for whatever reason the rape was not consummated he will not be liable for attempted rape.[70]

An accused is no longer deemed to be participating in the commission of an offence where he or she willingly abandons the wrongful conduct before the act is consummated and without any external intervention. Such abandonment must be a wholly voluntary act. This rule obviously applies to crimes that require completion in

---

[68]   Bantekas *Principles*, at 49, citing from the official records of ICC preparatory commissions.
[69]   Cassese, *International Criminal Law*, 220–25.
[70]   Ashworth, *Principles*, 448–49.

order for liability to arise (crimes of consequence). In such cases it is presumed that the objective and fault elements of the offence have not been fulfilled and hence the offence has never existed. The rationale for not criminalising the abandonment of an otherwise commenced crime is to provide a chance to the average offender to reconsider and give up the offence without further criminal repercussions. This rule, however, does not apply with regard to continuing offences; ie offences whose objective and fault elements have been duly satisfied and the duration of which are continuous in time and space against the same or other victims.[71] For example, an accused that has enslaved certain of his adversaries for an entire year is responsible for the crime of enslavement regardless if he later decides to release his victims. It should not also apply with respect to crimes of conduct. D uses prohibited chemical weapons against V and seeing him suffer immediately ceases its operation. He is certainly liable for that incident and his subsequent withdrawal will be employed as a mitigating circumstance.

The ICC Statute employs the test found in the US Model Penal Code in order to determine when the accused has commenced a crime, as opposed to simply be deliberating on it. Thus, it is required that he committed at the very least a 'substantial step' of the crime. This would exclude mere preparatory acts, but the exact fault lines between the two are a matter of degree that can only be assessed on a case-by-case basis.[72]

3.7 Aiding and Abetting

Aiding and abetting consists of all acts that are 'specifically directed to assist, encourage or lend moral support to the perpetration of a specific crime [a single crime, such as murder or rape and not a criminal design] and this support has a substantial effect upon the perpetration of the crime'.[73] Although it is accepted in domestic criminal justice systems generally it is not recognised in classic Islamic criminal law.[74] The *Blaškić* Appeal judgment, while noting that the *actus reus* of aiding and abetting requires a substantial effect upon the crime committed by the

---

[71] This defence of withdrawal or abandonment was not accepted in the US case of *People v Cooper* (Ill, App 1975) 332 N.E 2d 453. There, D entered the house of V with two others with an intention to burgle and proceeded to restrain V by tying her up. In the course of the burglary he had second thoughts and left the house without taking any loot. He was charged with murder because after leaving the house V was killed by his co-perpetrators and he did nothing to release V.

[72] Ashworth, *Principles*, 450–52.

[73] *ICTY Prosecutor v Vasiljević*, Appeals Chamber Judgment (25 Feb 2004), para. 102; *Blaškić* Appeal Judgment, para. 45.

[74] A person is liable under classic Islamic criminal law only if he has fulfilled all the elements of a crime. If he simply assists the principal he is not liable. Where a crime involves multiple perpetrators, the sequence of acts and blows must be established with precision, otherwise liability is ascribed only to the last in sequence perpetrator, provided his conduct could have alone caused death. Obviously, if it is found that all perpetrators simultaneously attacked the victim they are all deemed principals, in accordance with the Hanafi school. The Maliki school, on the other hand, views aiding and abetting as a form of co-perpetratorship and ascribes liability to all participants. See Peters, *Crime and Punishment in Islamic Law*, 28–29.

principal, no proof of a cause-effect relationship between the aider and the commission of the crime is required, nor proof that such conduct 'served as a condition precedent to the commission of the crime'.[75]

The acts of aiding and abetting while mostly positive in practice, may be perpetrated through an omission where a particular duty to act exists and the omission itself had a substantial effect on the commission of the crime, provided that the accused possessed the appropriate volitional and cognitive elements relative to the crime under consideration.[76] In the *Mrkšić* case the accused Šljivančanin was found vested with temporary *de jure* command over a regular military contingent that assisted him among others in detaining and safe-keeping prisoners of war in a hospital compound. When his superior issued an order for the evacuation of this contingent the accused was well aware that it would be replaced by personnel known for their brutality and mistreatment of enemy forces, yet he did nothing to prevent the regular contingent from departing. The POWs were subsequently subjected to murder and other ill-treatment and the accused was charged with aiding and abetting through omission. He argued that a crime of omission required proof of a legal duty stemming from the dictates of criminal law (to which he was ordinarily subjected, ie Yugoslav law), which at the time forbid him to question superior orders and that he possessed no command over the departing or the newly-arrived troops. The Appeals Chamber rightly held that his duty to act need not emanate from criminal law, but also from the laws and customs of war to protect POWs.[77] Equally, it must be shown that the accused had a material capacity to act and he failed to discharge all that was materially available to him.[78] In the circumstances of the case the accused could have exercised a *de facto* power, as a superior to the commander of the irregulars and could have made concrete attempts to shield the POWs, which he did not. Therefore he was found liable for aiding and abetting their death and mistreatment by his omission to act.

The *actus reus* of aiding and abetting does not require the presence of the aider at the location where the crime was perpetrated, nor proof of a plan or agreement. Equally, the mere presence of a person with superior authority at the crime scene is insufficient to determine whether that person in fact encouraged or supported the principal. A combination of superior authority and presence that may be deemed to have a significant legitimising or encouraging effect on the principal, may be taken as weighty circumstantial evidence of substantial encouragement and support.[79] The participation of the aider may occur before, during, or after the act is committed by the principal.[80]

---

[75] *Blaškić* Appeal Judgment, paras 1, 48; ICTY *Prosecutor v Brđanin*, Trial Chamber Judgment (1 Sep 2004), para. 271

[76] *Blaškić* Appeal Judgment, para. 47; ICTY *Prosecutor v Simić*, Trial Chamber Judgment (17 Oct 2003), para. 162; *ICTY Prosecutor v Orić*, Appeals Chamber Judgment (3 Jul 2009), para 43; *ICTY Prosecutor v Blagoević and Jokić*, Appeals Chamber Judgment (9 May 2007), para 127.

[77] *ICTY Prosecutor v Mrkšić and Šljivančanin*, Appeals Chamber Judgment (5 May 2009), paras148–51.

[78] Ibid, paras 153–54.

[79] *Brđanin* Trial Judgment, para 271; *Simić* Trial Judgment, para 165.

[80] *Blaškić* Appeal Judgment, para 48; *Simić* Trial Judgment, para 162.

As far as the *mens rea* for aiding and abetting is concerned, while it is not required that the aider shared the *mens rea* of the principal, it must be demonstrated that the aider 'was aware of the essential elements of the crime which was ultimately committed by the principal'.[81] In other words, the law is interested in ascertaining the particular intent of the aider as to the act of the principal and his participation therein and in this sense it is not necessary for the aider to know the precise crime that was intended and ultimately committed, as long as he is aware that one of a number of crimes will probably be, and are in fact, committed and has intended to facilitate the commission of any one of those crimes.[82] If, however, the aider facilitates only a single crime of the principal, he must be found to be aware of the essential elements of the principal's crime, including his relevant *mens rea*.[83] Unlike other forms of participation in crime, the *mens rea* for aiding and abetting requires only direct intent (*dolus directus* of the first and second degree) as to the act of the principal and awareness as to the significance of one's contribution. As a result, the relevant test is not satisfied with the demonstration of foreseeability as to the result or the effect of the contribution (*dolus eventualis* or recklessness). With regard to persecution, a specific intent crime, the *mens rea* for aiding and abetting requires not only awareness of the facilitated crime, but also of the discriminatory intent of the principal. The aider need not share the intent of the principal but must be 'aware of the discriminatory context in which the crime is to be committed and know that his support or encouragement has a substantial effect on its perpetration'.[84]

The same is obviously true for genocide, yet another specific intent crime,[85] but subject to a crucial distinction. The jurisprudence of the ad hoc tribunals rightly differentiates between persons that play a key co-ordinating role in the planning and execution of genocide and those that merely associate themselves with the implementation of the crime. The former are considered direct perpetrators (or principals), whereas the latter are viewed as accomplices. As a result, the general rule applies, whereby specific intent is only required for the principals. As far as accomplice liability is concerned all that needs to be demonstrated is knowledge of one's assistance and awareness of the principal's genocidal intent. In the circumstances of that case the Tribunal found the accused liable for aiding and abetting genocide because he knew that murders were occurring and he nonetheless permitted the Main Staff to use personnel and resources under his command to facilitate these killings. Crucially, however, the *Krstić* Appeals Chamber held that whereas mere awareness

---

[81] *ICTY Prosecutor v Aleksovski*, Appeals Chamber Judgment (24 Mar 2000), para 162; *Krnojelac* Appeal Judgment, para. 51.

[82] *Blaškić* Appeal Judgment, para 50; *ICTR Prosecutor v Ndindabahizi*, Appeals Chamber Judgment (16 Jan 2007), para 122.

[83] *Krnojelac* Appeal Judgment, para 51.

[84] *Krnojelac* Appeal Judgment, para 52. In *Public Prosecutor v Kouwenhoven*, Hague District Court Judgment (7 Jun 2006), the accused was a Dutch national who was allegedly involved in arms supplies to the regime of Charles Taylor in Liberia and was among other things charged with complicity in war crimes committed in Liberia's domestic armed conflict. He was acquitted of this charge because neither his involvement nor his awareness of the crimes and intent to commit war crimes through his arms trade could be established beyond reasonable doubt. In *Public Prosecutor v Van Anraat*, Hague District Court Judgment (23 Dec 2005), on the other hand, the accused was found complicit in war crimes for selling raw materials to the regime of Saddam Hussein in the knowledge of its use to manufacture chemical weapons which were later used to kill the Kurdish civilian population of Halabja.

[85] *ICTY Prosecutor v Krstić*, Appeals Chamber Judgment (19 Apr 2004), para 140.

was sufficient with respect to aiding and abetting, it was not for complicity to genocide, which it found to be broader than aiding and abetting this offence. Complicity to genocide – which must certainly consist of assistance that is very significant – was held to require the specific intent of genocide (ie the intention to destroy a group in whole or in part).[86]

A particular manifestation of aiding and abetting, the so-called 'approving spectator', was adapted from national legal systems and identified as such early on by the ad hoc tribunals. This is identical in all other respects with the generic form of aiding and abetting with the exception that it requires actual presence during the commission of the crime or at least presence in its immediate vicinity, such that is perceived by the actual perpetrator as approval of the accessory's conduct. Liability arises where the 'approving spectator' knows that his presence would be perceived by the perpetrator as encouragement or support, particularly where he occupies a position of authority.[87]

The ICTY has on a few occasions, following the 1999 *Tadić* Appeals Judgment in which the concept of joint criminal enterprise (JCE) was formulated, discussed the differences between aiding and abetting and JCE. Where a person substantially contributes to the commission of a crime committed by a single principal, or a plurality thereof, and this is all that he is aware of, he becomes an accomplice (by aiding and abetting) as regards those particular offences. This is so even if the principal is part of a JCE involving the commission of further crimes. Where, however, the aider is aware that his assistance is supporting the crimes of a group of persons involved in a JCE and shares that intent he may be held liable for the crimes committed in furtherance of that common purpose as a whole and not simply for the crimes in which he assisted.[88] His overall awareness of the criminal design and willing participation therein suffices to establish oblique intent as to the perpetration of the objectives of the design.

3.8 Ordering

An order is a command for action or omission that is issued by a superior to a subordinate, irrespective of whether the context of the relationship is military or civilian. The relationship itself need not be formally established, but could exist de facto, as long as the addressee perceives the order as a binding command.[89] It may be written or oral and addressed to either a specific individual or to unknown recipients and it may also be channelled to its addressees through a number of intermediaries. The *actus reus* of ordering consists of the transmission of an unlawful command to

---

[86] Ibid, para 142. See chapter 9.6.

[87] *ICTR Prosecutor v Semanza*, Trial Chamber Judgment (15 May 2003), paras 385–89.

[88] *Vasiljević* Appeal Judgment, para 102; *Krnojelac* Appeal Judgment, para 33; *Kvočka* Appeal Judgment, para 90.

[89] In *ICTR Prosecutor v Semanza*, Appeals Chamber Judgment (20 May 2005), para 363, it was held that the authority required for the purposes of ordering may be informal or of a purely temporary nature and distinguishable from the authority required to prove command responsibility.

one or more subordinates.[90] An order is unlawful where it violates international humanitarian or general international criminal law, even if it is in conformity with the domestic law of the State of the person that issued it. Although this conclusion is consistent with the customary principle that domestic law may not be invoked to justify violation of an international rule,[91] it does little to aid a superior who dutifully acted within the boundaries of his domestic law. As a result, domestic law should itself be characterised as an order, so that its implementing recipients may benefit from the international law relating to superior orders and duress, assuming that they satisfy all the other elements of said defences.

Equally, not all orders whose content is unlawful entail the liability of the person who issued or transmitted them. The general *mens rea* standard for ordering requires knowledge of the order's illegal character, coupled with direct or oblique intent to fulfil its content. Where the order was not known to the issuer to be unlawful, or where it was not manifestly unlawful that person will not be liable for the harm caused by the order because that person's cognitive awareness is deemed to have been negated.[92] This would, therefore, exclude negligence, which may be defined as lacking awareness as to an unlawful risk or a criminal consequence. Thus, where subsequent superiors are aware of the illegality of the order, or are reckless (ie they are conscious as to the taking of an unjustifiable risk) as to its consequences and nonetheless transmit it through the chain of command they are just as liable as the person who initially issued the order.[93] Liability for ordering should not encompass military personnel who simply transmit an order as part of their ordinary function, but which are not endowed with direct subordinates.

In the absence of a standard lower than direct intent in Article 7(1) of the ICTY Statute, the ICTY was forced to decide whether recklessness or *dolus eventualis* pertain to ordering. The methodology employed by the *Blaškić* Appeals Chamber involved an examination of the common law of recklessness and civil law *dolus eventualis* as a matter of general principle of domestic laws. It found that in common law jurisdictions the *mens rea* for recklessness – which attaches to serious crimes equivalent to ordering – incorporates 'the awareness of a risk that the result or consequence will occur or will probably occur [but it must not be virtually certain, otherwise it is oblique intent], and the risk must be unjustifiable or unreasonable. The mere possibility of a risk that a crime or crimes will occur as a result of the actor's conduct generally does not suffice to ground criminal responsibility', because it amounts to negligence.[94] The Appeals Chamber's findings with regard to the civil law conception of *dolus eventualis* make no significant departure from its reckless standard counterpart.[95] In general terms it requires that the accused perceived or foresaw the harm as possible, but not remote, and although he may not have intended

---

[90] This much has been established without controversy by all ICTY chambers. See, eg *Brdjanin* Trial Judgment, para 270; Bantekas, *Principles of Direct and Superior Responsibility*, 50–53.

[91] Art 3, ILC Articles on State Responsibility; see also *LaGrand* case (Germany v USA), Provisional Measures Order (3 Mar 1999), (1999) ICJ Reports 9, para 28.

[92] See Art 33 ICTY Statute, on the defence of superior orders.

[93] *USA v von Leeb* [*High Command* case] 11 Trials 510.

[94] *Blaškić* Appeal Judgment, para 38.

[95] For a thorough discussion of *dolus eventualis* and recklessness see chapter 2.4.

to bring it about he accepted the possibility that it may well occur.[96] Thus, besides direct and oblique intent, the Appeals Chamber expressly grounded in addition the existence of a lower *mens rea* standard that is more akin to common law recklessness, despite the civil law composition of the ad hoc tribunal, in the following terms:

> A person who orders an act or omission with the awareness of the substantial likelihood that a crime will be committed in the execution of that order, has the requisite *mens rea* for establishing liability under Article 7(1) [of the ICTY Statute]. Ordering with such awareness has to be regarded as accepting that crime.[97]

The matter is not clarified in the ICC Statute, Article 30(1)(b) of which states that a person has intent in relation to a consequence where 'that person means to cause that consequence or is aware that it will occur in the ordinary course of events'. Although Article 30 generally establishes the general rule that only direct intent (in the sense of *dolus directus* of the first and second degree) is the mental standard applicable to ICC crimes and forms of participation, the same provision also entertains a clause that allows for the importation of lower standards (ie recklessness and negligence) if this is explicitly stated in the definition of that crime or mode of participation. This exception is indicated by the words: 'unless otherwise provided'.[98] It is thus not out of the question for an ICC chamber to apply a standard lower than direct intent, but this has to be strenuously justified on the basis of other provisions in the ICC Statute. In the absence of written orders as evidence before a court, attribution by means of ordering may be inferred from a variety of circumstantial evidence, particularly the number of illegal acts, the number, identity and type of troops involved, the effective command and control exerted over these troops, the logistics, the widespread occurrence of the illegal acts, the tactical tempo of operations, the location of the superior and his knowledge of crimes committed under his command and others.[99] Equally, confusion may well persist as to the unlawful nature of a written order, as was the case in the *Blaškić* Appeals Judgment where a preventive attacking order against a village inhabited by civilians was initially found by the Trial Chamber to lack a military objective. In reversing the Trial Chamber's determination as to the nature of the order the Appeals Chamber held that in fact the village had a strategic significance because it was very close to a road linking two major cities and on which enemy combatants frequently travelled.[100]

The issuer of an illegal order who satisfies the requisite *actus reus* and *mens rea* is liable as if he himself had perpetrated the eventual crime.[101]

---

[96]   *Blaškić* Appeal Judgment, para 39.

[97]   Ibid, para 42; now firmly accepted as part of the ICTY's jurisprudence. See ICTY *Prosecutor v Kordić*, Appeals Chamber Judgment (17 Dec 2004), para 30.

[98]   G Werle, F Jessberger, 'Unless Otherwise Provided' (2005) 3 *Journal of International Criminal Justice* 35. We have already made reference in this chapter to the *Lubanga* Confirmation of Charges Decision, para 352, where it was held that *dolus eventualis* is compatible with Art 30 of the ICC Statute.

[99]   *ICTY Prosecutor v Galić* Trial Chamber Judgment (5 Dec 2003), para 171.

[100]   *Blaškić* Appeal Judgment, paras 330–32.

[101]   See R Cryer, 'General Principles of Liability in International Criminal Law' in D McGoldrick *et al*, *The Permanent International Criminal Court* (Oxford, Hart Publishing, 2004) 242–47, where he discusses the legal nature of liability incurred as a result of ordering.

3.9 Planning and Preparation

Several legal terms have been employed since the end of World War II to describe a concerted effort between multiple participants to commit one or more crimes. Article 6(a) of the Nuremberg Charter imposed liability for the planning, among others, of crimes against peace as well as for participation in 'a common plan or conspiracy' to commit war crimes and crimes against peace. Equally, Article 3(b) of the 1948 Genocide Convention refers to liability arising from a conspiracy to commit genocide, without making any reference to planning. Finally, while the concept of conspiracy is absent from the ICTY and ICC Statutes, planning exists in Article 7(1) of the ICTY Statute, but not in its ICC counterpart. Planning and conspiracy are distinct legal concepts. A significant difference between the two is that while the planning of a crime may be committed by a single person, conspiracy requires at least two.[102] In practice, planning involves 'one or several persons contemplating designing the commission of a crime at both the preparatory and execution phases'.[103] The existence of a plan, whether this is formal or informal, must be demonstrated by direct or circumstantial evidence.[104] The level of participation of the accused in the plan is an additional important factor. According to the *Brđjanin* Trial Judgment, planning liability arises only if it was 'demonstrated that the accused was substantially involved at the preparatory stage of that crime in the concrete form it took, which implies that he possessed sufficient knowledge thereof in advance'.[105] It is not a requirement, however, that the accused be intimate with every detail of the acts committed by the physical perpetrator.[106] Moreover, it is necessary that the accused devise the plan or be involved in the immediate preparation of the concrete crimes and not merely participate in its implementation by virtue of his authority.[107]

A person that plans a crime and moreover commits the planned crime will only be liable for its perpetration.[108] This factor demonstrates a further proximity with conspiracy/JCE in which participants in the conspiracy or common design are ultimately liable as perpetrators and not on account of their particular roles, which may not have involved perpetration of the crimes themselves. There is no guidance in the relevant international instruments or the jurisprudence of the ICTY/ICTR as to whether the planner is liable absent perpetration of the crime. It is probably imprudent to seek a solution to this query on the basis of general principles because planning liability has developed since its Nuremberg origins wholly within the realm of international law. In this light, since the conspiracy/JCE concepts do not require completion and given that planning belongs within this family of liability, it would be wise at least to provide for the liability of persons that are instrumental with regard to the formulation of a criminal plan that is dissolved against their will before being consummated.

---

[102] *Akayesu* Trial Judgment, para 480.
[103] Ibid.
[104] *ICTY Prosecutor v Naletilić*, Trial Chamber Judgment (31 Mar 2003), para 59.
[105] *Brđjanin* Trial Judgment, para 357.
[106] Ibid.
[107] Ibid, para 358.
[108] *ICTY Prosecutor v Blaškić*, Trial Chamber Judgment (3 Mar 2000), para 278.

The *mens rea* for planning requires that the accused intended the crime in question through the plan. Besides direct intent, the *Kordić* Appeals Judgment stated that in relation to planning, 'a person who plans an act or omission with the awareness of the substantial likelihood that a crime will be committed in the execution of that plan' has the requisite *mens rea* for planning, since this is regarded as accepting that crime.[109] This would refer to oblique intent rather than recklessness/*dolus eventualis*. Nonetheless, there is no obvious reason why D who plans the forceful evacuation of the inhabitants of a village should not be liable for the murder of V, an evacuee, who resisted and was killed by his evacuators. D could have clearly foreseen that such an eventuality was possible and as a result a reckless standard may be sketched into the *mens rea* of planning.

3.10   Instigation

Liability through instigation arises by prompting another to commit an offence through an action or omission.[110] The ICTY has held that omissions amount to instigation in circumstances where a commander has created 'an environment permissive of criminal behaviour by subordinates'.[111] The creation of such a delinquent environment gives rise to liability when the commander is aware of it and accepts that it may encourage his or her subordinates, thus excluding negligent-based liability for the purposes of instigation. Unlike ordering, which involves a superior-subordinate relationship, no such relationship is required for a charge of instigation to succeed and as a result the relationship between the instigator and the physical perpetrator may lack the elements of compulsion and command.[112] A causal link must, however, exist between the instigation and the perpetration of a crime, although it is not necessary to demonstrate that the crime would not have been perpetrated without the involvement of the accused.[113] The prosecution must show that the instigation 'was a factor substantially contributing to the conduct' of the principal.[114] If the instigation was one of many reasons that culminated in the harm then a solid causal relationship is lacking and the accused will incur liability as an aider or abettor.[115] What this also means in practice is that if the direct perpetrator was already considering committing the crime, the instigator remains liable where the crime was ultimately committed by reason of his persuasion or strong encouragement. However, if the direct perpetrator had definitely decided to commit the crime in question regardless of any external

---

[109]   *Kordić* Appeal Judgment, para 31.
[110]   *Akayesu* Trial Judgment, para 482.
[111]   *Blaškić* Trial Judgment, para 337; *Galić* Trial Judgment, para 168.
[112]   *ICTY Prosecutor v Orić*, Trial Chamber Judgment (30 Jun 2006), para 272.
[113]   *Kordić* Appeal Judgment, para 27; *Gacumbitsi* Appeal Judgment, para 127.
[114]   *Kordić* Appeal Judgment, ibid.
[115]   In *ICTR Prosecutor v Nahimana* [*Media* case], Appeal Chamber Judgment (28 Nov 2007), paras 513, 994, it was held that radio broadcasts transmitted prior to the critical start date of the Rwandan genocide did not establish a causal link. The Appeal Chamber took the position that the 'longer the lapse of time between a broadcast and the killing of a person, the greater the possibility that other events might be the real cause of such killing and that the broadcasts might not have substantially contributed to it'. Equally followed in *SCSL Prosecutor v Fofana and Kondewa*, Appeal Judgment (28 May 2008), para 55.

influences (and is therefore acting as *omnimodo facturus*) any further encouragement by the instigator would not qualify as instigation, but at best as aiding and abetting.[116]

Moreover, liability for instigation arises only where the offence has been committed, or attempted.[117] Where the crime has not been committed, the accused's conduct may be described as incitement, which does not generally entail liability, unless it concerns public and direct incitement to commit genocide.[118] In cases where instigation has not been followed by perpetration, the prosecution may well argue that the accused devised a plan or was a co-perpetrator in the context of a joint criminal enterprise, assuming all other relevant elements are duly demonstrated. Because of the lack of compulsion involved in instigation the physical perpetrator cannot invoke superior orders or duress to exculpate himself. The instigator may under particular circumstances invoke these defences, particularly where the instigation was the result of a binding order given to him by his superiors, provided that the other requisites for these defences are met.

The *mens rea* for instigation requires that the accused intended to provoke or induce the commission of the crime by the physical perpetrator (*dolus directus* of the first and second degree), or that he was aware of the substantial likelihood that the commission of the crime would be a probable consequence of his acts or omissions.[119] This suggests, as would logically be the case, that recklessness/*dolus eventualis* will suffice. Where D, an influential local businessman makes an emotional speech to a local civilian population to drive out with force from their locality all foreign workers because they will eventually steal their jobs, he must somehow foresee that his views will necessarily push some of his listeners to commit acts of violence. The basic principle in respect of serious violations of international law committed through ordering, instigating and planning is that no recklessness is an acceptable *mens rea* standard, at least as far as the ad hoc tribunals are concerned.[120]

Just like incitement to genocide where the particular perception of the message by the intended audience is critical only for determining the perpetrator's awareness as to how that audience understood the message, the same is true with regard to instigation. If that were not so, a court would be justified in imposing liability on the basis of reckless behaviour by the accused where he was aware that a possibility did exist that the message may be perceived as instigating criminal activity. Recklessness, however, finds no place in the *mens rea* definition of instigation, or indeed in the crime of genocide.

---

[116] Orić Trial Judgment, para 271.
[117] *Akayesu* Trial Judgment, para 482; *Brđjanin* Trial Judgment, para 269.
[118] Art 3(c) of the 1948 Genocide Convention; Art 25(3)(e) ICC Statute.
[119] *Blaškić* Appeal Judgment, para 42; *Kordić* Appeal Judgment, para 32.
[120] See *Orić* Trial Chamber, para 279.

3.11   International Corporate Criminal Liability

There is no doubt that general corporate criminal liability does not exist in international law. Its existence is fragmentary, context specific and subject to qualification. One could argue that because the concept is found in some legal systems, it may in fact amount to a general principle of criminal laws and thus a source of international law. This is not true, because not only does it not exist in every, or most, legal systems, but even where it does exist its objective and subjective elements are significantly divergent. An alternative argument as to the possible general applicability of corporate criminal liability could be predicated on Articles 9 and 10 of the Charter of the Nuremberg Tribunal, which gave authority to the Tribunal to assess and declare groups or organisations as being criminal in nature. These provisions, however, were intended to target membership therein and not the legal entity itself. Article 10 is instructive of the purposes of its drafters.

> In cases where a group or organisation is declared criminal by the Tribunal, the competent national authority of any signatory shall have the right to bring individuals to trial for membership therein before national, military or occupation courts. In any such case the criminal nature of the group or organisation is considered proved and shall not be questioned.

The fact that corporate criminality was not envisaged in the post-World War II international instruments may also be discerned from the fact that in the so-called *Industrialist* trials it was personal participation at the highest levels that was targeted and not the corporation itself.[121] The rejection of corporate criminality was rejected also in the context of the ICC Statute, although a proposal to that effect was lodged with the aim of attributing criminal liability to a person in a position of control and acting under the consent of the corporation.[122] The rationale of this proposal was not so much the criminal liability of the wrongdoer, as the possibility of achieving a substantial compensation from the corporation. Ultimately, the idea was dropped because not all member States recognise this type of liability, which would consequently risk rendering the principle of complementarity moot.

In the post-Cold War era, while it is true that legal persons have been the subject of suits before some national courts for extraterritorial offences, the impact of these suits has remained largely at the civil and not the criminal level.[123] The two are quite distinct and no arbitrary similarities may be inferred as to criminal implications from civil suits and the reach of the criminal law thereof. This conclusion is further reinforced by the plethora of non-binding international legal instruments pertaining to the role and function of corporations.[124]

---

[121]   *USA v Flick*, 6 Trials 1217.

[122]   UN Doc A/CONF. 183/C.1/WGGP/L.5 (1998); UN Doc A/CONF. 183/C.1/SR.26 (8 Jul 1998).

[123]   See I Bantekas, 'Corporate Social Responsibility in International Law' (2004) 22 *Boston University International Law Journal* 309.

[124]   2000 OECD Guidelines for Multinational Enterprises, OECD Doc OECD/GD(97)40 (2000); and the UN Norms on the Responsibilities of Transnational Corporations and other Business Enterprises with regard to Human Rights, U.N. ESCOR C.H.R., 55th Sess, 22nd mtg, UN Doc E/CN.4/Sub.2/2003/12/Rev.2 (2003).

What we do have, however, is the seed of exceptional corporate criminal liability at the regional level, or in respect of particular international offences. As regards the latter, recent Framework Decisions falling within the Third Pillar of the European Union (EU), while obliging member States to promulgate legislation entailing corporate liability, all that such instruments do is to harmonise the sanctions and leave the nature of the liability to the law of each member State.[125] This is understandable given the lack of uniformity in the member States' legal systems on this matter. Hence, criminal corporate liability in this context becomes a matter for national law and not an international obligation. With regard to crime-specific corporate criminality, some degree of liability is prescribed in anti-corruption treaties, such as Articles 2 and 3(2) of the 1997 OECD Convention and Article 26 of the 2003 UN Convention against Corruption. It is true that these provisions do not oblige member States to promulgate the criminal liability of legal persons, but only to adopt 'effective, proportionate and dissuasive' sanctions, whether of a civil, administrative or criminal nature in conformity with their legal systems. Nonetheless, the conventions do provide for the criminal liability of the natural persons who committed the offences, particularly where they were acting as agents of the legal person.[126] Therefore, as a result of treaty law – under which only signatories are bound – corporate criminal liability with respect to corruption entails: a) criminal liability of the legal person only where this is possible in the law of the signatory and under the terms of that law, and b) the criminal liability of corporate agents for the crime they committed (as principals or accomplices) as a matter only of international law.[127] Such agents would be subject to the usual rules of principal or accomplice liability and as such they could also be tried before the ICC in their personal capacity. Their link to the legal person, although not wholly relevant for ICC criminal proceedings except only for evidentiary purposes, could provide the backbone for a subsequent civil suit brought by victims and their families against the legal person.[128]

Moreover, a number of jurisdictions are applying criminal law against corporations in their pursuit of extraterritorial offences, almost all of which involve the offence of corruption.[129] The concept of corporate criminality is well known in the common law world. The Securities and Exchange Commission (SEC) and the US Department of Justice have for many years pursued corporations for extraterritorial acts of corruption in accordance with the Foreign Corrupt Practices Act. Whereas their early practice consisted of prosecuting together both the individuals involved and the corporation, their recent approach is to charge the two separately and in sequence with a view to exacting cooperation from one party against the other. As a result,

---

[125] For example, Arts 7 and 8 of Council Framework Decision of 28 May 2001 on Combating Fraud and Counterfeiting of Non-Cash Means of Payment, OJ L 149, 2 Jun 1981; Arts 8 and 9 of Council Framework Decision of 29 May 2000 on Increasing Protection by Criminal Penalties and Other Sanctions against Counterfeiting in connection with the Introduction of the Euro, OJ L 140, 14 Jun 2000; Art 4, Council Framework Decision of 19 Jul 2002 on Combating Trafficking in Human Beings (2002/629/JHA), OJ L 203, 1 Aug 2002.

[126] Art 26(3), 2003 UN Convention; Art 3(1), 1997 OECD Convention.

[127] For a discussion of corporate criminality in relation to the liability of the legal person's controlling agents in the field of marine pollution see chapter 14.6.

[128] See I Bantekas, 'Corruption as an International Crime and Crime against Humanity: An Outline of Supplementary Criminal Justice Policies' (2006) 4 *Journal of International Criminal Justice* 466.

[129] See chapter 11.5.

most of these cases have resulted in guilty pleas and the imposition of criminal fines to both the corporation and its agent.[130] In other less developed legal systems, while the courts acknowledge the principle of corporate criminality they do not always possess clear guidance as to a theoretical basis for attribution and of translating criminality into appropriate penalties.[131] At the same time some, mainly common law nations, are adopting unambiguous legislation that imposes criminal liability on legal entities for crimes against the person, such as homicides and not solely in respect of offences such as corruption.[132]

Overall, it maybe said that attribution to a legal person of a crime under international law is justified where the personal law (which may turn out to be the law of constitution, the law of incorporation, or other) of the legal person acknowledges corporate criminality, whether generally or in respect of the particular offence, in which case individual criminal responsibility rests with those that directed and knew, or should have known, about the crimes. The criminal liability of the legal entity itself is satisfied with the payment of compensation, the offer of apology, or other penalties of a similar nature.

---

[130] See Shearman & Sterling, 'Recent Trends and Patterns in the Enforcement of the Foreign Corrupt Practices Act' (1 Mar 2009) 2–4.

[131] In *Acres International Ltd v The Crown*, Lesotho High Court of Appeals Judgment [*Lesotho Highlands Development Authority* cases] (15 Aug 2003), paras 5–69. it was held that although the profit made by the corporation through the bribery was crucial when imposing a criminal monetary sanction, this should not be the only consideration. The court justified this approach on the basis that the corporation will already suffer from a reputational point of view and this factor alone will cause significant financial losses.

[132] Section 1 of the 2007 English Corporate Manslaughter and Homicide Act provides that 'an organisation [corporation, police force, partnership, trade union, employers' association and others] is guilty of an offence if the way in which its activities are managed or organised – a) causes a person's death, and b) amounts to a gross breach of a relevant duty of care owed by the organisation to the deceased'.

4

The Law of Command Responsibility

4.1 The Legal Nature of Command Responsibility

The doctrine of command responsibility is a particular creature of international law, although academic writings trace similarities with analogous concepts derived from domestic criminal laws. Its fundamental purpose is to concretise through criminal law the duty of superiors to supervise the activities of their subordinates (essentially to prevent or punish their crimes), to such a degree that the acts of subordinates are to be attributed in the same manner to the superior. However, if there did not exist any recognisable limits to the application of the command responsibility doctrine, then the liability of superiors for acts of subordinates would be tantamount to vicarious liability – where irrespective of the personal circumstances and efforts of the superior to avert the consequences of the crime, once the crime is committed by the subordinate it is also attributed to the superior.[1] It is obvious that command responsibility does not entail vicarious liability or mere attribution by virtue of the command element, given that the prosecuting authorities must prove that the superior intended or could have foreseen the consequences of subordinate criminality and that he failed to take any meaningful measures to prevent or punish. Equally, therefore, command responsibility is not a form of strict liability, since the mental element involving the knowledge of the accused must be well proven. Two theories on liability have been proposed with a view to formulating the theoretical underpinnings of the doctrine and particularly its legal nature. On the one hand, command responsibility has been approximated to what domestic criminal justice systems would term 'accomplice' liability, because of the assumption that the commander is liable in the same manner as the subordinate, just like an accomplice who would incur liability in equal manner to the perpetrator so long as his individual intent is amply demonstrated.[2] On the other hand, it is suggested that command responsibility is best described as a '*sui generis* form of liability for culpable omission'. This position is justified by reference to the fact that command responsibility requires a pre-existing legal obligation, whereas complicity results from moral or physical assistance and is devoid of an obligation. Moreover, whereas the basis of complicity rests on a contributory element to the underlying offence, command responsibility is premised

---

[1] See *ICTY Prosecutor v Halilović*, Trial Chamber Judgment (16 Nov 2005), paras 46–47, discussing the personal culpability element in command responsibility doctrine stemming from WW II jurisprudence.
[2] I Bantekas, 'The Contemporary Law of Superior Responsibility' (1999) 93 *American Journal of International Law* 573, 575–77.

on a culpable dereliction of duty. Finally, at the *mens rea* level, command responsibility necessitates the existence of an awareness on the part of the superior which relates to the functions of his duty and a knowledge as to the acts of his subordinates, which is alien to accomplice liability.[3]

The latter of the two positions seems to better conform to the criminal nature of command responsibility for an additional reason which possesses a practical dimension. Were command responsibility to be equated to a form of accomplice liability it would follow that the commander is liable for the underlying crimes committed by his subordinates. On the contrary, if command responsibility were not found to be an alternative form of accomplice liability the commander would be liable for his own actions and not for those of his subordinates. If we accept this second view, it is crucial that we investigate those individual acts of the superior that give rise to his liability; namely failure to prevent or punish subordinate crimes. This in turn gives rise to a gross dereliction of duty and also constitutes a quantifiable culpable omission. According to Mettraux, gross dereliction of duty and culpable omission to prevent and punish are distinct.[4] The first does not constitute an international crime[5] (although it is a crime under national laws), whereas the second is a *sui generis* form of liability under international law and not a distinct substantive crime. According to this rationale, the commander's liability arises from his criminal omission in relation to the actual crimes that subordinates committed and which the commander failed to prevent and punish.[6] This corresponds to the so-called 'derivative nature' of command responsibility because it is derived from crimes committed by perpetrators over whom the commander had a duty to act. This argument is certainly convincing for an additional reason. Command responsibility can only be charged against a superior if, and only if under ICTY jurisprudence, the underlying crime has actually been consummated by one's subordinates;[7] thus, command responsibility is inapplicable in cases of attempted, or merely planned, international crimes that have not come to fruition. On the contrary, accomplices are liable in respect of a pre-planned offence or where such an offence has been merely attempted.

Another particularity of command responsibility is that no proof of causality need be demonstrated between the commander's failure to prevent or punish and his subordinates' criminal activity.[8] This is alien to domestic criminal justice systems wherein some form of causality is required for the purposes of final attribution. It is because of the concept of causality that the law can ascribe criminal liability to the actor of particular behaviour when such behaviour results in the harm inherent in a

---

[3] G Mettraux, *The Law of Command Responsibility* (Oxford, Oxford University Press, 2009) 38ff.

[4] This distinction is well reflected in ss 13(1) and 14(1) of the 2002 German Code of Crimes against International Law. The Code distinguishes between a duty of supervision (s 13) where the commander failed to prevent subordinate crimes from a duty to report completed crimes, which is classified as an omission (s 14).

[5] *Halilović* Trial Judgment, para 53.

[6] Mettraux, *The Law of Command Responsibility*, 18–19, 80ff.

[7] *ICTY Prosecutor v Strugar*, Trial Chamber Judgment (31 Jan 2005), para 373; *ICTY Prosecutor v Orić*, Trial Chamber Judgment (30 Jul 2006), para 577; *ICTY Prosecutor v Hadžihasanović*, Appeals Chamber Decision on Interlocutory Appeal Challenging Jurisdiction in Relation to Command Responsibility (16 Jul 2003), para 204.

[8] *ICTY Prosecutor v Blaškić*, Appeals Chamber Judgment (29 Jul 2004), para 77.

given offence.[9] The nexus between act and resulting harm is imperative in order to establish liability, unless this has been broken by a subsequent intervening act. The early jurisprudence on command responsibility was clearly disinclined to raise any causality questions and generally failed to address the relevance of causality stemming from a superior's culpable omission which led to the subsequent crimes of subordinates. The ICTY in a sweeping judgment in the *Čelebići* case dismissed any causality requirement in the operation of the command responsibility doctrine[10] and this reasoning has been followed by other ICTY chambers without any jurisprudential consideration whatsoever.[11] The absence of causality as espoused in the ICTY sits uncomfortably with the practice of subsequent WWII tribunals,[12] as well as the express language of more recent instruments. Article 6 of the 1996 version of the ILC Draft Code of Crimes Against the Peace and Security of Mankind upholds the liability of the superior where he 'contributes directly' to the commission of crimes by subordinates. Equally, Article 28 of the ICC Statute postulates command liability only in respect of subordinate crimes committed 'as a result of' a commander's failure. It comes as no surprise therefore that in its early jurisprudence the ICC accepted that some causation is required between the commission of the underlying crimes and a superior's failure to exercise control properly.[13] *Prima facie* it seems that a superior can only cause subordinate criminality where he fails to prevent crimes and not subsequent to their consummation. Nonetheless, failure to punish may in certain circumstances encourage the perpetrators to commit more crimes, or otherwise increase the risk of their commission, and, as such, causation as to these further crimes may be attributed to the superior who failed to punish. Given that it is difficult to definitively prove what may have happened but for the superior's omission (direct causal link), the Trial Chamber suggested a more practical test under which the court must only determine whether the omission increased the risk of the commission of the particular crimes.[14]

Finally, the application of command responsibility is accepted not only during armed conflict, but also during peace time. This is true by logical implication because some of the most serious international offences, such as crimes against humanity and genocide, may be perpetrated outside an armed conflict context. The perpetration of these crimes requires a high degree of physical and logistical organisation, a clear hierarchy, a sustained operation and a level of hostilities that may not be all that different from regular armed conflicts. This observation should not be over-stretched and one should not take it for granted that the doctrine of command responsibility applies without restrictions, whether legal or practical, to all international offences.

---

[9] Here, of course, we are referring to legal causation. See M Bohlander, *Principles of German Criminal Law* (Oxford, Hart Publishing, 2009) 45–54.

[10] *ICTY Prosecutor v Delalić et al* [*Čelebići* case], Trial Chamber Judgment (26 Nov 1998), paras 398–400.

[11] See *Blaškić*, Appeal Judgment, para 77; *ICTY Prosecutor v Hadžihasanović*, Appeals Chamber Judgment (23 Apr 2008), paras 38–39.

[12] See Mettraux, *The Law of Command Responsibility*, 82–87.

[13] *ICC Prosecutor v Bemba*, Trial Chamber Decision on Confirmation of Charges, (15 Jun 2009), para 423.

[14] Ibid, paras 424–25.

The definition of command responsibility in Article 28 of the ICC Statute best encapsulates the finer points of the doctrine and fills the lacunae from the less detailed definition of Article 7(3) of the ICTY Statute. It reads as follows:

a)   A military commander or person effectively acting as a military commander shall be criminally responsible for crimes within the jurisdiction of the Court committed by forces under his or her effective command and control, or effective authority and control as the case may be, as a result of his or her failure to exercise control properly over such forces, where:

(i)   that military commander or person either knew or, owing to the circumstances at the time, should have known that the forces were committing or about to commit such crimes; and

(ii)   that military commander or person failed to take all necessary and reasonable measures within his or her power to prevent or repress their commission or to submit the matter to the competent authorities for investigation and prosecution.

b)   [In cases where a superior-subordinate relationship is not described in paragraph (a), but which is nonetheless subject to the same effective command and control, the superior is liable where:]

(i)   the superior either knew, or consciously disregarded information which clearly indicated, that the subordinates were committing or about to commit such crimes;

(ii)   the crimes concerned activities that were within the effective responsibility and control of the superior; and

(iii) the superior failed to take all necessary and reasonable measures within his or her power to prevent or repress their commission or to submit the matter to the competent authorities for investigation and prosecution.

Subparagraph (b) is a residual clause whose purpose is to encompass within its ambit non-military superior-subordinate relationships. Let us now examine in more detail the various aspects of the doctrine.

4.2   The Superior-Subordinate Relationship

From the civilian President or Prime Minister of a country to the soldier on the battlefield there exist a large number of command layers. Persons that possess some authority in any of these layers are not responsible for the actions of everyone in all the command layers directly below them up until the soldier on the battlefield. Instead, command responsibility requires that commanders are liable only for acts committed by persons who are their direct subordinates and over whom they possess a pre-existing duty to prevent and punish; that is, persons they enjoy direct and effective command and control over (effective control standard).[15] In order to numerically ascertain the persons subject to any given superior-subordinate relationship one must proceed on the basis of both fact (*de facto*) and law (*de jure*).

A *de jure* superior-subordinate relationship is determined on the basis of the official (*de jure*) allocation of specific subordinates to a particular commander,

---

[15]   *Čelebići* Trial Judgment, para 378; *Strugar* Trial Judgment, para 360.

whether in the context of a military or civilian administration. Proof of *de jure* command structures may be derived from constitutional documents, administrative laws, military hierarchical charts, military orders and others of this nature. It is of course possible that due to the exigencies of battle, or on account of other operational realities, the *de jure* relationship becomes inoperable or inactive. Take for example the Captain of a military unit is deemed 'weak' by his subordinates and does not command their respect in the same manner as one of his Lieutenants. The effect is that no subordinate obeys or looks up to his *de jure* commander, the Captain, and effectively command will have been ceded to the Lieutenant. The determination of the superior-subordinate relationship then becomes a matter of fact and not formal law and is to be assessed on the basis of the 'effective control' standard that must be proven by the prosecutor. Four general layers may be delineated to demonstrate *de jure* command:[16] a) policy; b) strategic; c) operational; d) tactical.[17] The person, or limited number of persons, exercising policy command are most typically the Head of State and/or the Head of government. This person makes the final decision to enter into war. This decision is then channelled to a War Cabinet (strategic command) that is composed of both civilians and military officers of the highest possible rank whose task it is to formulate a viable war plan. This plan is further channelled to high-ranking officers on the battlefield (operational command) in order to implement it through their subordinate units, divisions, corps, etc. Tactical command is the final frontier on the battlefield, encompassing every officer and non-commissioned officer (NCO) that is physically present in the theatre of operations and who possesses one or more direct subordinates. The ICRC Commentary to the 1977 Protocols correctly notes that for the purposes of command responsibility tactical command may be assumed even by a mere soldier/private where all the officers and NCOs in his unit have been killed or incapacitated by wounds and the soldier has assumed authority.[18] The latter would of course constitute a case of *de facto* command, unless that person is indeed the highest ranking among his peers, a fact that would render his authority *de jure*.

Since the doctrine of command responsibility requires direct subordination, particular knowledge on the part of the superior and a failure to act it is evident that the construction of superior-subordinate relationships on the basis of the four general layers cannot involve situations where a superior is far removed from the acts committed by an alleged subordinate. Thus, a person exercising policy command does not exercise direct authority over a platoon on the battlefield because he cannot apprise himself of their activities and has for this reason delegated this task to senior military officers who in turn have done the same to other officers, etc. The President's direct subordinates are certainly officials comprising strategic command, they themselves possessing direct authority over persons exercising operational command. It is not out of the question that strategic commanders are directly subordinate to policy commanders, particularly where the size of the army is small, or the magnitude of the

---

[16] A plethora of other sub-layers exist within each layer, particularly at the lower end of tactical military command.

[17] Bantekas, 'Contemporary Law of Superior Responsibility', 578–79.

[18] C Pilloud, *et al* (eds), *Commentary on the Additional Protocols of 8 June 1977 to the Geneva Conventions of 12 August 1949* (Geneva, Martinus Nijhoff, 1987) [*ICRC Commentary*] 1019.

military operations limited. Equally, staff commanders, ie high-ranking military officers that formulate battle plans, and who belong to the layer of strategic command, can never be subject to the doctrine of command responsibility because despite their rank they do not enjoy direct subordination over others.

While *de jure* command structures may be found with regard to the political and military branches of State entities, the same is not true in relation to paramilitary units whose command structures are *ad hoc*, flexible and ever-changing. Moreover, even in the case of regular armies, it is not uncommon to experience quick command successions on the battlefield where casualties are high, or even where authority has been usurped *ultra vires*. In such cases the determination of direct subordination is no longer a matter of law – because no such law exists – thus necessitating a determination on the basis of fact. Article 28(a) of the ICC Statute iterates customary international law, particularly that reflected in Article 87 of Protocol I of 1977 and the relevant jurisprudence of the ICTY, when it expressly states that subordination must be rooted in 'effective command and control'. The concept of command is much broader than that of control, in that whereas policy or operational commanders exercise command over all those in subordinate layers, they do not, however, necessarily exercise control over such persons, which is a more direct form of authority. Thus, it is the concept of 'control' that is determinative for the purposes of command responsibility, because it encompasses by its very nature direct subordination.[19] In every case, besides the directness of control, the control itself must be effective, otherwise a superior-subordinate relationship will not have been established, unless the superior intentionally renders the control ineffective to escape subsequent liability. The concept of 'effective control' is also particularly important in cases where *de jure* command structures are well known, but additional troops are added informally to the superior's forces. This may take place, for example, where a military unit loses its commander on the battlefield and as a result joins the first available allied or affiliated commander it comes across.[20] The *Čelebići* Appeals Judgment defined effective control as 'the material ability to prevent and punish criminal conduct'.[21]

One of the pervasive problems associated with the command responsibility doctrine concerns the time frame at which effective control is relevant. One school of thought posits that a superior is liable when his effective control persisted at the exact time his subordinates committed the crimes for which he is charged.[22] The opposing school argues that a superior's liability is sustained where he is found to possess effective control at such time that he failed to prevent or punish subordinate crimes.[23] The early jurisprudence of the ICC suggests a preference for the former of the two schools of thought.[24]

Besides the element of effective control, which constitutes a *sine qua non* requirement of command responsibility, it is unclear whether the commander need only

---

[19] *ICRC Commentary*, ibid, at 1013.
[20] Ibid.
[21] *Čelebići* Appeals Chamber Judgment (20 Feb 2001), para. 256.
[22] *Halilović* Appeal Judgment (16 Oct 2007), para 59; *ICTR Prosecutor v Bagosora and Others*, Appeals Chamber Judgment and Sentence (18 Dec 2008), para 2012.
[23] *SCSL Prosecutor v Sesay and Others*, Trial Chamber Judgment (2 Mar 2009), para 299.
[24] *Bemba* Trial Confirmation Decision, para 419.

satisfy a legal, as opposed also to a material, duty to act. If a commander is responsible only for the acts of subordinates over which he is incumbent with a formal legal competence to act, it follows that he is not liable in the absence of a legal duty, despite the fact that said commander may in fact possess more than ample material capacity to act in a particular circumstance, as would be the case with a civilian group that randomly pledges its subordination to a military commander. This is a totally different proposition from that concerning the genuinely material inability of a commander to prevent or punish, in which case he clearly bears no liability.[25] However, it defies all notions of justice to contend that a person who willingly assumed effective control over persons not formally assigned to him does not possess authority and responsibility over their actions. On the contrary, if said commander had expressly denied their request to join his forces and had avoided as a result to exercise any element of command or control over them, he would lack the element of subordination over such persons and would bear no liability.[26]

The case law of the ICTY suggests that the establishment of *de facto* effective control is extremely hard to prove and involves a rigorous process. Where direct evidence is unavailable, for example in the form of a signed document demonstrating hierarchical structures, circumstantial evidence has successfully been utilised in the *ad hoc* tribunals to achieve the same purpose. The evidence that is more likely to be produced and which carries the highest probative value in the proceedings of the *ad hoc* tribunals is written and oral. Written evidence, particularly in the form of orders signed by the accused, helps provide circumstantial evidence as to his power over other persons, not necessarily those to whom it is addressed.[27] It should not be thought, however, that the signing of orders in all cases demonstrates a superior-subordinate relationship. This is true, for example, with regard to orders relating to logistics and administration.[28] For the purposes of command responsibility an order must demonstrate the existence of direct subordinates, but obviously the existence of such orders do not automatically establish a superior-subordinate relationship. It is merely one of many indicators that may provide evidence of effective control.[29] Some tribunals have suggested that the traditional indicia for ascertaining effective control with respect to regular armies are not always helpful in determining effective control in the context of irregular armies and rebel groups. These judgments presume, perhaps rightly, that many rebel commanders expose their true nature by assuming a dictatorial function that is evidenced by appropriating most of the loot, intimidating vulnerable persons, controlling the means to wage war and others.[30]

---

[25] *ICTR Prosecutor v Bagilishema*, Appeals Chamber Judgment (13 Dec 2002), para 50; *ICTY Prosecutor v Hadžihasanović*, Decision on Joint Defence Interlocutory Appeal of Trial Chamber Decision on Rule 98*bis* Motions for Acquittal [*Rule 98bis* Decision] (11 Mar 2005), para 164; *Čelebići* Appeal Judgment, paras 196–98.

[26] Obviously, if in such a case the commander was under a legal duty to incorporate that unit into his own and refused to do so, he will be liable under his ordinary criminal and disciplinary law.

[27] *ICTY Prosecutor v Strugar*, Appeals Chamber Judgment (17 Jul 2008), para 195.

[28] *Čelebići* Trial Judgment, para. 658.

[29] *Strugar* Appeal Judgment, para 254.

[30] *SCSL Prosecutor v Brima and Others*, Trial Chamber Judgment (20 Jun 2007), paras 787–88.

One should not rule out the possibility that the possession of significant powers of influence may under certain circumstances establish a superior-subordinate relationship, although the ICTY clearly thought otherwise in the *Čelebići* case.[31] An influential individual that yields full respect and obeisance, whether out of fear or otherwise, can establish as a result effective control over his subjects, having intentionally placed himself in a position of authority. There is sufficient precedent for this from the *Ministries* case,[32] but it is also a conclusion based on reason, which legal rationale cannot ignore. Finally, oral evidence, particularly that provided by prisoners of war (POWs) and other camp detainees, has produced sufficient circumstantial evidence for the ICTY in order to substantiate the distribution of tasks within a POW camp and thus distinguish those who hold superior positions within the camp from those that do not.[33]

4.3   The Position of Civilian Commanders

It is taken for granted that non-military commanders may be prosecuted in the same manner as their military counterparts under the doctrine of command responsibility.[34] This rests on the assumption that civilian leaders are also under an obligation to prevent and punish the crimes of their 'subordinates'.[35] However, the legal basis of such practice has never been satisfactorily explained by the courts and tribunals entertaining these cases. The easiest solution would be to assess whether a given civilian satisfies the relevant criteria and thereafter apply the doctrine to him or her, with primary emphasis placed on the existence of command and control. The most reliable exegesis for extending command responsibility to civilians suggests that if they indeed exercise effective command and control, they are under an international legal duty to exercise it responsibly (ie the doctrine of responsible command). This justification is not without its fair share of problems. For one thing, it is not entirely clear that all civilian leaders are under a binding duty to act. Certainly, the State is under an obligation under international law to protect civilians, aliens, property etc,[36]

---

[31] *Čelebići* Trial Judgment, paras 658, 669; *Čelebići* Appeals Judgment, para 266; but see *Brima* Trial Judgment, para 787.

[32] *USA v von Weizsaecker* [*Ministries* case], reprinted in 14 *Trials of War Criminals before the Nuremberg Military Tribunals* [Trials] 684.

[33] *ICTY Prosecutor v Nikolić*, Review of the Indictment pursuant to Rule 61 of the Rules of Procedure and Evidence (20 Oct 1995), para 24.

[34] See the Report of 29 March 1919 by the Commission on Responsibility of the Authors of the War and on the Enforcement of Penalties, which did not exclude civilian authorities from superior responsibility; Art 6(3) SCSL Statute that specifically encompasses political leaders and civilian superiors; *Prosecutor v Ferreira*, East Timor Special Panel Judgment (5 Apr 2003), para 520; Report of the International Commission of Inquiry on Darfur to the UN Secretary-General, pursuant to Security Council Resolution of 18 September 2004 (25 Jan 2005) [Darfur Report], para 558.

[35] *ICTY Prosecutor v Brđanin*, Trial Chamber Judgment (1 Sep 2004), para 283; *ICTR Prosecutor v Ntakirutimana*, Trial Chamber Judgment (21 Feb 2003), para 819; *Čelebići* Appeal Judgment, para 196.

[36] This duty was certainly found to exist in respect of the alleged spontaneous acts of students that took over the US embassy in Tehran, following the deposition of the outgoing regime. See *Case concerning United States Diplomatic and Consular Staff in Tehran* (USA v Iran), Judgment of 24 May 1980, (1980) ICJ Reports 3, paras 67–70, 77ff.

but this role is not specifically assigned to any particular individual in a civilian hierarchy, nor is there anything equivalent to a strict and answerable chain of command in a civilian setting. By way of illustration, the deputies and employees of a Minister may resign or abandon their posts when their boss becomes autocratic or abusive with the resulting harm being the loss of their salary. On the other hand, a military subordinate cannot afford to abandon his post in time of war, lest he be tried for a very serious criminal offence. Secondly, the application of command responsibility to civilians that are not part of a governmental structure but which are otherwise prominent business or communal figures is equally problematic, particularly since the element of effective control is generally absent, as is consequently that of responsible command. It is therefore evident that on the basis of current practice no single formula is able to fully explain the application of the doctrine to civilians. Thirdly, although the duties of military commanders are generally ascertainable and delineated, what should the law reasonably expect from civilian leaders and influential business figures whose authority in the sense of effective control is less clear? Thus, although Article 28 of the ICC Statute rightly distinguishes between military and military-like commanders from civilian commanders it wrongly distinguishes between two different sets of *mens rea* standards; contrary to the long-standing position under customary international law.[37]

It is not the place of this chapter to construct a unified legal basis for the attribution of command responsibility to civilians – assuming this is indeed possible. The only sensible approach is to apply the general elements of the doctrine in analogy to the function and context exercised by the civilian concerned.[38] Thus, although the element of effective control must be demonstrated, its existence will not normally be substantiated by reference to a strict hierarchy. Instead, effective control can by analogy be found to exist in various affiliations, such as those encompassed in political parties. The ICTR has succinctly stated that 'to the extent that members of a political party act in accordance with the dictates of that party, or otherwise under its instruction, those issuing such dictates or instruction can and should be held accountable for their implementation'.[39] Clearly, effective control will not always be established through the coercive mechanisms inherent in military chains of command. In the same manner, a civilian industrialist who has been ordered to employ slave labour is susceptible to command responsibility because of the degree of effective control over the slave force entrusted to him.[40] The employment of analogy should not be limited in order to ascertain only the existence of effective control, but also the legal and material capacity to act that is pertinent to civilian leaders. The ICC Statute offers no guidance in this respect, albeit it clearly suggests that the duties

---

[37] Mettraux, *The Law of Command Responsibility*, at 101. In *ICC Prosecutor v Bemba*, Trial Chamber Decision on Confirmation of the Indictment (15 Jun 2009), para 408, it was held that the notion of military commander encompasses also those situations where the superior does not exclusively perform a military function. This refers particularly to those Heads of State, ceremonial or other, that are constitutionally designated as commanders-in-chief. Naturally, one would then have to determine whether in fact such persons possess effective control.

[38] *Bagilishema* Appeal Judgment, para 52. In every case, proof must always be rendered that such control exists in practice, regardless of how it has come about.

[39] *ICTR Prosecutor v Nahimana*, Trial Chamber Judgment (3 Dec 2003), para 976.

[40] *USA v Flick et al*, Opinion and Judgment, 6 *Trials* 1187; *Roechling et al*, [*Roechling* case], 14 Trials 1075.

of civilian and military commanders are different. This leaves open the situation of those persons that fall within both fault lines; ie by exercising elements of both civilian and military leadership.[41] What strand of Article 28 of the ICC Statute applies to such persons is unclear, although given that in the course of a criminal trial what is at stake is the degree of one's failure to act, the most sensible solution would be to examine each function within its own particular context and consequently whether the duty to act therein has been fulfilled.

With respect to the application of command responsibility to security firms and terrorists there is no shortage of views. As long as effective control is duly maintained and exercised – and there is no reason why it should not be under such circumstances – the principle of responsible command certainly warrants the application of command responsibility to private security firms in situations of armed conflict.[42] As concerns, however, terrorist commanders this author finds himself unable to contemplate a palpable legal basis of liability under the doctrine of command responsibility. While it may be true that terrorist organisations operate around a hierarchical structure similar to those employed by military or paramilitary groups, their lines of subordination are not always clear even to the leaders themselves, particularly where they operate in cells that on account of secrecy do not communicate with each other. In such cases, the elements of direct subordination and knowledge of subordinate activities are manifestly missing, which in turn renders any assessment of command responsibility of the leader of a small terrorist cell rather redundant. A discussion of command responsibility in respect of large and less secretive terrorist organisations, organised as mini-armies, such as the Colombian FARC or the Taliban in Afghanistan and Pakistan, is certainly a different matter.

4.4   The Mental Element

The mental element in the definition of command responsibility requires that the superior either knew (ie that he had direct knowledge), or had reason to know on the basis of the circumstances at the time, that his subordinate(s) was about to commit, or had committed, a crime. Command responsibility does not require the commander to possess the same mental state as the direct perpetrators. Thus, where D, the subordinate, desired to kill V and knew that by burning him he would die, it is not necessary that C, his superior, shared D's mental state. Article 28 of the ICC Statute seems to follow the *mens rea* standards contained in Article 7(3) of the ICTY Statute, albeit with some slight variations as will be discussed shortly.[43] None of the judgments of past and present have given us a thorough exposition of the theoretical

---

[41]   Mettraux, *The Law of Command Responsibility*, at 27.

[42]   See Montreux Document on Pertinent International Legal Obligations and Good Practices for States related to Operations of Private Military and Security Companies during Armed Conflicts (17 September 2008), para 27; EC Gillard, 'Business Goes to War: Private Military/Security and Military Companies' (2006) 88 *International Review of the Red Cross* 637.

[43]   It should be noted from the outset that the issue of *mens rea* in the ICC Statute is regulated as a general rule by Art 30, which requires only intent (ie *dolus directus* of the first and second degree) and knowledge, unless a different standard is stipulated with respect to a particular crime or mode of liability.

bases of *mens rea* for omissions entailing serious violations of international law. Domestic principles are of very little, if any, assistance, not only because of the divergence on omissions between common and civil law jurisdictions,[44] but more so because of the context and magnitude in which command responsibility is applied.

When we talk about the subjective element (*mens rea*) of an offence we are in fact examining two distinct mental phases: a) the perpetrator's knowledge as to a circumstance, or of a risk, and; b) the formation of a desire and will to bring about that consequence, or a will to engage in prohibited conduct. In the vast majority of offences the two elements are contemporaneous and simultaneous and are treated as such by the criminal laws and the courts. In the case of command responsibility, however, they are seldom contemporaneous, since for example the duty to prevent requires the commander to ascertain information as to an impending criminal activity before he can take any action. This, depending on the circumstances, can take days, weeks or months, during which time the commander's knowledge of the criminal circumstance or risk may be obscure or inadequate to justify prosecution for failing to prevent. As a result, knowledge and desire may in fact be distinct in time and space. Let us, therefore, first examine what degree of knowledge is sufficient and how this may be ascertained. In any event, for a superior to be liable under the doctrine of command responsibility it is not sufficient merely to demonstrate that he was aware of criminal proclivity generally or of the vague occurrence of crimes, but that he had knowledge or reason to know of all the material elements of the particular offence(s) committed by his subordinates.[45] Thus, if the subordinate offence was murder, it must be proven that the superior knew or had reason to know that murder had been, or was about to be committed, and that he failed to prevent or punish the perpetrators. Certainly, where the commander is found negligent in taking notice of his subordinates' criminal proclivity this may be used as circumstantial evidence to demonstrate that he was aware or should have been aware of a particular crime.

Direct knowledge is pretty straightforward, whereas the 'had reason to know' standard is less so. The latter derives its contemporary origin from Article 86(2) of Protocol I of 1977, where it is understood as 'being in possession of sufficient information, such as to be put on notice of subordinate criminality'.[46] According to settled ICTY jurisprudence a person incurs superior responsibility 'only if information was available to him which would have put him on notice of offences committed by subordinates'.[47] The superior may in fact demonstrate that he was not at all aware of subordinate crimes, but if the prosecutor shows that the accused did not take the

---

Art 28, which refers to command responsibility contains a particular exception to the general rule, which will be explored below. For a more thorough discussion of the mental standards in the ICC Statute see chapter 2.

[44] By way of illustration, under s 323(c) of the German Criminal Code (Strafgesetzbuch, St GB) it is an offence to omit to offer assistance during accidents or a common danger or emergency, if this does not cause any danger to the rescuer. On the contrary, such a general duty to bring about an easy rescue does not exist in English law.

[45] *ICTY Prosecutor v Krnojelac*, Appeals Chamber Judgment (17 Sep 2003), paras 178–79; *ICTY Prosecutor v Naletilić and Martinović*, Appeals Chamber Judgment (3 May 2006), para 114.

[46] *Čelebići* Trial Judgment, para 393; *Strugar* Trial Judgment, para 369.

[47] *Čelebići* Appeal Judgment, para 241; *Krnojelac* Appeal Judgment, para 151; *Blaškić* Appeal Judgment, para 62.

necessary and reasonable measures to apprise himself of available and specific information[48] his truthful ignorance would not constitute a valid defence. The information need not be such that 'by itself, suffices to compel the conclusion of the existence of [subordinate] crimes ... it is sufficient that the superior was put on further inquiry by the information'.[49] The jurisprudence of the ad hoc tribunals also clearly stipulates that a commander is liable if put on notice of impending or existing subordinate criminality, which implies that if he was not put on notice in any manner then he is under no duty to go out and seek such indicia of criminality.[50] This would constitute an impossible duty that international law cannot impose, especially under sanction of criminal liability. This then gives rise to the quest for an appropriate standard applicable under international law for failing to make the most of the information available. Given the duty of commanders to take notice in order to avert crimes, the standard for failing to make the most of available information must necessarily be a low one; that is, gross negligence. Gross negligence, however, is only employed to assess the commander's handling of the information or notice. It may not be used to test his knowledge of subordinate criminality, or as a basis of liability, as was expressly spelt out in the *Blaškić* Appeal judgment.[51] This is the meaning that should be ascribed to the application of a negligence standard in respect of the 'had reason to know' or 'should have known' knowledge tests.[52]

As a result of the above considerations it is evident that recklessness is also applicable in assessing a commander's perceived lack of knowledge that caused his failure to act, although negligence alone will suffice.[53] What is suggested is not in fact an imputation of knowledge for failing to discover clues and information, but recklessness (both advertent and inadvertent)[54] for failing to institute mechanisms required under international law and of equally failing to apprise oneself of other-wise available information. A commander, for example, who does not institute reporting mechanisms and makes no use of information available to him is either aware of the risk to some degree and yet does nothing (advertent recklessness or *dolus eventualis*), or consciously renders himself completely oblivious to the risk (couldn't care less attitude, or indifference), in which case he is truly not aware (inadvertent recklessness, or negligence) he is nonetheless culpable. Equally, where a commander is in possession of some information which clearly suggests that his subordinates have

---

[48]   The superior is not, however, liable for failing to acquire such information in the first place, if it is not available to him through the normal course of events. Thus, under international law a 'duty to know' that is incumbent on superiors does not exist. See *Blaškić* Appeal Judgment, para 62; *Čelebići* Appeal Judgment, para 226; *Strugar* Trial Judgment, para 369.

[49]   *Strugar* Trial Judgment, paras 369, 370.

[50]   *Čelebići* Appeal Judgment, para 226; *Blaškić* Appeal Judgment, para 62.

[51]   *Blaškić* Appeal Judgment, para 63. The relevant passage reads as follows: '... the Appeals Chamber recalls that the ICTR Appeals Chamber has on a previous occasion rejected criminal negligence as a basis of liability in the context of command responsibility. ... It expressed that "references to negligence in the context of superior responsibility are likely to lead to confusion of thought". The Appeals Chamber expressly endorses this view'.

[52]   *Bemba* Trial Confirmation Decision, para 429, along with others, which generally fail to make this distinction.

[53]   Equally, it is impermissible to presume that a commander was aware of a particular fact. *Orić* Trial Judgment, para 319; *Čelebići* Trial Judgment, para 386; *ICTY Prosecutor v Limaj et al*, Trial Chamber Judgment (30 Nov 2005), para 524.

[54]   For a discussion of recklessness and *dolus eventualis* see chapter 2.4.

an unstable or violent character or otherwise drink before going out to missions, said commander is considered as having sufficient knowledge and as having been put on notice.[55] For the purposes of this chapter, we shall treat this aspect of the 'had reason to know' standard as referring to gross negligence. A showing of recklessness is not required, but if proven would certainly constitute an aggravating factor.

The test of recklessness under the ICC Statute, Protocol I, as well as under customary international law, is clearly a subjective one ('circumstances at the time'). Paragraph (b)(i) of Article 28 of the ICC Statute, which refers to a 'conscious disregard of information' that clearly indicates subordinate criminality is somewhat problematic. It is not clear at first sight whether this is a particular manifestation of the 'had reason to know' standard, or whether it refers to the 'must have known' standard. Given the particular genre of Article 28 and the negligence standard concerning disregard of information, I am of the opinion that paragraph (b)(i) refers to the 'had reason to know' standard. The onus for proving the commander's negligence rests with the prosecutor, who will attempt to demonstrate that the commander did not have a mechanism in place through which to monitor the behaviour of his subordinates. The same is true even if a mechanism was in place but the incumbent superior failed to reinforce it, or took lukewarm measures to apprise himself of the results of said monitoring. Following from our discussion on the ICTY's rejection of duty dereliction as part of the 'had reason to know' standard, it would be inconsistent to hold a superior liable for 'disregarding available information' when there exists no duty to collect it in the first place. Where, therefore, superiors have a mechanism in place to monitor subordinate behaviour and apprise themselves accordingly, then even if crimes do occur, the said superiors will not be deemed to have behaved negligently.

Besides actual knowledge and negligence ('had reason to know' standard), a third test has surfaced, the normative value of which is under fierce debate and which has gained no support in the ICTY. This is the so-called presumption of knowledge standard, or otherwise known as the 'must have known' test. This test stipulates that whenever subordinate criminality is widespread and notorious it must be presumed that the incumbent superior knew about it (ie he had both knowledge and intent or foresight).[56] As a result, the burden of proof is shifted from the prosecutor to the accused superior, but this is a presumption that is subject to rebuttal. The 'must have known' standard has not received recognition in the ICTY, but this has nothing to do with its normative value as such, as with the rightly conservative mandate of the *ad hoc* tribunal, whose authority extends to the application of law that is beyond any doubt part of customary international law. In this light, the ICTY exercised caution in the *Čelebići* case when it rejected the customary nature of the 'must have known' test.[57] Evidence clearly suggests that the test has a normative history equal to that of its 'had reason to know' counterpart. One must keep in mind, however, that when these *mens rea* formulations were employed in the aftermath of World War II it was at

---

[55] *ICTY Prosecutor v Milutinović*, Appeals Chamber Judgment, (26 Feb 2009), para 120.
[56] Bantekas, 'Contemporary Law of Superior Responsibility', 588–89.
[57] *Čelebići* Trial Judgment, paras 384–85.

a time when command responsibility was a sketchy concept that was under development and thus it is not wise to expect neat categorisations, precise semantic formulations and exact legal constructions. What is of interest in the present analysis is not the legal expressions employed in the past, but what the tribunals actually meant when using them. Thus, in the *Yamashita* case before a US Military Commission, the widespread nature and notoriety of crimes perpetrated by Japanese forces prompted the Commission to conclude that the accused 'either knew or had the means of knowing'.[58] This presumption of knowledge was reaffirmed by another US military tribunal in the *Hostages* case, although the test employed there was not premised on widespread occurrence and notoriety, but on the superior's failure to acquire and obtain complete information.[59] Equally, in the *High Command* case, the superior's knowledge was found by the military tribunal to be presumed through numerous reports received at his headquarters. Moreover, the ICRC Commentary on Articles 86 and 87 of Protocol I of 1977 affirms that widespread, publicly notorious, numerous, geographically and temporarily spanned breaches 'should be taken into consideration in reaching a presumption that the persons responsible could not be ignorant of them'.[60]

Even if Article 28 of the ICC Statute is construed as excluding the presumption of knowledge standard – something that is not totally clear[61] – on the basis of the overwhelming aforementioned evidence, the standard can still validly be applied before other courts and tribunals, be they domestic or international. The major difficulty in applying this test lies in the subjective determination of what constitutes widespread and notorious, such as to trigger the presumption against the superior. Although it is impossible to remove all subjectivity from the domain of criminal law, in the present case there are simply insufficient compelling criteria available. In the *Yamashita* case, the accused was far removed from the field of operations where the crimes took place and his lines of communication had been severed by enemy forces. The crimes may indeed have been widespread and notorious, but under the specific circumstances of Yamashita he certainly had very little scope for obtaining information. This, after all, was the whole purpose of the severing of his communication lines! More than a century later it is evident that not only communications are better, but that the mass media has access to a significant amount of information that is available in the public domain, but also contemporary military operations are far less restricted in respect of location, with the exception of occupations.

---

[58]   *Trial of General Yamashita* (US Military Commission, Manila, 8 Oct – 7 Dec 1945), 4 Trials 1, at 34, 94.

[59]   *USA v List, et al* [*Hostages* case], 11 Trials 759, at 1281.

[60]   *ICRC Commentary*, para 3548.

[61]   Art 28(a)(i) of the ICC Statute employs a 'should have known' standard 'owing to the circumstances at the time'. Mettraux, *The Law of Command Responsibility*, at 77, 194ff and 210ff, produces a long list of references to argue that this standard is inconsistent with customary international law.

4.5 The Duty to Prevent or Punish

The doctrine of command responsibility requires the existence of three cumulative criteria: a superior-subordinate relationship, knowledge of subordinate criminal activity by the superior (whether actual or through recklessness or negligence) and a subsequent failure to prevent or punish such crimes. It is evident that the duties are disjunctive, requiring action in different temporal phases; ie the duty to prevent arises prior to the perpetration of crimes, whereas the duty to punish arises after a crime has been committed, or in the course of its commission. International law consistently obliges commanders to take only such measures as are within their powers; this refers to actual, physical powers,[62] as opposed to legal powers, since a commander may not have legal authority over the actions of subordinate units, but could at the same time possess sufficient physical power and influence upon them so as to punish or prevent their behaviour. Thus, the actual power of a superior will be determined by a court on the basis of the subjective circumstances of the accused.

The ICC Statute requires that the accused take all 'necessary and reasonable' measures to prevent or punish. Again, the test in this case concerns the specific person of the superior in question. One can imagine two different scenarios, in which a superior has been overshadowed by other subordinates and has lost his influence and authority and another where the accused is a dominant personality that yields fear and respect also from units other than his own. The law is, after all, applicable to natural persons, whose private circumstances are subject to continuous change and which are not presumed to be automated robots. What constitutes necessary and reasonable measures on the basis of actual power in the two situations is certainly very different. The duty to prevent arises upon the preparation or planning of a crime, which suggests that the superior's duty at this stage is supervisory and disciplinary. A superior cannot be expected to foil every plan of his subordinates to commit a crime, but only those for which he has acquired information or for which he has reasonable grounds to suspect that a crime is about to be committed.[63] The disciplinary component of the duty to prevent includes an obligation to maintain and impose general discipline, train one's troops on the laws of war and secure an effective reporting system. In cases where information exists that a crime is planned or is in progress the superior must issue and enforce orders to the contrary, protest against it and its protagonists, or criticise criminal action and/or insist before a superior authority that immediate action be taken.[64] If all these measures are diligently performed and one's subordinates nonetheless engage in violations of humanitarian law their superior will bear no liability for their actions. Therefore, the duty to prevent should not be conceived as a general police duty, particularly taking in mind the additional combat functions of the superior, but rather as a supervisory and disciplinary duty. The other aspect of the duty to prevent concerns preventing the crime when it is in the process of being attempted. It should be emphasised that

---

[62] *ICTY Prosecutor v Kordić and Čerkez*, Trial Chamber Judgment (26 Feb 2001), para 443; *Strugar* Trial Judgment, para 372.

[63] Appeal Judgment, para 83; *Strugar* Trial Judgment, para 373.

[64] *Strugar* Trial Judgment, para 374.

where a commander fails to discharge his duty to prevent subordinate criminality he cannot thereafter exonerate himself by punishing the culprits.[65]

On the contrary, the duty to repress or punish requires specific action. It arises not at the time a subordinate offence takes place, because even a diligent commander may not be aware of the offence, but from the time the offence becomes known to the superior, or at a time when the superior would have known about it, in accordance with the *mens rea* standards applicable to the command responsibility doctrine. Thereafter, depending on the exigencies of battle the superior is obliged to investigate the case with a view to submitting it further to his competent authorities. There may be situations in which superiors are physically unable to seize, detain or investigate a subordinate. Even so, they can at least notify their immediate superiors of the situation.[66] Thus, the duty to punish may merely require of commanders to put their immediate superiors on notice of subordinate criminality, if this is all they are materially able to do under the exigencies of battle. In the *Strugar* case, the accused was the commander of several units that were responsible for the shelling of Dubrovnik and its old city. The shelling was intense and so was the damage to the city that it attracted global media attention on account of its status as a global heritage site. Strugar's superiors, who was the immediate commander of the military forces surrounding and shelling Dubrovnik, staged a 'sham' investigation and this was well known to the accused. The object of this investigation was to avoid liability by demonstrating that they were prepared to sanction those that perpetrated the shelling. The accused Strugar was held liable for his failure to punish those officers responsible for the shelling of Dubrovnik because he was not only aware that the investigation ordered by his superiors was a sham, but also because he had the material ability to institute a parallel investigation and did not choose to do so.[67]

In the specific context of the ICC Statute the duty to punish has been given more precision and is defined as a duty to repress. It encompasses within its ambit a duty to stop ongoing crimes from being committed in order to avert a chain of similar events, as well as an obligation to punish one's subordinates subsequent to the commission of crimes.[68] This duty to repress has been artificially, but not in legal terms, distinguished from the duty to submit the matter to the competent authorities for investigation and prosecution. Both these duties are part of the customary duty to punish, albeit the rationale for their distinction in the ICC Statute is to clarify them in respect of would-be commanders.

---

[65] *Milutinović*, Appeal Judgment, para 116.
[66] *Kordić* Trial Judgment, para 446.
[67] *Strugar* Appeal Judgment, paras 236–38. Further evidence of his failure to punish was established by proof furnished by the Prosecutor by which the accused had subsequently promoted some of those that were implicated in the shelling.
[68] *Bemba* Trial Confirmation Decision, para 439.

4.6   The Question of Successor Superior Responsibility

This term is associated with the question as to whether a superior can incur liability for failing to punish subordinates in respect of crimes committed prior to his assumption of command. It is therefore obvious that the person primarily responsible for punishing such crimes is the superior under whose command the crimes took place. The question pertinent to this section is whether the new commander is incumbent under international law with a continuous duty to punish or if simply a failure to act under such circumstances constitutes merely a dereliction of duty punishable in accordance with domestic law.

The approach of the ICTY chambers has been divisive on the matter. By a slim majority of 3–2 the Appeals Chamber in the *Hadžihasanović* case held that a successor superior is not liable for crimes committed by his subordinates prior to his undertaking command.[69] The theoretical rationale for this approach, however, is elusive and the Appeals Chamber in the *Orić* case missed a golden opportunity to clarify and cement the position adopted in *Hadžihasanović*, given that it agreed with it on the basis of a yet another narrow majority of 3–2.[70] The *ratio* of the *Hadžihasanović* rejection of successor liability was further obscured by the fact that the two dissenting judges in *Orić* expressed their strong support for the minority view in *Hadžihasanović*.[71] Despite this apparent dichotomy of views[72] and the narrowly decided judgments one cannot ignore the reality of two appellate judgments that at the time of writing, at least, confirm the case against successor superior responsibility. This by no means excludes the prevalence of the opposing view in the near future, particularly since it augments the foundational principle of responsible command which is central to the doctrine of command responsibility.

---

[69] *Hadžihasanović* Decision on Interlocutory Appeal Challenging Jurisdiction in relation to Command Responsibility, para 51.

[70] *ICTY Prosecutor v Orić*, Appeals Chamber Judgment (3 Jul 2008), para 167.

[71] See *Orić* Appeal Judgement, ibid, Partially Dissenting Opinion and Declaration of Judge Liu, paras 11–34; *Orić* Appeal Judgement, ibid, Separate and Partially Dissenting Opinion of Judge Schomburg, paras 5–29.

[72] For support of the majority opinion, see C Greenwood, 'Command Responsibility and the Hadžihasanović Decision' (2004) 2 *Journal of International Criminal Justice* 598. In support of the minority position, see M Shahabuddeen, 'Does the Principle of Legality Stand in the Way of Progressive Development of Law?' (2004) 2 *Journal of International Criminal Justice* 1007 [who was one of the dissenting judges in the case) and A Cassese, *International Criminal Law* (Oxford, Oxford University Press, 2008) 246–47.

Part II

Defences and Excuses from Criminal Liability

5

Defences in International Criminal Law

5.1 Theoretical Underpinnings of Criminal Defences

The concept of 'defence' in international criminal law is neither self-evident, nor does it clearly possess an autonomous meaning. Instead, it derives its legal significance as a result of its transplantation from domestic criminal justice systems through the appropriate processes of international law. Nonetheless, its definition, elaboration, evolution or application do not depend on the relevant processes of any single criminal justice system – nor combinations thereof – although these may have persuasive value. This is even more so on account of the quantitively different nature of international crimes and offences committed in armed conflict. It is equally warranted in the context of a self-contained, highly elaborate and sophisticated legal system, such as the International Criminal Court (ICC), where reliance on domestic rules is the exception – or at least, a judicial act of last resort – rather than the norm.[1] Despite these observations, however, the fact remains that the underlying theoretical underpinnings of the concept of defences is premised on well established notions of criminal law, originating from both the common law and the civil law traditions. Despite the elaborate character of the ICC Statute, its drafters have been wise in detecting the inadequacy of the fledgling international criminal justice system, thus necessitating recourse to national legal concepts and constructs. This is well evident as far as defences are concerned.[2]

In its most simple sense, a defence represents a claim submitted by the accused by which he or she seeks to be acquitted of a criminal charge. The concept of defences is broad and may encompass a submission that the prosecution has not proved its case. Since a criminal offence is constituted by two cumulative elements, a physical act or omission (*actus reus*) and a requisite combination of volition and knowledge or foresight (*mens rea*), it would seem that the accused could succeed with a claim of defence by disproving or negating either the material or the mental element of the offence charged. Where the accused proceeds to disprove his desire or knowledge to bring about the harm with which he is charged he is not claiming a defence; he is simply negating the existence of a *mens rea* as far as his personal liability is concerned. This is true for example where D is claiming that although his firing of a pistol did kill V, he was in fact aiming at a firing range and V accidentally happened to pass by. As a result he did not desire to kill V, nor could he foresee this outcome.

---

[1] ICC Statute, Art 21(1)(c).
[2] Ibid, Art 31(3).

When raising a defence, however, D makes a very different kind of proposition. Thus, where D kills V by shooting him in the head under a state of duress he cannot seriously suggest that he has not satisfied the conduct and mental elements for the crime of murder. His conduct was both intentional and knowing. What he should be arguing is that although he did in fact satisfy the *actus reus* and *mens rea* of that offence he should be justified or excused because of his particular and unique circumstances. Some defences, nonetheless, may be directed at negating or disproving either the conduct element (eg automatism) or the mental element (eg insanity, intoxication) of the crime charged. D kills V with a single blow to the head while suffering from an acute type of schizophrenia which persisted at the time of the incident. D has not voluntarily formed the volition to kill V and is unable to understand the consequences of his actions. As a result, he is deemed as not having formed the appropriate *mens rea* for murder.

Domestic criminal law systems generally distinguish between defences that may be raised against any criminal offence (so-called general defences) and those that can only be invoked against particular crimes (so-called special defences).[3] Another poignant distinction is that between substantive and procedural defences. The former refer to the merits of the offence and the perpetrator's role in relation to it, while procedural defences are employed to demonstrate that certain criminal procedure rules have been violated to the detriment of the accused, with the consequence that the trial cannot proceed to its merits. This distinction is not always clear cut, but one may point to the following often claimed procedural defences: abuse of process,[4] *ne bis in idem*,[5] *nullum crimen nulla poena sine lege scripta*,[6] passing of statute of limitations,[7] retroactivity of criminal law.[8] This chapter will focus only on substantive defences. Although our analysis covers substantive defences as these have evolved through domestic and international developments, the detailed ICC legal framework will serve as the basis of our discussion.

Another seminal aspect of any discussion on defences relates to the allocation of the burden of proof. Article 66 of the ICC Statute postulates the principle of 'presumption of innocence' until proven guilty beyond reasonable doubt. This means that, and in accordance with universal standards of justice, the prosecution carries the onus of proving the material and mental elements constituting an offence. On the other hand, facts relating to a defence raised by the accused, and being peculiar to his or her knowledge, must be established by the accused himself.[9] Article 67(1)(i) of the

---

[3] An example of a special defence is that of the 'battered wife syndrome'. See C Wells, 'Battered Woman Syndrome and Defences to Homicide: Where Now?' (1994) 14 *Legal Studies* 266.

[4] *ICTR Prosecutor v Barayagwiza*, Appeals Chamber Decision (3 Nov 1999), as well as the reversal of parts of the latter decision by the Appeals Chamber in its decision of 31 Mar 2000.

[5] ICC Statute, Art 20.

[6] Ibid, Arts 22 and 23.

[7] Ibid, Art 29. The crimes contained in the ICC Statute are not subject to a statute of limitations under general international law. This is consistent with the 1968 United Nations (UN) Convention on the Non-Applicability of Statutory Limitations to War Crimes and Crimes Against Humanity, 754 UNTS 73.

[8] ICC Statute, Art 24.

[9] *ICTY Prosecutor v Delalić and Others* (*Čelebići* case), Judgment (16 Nov 1998), para 1172. In English law, the burden of proof is always on the prosecution even with regard to defences raised by the defendant, with the exception of insanity and certain statutory exceptions (including diminished responsibility). See R May, *Criminal Evidence*, (London, Sweet & Maxwell, 1999) 53–60.

ICC Statute at first glance seems to possibly attack the burden of proof set out in Article 66, by declaring that 'the accused shall be entitled .... not to have imposed on him or her any reversal of the burden of proof or any onus or rebuttal'. This would not be a correct interpretation, as it runs contrary to the object and purpose of the ICC Statute and general international law. The correct view is that Article 67(1)(i) should be read in conjunction with Articles 31(3) and 21, which give authority to the Court to introduce defences existing outside the Statute, only if they are consistent with accepted treaty and custom or general principles of domestic law. Thus, no defence introduced by the Court in the proceedings under Article 31(3) can ever override the burden of proof established in accordance with Article 66. Essentially therefore, while the accused has the burden of proving the particular claim invoked in his or her defence (for example, that he faced death if he did not execute the illegal order of his superior), the burden is on the Prosecutor to prove the overall guilt of the accused.

As already explained, all true substantive defences represent claims that both the conduct and cognitive elements of the offence have indeed been satisfied by the accused, but for a reason which is or should be acceptable under the relevant criminal justice system. In this respect, domestic legal systems distinguish between two types of defences in which the accused claims that had it not been for particular underlying circumstances he would not have perpetrated the criminal conduct and that his volition was not formed voluntarily. These are known as justifications and excuses. Defences operating as justifications usually regard the criminal conduct as harmful but not as wrong in its particular context, whereas excuses are grounded on the premise that although the particular conduct was indeed wrongful its surrounding special circumstances would render its attribution to the actor unjust.[10] Most of the defences explored in this chapter are not true defences because their essential claim is that the accused has to a smaller or larger degree not satisfied the *mens rea* of the underlying crime. This is certainly the case with superior orders, intoxication, insanity, mental incapacity and mistake of fact and law. The only true defences are duress and necessity.

Despite the existence of the aforementioned distinctions in both common and civil law traditions, they were not included in the ICC Statute, whose drafters agreed instead to use the general term 'exclusion of criminal responsibility', thus avoiding the need to insert terminology distinguishing between the two. Whether this intentional omission has any legal significance remains to be seen by reference to the appropriate sources of the Court's jurisdiction. The next section, therefore, explores the general conception of defences as these have been developed in the jurisprudence of the ad hoc tribunals and as enunciated in the ICC Statute, with particular emphasis on primary and secondary sources. It should, however, be emphasised that where a person is charged with an international crime before a local court he or she will have available all the range of defences available under that legal system.

---

[10] Several theories have been elaborated in this respect, such as the 'character theory' and the 'fair opportunity theory'. See W Wilson, *Criminal Law* (London, Longman, 1998) 206–19; Draft Code of Crimes against the Peace and Security of Mankind, Art 14 (Comment 2), in ILC Report on the Work of its Forty-Eighth Session, UN GAOR 51st Sess, Supp No 10, UN Doc A/51/10 (1996) 14.

5.2   Is there a Place for Domestic Defences in the ICC Statute?

During the negotiations of the Preparatory Committee (Prep Com) draft Statute there was strong divergence over the inclusion of an exhaustive or open list of defences. Naturally, the proponents of an exhaustive list were apprehensive of the Court's freedom and latitude were it to be authorised to determine defences beyond those enumerated in the Statute. The opposite side, however, stressed the impossibility of reaching precise definitions of all desired defences, thus necessitating an open list. There was considerable support for a middle ground; although an enumerated list of defences was eventually preferred, the Court could under special circumstances introduce viable defences existing outside the Statute in such a way that it would not make but rather apply the law.[11] Preference for this latter solution was finally reflected in Article 31(3), which reads:

> At trial, the Court may consider a ground for excluding criminal responsibility other than those referred to in paragraph 1 [ie, mental incapacity, intoxication, self-defence, duress] where such a ground is derived from applicable law as set forth in Article 21.

Article 21 sets out the sources available to the Court in respect of its adjudicatory function; in the same fashion this is prescribed for the International Court of Justice in Article 38 of its Statute. Article 21 is premised on a hierarchy of rules, on top of which lie the Statute, supplemented by the Elements of Crimes and the Rules of Procedure and Evidence. Where the aforementioned sources fail to produce an appropriate result the Court may turn to relevant treaties and the principles and rules of international law, failing which it may seek a legal solution by reference to general principles of law derived from the national laws of the world's legal systems. The examination of these sources does not fall within the purview of this chapter, but a brief discussion of the third source (that is, general principles) is warranted, because of the potential use by the Court of defences existing outside its Statute. General principles of municipal law consist of practices or legal principles common to a substantial number of nations encompassing the major legal systems (common, civil and Islamic law). Under customary international law reliance upon principles deriving from national legal systems is justified either when rules make explicit reference to national laws, or when such reference is necessarily implied by the very content and nature of the concept under examination. However, even within these confines, the freedom of courts to extrapolate general principles may be open to abuse, as was the case in the *Furundžija* judgment that was decided by a Chamber of the ICTY.[12] It is evident that if the Court possesses authority to freely employ general principles the theoretical underpinnings of the distinction between 'justifications' and 'excuses' (constituting part and parcel of any domestic discussion on defences) is pertinent when general principles are introduced.

As a result of a compromise reached during the 1998 conference, whereby some delegations insisted that domestic law, especially that of the accused's nationality or

---

[11]   UN Doc A/CONF 183/C 1/WGGP/L 4/Add 1/Rev 1 (1998), commentary to Art 31(3).

[12]   *ICTY Prosecutor v Furundžija*, Judgment (10 Dec 1998), paras 182–86. See I Bantekas, *Principles of Direct and Superior Responsibility in International Humanitarian Law* (Manchester, Manchester University Press, 2002) 28.

that of the territorial State should be directly applicable apart from general principles,[13] the Statute extended the range of sources available to the Court. The compromise was basically a middle ground, whereby such domestic law could, if the Court deemed it appropriate, be included in the pool of sources. Article 21(1)(c) articulates the following sources, failing paragraphs 2 and 3:

> [G]eneral principles of law derived by the Court from national laws of legal systems of the world, *including, as appropriate, the national laws of states that would normally exercise jurisdiction over the crime*, provided that those principles are not inconsistent with this Statute and with international law and internationally recognised norms and principles [emphasis added].

A logical and realistic interpretation of this clause suggests that in the event the Court is unable to answer a lacuna through the use of international law it may turn to individual legal systems. In respect of this process, the Court may not simply choose a particular law or provision for subsequent application or transplantation to its own judicial proceedings; rather, it is bound to extract relevant principles from the rules of the legal system under consideration. This is an exercise that may turn out to be so cumbersome that it finally negates the initial utility of recourse to a particular legal system. A more realistic interpretation would reflect ICTY practice by which the ad hoc tribunals take heed of the sentencing practices and legislation of the former Yugoslavia and Rwanda, unless these conflict with general international law.[14] The ICC could extend the direct application of domestic law to determination of procedural matters that have taken place on the territory of a State, where this is relevant to ICC proceedings (for example, in relation to testimony and other evidence taken by the surrendering State), as well as to elements of defences that are ill-defined in the Statute, as will become apparent in this chapter. Let us now proceed to examine in detail the substantive defences set out in the Statute, that is, superior orders, duress/necessity, self-defence, intoxication, mistake of fact and law, and mental incapacity.

As a matter of safeguard against abuse by the defendant of the rule enunciated in Article 31(3), the Rules of Procedure and Evidence require that the defence give notice to both the Trial Chamber and the prosecutor if it intends to raise a ground for excluding responsibility under Article 31(3). This must be done 'sufficiently in advance of the commencement of the trial'.[15] Following such notice the Trial Chamber shall hear the prosecutor and the accused before deciding whether the accused can raise a ground for excluding criminal liability. If the accused is eventually permitted to raise the ground the Trial Chamber may grant the prosecutor an adjournment to address that ground.[16]

---

[13] See P Saland, 'International Criminal Law Principles' in RS Lee (ed), *The International Criminal Court: The Making of the Rome Statute: Issues, Negotiations, Results*, (The Hague, Kluwer, 1999) 214–15.

[14] Art 24(1) of the ICTY Statute states that '[i]n determining the terms of imprisonment, the Trial Chambers shall have recourse to the general practice regarding prison sentences in the courts of the former Yugoslavia'.

[15] ICC Rules of Procedure and Evidence, r 80(1).

[16] Ibid, r 80(2) and (3).

5.3   Superior Orders

Since discipline is the cornerstone of military doctrine it follows that obedience to superior orders is paramount. But a subordinate receiving an order may find that the order conflicts with his or her duty to obey criminal or military law. From the point of view of a strict hierarchy of rules a neutral observer will have little problem in articulating an objection to the order. Nonetheless, for the ordinary military subordinate used to the discipline described the choice is not readily obvious. The dilemma is simple: submit to the illegal order and commit a crime, defy the order and face the wrath and penalties imposed by your superiors and the disciplinary law to which one is subject.[17] One should not forget that in time of war disobedience often carries a penalty of summary execution, with little time or credence given to the subordinate to make his or her claim during the exigencies of conflict. These thoughts represent personal moral imperatives. What sense does the law make of all this?

From the time that national authorities prosecuted violations of the *jus in bello* and were subsequently faced with claims of superior orders, they themselves first encountered the aforementioned dilemma of the military subordinate. As a result, two schools of thought emerged on the subject. The first, premising its argument primarily on notions of justice, opined the invocation of superior orders to constitute a complete defence,[18] while the second articulated a doctrine of 'absolute liability' which gave no merit to claims of obedience.[19] Between these two extremes a more conciliatory position was adopted at both the national and international level. From the 1845 Prussian Military Code to the *Leipzig* trials at the close of the First World War a consistent principle has emerged recognising the relevance of 'moral choice' in such circumstances. In accordance with the 'moral choice' principle a subordinate would be punished if in the execution of an order he or she went beyond its scope, or executed it in the knowledge that it related to an act which aimed at the commission of a crime and which the subordinate could avoid.[20] The German Supreme Court affirmed this principle at the *Leipzig* trials on the basis of Article 47 of the 1872 German Military Penal Code, which provided that superior orders were of no avail where subordinates went beyond the given order or were aware of its illegality.[21] In the *Dover Castle* case the defendant Karl Neuman, the commander of a German submarine, claimed he was acting pursuant to superior orders when he torpedoed the

---

[17]   Y Dinstein, *The Defence of Obedience to Superior Orders in International Law*, (Leiden, Sijthoff, 1965) 5–7. See generally MJ Osiel, 'Obeying Orders: Atrocity, Military Discipline, and the Law of War' (1998) 86 *California Law Review* 939; MJ Osiel, *Obeying Orders* (New Brunswick, Transaction, 1999).

[18]   1845 Prussian Military Code; see also the adoption of the doctrine of *respondeat superior* by Oppenheim in his early treatises: L Oppenheim, *International Law: Disputes, War and Neutrality*, (New York, Longmans, 1912) 264–70; H Kelsen, 'Collective and Individual Responsibility in International Law with Particular Regard to the Punishment of War Criminals' (1943) 31 *California Law Review* 556–58.

[19]   *R v Howe and Others* [1987] 1 AC 417, *per* Lord Hailsham, at 427. See also Dinstein, *The Defence of Obedience to Superior Orders*, 68–70. Contemporary expressions of this doctrine, but for varying reasons described below, are also Art 8 of the Charter of the International Military Tribunal at Nuremberg, Art II(4)(b) of Control Council Law No 10, as well as the ICTY and ICTR Statutes, Arts 7(4) and 6(4), respectively. In all these instruments, a successful plea of superior orders could serve to mitigate punishment.

[20]   *USA v Ohlendorf and Others* (*Einsatzgruppen* case) 15 ILR 656.

[21]   *USA v Von Leeb and Others* (*High Command* case) 15 ILR 376.

Dover Castle, a British hospital ship. It was discovered at trial that German orders to torpedo Allied hospital ships were premised on the fallacious assumption that Allied hospital ships were being used for military purposes in violation of the laws of war. The accused was acquitted because he was not found to have known that the *Dover Castle* was not used for purposes other than as a hospital ship.[22] In the *Llandovery Castle* case, however, which once again involved the torpedoing of a British hospital ship and the subsequent murder of its survivors, the court did not readily accept a defence of superior orders. It emphatically pointed out that although subordinates are under no obligation to question the orders of their superior officer, this is not the case where the 'order is universally known to everybody, including also the accused, to be without any doubt whatever against the law'.[23]

Thus, the 'moral choice' principle encompassed an objective test, whereby an order whose illegality was not obvious to the reasonable man and was executed in good faith could be invoked as a viable defence. This was later also termed as the 'manifest illegality' principle. Where the subordinate is aware of the unlawfulness of the order, although the order itself is not manifestly illegal, the subjective knowledge of the accused is relevant in the attribution of liability, as any other conclusion would lead to absurdity. It would, moreover, disregard the significance of *mens rea* in the definition of crimes. Similarly, no irrebuttable presumption exists in this field of law suggesting that universal knowledge of the order's illegality will automatically prove the accused's awareness of it.[24] Following the end of the Second World War, both the 'moral choice' and the 'manifest illegality' tests were abandoned by the Allies in their quest for swift military justice. As already mentioned, the doctrine of absolute liability prevailed in the Nuremberg Charter, Control Council Law No 10 and did not feature either in the Genocide Convention[25] or the 1949 Geneva Conventions.[26] On this basis alone, it has wrongly been asserted that since 1945 the defence of superior orders has been abrogated and abandoned.[27] The fallacy of this argument will be proven shortly. For one thing, international tribunals constitute self-contained systems whose sources of law do not necessarily follow the evolution of law outside of that system; rather, their legal mandate is drawn by their drafters and is particular to them and is therefore *lex specialis*. The Nuremberg Tribunal was not an exception to this rule, since the Allies did not want to be faced with mass claims of superior orders, all leading back to Hitler. As a result, the Tribunal took it for granted that all of the accused were fully aware of the orders received and stated:

[22] *Dover Castle* case, (1921) 16 *American Journal of International Law* 704. Clearly, therefore, the accused had not formed an appropriate *mens rea* for the offence.

[23] *Llandovery Castle* case, (1922) 16 *American Journal of International Law* 708.

[24] Dinstein, *Defence of Obedience to Superior Orders*, at 28.

[25] 1948 Convention on the Prevention and Punishment of the Crime of Genocide, 78 UNTS 277.

[26] Convention for the Amelioration of the Condition of the Wounded and Sick in Armed Forces in the Field (No I), 75 UNTS 31; Convention for the Amelioration of the Condition of the Wounded, Sick, and Ship-Wrecked Members of Armed Forces at Sea (No II), 75 UNTS 85; Convention Relative to the Treatment of Prisoners of War (No III), 75 UNTS 135; Convention Relative to the Protection of Civilian Persons in Time of War (No IV), 75 UNTS 287.

[27] P Gaeta, 'The Defence of Superior Orders: The Statute of the International Criminal Court Versus Customary International Law' (1999) 10 *European Journal of International Law* 172. For the better view that the ICC Statute provision on superior orders is in conformity with customary law, see C Garraway, 'Superior Orders and the International Criminal Court: Justice Delivered or Justice Denied' (1999) 836 *International Review of the Red Cross* 785.

The true test, which is found in varying degrees in the criminal law of most nations, is not the existence of the order, but whether *moral choice* was in fact possible [emphasis added].[28]

Similarly, subsequent Second World War military tribunals, especially those applying Control Council Law No 10, while upholding the validity of Article II(4)(b), did not also fail to mention that to plead superior orders one must show an excusable ignorance of the order's illegality.[29] The tribunals in these cases made it clear that if a defence was available to an accused under such circumstances this would be the defence of duress, which would be brought about as a direct consequence of the severity and force of the order. The concept of duress will be examined below in another section. Further evidence of the existence of the duress-related 'moral choice' doctrine reemerged in 1950 when the International Law Commission (ILC) codified, after a request by the General Assembly, the Principles of the Nuremberg Charter and Tribunal.[30] Principle IV provided, or more importantly reaffirmed, that obedience to superior orders did not relieve the subordinate from responsibility, provided a moral choice was in fact available. The concept of moral choice in Principle IV is somewhat removed from the defence of superior orders, constituting as it does a particular defence in its own context.[31] Unlike the manifest illegality principle associated with the defence of superior orders, where personal knowledge of the illegal nature of the order is crucial, the application of the 'moral choice' principle assumes from the outset such knowledge, predicating the defence instead on the factual possibility of action. After an intense Cold War period fuelled by endless disagreements the final version of the Draft Code of Crimes against the Peace and Security of Mankind,[32] finally shelved in 1996, reverted to the absolute liability doctrine.[33] Interestingly, the Draft Code, especially in its final stages from 1981 to 1996, was a significant influence on the ICC Statute, which, as shall be seen, did not eventually adopt the stringent absolute liability doctrine.[34]

The evolution of national case law since the end of the Second World War has seen the domination of the principle of 'manifest illegality'. This was clearly articulated in the judgment of the District Court of Jerusalem in the *Eichmann* trial, confirmed subsequently by that country's Supreme Court.[35] Moreover, the US, who is not a party to the ICC Statute, has consistently upheld the defence of superior orders under strict application of the manifest illegality test in both the Korean[36] and the Vietnam wars.[37] The 1956 US Military Manual, in fact, not only recognises the plea

---

[28] IMT Judgment, (1946) vol 22, at 466.
[29] *Einsatzgruppen* case; *Re Eck and Others (The Peleus)* 13 AD 248.
[30] Reprinted in Yearbook of the International Law Commission (2nd session, 1950), vol II, at 374.
[31] This is confirmed by the fact that while the first ILC rapporteur on the Draft Code of Crimes submitted his report in 1950 suggesting the viability of the defence of superior orders under certain circumstances, a subsequent report submitted in 1951 adopted the 'moral choice' principle found in Principle IV. See Dinstein, *Defence of Obedience to Superior Orders*, 241–51.
[32] UN Doc A/CN 4/L 522 (31 May 1996).
[33] Draft Art 5.
[34] ICC Statute, Art 33.
[35] *AG State of Israel v Eichmann* 36 ILR 277.
[36] *USA v Kinder* (1954) 14 CMR 742, at 776.
[37] *USA v Calley* (1973) 46 CMR 1131, aff'd, 22 USCMA 534, (1973) 48 CMR 19. See also JJ Paust, 'My Lai and Vietnam: Norms, Myths and Leader Responsibility' (1972) 57 *Military Law Review* 99.

of superior orders as a valid defence,[38] but moreover obliges courts to take into consideration the fact that subordinates 'cannot be expected, in conditions of war discipline, to weigh scrupulously the legal merits of the orders received'.[39] Similarly, the Canadian Supreme Court in the *Finta* case recognised the defence of superior orders to war crimes and crimes against humanity as having been incorporated in the Canadian criminal justice system and firmly accepted the manifest illegality rule.[40]

We have already made reference to the fact that Article 33 of the ICC Statute permits, subject to certain stringent conditions, a defence of superior orders. Because of the divergence of doctrine – from absolute liability to manifest illegality before international and domestic tribunals – it is worthwhile examining the process leading to the formulation of Article 33 from the purview of the participating States. During the 1996 Prep Com it was generally felt that the absence of the defence in three seminal contemporary instruments, that is, the ICTY and International Criminal Tribunal for Rwanda (ICTR) Statutes, as well as the Draft Code, rendered any discussion on the matter redundant. With the insistence of Canada and France as regards the requirement of knowledge, supplemented with the 'manifest illegality' criterion, discussions on superior orders gradually resurfaced.[41] By December 1997 the inclusion of the defence had gained strong support, albeit disagreement remained over the quantum of knowledge required and whether or not the defence should cover orders received from the Security Council.[42] There was strong support, however, in favour of excluding the defence vis-a-vis crimes against humanity and genocide.[43] During the Rome conference the two opposing schools of thought clashed for the final time. The US and Canada vehemently argued that the defence of superior orders, in those cases where the subordinate was not aware that the order was unlawful or where the order was not manifestly unlawful, was widely recognised in international law.[44] This proposal was particularly criticised by the UK, New Zealand and Germany who argued that in cases where superior orders could otherwise be invoked an accused could raise a plea of duress and mistake of fact or law. Although the parties came up with a compromise formula agreed by an informal working group, which became the basis of Article 33, the German as well as other delegations were still disatisfied as a matter of principle. Having thereafter the

---

[38] US Dept of Army FM 27–10, The Law of Land Warfare, 1956, US Dept of Army. In accordance with para 509(a) the defence exists as long as the accused 'did not know and could not reasonably have been expected to know that the act ordered was unlawful'.

[39] Ibid, para 509(b).

[40] *R v Finta* 104 ILR 284.

[41] Report of the Preparatory Committee, UN Doc A/51/22 (12–30 Aug 1996), Art Q, at 518, cited in M Scaliotti, 'Defences Before the International Criminal Court: Substantive Grounds for Excluding Criminal Responsibility (Part I)' (2002) 1 *International Criminal Law Review* 111, 135–36.

[42] During the March–April 1998 Prep Com the proposal absolving subordinates from liability for orders received by the Security Council was dropped. Ibid.

[43] Decisions Taken by the Preparatory Committee at its Session held from 1–12 October 1997, UN Doc A/AC 249/1997/L 9/Rev 1 (1997), Art M, 18–19, cited in Scaliotti, ibid.

[44] UN Doc A/CONF 183/C 1/WGGP/L 2 (16 June 1998), ibid, at 137; see *ICTY Prosecutor v Mrđa*, Trial Chamber Sentencing Judgment (31 Mar 2004), para 67, where the orders given to the accused were found to be so manifestly unlawful that he must have been well aware that they violated the most elementary laws of war and dictates of humanity.

support of the US and its NATO allies the US proposal was adopted by the Committee of the Whole by consensus and finally also by the plenary of the Diplomatic Conference.

What has now emerged as Article 33 of the ICC Statute recognises the defence of superior orders on the basis of the three qualifications that exist under customary international law. The first presupposes an existing loyalty or legal obligation, while the other two refer to the requisite standards of knowledge, consisting of both the subjective knowledge of the accused and an objective test based on the 'manifest illegality' rule. The article thus reads as follows:

1   The fact that a crime within the jurisdiction of the Court has been committed by a person pursuant to an order of a Government or of a superior, whether military or civilian, shall not relieve that person of criminal responsibility unless:

    (a)   The person was under a legal obligation to obey orders of the Government or the superior in question;

    (b)   The person did not know that the order was unlawful; and

    (c)   The order was not manifestly unlawful.

2   For the purposes of this article, orders to commit genocide or crimes against humanity are manifestly unlawful.

The presumption of knowledge inserted in paragraph 2 seems to be irrebuttable. However, since the commission of genocide and crimes against humanity involve large scale action, often requiring minor operations in which the offender cannot always be expected to be aware of the overall and eventual aim, justice necessitates this presumption to be a rebuttable one. Overall, where D is aware of the illegality of the order and proceeds to execute some criminal conduct he satisfies the cognitive elements of the underlying offence but has no excuse available to him, according to the superior orders doctrine. On the other hand, where knowledge as to the unlawfulness of the order is lacking the volitional element (ie the desire) of the *mens rea* is impaired and hence the invocation of superior orders does not operate as a defence; the accused has simply not satisfied the subjective elements of the crime under consideration. In conclusion, superior orders is not a defence (in the meaning of an excuse) to a crime in respect of which the accused has satisfied both its objective and subjective elements.

Let us now proceed to examine the defence of duress, which has a strong affiliation and is closely related to the defence of superior orders.

5.4   Duress and Necessity

Unlike the case of superior orders, necessity and duress are true defences since they are available when the material and mental elements of an offence have been satisfied. Necessity and duress involve a threat to life or bodily harm, such that require or thwart a person to commit a crime. This threat may originate from the victim's external environment, such as a fire, a natural catastrophe, or other (necessity), but it may also be derived from a third person who threatens the victim to commit the crime, lest he lose his life or suffer bodily harm (duress). As will be demonstrated both necessity and duress are accepted in the common law, but not as full exculpatory defences to murder and are acceptable so long as the victim (of the threat) acted proportionally and was not responsible for inflicting the threat upon himself. It is obvious, however, that the circumstances which give rise to necessity and duress generally are quantitively different from those arising in situations of armed conflict. In the *Einsatzgruppen* case, a US military tribunal rejected the view that a soldier with a pistol at his head must choose to die rather than commit an unlawful killing.[45]

The poor drafting of Article 31(1)(d) of the ICC Statute, which iterates the general position in customary international law has its roots not in the ignorance of its drafters, but rather in the divergent and inflexible views of the negotiating parties. It therefore reflects, like many provisions in the Statute, a clause founded among other things on compromise. What is not clear in the text of sub-paragraph (d) is primarily the definition of 'duress' and 'necessity' as two related but distinct concepts, as well as the question whether this defence is also available to a charge of murder. The legislative history of the Statute suggests that although initially the two concepts were included in a different provision, by 1998 they had been moved to a single article where moreover necessity had been subsumed within the concept of duress.[46] Furthermore, during discussions before the Committee of the Whole it was decided that the combined defence encompassed in Article 31(1)(d) was available also to a charge of murder, since the prior requirement necessitating an intention not to cause death had been deleted.[47] Some isolated proposals to the effect that duress/necessity apply also in cases of threats to the property of the accused were unanimously rejected.[48]

Sub-paragraph (d) offers a definition of an offence caused as a result of duress, where this 'result[s] from a threat of imminent death or of continuing or imminent serious bodily harm against that person or another person'. According to this provision, an accused is exculpated from the underlying offence where:

(a) the threat is not brought about by actions attributed to the accused, but by other persons, or as a result of circumstances beyond the control of the accused (necessity);
(b) the accused has taken all necessary and reasonable action to avoid this threat; and
(c) the accused does not intend to cause a greater harm than the one sought to be avoided.

The ICTY Trial Chamber in the *Erdemović* case confirmed the conclusion of the post-Second World War War Crimes Commission that duress constitutes a complete defence subject to the aforementioned conditions.[49] In fact, the ICTY recognised that one of the essential elements of the post-war jurisprudence was the 'absence or not of

---

[45] In such circumstances the threat is 'imminent, real and inevitable'. *USA v Ohlendorf and Others* [*Einsatzgruppen* case], 4 Trials of War Criminals before the Nuremberg Military Tribunals under Control Council Law No 10 [Trials] 411, at 480.

[46] Saland, 'International Criminal Law Principles', 207–08.

[47] Although under traditional English law duress may never excuse the killing of an innocent person. See *R v Howe* [1987] 1 AC 417 and *Abbott v R* [1977] AC 755. But we have already shown that this position is different in international law.

[48] Saland, 'International Criminal Law Principles', at 208.

[49] *ICTY Prosecutor v Erdemović* Trial Chamber Sentencing Judgment (29 Nov 1996), para 17. These were identified in the *Trial of Krupp and Eleven Others*, 10 Law Reports of Trials of War Criminals (LRTWC) 147.

moral choice'.[50] In the face of imminent physical danger a soldier may be considered as being deprived of his moral choice, as long as this physical threat (of death or serious bodily harm) is clear and present, or else imminent, real and inevitable.[51] The ICTY Chamber, moreover, spelt out certain criteria which must be employed in order to conclude whether or not moral choice was in fact available. These are the voluntary participation of the accused in the overall criminal operation and the rank held by the person giving the order as well as that of the accused, which includes the existence or not of a duty to obey in a particular situation.[52]

Cassese J has convincingly argued that since law is based on what society can reasonably expect of its members it 'should not set intractable standards of behaviour which require mankind to perform acts of martyrdom and brand as criminal any behaviour falling below those standards'.[53] This ethico-philosophical approach to duress merits consideration because of its practical implications. In the *Erdemović* Appeals Decision the Chamber, while agreeing that no special rule of international law existed regulating duress where the underlying crime was the taking of human life, its members strongly disagreed on whether the general rule on duress should apply or whether some other domestic principle must be introduced. Judges McDonald and Vohrah unsuccessfully argued that in the absence of a special rule on duress, common law (as it turned out) was applicable, concluding thus that duress does not afford a complete defence to homicides. Judges Cassese and Stephen made the case that the general rule applies, which based on a case-to-case examination does afford a defence of duress. The dissenting opinion of Cassese J that the general international law rule on duress be applied[54] was not only internationally respected but moreover influenced subsequent ICC developments.

One of the essential elements in a successful plea of duress is that of proportionality (doing that which is the lesser of two evils). In practical terms this will be the hardest to satisfy, the burden of proof being on the accused, and may never be satisfied where the accused is saving his own life at the expense of his victim. Conversely, where the choice is not a direct one between the life of the accused and that of his victim, but where there is high probability that the person under duress will not be able to save the life of the victim, the proportionality test may be said to be satisfied.[55] Although duress has been admitted as a defence against homicides,[56] post-Second World War case law suggests that courts have rarely allowed duress to succeed in cases involving unlawful killing, even where they have in principle admitted

---

[50] In *USA v Krauch and Others* [*I G Farben* case], 8 Trials 1081, 1175–95, a US military tribunal had charged several industrialists for their use of slave labour. They argued that they were forced to do so by reason of a Nazi decree. The tribunal accepted the applicability of the defence where a moral choice was possible, the defendant is not responsible for the threat and his conduct was absolutely necessary under the circumstances.

[51] *Erdemović* Trial Sentencing Judgment, para 18, citing the *Einsatzgruppen* dictum above.

[52] Ibid, paras 18–19. Nonetheless, in the particular circumstances of the accused the Trial Chamber, rather strangely given his predicament, emphasised that Erdemović was under a duty to disobey, save in the face of the most extreme duress.

[53] *Erdemović* Appeals Chamber Decision (7 Oct 1997), Dissenting Opinion of Judge Cassese, para 47.

[54] Ibid, paras 12, 40.

[55] Ibid, para 42.

[56] It was only in the *Holzer* case, cited ibid, para 26, that both the prosecutor and the Judge Advocate contended that duress can never excuse the killing of innocent persons, relying however, on English law.

the applicability of this defence. This restrictive approach has its roots in the fundamental importance of human life to law and society, from which it follows that any legal endorsement of attacks on, or interference with, this right will be very strictly construed and only exceptionally admitted.[57] The result would be different where the homicide would have been committed in any case by a person other than the one acting under duress.[58] This was the case with Erdemović who argued that had he not adhered to his superiors to execute Bosnian civilians, not only would he have been shot but others would have taken his place as executioners. In such cases the requirement of proportionality is satisfied because the harm caused by not obeying the illegal order is not much greater than the harm that would have resulted from obeying it.[59] This requirement of proportionality is clearly a subjective one, irrespective of whether the greater harm is in fact avoided.

The concept of necessity is broader than duress, encompassing threats to life and limb generally and not only when they emanate from another person.[60] There is a subjective element in the definition of necessity in that the person should reasonably believe that there is a threat of imminent or otherwise unavoidable death or serious bodily harm to him or to another person. This should be combined with an objective criterion, that the person acted necessarily and reasonably to avoid the threat and moreover did not voluntarily expose him or herself to the threat or danger. Since the defence of necessity is encompassed within the general concept of duress in sub-paragraph (d), it necessarily follows that it is used to merely qualify the 'threat or danger' giving rise to a defence of duress. Therefore, duress in sub-paragraph (d) is broader than the equivalent concept found in general international law. This is not, however, the end of the story, since as already noted Article 21(1)(c) of the ICC Statute empowers the Court to delve into domestic law in cases where all other sources have failed to extract satisfactory solutions. In cases where this exercise may be required the Court would find itself unable to extrapolate general principles because of the divergences in national legislations on the permissibility of necessity between the common law,[61] civil law[62] and Islamic legal systems.[63] Depending on

---

[57] *Erdemović* Appeals Decision, para 43; *Re A* (*Conjoined Twins* case), [2004] All ER 961, exemplifies the ethical tensions in the law of necessity where even in circumstances where the killing of one (already condemned) conjoined twin to save the life of the other did not readily satisfy the ordinary conditions for the defence of necessity.

[58] *Erdemović* Appeals Decision, para 43.

[59] Ibid.

[60] Ibid, para 14. See also 1958 British Manual of Military Law, 'The Law of War on Land', para 630, which puts forward the case of one who in extremity of hunger kills another person to eat him or her.

[61] The failure of this defence in English law is premised on unclear and ill-defined case law that requires reinterpretation. In the classic case of *Dudley and Stephens* (1884) 14 QBD 273, necessity was not upheld to a charge of murder where a cabin boy was eaten by other shipwrecked crew members. The justification for the decision, however, is not clear. That case did not say that a deliberate killing could not be justified, only that a person could not justifiably kill an innocent to save his life because there is never a necessity to live (at the expense of another), nor does any particular individual have the authority to determine who lives or dies. Nonetheless, although the two accused would ordinarily have received the death penalty instead received a much commutted sentence and as a result it is suggested that necessity may at the discretion of the courts serve to mitigate the effects of a crime, even homicides.

[62] Civil law systems generally allow this defence. See, for example, Arts 122–27 of the French Penal Code, and Art 54(1) of the 1930 Italian Penal Code, cited by Scaliotti, *Defences*, 143–45.

[63] Classic Islamic criminal law recognises the defence of duress under *ikrah*. This is accepted widely among all schools and serves to exculpate fully in respect of *hadd* crimes (those subject to corporal

relevant circumstances, and after deeming it appropriate, the Court in a scenario of this type might very well be inclined to decide that the application of the principles of a particular legal system be applicable before the case at hand.

5.5 Self-Defence

Self-defence is another example of a true defence, since it is not directed at disproving the *actus reus* or *mens rea* of the underlying offence. A contemporary international definition of self-defence is that propounded by the ICTY in the *Kordić* case. The Tribunal pointed out that the notion of self-defence:

> May be broadly defined as providing a defence to a person who acts to defend or protect himself or his property (or another person or person's property) against attack, provided that the acts constitute a reasonable, necessary and proportionate reaction to the attack.[64]

The Trial Chamber in that case noted that although the ICTY Statute did not provide for self-defence as a ground for excluding criminal responsibility, defences nonetheless form part of the general principles of criminal law that are binding on the Tribunal. It went on to note that the definition of self-defence enshrined in Article 31(1)(c) of the ICC Statute reflects relevant principles found in most national criminal codes and as such 'may be regarded as constituting a rule of customary international law'.[65]

Despite this general definition which is almost identical to that found in the ICC Statute, there are issues related to this defence that are not straightforward. These problem areas include the relationship between the UN Charter and self-defence,[66] the invocation of self-defence in respect of property, the relevance of proportionality and whether force can be used in cases of pre-emptive self-defence or only when the danger is present or imminent. We shall examine each of these issues individually.

Where a State entity commits an act of aggression in violation of Article 2(4) of the UN Charter that country will incur the type of responsibility pertaining to States. Moreover, when the crime of aggression in the ICC Statute becomes activated and a definition is agreed upon by the parties to the Statute[67] the initiators of an act of aggression will be held criminally liable. Since a definition of aggression is bound to be premised on the relevant provisions of the UN Charter, persons in the highest civilian and military echelons of a State apparatus resorting to the use of military force will be able to invoke self-defence (as a claim aiming to exclude criminal liability) only where the force used is lawful, that is, it is permitted under Articles 42 and 51 of the UN Charter. What is more, such force, even if lawful, will exclude

---

punishment). This includes all types of superior orders even if no specific threats were uttered. See R Peters, *Crime and Punishment in Islamic Law* (Cambridge, Cambridge University Press, 2005) 23.

[64] *ICTY Prosecutor v Kordić and Others*, Trial Chamber Judgment (26 Feb 2001), para 449.

[65] Ibid, para 451.

[66] Of particular relevance is the concept of unlawful use of force under Art 2(4) of the UN Charter, as well as legitimate responses to such force in accordance with Arts 42 (collective enforcement action) and 51 (unilateral or collective self-defence).

[67] ICC Statute, Art 5(2). See chapter 13.3.

criminal liability only where it satisfies the requirements for self-defence, that is, it is proportionate, the danger is present and the response does not constitute a crime against humanity or genocide. Article 31(1)(c) is clear that:

> The fact that the person was involved in a defensive operation conducted by forces shall not in itself constitute a ground for excluding criminal responsibility [under the rubric of self-defence].[68]

Although most delegations raised reservations as regards the availability of self-defence to defend property, at the insistence of the US and Israel reference to this effect was eventually accepted. Sub-paragraph (c) reflects the unanimous feeling of all delegates that the commission of crimes against humanity and genocide can never justify the protection of property. Self-defence in order to protect property can only be sustained where the defensive action involved the perpetration of war crimes and under circumstances where the property concerned 'is essential for the survival of the person or another person or property which is essential for accomplishing a military mission'. Thus, stringent and narrow criteria apply. The result is not a happy one, at least as far as the second part of the sentence is concerned, since under customary international law the concept of military necessity, which is akin to 'property that is essential for accomplishing a military mission',[69] does not permit the commission of war crimes.[70] The rule is clear and simple; while military necessity allows under strict conditions a limited amount of collateral damage it does not provide any authority to commit war crimes. Since the concept of belligerent reprisals is not encompassed within the notion of self-defence,[71] it stretches the imagination to conceive of a war crime committed in defence of property essential for military operations, which is moreover proportionate! The only possible scenario would be where an unlawful attack against military property was repelled with unlawful weapons used against the attackers – the defending party possessing no other or appropriate weaponry – or where protected property was counterattacked as a result. The use of unlawful weapons or the perpetration of attacks in defence of such property against innocent civilians is not only contrary to *jus cogens*, it is certainly not warranted by any construction of the principle of proportionality.[72]

As far as the decision to engage in defensive action is concerned (which includes the determination that force has been used), the test applied in sub-paragraph (c) is an objective one. The person must act reasonably. This will depend on relevant external circumstances, but the Court is not excluded from assessing the personal state and characteristics of the accused. As a result, it is my opinion that pre-emptive self-defence is permissible in the realm of criminal law as long as it is deemed

---

[68] Enunciated also in the *Kordić* Trial Judgment, para 452.

[69] Ibid, para 451.

[70] 1977 Protocol I to the Geneva Conventions of 1949 (International Armed Conflicts), Art 51(4) and (5), 1125 UNTS 3. Kalshoven has correctly argued that deviations from the rules contained in Protocol I cannot be justified with an appeal to military necessity, unless a given rule expressly admits such an appeal. See F Kalsnoven, *Constraints on the Waging of War*, (Geneva, International Committee of the Red Cross, 1987) 73. See chapter 7.4 and 7.5.

[71] It is unlawful to subject civilians to belligerent reprisals in accordance with the customary rule encapsulated in the 1977 Protocol I, Art 51(6).

[72] Y Sandoz *et al* (eds), *Commentary on the Additional Protocols of 8 June 1977* (Leiden, Martinus Nijhoff, 1987) 625–26.

reasonable under the circumstances. Similarly, the degree of force applied is predicated on the objective test of proportionality.

5.6 Intoxication

Intoxication is likewise not a true defence because it is successful as a claim only when the accused was unable to form the *mens rea* of the pertinent offence. Legal systems usually distinguish between voluntary and involuntary intoxication. English law on intoxication is very confusing so I will only present a brief exposition and elucidation that is relevant to this discussion. The fundamental starting point in English law is that even where the defendant is seriously intoxicated he is liable for the offence committed if he was nonetheless able to form a personal volition voluntarily. Thus, intoxication is never a valid defence where its effect is such that although the defendant understood what he was doing (and its possible consequences, where relevant) he had simply lost his self-restraint. This is true even if the defendant was intoxicated by mistake or by another person.[73] Equally, in those situations where an accused becomes self-intoxicated in order to derive so-called Dutch courage the defence is unavailable because he would have already formed an intent (*dolus directus* of either the first or second degree) as to the planned offence.[74] Some doubt exists as to whether a self-induced mistake renders intoxication involuntary, or whether the mistake must be induced by the unlawful acts of another person. Both causes should excuse as long as the accused is deprived of a fair opportunity to conform. In this manner therefore intoxication operates as a true defence.

The ICC Statute entertains this rationale. The terms of the defence of intoxication contained in Article 31(1)(b) of the Statute are simple enough and the provision does not distinguish between offences where proof of the defendant's mental state is required as opposed to offences of strict liability. An excuse is available under strict conditions, namely where the intoxication is so serious as to negate the perpetrator's cognitive and volitional faculties, in the sense that he is either unaware of his actions or is otherwise unable to comprehend their unlawful character. Equally, in cases of voluntary intoxication the accused is liable if he acknowledged the likelihood of subsequent criminality. The matter has only arisen briefly in the ICTY, in a case where a guard had proceeded to brutalise detained inmates, arguing that during many of the incidents he was under intoxication. At sentencing the Trial Chamber found the element of intoxication to be an aggravating, as opposed to a mitigating, factor,[75] refusing to examine intoxication as a defence.

---

[73] In *R v Kingston* [1995] 2 AC 355, the accused was drugged by a third person and proceeded to engage in unlawful sexual intercourse with a minor. The House of Lords sustained his liability by arguing that the intoxication merely removed the defendant's inhibitions, but throughout the duration of the incident he was aware of the situation and had formed intent. Lord Mustill even observed that 'a drunken intent is still an intent'.

[74] *A-G Northern Ireland v Gallagher* [1963] AC 349. Equally, loss of memory that is caused by drunkenness in situations where the accused had already formed the requisite *mens rea* for the offence does not allow for the defence of intoxication. *R v C* [1992] Crim LR 642.

[75] *ICTY Prosecutor v Kvočka and Others*, Trial Chamber Judgment (28 Feb 2005), para 748.

The aforementioned state of the law in England reflects in general terms the practice of most States and hence its inclusion in Article 31(1)(b) of the ICC Statute does not depart from these principles. Thus, involuntary intoxication will negate liability where the accused has not had a chance to direct his cognitive and volitional faculties to the consequence of his conduct, in which case he will not have satisfied the elements of the crime. In those situations where intoxication is voluntary the accused will incur liability if he knew, or disregarded the risk, that, as a result of the intoxication, he or she was likely to engage in conduct constituting a crime.[76] Given the reduced gravity of the offences to which it is raised it is unlikely that this 'defence' will be invoked before international criminal tribunals. Nonetheless, one should not dismiss the possibility of a military or civilian leader that is constantly under sedation,[77] the influence of drugs or is otherwise suffering from alcoholism.

5.7   Mistake of Fact or Mistake of Law

There were widely divergent views on this defence in the context of the ICC Statute. Two options were initially inserted and on the basis of which delegates were divided over whether mistake of law or fact should be a ground for excluding liability. Some delegations were of the view that mistake of fact was not necessary because it was covered by *mens rea*.[78] The view eventually accepted was that both mistake of fact and law constitute valid grounds for excluding criminal responsibility only where the mistake under consideration negates the mental element required by the crime.[79] Understandably therefore it is not considered a true defence. A mistake of law 'as to whether a particular type of conduct is a crime' shall not be a ground for excluding criminal responsibility.[80] While this result is wholly consistent with the range of crimes prescribed in the ICC Statute, it should not be readily accepted as a general principle applicable to all crimes, as will be more thoroughly explained in the next section. Paragraph 2 of Article 32, moreover, makes the necessary connection between mistake of law and superior orders. Where a subordinate receives an unlawful order which is not manifestly unlawful and which he or she is under an obligation to obey the subordinate will be exculpated where he or she believed the order to lie within the confines of legitimacy.

A situation not covered in Article 32 is that of the doctrines of 'transferred intent' and 'mistaken object'. Where D plans to kill B but mistakenly assumes C for B, yet

---

[76] During the preparatory discussions two approaches to voluntary intoxication surfaced: if it was decided that voluntary intoxication should in no case be an acceptable defence, provision should nonetheless be made for mitigation of punishment with regard to persons who were not able to form a specific intent, where required, towards the crime committed due to their intoxication. If, on the other hand, voluntary intoxication were to be retained as a valid defence, as was finally accepted, an exception would be made for those cases where the person became intoxicated in order to commit the crime in an intoxicated condition. UN Doc A/CONF 183/2/Add 1 (14 Apr 1998) 57.

[77] In English law sedative drugs have been found not to create unpredictable and dangerous behaviour and have as a result not been classified as intoxicants. *R v Hardie* [1984] 3 All ER 848.

[78] UN Doc A/CONF 183/2/Add 1 (14 Apr 1998) 57.

[79] ICC Statute, Art 32 and UN Doc, ibid, 56–57.

[80] ICC Statute, Art 32(2).

proceeds to kill C, D's mistake is irrelevant as far as his liability for murder is concerned. His mistake did not prevent him from forming *mens rea* in respect of the crime of murder. The mistaken object doctrine should also find application before the ICC in situations analogous to the conduct just described. As for the applicable test for either a mistake of fact or of law, the wording of the Statute suggests that this is a subjective one. This is in line with English law, for example, where mistakes as to justificatory/definitional defences[81] need only be honest.[82] In classic Islamic law, on the other hand, a mistake of fact and law in many cases serves to exculpate the accused. This is the so-called defence of *shubba*, which generally applies to homicide and *hadd* offences (ie those subject to corporal punishment). It is successfully raised where either a set of facts or a particular law is uncertain. In respect of uncertainty as to the precriptions of a law, the accused is not justified where his ignorance relates to 'essential' elements, such as stealing or drinking wine. Where, however, the ignorance concerns 'details' of the law, the conduct of the accused is always excused.[83]

5.8 Ignorance of Law

The Latin maxim *ignoratio leges non excusat* (ignorance of law is no defence), an underlying principle of national as well as international law, is probably not expressly incorporated in most criminal codes in the world; it is simply taken for granted.[84] It postulates that members of a given society cannot claim that they were unaware of the existence of a law in order to escape the consequences for violating that law. The application of this principle to most offences in the criminal justice system seems to be without much question. Thus, a person blowing up two people in a bus cannot claim that he was not aware that one cannot take the life of other persons, thus effectively claiming ignorance of the offence of murder. However, there certainly exist situations in domestic legal contexts where the fairness of this maxim may come under fire. Take for example a Muslim man raised in a legal regime that permits the practice of blood money (*diya*), which involves the payment of reparation by the perpetrator of crime to his victim (or family) in respect of a homicide.[85] If that person, having lived all his life in his country, were to visit a foreign land to which the concept of *diya* is entirely alien and perhaps repugnant, the legal system of that

---

[81] That is, defences operating within the parameters of the offence definition, such as consent.
[82] *R v Williams* (1984) 78 Cr App R 276; *Beckford v R* [1988] AC 130.
[83] Peters, *Crime and Punishment in Islamic Law*, 21–22.
[84] See *Bilbie v Lumley* (1802) 2 East 469, at 470, *per* Lord Ellenborough's famous dictum on ignorance of law, p 472; *Lansdown v Lansdown* (1730) Mosely 364; *Queen v Mayor of Tewkesbury* (1868) LR. 3 QB 629, *per* Blackburn, J, at 635; *Culbreath v Culbreath* (1849) 7 Ga. 64, *per* Nisbet J, at 71, where it was stated that: 'The idea of excuse, implies delinquency. No man can be excused upon a plea of ignorance of the law, for disobeying its injunctions, or violating its provisions, or abiding his just contracts. He is presumed to know the law, and if he does not know it, he is equally presumed to be delinquent. I remark, to avoid misconstruction, that it is of universal application in criminal cases. In civil matters, it ought not to be used to effectuate a wrong'.
[85] See USC-MSA Compendium of Muslim Texts [Hadiths narrated by Buhkari] on the applicability and function of blood money compensatory processes in Islamic *Shari'a*, available at: <http://www.usc.edu/dept/MSA/fundamentals/hadithsunnah/bukhari/083.sbt.html>.

country would laugh at any suggestion that the accused be allowed to pay the victim's family because he was not aware of the local criminal laws. The accused will be convicted for the substantive offence, so what is of interest to the prosecuting legal system is not actual ignorance of the law, which would certainly be a fact in this case; rather, criminal law sanctions ignorance even where it is real. There are two extremes, however, to this process. On the one hand, criminal justice systems cannot tolerate ignorance as a defence to serious crimes, in respect of which everyone is expected to know the relevant penalties, while on the other hand there exist offences of a less serious nature which the law cannot expect everyone to know with the same degree of certainty.[86] Moreover, the law in certain circumstances allows for people to demonstrate their ignorance of a particular rule.[87] Equally, in the pursuit of fairness some courts are willing to accept that the relatively young age of the offender is a significant factor in demonstrating ignorance of the law, even if the violation under consideration may have generally been well known.[88]

The ignorance of law defence does not presuppose that the ordinary citizen is fluent in all aspects of the criminal law or that one should keep pace with legal developments, although in reality this is to some degree necessary. In practice, we are asked to be social animals and even if we are less social than we like to admit, there exist so many communication channels in contemporary societies that it is impossible not to be appraised as to the basic requirements of social behaviour. Equally, it is presumed that lawful combatants taking part in domestic and international armed conflict have a basic knowledge of the laws of war and receive regular training by designated legal advisors.[89] This is in fact an obligation on States parties to the 1949 Geneva Conventions.[90] In the *Lubanga* case the accused argued that he was not aware that it was illegal to recruit children into the armed forces. The ICC Chamber, relying on evidence that the victims were well acquainted with this prohibition and that the Democratic Republic of Congo, the accused's country of nationality, had moreover ratified relevant conventions, was unable to entertain the argument that the ignorance of the accused negated his volition to commit the offence. This defence could only

[86] In *Lambert v California* (1957) 355 U.S. 225 the complainant was unaware of a Los Angeles city ordinance whereby she was required to register if she remained in the city for more than five days. The penalty was further augmented for every day she failed to register. The US Supreme Court held that only knowledge or probability of knowledge of a statute is required to convict someone of a notice offence. See AF Booke, 'When Ignorance of the Law Became an Excuse: Lambert and its Progeny' (1992) 19 *American Journal of Criminal Law* 279.

[87] *Ratlaf v USA* (1994) 510 US 135, in which the US Supreme Court in a split decision held that people who keep their cash transactions with banks to under $10,000 to evade federal reporting requirements cannot be convicted without proof that they knew such action is illegal.

[88] In *Maverick Recording Company et al v Harper*, Judgment of 7 August 2008 (unreported), the US Western District Court of Texas held that a minor that was illegally downloading music from an Internet sharing site could not have known of the infringement of copyright laws (the 1976 US Copyright Act) because the particular website did not alert its users to this possibility.

[89] In the *Trial of Karl Buck and Ten Others*, 5 LRTWC 39, the British Military Court seized of the case viewed the matter as to whether the accused were aware of the existence of POW rights as a matter of fact and not a presumption under law, as would be the case today.

[90] Arts 82 and 83 of Protocol I of 1977.

succeed, argued the Chamber, where the accused did not realise the social significance, or everyday meaning, of the objective elements of the crime, which could not
be sustained in this particular instance.[91]

When we apply this maxim to the international legal sphere we can see that it is
certainly not free from problems. For one thing, when we are schooled or go through
life we do not become active members of an international society but only of a local,
or national, environment. While it is true that this is an age of international
interaction through the openness of frontiers and worldwide travel, this is by
necessity only a minor part of one's life, which is generally consumed by day-to-day
affairs within a single jurisdiction. Although this is true for the average person, it does
not mean that the average citizen does not possess the capacity to reason and
distinguish between right and wrong when asked to partake in crimes against
humanity or genocide. However, these are not the only crimes in international law.
Imagine, for example, the situation of a country that is not a party to the 1997 OECD
Transnational Bribery Convention[92] and where corrupt practices are either allowed
because the country lacks an anti-corruption law, or because in practice such
practices are openly carried out by all government officials. A national of this
country that was schooled throughout his life in this environment of corruption,
which is fuelled also by the active bribery committed by nationals of other nations,
may well think this practice to be the norm, even if he perceives it as morally wrong.
If he commits an international corruption offence in a country where this is
prohibited, should he not be able to invoke the ignorance of law maxim on the
ground that he was not schooled in an environment that taught him to distinguish the
wrongfulness of corruption?

I can furnish numerous other examples of otherwise serious crimes whose perpetrators have never been taught otherwise. Among these one may find the practice of
female genital mutilation (FGM), which absent medical authorisation would amount
to an offence of grievous bodily harm in the UK.[93] Equally, certain tribal practices in
parts of the world may be tantamount to acts similar to slavery (inheritance of family
members upon the death of the husband)[94] or torture (in respect of initiation rituals).
The international community tries to banish these practices mainly through the
United Nations and via multilateral treaties, such as the 1957 Convention on
Slavery-Like Practices,[95] but there is a growing resistance from many developing
States. They argue that many of these practices are deeply rooted in their cultural

---

[91] *ICC Prosecutor v Lubanga*, Trial Chamber Decision on Confirmation of Charges (29 Jan 2007),
para 316.

[92] OECD Convention on Combating Bribery of Foreign Public Officials in International Business
Transactions, (1997) 37 ILM 1.

[93] UK Female Genital Mutilation Act 2003, s 1. Under s 3 of the Act the offence is punishable in the
UK even where it is committed abroad, subject to certain conditions. In fact, the very purpose of the Act
was to prevent and punish extraterritorial infringements by persons with a UK connection.

[94] These are known as 'levirate' marriages, in which the brother of the deceased inherits his spouse.
Obviously, the origins of this practice related to the protection of the woman, but its contemporary
application is abhorrent and a violation of fundamental human rights. See B Potash, *Women in African
Societies* (Palo Alto, Stanford University Press, 1988) 77–78.

[95] Supplementary Convention on the Abolition of Slavery, the Slave Trade and Institutions and
Practices Similar to Slavery, 226 UNTS 3.

identities, which western societies have no way of understanding, or indeed appreciating. They further argue that local culture should validate the normativity of the universal human rights system and that the UN system should not be self-referential and self-validating. In this manner they are rejecting the universality of human rights and are instead claiming that human rights are relevant only in each particular culture. For good reason, the universal human rights movement is adamantly opposed to any such assertions.[96] This discussion is meant to provide food for thought and is in no way meant to challenge the applicability of the various principles of jurisdiction or the applicability of defences generally.

Werle argues that a mistake of international criminal law is relevant if it concerns the normative elements of a crime, but not the core substance of the crime itself. By way of illustration, an excusable mistake of law exists where the perpetrator deems the trial of a prisoner of war as encompassing fundamental hearing guarantees when in fact it does not.[97] This mistake does not constitute a defence, however, because in and of itself it negates the *mens rea* of the accused in relation to the offence charged. In all other respects, it is contended that ignorance of the law may exceptionally constitute an excuse where such ignorance culminates in duress, in accordance with Articles 32(2) and 33 of the ICC Statute.[98] In the case of the defence of superior orders the defendant may claim ignorance as to the illegality of the orders given him, except where such orders related to the crime of genocide. If one views superior orders as constituting domestic law by reason of the formal hierarchical delegation involved then ignorance as to their legality is only a matter of fact for the purposes of international law. If, however, the legality of the orders is determined solely in accordance with international law then their observance is not a matter of fact but a matter of law.

5.9 Mental Incapacity

A defence of mental incapacity necessarily develops and evolves alongside medical/psychiatric advances. Although this is recognised in domestic legal systems, in essence because serious mental incapacity negates the mental element of crime, law-making institutions and courts are not bound in incorporating such scientific evidence into the criminal law. Article 31(1)(a) of the ICC Statute exculpates an accused from criminal responsibility where the 'defence' of mental incapacity is proven. However, besides a general qualification of the scope of mental incapacity none of the variants recognised in the different legal systems are employed; and for good reason. In the limited spatial confines of the Prep Com, agreement would have been impossible and by that time paragraph 3 of Article 31 had been inserted, or was imminent, according to which the Court could *proprio motu* derive any additional appropriate defence by reference to general principles of law. In fact, it is very likely that the elaboration of

---

[96] See generally, J Donnelly, 'Cultural Relativism and Universal Human Rights' (1984) 6 *Human Rights Quarterly* 400.
[97] G Werle, *Principles of International Criminal Law* (The Hague, TMC Asser Press, 2005) 152.
[98] Ibid.

this defence before the ICC will depend almost exclusively on such principles,[99] given the lack of an international body of jurisprudence on the legal effects of psychiatric conditions.

The defence was raised in the *Čelebići* case, where an ICTY Trial Chamber established a two-tier test of 'diminished responsibility'. This consists of an 'abnormality of mind' from which the accused must be suffering at the time of the crime and which must moreover 'substantially impair' the ability of the accused to control his or her actions.[100] This test was essentially constructed on the basis of English law.[101] On the facts of the case the ICTY, although recognising that the accused Landzo suffered from an abnormality of mind, rejected his claim because in its opinion he failed to prove that the impairment was substantial. The basis of this judgment does represent at a minimum the incorporation of the defence in the various legal systems and as such was deemed appropriate for the purposes of the ICC Statute. It may successfully be raised where:

> The person suffers from a mental disease or defect that destroys that person's capacity to appreciate the unlawfulness or nature of his or her conduct, or capacity to control his or her conduct to conform to the requirements of law.[102]

If successfully raised a defence of insanity would constitute a full defence and lead to acquittal.[103] Yet, in the context of the ICTY Statute the admission of mental incapacity cannot follow its status in domestic law because while therein it serves to reduce murder to manslaugher, with respect to the ICTY no such sub-categorisations exist. As a result, all pleas of insanity have been treated merely as mitigating factors before the ICTY for purely practical purposes.[104] As for the burden of proof, based on discussions in previous sections of this chapter, this is an affirmative defence whose elements must be raised and satisfied by the accused on a balance of probabilities.[105]

In its determination of the factual criteria relating to this defence the ICC will have recourse to expert witnesses provided by both parties[106] or by the Registrar from a list approved by it. Conversely, it may also have recourse to an expert approved by the Court at the request of a party.[107] This intricate interplay between law and psychiatry/forensics, coupled with: (a) the relatively wide definition of Article 31(1)(a), and (b)

---

[99] The lack of international jurisprudence was also evident during the drafting of the ICTY Statute, where the UN Secretary General's report, although silent on the specific issue, left it to the Tribunal to decide the fate of 'mental incapacity, drawing upon general principles of law recognised by all nations'. UN Doc S/25704 (1993), reprinted in (1993) 32 ILM 1159, para 58.

[100] *ICTY Prosecutor v Delalić and Others* (*Čelebići* case), Trial Chamber Judgment (16 Nov 1998), paras 1165–70. Where the effect of the abnormality is of this nature, is it not best to argue that the accused did not commit the criminal act and that the criminal conduct was performed through him?

[101] *R v Byrne* [1960] 3 All ER 1, at 4 and s 2(1) of the 1957 Homicide Act of England and Wales, where it is, however, only a partial defence in that it reduces a charge of murder to one of manslaughter.

[102] The *Čelebići* Appeals Judgment (20 Feb 2001), para 587, held that the ICC defence is akin to the defence of insanity.

[103] Ibid, para 582.

[104] Ibid, para 590.

[105] *Čelebići* Trial Judgment, paras 78, 1160, 1172.

[106] ICC Rules of Procedure and Evidence, r 135(1).

[107] Ibid, r 135(3).

the liberal rules on the production of evidence (as long as probative value can be demonstrated), ensures that technical consultants will be a substantial guide for the Court were such a defence to arise.[108]

5.10 *Tu Quoque*

It should be stated from the outset that this is no longer,[109] and under any circumstances, a successful defence, although from a structural point of view it is a true defence because its aim is not to negate the *actus reus* or the *mens rea* of the underlying crime, but to justify or excuse the otherwise criminal conduct of the accused. It literally means 'you too', implying that one may be permitted to perpetrate a violation of humanitarian law against his adversary as a means of retaliation because said adversary committed a similar or other violation and went unpunished. *Tu quoque* claims should be distinguished from claims of belligerent reprisals, since although a reprisal does indeed constitute an illegal act, its purpose is to persuade one's adversary to comply with the laws of war and, or, to cease his violations. Thus, the difference between the two is predicated on the intent and knowledge of the accused. It is obvious that were this defence to be accepted it would defeat the very purpose of the laws of war (because it assumes that this corpus of law is premised on reciprocity),[110] but it is equally unsettling for victors to prosecute their adversaries for offences which they themselves remain unpunished.

Tu quoque claims invoked as defences should be distinguished from claims the aim of which is to assist the preparation of the accused in demonstrating that a particular incident is far more extensive than originally conceived. Thus, in the *Lubanga* case before an ICC pre-Trial chamber the accused requested the admission of evidence showing that the recruitment of child soldiers was endemic in the Ituri region and undertaken by all parties to the conflict.[111]

---

[108] See generally, P Krug, 'The Emerging Mental Incapacity Defence in International Criminal Law: Some Initial Questions of Implementation' (2000) 94 *American Journal of International Law* 317, 322–35.

[109] Not that it was ever confirmed as such. It was specifically rejected in the *High Command* case, 12 LRTWC 1, at 64.

[110] *ICTY Prosecutor v Kupreškić*, Appeals Chamber Judgment (14 Jan 2000), paras 515–17; discussed also and rejected in *ICTY Prosecutor v Kunarac and Others*, Appeals Chamber Judgment (Jan 2002), para 87.

[111] *ICC Prosecutor v Lubanga*, Decision on the Prosecution's Request for an Order on the Disclosure of Tu Quoque Material Pursuant to Rule 77 (2 Oct 2009), para 18.

6

Immunities from Criminal Jurisdiction

6.1 General Conception of Immunity in International Law

As a general rule a State enjoys absolute and complete authority over persons and property situated on its territory. Indeed, without directly intervening in the internal affairs of another country it is difficult to see how a sovereign may otherwise assert authority over persons or property situated in a foreign land. Even before the establishment of the modern sovereign States it was recognised that if State-like entities were effectively to interact in commercial, diplomatic and other fields they required normative assurances that their official representatives would be free from arrest or suit in the receiving State. This freedom from suit before a foreign court, which represents the heart of the concept of immunity, no doubt constitutes a limitation on State sovereignty. Nonetheless, it is a welcome limitation because it is of a reciprocal nature that may also be invoked by the receiving State in the exercise of its own foreign relations.

If it is agreed that a State enjoys absolute territorial competence, immunity from civil or criminal suit is possible only by the forum's waiver of competence in respect of persons or property located on its territory. This also means that immunity is an exception to a normative rule that would otherwise apply [ie to the ordinary criminal or civil jurisdiction of States].[1] This State-centred concept can be discerned as early as *Schooner Exchange v McFaddon*,[2] where Marshall J explained that a foreign public vessel would not dare enter the ports of another State if it was not satisfied that it benefited from not being sued in the courts of the coastal State. This voluntary waiver of jurisdiction by the forum/territorial State amounts to an 'implied licence' from its judicial, executive and enforcement claws. This is the primary legal basis for the concept of immunity, which through the consistent practice of each State has developed into a rule of customary law. The fact that sovereign States are juridically equal under international law does not alone suffice as a basis for granting this implied licence, despite the maxim *par in parent non habet imperium*.[3] In an era where a significant number of human rights and humanitarian norms have attained *jus cogens* and *erga omnes* character, equality has not prevented suits against States and

---

[1] *Arrest Warrant of 11 April 2000* (Democratic Republic of Congo v Belgium) Judgment (14 Feb 2002), (2002) ICJ Reports 3, Separate Opinions of Judges Higgins, Kooijmans and Buergenthal, para 71.
[2] *Schooner Exchange v McFaddon* (1812) 7 Cranch 116.
[3] One sovereign cannot exercise authority over another by means of its legal system.

their officials before municipal courts for both tort and criminal cases,[4] although as will become evident in this chapter most of these have not generally succeeded. Similarly, although designed to enhance inter-State relations and limit the reach of the receiving State's judicial and executive machinery the concept of State immunity is not based on comity. State practice at the international level suggests that what was once an implied licence has now evolved into an international obligation on the part of the receiving sovereign.

The fact that litigation before a domestic court raises issues of policy pertinent to a foreign State[5] may explain why national courts have on many occasions been reluctant to exercise jurisdiction over foreign sovereigns. Moreover, the nature of most sovereign acts cannot become the subject of municipal judicial proceedings because it would entail the imposition of one's law over a foreign State.[6] In this light, in *Buck v AG*[7] the English Court of Appeal refused to make a declaration on the validity, or otherwise, of the Constitution of Sierra Leone. Sovereign acts that would otherwise be excluded from the consideration of national courts have included governmental conduct dealing with purely internal issues or external affairs.[8] These issues have fallen under the umbrella of non-justiciable acts and have precluded national courts from asserting their jurisdiction. Immunity is not strictly speaking a personal plea of defence on account of two seminal reasons. Firstly, in those situations where it is invoked by the State in favour of the accused it lacks the status of a personal claim. Secondly, by invoking immunity the accused does not seek to excuse or justify his conduct by reference to an extraneous substantive factor (ie duress, superior orders); rather, he or she is invoking a procedural limitation that bars a national court from entertaining a suit because of the particular status of the accused. It seems doubtful, however, that all traditional non-justiciable acts are beyond the ambit of national courts, since if the prevention or punishment of specific conduct is classified as a peremptory norm of international law (*jus cogens*) it would need to be subject to some judicial enforcement irrespective of the status of the perpetrator. For example, if a case comes before the courts of State A, whereby an alien has acted in accordance with a law in State B allowing the practice of torture the courts of State A may reasonably declare that law to be contrary to international law and invalidate any legal effects arising within the territory of State A. The

[4] *Re Pinochet (No 3)* (1999) 17 ILR 393; *Prefecture of Voiotia and Others v Federal Republic of Germany* (1998) 92 *American Journal of International Law* 765, where acts of atrocity committed by German troops during their occupation of Hellas in the Second World War were held to constitute violations of *jus cogens* norms, hence susceptible to the civil jurisdiction of Hellenic courts. This result was subsequently sustained in cassation by the Court of Cassation. Reported in (2001) 95 *American Journal of International Law* 375. A similar result was confirmed in *Ferrini v Repubblica Federale di Germania* by the Italian Court of Cassation in its Judgment No 5044/2004 (11 Mar 2004), (2004) 128 ILR 658, where it was claimed that the *jus cogens* character of crimes justifies universal jurisdiction and deprives not only the culprit State of immunity, but also the agent of his functional immunity. The *Ferrini* rationale was subsequently concretised by the Court of Cassation in *FRG v Mantelli and Others*, Judgment No 14199 (29 May 2008).

[5] *Rahimtoola v Nizam of Hyderabad* [1958] 3 All ER 961.

[6] H Fox, *The Law of State Immunity* (Oxford, Oxford University Press, 2008) 87.

[7] *Buck v AG* [1965] Ch 745; 42 ILR 11. The same has been sustained as regards the validity of treaties in situations where the issue at hand does not raise questions of national law. *Ex p Molyneaux* [1986] 1 WLR 331.

[8] See *Kuwait Airways Corp v Iraqi Airways Co* [1995] 1 WLR 1147.

invocation of immunity as a procedural bar cannot preclude such a legitimate result. In *Oppenheim v Cattermole,* for example, one of the salient issues of the case was whether a decree adopted in Nazi Germany in 1941 depriving those Jews who had emigrated from Germany of their citizenship should be recognised by the English court. Lord Chelsea pointed out that although the courts should generally be very reluctant to pass judgment on foreign sovereign acts, by reason of the fact that the particular Nazi statute was not only discriminatory but deprived German Jews of their property and citizenship he emphatically asserted that: 'a law of this sort constitutes so grave an infringement of human rights that the courts of this country ought to refuse to recognise it as a law at all'.[9]

Under the classical law of immunity there was little or no distinction between the entity of the State and its agents or officials. Moreover, until very recently States could not be sued at all before the courts of other nations. This rule of absolute immunity rested on the customary assimilation of the sovereign and its officials with the represented State, regardless of the function served in each particular case. Before the 1920s this rule of absolute immunity suggested that every State act was immune from scrutiny in the courts of other nations. With the rapid growth of inter-State commerce, however, private traders and merchants demanded definite guarantees that in their transactions with governmental entities they would not be disadvantaged by the unlimited and abusive operation of immunity. Indeed, the erosion of absolute immunity seems to have rested on trading considerations. As a result, the absolute nature of immunity gave way to a more restricted model whereby only governmental acts that were genuinely public in nature (acts *jure imperii*) would benefit from immunity. Conversely, conduct that was quintessentially private, such as government trading or purchasing of land and other commercial transactions (acts *jure gestionis*) were gradually excluded from the entitlement of immunity. With the dissolution of the USSR and the communist system generally in Europe only China and a few South American States continue to hold on to the doctrine of absolute immunity. Given that immunity pleas are raised as procedural bars before domestic courts it is reasonable that the criteria for determining whether an act is performed in a public or private capacity be developed by the laws of each forum. Such criteria are usually incorporated in specific statutes, such as the UK State Immunity Act (SIA) 1978. Since the distinction is not always clear-cut several theories have subsequently been adopted through the case law and by theorists with a view to elucidating the correct boundaries between public and private acts. These have given rise to the following considerations: a) examination of the 'purpose of the act', that is whether or not it was intended for a commercial or a public transaction. This approach has not attracted favour from UK and US courts.[10] It was, nonetheless, incorporated in a subsidiary role in Article 2 of the International Law Commission's (ILC) Draft Articles on Jurisdictional Immunities. This was principally justified because its role as

---

[9] *Oppenheim v Cattermole* [1976] AC 249, at 277; in *The Queen on the Application of Abbasi and Another v FCO Secretary of State and Others,* Judgment [2002] EWCA Civ 1598, the Court of Appeal agreed with this position, but on the facts of the case it had no power to compel the US to grant *habeas corpus* relief to the applicant, who was a British national held at Guantanamo Bay as a suspected Al-Qaeda member.

[10] *Trendtex Trading Corp v Central Bank of Nigeria* [1977] 1 All ER 881; *I Congreso del Partido* [1981] 2 All ER 1064; *Victory Transport Inc v Comisaria General De Abastecimientos y Transportos,* 35 ILR 110.

a complementary test in a number of jurisdictions could not be overlooked;[11] b) the 'nature of the act' test has found some support[12] but it is unambiguous that certain commercial contracts can only be made by States and not by private parties, such as the supply of military material; c) the more common approach seems to suggest that a list of detailed exceptions was preferred by municipal courts in order to avoid making personal determinations on the basis of either test.[13] This, to a large extent, is reflected in section 3 of the UK SIA 1978. The 1978 Act represents a good example of a restrictive immunity statute since it is not only similar to the US Foreign Sovereign Immunities Act (FSIA) 1976, but it also implements the 1972 European Convention on State Immunity.[14]

A foreign sovereign may waive its immunity privileges either expressly or by conduct. Such waiver need not necessarily extend to measures of execution.[15] US and UK courts require genuine submission to the competence of their judiciary and have rejected the invocation of implied waivers, even with respect to conduct constituting a violation of *jus cogens*.[16]

6.2   Act of State Doctrine

This doctrine has been developed mainly by common law courts, which have generally refused to pass judgment on the validity of acts of foreign governments performed within their national territory.[17] This doctrine is akin to the concept of 'non-justiciability', having been viewed as a function of the separation of powers with the aim of avoiding judicial interference in the executive's conduct of foreign relations.[18] The difference between the doctrines of State immunity and act of State is that the former being a procedural bar to the jurisdiction of a court can be waived, while the latter being a substantial bar cannot. Although it is not raised as a defence against criminal prosecution of foreign officials, generally involving tort and compensation claims, it is nonetheless important for the purposes of this book because if

---

[11]   *USA v The Public Service Alliance of Canada* (1993) 32 ILM 1.

[12]   *Trendtex* [1977] 1 All ER 881.

[13]   In the *Victory Transport* case, 35 ILR 110, the District Court of Appeals listed as acts *jure imperii*, internal administrative measures, such as the expulsion of aliens and the passing of national laws, acts concerning military and diplomatic affairs and public loans.

[14]   ETS 74.

[15]   I Brownlie, *Principles of Public International Law,* (Oxford, Oxford University Press, 1998) 343; J Crawford, 'Execution of Judgments and Foreign Sovereign Immunity' (1981) 75 *American Journal of International Law* 75, at 86.

[16]   *Hirsch v State of Israel and State of Germany* (1997) 113 ILR 543; in *Smith v Socialist People's Libyan Arab Jamahiriya* (1997) 113 ILR 534, the Court of Appeals stated further that FSIA, § 1605, did not contemplate a dynamic expansion whereby immunity could be removed by action of the UN Security Council; *Kahan v Pakistan Federation* [1951] 2 KB 1003, rejecting a claim that a waiver had been established from a prior contract to submit to the jurisdiction of UK courts.

[17]   For a discussion of a civil law approach, see *Border Guards Prosecution* case, 100 ILR 364, where the German Federal Supreme Court found the act of State doctrine to be a rule of domestic law encompassing the extent to which the acts of foreign States were assumed to be effective. See also JC Barker, 'State Immunity, Diplomatic Immunity and Act of State: A Triple Protection against Legal Action?' (1998) 47 *International & Comparative Law Quarterly* 950.

[18]   See *Kirkpatrick v Environmental Tectonics* (1990) 493 US 403.

unsuccessfully raised it exposes crimes guised as governmental acts. Moreover, it forms part of the process for the pursuit of civil remedies by victims of international crimes and may lead to so-called universal tort jurisdiction in respect of international crimes or serious human rights violations.

The classic expression of the doctrine was stated in *Underhill v Hernandez*[19] in which the US Supreme Court refused to assess the legality of the detention incurred by the plaintiff in the hands of an insurrectionist movement that was later recognised as the successor government of Venezuela. In *Banco Nacional de Cuba v Sabbatino*[20] the US Supreme Court equally refused to examine the legality of the Cuban Government's expropriation of US property in that country, but the case served as a precursor for two of the three exceptions to the doctrine. These relate to: a) illegal takings of property in violation of international law; b) violation of a treaty obligation relating to expropriation, and; c) foreign laws and decrees that purport to violate fundamental human rights.[21] The doctrine requires the defendant to establish that the performed activities were undertaken on behalf of the State and not in a private capacity. While any personal commercial transactions would clearly not be attributable to the State,[22] the extent to which individuals may purport to be acting for their sovereign has been limited in recent years. What is relevant for the purposes of the present analysis is the refusal of courts to accept the sovereign character of criminal acts in furtherance of personal aims. In *Jimenez v Aristeguieta*[23] the accused had used his position as former President and dictator of Venezuela to commit financial crimes for his own benefit. He claimed that criminal though these actions may have been they were, nonetheless, acts that should be attributable to Venezuela. The Fifth Circuit rejected this claim stating that offences perpetrated for private financial benefit constitute 'common crimes committed by the Chief of State in violation of his position and not in pursuance of it. They are as far from being an act of State as rape'.[24]

Similarly, in *USA v Noriega*[25] a district court held that acts of drug trafficking committed even by a *de facto* leader of a country do not constitute sovereign acts, relying on *Jimenez*. The district court further correctly noted that because the doctrine was designed to preclude the hindrance of foreign relations it was not applicable to situations where the US federal government had already indicted the claimant, as was the case with Noriega. US courts have demonstrated significant judicial activism in limiting the effects of the act of State doctrine. In *Doe v Unocal* it was held that the act of State doctrine did not preclude US courts from considering

---

[19]   *Underhill v Hernandez* (1897) 168 US 250, at 252; see also the earlier decision *of Hatch v Baez* (1876) 7 Hun 596, where the New York Supreme Court was prevented from reviewing acts of the former President of the Dominican Republic in his official capacity.

[20]   *Banco Nacional de Cuba v Sabbatino* (1964) 376 US 398.

[21]   Fox, *The Law of State Immunity*, 106–07.

[22]   *Alfred Dunhill of London Inc v Republic of Cuba* (1976) 425 US 682.

[23]   *Jimenez v Aristeguieta* (1962) 311 F 2d 547.

[24]   Ibid, 557–58; similarly, in *Sharon v Time Inc* (1984) 599 F Supp 538, it was held that the Israeli Defence Minister's alleged support of a massacre could not constitute the policy of the Israeli Government and, therefore, an act of State.

[25]   *USA v Noriega*, 99 ILR 143.

claims based on legal principles on which the international community had reached unambiguous agreement, such as slavery.[26]

Thus far, a thorough, yet necessarily brief, discussion of the general conception of immunity in international law was undertaken. These rules are useful in discerning whether or not a foreign State may be impleaded in civil suits before the courts of other nations. I will now proceed to examine the international law of immunity from criminal jurisdiction, as this is specifically afforded to natural persons.

6.3   Immunity from Criminal Jurisdiction

In general terms, immunity from jurisdiction means that a court cannot entertain a particular suit, not that the defendant is discharged from criminal liability altogether or that the jurisdiction of the court is extinguished.[27] This means that once the procedural bar of immunity is removed (eg because the person benefiting from it is no longer an active office holder) the criminal liability of the accused re-emerges and that person becomes once again susceptible to criminal prosecution. Under customary law aliens have been granted immunity from municipal courts in respect of alleged international or transnational offences on two grounds. The first relates to the particular status of certain persons. Thus, it is recognised that individuals who hold the highest public offices enjoy absolute immunity from criminal prosecution before domestic courts. Its basis is not the nature of the action but the official status of the person concerned. This type of immunity is known as personal or *ratione personae* and is available to a limited number of individuals: serving Heads of State, heads of diplomatic missions, their families and servants.[28] It should be pointed out that personal immunity is not available to serving Heads of Government who are not also Heads of State, military commanders and their subordinates. The rationale is to facilitate international relations through travel, lest a contrary result would lead to isolation and a break-down of inter-State communication. Despite the occasional abuses that the granting of such immunity may entail it is far more preferable to the potentiality of armed conflict as a result of an aggrieved sovereign. If the Security Council were to decide that the actions of said sovereign are so severe as to merit prosecution then it is free to refer him or her to the ICC or set up an ad hoc or other criminal tribunal. Equally, once persons enjoying personal immunity are removed from office they are susceptible to criminal prosecution.

Immunity *ratione materiae* (otherwise known as functional immunity), on the other hand, serves to protect not any particular person but the governmental function bestowed upon government agents. There is thus no pre-determined restriction as to

---

[26]   Doe v UNOCAL (1997) 963 F Supp 880.

[27]   *Dickinson v Del Solar* [1930] 1 KB 376, at 380, *per* Lord Hewart CJ; similarly, ICJ *Belgian Arrest Warrant* judgment, paras 47–55.

[28]   SIA 1978, s 14(1) extends immunity *ratione personae* to: (a) the sovereign or other Head of that State in his public capacity; (b) the government of that State; and (c) any department of that government [but not every executive entity]. In *Propend Finance Pty Ltd and Others v Sing and Others* (1998) 111 ILR 611, the UK Court of Appeals held that the correct interpretation of the word 'government' in s 14(1) be in light of the concept of sovereign authority, thus encompassing police functions.

the range of persons entitled to functional immunity. It serves to protect governmental acts of one State from being assessed before the courts of another and therefore only incidentally confers immunity on the individual carrying out such tasks. Subsequently, it is open to any person exercising official functions, from a former Head of State to the lowest public official. The reason for granting this type of immunity is to protect the person of the foreign dignitary in order to carry out his or her State functions and to represent that country abroad without any hindrance, much like personal immunity. This means that once the person is removed from office and no longer represents State interests abroad he or she may thereafter become subject to criminal prosecution for offences committed during his or her office. The fact that such immunity may be abused while the holder is in office is regrettable, but does not alter that person's protected status, as this remains a well established rule of international law. In the *Belgian Arrest Warrant* case Belgian courts had asserted universal jurisdiction over the Congolese Foreign Minister in respect of alleged international crimes (namely crimes against humanity). In a heavily split judgment the ICJ confirmed that no distinction could be drawn between acts undertaken in an official or private capacity because his immunity was *ratione materiae*. The Court clearly emphasised that customary international law did not provide an exception to the granting of immunity *ratione materiae,* even in respect of war crimes and crimes against humanity.[29] The case would obviously be different where such immunity to be removed by the State of the protected person's nationality, or by treaty – including Security Council resolutions – as was the case with the prosecution of former President Milosevic before the ICTY.

The reader will no doubt appreciate that whereas immunity serves international relations well it is counter-productive in respect of leaders and governmental officials who plan and execute serious and widespread international crimes. Obviously, very few serious crimes are perpetrated by leaders and other State officials at a global level and it would be absurd to suggest an overhaul of the international law of immunity for the few deplorable culprits, particularly since the Security Council may otherwise subject these to the jurisdiction of international criminal tribunals. Yet, it is also evident that the abuse of the concept is threatening the rubric of international legitimacy.

6.3.1   The Application of Functional and Personal Immunity in Practice

As explained above, foreign Heads of State have customarily enjoyed immunity from criminal prosecution by reason of the respect afforded to their person and the State they represent.[30] This is generally true irrespective of the criminal offence they are alleged to have committed. Certainly, the rule against non-intervention, which is also enshrined in Article 2(7) of the UN Charter, has played a large part in the

---

[29] ICJ *Belgian Arrest Warrant* judgment, paras 47–55.

[30] In *Lafontant v Aristide* (1994) 103 ILR 581, the Eastern District Court of New York held that a recognised Head of State enjoys absolute immunity even in exile, unless such immunity has been explicitly waived.

contemporary consolidation of the law of immunity. This principle, however, has come under intense scrutiny in the years following the end of the Cold War and has been significantly eroded by the Security Council and the flourishing of international human rights law and its judicial or quasi-judicial institutions. The majority of the House of Lords in the *Pinochet (No 3)* case[31] admitted that while the immunity of a former Head of State persists with respect to official acts the determination of what constitutes an official act is to be made in accordance with customary law. As a result, it held that international crimes such as torture cannot constitute the official acts of a former Head of State.[32] This represents a marked progression in comparison with past practice, despite its otherwise obvious nature. Indeed, since Article 1(1) of the 1984 Torture Convention defines torture as conduct that can only be inflicted by a public official the mere invocation of immunity *ratione materiae* would necessarily render the criminal provisions of the Torture Convention redundant. Article 1(1) has to be read, hence, as excluding such functional immunity. This conclusion has not always been self-evident. The situation is different in relation to an acting Head of State, who continues to enjoy absolute immunity from criminal prosecution before national courts [but not international tribunals sanctioned by the UN Security Council] irrespective of the crimes committed.

The few prosecutions that have taken place before national courts do not in my view support a proposition that the community of nations has decided to altogether abandon immunity (both functional and personal) in respect of serious international crimes.[33] Interestingly, a very split European Court of Human Rights in the *Al-Adsani* case took the view that even *jus cogens* norms such as the prohibition against torture must be construed as existing in harmony with other recognised principles of international law with which they may at first sight seem to conflict, namely State immunity. The applicant was tortured by government agents in Kuwait and pursued civil claims before British courts for a period of 10 years, all of which were rejected on the basis of the immunity afforded under the Sovereign Immunities Act (SIA) 1978 to Kuwait. The claimant ultimately applied to the European Court of Human Rights, arguing that the SIA violated his right of access to judicial remedies. The Court rejected his claim by suggesting that immunity is inherent in the operation of international law and cannot be regarded as imposing a disproportionate restriction on the right of access to court.[34] One cannot help but sense the immensity of the injustice to the claimant, as well as the lamentable reality in situations where immunity is flagrantly abused. Nonetheless, this case only upholds the immunity of the State, not the functional immunity of the perpetrator of a serious international crime.[35]

---

[31] *Pinochet (3)* case [1999] 2 WLR 827, at 880, 906.

[32] See G Garnett, 'The Defence of State Immunity for Acts of Torture' (1997) 18 *Australian Yearbook of International Law* 97.

[33] Equally, it may be argued that the absence of a significant body of case law on immunities from criminal jurisdiction is evidence that States and their courts are reluctant to prosecute foreign public dignitaries.

[34] *Al-Adsani v UK*, Judgment (21 Nov 2001) (2002) 34 EHRR 11, paras 55–66; for an overview, see E Voyakis, 'Access to Court v State Immunity' (2003) 52 *International & Comparative Law Quarterly* 279.

[35] My proposition is not fully supported in the case law. In *Jones and Others v Saudi Arabia*, [2006] UKHL 26, paras 30–31, the House of Lords dismissed the argument upheld by the Court of Appeals,

In respect of personal immunity case law and State practice continue unabated in favour of the absolute rule.[36] The only acting Head of State to be prosecuted before national courts was Noriega. In order to bypass the thorny issue of personal immunity it was accepted by the court that the illegitimate assumption of power by a dictator such as Noriega does not carry immunity benefits.[37] If this was generally true half the leaders of the planet would be susceptible to criminal prosecution. The *Noriega* case should best be seen as an exceptional case. Moreover, one should note that the lack of prosecution of persons otherwise enjoying personal immunity is a significant indication of State practice in favour of the general rule.

The situation in respect of persons enjoying functional immunity is different. Their immunity is by no means absolute and is subject to two erosions. On the one hand acts *jure imperii* (official conduct) are construed narrowly and exclude international crimes, while on the other hand persons who no longer hold office may be legitimately prosecuted for past conduct. Former Heads of State have certainly realised the veracity of this observation, beginning with the *Pinochet* case where the House of Lords took it for granted that the former Chilean leader no longer enjoyed immunity.[38] Equally, a court in Senegal indicted Hissène Habré, the Head of State in Chad from 1982–90, for acts of torture during his reign in that country. Despite the fact that the Senegalese Court of Cassation on 20 March 2001 decided that the accused could not be tried under torture charges in Senegal[39] this was on account of a technical reason and concerned the lack of implementing legislation for the UN Torture Convention, which Senegal had otherwise ratified. As a result, in 2008 the Constitution of Senegal was amended and a statute was passed according to which persons like Habré would be susceptible to universal jurisdiction for genocide, crimes against humanity and war crimes.[40]

As to the process of de-characterisation of conduct as an official act it is now generally accepted that where this constitutes a serious human rights violation it is not attributable to the State because international law does not recognise that one of

---

whereby the State enjoys immunity but not the agent. Equally, in *Bouzari v Islamic Republic of Iran* (2004) 124 ILR 427, the Ontario Court of Appeals could find no exception to the general rule of immunity for acts of torture committed outside the forum State.

[36]   *Re Castro*, Order No 1999/2732 (4 Mar 1999), where the Spanish Audencia Nacional upheld the immunity of the Cuban leader, regardless of the crimes charged (genocide and terrorism). Similarly, the French Court of Cassation in the *Gaddafi* case, 125 ILR 490, had no hesitation in affirming the Libyan leader's personal immunity despite the fact that his formal title is 'Leader of the 1st September Great Revolution of the Socialist People's Libyan Arab Jamahirya'. His recognition as Head of State by de facto means was sufficient for the Court.

[37]   *USA v Noriega*, 99 ILR 143, 162–63.

[38]   The House of Lords in the *Pinochet (No 3)* case in some respect adopted a conservative view by upholding its jurisdiction only over acts of torture committed after 1988 when the Torture Convention was enacted into British law. Another route would have been to recognise the prohibition of torture under customary law and avoid limiting the temporal scope of the charges.

[39]   F Kirgis, 'The Indictment in Senegal of the Former Chad Head of State' (Feb 2000) ASIL Insights. In the *Honecker Prosecution* case, 100 ILR 393, the issue of the criminal liability of a former Head of State for human rights violations authorised by him while in office was not considered because of the ill health of the accused.

[40]   Eventually, Senegal decided not to extradite Habré for trial elsewhere under the universality principle. Belgium, a requesting State, subsequently commenced proceedings against Senegal before the ICJ, alleging that Senegal had violated its obligation to prosecute or extradite under the 1984 Torture Convention. The case is pending at the time of writing.

the functions of statehood is to commit crimes. In *Forti v Suarez-Mason* acts of torture and disappearances committed by an Argentine General, who was an official of the military regime, could not be assimilated to Argentina.[41] This supplements the recent jurisprudence in which we have already determined that the act of State doctrine has eroded the range of conduct that can be considered *jure imperii*. The conclusion is therefore that it is legitimate and reasonable for domestic courts to assume jurisdiction and deny immunity to those agents of foreign States – other than persons entitled to personal immunity – that have committed international crimes in the course of their official duties.

6.4   Diplomatic and Consular Immunities[42]

According to the more correct view the immunity enjoyed by diplomatic envoys is functional, its rationale being to allow them to perform their duties without interference or other hindrance.[43] In fact, under Article 29 of the 1961 Vienna Convention on Diplomatic Relations (Vienna Convention)[44] the receiving State has an obligation to safeguard the freedom and dignity of diplomatic agents.[45] Their immunity from local criminal jurisdiction under Article 32 of the 1961 Vienna Convention does not release them from liability under the law of the receiving State, nor is the jurisdiction of the latter's courts extinguished.[46] The practical significance of this observation is that if the sending State waives the diplomatic immunity of its agent, as it may under Article 32 of the 1961 Vienna Convention, criminal liability may thereafter arise and the exercise of jurisdiction becomes legitimate.[47]

Diplomatic immunity, in accordance with Article 39(1) and (2), exists from the moment the person enters the territory of the receiving State until such time as the privileges and immunities are revoked by the sending State. Under Article 39(2) the diplomatic agent enjoys continuing immunity for acts performed 'in the exercise of his or her functions as a member of the mission'. Such immunity does not, however, produce legal effects against all nations and at all times. The correct view is that since the conferral of diplomatic immunity is dependent on the consent of the receiving State any immunity granted by the latter will not bind third States. As a result, if diplomatic agent A, who is accredited in country X, commits an offence in country Y

---

[41]   *Forti v Suarez-Mason* (1987) 672 F Supp 1531. These cases have been brought under the Aliens Tort Claims Act 1789, 18 USC § 1350, and so the criminal elements involved are incidental to the principal character of such claims, which are of a tort nature.

[42]   See J Brown, 'Diplomatic Immunity: State Practice under the Vienna Convention on Diplomatic Relations' (1988) 37 *International & Comparative Law Quarterly* 53.

[43]   See SE Nahlik, 'Development of Diplomatic Law: Selected Problems' (1990) 222 *Revue des Cours Academie de Droit International* (RCADI) 187.

[44]   500 UNTS 95.

[45]   Affirmed by the ICJ in *USA Diplomatic and Consular Staff in Tehran (*USA v Iran*)* (1980) ICJ Reports 3.

[46]   *Dickinson v Del Solar* [1930] 1 KB 376, at 380, *per* Lord Hewart CJ; similarly, *Empson v Smith* [1966] 1 QB 426.

[47]   Art 32(2) of the 1961 Vienna Convention requires that the waiver be express. See Diplomatic Privileges Act 1964, s 2(3); *Engelke v Musmann* [1928] AC 433; *R v Madan* [1961] 2 QB 1.

he does not enjoy immunity from criminal prosecution before the courts of Y. In the *Former Syrian Ambassador to the GDR* case, the German Federal Constitutional Court found no general rule of customary international law whereby this principle of continuing immunity would be binding on third States, other than the receiving one. It naturally came to the logical conclusion that diplomatic immunity does not generate *erga omnes* effects.[48] This immunity *ratione materiae*,[49] the court further held, was effective in the receiving State even after the termination of diplomatic status, but only in respect of acts performed in the exercise of official duties. Nonetheless, it held that conduct involving the provision of assistance within the framework of a terrorist operation would not be considered as constituting an official function.

It is not rare for persons entitled to diplomatic immunity under Article 37 of the 1961 Vienna Convention to abuse their status by committing crimes that offend the laws of the territorial State.[50] In these cases the receiving State is free to declare such persons *non grata* and effectively expel them from its territory. Things become problematic when diplomatic agents are known to be in the course of committing an offence injurious to the interests of the receiving State, given that Article 29 of the 1961 Vienna Convention prohibits any arrest or detention of diplomatic agents. What action is therefore available to the authorities of the receiving State when facing such a dilemma? Although the person of the diplomat is inviolable there does not exist any rule under international law curtailing the inherent authority of the receiving State from maintaining internal order through the arrest or detention of diplomatic agents. No doubt, such measures must not only be reasonable but absolutely necessary and proportionate. This inherent authority does not subsequently give license to the receiving State to investigate or prosecute the person of the diplomat. Its only avenue following his or her arrest is to expel such person.[51]

The law applicable to consular agents, who as a rule perform purely administrative functions, is quite different from that applied to their diplomatic counterparts.[52] Under Article 41 of the 1963 Vienna Convention on Consular Relations[53] consular agents do not enjoy absolute immunity from the criminal jurisdiction of the receiving State, since in cases of 'grave crimes' they are susceptible to arrest and other judicial proceedings. Nonetheless, under Article 43 of this Convention they are entitled to immunity in respect of acts performed in the exercise of consular functions.[54]

Persons attached to special international missions are also subject to a regime of privileges and immunities. This is dependent on the consent of the receiving State either on an *ad hoc* basis, or as a result of a relevant treaty obligation. In its *Advisory*

---

[48] *Former Syrian Ambassador to the GDR* case 115 ILR 597, 605–12.

[49] As already noted, heads of diplomatic missions enjoy personal immunity.

[50] See R Higgins, 'The Abuse of Diplomatic Privileges and Immunities: Recent United Kingdom Experience' (1985) 79 *American Journal of International Law* 641; JS Parkhill, 'Diplomacy in the Modern World: A Reconsideration of the Bases for Diplomatic Immunity in the Era of High-Tech Communications' (1998) 21 *Hastings International & Comparative Law Review* 565.

[51] JS Beaumont, 'Self-Defence as a Justification for Disregarding Diplomatic Immunity' (1991) 29 *Canadian Yearbook of International Law* 391.

[52] CJ Milhaupt, 'The Scope of Consular Immunity Under the Vienna Convention on Consular Relations: Towards a Principled Interpretation' (1988) 88 *Columbia Law Review* 841.

[53] 596 UNTS 261.

[54] *Waltier v Thomson* (1960) 189 F Supp 319; see *Honorary Consul of X v Austria,* 86 ILR 553.

Opinion on Interference Relating to Immunity from Legal Process of a Special Rapporteur of the Commission on Human Rights[55] the ICJ held that a UN rapporteur was immune from the criminal jurisdiction of the receiving State for the contents of an interview premised on the subject matter of his investigation. The obligation incumbent on Malaysia to recognise the immunity of the rapporteur was based on Article VI(22)(b) of the 1946 Convention on the Privileges and Immunities of the United Nations.[56]

6.5 Immunity from International Criminal Jurisdiction

The jurisdiction of an international judicial body is dependent on its constitutive instrument. Although this instrument will typically adhere to international human rights and fundamental principles of international law it need not follow those principles that although firmly established generally bind only national institutions, such as immunities and other privileges. As will be explained in the chapter dealing with jurisdiction, the five bases of jurisdiction are inapplicable to international criminal tribunals because they are inextricably associated with qualities pertinent to States (ie active personality jurisdiction requires the conferral of nationality, which a tribunal cannot perform). Personal and functional immunities are, too, associated with statehood, but are not exclusive to it because State practice has afforded functional immunities to the employees of international organisations. Given that the purpose of immunities is to facilitate the conduct of international relations the community of States may decide to remove them in particular instances where they no longer serve this purpose and moreover endanger international peace and security. Whereas the unilateral removal of immunities would contravene the general rule established through global consensus, common action would be legitimate because the origin of the rule lays in common action. Such common action is typically established in two ways: either by reason of multilateral agreement, as was the case with the Charter of the Nuremberg Tribunal, or as a direct result of a Security Council resolution establishing an ad hoc tribunal. State practice clearly demonstrates that the drafters of the statutes of contemporary international criminal tribunals removed both functional and personal immunities therein. Not only is there no room for immunities in the statutes of international tribunals, because it would render them redundant *a priori*, but moreover such tribunals constitute exceptions to the persistence of immunities in the bilateral relations between States. The first contemporary rejection of immunity before an international tribunal was achieved through Article 7 of the Charter of the International Military Tribunal at Nuremberg, which read as follows:

---

[55] *Advisory Opinion on Interference Relating to Immunity from Legal Process of a Special Rapporteur of the Commission on Human Rights* (1999) ICJ Reports 62.
[56] 1 UNTS 15.

The official position of defendants, whether as Heads of State or responsible officials in Government Departments, shall not be considered as freeing them from responsibility or mitigating punishment.[57]

This position was also adopted in Article II(4)(a) of the 1945 Control Council Law for Germany No 10, which served as the legislation utilised by Allied military tribunals operating in Germany at the end of the Second World War. The ILC's formulation of the Nuremberg Principles and the 1996 Draft Code of Crimes against the Peace and Security of Mankind also iterated this approach, although it is true that the Nuremberg Principles did not explicitly preclude this defence when used to support mitigation of punishment.[58] Similarly, Articles 7(2) and 6(2) of the Statutes of the ICTY and ICTR respectively rejected this plea as a defence.[59] It is clear that in the ad hoc tribunals the official status of the claimant is perceived not in jurisdictional terms but as a substantive defence, which is nonetheless rejected. Thus, if the status of the accused was relevant under the statutes of the ad hoc tribunals, its successful invocation would have led to relief from criminal responsibility.

On the contrary, Article 27 of the ICC Statute distinguishes between a plea grounded on official status from that based on immunity. The former, if successful, would have served as a substantive defence, but is outright rejected.[60] Immunities, on the other hand, function as a procedural bar to the exercise of jurisdiction under Article 27(2) of the ICC Statute, much like their function before domestic courts. The Statute adopts a middle ground on the application of immunities. Although as a general rule they are not to be sustained as a procedural bar, exceptionally the Court, in the case of referrals by member States, is obliged to adhere to that member's pre-existing treaty obligations by which immunity is afforded to a particular class of persons.[61] No doubt, the Court would have to assess whether the immunity offered in the agreement is relevant in its contemporary setting, reasonable and consistent with general international law. If it is simply in conflict with the Statute, the latter will not prevail. Finally, the exceptional rule contained in Article 98 of the Statute is inapplicable where a situation has been referred to the Court by reason of a Security Council resolution. As a result, where a situation has been referred to the ICC by the Security Council, any immunity afforded to the accused by reason of a pre-existing treaty is inapplicable.

---

[57] Art 6 of the Charter of the International Military Tribunal for the Far East provided that although an individual's official position did not constitute a defence it could be used in mitigation of punishment.

[58] See M Ratner and J Abrams, *Accountability for Human Rights Atrocities in International Law*, (Oxford, Oxford University Press, 1997) 124–25.

[59] Similarly rejected in the 1948 Genocide Convention, Art IV.

[60] A person's official status may, but does not necessarily, serve to simply confer immunity. It may be employed for example to shield an accused from a particular type of liability which is attributable only to a limited number of individuals, as would be the case with command responsibility. This may be at conflict with the constitutional requirements of those States that do not acknowledge that the status of certain individuals gives rise to particular forms of liability. In *Ruling on Compatibility of the ICC Statute with the Colombian Constitution*, Judgment No C-578/2002 the Colombian Constitutional Court held that the concept of command responsibility is consistent with the Constitution of that country, even in respect of persons that enjoy domestic immunity or similar privileges under this instrument.

[61] Art 98, ICC Statute. See chapter 19.6 and 19.7.

Part III

Substantive Crimes

7

War Crimes and Grave Breaches

7.1 Grave Breaches of the 1949 Geneva Conventions

The *jus in bello* has conventionally been categorised as 'Geneva law', that is, international humanitarian law, and 'Hague law', the latter of which is concerned with the regulation of the means and methods of warfare. International humanitarian law is itself concerned with the protection of victims of armed conflict, which includes those rendered *hors de combat* by injury, sickness or capture, as well as civilians. This division is purely artificial and there is a wide measure of overlap between the two.[1] The Geneva Conventions recognise two types of violations, in accordance with the gravity of the condemned act, namely, 'grave breaches'[2] and other prohibited acts not falling within the definition of grave breaches. Although both grave breaches and all other infractions of the Conventions are outlawed under international humanitarian law, the distinguishing feature of grave breaches is that they can only be committed in international armed conflicts against protected persons or property as designated by the Conventions and are moreover subject to universal jurisdiction.[3] As a result, they entail the criminal responsibility of the perpetrator under international law. The same is not *ipso facto* true with regard to infractions that are not grave breaches and this is true also in respect of violations against 'the laws and customs (usages) of war'. There is no clear criminal basis for these in the Geneva Conventions and criminalisation will only accrue where such violations are penalised in any domestic legal order or in the Statute of an international tribunal. Equally, and this is in fact the case, violations against the laws and customs of war were criminalised by virtue of the general criminalisation processes of international law, particularly through the operation of customary consensus.

The 'grave breaches' provisions are applicable where the victims are clearly defined as 'protected persons' under the relevant Geneva Conventions.[4] In the ICTY context, for example, civilian populations during the Yugoslav conflicts were made the target of attacks with a view to either being exterminated or expelled from their ancestral

---

[1] H McCoubrey, *International Humanitarian Law: The Regulation of Armed Conflicts* (Aldershot, Dartmouth Publishing, 1990) 1–2.

[2] Convention I, Art 50; Convention II, Art 51; Convention III, Art 130; Convention IV, Art 147.

[3] 1977 Protocol I, Additional to the 1949 Geneva Conventions, added new grave breaches to the list of the 1949 Geneva Conventions and further introduced a new set of such breaches; C van den Wyngaert, 'The Suppression of War Crimes under Additional Protocol I' in AJM Delissen and GJ Tanja (eds), *Humanitarian Law of Armed Conflict*, (The Hague, Martinus Nijhoff, 1991) 197.

[4] Art 13, Convention I; Art 13, Convention II; Art 4, Convention III; Art 4, Convention IV.

homes. Article 4 of Geneva Convention IV provides that protected persons are those belonging to another party to the conflict. When this provision was drafted in 1949 it did not envisage the unprecedented eruption of internal or mixed armed conflicts in their contemporary form and its purpose was to protect civilian persons held by the adversary, these being in their majority enemy nationals. The concept of nationality by which the status of 'enemy national' can be determined, itself belying a formal legal bond between an individual and a State, clearly does not serve the protective function of Geneva Convention IV in those situations where the victim and the perpetrator possess the same nationality, irrespective of the fact that a particular conflict may be largely international in nature. This was undoubtedly the situation in the former Yugoslavia and this fact alone posed a significant legal problem for the judges. The *Tadić* Appeals judgment correctly observed that since 1949 the legal bond of nationality had not been regarded as crucial in determining protected person status, further adding that, in the particular case of the former Yugoslavia, it was 'allegiance' to a party or 'control' over persons by a party that was perceived as crucial for the purposes of otherness or membership.[5] In a nation that had crumbled, ethnicity became more important than nationality in determining loyalties.[6] Therefore, civilian persons in Bosnia who fell into the hands of belligerents possessing the same nationality as they did, but who associated themselves with a different ethnic group, were entitled to protected status under Article 4 of Geneva Convention IV. The *Tadić* Appeals judgment further identified as recipients of the same protection persons in occupied territory who, while possessing the nationality of their captor, were in fact refugees and thus no longer benefited from the protection of Geneva Convention IV.[7] A possible scenario would be that of German Jews fleeing to France before 1940 to avoid persecution and who subsequently fall into German hands when Germany occupies France. It should be noted that whatever the defining element of loyalty may be in each particular case, under Article 4(2) of Geneva Convention IV 'nationals' of co-belligerent States are not entitled to benefit from protected status. In the case of the fragile and, on many occasions, interrupted alliance between the Bosnian Croats and the Bosnian Moslems, the *Blaškić* judgment found the two parties not to be co-belligerents.[8] Although the Trial Chamber in the latter case rebuffed the existence of an alliance *in toto,* at least as this was relevant to determining protected status, this alliance undoubtedly existed on various occasions despite its instability, and on this basis co-belligerency must be formally recognised as a fact.

It has already been briefly mentioned that a war crime is a crime that takes place in the particular context of an armed conflict, is sufficiently linked to the conflict and the perpetrator intended or foresaw the results of his or her action. This does not, however, tell us who may commit a war crime. Obviously, those taking a direct part in hostilities incur liability for a war crime by either intentionally attacking protected persons, employing prohibited weapons or employing prohibited means and methods of combat, or by altering the status of civilians (such as by altering the demographics

---

[5] *ICTY Prosecutor v Tadić*, Appeals Chamber Judgment (15 Jul 1999), paras 165–66.
[6] *ICTY Prosecutor v Blaškić*, Trial Chamber Judgment (3 Mar 2000), paras 125–33.
[7] *Tadić* Appeals Judgment, para 164.
[8] *Blaškić* Trial Judgment, paras 137–43.

of occupied territories), or by engaging in any other activity that is deemed as criminal by the laws of war. Civilians in occupied territory who intentionally attack the enemy and who do not satisfy the four criteria for lawful combatant status[9] also commit a war crime because they act in a perfidious manner,[10] in addition to losing their status as civilians for the duration of their engagement.[11] Their status when engaged in hostilities is explained in more detail in a subsequent section of this chapter dealing with prohibited targeting crimes.

According to the by-now classic definition adopted by the *Tadić* Appeals jurisdiction decision, an armed conflict exists where there is 'resort to armed force between States or protracted armed violence between governmental authorities and organised groups or between such groups within a State'.[12] The fundamental criteria, therefore, as to the existence of an armed conflict are its intensity and organisation of the parties. Anything below this threshold would amount to a short-lived insurrection, acts of banditry or terrorism, and would not bring into application international humanitarian law.[13] The Appeals Chamber further affirmed that the temporal and geographical scope of an armed conflict extends beyond the exact time and place of hostilities and covers the entire territory or territories in which an armed conflict is taking place.[14] This means that although actual fighting may not be taking place in certain parts of a territory plagued by war, any breaches committed in these locations against protected persons or property may warrant the application of humanitarian law if the breaches are connected in some way to the armed conflict. What are the criteria for determining such a nexus to the armed conflict when the alleged violation did not occur at a time and place where fighting was taking place? According to the ICTY, it would be sufficient that alleged war crimes were closely related to hostilities 'occurring in other parts of the territories controlled by the parties to the conflict' and despite the fact that the armed conflict 'need not have been causal to the commission of the crime', it must at a minimum have played a substantial part in the perpetrator's intention or ability to commit it.[15] Equally, the nexus requirement is satisfied where the accused acted in furtherance of, or under the guise of the armed conflict; this obviously excludes crimes that are merely incidental to an armed conflict.[16] Thus, where D, a civilian, kills A, his civilian neighbour, in occupied territory, this conduct would not be linked to the armed conflict (by reason of the occupation). If D, however, were to kill B, a person attached to the occupying power, as a matter of resistance against the occupier, his conduct would be sufficiently linked to the conflict.

---

[9] In accordance with Art 4(2) of Geneva Convention III these consist of: being commanded by a responsible superior; having a fixed distinctive sign recognisable at a distance; carrying arms openly; conducting overall operations in compliance with humanitarian law.

[10] Art 37, Protocol I.

[11] Art 51(3), Protocol I.

[12] *ICTY Prosecutor v Tadić*, Appeals Chamber Interlocutory Decision on Jurisdiction (2 Oct 1995), para 70; *ICTY Prosecutor v Kovac, et al*, Appeals Chamber Judgment (12 Jun 2002), para 57.

[13] *Tadić* Trial Judgment, para 562; *ICTY Prosecutor v Limaj et al*, Trial Chamber Judgment (30 Nov 2005), paras 84, 89.

[14] *Tadić* Appeals Jurisdiction Decision, para 67.

[15] *ICTY Prosecutor v Kunarac*, Appeals Chamber Judgment (12 Jun 2002), paras 57–58.

[16] Ibid, para 58; *ICTR Prosecutor v Rutaganda*, Appeals Chamber Judgment (26 May 2003), para 570.

7.1.1 Classification of Armed Conflicts

An armed conflict may be classified as being international and to have commenced in accordance with the requirements of common Article 2 of the 1949 Geneva Conventions, where in addition to armed violence between two or more States, there has been a declaration of war – even without any hostilities – or partial or total occupation even if it meets with no resistance. Moreover, an international armed conflict exists in situations of *levee en masse*, that is where the inhabitants of a non-occupied territory spontaneously take up arms against an approaching enemy.[17] Equally, for those States that have ratified the 1977 Protocol I, an international armed conflict arises in cases of protracted armed violence in which peoples are fighting against colonial domination, alien occupation and racist regimes, in accordance with Article 1(4) of the Protocol. Besides these situations described in treaty law, an international armed conflict exists where a State directly intervenes militarily in a non-international armed conflict on the side of either party, or when a State exercises 'overall control' over a rebel entity as to justify attributing its actions to the controlling State. The Appeals Chamber in its judgment in the *Tadić* case rebuffed the 'effective control' test propounded by the International Court of Justice (ICJ) in the *Nicaragua* case, which held that organised private individuals whose action is co-ordinated or supervised by a foreign State and to whom specific instructions are issued are considered *de facto* organs of the controlling State. Although this test had found application by the ICJ in respect of 'Unilaterally Controlled Latino Assets' who were non-US nationals, but acting while in the pay of the US, on direct instructions and under US military or intelligence supervision to carry out specific tasks, it was not applied to the contra rebels because they had not received any instructions.[18] The ICTY Appeals Chamber held that the ICJ's 'effective control' test was at variance with both judicial and State practice, and could only apply with regard to individuals or unorganised groups of individuals acting on behalf of third States, but was generally inapplicable to military or paramilitary groups.[19] It should be emphasised that whereas the ICJ's purpose in employing the effective control test was to determine State responsibility, the ICTY's objective was to apply international humanitarian law and to enforce the criminal liability of the perpetrators. The ICTY's departure from the stringent 'effective control' test was duly replaced with an 'overall control test' which simply requires co-ordinating or helping in a group's general military planning, besides equipping or possibly financing the group, in order to establish a relationship of agency between the group and the aiding State.[20] Thus, in overturning the much criticised Trial Chamber's judgment which had found the Bosnian Serb Army (VRS) not to be an agent of the Federal Republic of Yugoslavia (FRY),[21] the Appeals Chamber held the VRS to constitute a military organisation under the overall control of the FRY, finding the latter not only to have equipped and financed the VRS, but to have also

---

[17] Art 1(2), Regulations attached to the 1907 Hague Convention No IV [Hague Regulations].
[18] *Tadić* Appeals Judgment, paras 109, 114.
[19] Ibid, para 124.
[20] Ibid, para 131.
[21] T Meron, 'Classification of Armed Conflicts in the Former Yugoslavia: Nicaragua's Fallout' (1998) 92 *American Journal of International Law* 236.

participated in the planning and supervision of its military operations.[22] Until the *Tadić* Appeals judgment in 1999, the various ICTY Chambers had, as a direct result of interpreting differently in each case the test propounded in the *Nicaragua* judgment, reached inconsistent determinations as to the nature of the Bosnian armed conflicts. The 'overall control' test, correct on its merits, certainly set a precedent and has subsequently been accepted as good law by ICTY Chambers in their evaluation of both FRY and Croat intervention on behalf of rebel entities.[23]

7.1.2 Types of War Crimes in International Armed Conflicts

When the ICTY Statute was set up its drafters were mindful that the list of offences prosecutable therein be strictly circumscribed by customary international law. While this policy requirement was satisfied in respect of war crimes perpetrated in international armed conflicts, the Security Council was also cognisant of the fact that in the course of the proceedings many crimes may be deemed as having been committed in non-international armed conflict. Given the indeterminate nature of individual criminal responsibility for infractions committed in non-international armed conflicts in 1993, when the ICTY was established, any criminalisation of such infractions would by necessity fail to satisfy the aforementioned policy applicable to international armed conflicts. Thus, while Article 2 of the ICTY Statute provides for criminal jurisdiction over grave breaches of the Geneva Conventions, in line with customary law, the scope of Article 3 is at first glance unclear. As the *Tadić* Appeals Jurisdiction Decision later explained, Article 3 of the ICTY Statute, entitled 'Violations of the laws or customs of war', is a residual clause that covers international armed conflict war crimes other than grave breaches, as well as certain violations committed in non-international armed conflicts.[24] Although the International Committee of the Red Cross (ICRC) commentary to the 1949 Geneva Conventions states that the list of grave breaches therein is not exhaustive and that criminality itself may extend beyond grave breaches,[25] such construction cannot have any application to Article 2 of the ICTY Statute whose list of grave breaches is exhaustive. The same is, however, not true with regard to Article 3 thereto.

In general terms four broad categories of war crimes, including grave breaches, may be said to exist: targeting crimes; those involving prohibited weapons; prohibition of particular means of combat, and; altering the status of civilians. Article 8(2)(b) of the ICC Statute aptly reflects these categorisations. Targeting crimes (paras (i) (ii), (iii), (iv), (v), (ix), (xii) and (xxiv)) are premised on the customary principle

---

[22] *Tadić* Appeals Judgment, para 131.

[23] *ICTY Prosecutor v Aleksovski*, Appeals Chamber Judgment (24 Mar 2000), para 145; *Blaškić*, Trial Judgment, para 100.

[24] *Tadić* Appeals Jurisdiction Decision, paras 87–92.

[25] JS Pictet, Commentary: IV Geneva Convention Relative to the Protection of Civilian Persons in Time of Armed Conflict, (Geneva, International Committee of the Red Cross Publishing, 1958) [Pictet Commentary] 305.

that the warring parties should distinguish between civilians/civilian objects[26] and combatants/military objects and must only target the latter.[27] These issues will be explored more fully in our analysis of prohibited attacks in a later section of this chapter.

As regards prohibited weapons, there is some agreement under customary law as to which are prohibited, whereas in respect of others there is substantial dissention. This is aptly reflected in the ICC Statute, which criminalises the employment of poison or poisoned weapons,[28] asphyxiating or poisonous gases and other analogous materials,[29] expanding bullets[30] and finally 'some' weapons that are inherently indiscriminate, or which are of a nature to cause superfluous injury or unnecessary suffering.[31] The latter category, while valid without any reservations under international law for the majority of conventional weapons, is explicitly conditioned in the context of the ICC Statute by the existence of a comprehensive prohibition and a yet to be formulated annex. This leaves out of the Rome Statute, therefore, bacteriological weapons,[32] anti-personnel mines,[33] blinding laser weapons[34] and nuclear weapons. This policy of particular, as opposed to general, weapons prohibition is consistent with treaty and other State practice, as well as the ICJ's *Advisory Opinion on the Legality of the Threat or Use of Nuclear Weapons*. This Opinion, however, stressed the irreconcilable conflict, from a practical perspective, between the principles of discrimination and prohibition of unnecessary suffering on the one hand and the non-prohibition of inherently indiscriminate weapons.[35] War crimes predicated on prohibited weapons will be analysed in a distinct section later on in this chapter.

Let us now proceed to examine each of these war crimes in more detail on the basis of their enumeration in Article 8 of the ICC Statute, but under more workable thematic categories. It should be strongly emphasised from the outset that as a general rule the ad hoc tribunals require at least a mental standard of recklessness for all violations of international humanitarian law. This approach is wholly antithetical to the position adopted in the ICC Statute, Article 30 of which demands that the Court apply only intent and knowledge to the crimes within its jurisdiction. As has already been explained this amounts to *dolus directus* of the first and second degree

---

[26] This includes also widespread, long-term and severe damage to the natural environment, in accordance with Art 8(2)(b)(iv) ICC Statute; Art 55, Protocol I.

[27] Arts 51, 52, Protocol I.

[28] Art 8(2)(b)(xvii), ICC Statute; Art 2(3), 1907 Hague Regulations.

[29] Art 8(2)(b)(xviii), ICC Statute; 1925 Protocol for the Prohibition of the Use in War of Asphyxiating, Poisonous or Other Gases and of Bacteriological Methods of Warfare [1925 Gas Protocol].

[30] Art 8(2)(b)(xix), ICC Statute; 1899 Hague Declaration No III Concerning Expanding Bullets.

[31] Art 8(2)(b)(xx), ICC Statute.

[32] But see the relevant parts of the 1925 Gas Protocol and the 1972 Convention on the Prohibition of the Development, Production and Stockpiling of Bacteriological and Toxic Weapons and on their Destruction.

[33] Nonetheless, many States are parties to either the 1997 Ottawa Convention on the Prohibition of the Use, Stockpiling, Production and Transfer of Anti-Personnel Mines and on their Destruction or the 1980 Protocol II on Prohibitions or Restrictions on the Use of Mines, Additional to the UN Convention on Prohibitions on the Use of Certain Conventional Weapons (CCW).

[34] 1995 CCW Protocol IV on Blinding Laser Weapons.

[35] See Art 35, Protocol I (1977).

(ie direct and oblique intent). This general rule in Article 30 of the ICC Statute is inapplicable to those crimes whose definition demands a mental standard lower than intent.[36]

7.2 War Crimes against Protected Persons and of Property in the Hands of the Adversary

7.2.1 Wilful Killing

The elements of the crime of wilful killing in international law are the same as those for the crime of murder.[37] These elements have been mostly extrapolated from domestic laws, where it must be admitted there exist differences among the various legal systems. For a person to be liable it is required that a) the victim is dead;[38] b) the death was caused by an act or omission of the accused, or of a person or persons for whose acts or omissions the accused bears criminal responsibility; c) that act was done, or that omission was made, by the accused, or a person or persons for whose acts or omissions he bears criminal responsibility, with an intention: to kill, or to inflict grievous bodily harm, or to inflict serious injury in the reasonable knowledge that such act or omission was likely to cause death.[39] The above definition also makes it clear that the act of the accused must have directly caused (or otherwise had a causal effect) as to the death of the victim. In this manner, and more specifically in the context of international law, it is not only the person who physically killed or who ordered the killing of another that is liable for murder;[40] rather, an accused participating in a joint criminal enterprise is also liable if he shared the intent of the group for the particular murder, or where this was otherwise reasonably foreseeable.[41]

Although the ICTY chambers have at times employed differing terminology to explain the mental standards that pertain to murder, it is clear that besides direct intent (*dolus directus* of the first and second degree), the mental element of the crime is fulfilled if the accused is reckless as to the outcome of his or her action; moreover,

---

[36] See chapter 2.3 for a discussion of *dolus directus*.

[37] *ICTY v Delalićet al* [*Čelebići* case], Appeals Chamber Judgment (20 Feb 2001), para 423. Moreover, in *ICTY Prosecutor v Stakić*, Trial Chamber Judgment (31 Jul 2003), para 586, it was held that murder should be equated with 'killings', thus coinciding with the French term 'meurtre'. The term 'wilful killing' appears in the grave breaches provisions of the Geneva Conventions and Art 8(2)(a)(i) ICC Statute. The corresponding crime for non-international conflicts is contained in Art 8(2)(c)(i) ICC Statute, which employs the term 'murder', reflecting common Article 3(1)(a) of the 1949 Geneva Conventions. See also *ICTR Prosecutor v Akayesu*, Trial Chamber Judgment (2 Sep 1998), para 500–01.

[38] Although for the purposes of the ICTY the recovery of a dead body is not imperative, so long as the fact of death is established circumstantially. See *ICTY Prosecutor v Krnojelac*, Trial Chamber Judgment (15 Mar 2002), para 326.

[39] *ICTY Prosecutor v Vasiljević*, Trial Chamber Judgment (29 Nov 2002), para 205; see the early case law that was the forerunner to this consistent definition, particularly *ICTR Prosecutor v Akayesu*, Trial Chamber Judgment (2 Sep 1998), paras 587–89 and *Čelebići* Trial Chamber Judgment (16 Nov 1998), paras 422, 439.

[40] In fact, the suicide of a person may be attributable to another as murder, if he intended this result or if it was foreseeable. *Krnojelac* Trial Chamber Judgment, para 329.

[41] See chapter 3.2.

premeditation is not required.[42] Recklessness of this type is manifest where the accused undertakes life-threatening action and reconciles himself with the likelihood of death.[43] As far as establishing recklessness for murder the magnitude of the risk is not always of paramount importance in establishing whether the accused accepted the consequence of death; manifest indifference to human life – in which case even a minor risk may suffice – is also a potent factor.[44] This is exceptional, however, and under ordinary circumstances knowledge of a 'higher degree of risk' is required.[45] Manifest indifference to human life does not amount to negligence or gross negligence. Both of these mental elements are insufficient to substantiate a charge of murder.[46] Finally, in some domestic criminal justice systems, where the accused intends to inflict grievous bodily or mental harm or a great degree of suffering on a person and the latter dies as a result the accused is liable under the charge of murder.[47] This may be useful as a general principle of criminal laws.

7.2.2   Torture as a War Crime

The war crime of torture has taken on a distinct life from its namesake counterpart found in Article 1(1) of the 1984 Convention against Torture and Other Cruel, Inhuman or Degrading Treatment or Punishment.[48] The two offences are now distinguished by the absence of the 'public official requirement' and the non-specificity of the perpetrator's objective in the offence's war crime manifestation. Traditionally, on the basis of the 1984 Convention and practice, torture required that the underlying act be committed by a State official or an agent thereof. This was meant to differentiate similar acts of violence inflicted by private actors and in respect of which the perpetrators could not make demands to the victim that generally pertain to the State, such as confessions. Such instances of physical violence could be dealt with by other provisions of domestic criminal law. Hence, torture was designated a State crime. This state of affairs was abruptly reconsidered in the midst of the ICTY's proceedings on account of the fact that many cases involving non-State officials – particularly members of paramilitary groups – had inflicted severe physical and mental pain to victims in much the same manner as one would expect from State officials. In order to avoid the characterisation of these crimes as inhuman treatment or as causing great suffering, the Trial Chamber in the *Kunarac* case distinguished between torture in international human rights law and IHL. Whereas the role of the State in human rights law is paramount and it is in fact the sole violator of rights, in the context of IHL the purpose of the law is to minimise the effects of warfare on

---

[42]   *Krnojelac* Trial Chamber Judgment, para 235; *Blaškić* Trial Judgment, para 216.
[43]   *ICTY Prosecutor v Stakić*, Trial Chamber Judgment (31 Jul 2003), para 587.
[44]   Ibid.
[45]   *ICTY Prosecutor v Strugar*, Trial Chamber Judgment (31 Jan 2005), para 235.
[46]   *Stakić* Trial Judgment, para 587.
[47]   This is the position in English criminal law. See *R v Moloney* (1985) 1 ALL ER 1025 and *R v Woolin* (1999) AC 82.
[48]   See the discussion on torture as a crime under international law in chapter 10.2, which is somewhat distinct as opposed to its counterpart as a war crime.

combatants and protected persons and as a result the State is not the only possible violator of rights.[49] Consequently, the existence of a public official was declared not to be a requirement in the definition of torture as a war crime, not only under the relevant instruments but also in accordance with customary international law.[50]

The next leap of differentiation from the Torture Convention was not far away. Given the exigencies of armed conflict, the list of 'prohibited purposes' by which to attain a certain result or purpose under the Convention was also up for reconsideration, thus leaving only the severity of physical or mental pain as the sole common element. In order to avoid encompassing every infliction of pain as torture, ICTY chambers held that it does not include 'gratuitous act[s] of violence; it [must] aim, through the infliction of severe mental or physical pain, to attain a certain result or purpose',[51] which represents the special intent of torture. The idea of a list of objectives does not feature in the ICC Statute and the Elements of Crimes, where the small list included is merely indicative and certainly not conclusive.[52] It is fair to say that since in the context of an armed conflict all violence against one's enemy is discriminatory and no infliction of pain is aimless but is premised on a particular purpose, most inflictions of mental and physical pain can amount to torture as a war crime.[53] It is therefore prudent to consider each event on a case-by-case basis.[54]

7.2.3 Inhuman and Cruel Treatment

In theory, inhuman and cruel treatment, constitute distinct offences. The former is a grave breach, whereas cruel treatment is a common Article 3 offence. This distinction is also reflected in the ICC Statute.[55] In terms of gradation of suffering, torture stands at the apex, followed by the war crime of causing great suffering and serious injury, while at the bottom lies the crime(s) of inhuman and cruel treatment. The legal basis of the distinction between cruel and inhuman treatment – ie their particular position in the text of the Geneva Conventions – is certainly not determinant of the level of gravity attached to each. It is of no wonder therefore that the Čelebići Trial Chamber suggested that the two in fact have the same meaning.[56] Cruel treatment is thus residual to torture where the purposive element is lacking and is

---

[49] *ICTY Prosecutor v Kunarac and Others*, Trial Chamber Judgment (22 Feb 2001), paras 466ff.

[50] Ibid, paras 490–92, 497; confirmed in *Kunarac* Appeals Judgment, paras 145–48.

[51] *Krnojelac* Trial Judgment, para 180.

[52] ICC Elements of Crimes, Art 8(2)(a)(ii)–1, num 2, which requires that the perpetrator inflicted the pain or suffering for such purposes as: 'obtaining information or a confession, punishment, intimidation or coercion or for any reason based on discrimination of any kind'.

[53] *ICTY Prosecutor v Mrkšić and Others*, Trial Chamber Judgment (27 Sep 2007), paras 513, 515.

[54] *ICTY Prosecutor v Naletilić and Martinović*, Appeals Chamber Judgment (3 May 2006), para 299; *ICTY Prosecutor v Brđanin, Appeals Chamber Judgment* (3 Apr 2007), para 251.

[55] Thus, 'inhuman treatment' is reserved in Art 8(2)(a)(ii) as a grave breach, whereas 'cruel treatment' features in Art 8(2)(c)(i) as a common Art 3 violation.

[56] *Čelebići* Trial Chamber Judgment, para 443.

defined as an intentional act that causes severe physical or mental pain and moreover constitutes a serious attack on human dignity.[57]

The meaning of human dignity in the context of cruel treatment as a war crime does not wholly correspond to its popular lay meaning.[58] Certainly, an affront to human dignity exists where a person is inflicted with pain in order to entertain his tormentor, but this is not obvious under circumstances of beatings, or where a person is forced to stand for hours. Thus, the meaning attached to the concept in IHL is broader in relation to all its other usages. The above instances of harm qualify as cruel and inhuman treatment so long as the victim has endured physical or mental pain and suffering.

As for the *mens rea*, once again either intent or recklessness will suffice in the jurisprudence of the ad hoc tribunals.[59]

7.2.4 Biological Experiments

The prosecution of this war crime became imperative in the aftermath of WWII whereby it was discovered that the Nazi regime was using prisoners in order to conduct biological and medical experiments. Convictions were handed out in all cases where the experiment at hand was not intended to directly contribute to the best interests of the patient and which was not therapeutic in nature or orientation. This would include experiments conducted with sole intent to gain new knowledge, even if it meant curing long-standing illnesses.[60] In the context of the ICC Statute, the crime is a sub-species of inhuman treatment and therefore one would have thought that some physical harm would have been required. Instead, what needs to be demonstrated is only that the particular act seriously endangered the physical or mental integrity of the victim. Article 11 of Protocol I of 1977 is more instructive than the cursory description in Article 8(2)(a)(ii) of what medical action is permissible under IHL. More specifically:

> It is prohibited to subject [protected persons] to any medical procedure which is not indicated by the state of health of the person concerned and which is not consistent with generally accepted medical standards which would be applied under similar medical circumstances to persons who are nationals of the Party conducting the procedure and who are in no way deprived of liberty.
>
> 2.   It is, in particular, prohibited to carry out on such persons, even with their consent:

---

[57] *Čelebići* Trial Chamber Judgment, para 552; *Blaškić* Trial Chamber Judgment, para 186; ICC Elements of Crimes, Art 8(2)(a)(ii)–2, num 1 and Art 8(2)(c)(i)–3, num 1.

[58] Although the fundamental concepts of humanity are inherent in the operation of IHL and are prominent for example in the Martens clause, it is the opinion of this author that they should not be utilised excessively in determining its namesake term of inhuman treatment, lest one removes the offence from the boundaries of specificity required by the criminal law.

[59] *Strugar* Trial Chamber Judgment, para 261; *Limaj* Trial Judgment, para 231.

[60] See *USA v Milch*, Judgment (17 Apr 1947), in 7 Trials of War Criminals before the Nuremberg Military Tribunals under Control Council Law No 10 [Trials], at 355ff; *USA v Brandt* [Medical Trial], Judgment (20 Aug 1947), 2 Trials 171ff.

(a)   physical mutilations;

(b)   medical or scientific experiments;

(c)   removal of tissue or organs for transplantation, except where these acts are justified in conformity with the conditions provided for in paragraph 1.

3.   Exceptions to the prohibition in paragraph 2 (c) may be made only in the case of donations of blood for transfusion or of skin for grafting, provided that they are given voluntarily and without any coercion or inducement, and then only for therapeutic purposes, under conditions consistent with generally accepted medical standards and controls designed for the benefit of both the donor and the recipient.[61]

Violations of the prescriptions enshrined in Article 11 of the Protocol constitute grave breaches. Despite the fact that this extensive description of what is permissible medical experimentation was not included in the ICC Statute, the basic principle is in fact the same in both instruments (ie the treatment must have been carried out in the person's [best] interest and justified by medical reasons).[62] In the opinion of this author the additional criterion contained in Protocol I, whereby treatment is permissible if 'applied under similar circumstances to [one's own nationals]' was rightly excluded from the ICC Statute. There is always the risk of a despotic regime committing the same sort of crimes to its own people as it does to its enemies.

As far as mutilations are concerned, this requires the infliction of permanent disfigurement, permanent disablement, or the removal of an organ or appendage. Such actions must moreover not be dictated by medical necessity or carried out in the patient's best interests and the accused intended that said mutilations take place or possessed reasonable knowledge of this eventuality.[63] Despite the fact that common Article 3 and Article 4(2) of Protocol II do not expressly exculpate the accused by reason of medical necessity, the Trial Chamber in the *RUF* case emphasised that this should be logically inferred.[64] It is not required that the Prosecutor establish that the mutilation seriously endangered the physical or mental health of the victim.[65]

7.2.5   Wilfully Causing Great Suffering or Serious Injury

The war crime of wilfully causing great suffering or serious injury to body or health is found in Article 8(2)(a)(iii) of the ICC Statute. It involves an intentional act or omission causing serious bodily or mental suffering.[66] The gravity of the suffering must be severe, but the harm suffered need 'not cause permanent and irremediable

---

[61]   See also Art 13, Geneva Convention III.

[62]   ICC Elements of Crimes, Art 8(2)(a)(ii)–3, nums 2 and 3. In accordance with the Pictet Commentary to Geneva Convention III, at 628, it is permissible for a doctor to use new methods of treatment if justified by medical reasons.

[63]   ICC Elements of Crimes, Art 8(2)(c)(i).

[64]   *SCSL Prosecutor v Sesay, Kallon and Gbao* [RUF case], Trial Chamber Judgment (25 Feb 2009), para 181.

[65]   *SCSL Prosecutor v Brima, Kamara, Kanu* (AFRC case], Trial Chamber Judgment (20 Jun 2007), para 725; *RUF* Trial Judgment, ibid, para 182.

[66]   *Čelebići* Trial Chamber Judgment, para 511; *ICTY Prosecutor v Krstić*, Trial Chamber Judgment (2 Aug 2001), para 513.

harm, but it must involve harm that goes beyond temporary unhappiness, embarrassment or humiliation'.[67] It must result in a 'grave and long-term disadvantage to a person's ability to lead a normal and constructive life'. Thus, the mental trauma inflicted upon a mass executions survivor does amount to this war crime.[68] Causing great suffering and injury must be distinguished from torture where there exists no specific purpose behind the infliction of harm.[69] Thus, unlike torture, wilfully causing great suffering is not a special intent crime. It must also be distinguished from that of inhuman treatment because the latter does not require a showing of serious physical or mental injury; equally, offences that pertain solely to the victim's dignity are also excluded from this category, despite their effects on the mental health of the victim.[70]

The term 'wilfully' in the jurisprudence of the ad hoc tribunals and the official ICRC Commentary stipulate the application of a *mens rea* standard that encompasses intent and recklessness.[71]

7.2.6 Extensive Destruction and Appropriation of Property

This war crime, as enunciated in Article 8(2)(a)(iv) of the ICC Statute, is derived from the verbatim wording encountered in the grave breaches provisions of Geneva Conventions I, II and IV (Articles 50, 51 and 147 respectively). It applies only to such property that is in the hands, or the power, of the enemy. Certainly, it is permissible for a warring party to attack the property of its adversary, but this entitlement is subject to particular limitations. Firstly, the object, or property, under consideration must be a legitimate military objective, in conformity with Article 52 of Protocol I. Consequently, attacks against civilian properties and dwellings are prohibited, unless used for military purposes by the enemy, or imperative as a matter of military necessity.[72] The same applies to hospitals and institutions of this nature.[73] Secondly, the destruction or appropriation of such property must be dictated by military necessity.[74] The concept of military necessity, however, entails recognition that an otherwise legitimate attack may have negative repercussions on the civilian population if this is absolutely necessary to achieve one's objective under three strict

---

[67] *Krstić* judgment, ibid; *Akayesu* Trial Chamber Judgment, para 503.

[68] *Krstić* judgment, ibid. In fact, this war crime seems to have been derived in its more contemporary form by the District Court of Jerusalem, in *A-G Israel v Eichmann*, 36 ILR 277, at 340, where it was stated that all the inhuman conditions suffered by Jews in concentration camps were designed to cause, *inter alia*, great suffering to the victims.

[69] Although the Pictet Commentary to Geneva Convention IV, at 599, distinguishes between this offence and torture, it rather confusingly states that the crime of wilfully causing great suffering 'would therefore be inflicted as a punishment, in revenge or for some other motive, perhaps out of pure sadism'.

[70] *ICTY Prosecutor v Kordić and Čerkez*, Trial Chamber Judgment (26 Feb 2001), para 245.

[71] 'Wilful' has been interpreted by the ICTY as an act or omission that is intentional, deliberate and by no means accidental. See *Krstić* Trial Chamber Judgment, para 511; *Čelebići* Trial Chamber Judgment, para 511.

[72] Art 53 Geneva Convention IV.

[73] Arts 18, 19, ibid.

[74] The destruction of property in occupied territory in order to prevent enemy incursions thereto was found not to conform to the precepts of military necessity. *Jodl* case (1948) 16 Trials of German Major War Criminals (TGMWC) 415.

constraints: a) the attack's primary and foremost objective must be to defeat the enemy – as perhaps opposed to terrorising the civilian population; b) even such a military attack must not cause harm to civilians or civilian objects in a manner that is excessive to the particular military advantage anticipated; c) military necessity can never justify the violation of the laws of war.

Despite the fact that either intent or recklessness suffice for this offence under the jurisprudence of the ad hoc tribunals, it should be noted that the ICTY in the *Brđanin* case distinguished between 'destruction' and 'appropriation', holding that the latter requires only intent.[75] Non-extensive destruction or appropriation – and consistent with the above analysis – remains a war crime, but does not constitute a grave breach.[76]

7.2.7 Pillage

The war crime of pillage entails an act of appropriation of property belonging to another without that person's consent and under circumstances where the perpetrator intended to deprive the owner of the property and to appropriate it for private or personal use.[77] Its legal basis may be found primarily in Articles 28 and 47 of the 1907 Hague Regulations, as well as Articles 33 of Geneva Convention IV and 4(2)(g) of Protocol I. Historically, the term 'pillage' has been associated also with other terms, such as plunder, spoliation, looting and sacking. To a very large degree all of these terms reflect the definition of the crime of pillage and should all be viewed as synonymous.[78] Given that pillage requires an act of appropriation, this term has been the subject of some debate and ultimately construed restrictively by some international tribunals. Thus, the Sierra Leone Special Court has ruled that the burning of civilian property cannot constitute pillage under international law.[79]

It should not be thought that every act of appropriation of property belonging to the enemy or its civilian population constitutes pillage. International humanitarian law recognises the right of belligerents to requisition and seizel[80] enemy property with a view to utilising it for the benefit of their armed forces, as long as by doing so the

---

[75] *ICTY Prosecutor v Brđanin*, Trial Chamber Judgment (1 Sep 2004), paras 589–90.

[76] Elements of Crimes, Art 8(20(a)(iv), num 3, which states that the destruction or appropriation 'was extensive and carried out wantonly'.

[77] Elements of Crimes, Art 8(2)(b)(xvi).

[78] *Čelebići* Trial Chamber Judgment, paras 587ff. See K Dormann, L Doswald-Beck, R Kolb, *Elements of War Crimes under the Statute of the International Criminal Court* (Cambridge, Cambridge University Press, 2002) [hereinafter Dormann, *Elements of War Crimes*] 272ff.

[79] *SCSL Prosecutor v Fofana and Kondewa* (CDF case), Appeals Chamber Judgment (28 May 2008), para 409; *RUF* Trial Judgment, para 212; this is contrary to the meaning given to 'appropriation' in the law of theft of numerous jurisdictions. In England, eg, s 3(1) of the 1968 Theft Act states that appropriation comes out through 'any assumption by a person of the rights of ownership'. Thus, appropriation encompasses touching, selling or destroying another's property. *Pitham and Hehl* (1976) 65 Cr App R 45 (CA); *Briggs* [2004] Crim LR 495.

[80] Art 34(2) GC I; Art 55(2) GC IV.

civilian population is not starved of food and medical treatment.[81] Thus, although pillage refers to both an individual crime and an offence committed under orders 'within the framework of a systematic economic exploitation of occupied territory',[82] international tribunals will only prosecute the latter given its gravity.

7.2.8 Compelling Prisoners of War or Protected Persons to Serve with the Hostile Power

This prohibition has a long history, stretching back to Article 23 of the 1907 Hague Regulations, whereby it is forbidden to compel the nationals of a hostile party 'to take part in the operations of war directed against their own country, even if they were in the belligerent's service before the commencement of the war'. The rationale was not only to prohibit belligerents forcing enemy nationals generally taking up arms against their own country, but also to avoid rendering such persons subject to the military and criminal law of the enlisting State – a fact that would make them legally susceptible to extremely harsh measures where they failed to obey orders contrary to their conscience. Whereas Article 23 of the Hague Regulations confines illegal enlistment to military operations against one's own country, the grave breaches provisions of GC III and IV (Articles 130 and 147 respectively) are broader and are content to criminalise merely the act of compelling a protected person to serve with the enemy. It must be presumed that the nature of the particular unit in which the protected person is compelled to enlist – as far as the Geneva Conventions and the ICC Statute is concerned – is irrelevant, as long as it is part of the broader corpus of a nation's armed forces. This would include paramilitary groups and even code-breaking units that are not involved in actual fighting, because their work directly aids the armed forces. On the contrary, work undertaken by prisoners of war in the ordinary course of their captivity would not satisfy the criteria for this war crime.[83] In the course of the ICC Statute it must also be accepted that compelling a protected person to join the enemy's armed forces against nations other than one's own suffices to satisfy the offence because of the word 'otherwise' in the Elements of Crimes.[84]

Articles 8(2)(a)(v) and (2)(b)(xv) of the ICC Statute reflect the grave breaches of the Geneva Conventions and Article 23 of the Hague Regulations respectively. The

---

[81] Equally, the practice of booty is no longer acceptable practice and if it entails unlawful appropriation in the manner described above it will constitute pillage. *Menzel v List* (Sup Ct, 1966) 267 N.Y.S. 2d 809. See generally WG Downey, 'Captured Enemy Property: Booty of War and Seized Enemy Property' (1950) 44 *American Journal of International Law* 488.

[82] *Čelebići* Trial Judgment, para 590.

[83] Arts 49–57 Geneva Convention III. See *Naletilić and Martinović* Trial Chamber Judgment (31 Mar 2003), paras 255–61, where the tribunal discusses the legitimate boundaries of the crime of forced labour, but which has an impact on the present analysis.

[84] ICC Elements of Crimes, Art 8(2)(a)(v) num 1 'or otherwise serve in the forces of a hostile power'. For support of this position, see O Triffterer (ed), *Commentary on the Rome Statute of the ICC* (Oxford, Hart Publishing, 2008) [Triffterer Commentary] 314.

actus reus of the offence is defined in the Elements of Crimes as 'coercing one or more persons, by act or threat, to take part in military operations …'[85]

7.2.9 Wilfully Depriving Protected Persons of Rights to Fair and Regular Trial

In the WWII landmark case of *In Re Alstotter and Others* (the Justice Trial), the accused were high-ranking officials of the Reich Justice Ministry who orchestrated the promulgation of laws and decrees in order to set up special courts by which to distort and deny judicial process to internal enemies of the Nazi regime. These special courts inflicted a reign of terror on their opponents and applied retroactive and discriminatory laws without offering any judicial guarantees to the accused.[86] This war crime is articulated in the grave breaches provisions of Geneva Conventions III and IV (Articles 130 and 147 respectively). What is ultimately at stake is the denial of judicial guarantees.[87] Although the ICC Elements of Crimes criminalise the removal of those judicial guarantees encompassed in the Geneva Conventions, the inclusion of the wording 'in particular' was aimed at rendering the provision broader, thus including the customary law guarantees found in Article 75 of Protocol I.[88] These include:

- the right of an accused to be judged by an independent and impartial court (Art 84(2) GC III; Art 75(4) Protocol I)
- the right of the accused to be promptly informed of the offences with which he is charged (Art 104 GC III; Art 71(2) GC IV; Art 75(4)(a), Protocol I)
- the rights and means of defence, such as the right to be assisted by a qualified lawyer chosen freely and by a competent interpreter (Arts 99, 105 GC III; Arts 72, 74 GC IV; Art 75(4)(a) and (g) Protocol I)
- the principle of individual criminal responsibility (Art 87 GC III; Art 33 GC IV; Art 75(4)(b) Protocol I)
- the principle *nullum crimen sine lege* (ie no crime without law) (Art 99(1) GC III; Art 67 GC IV; Art 75(40(c) Protocol I)
- the presumption of innocence (Art 75(4)(d) Protocol I)
- the right of the accused to be present at his trial (Art 75(4)(e) Protocol I)
- the right of the accused not to testify against himself or to confess guilt (Art 75(4)(f) Protocol I)
- the principle of *non bis in idem* (ie no punishment more than once for the same act) (Art 86 GC III; Art 117(3) GC IV; Art 75(4)(h) Protocol I)
- the right of the accused to have the judgment pronounced publicly (Art 75(4)(i) Protocol I)
- the right of the accused to be informed of his rights of appeal (Art 106 GC III; Art 73 GC IV; Art 75(4)(j) Protocol I)[89]

---

[85] Elements, ibid.
[86] *In Re Alstotter and Others* [Justice Trial] 14 AD 278.
[87] ICC Elements of Crimes, Art 8(2)(a)(vi) num 1.
[88] Triffterer Commentary, at 314.
[89] Dormann, *Elements of War Crimes*, 101.

In situations where the prosecuting State does not genuinely have the means to pursue trials in conformity with these guarantees and in fact is unable to apply them to its own people, this cannot constitute a valid excuse for withholding them from enemy protected persons. This conclusion is drawn out from the fundamental and customary nature of the guarantees.

7.2.10   Unlawful Deportation or Transfer of Protected Persons

This war crime pertains to the actions of an occupying power because it entails the deportation and transfer of protected persons in occupied territory to another State or to another location from that in which they were found to habitually reside.[90] Consequently, it is a grave breach under Article 147 of Geneva Convention IV.[91] For the deportation and transfer to become criminal it must be unlawful; this takes place where it is involuntary and the person is moved outside his country's borders (deportation) or within that country's borders (transfer). In all other respects the two are synonymous[92] and this is true as regards the ICC Statute. However, other ICTY chambers have held that under customary law there exists a sharp distinction between deportation and unlawful transfer. According to this jurisprudence, deportation relates to involuntary transfer across national borders, while forcible transfer relates to involuntary transfers within a State.[93] There is no need for a multiplicity of victims for the offence to materialise; a single deportation or transfer will suffice.

Quite rightly, not all deportations must be deemed criminal, even if they do import the element of force and compulsion. Departures motivated by the fear of discriminatory attacks against a particular group are not in violation of international law.[94] It may also prove expedient for a belligerent power to evacuate an area of its civilian population where this presents itself as a distinct military advantage. For the purposes of civilian deportations, military necessity has been interpreted narrowly. In *Re von Lewinski* (von Manstein) the accused, a high-ranking German Army officer in Ukraine argued that in a country so densely populated as the Ukraine it was necessary for the security of his troops to remove the population from the combat zone, lest he invite espionage; an argument rejected by the tribunal.[95] Exceptions to the general rule against compulsory deportations and transfers are subject to a list of constraints as found in Article 49 of Geneva Convention IV. Thus, they are permissible only: a) in the security interests of the civilian population, or if 'imperative military reasons so demand'; b) 'when for material reasons it is impossible to

---

[90]   ICC Elements of Crimes, Art 8(2)(a)(vii)–1, nums 1 and 2; see *In Re Milch*, 14 AD 299, where the accused was held liable for his part in the forcible transfer of civilians in occupied territory and POWs to slave labour.

[91]   The *Kupreškić* Trial Judgment, para 566, found forcible displacement to constitute an inhumane act as part of a crime against humanity.

[92]   *Krstić* Trial Chamber Judgment, para 521.

[93]   *ICTY Prosecutor v Slobodan Milošević*, Trial Chamber Decision on Motion for Judgment of Acquittal, (16 Jun 2004), para 68.

[94]   *Krstić* Trial Chamber Judgment, para 528.

[95]   *In Re von Lewinski (von Manstein case)* 16 AD 509, 521–23.

avoid such displacement'; c) evacuated persons shall be transferred back to their homes as soon as hostilities in the area cease; d) evacuees shall be cared for by the occupying power; e) detained persons shall not be exposed to the dangers of war, subject to military necessity, and; f) the occupying power shall not deport or transfer parts of its own civilian population into the territory it occupies, which in itself constitutes a distinct war crime.[96]

7.2.11 Transferring Own Population into Occupied Territory

This is a particularly egregious offence that requires significant planning and yet despite the general prohibition in Article 49(6) of Geneva Convention IV it was not included as a grave breach in Article 147 of that convention. In order to dispel any doubts as to whether it constitutes a crime under international law, it was expressly mentioned as such in Article 85(4)(a) of Protocol I and Article 8(2)(b)(viii) of the ICC Statute. The *actus reus* of the offence entails a transfer by the occupying power of its own civilian population (or parts thereof) into occupied territory. The rationale of such practice is that it may lead to effective annexation and in any event it maintains a status quo that cannot easily be reversed through subsequent measures of restitution.[97] A poignant example is that of the occupied part of Cyprus in which the Turkish authorities have transferred large civilian populations from mainland Turkey since the occupation commenced in 1974 and which have severely imbalanced the island's demographics to the detriment of any proposed peace solutions.[98]

The offence requires that only a part of the occupant's civilian population need be transferred; additionally, there is no requirement that such transfer be preceded by an unlawful deportation of the local population, as this is a separate offence. During the ICC negotiations two major issues emerged. Firstly, it was queried how this offence may for practical purposes translate into personal responsibility and secondly whether occupying powers may conceivably transfer their own civilian population other than by a clear and direct mandate. The latter issue was resolved through the express requirement that the transfer be either 'direct or indirect', thus encompassing those situations where the occupier induced or otherwise encouraged and facilitated the transfer.[99] As regards the attribution of liability, a proposal championed by Switzerland stood out among its rivals, which essentially replaced the wording of the ICC Statute 'the occupying power' by 'the perpetrator'.[100] Although this may seem

---

[96] See also Art 85(4)(a) Protocol I.

[97] The E Ct HR in *Loizidou v Turkey* (1996) 23 EHRR 153, pointed out that an occupying power that ultimately causes the deportation of the local population and the transfer of its own civilian population in the occupied territory violates, among others, the right to enjoyment of property rights, in addition to the illegality of the transfer itself.

[98] In *Apostolides v Orams*, Case 420/07, Judgment (28 Apr 2009), the ECJ ruled that the rights of ownership over private property in the occupied part of Cyprus could not be conveyed to the occupying power or the civilian population it transferred there.

[99] Triffterer Commentary, 365–66.

[100] Ibid, at 367.

nonsensical because the perpetrators do not possess a civilian population, it encompasses within the scope of the offence all relevant actors that directly or indirectly contributed to the transfer. It is clear, therefore, that the influx of a refugee wave in the occupying territory as a result of the armed conflict, such that could not reasonably have been foreseen, would be insufficient to produce any criminal liability.

7.2.12   Unlawful Confinement

Although unlawful confinement was considered a war crime prior to WWII, it was on account of the well-documented mass internment of civilians, by both sides, during that war which prompted the need for greater safeguards. As a general rule, the occupying power and/or a detaining force does have the right to intern enemy combatants as well as elements of the occupied civilian population.[101] Our concern here is with the latter, in respect of which the general rule is subject to a number of limitations in accordance with Articles 27(4) 42, 43 and 78 of Geneva Convention IV. Thus, all measures of control and security must be 'necessary as a result of the war' and 'only if the security of the detaining power makes it absolutely necessary'. The degree of the security risk required is not specified, but the *Čelebići* Trial Chamber defined it as follows:

> Subversive activity carried on inside the territory of a party to the conflict, or actions which are of direct assistance to an opposing party may threaten the security of the former, which may, therefore, intern people or place them in assigned residence if it has serious and legitimate reasons to think that they may seriously prejudice its security by means such as sabotage or espionage.[102]

Given that the aim of such confinement is to prevent particular individuals from aiding the enemy, it does not follow that every person that is a national of the enemy – in occupied territory this would include almost everyone – may be subjected to internment; this is possible only in respect of enemy nationals that pose a real threat to security by virtue of 'their activities, knowledge, or qualifications'.[103] Thus, mass internment would constitute a war crime and perhaps even a crime against humanity. The same is true where it is done as a reprisal or as a means of collective punishment.[104]

The other limitation on the occupying/detaining power concerns the duration and quality of confinement. In accordance with Articles 43(1) and 78 of Geneva Convention IV, the duration of internment can only persist as long as the claimed security threat is present and reviewed regularly, while those subject to this measure must have access to a process of appeal. As a result, where no serious security threat

---

[101] Arts 27(4) and 78 of Geneva Convention IV.
[102] *Čelebići* Trial Chamber Judgment, para 575.
[103] Ibid, para 577.
[104] Ibid, para 578.

exists, or where the process of confinement is not subject to any of the aforementioned controls, it is considered unlawful.[105]

7.2.13 Taking of Hostages

The grave breach of hostage taking in Article 8(2)(a)(viii) of the ICC Statute is predicated on Articles 34 and 147 of Geneva Convention IV, as well as Article 1(1) of the 1979 International Convention against the Taking of Hostages.[106] The practice was fiercely condemned at the close of WWII by the subsequent military tribunals, particularly because it was employed by the German armed forces in order to compel guerrillas to surrender themselves lest entire villages be burnt to the ground.[107] What, therefore, distinguishes hostage taking from the war crime of unlawful confinement is the fact that in addition to the unlawful character of the taking:

2. The perpetrator threatened to kill, injure or continue to detain such person or persons;
3. The perpetrator intended to compel a State, an international organisation, a natural or legal person or a group of persons to act or refrain from acting as an explicit or implicit condition for the safety or the release of such person or persons.[108]

As a result, the taking of hostages with a view to their utilisation as human shields,[109] or in order to compel enemy combatants to lay down their arms is unacceptable as a means and method of warfare and is moreover a serious criminal violation of international law. The so-called Early Warning procedure used by the Israeli armed forces was also found to be illegal by the Israeli Supreme Court. This consisted of forcing Palestinian residents to patrol with Israeli troops and enter buildings thought to hide Palestinian suspects with a view to providing an early warning to occupants, enabling innocent persons to leave and for wanted persons to give themselves up. The Court found that the use of Palestinians in this manner, particularly in the knowledge that some buildings were booby trapped, was tantamount to using them as human shields, contrary to Articles 28 of Geneva Convention IV and 51(7) of Protocol I.[110]

The perpetrator must necessarily possess intent and recklessness as to both substantive strands of the offence.

---

[105] Art 8(2)(a)(vii) ICC Statute.
[106] See chapter 12.3.2.
[107] *USA v List et al* [Hostages case], 11 Trials 759.
[108] ICC Elements of Crimes, Art 8(2)(a)(vii), nums 2 and 3.
[109] *USA v von Leeb and Thirteen Others* [High Command case], 12 Law Reports of Trials of War Criminals (LRTWC), which underlined the illegality of using POWs as human shields, while omitting to make the same ruling to civilians. In the *Blaškić* Trial Judgment, para 716, the ICTY held that employing villagers as human shields was tantamount to inhuman and cruel treatment. In the *Aleksovski* Trial Judgment, para 229, the same act was characterised as an outrage upon personal dignity under Common Art 3.
[110] *Adalah et al v Commander of the Central Region* [Early Warning case], Judgement (23 Jun 2005), paras 21–22. See R Otto, 'Neighbours as Human Shields? The Israel Defence Forces' Early Warning Procedure and International Humanitarian Law' (2004) 86 *International Review of the Red Cross (IRRC)* 771.

7.2.14   War Crime of Depriving the Nationals of the Hostile Party of Rights or Actions

The origins of this war crime are found in Article 23(h) of the 1907 Hague Regulations. Its precise boundaries, however, have never satisfactorily been spelt out.[111] According to Article 8(2)(b)(xiv) of the ICC Statute it is a war crime to declare abolished, suspended or inadmissible in a court of law the rights and actions of the nationals of a hostile party. As originally conceived, the prohibition related to the suspension of civil, contractual and commercial rights and the effective access of right-holders before the courts. Contemporary scholars argue that the prohibition encompasses not only commercial and property rights, but also other discriminatory measures and restrictions.[112] This does not mean that the occupying power does not have the right to amend existing laws or introduce new ones in the occupied territory. This prerogative is generally permissible only in order to restore and ensure as far as possible public order and safety in accordance with Article 43 of the 1907 Hague Regulations. Thus, it does not apply in order to amend laws from which the occupying power or its nationals can draw direct or indirect benefits The war crime is not only applicable in situations of occupation, given that the relevant provisions do not pose such a limitation, but in practice they will be predicated on a subsequent act of occupation. Thus, the annulment of public contracts entered into between Iraq and its nationals would *prima facie* satisfy the material elements of this war crime, whereas similar action with respect to nationals of the occupying force would not.[113]

7.2.15   Using, Conscripting or Enlisting Children

The Security Council had since 30 August 1996 condemned the recruitment, deployment and training of children for combat in Resolution 1071 in connection with the civil conflict in Liberia. It was only in 1999 that the Council not only took up the matter annually on its agenda but condemned all forms of recruiting and deployment of children in armed conflict as a war crime.[114] Although children are protected persons under Geneva Convention IV, it was not clear until the late 1990s whether it was also a war crime to recruit them into active military service. Article 4(3)(c) of Additional Protocol II (1977) states that:

> Children who have not attained the age of fifteen years shall neither be recruited in the armed forces or groups allowed to take part in hostilities.

---

[111]   See Triffterer Commentary, at 401.
[112]   Ibid, 403–04.
[113]   KH Kaikobad, 'Problems of Belligerent Occupation: The Scope of Powers Exercised by the Coalition Provisional Authority in Iraq' (2005) 54 *International & Comparative Law Quarterly* 253.
[114]   SC Res 1261 (30 Aug 1999).

A similar provision was also inserted in Article 77(2) of Additional Protocol I (1977) and Article 38(3) of the 1989 Convention on the Rights of the Child (CRC).[115] By the time of the adoption of the ICC Statute in 1998, the Sierra Leone Special Court was of the opinion that the particular behaviour had culminated to a war crime under customary international law, on account particularly of the almost universal ratification of the CRC and the adoption of national laws criminalising child recruitment.[116] The Secretary General pointed out in his 2000 Report on Article 4 of Protocol II, and in relation to the criminality of child recruitment, that although the prohibition on child recruitment had acquired customary international law status, it was not clear at the time to what extent it was recognised as a war crime entailing individual criminal responsibility.[117] By 1998 there was no doubt that such practices were indeed universally recognised war crimes. Article 8(2)(b)(xxvi) of the ICC Statute and Article 4 of the SLSC Statute are identical in this respect. This new crime of child recruitment is defined as follows:

> Conscripting or enlisting children under the age of 15 years into armed forces or groups using them to participate actively in hostilities.

The Special Court went a step further, arguing that by the time of the adoption of the 2000 CRC Optional Protocol on the Involvement of Children in Armed Conflict, the discussion of criminalisation of child recruitment below the age of 15 had been settled and the matter had shifted to raising the standard to include all children below the age of 18.[118] This is a plausible argument. There is no contention of course that the recruitment of all persons above the age of 15 constitutes an international offence under customary law, since a significant number of countries enlist persons who are at least 17, although admittedly they are not always deployed to combat zones.[119]

The ICC Statute criminalises all forms of 'active' participation of children in hostilities, as opposed to 'direct' participation contained in Article 77(2) of Protocol I. The former is considerably broader in scope as it not only encompasses combat situations but also a broader range of participation, such as working in a munitions factory. It has been suggested that despite the injunction in the ICC Statute that recruitment and enlisting be undertaken in the context of an armed conflict, this nexus is not in fact required under customary law or the Statute itself.[120]

---

[115] 1577 UNTS 3.

[116] *SLSC Prosecutor v Norman*, Appeals Chamber Decision on Preliminary Motion based on Lack of Jurisdiction (Child Recruitment) (31 May 2004), paras 34, 53. On the basis of its findings of State practice, the SLSC asserted that 'child recruitment was criminalised before it was explicitly set out as a criminal prohibition in treaty law and certainly by November 1996'.

[117] The Secretary General had initially proposed the more precise and restrictive offence of 'conscripting or enlisting children', being unsure as to whether the ICC Statute formulation was consistent with customary international law. Report of the Secretary General on the Establishment of a Special Court for Sierra Leone, UN Doc S/2000/915 (4 Oct 2000), para 18.

[118] *Norman* Decision on Child Recruitment, para 34.

[119] See generally M Happold, *Child Soldiers in International Law*, (Manchester, Manchester University Press, 2005).

[120] See Triffterer Commentary, 467–474.

The term 'recruitment' should be understood as having the same meaning with the terms 'conscription' and 'enlistment'. While forced enlistment constitutes the aggravated form of this war crime, voluntary enlistment of children is of equal value.[121] Naturally, the *actus reus* of enlistment cannot be predicated on the same formal methods relating to the recruitment of adults. The CDF Appeals Chamber held that an act of enlistment requires a nexus between the acts of the accused and the child joining the group, coupled with knowledge of the child's age and his or her use in armed combat.[122] In the case at hand, the accused had organised 'initiation' rituals where the boys were told 'that they would be made powerful for fighting and were given a potion to rub on their bodies as protection . . . before going [into] war'. Although the Appeals Chamber did not specifically address the nature of such initiation, it held that where an armed group is not a conventional organisation 'enlistment cannot narrowly be defined as a formal process . . . [This includes] any conduct accepting the child as a part of the militia'.[123] On the other hand, intentionally using children to actively participate in the hostilities, although not a form of recruitment, is also considered a war crime under customary international law. This prohibition in all probability does not cover mere support functions outside the front line.[124]

The prosecution of children for war crimes and crimes against humanity has presented a 'difficult moral dilemma' for a number of reasons.[125] In the context of the Sierra Leone Special Court, although children were feared for their brutality, the Secretary General noted that they had been subjected to a process of psychological and physical abuse and duress that had transformed them from victims into perpetrators.[126] In a balancing act catering on the one hand for the concerns of humanitarian organisations responsible for rehabilitation programmes, who objected to any kind of judicial accountability for children below 18 years of age, and on the other adhering to vociferous popular feeling demanding punishment of offenders, the Secretary General decided in favour of prosecuting juveniles above 15 years of age, but instructed the prosecutor in cases of juvenile offenders to:

> ... ensure that the child rehabilitation programme is not placed at risk and that, where appropriate, resort should be had to alternative truth and reconciliation mechanisms, to the extent of their availability.[127]

Besides the direct consequences on the mental and physical health of the children, the endemic, in certain countries, forceful recruitment of children on the side of rebel groups constitutes one of the main causes of internal displacement.[128]

---

[121] *CDF* Trial Judgment, paras 191–92; Y Sandoz *et al*, Commentary on the Additional Protocols of 8 June 1977 to the Geneva Conventions of 12 August 1949 [ICRC Commentary], (Geneva, Martinus Nijhoff, 1987) 1380; *ICC Prosecutor v Lubanga*, Decision on Confirmation of Charges (29 Jan 2007), para 47.

[122] *CDF* Appeals Judgment (28 May 2008), para 141.

[123] Ibid, paras 128, 144.

[124] *CDF* Trial Judgment, paras 193, 196.

[125] Report of the Secretary-General, above n 117, para 32.

[126] Ibid.

[127] SLSC Statute, Art 15(5).

[128] Colombian Constitutional Court Judicial Decree 251 (2008).

7.3   Sexual Crimes

7.3.1   Outrages upon Personal Dignity

This was initially conceived as an offence that was largely designed to be residual to those acts encompassed within the larger category of rape.[129] Nonetheless, as this section will demonstrate it also encapsulates distinct criminal behaviour. Its legal basis is found in Common Article 3(1)(c) to the Geneva Conventions, Article 75(2)(b) of Protocol I and Article 4(2)(e) of Protocol II. The definition contained therein provides merely a glimpse of the *actus reus* of the offence, 'particularly humiliating and degrading treatment, rape, enforced prostitution and any form of indecent assault'. Given that the contemporary definition of rape is significantly broad, there is no reason why rape-related offences should be charged as outrages upon personal dignity. The statutes of the ad hoc tribunals and of the other hybrid tribunals have similarly followed verbatim the aforementioned definitions.[130] The Elements of Crimes to Article 8(2)(b)(xx) of the ICC Statute detaches the crime from its residual (to rape) character by requiring that:

> The perpetrator humiliated, degraded or otherwise violated the dignity of one or more persons.

> The severity of the humiliation, degradation or other violation was of such degree as to be generally recognised as an outrage upon personal dignity.

To be sure, an enumeration of specific acts that constitute this offence would be counter-productive and this approach is well reflected in the ICRC Commentary to Article 75(2)(b) of Protocol I, which agrees with the above definition in the Elements of Crimes and which moreover does not require direct physical or mental harm to the victim.[131] It is the *mens rea* (especially its particular special intent) of the offence that essentially distinguishes it from other similar acts. The aim of the perpetrator must be to ridicule, degrade or humiliate the victim,[132] but there need not exist any discriminatory intent.[133] In this manner, there need not be any physical contact with the victim's body, as where the victim is ordered to undress in front of a crowd.[134]

The accused must intend or be reckless as to the fact that his act or omission has the effect of serious humiliation.[135] The fact of humiliation itself is assessed objectively, rather than subjectively, requiring that the act or omission of the accused is

---

[129] The ICTY continues to apply this offence to discrete instances of rape. See *Kunarac* Trial Chamber Judgment, para 159.

[130] See Art 3(e) SLSC Statute; Art 4(e) ICTR Statute.

[131] ICRC Commentary, paras 3047–50.

[132] This does not, however, mean that this particular aim adds a specific intent to the offence; it simply describes the conduct. *ICTY Prosecutor v Aleksovski*, Appeals Chamber Judgment (30 May 2001), para 27.

[133] *Aleksovski*, ibid, para 28. Where, nonetheless, proof of discrimination is established, it may well contribute to proving the perpetrators' intent and knowledge, ibid, at para 27.

[134] *Akayesu* Trial Chamber Judgment, para 688; equally, in *ICTY Prosecutor v Furundžija*, Trial Chamber Judgment (10 Dec 1998), para 183ff it was held that forcing a detained person to eat human excrement before a crowd amounted to an outrage upon personal dignity.

[135] *Kunarac* Appeals Chamber Judgment, para 512.

'generally considered to cause serious humiliation, degradation or otherwise be a serious attack on human dignity' and that the accused knew it would have that effect.[136]

7.3.2 Rape and Sexual Violence

Although in the past rape had been explicitly[137] or implicitly[138] prohibited under international humanitarian law, until the establishment of the ICTY it had never been defined in any of the instruments in which it was contained. It was not elucidated even when prosecuted as a war crime at the International Military Tribunal for the Far East or its Charter.[139] Lack of specificity was not a pressing issue to the post-war tribunals because not only did rape not play a significant role in prosecutorial agendas that were then working under severe time constraints, but where reference to rape was made in the Tokyo Trials, its elements must have seemed to all parties as self-proven and in no need of further elaboration.[140] There is no doubt that Nazi and Japanese licence to commit rapes and forced prostitution (the so-called practice of comfort women) was intended to both encourage soldiers and serve as an instrument of policy.[141] In any event, neither the relevant provisions of the 1949 Geneva Conventions nor of the 1977 Additional Protocols listed rape amongst their grave breaches provisions.

The practice and variety of rape in the conflicts occurring in the former Yugoslavia was both widespread and deliberate.[142] The special rapporteur of the UN Commission on Human Rights clearly pointed out the purpose of rape therein as constituting an individual attack and a method of ethnic cleansing designed to degrade and terrify the entire ethnic group.[143] Indiscriminate and widespread rape was also practised in the Rwandan genocide. Any assessment of rape must be viewed particularly in the context of gender-based crimes, that is, whereas 'sex' refers to biological differences, 'gender' refers to socially constructed differences, such as power imbalances, socio-economic disparities and culturally reinforced stereotypes.[144]

Rape is a particular offence contained in the list of crimes encompassing crimes against humanity in both the ICTY[145] and ICTR Statutes,[146] and a war crime of

---

[136] *Kunarac* Trial Chamber Judgment, para 514.

[137] Art 27, Geneva Convention IV; Art 76(1), Protocol I; Art 4(2)(c), Protocol II.

[138] Art 46, Hague Regulations; Art 3, Geneva Conventions; Art 147, Geneva Convention IV; Art 85(4)(c), Protocol I; Art 4(1) and 2(a), Protocol II.

[139] 4 Bevans 20.

[140] Control Council Law No 10, Art II(1)(c) included rape as a crime against humanity.

[141] T Meron, 'Rape as a Crime under International Law' (1993) 87 *American Journal of International Law* 424, at 425.

[142] C Niarchos, 'Women, War and Rape: Challenges Facing the International Tribunal for the Former Yugoslavia' (1995) 17 *Human Rights Quarterly (HRQ)* 649.

[143] Report on the Situation of Human Rights in the Territory of the Former Yugoslavia, UN Doc A/48/92-S/ 25341, Annex (1993), at 20, 57; *Karadžić* Decision (11 Jul 1996), para 64.

[144] K D Askin, 'Sexual Violence and Indictments of the Yugoslav and Rwandan Tribunals: Current Status' (1999) 93 *American Journal of International Law* 97, at 107.

[145] ICTY Statute, Art 5(g).

[146] ICTR Statute, Art 3(g).

internal conflicts under the ICTR.[147] Notwithstanding the absence of explicit reference to rape in the definition of other offences within the jurisdiction of the Tribunals, this egregious violation may also be prosecuted as a war crime, a grave breach under 'inhuman treatment' or 'torture', genocide and as a crime against humanity.[148] Although the two ad hoc tribunals basically agree on the definition of rape as a physical invasion of a sexual nature committed on a person under coercive circumstances,[149] there has been a substantial difference of opinion as to the sources of this definition and its scope. The *Akayesu* judgment viewed rape as a form of aggression and a violation of personal dignity whose central elements could not be captured in a mechanical description of objects and body parts.[150] Variations of rape, the Rwanda Tribunal held, may include acts involving the insertion of objects and/or the use of bodily orifices not considered to be intrinsically sexual. This conceptual and flexible definition of rape, having subsequently been followed by other ICTR Chambers,[151] is in contrast with the *Furundžija* judgment which, in fact, relied on a detailed description of objects and body parts.[152] In inquiring into the precise ambit encompassed by the term 'rape' and, specifically, whether this included 'forced oral penetration', the Trial Chamber in the *Furundžija* case highlighted the lack of a definition in international law, but found that the various relevant international instruments distinguished between rape and indecent assault. Unable to discover any relevant customary law or other definition based on general principles of public international or international criminal law, the judges turned their attention to general principles of criminal law common to the major legal systems. Although they ascertained that the forcible sexual penetration by the penis or similar insertion of any other object into either the vagina or anus is considered as constituting rape in all the examined legal systems, there was still some discrepancy concerning 'oral penetration', as in some countries it was classified as rape while in others as sexual assault.[153] The court ruled, nonetheless, that the principle of respect for human dignity dictated that extremely serious sexual outrage such as forced oral penetration could be classified as rape, amply outweighing any concerns the perpetrator might have of being stigmatised as a rapist rather than as a sexual assailant.[154] Although the *Furundžija* approach purports to be specific in its orientation, in reality it does not seem to differ much from the conceptual position adopted in *Akayesu*, especially since it is obliged to employ a non-specific principle to categorise forced oral

---

[147]   Ibid, Art 4(e).
[148]   The use of rape as a process of 'slow death' was recognised as a means of deliberately inflicting on a group conditions of life calculated to bring about its physical destruction, thus, constituting genocide. *ICTR Prosecutor v Kayishema*, Trial Chamber Judgment (21 May 1999), para 116. SC Res 1820 (19 Jun 2008), para 4, states that rape and other forms of sexual violence can constitute war crimes, crimes against humanity and a constitute act of humanity and genocide and should never be the subject of amnesties.
[149]   *Akayesu* Trial judgment, para 598; *ICTY Prosecutor v Furundžija*, Trial Chamber Judgment (10 Dec 1998), para 181.
[150]   *Akayesu* Trial Judgment, paras 596–98.
[151]   *ICTR Prosecutor v Musema*, Trial Chamber Judgment (27 Jan 2000), para 228.
[152]   *Furundžija* Trial Judgment, paras 175–84.
[153]   Ibid, paras 175–82.
[154]   Ibid, paras 183–84.

penetration. The *Furundžija* judgment adopted, therefore, the following definition of the *actus reus* of rape under international law:

    (i)   the sexual perpetration, however slight:

        (a) of the vagina or anus of the victim by the penis of the perpetrator or any other object used by the perpetrator; or

        (b) of the mouth of the victim by the penis of the perpetrator;

    (ii) by coercion or force or threat of force against the victim or a third person.[155]

The *Kunarac* judgment, although agreeing with this definition, argued that element (ii) of the definition is narrower than what is required under international law, since it omits any reference to factors that do not involve some form of coercion or force, especially factors that 'would render an act of sexual penetration non-consensual or non-voluntary on the part of the victim'.[156] Finding that the common denominator underlying general principles of law with regard to the criminalisation of rape is the violation of 'sexual autonomy', it added two further components to the *Furundžija* definition. These are that:

    (a) the sexual activity be accompanied by force or a variety of other specified circumstances which made the victim particularly vulnerable or negated her ability to make an informed refusal, or:

    (b) the sexual activity occurs without the consent of the victim.[157]

These specified circumstances, explained the Chamber, may include situations where the victim is put in a state of being unable to resist, particular vulnerability, or incapacity of resisting because of physical or mental incapacity, or because she was otherwise induced into the act by surprise or misrepresentation. These factors clearly rob the victim of the opportunity for an informed or reasoned refusal.[158] These considerations have found their way in Article 8(2)(b)(xxii) of the ICC Statute and the Elements of Crimes which state that the invasion of the body of the victim must have been committed:

> ... by force, or by threat of force or coercion, such as that caused by fear of violence, duress, detention, psychological oppression or abuse of power, against such person or another person, or by taking advantage of a coercive environment, or the invasion was committed against a person incapable of giving genuine consent.[159]

To the extent that an act of rape carries the attributes of the crime of torture – that is, infliction of severe physical or mental suffering by a State official whether for imparting a confession, rendering of punishment, intimidation, coercion or discrimination – it may be characterised as torture.[160] 'Outrages upon personal dignity' as a species of 'inhuman treatment' under Article 2 of the ICTY Statute, comprising acts animated by contempt for another person's dignity and whose aim is to cause serious

---

[155] Ibid, para 185.
[156] *Kunarac* Trial Judgment, para 438.
[157] Ibid, para 442.
[158] Ibid, paras 446–60; see concurring decisions adopted in the *Kvočka* Trial Judgment, para 177.
[159] ICC Elements of Crimes, Art 8(2)(b)(xxii)–1, num 2.
[160] *Furundžija* Trial Judgment, para 163.

humiliation or degradation to the victim, can also include rape.[161] Physical harm in this case is not necessary as long as the humiliation has caused 'real and lasting' suffering on the victim. The same is true where the perpetrator perceived this result as foreseeable.[162]

The inherently personal and sensitive object which rape violates should not allow for the use of regular principles of evidence pertaining to other offences. This notion was reflected in the Tribunals' Statutes, which provide guarantees for the protection of victims and witnesses,[163] further implemented by the Rules of Procedure, which do not require corroboration in cases of sexual assault.[164] This influence is evident in the ICC context, where rule 70 of its Rules of Procedure and Evidence provides that consent cannot be inferred by words or conduct under situations that undermined the victim's ability to give voluntary and genuine consent, nor by silence or lack of resistance. As a result, international tribunals seem to concur that in egregious and sustained situations of armed conflict and where rapes take part on a large scale, the non-consent of the victim and the *actus reus* of the offence may validly be adduced through circumstantial evidence.[165] Moreover, the victim's prior sexual life or character will not be admitted as evidence. Nonetheless, in the ICTY Rules of Procedure (rule 96) the description of 'consent' as a defence is used in a non-technical sense. Thus, the burden of proof is not shifted to the accused.[166]

7.3.3 Sexual Slavery

During the invasion of China and its subsequent hostilities in the Pacific theatre of operations, the Japanese armed forces institutionalised sexual slavery for their troops through the practice of so-called 'comfort women'. Much like the crime of rape, sexual slavery was recognised rather late as an international offence in the context of the ad hoc tribunals and the ICC. Its definition in the ICC Elements of Crimes is predicated on the legal notion of slavery as enshrined in the 1929 Slavery Convention, involving the exercise of powers of ownership, in whole or in part, over one or more persons. Given the many ways under which enslavement may come about, the Elements spell out some indicative, but by no means conclusive, ways through which this condition can be achieved by the perpetrator:

---

[161] *ICTY Prosecutor v Aleksovski*, Trial Chamber Judgment (25 Jun 1999), paras 54–56. The application of this particular ruling was unrelated to acts of rape.

[162] Ibid.

[163] ICTY Statute, Art 22; ICTR Statute, Art 21. Such measures include, but are not limited to, the conduct of *in camera* proceedings and the protection of the victim's identity. M Leigh, 'The Yugoslav Tribunal: Use of Unnamed Witnesses Against Accused' (1996) 90 *American Journal of International Law* 235; C Chinkin, 'Due Process and Witness Anonymity' (1997) 91 *American Journal of International Law* 75.

[164] ICTY Rules, r 96(1); see *Tadić* Appeals Opinion and Judgment (7 May 1997), para 536.

[165] *ICTR Prosecutor v Gacumbitsi*, Appeals Chamber Judgment (7 Jul 2006), para 115; *ICTR Prosecutor v Muhimana*, Appeals Chamber Judgment (21 May 2007), para 49; *RUF* Trial Judgment, para 149.

[166] *Kunarac* Trial Judgment, para 463.

... by purchasing, selling, lending or bartering such a person or persons, or by imposing on them a similar deprivation of liberty.[167]

Although all of the above elements suggest a pecuniary requirement to sexual slavery, this is not the case at all.[168] Equally, one need not satisfy the requirement of exercising ownership, since other lesser forms of slavery suffice,[169] particularly the four offences under the 1956 Supplementary Slavery Convention, ie serfdom, debt bondage, bride-price and the illegal transfer of children.[170] The same is true in those situations where people are trafficked.[171]

The definition in the ICC Statute and its Elements is not particularly helpful as it does not provide a meaningful distinction between general unlawful enslavement and sexual slavery. Certainly, therefore, sexual slavery encompasses both proof of slavery or slavery-related practices and deprivation of the victim's sexual autonomy. In this manner, depriving the victim of sexual intercourse without other physical invasion of the body would constitute the element of the offence – although quite rare in egregious contexts analysed in this book. While some practices may be clear demonstrations of sexual slavery, such as prostitution and trafficking, the vulnerability of the victim, psychological control, coercion, assertion of exclusivity, control of sexuality and forced labour may not render clear the sexual nature of the offence or the element of enslavement; yet it is very much the same offence.[172]

7.3.4   Enforced Prostitution

This is in fact similar in many ways to the crime of sexual slavery, given that the 'enforced' nature of the prostitution suggests a degree of ownership over the victim. In any event, the distinction is crucial not so much for legal purposes but in order to highlight its heinous character and its devastating effect on women in the course of twentieth century armed conflicts. Besides Article 8(2)(b)(xxii) of the ICC Statute, it was also specifically prohibited under Article 76(1) of Protocol I.

Unlike the war crime of sexual slavery where a pecuniary intent is not a *sine qua non* condition of the offence, the opposite is true in respect of enforced prostitution.[173] The perpetrator must have caused:

one or more persons to engage in one or more acts of a sexual nature by force, or by threat of force or coercion, such as that caused by fear of violence, duress, detention, psychological

---

[167]   ICC Elements of Crimes, Art 8(2)(b)(xxii)–2, num 1.
[168]   *Kunarac* Trial Judgment, para 542.
[169]   ICC Elements of Crimes, Art 8(2)(b)(xxii)–2, num 1, note 53 thereof.
[170]   See chapter 10.1.
[171]   Ibid.
[172]   *Kunarac* Trial Judgment, para 543; *RUF* Trial Judgment, para 160.
[173]   ICC Elements of Crimes, Art 8(2)(b)(xxii)–3, num 2.

oppression or abuse of power, against such person or persons or another person, or by taking advantage of a coercive environment or such person's or persons' incapacity to give genuine consent.[174]

The fact that the victim is forced to solicit clients does not detract from the criminal liability of the perpetrator, since the circumstances described above serve to fully remove the victim's consent to the prostitution.

7.3.5 Forced Pregnancy

The war crime of forced pregnancy differs from that of rape and other rape-related offences in that it contains a special intent that is absent elsewhere. Thus, besides the physical violation of the victim and the additional element of unlawful confinement, the perpetrator must act 'with the intent of affecting the ethnic composition of any population or [in order to carry out] other grave violations of international law'.[175] It is difficult to see how a lone individual can realistically aim to satisfy this special intent, unless he is party to a criminal enterprise or a conspiracy. The second alternative of the special intent suggests a frame of mind whereby the perpetrator seeks to commit torture, unlawful medical experimentation and similar offences through the act of forced pregnancy. In terms of the *actus reus* the nature of the offence necessarily requires that the perpetrator either raped the victim, or that he subjected the victim to a forced maternity (ie up to the point of giving birth), irrespective of whether the rape was committed by him or another person.

7.3.6 Enforced Sterilisation

The *actus reus* of this offence requires the deprivation of one's 'biological reproductive capacity', absent any medical reason or the victim's genuine consent.[176] The deprivation must be of a permanent nature; hence, birth-control measures that have a non-permanent effect do not fall within the ambit of the offence.[177] It is therefore evident that the fundamental purpose behind this war crime is the motivation of the perpetrator to achieve a result similar to that of forced pregnancy (ie to affect an ethnic composition, or to commit other grave violations). Given that enforced sterilisation may succeed in altering the ethnic composition of a population, it is curious why the ICC Statute did not attach a special intent to this offence. In the opinion of this author this war crime concerns minor executioners of a larger plan that consists of either a crime against humanity or genocide.

---

[174] Ibid, num 1.
[175] ICC Elements of Crimes, Art 8(2)(b)(xxii)–4, num 1.
[176] Ibid, Art 8(2)(b)(xxii)–5, nums 1 and 2.
[177] Ibid, footnote 54 to num 1.

7.4 Prohibited Targeting Crimes

The protection of civilians in international humanitarian law is predicated on two fundamental and inextricably linked rules; that of distinction[178] and the absolute prohibition against the targeting of civilians. The rule of distinction postulates that at all times the parties to a conflict must distinguish between the civilian population and combatants and between civilian objects and military objects and must accordingly direct their attacks against combatants and military objects.[179] The absolute nature of the prohibition of attacks against civilians, which includes also acts or threats of violence the objective of which is to spread terror to a civilian population, is clearly spelt out in Article 51(2) of Protocol I. Given this absolute nature, it is wrong to argue that the invocation of military necessity can justify such an attack against civilians, or otherwise be employed as a viable defence.[180] Military necessity can only be invoked where the attack is otherwise lawful but under the particular circumstances there is a danger of killing or wounding civilians or of damaging civilian property.[181] The sole exception to the aforementioned strict rule is where a civilian abandons his or her protected status by taking a direct part in hostilities. Even so, the loss of civilian status is temporary since it persists only 'for such time as they take a direct part in hostilities'.[182]

Two matters require clarification before proceeding further with our analysis of the various crimes; the definition of civilians and the meaning of the term 'taking a direct part in hostilities'. A civilian is any person who is not a member of the armed forces, militia, paramilitary group, resistance movement and other similar outfits in the sense of Articles 4(A)(1)–(3) and (6) of Geneva Convention III[183] and 43 of

---

[178] *Legality of the Threat or Use of Nuclear Weapons*, Advisory Opinion (8 July 1996), (1996) ICJ Reports 226, paras 78–79; see JF Quéguiner, 'Precautions under the Law Governing the Conduct of Hostilities' (2006) 88 *IRRC* 793;

[179] Art 48, Protocol I; ICJ Advisory Opinion on Nuclear Weapons, para 78.

[180] *ICTY Prosecutor v Galić*, Trial Chamber Judgment (5 Dec 2003), para 44.

[181] See WJ Fenrick, 'The Rule of Proportionality and Protocol I in Conventional Warfare' (1982) 98 *Military Law Review* 91. This reality is recognised as a distinct offence in Art 8(2)(b)(iv) of the ICC Statute, which criminalises the intentional launching of an attack against a civilian population in the knowledge of its excessive consequences to civilians or to the natural environment. The excessive nature of the attack is measured against the concrete and direct overall military advantage anticipated. In a footnote to Art 8(2)(b)(iv) of the ICC Elements of Crimes, the expression concrete and direct military advantage refers to 'a military advantage that is foreseeable by the perpetrator at the relevant time. Such advantage may or may not be temporally or geographically related to the object of the attack. The fact that this crime admits the possibility of lawful incidental injury and collateral damage does not in any way justify any violations of the law applicable in armed conflict'. The offence in the ICC Statute was adopted verbatim from Art 51(5)(a) of Protocol I.

[182] Art 51(3), Protocol I.

[183] A person is considered a member as such where the following conditions are satisfied: a) the group is structured under an authority of responsible command; b) its members distinguish themselves from the civilian population through a distinct emblem; c) arms are carried openly; d) the group conducts its operation in accordance with the laws and customs of war. Persons belonging to a group that satisfies these criteria are considered lawful combatants and enjoy prisoner of war status if captured. The same status is enjoyed also by persons falling under the category of levée en masse, which is described in Art 4(A)(6) of Geneva Convention III and Art 2 of the 1907 Hague Regulations. The concept refers to the spontaneous taking of arms by inhabitants of a non-occupied territory at the approach of the enemy. In this case, although such persons would normally fail to satisfy the conditions of responsible command and of sufficient distinction, they still enjoy combatant status where they satisfy the remaining two criteria.

Protocol I.[184] Moreover, the civilian population comprises all persons that are civilians.[185] Equally, the presence of combatants within the midst of a civilian population does not alter the civilian character of the group.[186] Equally, it is also fair to argue that a person or a group that engages in armed violence against a party to a conflict, without however belonging to another party in that same conflict cannot be considered as being members of the armed forces of a party to the conflict.[187] Such groups are, therefore, considered as being engaged in a distinct non-international armed conflict with their rival government forces.

It has already been stated that a civilian forfeits his status as such where he takes a direct part in hostilities.[188] This term is not defined in a binding legal instrument, but it is taken to encompass 'any acts of war which by their nature or purpose are likely to cause actual harm to the personnel or equipment of the enemy armed forces'.[189] When such circumstances arise an otherwise civilian becomes a legitimate object of attack, irrespective of his motives for taking up arms against the adversary.[190] Experts, both academic and military, have argued for a while whether certain activities carried out by civilians may be excluded from direct participation in hostilities. Thus, the cases of civilian contractors working on projects in the battle-field, as well as civilian workers in munitions factories or in other installations the work of whom contributes directly or indirectly to the war effort are thought to fall within a grey zone of humanitarian law. The ICRC's position on whether particular conduct qualifies as direct participation in hostilities is predicated on the following cumulative criteria:

(a) The act must be likely to adversely affect the military operations or military capacity of a party to an armed conflict or, alternatively, to inflict death, injury, or destruction on persons or objects protected against direct attack (*threshold of harm*), and

(b) there must be a direct causal link between the act and the harm likely to result either from that act, or from a coordinated military operation of which that act constitutes an integral part (*direct causation*), and

---

[184] Art 50(1), Protocol I.

[185] Art 50(2), Protocol I. The *Blaškić* Trial Judgment, para 180, also defined them as 'persons who are not, or no longer are, members of the armed forces'.

[186] Art 50(3), Protocol I.

[187] See *The Public Committee Against Torture et al v The Government of Israel et al*, (HCJ 769/02), Judgment (13 Dec 2006), para 26, where the Israeli Supreme Court held that independent Palestinian groups operating within a framework of belligerent occupation should be classified as civilians.

[188] One school of thought is of the opinion that under such circumstances civilians not only lose their civilian status but moreover become unlawful combatants. The chief proponent of this view, which is shared by this author, is Dinstein and the US government. See Y Dinstein, *The Conduct of Hostilities under the Law of International Armed Conflict* (Cambridge, Cambridge University Press, 2004) 27–33; *Hamdi v Rumsfeld* (2004) 124 S Ct 2633, 2640 and *Hamdan v Rumsfeld* (2006) 126 S Ct 2749, 2824. For an opposite point of view see K Dormann, 'The Legal Status of Unlawful/Unprivileged Combatants' (2003) 85 *IRRC* 45. In much the same terms in *Public Committee Against Torture in Israel and Others v The State of Israel and Others*, Israel Supreme Court Judgment (13 Dec 2006), HCJ 769/02, a case concerning the legality of targeted killings, it was held that civilians taking a direct part in hostilities, as is the case with Palestinian civilians who become members of alleged terrorist organisations, are not to be considered unlawful combatants. By doing so, however, they do not enjoy full protection from hostilities. According to the Court it is one's function that determines his direct participation in hostilities. Ultimately the legality of targeted killings of civilians engaged in terrorist activities was upheld but under very strict circumstances.

[189] *Galić* Trial Judgment, para 48, citing the ICRC Commentary, para 1944.

[190] *Kupreškić* Trial Judgment, para 522; *Abella v Argentina* [Tablada case], IACHR Report No. 55/97, Case No. 11.137, OEA/Ser/L/V/II.97, Doc 7, rev at 271 (30 Oct 1997).

(c)   the act must be specifically designed to directly cause the required threshold of harm in support of a party to the conflict and to the detriment of another (*belligerent nexus*).[191]

As a result of the above it is a grave breach to intentionally direct an attack against civilians not taking direct part in hostilities.[192] Moreover, indiscriminate attacks against civilians will also bring about the same result.[193] Whereas Protocol I requires the occurrence of a specific result to accompany the unlawful attack against civilians, ie causing death or serious injury to body or health,[194] this is not the case in respect of the ICC Statute. Nonetheless, the weight of opinion seems to suggest that the requirement of this specific result is an intrinsic element of customary international law, regardless of its absence in the ICC Statute.[195]

The intentional nature of the attack in the ICC Statute relates not only to the act of directing the attack, but also to the object of the attack.[196] ICTY chambers have consistently interpreted the 'wilful' nature of the offence of directing and launching attacks against civilians in Article 85(3) of Protocol I as encompassing both intention and recklessness.[197] In every case, the 'Prosecution must show that the perpetrator was aware or should have been aware of the civilian status of the persons attacked'.[198]

Articles 52(2) of Protocol I and 33 of Geneva Convention IV criminalise the infliction and spreading of terror upon a civilian population where this constitutes the primary purpose of the accused and is achieved through acts or threat of violence.[199] Whereas acts of terror may be perpetrated through unlawful internment, torture and other crimes, we are here interested in its infliction as part of an attack against a civilian population[200] and need not necessarily involve acts that are otherwise criminal under international law.[201] In the former Yugoslavia, it was common for cities to be shelled for a prolonged duration and for civilians to be the victims of long-running sniping campaigns with a view to terrorising them and forcing them to abandon their ancestral homes. The Trial Chamber in the *Galić* case, required the following characteristics for this facet of the offence to take place:

1.   Acts of violence directed against the civilian population or individual civilians not taking direct part in hostilities causing death or serious injury to body or health within the civilian population.

---

[191] ICRC, Interpretive Guidance on the Notion of Direct Participation in Hostilities (Geneva, ICRC, 2009) 46ff, available at: <http://www.icrc.org/Web/eng/siteeng0.nsf/htmlall/direct-participation-report_res/$File/direct-participation-guidance-2009-icrc.pdf>.

[192] Art 8(2)(b)(i), ICC Statute; Art 85(3)(a), Protocol I.

[193] *ICTY Prosecutor v Martić*, Rule 61 Decision (8 Mar 1996), paras 23–31; *Galić* Trial Judgment, para 57.

[194] Art 85(3), Protocol I.

[195] *Kordić and Čerkez* Appeals Judgment, para 67; Triffterer Commentary, 325–26.

[196] ICC Elements of Crimes, Art 8(2)(b)(i).

[197] *Galić* Trial Judgment, para 54.

[198] Ibid, para 55.

[199] The same is explicitly prohibited under Arts 4(2)(d) and 13(2) of Protocol II (1977). Art 3(d) of the SLSC Statute is taken verbatim from Art 4(2)(d) of Protocol II.

[200] The ICRC Commentary, at 1375, views it as a special form of terrorism, which covers not only 'acts directed against people, but also acts directed against installations which would cause victims as a side-effect'.

[201] *CDF* Appeals Judgment, para 359; however, given that even legitimate military operations may well spread terror to a civilian population, such operations are excluded from the ambit of the relevant offence. See *RUF* Trial Judgment, para 120.

2. The offender wilfully made the civilian population or individual civilians not taking direct part in hostilities the object of those acts of violence.

3. The above offence was committed with the primary purpose of spreading terror among the civilian population.[202]

It was held that the actual infliction of terror is not a material element of the offence.[203] Moreover, readers should distinguish between the mental elements for committing acts or threats of violence against the civilian population, which includes intent and recklessness, from the requirement that the spreading of terror was the 'primary purpose of the perpetrator', which must be specifically intended, thus necessarily excluding *dolus eventualis* or recklessness even in the context of the ad hoc tribunals.[204] Clearly, it is a specific result crime.[205]

The status of civilians in international armed conflicts is also shared by the personnel of humanitarian assistance and peacekeeping missions, to the extent that they are entitled at any given time to the protection available to civilians and civilian objects; ie on the basis that they do not take a direct part in hostilities.[206] Personnel of humanitarian assistance missions may encompass members of non-governmental organisations, as well as of specially protected entities, such as the ICRC, as well as of international organisations engaged in a purely humanitarian capacity, such as the UNHCR and the OSCE. On the other hand, peacekeeping missions are mandated and specifically sanctioned by the UN Security Council, or at times by the UN General Assembly, and this authority is also delegated to regional international organisations, such as ECOWAS.[207] The legal basis of peacekeeping missions is generally understood to be Chapter VI of the UN Charter, but they may also be constituted under Chapter VII, as long as their mandate does not emanate from Article 42 of the Charter.[208] Under Article 8(2)(b)(iii) of the ICC Statute, such attacks on humanitarian assistance and peacekeeping personnel constitute war crimes against civilians, as the personnel of such entities are treated for the purposes of the *jus in bello* as civilians (as long as they do not take a direct part in hostilities).[209] This is not the case with the personnel of peace-enforcement operations whose mandate includes not only a right to use force in self-defence, which applies anyway to humanitarian and peacekeeping missions, but a right to employ

---

[202] *Galić* Trial Judgment, para 133.

[203] Ibid, para 134.

[204] *CDF* Appeals Judgment, paras 355–57.

[205] *Galić* Trial Judgment, para 136.

[206] See *ICTY Prosecutor v Karadžić and Mladić*, Rule 61 Decision (11 Jul 1996), para 14; *SCSL v Sesay, Kallon, Gbao* (RUF case), Trial Chamber Judgment (2 Mar 2009), para 215.

[207] A Abass, *Regional Organisations and the Development of Collective Security: Beyond Chapter VII of the UN Charter* (Oxford, Hart Publishing, 2004).

[208] *RUF* Trial Judgment, paras 233–35.

[209] ICC Elements of Crimes, Art 8(2)(b)(iii), num 4; see RUF Trial Judgment, paras 116–20, which concluded that attacks against such missions constitute international crimes under customary law in both internal and international armed conflicts and relied on the ICC Elements of Crimes in order to substantiate the contours of the offence.

force in order to carry out the terms of their mandate.[210] Members of peace-enforcement operations are thus treated as parties to the conflict and not as civilians and an unlawful attack against them would fall under the relevant provisions of the Geneva Conventions and Protocol I.[211]

The Security Council has not always treated unlawful attacks against peacekeeping and humanitarian assistance missions as international crimes, despite vociferously condemning them;[212] nonetheless, in certain instances it has not hesitated to condemn these explicitly as criminal acts.[213] Following, however, the unlawful attack against the UN's Baghdad headquarters on 19 August 2003, the Security Council adopted resolution 1502 through which it emphasised that such attacks 'constitute war crimes in situations of armed conflict' and recalled 'the need for States to end impunity for such criminal acts'.[214] The resolution further emphasised that member States must enforce their criminal jurisdiction against such crimes, strongly urging therefore for the application of universal jurisdiction. It is not clear, however, that resolution 1502 is consistent with relevant customary law. Given that an attack against peacekeepers must be distinguished from an attack against a peace enforcement mission consti-tuted under Article 42 of the UN Charter, and that moreover the attacker must have intended to attack the latter in the knowledge or belief that it was directly partaking in hostilities, it is wholly likely that the perpetrators of the offence believed the UN HQ to be part of the wider peace enforcement mission in Iraq.

Criminal jurisdiction for such attacks is additionally available under the 1994 Convention on the Safety of United Nations and Associated Personnel,[215] on the basis of the territorial, nationality and passive personality principle, or where the attack was an attempt to compel that State to do or abstain from doing any act. Moreover, each State party in whose territory an alleged offender is present is required to take appropriate measures under its national law to ensure that person's presence for prosecution or extradition, thus permitting the exercise of universal jurisdiction.

After having examined the criminalisation of unlawful attacks against civilians, let us now proceed to analyse the criminality of unlawful attacks against civilian, or otherwise protected, objects. The general rule is enshrined in Article 52(1) of Protocol I and holds that civilian objects (ie non-military objectives) shall not be the object of attack or of reprisals. Failure, therefore, to apply the rule of distinction gives rise to a grave breach, for which the defence of military necessity is inapplicable.[216] A military objective is defined in Article 52(2) of Protocol I as follows:

> those objects which by their nature, location, purpose or use make an effective contribution to military action and whose total or partial destruction, capture or neutralisation, in the circumstances ruling at the time, offers a definite military advantage.

---

[210] eg SC 678 (29 Nov 1990); SC 1529 (29 Feb 2004).

[211] See C Greenwood, 'International Humanitarian Law and United Nations Military Operations' (1998) 1 *Yearbook of International Humanitarian Law* 3; U Palwankar, 'Applicability of International Humanitarian Law to United Nations Peacekeeping Forces' (1993) 294 *IRRC* 227.

[212] SC Res 788 (19 Nov 1992); SC Res 813 (26 Mar 1993); SC 987 (19 Apr 1995).

[213] SC Res 865 (22 Sep 1992); SC Res 837 (6 Jun 1993); SC Res 1099 (14 Mar 1997).

[214] SC 1502 (26 Aug 2003).

[215] 2051 UNTS 363, Art 10.

[216] *Strugar* Trial Judgment, para 280.

The term 'military advantage' must be qualified further as being concrete, imminent and finite and not merely hypothetical or applicable to the general armed conflict as a whole. Rather, a military advantage is both restricted in time and space and concerns only a particular military operation.[217] The concept of reprisals is, however, treated differently than that of other attacks against civilian objects in the context of Article 8(2)(b)(ii) of the ICC Statute, despite making no reference to this concept. Reprisals have been excluded from the general rule enunciated in Article 52(1) of Protocol I by virtue of several reservations entered into by some States upon ratification of the Protocol, but only in respect of such reserving States.[218] This exception is predicated on Article 8(2)(b) of the ICC Statute which purports to criminalise the various types of unlawful behaviour 'within the established framework of international law', which encompasses the aforementioned reservations to Protocol I, on which the relevant ICC Statute provision is premised.

A particular form of unlawful attack is that launched against an undefended locality.[219] An undefended locality shall fulfil the following criteria in order to qualify for special protection:

(a) all combatants, as well as mobile weapons and mobile military equipment must have been evacuated;
(b) no hostile use shall be made of fixed military installations or establishments;
(c) no acts of hostility shall be committed by the authorities or by the population, and;
(d) no activities in support of military operations shall be undertaken.[220]

Article 8(2)(b)(v) of the ICC Statute, which enshrines the rule against attack or bombardment of towns, villages and dwellings that are undefended, incorporates an additional requirement that is absent in the relevant provision of Protocol I; that the undefended locality be not at the same time an objective subject to military necessity. If its acquisition is justified by military necessity it can be made the object of attack. An undefended locality is to be distinguished from a demilitarised zone.[221] Although the two are otherwise identical in respect of their constitutive elements, whereas demilitarised zones require an agreement between the parties,[222] an undefended locality may be unilaterally proclaimed and notified.[223]

Similarly, attacks against protected objects and buildings, particularly those dedicated to religion, education, art, science or charitable purposes, historic monuments, hospitals or places where the sick and wounded are collected are considered war

---

[217] Dinstein, *The Conduct of Hostilities*, at 87.
[218] These reservations are applicable only vis-a-vis reprisals directed against civilian objectives and are inapplicable against the rule in Article 51(6) of Protocol I which prohibits at all times reprisals against civilians.
[219] Art 8(2)(b)(v) ICC Statute; Art 59 Protocol; Art 25, 1907 Hague Regulations.
[220] Art 59(2)(a)–(d) Protocol I.
[221] These are defined in Arts 15 and 60 of the 1907 Hague Regulations and Protocol I respectively.
[222] Although in practice the Security Council has established these in the absence of an agreement between the relevant States, eg SC Res 687 (3 Apr 1991).
[223] See SD Bailey, 'Non-Military Areas in UN Practice' (1980) 74 *American Journal of International Law* 3.

crimes.[224] In the case of the ICC Statute, just like undefended localities, such an attack constitutes a criminal offence where the objects or buildings under consideration were not also military objectives.[225] Although this offence overlaps with its counterpart concerning unlawful attacks against civilian objects, it should be treated as *lex specialis*.[226] Whereas in the ICTY context, and particularly Article 3(d) of its Statute, actual damage is a requirement of the offence, this is not so as regards the ICC Statute.[227] The accused must have known about the protected status of the object or building and must have intended to direct an attack against it.

Finally, the intentional starvation of civilians as a method of warfare falls within the broad category of unlawful attacks, to the degree that the perpetrator is targeting objects indispensable for one's survival, such as food, foodstuffs and water.[228] The general rule is clearly enunciated in Article 54(1) of Protocol I, which strictly forbids the starvation of civilians. The scope of this offence, however, is much broader than starvation in the strict sense, because it encompasses in addition the deprivation of objects that are indispensable to the survival of civilians, which may include clothing, medical supplies, other essential commodities, impediment of relief supplies, as well as machineries that are required for farming, etc.[229] The list is certainly open-ended. Four exceptions permeate the general law such that justify the taking of objects indispensable for civilian survival. These are:

(a) as sustenance solely for the members of its armed forces, or;
(b) if not as sustenance, then in direct support of military action, provided, however, that in no event shall actions against these objects be taken which may be expected to leave the civilian population with such inadequate food or water as to cause its starvation or force its movement
(c) in recognition of the vital requirements of any party to the conflict in the defence of its national territory against invasion.[230]

Additionally, where the starvation is incidental to an otherwise lawful attack, provided that such result is not excessive to the benefits accruing from the attack, it will not constitute a war crime.[231] As regards the *mens rea* of this offence it is clear that it requires a specific intent to starve civilians as a method of warfare.[232]

---

[224] Arts 27 and 56, 1907 Hague Regulations; Arts 19–23 Geneva Convention I; Arts 22–23, 34–35, Geneva Convention II; Arts 18–19, Geneva Convention IV; Arts 12 and 53, Protocol I; 1954 Hague Convention for the Protection of Cultural Property in the Event of Armed Conflict, particularly Art 1 which defines cultural property.

[225] Art 8(2)(b)(ix).

[226] *Kordić and Čerkez* Trial Judgment, para 361.

[227] *Strugar* Trial Judgment, para 307; Art 8(2)(b)(ix), num 1 of the ICC Elements of Crimes requires merely that the perpetrator 'directed' an attack.

[228] Art 8(2)(b)(xxv) ICC Statute.

[229] Triffterer Commentary, 460–61. See Art 54(2), Protocol I.

[230] Art 54(3) and (5), Protocol I.

[231] Triffterer Commentary, 464.

[232] Ibid, 465–66.

7.5   War Crimes against Combatants and *Hors de Combat*

These war crimes concern the employment of means and methods of warfare that are prohibited under international humanitarian law and offences against *hors de combat*. The basic rule is that perfidious acts are forbidden as war crimes,[233] whereas persons that are recognised or who, in the circumstances should be recognised as *hors de combat* shall not be made the object of attack.[234] A person is *hors de combat*, in accordance with Article 41(2) of Protocol I, if:

(a)   he is in the power of an adverse party;
(b)   he clearly expresses an intention to surrender; or
(c)   he has been rendered unconscious or is otherwise incapacitated by wounds or sickness, and therefore is incapable of defending himself,

provided that in any of these cases he abstains from any hostile act and does not attempt to escape.

Thus, persons that are *hors de combat* are generally physically incapable of attacking the enemy and should be spared from the evils of warfare and never regarded as combatants, which in fact they are not, even if they once were. This prohibition, which is very well entrenched in customary international law, is derived from considerations of chivalry. As a result, WWII military tribunals had no problem declaring that the killing of prisoners of war[235] as well as the killing of survivors-at-sea of a torpedoed ship were war crimes against such protected persons.[236] Consequently, Article 85(3) of Protocol I makes it a grave breach to cause death or serious injury by wilfully 'making a person the object of attack in the knowledge that he is *hors de combat*'.[237]

A specific grave breach of this nature is that relating to the denial to provide quarter to persons that have laid down their arms and have surrendered, to survivors, or to existing prisoners of war.[238] The meaning of denial of quarter itself must be understood as referring to the denial of life, or of leaving no survivors,[239] or exposing a protected person to the elements under circumstances that death is foreseeable.[240] There does exist, however, a discrepancy between the relevant provisions in Protocol I and the ICC Statute. Whereas both agree that the perpetrator's liability is engaged where he or she declares or orders the denial of quarter, this is understood in the ICC Statute in narrow temporal terms. On the contrary, Protocol I recognises that the conduct of hostilities generally on the basis that no quarter will be given to members of the adversary – which acts also as a scare tactic – is additionally punishable under

---

[233]   Art 37, Protocol I.
[234]   Art 41(1), Protocol I; Art 23(c), Hague Regulations.
[235]   *Re Kurt Meyer*, 4 LRTWC 107ff.
[236]   *In Re Eck and Others (The Peleus)*, 13 AD 248.
[237]   The same is true in respect of Art 8(2)(b)(vi), ICC Statute.
[238]   Art 23(d), Hague Regulations; Art 40, Protocol I; Art 8(2)(b)(xii), ICC Statute.
[239]   In *Re Dostler*, 13 AD 281, at 290, a US military commission found that Hitler's Commando Order, which called for the extermination of all enemy commandos, was a war crime of this nature.
[240]   A poignant example is the Laconia Order, which forbade members of submarine crews to rescue crews of sunken ships, or to provide them with food, water or lifeboats. See *In Re Moehle*, 13 AD 246.

the same category.[241] Although the ICC Elements of Crimes employ verbatim the wording of Article 40 of Protocol I, it is doubtful that it can be interpreted in the same manner as Article 40 because a Swiss proposal to that effect during the ICC's preparatory conferences did not gather sufficient support.[242] In any event, it may additionally be classified as an unlawful act against an *hors de combat*.

As regards war crimes against combatants, two things should be noted from the outset. The first is that it is lawful to intend to kill other combatants, provided they have not been rendered *hors de combat*, and equally it is permissible to deceive the enemy as a matter of ruse.[243] It is therefore imperative to ascertain under what circumstances a ruse of war is prohibited. Article 23(b) of the Hague Regulations and Article 8(2)(b)(xi) of the ICC Statute criminalise the treacherous killing or wounding of persons belonging to the hostile nation or army. Article 37 of Protocol I, on the other hand, employs the term 'perfidy' to convey the same meaning. Thus, both perfidy and treachery should be treated as synonymous for legal purposes. Perfidy is defined in Article 37(1) of Protocol I as encompassing:

> Acts inviting the confidence of an adversary to lead him to believe that he is entitled to, or is obliged to accord, protection under the rules of international law applicable in armed conflict, with intent to betray that confidence.

Whereas the underlying notions of chivalry imbued in the nature of warfare allow combatants to trick and betray the good faith of their adversary, this is permissible only to the degree that it does not implicate or violate other mandatory rules of the *jus in bello*; if it does, such betrayal constitutes a war crime. Article 37(2) of Protocol I defines permissible ruses as encompassing those acts:

> which are intended to mislead an adversary or to induce him to act recklessly but which infringe no rule of international law applicable in armed conflict and which are not perfidious because they do not invite the confidence of an adversary with respect to protection under that law. The following are examples of such ruses: the use of camouflage, decoys, mock operations and misinformation.

Thus, deceiving the enemy by wearing his uniform or feigning an injury is permissible if it is used to escape detention or in order to flee. If, however, such deception is employed with the intention of wounding or killing the enemy it constitutes a war crime.[244] As examples of perfidy, Article 37(1) includes:

(a) the feigning of an intent to negotiate under a flag of truce or of a surrender;
(b) the feigning of an incapacitation by wounds or sickness;
(c) the feigning of civilian, non-combatant status, and;
(d) the feigning of protected status by the use of signs, emblems or uniforms of the United Nations or of neutral or other States nor parties to the conflict.

---

[241] This interpretation is based solely on the wording of Art 40, since the ICRC Commentary, 473–77, makes no reference to this issue.

[242] Triffterer Commentary, 392–93.

[243] Art 37(2), Protocol I. See JC Dehn, 'Permissible Perfidy? Analysing the Colombian Hostage Rescue, the Capture of Rebel Leaders and the World's Reaction' (2008) 6 *Journal of International Criminal Justice* 627; GP Politakis, 'Stratagems and the Prohibition of Perfidy with a Special Reference to the Law of War at Sea' (1993) 45 *Austrian Journal of Public International Law* 253.

[244] ICC Elements of Crimes, Art 8(2)(b)(xi), nums 3–4.

Article 8(2)(b)(vii) of the ICC Statute echoes this provision in criminalising the improper use of a flag of truce, a flag, insignia or uniform of the hostile party[245] or of the United Nations,[246] or of the distinctive emblems of the Geneva Conventions.[247] Perfidy should not be confused with acts of treason and espionage, which are not treated as war crimes under international law,[248] albeit persons engaging therein are susceptible to severe punishment under the domestic law of the harmed State.[249]

7.6 War Crimes related to the Use of Illegal or Prohibited Weapons

The regulation of weaponry in international humanitarian law is undertaken in three ways: a) through the basic rule that the right of the parties to a conflict to 'choose methods or means of warfare is not unlimited' and in any event weapons are prohibited at all times where they are of a 'nature to cause superfluous injury or unnecessary suffering';[250] b) certain weapons have been barred, for all or some States, through the conclusion of specific multilateral treaties, and; c) where a weapon does not fall in categories (a) or (b) the legality of its use is predicated on general international law. This may include custom, the *Lotus* rule (ie it is not negated by a conflicting rule), the principle of distinction[251] and others.[252]

It should be pointed out that the list of prohibited weapons in the ICC Statute is not wholly consistent with the position in general international law. For one thing, nuclear powers did not wish to give up the right to possess and use their arsenal, particularly following the *Nuclear Weapons* Advisory Opinion of the ICJ. Equally, they naturally opposed the inclusion of an open, general, clause that may potentially prompt the judges in the future to rule that nuclear and similar weapons were contrary to customary international law.[253] Yet, other States posited their own particular interests in respect of these and other weapons. Given the impasse until the final day of negotiations, a compromise, take-it-or-leave-it, was put forward, which did not criminalise nuclear, biological and chemical weapons, nor also blinding laser weapons and anti-personnel mines.[254] Whereas chemical weapons are prohibited

---

[245] See also, Art 39(1)–(2), Protocol I. A combatant may wear the uniform of the adversary but cannot engage the adversary while wearing it. This rule is particularly significant in respect of special forces operations.

[246] Ibid, Art 38(2).

[247] Ibid, Art 38(1).

[248] Ibid, Art 39(3).

[249] See *Joyce v DPP* [1946] AC 347.

[250] Art 35(1) and (2), Protocol I.

[251] Judge Higgins offered a definition of what constitute indiscriminate weapons in the ICJ's *Nuclear Weapons* Opinion, Dissenting Opinion, para 24. These encompass weapons that are 'incapable of being targeted at a military objective only, even if collateral harm occurs. ... To the extent that a specific nuclear weapon would be incapable of this distinction, its use would be unlawful'.

[252] For a review of State practice on weapons see JM Henckaerts, L Doswald-Beck (eds.), *Customary International Humanitarian Law* (Cambridge, Cambridge University Press, 2005), vol II, part I, at 1505ff [hereinafter Customary Humanitarian Law].

[253] Triffterer Commentary, 412.

[254] Ibid.

under customary international law,[255] all the aforementioned are barred *inter partes* on the basis of relevant conventions. For what it is worth, Article 8(2)(b)(xx) of the ICC Statute does not exclude the possibility that these and other weapons may be criminalised in the future through the conclusion of an annex by the State parties and attached to the Statute.

In accordance with customary law,[256] Article 8(2)(b)(xvii) prohibits the employment of poison or poisoned weapons. It is not limited to weapons *per se*, but encompasses also the use of poison to contaminate potable water, although in this case the offence may well overlap with the intentional starvation of civilians or the destruction of civilian objects. It is required that the substance released from the weapon or the poison 'cause death or serious damage to health in the ordinary course of events, through its toxic properties'.[257] Some controversy as to the scope of the term 'poison' does exist, given that some chemical weapons release toxic properties. It is argued that the ICC definition includes gas, but excludes biological weapons.[258]

A similar discrepancy is encountered in relation to Article 8(2)(b)(xviii) of the ICC Statute, which criminalises the employment of prohibited gases, liquids, material or devices. This provision does not directly encompass biological weapons and herbicides (the toxic effects of which affects plants), nor non-lethal riot control agents.[259] Instead, it is directed against all other gases, substances or devices such that 'cause death or serious damage to health in the ordinary course of events, through its asphyxiating or toxic properties'.[260] Former and current inter-State treaties forbid the employment of all chemical weapons, asphyxiating or other deleterious gases, namely the 1899 Hague Declaration concerning Asphyxiating Gases, Article 171 of the 1919 Versailles Peace Treaty, Article 5 of the 1922 Washington Treaty on the Use of Submarines and Noxious Gases in Warfare, the 1925 Geneva Gas Protocol,[261] Article 1(1) of the 1990 US-Soviet Chemical Weapons Agreement and Article I of the 1993 Chemical Weapons Convention. Despite some reservations to the 1925 Geneva Convention, this rule seems by now to be absolute and in fact the 1993 Convention[262] prohibits the use of all chemical weapons in any circumstances and forbids reservations.[263] Contrary to the ICC Statute, under general international law it must be

---

[255] *Customary Humanitarian Law*, vol II, Part 1, 1658–1741.

[256] Art 23(a), Hague Regulations; Art 13(a), 1874 Brussels Declaration; Art 8(a), 1880 Oxford Manual; Art 16(1), 1913 Oxford Manual of Naval War; Art 3(a), ICTY Statute; Art 20(e)(i), 1996 ILC Draft Code of Crimes. See *Customary Humanitarian Law*, 1591–1603

[257] ICC Elements of Crimes, Art 8(2)(b)(xvii), num 2.

[258] Triffterer Commentary, 414–18.

[259] Triffterer Commentary, 418–20.

[260] ICC Elements of Crimes, Art 8(2)(b)(xviii), num 2. A footnote to this section makes it clear that the relevant ICC provision is the result of compromise and is not meant to limit or narrow existing or future regulation of gaseous weapons.

[261] Protocol for the Prohibition of the Use in War of Asphyxiating, Poisonous or Other Gases, and of Bacteriological Methods of Warfare.

[262] Art XXII.

[263] See also GA Res 2603 A (XXIV) (16 Dec 1969), which, with a great majority, extended the prohibition contained in the 1925 Gas Protocol to all biological and chemical weapons of warfare; UN Doc A/44/561 (4 Oct 1989), by which the GA asked the Secretary-General to investigate instances where chemical and bacteriological weapons had been used and reiterated that such weapons were illegal; SC Res 612 (9 May 1988) and 620 (26 Aug 1988), whereby the Council condemned Iraq for its use of chemical weapons as being contrary to the 1925 Gas Protocol and customary international law. See *Customary Humanitarian Law*, vol II, part 1, 1725–35.

assumed that the use of riot control agents as a method of warfare is prohibited, albeit the customary nature of this rule is doubtful. This prohibition must be distinguished from the use of agents to disperse crowds during peace time, where they are generally allowed.[264] Their prohibition as a method of warfare is derived from Article I(5) of the 1993 Chemical Weapons Convention and customary law.[265] The divergence between the ICC Statute and general international law is also evident with regard to biological weapons. Their use is expressly prohibited under all circumstances by reference to discrete multilateral treaties, particularly the 1925 Gas Protocol and the 1972 Convention on the Prohibition of the Development, Production and Stockpiling of Bacteriological (Biological) and Toxin Weapons and on their Destruction,[266] as well as on the basis of universal State practice.[267] These international instruments and State practice give rise to individual responsibility irrespective of the nature of the conflict.

Incendiary weapons,[268] which are not prohibited *per se* under the ICC Statute, constitute an instructive example of regulation by two non-conflicting general rules; they may be employed against combatants, to the degree, however, that they do not cause superfluous injury or unnecessary suffering. In practice, this means that they may not be employed directly against a combatant, but the legislation of a significant number of countries does not prohibit this out of hand.[269] Thus, with the exception of the illegality of incendiary weapons against civilians and civilian objects, their direct use against other combatants is not generally unlawful, unless the perpetrator intended solely to cause unnecessary suffering when other means of incapacitation were clearly available.

Certain types of bullets have long been the subject of prohibition because of the unnecessary suffering they entail for the victims. Article 8(2)(b)(xix) of the ICC Statute criminalises only those bullets that expand or flatten easily in the human body.[270] It does not also criminalise the use of exploding bullets and this result is confirmed by the ICC's Elements of Crimes.[271] Bullets whose casing is not sufficiently hard, those which do not entirely cover their exploding power charge, or those pierced with incisions have this effect upon impact with the human body. Exploding bullets, on the other hand, were outlawed through the 1868 St Petersburg Declaration Renouncing the Use, In Time of War, of Explosive Projectiles under 400 Grammes Weight, which as the name suggests stated that explosive or inflammable projectiles with a weight of less than 400 grams were prohibited from use in armed conflict.

---

[264] Art II(9)(d), 1993 Chemical Weapons Convention.

[265] See *Customary Humanitarian Law*, vol II, part 1, 1744–62.

[266] Art 1(2) of the 1972 Convention obliges States, *inter alia*, never to produce or employ weapons designed to use biological agents or toxins for hostile purposes or in armed conflict.

[267] *Customary Humanitarian Law*, vol II, part 1, at 1607ff.

[268] These are defined in Art 1(1) of the 1980 Protocol III on Prohibitions or Restrictions on the Use of Incendiary Weapons Additional to the 1980 Certain Conventional Weapons Convention [CCW Convention], (1980) 19 ILM 1523, as any 'weapon or munition which is primarily designed to set fire to objects or to cause burn injury to persons through the action of flame, heat, or combination thereof, produced by a chemical reaction of a substance delivered on the target'.

[269] *Customary Humanitarian Law*, vol II, part 1, at 1917ff.

[270] Early outlawed by the 1899 Hague Declaration (3) Concerning the Prohibition of Using Bullets which Expand or Flatten Easily in the Human Body, now considered to be part of customary international law.

[271] ICC Elements of Crimes, Art 8(2)(b)(xix), num 2.

Although this prohibition applies strictly in respect of land and sea warfare against civilians and combatants, under customary law it is deemed not to apply in situations concerned with air warfare.[272]

As to other specific weapons, particularly blinding laser weapons,[273] weapons primarily injuring by non-detectable fragments,[274] booby traps[275] and land mines,[276] the legality of their use is regulated by their respective conventions as well as by the basic rules of international law in each case. These are not prohibited under customary international law, so long as they do not conflict with the basic rules of international humanitarian law as analysed above. Criminal liability that arises as a result of *inter-partes* prohibitions is somewhat problematic from a jurisdictional perspective, but more importantly given that such weapons will have been provided to military personnel from the highest echelons of the military and government it is questionable whether criminal liability, rather than State responsibility, is best suited to deal with these infractions.

7.7   Violations of the Laws or Customs of War in Internal Armed Conflicts

Non-lawyers are astounded by the fact that different sets of rules regulate the conduct of hostilities and war crimes occurring in international and non-international conflicts. What is more, whereas offences perpetrated in international conflicts were long perceived as international crimes, their domestic conflict counterparts were viewed under the lens of municipal criminal law. Until the promulgation of Article 4 of the ICTR Statute in 1994 that criminalised violations committed in internal armed conflicts, the possibility that individual criminal responsibility may arise from infractions committed in the course of non-international armed conflicts was deemed contrary to the principle of non-interference in the domestic affairs of States and the case of Rwanda was considered somewhat exceptional. This view was even more reinforced by the fact that Article 3 of the ICTY Statute, a possible basis for internal armed conflict criminalisation, was unclear as to this eventuality.

---

[272] Art 18, 1923 Hague Rules of Air Warfare, which provides that 'the use of tracer, incendiary or explosive projectiles by or against aircraft is not prohibited'. See for State practice, *Customary Humanitarian Law*, vol II, part 1, 1787–94.

[273] 1995 Protocol IV on Blinding Laser Weapons, Additional to the CCW Convention, (1996) 35 ILM 1218, Art 1 of which prohibits the use of lasers the sole, or parallel, combat function of which are to cause permanent blindness. See BM Carnahan, M Robertson, 'The Protocol on Blinding Laser Weapons: A New Direction for International Humanitarian Law' (1996) 90 *American Journal of International Law* 484.

[274] Protocol I to the CCW Convention on Non-Detectable Fragments, 1342 UNTS 168, contains a single article, which prohibits any weapon the primary effect of which is to injure by fragments which in the human body escape detection by X-rays.

[275] Protocol II (as amended in 1996) to the CCW Convention on Prohibitions or Restrictions on the Use of Mines, Booby Traps and Other Devices, 2048 UNTS 133.

[276] Two sets of treaty obligations apply with respect to anti-personnel mines. Parties to the 1997 Ottawa Convention on the Prohibition of the Use, Stockpiling, Production and Transfer of Anti-Personnel Mines and on their Destruction, (1997) 36 ILM 1507, are bound under all circumstances never to use, develop, produce or acquire such weapons. On the other hand, parties solely to Protocol II to the CCW Convention are only prevented from employing mines which are designed or are of a nature to cause superfluous injury or unnecessary suffering and which are also undetectable or non self-destructing. See L Maresca, S Maslen (eds.), *The Banning of Anti-Personnel Landmines* (Cambridge, Cambridge University Press, 2000).

Although the title of Article 3 of the ICTY Statute, 'Violations of the laws or customs of war' suggests that the intention of its drafters was to limit this provision to the 1907 Hague Convention IV and the Regulations annexed to it, the Appeals Chamber in the *Tadić* jurisdiction decision held that Article 3 in fact covers all violations of international humanitarian law other than grave breaches. This therefore includes the 1907 Hague Convention, non-grave breaches provisions of the 1949 Geneva Conventions, violations of common Article 3 of the four Geneva Conventions, as well as other customary law applicable to internal conflicts and violations contained in agreements entered into by the parties to the conflict.[277] The implication of this construction of Article 3 of the ICTY Statute, which is nonetheless consistent with relevant Security Council deliberations, has been the recognition for the first time by an international judicial institution of individual criminal responsibility for offences committed in the context of non-international armed conflicts.

The *Tadić* Appeals Chamber did not hesitate to assert that violations of common Article 3 of the 1949 Geneva Conventions entail individual criminal responsibility under customary international law.[278] It is true, as categorically noted by the ICJ, that the norms prescribed in common Article 3 constitute minimum considerations of humanity.[279] Similarly, the ICTY Appeals Chamber found at the time that customary international law prohibited all attacks against civilian objects and persons no longer taking part in hostilities, as well as certain means and methods of warfare applicable to internal armed conflicts.[280] Although the international community's concern over such issues seemingly violates the rule against interference in the domestic affairs of States, it is evident that a State sovereignty-oriented approach has been gradually superseded by a human being-oriented approach.[281] Notwithstanding this universal character of international humanitarian norms governing internal conflicts, it seems unlikely that there ever existed a customary rule entailing the penalisation of these norms under international law, especially since both common Article 3 and the 1977 Protocol II were drafted purposively, that is, as minimum humanitarian considerations whose criminal aspects and prosecution would be determined exclusively at a domestic level.[282] In fact, the drafting history of the 1949 Geneva Conventions demonstrates that ICRC proposals to apply the Conventions to non-international armed conflicts were almost unanimously rejected by participating delegates. The ICRC then proposed that Convention No. IV (the Civilians Convention) be applied to internal conflicts in order to better protect civilians, but delegates noted the

---

[277] *Tadić* Appeals Jurisdiction Decision, paras 87, 89.

[278] Ibid, para 134.

[279] *Military and Paramilitary Activities in and Against Nicaragua* (Nicaragua v USA), Merits (1986) ICJ Reports 14, para 218.

[280] *Tadić* Appeals Jurisdiction Decision, para 127.

[281] Ibid, para 97.

[282] The view common among jurists is that by 1994 there was no such consensus at the inter-State level. See D Plattner, 'The Penal Repression of Violations of International Humanitarian Law Applicable in Non-International Armed Conflicts' (1990) 20 *IRRC* 414; T Meron, 'The Case for War Crimes Trials in Yugoslavia' (1993) *Foreign Affairs* 124, at 128; 'Letter dated 24 May 1994 from the Secretary General to the President of the Security Council', UN Doc S/1994/674 (1994), para 52, which reads: 'It must be observed that the violations of the law or customs of war ... are offences when committed in international, but not in internal armed conflicts', in JV Mayfield, 'The Prosecution of War Crimes and Respect for Human Rights: Ethiopia's Balancing Act' (1995) 9 *Emory International Law Review* 573.

political and technical difficulties this would entail. The conference rejected a considerable number of alternative drafts and after much effort adopted common Article 3.[283] The aforementioned discussion seeks merely to highlight the fact that contrary to the Appeals Chamber conclusion, customary international law had not until 1995 penalised violations of the laws or customs of war occurring in internal conflicts. This notwithstanding, it is undeniable that the pronouncement of such liability is laudable and is in fact now supported by a much larger number of States than prior to the establishment of the ICTY. Whatever the merits of the Appeals Chamber ruling on the criminal nature of common Article 3 in October 1995, that decision has subsequently been relied upon as authoritative by both ICTY and ICTR Chambers;[284] it has influenced the national prosecution of common Article 3 offences committed abroad and has culminated in the incorporation of an analogous and much more extensive provision in the Statute of the International Criminal Court (ICC).[285]

Under international law, there exist two types of non-international armed conflicts: internal armed disputes of any kind attaining the threshold of armed conflicts (common Article 3 conflicts) and armed disputes under Article 1(1) of the 1977 Protocol II which require that rebels occupy a substantial part of territory, attain a sufficient degree of organisation and that hostilities reach a certain degree of intensity.[286] Conflicts, even sustained, which are waged between otherwise anarchic armed groups with no responsible command, as was the case at the time of the UNOSOM II peacekeeping mission in Somalia in 1993 will not be considered as domestic armed conflicts at all. Consequently, crimes perpetrated therein will not amount to war crimes.[287] Although the 1977 Protocol II was purposely excluded from the ambit of the ICTY, it was expressly included in Article 4 of the ICTR Statute. The application of common Article 3 and Protocol II as criminal provisions is triggered by the cumulative existence of a non-international armed conflict, a link between the accused and the armed forces, the civilian nature of the victims and a nexus between the crime and the armed conflict. The accused need not necessarily be a member of the armed forces, since 'individuals legitimately mandated and expected as public officials or agents or persons otherwise holding public authority or *de facto* representing the government in support of the war effort' are deemed to be sufficiently linked to the armed forces.[288] As for the victims, although the definition of

---

[283] See DE Elder, 'The Historical Background of Common Article 3 of the Geneva Conventions of 1949' (1979) 11 *Case Western Reserve Journal of International Law* 37.

[284] *Akayesu*, Trial Judgment, para 617.

[285] Art 8(2)(c) and (e), ICC Statute. Significantly, it also influenced other treaty developments, namely the inclusion of individual criminal responsibility in non-international armed conflicts in the context of the Amended Protocol II to the CCW (Art 14), Protocol II to the Hague Convention for the Protection of Cultural Property (Arts 15 and 22), the Ottawa Convention Banning Anti-Personnel Mines (Art 9) and the Optional Protocol to the Convention on the Rights of the Child on the Involvement of Children in Armed Conflict (Art 4).

[286] See D Turns, 'War Crimes Without War? The Applicability of International Humanitarian Law to Atrocities in Non-International Armed Conflicts', (1995) 7 *African Review of International & Comparative Law* 804; HP Gasser, 'International Non-International Armed Conflicts: Case Studies of Afghanistan, Kampuchea and Lebanon' (1982) 31 *American University Law Review* 911.

[287] *Ministére Public and Others v C and B*, Brussels Military Court Judgment (17 Dec 1997).

[288] *Akayesu* Trial Judgment, para 631; *ICTR Prosecutor v Kayishema and Ruzindana*, Trial Chamber Judgment (21 May 1999), para 175.

'civilian population' is usually given negatively as consisting of persons who are not members of the armed forces,[289] the concept of 'civilians' includes those accompanying armed forces, those who are either attached to them, or those who are among combatants engaged in hostilities.[290] In accordance with Article 13(3) of Protocol II, 'civilians' enjoy protection unless and for such time as they take a direct part in hostilities. 'Civilian populations' by their very nature are presumed not to take part in hostilities and are, therefore, entitled to general protection. Thus, the legal status of civilians is the same as that encountered in international armed conflicts, *mutatis mutandis*.

In the *Kayishema* case, the ICTR ascertained the existence of a Protocol II type conflict between governmental Rwandan forces (FAR) and dissident armed forces (RPF). It found the RPF to be under the responsible command of General Kagame, to have exercised control over part of Rwanda, and to have been able to carry out sustained and concerted military action, as well as implement international humanitarian law.[291] It found, however, the Tutsi victims of the specific assault not to have been attacked by either the FAR or the RPF at the localities they sought refuge in Kibuye prefecture. It held the massacres to have been undertaken by civilian authorities as a result of an extermination campaign against the Tutsis, with no proof that either the victims or the offences against them were directly related to the conflict, and thus concluded that Protocol II was inapplicable in that case.[292]

7.7.1 Specific Internal Armed Conflict War Crimes

Having overcome the obstacle of international criminal liability in the context of international armed conflicts, one is next concerned with the range of applicable crimes. A wholesale importation of grave breaches and other war crimes into the realm of non-international armed conflicts is precluded by the following considerations: a) treaty limitations, particularly the specific applicability of grave breaches to international conflicts. The same is true for the majority of pre-1995 treaties[293] or lack thereof, none of which categorically provides for criminal liability. Thus reliance can only be placed on the existence of customary war crimes, or a revision of these treaties, or their re-interpretation by States – which would probably amount to a new custom anyway; b) the status of participants and the general legal context of international armed conflicts are determined solely by international law. In domestic conflicts these elements are determined to a very large degree by domestic law. Thus, in a domestic conflict, while government forces are obliged to treat members of the dissident group humanely, they may validly declare the dissident cause, armed fight and participation therein as a criminal offence, irrespective of whether dissident forces satisfy the four criteria of combatant status enunciated in Article 4 of Geneva

---

[289] 1977 Protocol I, Art 50.
[290] *Kayishema* Trial Judgment, para 180.
[291] Ibid, para 172.
[292] Ibid, paras 602–03.
[293] One notable exception is Art 1 of the 1993 Chemical Weapons Convention.

Convention III. As a result, whereas such persons would be lawful combatants and benefit from prisoner of war (POW) status in international armed conflicts, they would not benefit from POW status while engaged in non-international conflicts. Thus, the largest part of Geneva Convention III (POW Convention) is automatically inapplicable to domestic conflicts.[294] Equally, the international law of occupation cannot apply to government forces anywhere in the territory of the State; c) finally, dissident forces are unlikely to be able to establish lawfully constituted and impartial tribunals, because for reasons noted above they have no authority to establish tribunals under domestic law. Equally, they cannot occupy territory for the purposes of the law of occupation and as such, for example, cannot commit the offence described in Article 49 of Geneva Convention IV, which concerns the transfer of one's own population to change the demographics of a particular area.

The aforementioned considerations, therefore, severely restrict the importation of the whole range of international conflict war crimes into domestic armed disputes. The drafters of the ICC Statute wisely balanced these realities with the need to protect all human beings from the calamities of war and the corruption of authority where impunity is present. Much like other war crimes, therefore, the ICC Statute recognises two types of internal armed conflict war crimes, depending on their source in law: a) common Article 3 violations,[295] and; b) 'other serious violations of the laws and customs' applicable to non-international armed conflicts.[296] As these two categories are meant to be exhaustive in their enumeration of war crimes, it is sensible from a purely legal point of view that there are no prohibited weapons provisions analogous to those applicable in international conflicts. The other three categories are, nonetheless, present. In all other respects, the ICC Statute has implemented what is logical after all. Thus, it has generally criminalised existing portions of the *jus in bello* applicable to internal armed conflicts and has moreover imported those international conflict war crimes that by logical extension should apply in domestic conflicts.

Targeting crimes comprise those in Article 8(2)(e), subparagraphs (i), (ii), (iii), (iv), while means and methods of combat crimes include Article 8(2)(c), subparagraphs (i), (ii), (iii), (e)(v), (e)(vi), (e)(vii), (e)(ix), (e)(x), (e)(xi), (e)(xii). War crimes against civilian populations encompass the following: passing of sentences and executions without previous judgment of a lawfully constituted court affording all judicial guarantees;[297] ordering the displacement of the civilian population for reasons related to the conflict, unless this is demanded by imperative military necessity and the security of the civilians.[298] Before the close of this chapter it is sensible to view in more detail one particular war crime that does not feature in the Statutes of the ICC, the ICTY or the ICTR, but is instead a prominent offence within the framework of

---

[294] However, Rowe correctly suggests that due to the lack of combatant status in domestic armed conflicts, a member of a dissident group detained by his own side will benefit from the relevant provisions and any harm caused to him will be deemed a war crime. P Rowe, 'War Crimes' in D McGoldrick *et al*, *The Permanent International Criminal Court* (Oxford, Hart Publishing, 2004) 229.

[295] Art 8(2)(c), ICC Statute.
[296] Art 8(2)(e), ICC Statute.
[297] Art 8(2)(c)(iv), ICC Statute.
[298] Art 8(2)(e)(vii), ICC Statute.

the Sierra Leone Special Court; this is the war crime of inflicting collective punishments. Although it is also a crime under customary international law applicable in international armed conflicts, its more recent utilisation has been in non-international armed conflicts.

7.7.2   The War Crime of Inflicting Collective Punishments

The imposition of collective punishments on mainly civilian populations has existed for some time as a tactic aimed at forcing such populations to either give up combatants affiliated to them or in order to punish them for supporting the enemy, whether morally or physically. In fact, during WWII this was extensively practiced by German armed forces in occupied territory and civilians were routinely executed for acts of sabotage committed by guerrillas.[299] The defence put forward by the perpetrators was that such acts were reprisals in retaliation to the killing of German soldiers by the local population – this defence would be unavailable today because reprisals against civilians are prohibited at all times. Military tribunals acknowledged the legality of reprisals at the time, but found that in all cases the perpetrators had by far exceeded all sense of proportionality, necessity and fundamental considerations of humanity (essentially the Martens clause).[300] This absolute prohibition was subsequently recognised in Article 33 of Geneva Convention IV,[301] which criminalised both collective punishments, for offences not personally committed, 'and likewise all measures of intimidation or of terrorism'. There is thus a clear nexus between the infliction of collective punishment and terrorism in the broad armed conflict sense, the ultimate aim of which is the intimidation of a civilian population. Collective punishments were equally outlawed in Article 4(2)(b) of Protocol II (1977).[302] The ICRC Commentary in explaining the position of the drafters noted that the prohibition against collective punishments:

> ... should be understood in its widest sense, and concerns not only penalties imposed in the normal judicial process, but also any other kind of sanction (such as confiscation of property) ... In fact, to include the prohibition on collective punishments amongst the acts unconditionally prohibited by Article 4 is virtually equivalent to prohibiting reprisals against protected persons.[303]

---

[299] *USA v List* (Hostages case), 11 Trials 759; *In Re von Mackensen and Maelzer*, 13 AD 258; *In Re Kappler*, 15 AD 471. R Provost, *International Human Rights and Humanitarian Law* (Cambridge, Cambridge University Press, 2002) 185–95.

[300] *Haas and Priebke* case, Rome Military Court of Appeal, Judgment (7 Mar 1998), at 1.1.4. In the case at hand, the accused executed 335 civilians in retaliation for the killing of 33 German military personnel.

[301] Although it was also iterated in Art 50, Hague Regulations. Moreover, Art 87 of Geneva Convention III prohibits the imposition of collective punishment against POWs in retaliation to individual acts.

[302] Art 75(2)(d) of Protocol I (1977) lists among its fundamental guarantees the prohibition of collective punishments.

[303] ICRC Commentary, at 1374.

Article 3(b) of the Special Court of Sierra Leone (SLSC) Statute incorporates verbatim its counterpart from Protocol II. The Special Court has defined 'punishment' for the purpose of collective punishment:

> as an indiscriminate punishment imposed collectively on persons for omissions or acts which some or none of them may or may not have been responsible. As such, a 'punishment' is distinct from the targeting of protected persons as objects of attack. The targeting of protected persons as objects of war crimes and crimes against humanity may not necessarily be predicated upon a perceived transgression by such persons and therefore does not constitute collective punishments. Thus, the *mens rea* element of collective punishments represents the critical difference between this crime and the crime of targeting. While targeting takes place on account of who the victims are, or are perceived to be, the crime of collective punishments occurs in response to the acts or omissions of protected persons, whether real or perceived.[304]

As a result, the fact that the perpetrator has committed other crimes, such as murder or pillage, against a particular group of persons, does not mean that the offence of collective punishments has been subsumed within these. Rather, because the crime of collective punishments requires proof of an intention to punish collectively, whereas other crimes do not, it can be charged cumulatively with other offences.[305]

---

[304] *SCSL Prosecutor v Fofana and Kondewa*, Appeals Chamber Judgment (CDF case) (28 May 2008), para 223; *RUF* Trial Judgment, paras 125–27.
[305] *CDF* Appeals Judgment, para 225.

8

Crimes Against Humanity

8.1 Origins of the Concept

The concept of crimes against humanity was first articulated as an international offence in Article 6(c) of the Charter of the Nuremberg Tribunal in 1945.[1] This read as follows:

> Crimes against Humanity: namely, murder, extermination, enslavement, deportation, and other inhumane acts committed against any civilian population, before or during the war,[2] or persecutions on political, racial or religious grounds in execution of, or in connection with any other crime within the jurisdiction of the Tribunal, whether or not in violation of the domestic law of the country where perpetrated.

Prior to the Nuremberg Charter, reference to the 'laws of humanity' and the 'dictates of public conscience' was expressly made in the preamble to the 1907 Hague Convention IV – otherwise known as the Martens clause – the aim of which was to extend additional protection to both combatants and civilian populations where the law was silent or in development until such time as more comprehensive rules were adopted. Following the massacre of a large part of the Armenian population under orders of what was then the Ottoman Empire, the Governments of Great Britain, France and Russia issued a declaration denouncing the atrocities as 'crimes against humanity and civilisation', further noting the criminal culpability of all members of the Turkish Government and its agents.[3] This formulation, however, was not the result of normative considerations and the initial Russian proposal was to treat the offences as 'crimes against Christianity', to which France objected on the grounds that it would offend the Muslim subjects of itself and Britain. The 1920 Peace Treaty of Sèvres which made provision for the trial of those Turkish officials responsible for violating the laws and customs of war and of engaging in the Armenian massacres

---

[1] 1945 Agreement for the Prosecution and Punishment of the Major War Criminals of the European Axis, 82 UNTS 279. See E Schwelb, 'Crimes Against Humanity' (1946) 23 *British Yearbook of International Law* 178; B Van Schaack, 'The Definition of Crimes Against Humanity: Resolving the Incoherence' (1999) 37 *Columbia Journal of Transnational* Law 787.

[2] The original text of Art 6(c) included a semicolon between the words 'war' and 'or', which conveyed a meaning that was not intended by the drafters (ie that crimes against humanity were a particular manifestation of the offence of persecution). As a result, a Protocol Rectifying the Discrepancy in the IMT Charter was adopted on 6 October 1946, which replaced the semicolon with a comma.

[3] R Clark, 'Crimes Against Humanity at Nuremberg' in G Ginsburg, VN Kudriavtsev (eds) *The Nuremberg Trial in International Law,* (The Hague, Kluwer, 1990) 177. See also the discussion in chapter 9.1 where the Armenian massacres are related to the crime of genocide.

during the war, but excluding reference to the 'laws of humanity',[4] was superseded by the 1923 Treaty of Lausanne which contained a declaration of amnesty for all offences committed between 1914 and 1922.[5] However, as Cherif Bassiouni points out, the political motivations behind this compromise could not guise the fact that amnesties are only granted for crimes, which even if not prosecuted does not negate their existence in both law and fact.[6] It is true, nonetheless, that up to that point the term 'humanity' and its link to 'crime' had no fixed legal meaning. 'Humanity' was employed in a non-technical sense and was meant to convey a rather vague array of sentiments and denote the existence of a large number of underlying victims, rather than refer to a punishable offence as such.

Immediately upon conclusion of the First World War the Allied and Associated Powers established in 1919 a Commission on the Responsibility of the Authors of the War and Enforcement of Penalties.[7] The majority of the Commission supported the establishment of a tribunal with criminal jurisdiction over all persons belonging to enemy countries that were found to have violated the laws of war or the laws of humanity.[8] United States' dissent over the precision and uncertain scope of the term laws of humanity prevailed against endorsing the Commission's position and so the 1919 Peace Treaty of Versailles excluded reference to crimes against humanity.[9] Given our previous analysis about the indeterminate and non-technical invocation of this particular construction, such dissent was certainly legally sustainable, even if it served to preclude the development of the law in respect of mass scale atrocities.

The rationale for constructing this particular international offence stems from the fact that in the aftermath of the Second World War the victorious nations came to the realisation that international law failed to criminalise the perpetration of large-scale offences against one's own population – not that extermination of enemy populations was treated with anything more than a charge of war crimes. In the case at hand, the Nazi regime had instituted laws and policies that were designed to persecute its Jewish population, or at best drive them out of Germany and confiscate their properties. Moreover, during the war from 1939 until 1945, it is well known that the German government put forward a well-designed mechanism to decimate the Jewish population from occupied territories, as well as within Germany and towards this aim set up extermination camps. Extermination policies also took place against other German nationals, namely certain members of the Church, the invalid or mentally sick, Gypsies and dissenters. Crimes against one's own population, although generally subject to severe condemnation, were not considered international crimes prior to 1939 and thus did not incur the liability of their perpetrators. Equally,

---

[4] Treaty of Peace between the Allied Powers and Turkey (Treaty of Sèvres), Arts 226, 230, (1921 Supp) 15 *American Journal of International Law* 179.

[5] Treaty of Peace between the Allied Powers and Turkey (Treaty of Lausanne), 28 LNTS 12.

[6] CM Bassiouni, *Crimes Against Humanity in International Criminal Law* (Leiden, Martinus Nijhoff, 1992) 175–76.

[7] Commission on the Responsibility of the Authors of the War and on Enforcement of Penalties, Report Presented to the Preliminary Peace Conference (Versailles, 29 March 1919), reprinted in (1920) 14 *American Journal of International Law* 95.

[8] 'All persons belonging to enemy countries, however high their position may have been, without distinction or rank, including Chiefs of Staff, who have been guilty of offences against the laws and customs of war or the laws of humanity, are liable to criminal prosecution'. Ibid, at 123.

[9] 2 Bevans 43.

international humanitarian law at the time only criminalised, if at all, war crimes committed in international armed conflicts and then only when inflicted against enemy combatants and civilians, thus excluding one's own civilian population. As a result, Nazi atrocities against German Jews and other civilians could only be tried as individual or collective murders under German criminal law. This outcome would have been absurd, given that the Holocaust was by far the most serious collective act of brutality of the war and as such could not be left to the device of ordinary criminal law. It was no wonder, therefore, that this *new* international crime was created, which although failed to strictly satisfy the requirements against retroactive penal legislation, was certainly foreseeable to its authors.[10] Moreover, it is obvious that the creation of this offence did not only serve the purposes of fair labelling or of stigmatisation, which is the very purpose of genocide, the gravity of which can equally be served by crimes against humanity; rather, its drafters had a very real and practical situation in mind.

The original definition in Article 6(c) of the IMT Statute was limited in certain respects. It was conditioned on the existence of other crimes, namely war crimes and crimes against peace, in the sense that if acts otherwise amounting to crimes against humanity were not undertaken within the context of the two aforementioned offences their authors could not be prosecuted by the IMT. This was merely a contextual element in its definition and not one pertaining to its subjective or objective elements. As a result, in order to substantiate a charge of crimes against humanity from the time it was alleged that a plan to exterminate the Jewish people was being formulated, that is in the early 1930s, it was imperative that the prosecutors put forward evidence showing that a war of aggression was also being planned during the same time. However, the Tribunal opined that such evidence was not available so as to allow it without doubt to make a determination of this nature and subsequently confined its jurisdiction for crimes against humanity to events taking place on or after the invasion of Poland, ie September 1939. Even so, the requirement that crimes against humanity be linked to war crimes necessarily entails the existence of war or armed conflict, which constitutes yet another contextual limitation in the definition of this new offence. Both of these contextual limitations (ie the link to war crimes and crimes against peace) soon disappeared and the so-called nexus to armed conflict was never again required in treaty and customary law,[11] save much later in Article 5 of the International Criminal Tribunal for Yugoslavia (ICTY) Statute, albeit its chambers were quick to emphasise its discrepancy with customary law. The definition in Article 6 of the IMT Charter in respect of the enumerated acts that may give rise to crimes

---

[10] For a discussion against retroactivity of criminal laws, see chapter 1.7.2.

[11] Unlike the Nuremberg Charter, Control Council Law No 10, enacted by the Allied Control Council for Germany (hence, it did not have the attributes of a treaty), excluded the requirement that crimes against humanity be committed in execution of or in connection with war crimes or crimes against peace. While some military tribunals entertaining cases pursuant to Control Council Law No 10 accepted that crimes against humanity could also be committed in time of peace, others did not. See WJ Fenrick, 'Should Crimes Against Humanity Replace War Crimes?' (1999) 37 *Columbia Journal of Transnational Law* 767, at 775; both the 1968 UN Convention on the Non-Applicability of Statutory Limitations to War Crimes and Crimes Against Humanity, 754 UNTS 73, as well as the 1974 European Convention on the Non-Applicability of Statutory Limitations to Crimes Against Humanity and War Crimes, ETS 82, referred to the definitions of the Nuremberg Charter and the 1948 Genocide Convention respectively. To this date they are sparsely ratified.

against humanity has equally expanded significantly since its adoption and now includes conduct such as enforced disappearances, apartheid, torture, rape and others, as will be explained in another section of this chapter. This means that persecution is but one type of conduct that may constitute crimes against humanity and not the only. As a result of these observations it is fair to say that the definition of crimes against humanity has moved on significantly from its original construction.

Unlike other international crimes, such as genocide, war crimes and torture that are defined at least in one multilateral treaty – in addition to regional treaties – crimes against humanity were not defined in this manner until their incorporation in 1998 in the ICC Statute. In the interim period reliance was placed on the IMT Charter and the jurisprudence of the Nuremberg Tribunal – particularly in respect of persons accused of WW II-related offences, although these judgments were not always in conformity with customary international law[12] – and soft law, such as the ICL Draft Code of Crimes against the Peace and Security of Mankind and Security Council resolutions setting up the ad hoc tribunals, such as the ICTY and ICTR. However, given the absence of a single and universally accepted definition, all of these instruments and national judgments eroded, expanded and bypassed many of the limitations of Article 6 of the Nuremberg Charter. Hence, in some respects the absence of a concrete treaty formulation following the IMT Charter paradigm was more of a blessing than a curse, particularly if one contrasts this state of affairs with the rigid definition of genocide that has placed significant limitations on international courts and law-makers, as is the case with its narrow range of potential victim groups. Even the ICC Statute formulation, given the political considerations underpinning its adoption, cannot be said to definitively represent the last word on crimes against humanity, although it is certainly closer than any other international instrument in this regard. As already explained, this lack of rigidity is not necessarily a bad thing, since the concept is able to adapt itself to new forms of mass criminality, some of which are not always evident. Let us now proceed to examine its constitutive elements.

8.2   The Fundamental Elements of the Offence and the Meaning of 'Attack'

The crime against humanity provision in Article 5 of the ICTY Statute was the first new post Cold War international normative formulation of the offence. The relevant

---

[12]   In the *Barbie* case, French Court of Cassation Judgment (1988) 100 ILR 330, at 332, 336, the accused who was the Head of the Gestapo in Lyon from 1942 to 1944 was convicted of crimes against humanity for his role in the deportation and extermination of Jewish civilians. The court held that the definition of crimes against humanity within the meaning of the Nuremberg definition consisted of enumerated inhumane acts against civilians 'performed in a systematic manner in the name of the State practising by those means a policy of ideological supremacy'. The Court of Cassation thus viewed crimes against humanity as being premised on persecution; see also *Touvier* case, French Court of Cassation Judgment (1992) 100 ILR 337, and *R v Finta,* Canadian Supreme Court Judgment (1994) 104 ILR 284, which agreed on this point. This requirement of persecutory intent recognised in the *Finta* judgment was subsequently overturned by the Supreme Court in *Mugesera v Canada (Minister of Citizenship and Immigration)* (2005) SCC 40, because it was no longer in conformity with ICTY/ICTR jurisprudence, which as will become evident later on in this chapter was confined only to the crime against humanity of persecution.

ICTY and ICTR jurisprudence has been largely responsible for its rapid evolution and detailed elaboration. In the present section of this chapter we shall confine our analysis to the ad hoc tribunals' articulation of the offence and in the latter part of the chapter we shall analyse the particularities of the ICC definition. By and large these elements are common under customary international law, save for one notable exception that will be duly pointed out.

Article 5 of the ICTY Statute requires that crimes against humanity be committed in the context of an on-going armed conflict, whether international or internal in character, of which the particular attack on the targeted civilian population is an integral feature. Hence, the five elements that comprise this offence under the ICTY Statute are: (a) the existence of an overarching attack; (b) the perpetrator's conduct must be part of the attack; (c) the attack must be directed against any civilian population; (d) the attack must be widespread or systematic; and (e) the perpetrator must know of the wider context in which his conduct occurs and as a result must be aware that his conduct constitutes part of the attack.

As already explained, the ICTY definition curiously required demonstration of the contextual element of a nexus between crimes against humanity and that of an armed conflict, in similar manner with the Nuremberg Charter, regardless however of the nature of the conflict. The ICTY Appeals Chamber in the *Tadić* Interlocutory Decision on Jurisdiction held that Article 5 was narrower than customary international law, which no longer requires any nexus to armed conflict.[13] This aspect of customary law (that is, the absence of a nexus to armed conflict) is reflected in Article 3 of the ICTR Statute, which, however, requires the existence of a discriminatory intent on national, political, ethnic, racial or religious grounds. Discriminatory intent in Article 5 of the ICTY Statute is required only with regard to the specific offence of persecution. Finally, unlike Article 6(c) of the Nuremberg Charter, Article 5 of the ICTY Statute does not require that crimes against humanity be connected to any other offences, as is also the case with the ICTR and the statutes of all subsequent tribunals, ad hoc, permanent and hybrid.

Within a year following the adoption of the ICTY Statute the drafters of the ICTR Statute realised that the customary elements of the definition of the offence required explicit elaboration. As a result, Article 3 of the ICTR Statute qualifies an attack as constituting a crime against humanity when it is perpetrated in either widespread or systematic fashion. This 'widespread or systematic' requirement that pertains to the nature of attacks, although not expressly articulated in Article 5 of the ICTY Statute, is consonant with the long-standing customary definition of crimes against humanity and was early elaborated by ICTY chambers.[14] It should be pointed out that the concept of 'attack' in the definition of crimes against humanity is significantly broader than that used in the context of the laws of war, and particularly Article 49(1) of the 1977 Additional Protocol I, since it 'may also encompass situations of mistreatment of persons taking no active part in hostilities, such as someone in detention',[15] in addition to purely civilian populations. It is also distinct from its counterpart in the *jus in bello* from the fact that it does not relate to a single incident

---

[13] *ICTY Prosecutor v Tadić*, Appeals Jurisdiction Decision (2 Oct 1995), paras 140–41.
[14] *ICTY Prosecutor v Nikolić*, R 61 Decision (20 Oct 1995), para 26.
[15] *ICTY Prosecutor v Kunarac and Others*, Trial Chamber Judgment (22 Feb 2001), para 416.

or military targeting, as the ordinary meaning of the term may otherwise suggest. An attack for the purposes of crimes against humanity presupposes a number of underlying offences that taken as a whole give form and existence to a campaign against a targeted group. Whereas each underlying offence would individually amount to a war crime, taken cumulatively they give rise to an 'attack'. The underlying offence does not need to constitute an attack (ie it need not be widespread or systematic), but must form part of, or be linked with the attack, which itself is the crime against humanity and not the underlying offences *per se*.[16] An 'attack' is therefore an accumulation of various crimes, not necessarily perpetrated at the same time and place, but which taken individually are an integral part of a policy or widespread occurrence. An individual offence, no matter its gravity, does not amount to a crime against humanity if it is not connected to an ongoing attack, in the manner described. It is interesting to note that in terms of ICTY temporal jurisdiction, although the attack must be part of the armed conflict, it can outlast it.[17]

Let us proceed to examine each of the constitutive elements of the offence of crimes against humanity in more detail. Following our assessment of the concept of 'attack' it is only prudent to delve into the list of underlying crimes through which a crime against humanity can be substantiated.

8.2.1 The Underlying Offences

The list of underlying offences that constitute an 'attack' for the purposes of the concept of crimes against humanity is exhaustive in the statutes of the ICTY, ICTR and the ICC; moreover, they are identical in the first two. As a result, we shall proceed to first examine those found in the ICTY and ICTR statutes, followed by the two residual offences enumerated in the ICC Statute.[18] As regards the underlying crimes that are common to all three statutes, any differences found in the ICC context will be pointed out. The reader should also refer to the analysis in the chapters dealing with war crimes and offences against the person, where these underlying offences are elaborated in more detail. The remainder of the section will offer an analysis of other offences not listed in any of these instruments, which nonetheless have the capacity to bring about the same result.

(a) **Murder**. This offence necessitates as a matter of result the death of the victim, caused by an act or omission of the accused, or of a person or persons for whose acts or omissions the accused bears criminal responsibility. The accused is liable not only where he acted with *dolus directus* of the first and second degree to kill the victim, but

---

[16] *ICTY Prosecutor v Mrkšić [Vukovar Hospital* case], R 61 Decision (3 Apr 1996), para 30; *ICTY Prosecutor v Tadić*, Appeal Chamber Judgment (15 Jul 1999), para 248; *ICTY Prosecutor v Kunarac*, Appeal Chamber Judgment (12 Jun 2002), para. 96; *ICTY Prosecutor v Blaškić*, Appeal Chamber Judgment (29 Jul 2004), para 102.

[17] *Kunarac* Trial Judgment, para 420.

[18] Given the particular mental element requirements in Art 30 of the ICC Statute, the following analysis is limited to the ICTY jurisprudence. For a better understanding of the mental element in the ICC Statute see chapter 2.

also in circumstances where he intended to inflict serious harm and the victim died as a result of his or her wounds. Therefore, a degree of recklessness is inherent in the customary definition of murder.[19]

(b) **Extermination**. Unlike murder where the killing of a single person suffices for liability to arise, extermination may be defined as 'killing on a large scale', which includes, other than direct acts of killing, subjecting a widespread number of people, or systematically subjecting a number of people, to conditions of living that would inevitably lead to their death.[20] This may encompass the withdrawal of food or other necessary items or consumables that sustain life.[21] Liability for extermination arises only in respect of persons whose conduct contributes to killing on a large scale, even if their part was indirect. Thus, the killing of a single person would not amount to extermination, but murder.[22] Hence, like persecution, this is a collective crime in terms of the multiplicity of victims. Whereas the ICTY/ICTR jurisprudence rightly do not require that the aim or effect of an extermination must have been to destroy a group in whole or in part – as is the case with genocide – Article 7(2)(b) of the ICC Statute does, albeit this requirement is not in conformity with customary law. As for the applicable *mens rea*, the accused must have intended to kill a large number of individuals or intentionally expose them to conditions of life, or inflict upon them serious bodily harm, in the reasonable knowledge that in both situations the death of the victims was likely.[23]

(c) **Enslavement**. This offence is the same as that of slavery and consists of the intentional exercise of any, or all, of the powers of ownership over a person.[24] This includes a significantly broad range of conduct. The ICC Elements of Crimes indicatively encompass the purchase, sale, lending or bartering of persons by imposing on them a similar deprivation of liberty. This includes not only trafficking in persons, particularly women and children, but also forced labor as well as the range of offences found in the 1957 Supplementary Slavery Convention, namely debt bondage, bride-price, illegal adoptions and serfdom.[25]

(d) **Deportation**. This offence entails 'the forced displacement of persons by expulsion or other forms of coercion from the area in which they are lawfully present, across a *de jure* State border or, in certain circumstances, a *de facto* border, without grounds permitted under international law'.[26] On the other hand, 'forcible transfer' refers to displacement within national boundaries. Under the ICC Elements of Crimes the 'forced' nature of deportation is not limited to physical force, but may

---

[19] See *ICTY Prosecutor v Delalić et al* [*Čelebići* case] Trial Chamber Judgment, (16 Nov 1998), para 439; *ICTY Prosecutor v Kupreškić et al*, Trial Judgment (14 Jun 2000), para 561.

[20] See *ICTY Prosecutor v Krstić*, Trial Chamber Judgment (2 Aug 2001), para 503. *ICTR Prosecutor v Ntakirutimana*, Appeals Chamber Judgment (13 Dec. 2004), paras 516, 522; *ICTY Prosecutor v Stakić*, Appeals Chamber Judgment (22 Mar 2006), paras 259–60; *ICTY Prosecutor v Vasiljević*, Trial Chamber Judgment (29 Nov 2002), para 229.

[21] Art 7(2)(b) ICC Statute.

[22] *Vasiljević* Trial Judgment, para 227; *ICTR Prosecutor v Kajelijeli*, Trial Chamber Judgment (1 Dec 2003), para 893.

[23] *Vasiljević* Trial Judgment, paras 228–29; *ICTY Prosecutor v Stakić*, Trial Chamber Judgment (31 Jul 2003), para 641.

[24] See *ICTY Prosecutor v Krnojelac*, Trial Chamber Judgment (15 Mar 2002), para 350; *Kunarac* Trial Judgment, paras 515ff.

[25] ICC Elements of Crimes, Art 7(1)(c), num 1.

[26] Art 7(1)(d) ICC Statute.

include 'threat of force or coercion, such as that caused by fear or violence, duress, detention, psychological oppression, or abuse of power against such person or another person, or by taking advantage of a coercive environment'.[27] Naturally, if an act of forced displacement is committed on discriminatory grounds it also constitutes persecution.[28] The accused must intend to remove the target population by means of force. The relevant jurisprudence suggests, although not uniformly, that the perpetrator need not intend to render the displacement permanent.[29] This is certainly the right approach, given that whether or not the perpetrator intends the displacement to be permanent is irrelevant, because it is not something he or she can definitely control. It is sufficient that in any particular circumstances the accused intended to bring about the displacement.

(e) **Imprisonment**. The ICTY jurisprudence has found the following elements as essential for a finding of the crime of imprisonment: a) deprivation of liberty; b) such deprivation is imposed arbitrarily, that is without any legal justification; c) the act or omission leading to such deprivation of physical liberty is performed with the intent to deprive a person arbitrarily of his or her physical liberty, or in the reasonable knowledge that his act or omission is likely to cause arbitrary deprivation of physical liberty.[30]

(f) **Torture**. This offence is described elsewhere in this book as a war crime and as a distinct crime under international law.[31] In short, it 'means the intentional infliction of severe pain or suffering, whether physical or mental, upon a person in the custody or under the control of the accused; torture [does] not include pain or suffering arising [inherently or incidental] from lawful sanctions'.[32]

(g) **Rape**. Rape, sexual slavery, enforced prostitution, forced pregnancy and enforced sterilisation, as opposed to lesser forms of sexual abuse, is described in detail as a war crime.[33] In each case, the invasion of the body, liberty, or one's sexuality is accomplished under coercion. It should be stressed that the ambit of offences of a sexual nature comprising crimes against humanity has been considerably expanded in the ICC Statute in comparison to the ICTY and ICTR, including besides rape, 'sexual slavery, enforced prostitution, forced pregnancy, enforced sterilisation, or any other form of sexual violence of comparable gravity'.[34] Fears from western countries that reference to 'forced pregnancy' might be interpreted as affecting national laws relating to the right to life of the unborn or that of a mother regarding the termination of her pregnancy were removed with the addition of paragraph 2(f).

[27] ICC Elements of Crimes, Art 7(1)(d), num 1.

[28] *ICTY Prosecutor v Blaškić*, Appeal Chamber Judgment (29 Jul 2004), paras 152–53. Equally, forcible transfer may amount to 'other inhumane acts'; confirmed in *ICTY Prosecutor v Blagoević and Jokić*, Trial Chamber Judgement (17 Jan 2005), paras 629–30.

[29] See *Stakić* Appeals Judgment, para 278. In *ICTY Prosecutor v Simić, Tadić and Zarić*, Trial Chamber Judgment (17 Oct 2003), para 134, it was held, contrary to the *Stakić* judgment, that deportation requires an intent to permanently remove the victims.

[30] . See *Krnojelac* Trial Judgment, para 15; *ICTY Prosecutor v Kordić and Čerkez*, Trial Chamber Judgment (26 Feb 2001), paras 302–03. These elements are unchallenged in the ICC Statute and its Elements of Crimes, Art 7(1)(e).

[31] See chapters 7.2.2 and 10.2.

[32] Art 7(29)(e) ICC Statute.

[33] See chapter 7.3.2.

[34] Art 7(1)(g), ICC Statute.

Similarly, to allay the concerns of Moslem countries that the definition of torture might affect their practice of corporal punishment, paragraph 2(e) excludes pain or suffering arising from lawful sanctions.

(h) **Persecution** on political, racial and religious grounds. The *actus reus* of persecution in the ICTY jurisprudence consists of an act or omission that discriminates in fact and which denies or infringes upon a fundamental right laid down in international customary or treaty law[35] by reason of the identity of a group or collectivity.[36] Thus, the violation of a fundamental right is a strict requirement of the offence. Besides the three traditional bases of discrimination under customary international law, Article 7(1)(h) of the ICC Statute has added four new ones; namely, ethnic, national, cultural and gender grounds. Moreover, the same provision makes it clear that the list is not exhaustive and the discriminatory purpose covers any 'other grounds that are universally recognised as impermissible under international law'.[37] The *Kupreškić* judgment held that the *actus reus* for persecution in the ICTY Statute does not require a link to crimes enumerated elsewhere in the Statute, albeit by reason of it being a broad offence, its definition may encompass crimes not listed in the Statute. However, there must be 'clearly defined limits on the expansion of the types of acts which qualify as persecution'.[38]

The discrimination has to be manifested through an external act that itself must amount to a criminal offence. Should this be limited to violent crimes such as murder, or can it also encompass non-violent crimes? The jurisprudence of the ICTY clearly suggests that persecutory acts are not confined to physical or violent acts; rather, they consist also of conduct of an 'economic or judicial nature that violates an individual's right to the equal enjoyment of his basic rights'.[39] Naturally, not every economic or property-related offence that is perpetrated on discriminatory grounds should amount to persecution. For example, the discriminatory confiscation or destruction of property will only be defined as persecution if its effects are tantamount to a forced transfer or deportation.[40] The *mens rea* requires that the act was carried out deliberately with the intention to discriminate on the basis of anyone of the grounds already listed. The subjective element for the particular act of persecution is higher than ordinary offences falling within the ambit of crimes against humanity, but lower than genocide. In the crime of persecution, the discriminatory intent may take many inhumane forms, while in genocide it must strictly be accompanied by the specific intent *(dolus specialis)* for genocide, that is, to destroy in whole or in part a specific group.[41]

As regards the place of persecution in the ICC Statute, it has to be noted that many delegates at the Rome conference expressed concern that this provision could be used to criminalise all forms of discrimination. To alleviate such fears it was finally agreed that persecution as a crime against humanity in the ICC context refers only to

---

[35] See *Krnojelac* Trial Judgment, para 431; *Blaškić* Appeals Judgment, para 131.

[36] Equally, in Art 7(2)(g) ICC Statute.

[37] This general expansive interpretation of the applicable discriminatory bases was also accepted in the ICTY jurisprudence. See *Blaškić* Appeal Judgment, para 139, albeit they must be of such gravity that is equal to other crimes under Art 5 of the ICTY Statute. *Krnojelac* Appeal Judgment, para 221.

[38] *Kupreškić* Trial Judgment, paras 581, 618; *Kordić and Čerkez,* Trial Judgment, paras 193–94.

[39] *ICTY Prosecutor v Tadić*, Trial Chamber Judgment (7 May 1997), para 710.

[40] *Kupreškić* Trial Judgment, para 631.

[41] See *Kupreškić* Trial Judgment, ibid, paras 627, 636.

extreme forms of discrimination with a clear criminal character. Furthermore, persecution can only be characterised as a crime against humanity if it is connected to any of the other ten enumerated acts articulated in Article 7 or any other offence within the court's jurisdiction (that is, war crimes, genocide, or aggression), notwithstanding that such nexus is not required by the ICTY and ICTR or customary law.[42] There is no need to prove that the connected acts themselves were committed on a widespread or systematic scale; however, if found to be connected to severe criminal persecution, this, in effect, furnishes evidence of either widespread crimes or a particular policy.

(i) **Other inhumane acts**. This was designed deliberately as a residual category whose drafters felt did not require exhaustive enumeration because its purpose was to encompass all serious conduct that was not otherwise found within the list of acts that give rise to crimes against humanity. This open-endedness, however, was rightly construed as offending the principle of specificity in domestic and international criminal law because it is lacking in precision, to say the least.[43] The offence was retained in the ICC Statute (Article 7(1)(k)) and together with the ICTY reached a compromise solution that this crime consists of conduct that is of a similar character to other crimes in their respective statutes by which the perpetrator intentionally causes great suffering, or serious injury to body, or to mental or physical health. As a result, other inhumane acts (as a crime against humanity) – subject to all the other contextual elements – must satisfy the following conditions: a) the victim must have suffered serious bodily or mental harm; b) the suffering must be the result of an act or omission of the accused or his subordinate, and; c) when the offence was committed, the accused or his subordinate must have been motivated by the intent to inflict serious bodily harm or mental harm upon the victim.[44]

The ICC Statute has additionally included two other crimes in its list of unlawful acts that give rise to crimes against humanity. These are the crimes of apartheid and enforced disappearances.

(j) **Apartheid**. This crime is discussed in detail in the chapter relating to offences against the person. In brief, it refers to 'inhumane acts committed in the context of an institutionalised regime of systematic oppression and domination by one racial group over any other racial group or groups and committed with the intention of maintaining that regime'.[45] Although apartheid could, and does in the context of the ICC, fall within the ambit of 'other inhumane acts', it was purposely included as an individual offence in order to reaffirm universal condemnation of this practice.[46]

(k) **Enforced disappearances**. This is equally discussed in the chapter relating to offences against the person. It is defined in Article 7(2)(i) of the ICC Statute as encompassing the 'arrest, detention or abduction of persons, by, or with the authorisation, support or acquiescence of, a State or a political organisation,

---

[42] D Robinson, 'Defining Crimes Against Humanity at the Rome Conference' (1999) 93 *American Journal of International Law* 43, 53–55.

[43] Ibid, para 563; *Stakić* Trial Judgment, para 719.

[44] See *ICTY Prosecutor v Kordić and Čerkez*, Appeals Chamber Judgment (17 Dec. 2004), para. 117; ICC Elements of Crimes, Art 7(1)(k), nums 1 and 2.

[45] Art 7(2)(h) ICC Statute.

[46] See RC Slye, 'Apartheid as a Crime Against Humanity: A Submission to the South African Truth and Reconciliation Commission' (1999) 20 *Michigan Journal of International Law* 267.

followed by a refusal to acknowledge that deprivation of freedom or to give information on the fate or whereabouts of those persons, with the intention of removing them from the protection of the law for a prolonged period of time'.

Besides the aforementioned enumerated list of underlying offences that may give rise to a crime against humanity, all of which should be considered as being customary in nature, it is logical to assume that other non-listed crimes can produce the same result. Given the context of the ad hoc tribunals and the ICC, these other crimes could not have been included therein. For the purposes of this section I shall only briefly touch on two of these in order to make the point more obvious; terrorism and corruption. By their very nature, acts of terrorism aim to spread terror to a civilian population with a view to achieving a political, military or other advantage. This may encompass killing some, or many, members of the civilian population and terrorising the rest. Conduct that amounts to terrorism need not necessarily aim to kill civilians, but may instead be employed simply with a view to instilling mass fear, the effect of which is to hamper one's livelihood in numerous ways. It is now evident that transnational terrorist groups operate in cells and under elaborate planning and their illegal conduct is widespread and global in orientation. Their immediate victims are civilians, irrespective of the fact that terrorist groups claim that governments are their sole targets.[47] In this manner the effects of the attack against civilians (ie killing) is premised on *dolus directus* of the second degree (or oblique intent), which is still intent, and not recklessness.[48]

Corruption is not an obvious candidate for a crime against humanity.[49] Nonetheless, in cases where the leaders of a despotic regime accumulate public wealth illegally at the expense of the survival of their people, the consequence of their actions, even if not directly intended or desired, may be to cause widespread famine or to otherwise make conditions of life unsustainable. If this argument is accepted, its logical extension is to attribute liability to persons acting on behalf of legal entities or corporations in their role as active corruptors, in the reasonable knowledge of said outcome. Depending on the assessed degree of their contribution to the criminal consequence their liability may be that of an accomplice, aider or abettor, co-principal or indirect perpetrator. It is absurd to charge a corrupt leader and his entourage with corruption or grand corruption as an offence under ordinary criminal law when the effect of the corruption has a direct bearing on the survival and livelihood of a large part of a civilian population.[50] It may also be possible to subject corruption, terrorism and similar offences to the regime of other inhumane acts on

---

[47] See SC Res 1566 (8 Oct 2004), para 3, which does not, however, define these as crimes against humanity, but does not exclude this possibility either.

[48] See generally, R Arnold, 'Terrorism as a Crime against Humanity under the ICC Statute' in G Nesi (ed.), *International Co-operation in Counter Terrorism: The United Nations and Regional Organisations in the Fight against Terrorism* (Dartmouth, Ashgate, 2006) 121ff; A Cassese, 'The Multifaceted Criminal Notion of Terrorism in International Law' (2006) 4 *Journal of International Criminal Justice* 933.

[49] For a more detailed exposition of corruption as a transnational offence, see chapter 11.5.

[50] I Bantekas, 'Corruption as an International Crime and a Crime Against Humanity, (2006) 4 *Journal of International Criminal Justice* 466; S Starr, 'Extraordinary Crimes at Ordinary Times: International Justice Beyond Crisis Situations' (2007) 101 *Northwestern University Law Review* 1257, at 1282ff.

account of the widespread suffering they cause to a large number of targeted civilians. An elaboration of this eventuality is beyond the narrow scope of this section.

8.3   The Widespread or Systematic Element

As already observed, the underlying offences enumerated above constitute crimes against humanity when they are perpetrated against any civilian population in a widespread or systematic manner. Evidence of either a 'widespread' or 'systematic' element suffices, although in practice it will not be unusual for both to co-exist. International law requires that only the overall attack, and not the underlying offences, be widespread or systematic – save for the ICC Statute. This means that a single offence can only be regarded as a crime against humanity if it takes place under the umbrella of a widespread or systematic attack against a civilian population.[51]

The *Blaškić* judgment held that the term 'systematic' requires the following ingredients: (a) the existence of a political objective, a plan pursuant to which the attack is perpetrated or an ideology that aims to destroy, persecute or weaken a community; (b) the perpetration of a crime on a large scale against a civilian group, or the repeated and continuous commission of inhumane acts linked to one another; (c) the preparation and use of significant public or private resources, whether military or other; and (d) the implication of high-level political and/or military authorities in the definition and establishment of the plan.[52] The *Akayesu* judgment defined a systematic attack as one that is 'thoroughly organised and following a regular pattern on the basis of a common policy involving substantial public or private resources'.[53] Unlike the French Cassation judgments, the ICTR affirmed that there is no requirement that such policy be formally adopted as the policy of the State.[54] Obviously, there is no requirement that the planners intend to destroy the group in whole or in part as would be the case with genocide. Thus, there is no *dolus specialis* associated with crimes against humanity.

Moreover, the existence of a plan does not have to be expressly declared, nor clearly and precisely stated in order to prove the 'systematic' element of crimes against humanity, although if such is found it will be useful from an evidentiary point of view.[55] This does not mean that crimes against humanity may be the work of private individuals acting alone, but they can be orchestrated and executed by organised non-State entities.[56] This was the conclusion reached by an ICTY Trial

---

[51]   *Kupreškić* Trial Judgment, para 550; *Kunarac* Trial Judgment, para 431.

[52]   *ICTY Prosecutor v Blaškić*, Trial Chamber Judgment (3 Mar 2000), para 203; *Kordić and Čerkez* Trial Judgment, para 179.

[53]   *ICTR Prosecutor v Akayesu*, Trial Chamber Judgment (2 Sep 1998), para 580.

[54]   Ibid; *Nikolić*, R 61 Decision, para 26; *Kupreškić* Trial Judgment, para 551.

[55]   *Blaškić* Trial Judgment, para 204; *Kordić and Čerkez* Trial Judgment, para 181; *Kunarac* Appeals Judgment, para 98; *Blaškić* Appeals Judgment, para 120.

[56]   ILC Report, Draft Code of Crimes Against the Peace and Security of Mankind, UN Doc A/51/10 (1996) Supp No 10, at 94; in *ICTR Prosecutor v Kayishema*, Trial Chamber Judgment (21 May 1999), para

Chamber in its r 61 Review of the evidence against the leader of the Bosnian Serbs, Radovan Karadžić. The ICTY ascertained the existence of a policy of 'ethnic cleansing' by this non-State actor as consisting of a systematic separation of non-Serbian men and women with subsequent internment in detention facilities, extensive damage to sacred symbols with intent to eradicate them, shelling of Sarajevo in order to expel non-Serbian residents, and establishment of camps devoted to rape, enforced pregnancy and enforced prostitution of non-Serbian women. The purpose of these camps and the policy of sexual assaults in general were found to be the displacement of civilians and the infliction of shame and humiliation upon the victims and their communities, thus, forcing them to abandon their homelands.[57]

As evidence of plans of this nature will seldom be retrieved in writing, it suffices if such planning can be inferred from relevant circumstances, even if not expressly declared or stated clearly and precisely. Such circumstances include the overall prevailing political background, the general content of a political programme, the role of the media and incendiary propaganda, intentional alterations to ethnic compositions, the imposition of discriminatory measures and the sheer scale of acts of violence.[58] Since the concept of crimes against humanity refers not to a particular act, but to a 'course of conduct', a single act may constitute a crime against humanity when the perpetrator has the requisite *mens rea* and the offence is part of either a widespread or systematic attack against a civilian population.[59] The plan may moreover be inferred by reference to the duration of criminal acts and the systematicity of events associated with them. In the *Al-Bashir Warrant* Decision, an ICC Pre-Trial Chamber noted that the Sudanese government's campaign of violence against villages and towns inhabited by the Fur, Masalit and Zaghawa peoples lasted for a period of five years. During this time the attackers encircled the targeted village or approached it with tens or hundreds of vehicles and camels forming a wide line. Ground attacks were routinely preceded by aerial bombings, followed by ground camel assaults from Janjaweed militias.[60]

The 'widespread' element of crimes against humanity is probably easier to substantiate, as it necessarily refers to the scale of the acts perpetrated and the number of victims.[61] The *Akayesu* judgment defined the element of 'widespread' as 'massive, frequent, large scale action, carried out collectively with considerable seriousness and directed against a multiplicity of victims'.[62] The widespread occurrence of crimes need not involve only one type of underlying crime, such as murder or rape, but may consist of an accumulation of multiple offences against numerous victims at different times and places. Thus, the 9/11 terrorist attack constitutes an example of a crime against humanity involving a large number of victims and committed on the same

---

125, the ICTR convicted the accused Ruzindana, a local businessman, of crimes against humanity because he partook in the overall Hutu extremist policy to exterminate the minority Tutsi.

[57] *ICTY Prosecutor v Karadžić and Mladić*, R 61 Decision (11 Jul 1996), paras 60–64.

[58] *Blaškić* Trial Judgment, para 204; *Prosecutor v Jelisić*, Trial Chamber Judgment (14 Dec 1999), para 53.

[59] *Kupreškić* Trial Judgment, para 550.

[60] *ICC Prosecutor v Al-Bashir*, Decision on the Prosecution's Application for a Warrant of Arrest against Omar Al-Bashir (4 Mar 2009), paras 84–85.

[61] *Blaškić* Trial Judgment, para 206.

[62] *Akayesu* Trial Judgment, para 580.

day through the employment of a single underlying offence. A different exposition of a widespread crime against humanity relates to the Bosnian ethnic cleansing, which was also premised on a policy. There, the victims were forced to abandon their ancestral homelands through a series of murders, deportations, rapes, forced impregnations, torture and other heinous acts committed against the targeted civilian population over a period of several years. From an evidential point of view the 'widespread' element requires proof of a significant number of offences before a charge of crimes against humanity can be substantiated. On the other hand, proof of a plan that demonstrates an intent to undertake such an attack is sufficient to ground a charge, even if only a single crime has been committed.

8.4   The Nature of the Targeted 'Civilian Population'

The status and nature of the civilian population that is the target of an attack is very important, since it is this which differentiates crimes against humanity from random attacks against civilian populations without any defining characteristics in the mind of the attacker. Civilian populations, defined generally as people not taking active part in hostilities, can never become legitimate objects of attack. The *Kunarac* Appeals Judgment further elaborated on the fact that an attack could still be classified as systematic even where not every member of a particular civilian population were targeted, by stating that:

> ... the use of the word 'population' does not mean that the entire population of the geographical entity in which the attack is taking place must have been subjected to that attack. It is sufficient to show that enough individuals were targeted in the course of the attack, or that they were targeted in such a way as to satisfy the Chamber that the attack was in fact directed against a civilian 'population', rather than against a limited and randomly selected number of individuals.[63]

The possible presence of non-civilians within the midst of such populations does not deprive them of their civilian character,[64] provided that these are not regular units with fairly large numbers.[65] The general approach in the ICTY has been to construe the term 'civilian population' broadly, encompassing persons who have been involved in resistance movements and also former combatants who no longer take part in hostilities at the time the attack against the civilian population took place, either because they had decided to abandon their units, no longer bore arms, or because

---

[63]   *Kunarac* Appeals Judgment, para 90.

[64]   1977 Protocol I, Art 50. See Y Sandoz, *et al, Commentary on the Additional Protocols of 8 June 1977 to the Geneva Conventions of 12 August 1949* (Geneva, Martinus Nijhoff, 1987) [*ICRC Commentary*], para 1922; affirmed in *Akayesu* Trial Judgment, para 582.

[65]   *ICRC Commentary*, ibid; *Blaškić* Appeals Judgment, para 116. Even so, the commander that engages in a military attack against such military units should take every possible precaution to avoid casualties not only among the civilian population, but also to minimise its effects on combatants. This is in accordance with the customary principle prescribed in Art 35 of Protocol I 1977 that the choice of methods of warfare are not unlimited and the employment of weapons must be such as to avoid causing unnecessary suffering or superfluous injury.

they had been rendered *hors de combat*.[66] This is certainly the contemporary position in customary international law, which itself is reflected in Article 7 of the ICC Statute. Nonetheless, the *Blaškić* Appeals Judgment placed a very logical limitation to the broad construction of civilian populations for the purposes of crimes against humanity. The Trial Chamber had suggested that the assessment of civilian status depends on the 'specific situation of the victim at the moment the crimes were committed, rather than his status'.[67] The implication of this suggestion is that a combatant under Article 4(A) of Geneva Convention III and Article 50 of Protocol I (1977) switches to a civilian every time he is not engaged in active combat (eg during sleep, dinner, breaks, etc). The Appeals Chamber expressly refuted this suggestion, adding that if a person is 'indeed a member of an armed organisation, the fact that he is not armed or in combat at the time of the commission of crimes does not accord him civilian status'.[68] Unlike the Nuremberg definition which required that the civilian population be composed of nationals or allies of the offending State, the contemporary stance is that – and given that the ICC Statute no longer requires any link to an armed conflict – crimes against humanity may be committed against all civilian populations (whether nationals or non-nationals).

Cassese argues that customary international law no longer limits the possible range of victims of crimes against humanity to purely civilian populations. He contends that besides *hors de combat* widespread or systematic attacks against active combatants could amount to crimes against humanity. He bases his contention on the absence of an armed conflict nexus in respect of this international crime and on the application of human rights and international criminal law to all areas of inter and intra-State relations.[69] The effect of this argument is to bypass the very definition of the offence and to blur the necessary distinction between crimes against humanity and war crimes; I therefore find it untenable.[70] A basic difference between civilians/ *hors de combat* and combatants rests in the fact that the former have no capacity to resist their attackers. This makes an attack against them all the more heinous. On the other hand, an attack against combatants is susceptible to some or significant opposition and resistance. Where such an attack against combatants is conducted with illegal weapons or through the infliction of unnecessary suffering, or in violation of the international law of targeting, it is regulated by humanitarian law and constitutes a grave breach.

---

[66] *Vukovar Hospital* R 61 Decision, paras 29–32; *Blaškić* Trial Judgment, paras 210, 216; *Kayishema* Trial Judgment, para 127; *ICTY Prosecutor v Martić*, Appeals Chamber Judgment (8 Oct 2008), para 307.

[67] *Blaškić* Trial Judgment, para 214.

[68] *Blaškić* Appeals Judgment, para 114.

[69] A Cassese, *International Criminal Law* (Oxford, Oxford University Press, 2008) 122–23.

[70] This position is equally unsupported by the most recent ICTY case law, particularly *ICTY Prosecutor v Mrkšić et al*, Appeals Chamber Judgment (5 May 2009), paras 29ff, where although the Appeals Chamber accepted that the term 'civilians' was much broader than its counterpart in the *jus in bello*, it did not go as far as saying that an attack, for the purposes of crimes against humanity, could encompass active combatants.

8.5   The Subjective Element

Crimes against humanity differ from other war crimes from the fact that their perpetrators are engaging in particular unlawful conduct with the knowledge and approval that such acts are committed on a widespread scale or based on a policy against a specific civilian population. Hence, it is the knowledge and awareness of the 'overall context' within which an underlying crime is committed that makes a perpetrator criminally liable for a crime against humanity, combined with his intent to contribute thereto through the commission of an underlying crime. It is the widespread or the policy elements that establish this overall context and not the perpetrator personally through multiple acts of violence and hence the perpetrator need not share or be identified with the ideology or plan that supports the attack against the targeted population. However, it would be absurd to require each and every mid-level executioner of a well-organised crime against humanity to possess full knowledge of all characteristics of the attack or the precise details of the plan or policy of the State or organisation.[71] If this were not so, only the planner and his immediate entourage would incur liability for this offence. The *Kunarac* Appeals Judgment succinctly stated that:

> It is irrelevant whether the accused intended his acts to be directed against the targeted population or merely against his victim. It is the attack, not the acts of the accused, which must be directed against the target population and the accused need only know that his acts are part thereof.[72]

Therefore, as explained above, a single unlawful act perpetrated within an overall context of an attack against a civilian population constitutes a crime against humanity by reason of the perpetrator's knowledge of the overall context. In the *Jelisić* case, the accused was the commandant of a Bosnian Serb POW camp in the municipality of Brčko. He was eventually convicted of serious offences against prisoners and other detainees under his authority, all of which were found to be part of a crime against humanity. The ICTY Trial Chamber inferred Jelisić's knowledge of a Bosnian Serb policy of annihilation of non-Serb populations in the Brčko area on the basis of his appointment to the Brčko camp and his active participation in the operations against Moslems in the region.[73] Knowledge of the attack (ie the overall context) is the defining element that distinguishes a crime against humanity from other crimes. If D kills ten villagers under orders that they were allegedly responsible for the death of some of his comrades he is not liable for a crime against humanity, even if his superiors were in fact engaging in a campaign to drive out all enemy civilians from a particular territory. Although D's knowledge of the overall context may be otherwise inferred by reason of the widespread occurrence of offences, his liability will generally arise in respect of crimes such as murder and extermination. If under the same set of circumstances A was D's co-perpetrator, with the difference

---

[71]   *ICC Prosecutor v Al-Bashir*, Decision on the Prosecution's Application for a Warrant of Arrest against Omar Al-Bashir (4 Mar 2009), para 89.

[72]   *Kunarac* Appeals Judgment, para 103.

[73]   *Jelisić* Trial Judgment, para 57.

that A was fully aware of the overall context but refused to reveal it to D out of fear that he would not follow along, then whereas A is liable for crimes against humanity, D is not.

Finally, some mention should be made to persecution as a contextual element in the definition of attack, as opposed to persecution as an underlying offence for the purposes of crimes against humanity. Contrary to customary international law, Article 3 of the ICTR Statute requires a discriminatory intent in the definition of the overall attack. This requirement does not exist in respect of the ICTY Statute.

8.6   Crimes Against Humanity in the ICC Statute

The definition of this offence under Article 7 of the ICC Statute is different in a number of respects from that found in the statutes of the ICTY and ICTR, as a result of a compromise in accommodating varying demands regarding the threshold standard for this offence. The general threshold for crimes against humanity is set out in Article 7(1), comprising any act contained in an exhaustive list of offences when committed 'as part of a widespread or systematic attack' against any civilian population. Up to this point the definition is identical to the jurisprudence of the ad hoc tribunals. However, since it was agreed by all participants at the Rome Conference that not every inhumane act should amount to a crime against humanity – as the Court should only accept the most serious cases – the concept of an 'attack' in the ICC Statute is elaborated in Article 7(2)(a), meaning a 'course of conduct involving the multiple commission of acts pursuant to or in furtherance of a State or organisational policy to commit such attack'. To substantiate a charge of crimes against humanity the Prosecutor would have to demonstrate that an attack against a civilian population involves multiple crimes, each being either widespread or systematic, in addition to the requirement that the overall attack be naturally widespread or systematic.[74] This is a significantly high threshold, designed to allow the Court to address serious situations. In practice, it brings within the Court's jurisdiction situations where although multiple persons commit offences in the knowledge that they are part of an overall context of widespread or systematic conduct, only those perpetrators whose particular crimes are themselves widespread or systematic are susceptible to prosecution. Thus, if D commits a single act of murder in the knowledge that this is part of a campaign of crimes against humanity against a particular civilian population he would not fall within the jurisdiction of the ICC, albeit he may obviously be prosecuted elsewhere in respect of this offence.

The *mens rea* for crimes against humanity in Article 7(1) of the ICC Statute requires that the perpetrator act with knowledge that his or her particular underlying offence was part of an overall widespread or systematic attack against a civilian population. While the perpetrator must be aware of the overall attack, it is also necessary that the elements of the particular offence be proven. For example, a person killing two civilians from group A is guilty for a crime against humanity only

---

[74] Robinson, 'Defining Crimes Against Humanity', at 51.

if it can be proven that the *mens rea* elements for the offences of extermination or murder have been satisfied, and also that either of these offences was committed with the knowledge that group A was specifically targeted by the perpetrator's affiliate organisation. It must also be demonstrated that the murders and exterminations were themselves either widespread or systematic. Likewise, and following the jurisprudence of the ad hoc tribunals, crimes against humanity can be committed by State entities and their agents, as well as by non-State entities. However, unlike the ICTY and ICTR Statute, Article 7 of the ICC Statute does not require a nexus to an armed conflict, or a discriminatory intent.

9

The Crime of Genocide

9.1 Early Perceptions and the Duties of States to Prevent and Punish Genocide

Genocide has been described as the 'ultimate crime'.[1] The first widely assumed genocide of the twentieth century was that of the Armenian population of the Ottoman Empire in 1915, most probably out of fear that they would join an impending Russian assault against the then crumbling Empire. Despite the issuance of a severe note on 28 May 1915 by Britain, France and Russia that held the perpetrators liable for the crimes committed on account of their impact on 'humanity and civilisation' and Article 230(1) of the 1920 Treaty of Sèvres,[2] which called for the surrender of persons responsible for massacres or violations of the law of war – albeit without expressly naming the Armenian massacres as such[3] – no international criminal proceedings ever took place.[4] This was the result of a subsequent fortunate politico-military situation for the successor to the Ottomans, Turkey,[5] which led to the replacement, and effective abrogation, of the relevant provisions in the Sèvres

---

[1] P Akhavan, 'Enforcement of the Genocide Convention: A Challenge to Civilization' (1995) 8 *Harvard Human Rights Journal* 229.

[2] Treaty of Peace between the Allied and Associated Powers and Turkey, signed in Sèvres, 28 LNTS 244.

[3] This was because the Armenians were not the only ethnic or religious group targeted for persecution. Greeks and Christians in particular were severely persecuted, suffering mass killings, expulsion, taking of properties and forced conversions to Islam. In fact, the genocide of 400,000 Pontus Greeks who lived adjacent to the Black Sea has gone largely unnoticed, despite its notoriety at the time, due in large part to the annihilation of other ethnic groups. Arts 142 and 144 of the Treaty of Sèvres specifically denounced the validity of the forced conversions and demanded of the Turkish authorities to release detained and disappeared persons and return properties to their rightful owners. These violations were deemed as having been 'inflicted on individuals in the course of the massacres perpetrated in Turkey during the war'. See NC Brown, TP Ion, *Persecutions of the Greeks in Turkey since the Beginning of the European War* (Oxford, Oxford University Press, 1918).

[4] VN Dadrian, 'Genocide as a Problem of National and International Law: The World War I Armenian Case and its Contemporary Legal Ramifications' (1989) 14 *Yale Journal of International Law* 221. It should be noted however that a number of court martials were instituted by the Ottoman Empire, which overall demonstrated the recognition of the fact that the incumbent political party at the time had set up a special branch for the annihilation of the Armenians. VN Dadrian, 'The Documentation of the World War I Armenian Massacres in the Proceedings of the Turkish Military Tribunal' (1991) 23 *International Journal of Middle East Studies* 549.

[5] By 1922 Turkey had achieved significant military successes on the battlefield and had placated its place in the community of nations on the basis of western values, having by that time become a republic. The emergence of political considerations that provided disincentives to avert the Rwandan genocide almost a century later are reported grimly by the OAU Report Regarding the Rwandan Genocide, (2000)

Treaty by the 1923 Treaty of Lausanne.[6] What is important, however, about the Armenian and Greek massacres for the purposes of this chapter is that the international community recognised for the first time that States are not permitted to commit crimes of a mass scale upon their population, which constitutes a break with international law at the time – at least, as far as the criminal liability of the perpetrators was concerned. Despite the fact that the legal notion of genocide had not yet been conceived in the years following the Armenian massacres these events have been officially proclaimed as constituting genocide by the legislative bodies of numerous countries.[7] Understandably, this is a matter of much political contestation.

It was not until a good thirty years later that the need to devise an international offence capable of encapsulating the massive scale of annihilation and destruction of a particular group had been solidified. Alas, the revulsion caused by the Jewish Holocaust eventually led to the adoption in 1948 of the Genocide Convention,[8] even though the term had been in use in the Nuremberg Tribunal proceedings to underline the depravity of crimes of persecution despite the fact that genocide had not been recognised therein as a distinct crime under international law.[9] Although the acts covered by the Convention could just as well be encompassed under the definition of crimes against humanity (as a form of persecution thereto) – or even that of extermination – there was a compelling reason to distinguish between the two offences. This reason was wholly unrelated to any legal considerations. The drafters of the crime of genocide desired to emphasise the particular gravity of targeting members of a specific group with a view to their intentional physical or biological extermination. Emphasis is therefore placed on the destruction of the group, whereas the victimisation of group members in their individual capacities takes second place. Moreover, unlike other mass crimes, genocide requires that the perpetrators intended to destroy the group in whole or in part. It therefore stands out not only because of the scale of the crimes, but more importantly because of the particularly repugnant *mens rea* of the perpetrators.

Given its seriousness the prohibition of genocide as a matter of *jus cogens* by the ICJ is hardly surprising.[10] Neither is the recognition of the Genocide Convention's non contractual character, that is, its capacity in creating obligations even vis-a-vis non-affected States (*erga omnes* obligations) – including States whose nationals are not victims of genocide – on the basis of its compelling humanitarian nature.[11] The

---

94 *American Journal of International Law* 692, which attributed the USA's passive role to the loss of 18 soldiers in the course of its Somalia campaign a year prior to the genocide and was therefore afraid of a 'domestic political backlash', p 693.

    [6] Treaty of Peace between Turkey and the British Empire, France, Italy, Japan, Greece, Romania and the Serb-Croat-Slovene State, 28 LNTS 11.

    [7] See eg the French Loi No 2001–70 du 29 January 2001 Relative à la Reconnaissance du Génocide Arménien de 1915, J.O. No 25 (30 Jan 2001).

    [8] 78 UNTS 277.

    [9] *Prosecutor v Göring*, XXII Trial of the Major War Criminals before the IMT (1946), at 497 and 531, as per the closing statements of the British and French prosecutors respectively.

    [10] *Advisory Opinion Concerning Reservations to the Genocide Convention* (1951) ICJ Reports 15, at 23; *Barcelona Traction Light and Power House Co Ltd* [*Barcelona Traction* case] (Belgium v Spain), Second Phase Judgment (1970) ICJ Reports 3.

    [11] *Barcelona Traction* case, ibid, paras 33–34. See R Provost, 'Reciprocity in Human Rights and Humanitarian Law' (1994) 65 *British Yearbook of International Law* 383.

real vexing question is to determine how best the international community may set about to prevent and punish genocide. The primary basis for prevention necessarily rests with each State, unless the doctrines of humanitarian intervention and the responsibility to protect (R2P) give rise to a rule or formal mechanism whereby acts amounting to genocide may be pre-empted or countered through collective action. So far in international relations this prospect has never materialised in the form of a normative expectation. With the exception of the Vietnamese invasion of Cambodia and the conviction of former Prime Minister Pol Pot by a people's revolutionary tribunal of genocide *in absentia,* there have been no other cases of humanitarian intervention in order to suppress the occurrence of genocide,[12] even though a rapporteur of the UN Sub-Commission on Prevention of Discrimination and Protection of Minorities pointed out in his 1985 report on genocide that a significant number of genocidal incidents had taken place after 1945, namely, the Hutu massacres by Tutsis in Burundi in 1965 and 1972, the 1974 Paraguayan eradication campaign of the Ache Indians, the Khmer Rouge massacres in Cambodia in 1975 and 1978 as well as the extermination of Baha'is in Iran – although in the case of the Baha'is their persecution commenced in the mid nineteenth century when they were first established as a religious minority.[13] One should also recall other more contemporary events in Africa, particularly in the Congo and Darfur in Sudan.

Where preventative mechanisms have failed to avert a genocide one must consider the application of penal processes. In order to be successful, these processes must be capable of producing consistent and coherent results. It is no accident that the Security Council refrains from characterising particular situations as genocide, deeming this to be a function that falls within the exclusive ambit of judicial or quasi-judicial determination.[14] Imagine a situation where the Council classified a situation as genocide, only later to be described as a crime against humanity by a judicial body. Consistency is also lacking in the definition of the offence, given the passage of almost fifty years since the adoption of the Genocide Convention and despite the verbatim iteration of the definition encountered therein in the statutes of international criminal tribunals. It is now evident that the practice of national and international criminal tribunals has evolved in latitude significantly in relation to the original text of the Genocide Convention. It is also felt that a good number of genocidal campaigns are now known to have targeted groups organised around a political idea or affiliation; however, political groups are outside the scope of the Convention, albeit some national prosecutions have succeeded in attributing liability to persons that targeted political groups as such.[15] No doubt, such persecution may

---

[12] See H Hannum, 'International Law and Cambodian Genocide: The Sounds of Silence' (1989) 11 *Human Rights Quarterly* 82.

[13] Question of the Prevention and Punishment of the Crime of Genocide, UN Doc E/CN4/Sub2/ 1985/6 (2 July 1985) 9.

[14] The Council has, however, consciously excluded genocide from the jurisdiction *ratione materiae* of international tribunals, such as those of Sierra Leone and Lebanon, expressly considering in advance that no genocide had taken place in respect of these situations.

[15] This is true, for example, in respect of massacres that took place in Ethiopia against political groups that were labelled as anti-unity or counter-revolutionary, on the basis of Art 281 of the 1957 Ethiopian Penal Code. This provision included political groups as possible targets of genocide and the country's former president and his co-accused were held liable for genocide for their so-called 'Red Terror' campaign between 1977–78. *Special Prosecutor v Mengistu Hailemariam and Others,* Ethiopian Federal High Court

just as well be classified as a crime against humanity, but its absence from the genocide definition is viewed in many circles as unfortunate and as a disadvantage of the Convention; even so, this 'deficiency' in the best of my knowledge has not been remedied by customary international law.

Finally, the dictates of coherence require that the consequences of genocide are not inconsistent in respect of the liabilities of its principal actors. This is simple enough when assessing individual liability among a multitude of physical actors, but is quite problematic when we consider the right balance between individual and State responsibility. If principal responsibility for genocide is ascribed to a State as the organiser of a particular policy, the impression may perhaps be given that criminal liability is only of residual importance. The ICJ in the *Bosnia Genocide* case failed to allay this apprehension. The Court contended that the Genocide Convention imposes obligations on both individuals as well as States.[16] Although it should have been clear that States can only incur liability for failing to prevent and punish genocide, the Court proceeded to interpret the obligation in Article III of the Convention – which spells out the various modes of committing genocide – as applicable also to States.[17] Such an interpretation unnecessarily blurs the distinction between personal and State responsibility and risks apportioning blame in a disproportionate manner.

9.2 Destruction of the Group 'in Whole or in Part'

The definition of genocide and the enumeration of punishable acts under Articles 2 and 4 of the ICTR and ICTY Statutes respectively constitute a *verbatim* reproduction of Articles II and III of the 1948 Genocide Convention. Article II of this Convention defines genocide as:

> ... any of the following acts committed with intent to destroy, in whole or in part, a national, ethnical, racial or religious group, as such:
>
> (a) killing members of the group;
> (b) causing serious bodily harm or mental harm to members of the group;
> (c) deliberately inflicting on the group conditions of life calculated to bring about its physical destruction in whole or in part;
> (d) imposing measures intended to prevent births within the group;
> (e) forcibly transferring children of the group to another group.

Judgment (12 Dec 2006). For a thorough analysis, see FK Tiba, 'The Mengistu Genocide Trial in Ethiopia' (2007) 5 *Journal of International Criminal Justice* 513.

[16] *Application of the Convention on the Prevention and Punishment of the Crime of Genocide* (Bosnia and Herzegovina v Serbia and Montenegro) [*Bosnia Genocide* case], Judgment (26 Feb 2007), paras 162–66. It should be noted that despite the ICJ's finding that the Srebrenica massacre was the only instance that amounted to genocide – on the basis of the available evidence – the Court additionally stated that there was no proof that Serbian leaders had prepared plans, or participated, to carry it out. Serbia was only held liable for its failure to punish genocide, albeit only in respect of its failure to at times cooperate with the ICTY.

[17] Ibid, para 167.

Article III penalises, besides principal participation in genocide, conspiracy, direct and public incitement, attempt and complicity in acts of genocide. These constitute inchoate crimes – in that it is not required that they culminate in subsequent physical acts of genocide – and not mere modes of liability in respect of genocide. What is evident from this definition is that it is exhaustive and much more specific than that articulated for other grave offences, namely, crimes against humanity, whose list of underlying prohibited conduct varies from statute to statute and is not seen as static. The specificity of genocide is not exhausted solely on account of the four groups that may become the target of genocide, but is more importantly based on the particular *mens rea* of the perpetrator, whose intention must be to destroy in whole or in part anyone of the enumerated groups. This element renders genocide a specific intent crime *(dolus specialis)* and differentiates it from other offences of mass destruction and extermination.

As already stated, the *actus reus* of genocide requires the perpetration of acts that aim to destroy a group in whole or in part. The 'in part' element does not characterise the destruction of the group, but refers instead to the intent of the perpetrator in destroying the group within the confines of a limited geographical area.[18] Thus, if an individual possesses the intent to destroy a distinct part of a group within a limited geographical area, as opposed to an accumulation of isolated individuals within it, that person would be liable for genocide. Thus, genocide does not require that the perpetrator must intend to kill each and every member of the group. On this basis the ICTY Trial Chamber convicted General Krstić of genocide for his participation in the extermination of thousands of Bosnian Moslem males in the area of Srebrenica in 1995.[19] In that unfortunate incident that was not discovered until a few years later the Muslim male population of the area around Srebrenica was rounded up under the guise of an exchange agreement but was instead taken to an isolated field where up to 8,000 souls were brutally executed. Given that the accused could not reasonably expect to annihilate the entire Muslim population of Bosnia, genocide must certainly be sustained where he had intended to physically destroy the entire male population of the target group in the geographical vicinity under his military command.

Since genocide is a mass-victim offence, the part targeted must be a substantial part of the group. In terms of victim numbers, ICTY and ICTR jurisprudence suggest that the intent to destroy a part of the group must affect a considerable number of individuals that make up a 'substantial' part of that group.[20] In such cases the prosecutor must prove both the intent to destroy the targeted group in the particular geographical area, as well as the intent to destroy a substantial part of that group as such.[21] In the *Krstić* case, the accused argued that the Bosnian Muslim population of

---

[18] *ICTY Prosecutor v Krstić*, Trial Chamber Judgment (2 Aug 2001), paras 582–84.

[19] This view was adopted by two German judgments relating to offences perpetrated in the context of the Bosnian conflicts: the *Jorgić* case, Dusseldorf Supreme Court, 3 StR 215/98 (30 Apr 1999), upheld by the FRG Federal Constitutional Court, and the *Djajic* case, Bavarian Appeals Court (23 May 1997), (1998) 92 *American Journal of International Law* 528, cited with approval in the *Krstić* Trial Judgment, ibid, para 589. The *Jorgić* case is analysed further in subsequent sections of this chapter.

[20] *ICTR Prosecutor v Kayishema and Ruzindana*, Trial Chamber Judgment (21 May 1999), para 97; *ICTR Prosecutor v Bagilishema*, Trial Chamber, Judgment (7 Jun 2001), para 64; *Krstić* Trial Judgment, paras 586–88; *ICTY Prosecutor v Krstić*, Appeals Chamber Judgment (19 Apr 2004), paras 8–12.

[21] *ICTY Prosecutor v Sikirica* . Trial Chamber Judgment (3 Sep 2001), para 61.

Srebrenica did not constitute a significant part of the overall Muslim population in Bosnia. The ICTY Appeals Chamber pointed out, however, that in the present instance this was not an overriding consideration on account of the following two reasons: a) Srebrenica was of huge strategic importance to the Bosnian Serbs, because it was an obstacle to an ethnically pure Bosnian Serb State; b) Srebrenica was the only area in that region which the Serbs were able to control and thus extermination of other Muslims elsewhere was not physically possible under the circumstances.[22]

It is possible in some cases for the accused to validly argue that although many members of the targeted group were killed while under his authority, many others under similar authority were allowed to leave. In the context of the Srebrenica massacre, while the Bosnian Serbs rounded up and executed all Bosnian Muslim male civilians, they transferred all other women, children and the elderly to Muslim armed forces. The *Krstić* Appeals Chamber gave no significance to this act, putting it down to the fact that such an action could not have been kept an eternal secret or disguised as a military operation and thus carried an increased risk of international exposure.[23] It was sufficient that the intent to exterminate a part of the group without being detected existed, further making sure that without its males the Srebrenica female community would not be able to reconstitute itself. The rationale of the ad hoc tribunal rests on the ultimate aim of the particular acts of destruction and as a result disregards other factors. This is in contrast to the report of the UN Commission of Inquiry for Darfur, which as will be explained, rejected claims of genocide on the basis that many civilians from the targeted group had been spared. The real test in any case is whether the perpetrator, even if he or she chose not to kill or otherwise harm every member of the group under his or her control, intended nonetheless to destroy the group in part and if he or she reasonably believed that the partial destruction of the group would come about as a result of such action.

9.3   The Specific Intent (*Dolus Specialis*) Required for Genocide

The ICTY had not, until January 2001, made a finding on the occurrence of genocide with regard to the former Yugoslavia nor, of course, did it convict any accused of this offence.[24] It did, however, urge the Prosecutor in the *Nikolić* case to consider charging the accused also of genocide[25] and inferred Karadzic's genocidal intent from a variety of factors.[26] In the *Jelisić* case, the accused was the commandant of a Bosnian Serb camp that was charged, *inter alia,* with participating in a campaign of genocide against Moslems. The Trial Chamber initially acquitted him of genocide on the

---

[22]   *Krstić* Appeals Judgment, paras 15–17.

[23]   Ibid, para 31.

[24]   On 2 August 2001, Bosnian-Serb General Krstić was convicted at first instance of genocide for his role in the planning and execution of the Srebrenica massacre in 1995. On appeal, his conviction was upheld in relation to aiding and abetting genocide.

[25]   *ICTY Prosecutor v Nikolić*, R 61 Decision (20 Oct 1995), para 34.

[26]   *ICTY Prosecutor v Karadžić*, R 61 Decision (11 Jul 1996), para 95.

grounds that the Prosecutor had failed to prove Jelisić's genocidal intent beyond reasonable doubt.[27] It had reached this conclusion because the evidence (random acts of violence, albeit against Bosnian Moslems) and the disturbed personality of the accused (for example, narcissistic tendencies) did not demonstrate a *dolus specialis* against Moslems living in the area of Brčko beyond a reasonable doubt. The Appeals Chamber disagreed with this evaluation of the evidence, finding instead that genocidal intent clearly existed, but did not see it in the interests of justice to order a retrial and thus declined to reverse the acquittal.[28] The ICTY has generally been reluctant to convict lower-ranking personnel of genocide, despite the large number of victims in particular cases.[29] In the chapter dealing with the legal nature of specific intent in international criminal law and in particular its application to genocide we examined the so-called knowledge-based theory.[30] According to this, mid-level and lowly executioners of genocide who although aware of the genocidal plan have not formed the special intent for the crime itself should be deemed principals. The ICC has rejected the application of this position in its early jurisprudence, viewing it as inconsistent with the literal interpretation of its Statute and Elements of Crimes, which require that a person is liable as a principal to genocide only if he or she possesses the requisite specific intent. Persons that are simply aware of the genocide are considered accessories.

Unlike the ICTY, the ICTR was established primarily to address the issue of genocide and early on in its case load, in the *Akayesu* case, it authoritatively determined that genocide against the Tutsi did, in fact, take place in Rwanda in 1994.[31] The judicial assessment of the *dolus specialis* by the ad hoc tribunals begins by first examining the existence of a genocidal plan and the commission of genocide and then by inquiring into the genocidal intent of the accused, which is distinct but yet interrelated to that of the underlying plan.[32] It should be pointed out that the existence of a genocidal plan is not a normative ingredient of the crime of genocide, but ICTY Chambers have consistently argued that it could nonetheless provide evidential assistance in proving the intent of the authors.[33] It is therefore of evidentiary value. This consideration notwithstanding the language of the Genocide Convention implicitly suggests that whereas the existence of a policy or plan is not required in respect of killing members of the group or causing serious or bodily mental harm, it is necessary when considering other forms of conduct. Thus, 'deliberately' inflicting conditions of life calculated to bring about a group's physical destruction, imposing birth prevention measures and forcibly transferring the group's children necessitates a certain degree of planning and organisation.[34] It is unlikely

---

[27] *ICTY Prosecutor v Jelisić*, Trial Chamber Judgment (14 Dec 1999), paras 97–98.

[28] *ICTY Prosecutor v Jelisić*, Appeals Chamber Judgment (5 Jul 2001), paras 70–77.

[29] *ICTY Prosecutor v Sikirica and Others*, Trial Chamber Judgment on Defence Motions to Acquit (3 Sep 2001).

[30] See chapter 2.6.

[31] *ICTR Prosecutor v Akayesu*, Trial Chamber Judgment (2 Sep 1998), para 126.

[32] G Verdirame, 'The Genocide Definition in the Jurisprudence of the Ad Hoc Tribunals' (2000) 49 *International & Comparative Law Quarterly* 578, at 588.

[33] *Krstić* Trial Judgment, para 572; *Jelisić* Appeals Judgment, para 48.

[34] A Cassese, *International Criminal Law* (Oxford, Oxford University Press, 2008) 141.

that such acts can be committed with the requisite intent by a mere group of individuals that are not acting under the authority of government.

In the context of the ICC Statute, on the other hand, the existence of a plan as a constitutive element of the crime is expressly required. This requirement is evident in the Elements of Crimes pertinent to genocide, which require that said acts take place 'in the context of a manifest pattern of similar conduct directed against that group or conduct that could itself effect such destruction'.[35] The validity of this contextual element was confirmed in the *Al-Bashir* Warrant Decision. Not only is a clear pattern of conduct necessary, but moreover the 'relevant conduct must present a concrete threat to the existence of the targeted group, or a part thereof'.[36] Thus, unlike genocide under general international law, the same offence under the ICC Statute is only triggered when the threat of destruction becomes 'concrete and real'.[37]

The *dolus specialis* of genocide necessitates that the intention to commit this crime be formed prior to the execution of genocidal acts, although the individual offences themselves do not require any such premeditation.[38] This requirement serves to exclude the possibility that genocide may ever be committed by reason of spontaneous impulse. The execution of genocide involves two levels of intent: that of the criminal enterprise as a collectivity and that of the participating individuals. In such cases of joint participation the intent to commit genocide must be discernible in the criminal act itself, apart from the intent of particular perpetrators. The next step is to establish whether the accused shared the intention that genocide be carried out.[39] The *Jelisić* judgment opined that genocidal intent may manifest itself through a desire to exterminate a very large number of group members, or by killing a more limited number of persons selected for the impact their disappearance or extermination will have upon the survival of the group as such.[40] In most cases, there will be no direct proof of genocidal intent and so this result must be inferred through circumstantial evidence. Jean Paul Akayesu, the first person to be convicted of genocide by the ICTR, was the Bourgmestre of Taba commune, a position that afforded him a very significant amount of influence and authority over all the public institutions of the commune. The accused had delivered passionate speeches against the Tutsi and moderate Hutus, whereby he advocated their extermination and was found to have ordered other acts of violence against his victims. These actions could only be classified as genocide if discriminatory intent could be demonstrated with the aim of destroying the targeted group in whole or in part. The ICTR reached this inference on the basis of the general context of other culpable acts systematically directed against the Tutsi, the multiplicity of offenders across Rwanda, the general nature and distinct genre of the crimes and the deliberate targeting of victims on account of their particular membership, while excluding others.[41] The *Kayishema* judgment added

---

[35] ICC Elements of Crimes, Art 6(a), num 4, ICC Doc PCNICC/2000/1/Add.2 (2 Nov 2000).

[36] *ICC Prosecutor v Al-Bashir*, Decision on the Prosecution's Application for a Warrant of Arrest against Omar Al-Bashir (4 Mar 2009), paras 121, 123.

[37] Ibid, para 124.

[38] *Kayishema* Trial Judgment, para 91.

[39] *Krstić* Trial Judgment, para 549.

[40] *Jelisić* Trial Judgment, para 82.

[41] *Akayesu* Trial Judgment, para 523; reaffirmed in *ICTR Prosecutor v Rutaganda*, Trial Chamber Judgment (6 Dec 1999), para 399.

further elements, such as the use of derogatory language towards group members, methodical planning and systematic killing and the number of victims exterminated.[42] None of these factors alone can provide credible proof of genocidal intent; what is needed is a combination demonstrating the overall context of atrocities against a specific group of which the accused can only have been a substantial actor on account of his or her unlawful conduct against the targeted group.

In other cases, however, the widespread nature and massive scale of acts of murder, rape and annihilation have not given rise to a conclusion that genocide in fact occurred, nor an inference of specific intent. The International Commission of Inquiry on Darfur (ICID), mandated by the Security Council with ascertaining the range of offences committed in Sudan's Darfur region, and of assessing whether genocide had taken place,[43] noted that on the basis of the material collected by it the evidence:

> ... tends to show the occurrence of systematic killing of civilians belonging to particular tribes, of large-scale causing of serious bodily or mental harm to members of the population belonging to certain tribes, and of massive and deliberate infliction on those tribes of conditions of life bringing about their physical destruction in whole or in part (for example by systematically destroying their villages and crops, by expelling them from their homes, and by looting their cattle).[44]

The Commission went on to say nonetheless that genocidal intent was lacking. For one thing, in respect of villages burned and attacked by militias and government forces the culprits did not kill everyone but selectively murdered groups of young men.[45] Equally, persons forcibly dislodged from their villages were collected in internally displaced persons camps.[46] As a result, the Commission concluded that despite the high death toll and the sheer scale of criminal activity the intention of the militias and government forces 'was to murder all those men they considered as rebels, as well as forcibly expel the whole population so as to vacate the villages and prevent rebels from hiding among, or getting support from, the local population'.[47] Whatever criticism one may invoke against the Report, it is not inconsistent with the aforementioned conservative view of international law-makers as to the existence of genocide, albeit it seems to disregard the clear jurisprudence of the ICTR, as noted above. It should also be mentioned that the ICC and other national courts engaged with the events in Darfur are free to make a different finding.[48]

[42] *Kayishema* Trial Judgment, para 93; a chamber of the ICTY in the *Karadžić* R 61 Decision, para 95, inferred the accused's genocidal intent from the combined effect of his speeches and the massive scale of crimes, all of which were aimed at undermining the foundation of the group; the *Krstić* Appeals Judgment, para 35, inferred genocidal intent from the scale of killings, the awareness of senior military staff and the actions of senior staff to ensure the targeted group's physical demise.

[43] SC Res 1564 (18 Sep 2004).

[44] Report of ICID (25 Jan 2005), UN Doc E/CN.4/2005/3 (11 Feb 2005), para 507.

[45] Ibid, para 513.

[46] Ibid, para 515.

[47] Ibid, para 514.

[48] In fact, in the 2009 *Al-Bashir Warrant* Decision, paras 202–08, the Pre-Trial Chamber examined the Prosecutor's evidence which claimed the inference of a genocidal policy by the Sudanese President Al-Bashir and the Government of Sudan (GoS) against three tribal groups. Nonetheless, on the basis of the evidence available by early 2009 the Chamber was unable to accept that there were 'reasonable grounds' that the accused and GoS had formulated such a genocidal plan. This part of the Pre-Trial Decision was

9.4   Membership of the Targeted Group

Article II of the Genocide Convention only penalises the destruction of four particular groups; namely, national, ethnical, racial or religious. Although other groups may certainly be protected under international or human rights law, particularly those with a political or cultural affiliation, they do not fall within the strict ambit of the Genocide Convention. Although the crime of genocide requires that the accused intended to destroy any of the enumerated groups, it is silent as to membership and admission therein. Moreover, there is no guidance as to whether membership of a group should be viewed objectively – that is, by reason of external and general criteria – or on the basis of subjective criteria, especially through the particular lens of the accused, regardless if such perception is correct according to objective standards. Quite obviously, to the drafters of the Convention at the time it was clear that membership to the various groups was subject to neat categorisations that were discernible through objective deliberations. In this manner, a national group is premised on the formal bond of nationality or the informal notion of national origin. Membership on the basis of race was obviously not intended to take into account one's DNA composition, but rather external traits, such as skin colour, facial and cranial features and others. Religious characteristics are generally self-explanatory, albeit it is uncertain whether they encompass agnostics and atheists. Finally, ethnicity is defined by reference to shared values, such as language and cultural traditions – although it is unusual for each member of a large group to share all the perceived values of the group.[49] This led an ICC Pre-Trial Chamber in the *Al-Bashir* Warrant Decision to claim that three Sudanese tribal groups living in the same area, namely the Fur, the Masalit and the Zaghawa constituted distinct ethnic groups because each possesses its own language, tribal customs and traditional links to its lands.[50] This objective categorisation is consistent with the case law of the Permanent Court of International Justice and the early jurisprudence of the ICJ, all of which suggested that membership of a specific group was a question of fact and therefore objective in nature.[51]

---

subsequently overturned by the ICC Appeals Chamber in a judgment rendered on 3 February 2010, which correctly ruled that the Pre-Trial Chamber had erred in its reading of Art 58(1)(a) of the ICC Statute. This provision requires that in order to issue an arrest warrant for a particular crime – in this case, genocide – the chamber must be convinced that there are 'reasonable grounds to believe' that the person has committed the crime. The Pre-Trial Chamber had instead confused this with the 'beyond reasonable doubt' standard, which is applicable at trial to demonstrate the guilt of the accused.

[49]   The term 'ethnic' is derived from the Greek word ἔθνος, which corresponds to the notion of 'nation'. Thus, although the terms 'ethnic' and 'national' appear to be identical, the contemporary semantic designation of the word 'ethnic', especially in the context of minority law, refers to a category of people possessing some degree of coherence, while at the same time being aware of their common origin and cultural interests. 'National', on the other hand, refers to the bond of nationality. See G Welhengama, *Minorities' Claims: From Autonomy to Secession, International Law and State Practice,* (Dartmouth, Ashgate, 2000) 64–65.

[50]   *Al-Bashir Warrant* Decision, para 137.

[51]   *Rights of Minority Schools in Upper Silesia* (Germany v Poland), (1928) Permanent Court of International Justice (PCIJ) Reports, Ser A, No 15; *Nottebohm* case (Liechtenstein v Guatemala), Judgment on Merits, (1955) ICJ Reports 4.

This deceptively minor aspect of the Genocide Convention gave rise to a make-or-break debate in the ICTR regarding the distinct racial or ethnic make-up, if any, between the Hutu and the Tutsi in Rwanda. No doubt, there existed a well organised campaign to exterminate and eradicate the Tutsi; but did they constitute a distinct group from that which their exterminators claimed affiliation? The anthropological evidence furnished before the ICTR did not demonstrate any differences. In fact, the two shared a common race, religion, language and culture, had lived in the area since time immemorial and had engaged in extensive intermarriages. The use of the two terms (ie Hutu and Tutsi) were not employed to designate a group as such, but rather to denote individual lineage and it was not until 1931 that the Belgian colonisers formalised distinct Hutu and Tutsi clanship through the introduction of identity cards that these designations received any prominence.[52] Strictly speaking, therefore, given the common characteristics between the two a finding of genocide would be absurd because it would entail the destruction of a group as such by its very own members; it would thus amount to a claim of self-destruction. Equally, an expansion of the ambit of the enumerated groups in Article II would conflict with the dictates of the Convention's drafters. Clearly, any international tribunal enforcing the Convention could not arbitrarily introduce new groups into Article II.

The ICTR therefore engineered a position that was not directly in conflict with the Genocide Convention. The *Akayesu* Trial Chamber assessed membership solely on subjective criteria, in accordance with recent developments in human rights law.[53] That is, a person is deemed to belong to a particular group because not only does he identify himself as a member thereof, but also because all other relevant actors perceive him in the same light. To achieve this result the tribunal considered not the ethnic or racial characteristics of the two groups, but the particular perception of the members of each group, which considered themselves distinct from the members of the other group.[54] This approach is desirable in the construction of membership with regard to genocide, since each specific culture and society maintains its own distinct perception of membership that is not easily visible to outside observers. In my opinion this also conforms to customary international law in the sense that it follows scientific advances that demonstrate the fallacy of clean race, at least from a genetic point of view. As a result, it is not inconsistent with the spirit of the Genocide Convention, which certainly cannot be construed in defiance of scientific evidence that is not in direct conflict with its spirit. The Trial Chamber in the *Akayesu* case, based on its aforementioned approach, resorted to an interpretation of particular membership on the basis of the preparatory works of the Genocide Convention, which in its opinion intended to ensure the protection of only 'stable' groups.[55] This interpretation was probably a step too far in respect of the boundaries of the Genocide Convention, albeit the subjective determination of membership was unanimously recognised in later

---

[52] *Akayesu* Trial Judgment, paras 81–83.
[53] See *Lovelace v Canada*, UN Human Rights Committee (1981) 68 ILR 17.
[54] *Akayesu* Trial Judgment, para 702.
[55] *Akayesu* Trial Judgment, paras 510–11, 516. In fact, the 1948 Genocide Convention has come under increased criticism for excluding from its ambit political and other socially vulnerable groups.

judgments and stands for good and reasonable law.[56] Some national statutes and courts have shown defiance to the general conservatism of group membership. In the *Jorgić* case the German Federal Constitutional Court accepted that Article 220(a) of the Criminal Code in force in 1997 was consistent with international law and constitutional safeguards, despite encompassing within its meaning of group destruction: 'a group as a social unit in its distinctiveness and particularity and its feeling of belonging together'.[57] This interpretation is actually wholly consistent with the aim of the Genocide Convention whose focus is on the destruction of the group 'as such', rather than its individual members. Destruction of a protected group's social cohesion renders individual membership meaningless, which is exactly what the Convention aims to prevent and punish. This is not an isolated case that goes beyond the letter of the Genocide Convention. We have already seen that the ex-President of Ethiopia was convicted of genocide for his part in the destruction of a political group. Moreover, the Spanish Central Criminal Court (*Audienca Nacional*) in the *Scilingo* case held that Article 137 of the Spanish Criminal Code, which refers to genocide, is broader than the Genocide Convention and encompasses political opponents as possible victims of genocide.[58]

What, however, of the proposition that within the ambit of the subjective approach to membership the perpetrator may target members of a group by reference to negative inferences? A negative inference is viewed from the perspective of what the victims are not, as opposed to what they are or may be. For example, an attack against anyone perceived as non-black or as non-British, or as non-Christian is certainly distinguishable from attacks against black people, British and Christians in that the latter are targeted precisely because of the characteristics of a particular group. Some ICTY and ICTR chambers have given normative credence to the accused's personal assessment of membership on the basis of negative criteria.[59] In the *Stakić* case, the ICTY Appeals Chamber was faced with a situation that possessed all the elements of genocide, but where the accused did not target any particular group as such; he simply sought to target anyone who was not a Serb. This negative approach by the accused, although admitted in the *Jelisić* case to demonstrate that the accused possessed genocidal intent against a prescribed group, was expressly rejected by the *Stakić* Appeals Chamber, which stated as follows:

> Given that negatively defined groups lack specific characteristics, defining groups by reference to a negative would run counter to the intent of the Genocide Convention's drafters. ... Unlike positively defined groups, negatively defined groups have no unique distinguishing characteristics that could be destroyed.[60]

---

[56] *Jelisić* Trial Judgment, para 70; *Krstić* Trial Judgment, paras 556–57; *Rutaganda,* Trial Judgment, para 56; *Kayishema and Ruzindana* Trial Judgment, para 98; *ICTR Prosecutor v Musema*, Trial Chamber Judgment (27 Jan 2000), paras 161–63.

[57] The relevant passages are cited in *Jorgić v Germany*, Eur Ct HR Judgment (12 Jul 2007), paras 18, 23, 27 and 36, which were approved by the Eur Ct HR, which stated that this particular construction of genocide, although not followed by the ICTY and ICTR, was nonetheless foreseeable as far as the accused was concerned. Although the conclusion is laudable, the Court's reasoning is very weak, albeit one cannot expect it to pronounce on the validity of customary expressions of genocide as found in domestic statutes.

[58] *Re Scilingo*, Judgment No 16/2005 (19 Apr 2005).

[59] *Jelisić* Trial Judgment, paras 70–71; *Rutaganda,* Trial Judgment, para 56.

[60] *ICTY Prosecutor v Stakić*, Appeals Chamber Judgment (22 Mar 2006), paras 22–23.

Despite the fact that the subjective approach may be employed to stigmatise a group by reference to positive characteristics, with a view to ascertaining the target group, this approach is not the sole determinant as to the existence of the group. Although national, ethnic, racial and religious identity is largely accepted as conforming to subjective criteria, the ad hoc tribunals have not abandoned the Genocide Convention's seemingly objective test, holding that a subjective definition alone is insufficient to determine the existence of a victim group.[61] This clarification was meant to dispel fears that the subjective approach can open the floodgates to anyone to argue genocide victimhood on the basis of a personally perceived membership that is not supported by any contextual or other underpinning. As a result, the veracity of subjective self-determination is always conditioned on its recognition by the court and is not taken for granted simply because a victim thinks as much.

9.5 Acts Constituting Genocide

Genocide, at least in the jurisprudence of international criminal tribunals, is limited to any act seeking the physical or biological destruction of all or part of the group and thus 'an enterprise attacking only the cultural or sociological characteristics of a human group in order to annihilate these elements which give to that group its own identity distinct from the rest of that community' would not fall under the definition of genocide.[62] We have already seen, however, that the German Federal Constitutional Court in the *Jorgić* case accepted that the destruction of a group's social cohesiveness may amount to genocide and in this manner physical or biological destruction is irrelevant. Contrary to the rationale of this position, international courts and tribunals generally agree that the practice of ethnic cleansing as such (ie the forced expulsion or displacement of a group from its habitual territory with a view to achieving ethnic homogeneity) does not *ipso facto* amount to genocide. The ICJ noted that not only was a proposal to this effect rejected during the drafting of the Genocide Convention[63] but moreover an ethnic cleansing policy does not give rise to the specific intent of genocide, nor is it necessarily equivalent to the destruction of the group.[64] This does not of course mean that ethnic cleansing can never constitute genocide; rather, if such a policy implicates any of the objective elements of the offence and is moreover committed with the requisite *dolus specialis* it will no doubt amount to genocide.[65]

---

[61] *Rutaganda* Trial Judgment, paras 56–57; *Stakić* Appeals Judgment, ibid, para 25.
[62] *Krstić* Trial Judgment, para 580; cited with approval by the *Krstić* Appeals Judgment, para 25.
[63] *ICJ Bosnia Genocide* Judgment, para 190.
[64] Ibid.
[65] *Al-Bashir Warrant* Decision, para 145; in *Presbyterian Church of Sudan v Talisman Energy Inc* (SDNY, 2003) 244 F Supp 2d 289, at 299, 300–01, which concerned the expulsion of southern Sudanese tribal peoples (the Dinka, Nuer and Nuba) from their ancestral homelands in order to make way for natural resources exploitation, the court acknowledged the existence of a 'low intensity ethnic cleansing' that was implicitly similar to genocide. These events predate the Darfur massacres. The view that under such circumstances ethnic cleansing amounts to genocide was accepted in *ICTY Prosecutor v Blagoević and*

The enumerated criminal acts against members of a group on the basis of their
membership in the group as such are exhaustive, but their ambit had not prior to the
ICTR's jurisprudence been tested in practice. 'Killing members of the group'[66]
encompasses only homicides committed with intent to cause death.[67] 'Causing
serious bodily or mental harm'[68] to members of the group does not require, contrary
to what the USA has been arguing since the adoption of the 1948 Genocide
Convention,[69] that the harm be permanent or irremediable.[70] This provision is not
limited to specific and well known practices causing bodily or mental harm, such as
torture, but is open, as the Israeli Supreme Court pointed out in the *Eichmann* case,
to any acts designed to cause degradation, deprivation of humanity and physical or
mental suffering.[71] 'Deliberately inflicting upon a group conditions of life calculated
to bring about its physical destruction'[72] has been described as a method of slow
death, of which rape can constitute a means for its accomplishment.[73] The *Akayesu*
judgment stated that this category comprises the methods of destruction that are not
immediately aimed at killing the members of the group, but which do so ultimately.
This includes, *inter alia,* subjecting a people to 'a subsistent diet, systematic expulsion, and the reduction of essential medical services below a minimum requirement'.[74] 'Imposing measures intended to prevent births within a group'[75] includes,
but is not limited to, obvious practices such as sexual mutilation, sterilisation, forced
birth control, separation of sexes, or prohibition of marriages. As was noted by the
ICTR, in patriarchal societies children follow the lineage of the father. Thus,
impregnation of a woman by a rapist belonging to another group with the intention
that the victim bear a child from his group may constitute genocide. Likewise, the
mental effect of rape by which a woman is so traumatised that she refuses to
procreate would also amount to genocide.[76] 'Forcibly transferring children of the

---

Jokić, Trial Chamber Judgment (17 Jan 2005), paras 665–66, on the ground that a group is comprised of its
history, traditions, relationships between its members and other groups and its land. The Chamber was
relying on the *Jorgić* judgment.

[66] ICTR Statute, Art 2(2)(a).
[67] *Akayesu* Trial Judgment, paras 500–01; *Musema,* Trial Judgment, para 155.
[68] ICTR Statute, Art 2(2)(b).
[69] Verdirame, 580–81.
[70] *Akayesu* Trial Judgment, paras 502–04.
[71] *Public Prosecutor v Eichmann*, Judgment (1962) 36 ILR 277, at 340. This passage from the court's
judgment refers to the charge of 'crimes against the Jewish people', which is equivalent to that of genocide
in terms of scope. The judgment rendered by the District Court of Jerusalem was subsequently upheld by
the Israeli Supreme Court.
[72] ICTR Statute, Art 2(2)(c).
[73] *Kayishema* Trial Judgment, para 116. Nonetheless, the ICC Elements of Crimes, Art 6(b), num 1,
stipulate that rapes can constitute genocide under the category of causing serious bodily or mental harm.
See also AA Miller, 'From the International Criminal Tribunal for Rwanda to the International Criminal
Court: Expanding the Definition of Genocide to Include Rape' (2003) 108 *Dickinson Law Review* 349.
[74] *Akayesu* Trial Judgment, paras 505–06; iterated with approval in the ICC Elements of Crimes, Art
6(c), num 4.
[75] ICTR Statute, Art 2(2)(d).
[76] *Akayesu* Trial Judgment, paras 507–08.

group to another group'[77] concerns not only forceful physical transfer, but also the causing of serious trauma to the parents or guardians that would necessarily lead to such transfer.[78]

In the *Krstić* Trial judgment, the ICTY noted that besides the physical destruction of a group the same result may also be achieved by a 'purposeful eradication of [the group's] culture and identity, resulting in the eventual extinction of the group as an entity distinct from the remainder of the community'.[79] Although the Trial Chamber found that cultural genocide was excluded from the ambit of the Genocide Convention it nonetheless pointed to some recent developments outside the ICTY/ICTR context that support criminalisation of this form of genocide. It finally determined that cultural genocide was not part of customary international law and thus did not fall within the ICTY Statute, but since acts of genocide usually involve attacks against cultural and religious property, such attacks may at least be seen as evidence of genocide.[80]

9.6   The Problematic Nature of Aiding and Abetting Genocide

Article III of the Genocide Convention enumerates the various modalities through which a person may be convicted of this offence. These include: direct perpetration of genocide, conspiracy, direct and public incitement, attempt and complicity to commit genocide. Whereas these would otherwise constitute different forms by which a person participates in a criminal offence, in the Genocide Convention they play the role of inchoate crimes – apart from direct perpetration and complicity which requires the existence of either direct perpetration or an inchoate offence. Given the scale of planning and execution that are involved in genocide every participant can be treated as a direct perpetrator, in which case there would be no role for complicity. The practice of the ad hoc tribunals is to distinguish between persons that fulfil a 'key co-ordinating role' and whose participation is significant for the planning and implementation of the genocide,[81] from those that simply associate themselves to the crime and the direct perpetrators.[82] What is unclear in the statutes of the ad hoc tribunals is whether the general modes of complicity (Articles 7(1) and 6(1) of the ICTY and ICTR respectively), particularly aiding and abetting, apply to genocide. The question is not rhetorical, but crucially practical, for complicity in genocide may be narrower or broader than aiding and abetting generally and moreover the *mens rea* for complicity in genocide may require proof of specific intent to destroy, whereas this is not necessary in respect of aiding and abetting. Let us examine these matters in more detail.

---

[77]   ICTR Statute, Art 2(2)(e).
[78]   *Akayesu* Trial Judgment, paras 509–10.
[79]   *Krstić* Trial Judgment, para 574.
[80]   Ibid, paras 576–80.
[81]   *Stakić* Trial Judgment, para 533; *Krstić* Trial Judgment, paras 642–44.
[82]   *ICTY Prosecutor v Brđanin*, Trial Chamber Judgment (1 Sep 2004).

In the context of the ICC Statute general and specific (to genocide) complicity are considered complementary, albeit in the case of the ad hoc tribunals the relation between the two remained for some time problematic and subject to two differing interpretations.[83] The position has now been clarified and it is now accepted that the general modes of participation, including aiding and abetting, may be read into the genocide provision of the statutes of the ad hoc tribunals,[84] although the concept of complicity is broader than the forms of assistance encompassed within the meaning of 'aiding and abetting'.[85] We have already examined the rejection of the knowledge-based theory in the construction of the *mens rea* for genocide. As a result, the appropriate mental state required to convict a person as an aider and abettor to genocide is knowledge that one's acts will assist in the commission of genocide and awareness of the principal's specific intent to commit genocide.[86] Thus, the aider must be found to be aware of the impending genocide as an event in and of itself and not by mere reference to disparate crimes that give rise to the genocide but in respect of which the aider cannot see the full picture. In the *Blagoević and Jokić* case, which concerned the Srebrenica genocide, the accused was cleared of complicity because the event which his principal committed involved the forceful expulsion of the civilian population (ie ethnic cleansing), which as already explained is not considered as genocide. Hence, it was presumed that on the basis of this act alone the accused was not aware of the genocide, having already demonstrated that he was not aware of the other mass killings.[87]

Where, however, complicity in genocide consists of conduct that is broader than aiding and abetting, it must be shown that the accomplice was not simply aware of the principal's specific intent but that additionally he himself possessed this specific intent required for genocide.[88] The *Krstić* Appeals Chamber explained that this conclusion was uncontested during the deliberations for the Genocide Convention, but did not proceed to explain how it would be applied in practice, deeming the matter to have been discussed by it merely *obiter dictum*.[89] If we accept this distinction between aiding/abetting and complicity, the latter must possess character-istics that are quantifiably more significant than the former. Thus, D aids genocide where he drives the vehicle that transports the victims to their place of execution, or where he arrests and detains them. He also aids the principal if he allows him to kill or rape members of the group that are under his protection. In these cases it is not necessary that D possesses the *dolus eventualis* for genocide, which already resides in the principal. Where, however, D receives an order from the key planners to burn down a village or to execute a large number of civilians and he implements this order in the knowledge that it is part of a wider genocidal campaign, he will have formed the intention to destroy that group in whole or in part and is thus liable as an accomplice to genocide. As a result, it is fair to argue that an accomplice to genocide

---

[83]   See C Eboe-Osuji, 'Complicity in Genocide versus Aiding and Abetting Genocide: Construing the Difference in the ICTR and ICTY Statutes' (2005) 3 *Journal of International Criminal Justice* 56.

[84]   *Krstić* Appeals Judgment, para 138.

[85]   Ibid, para 139.

[86]   *Akayesu* Trial Judgment, para 485; *Brđanin* Trial Judgment, para 730.

[87]   *ICTY Prosecutor v Blagoević and Jokić*, Appeals Chamber Judgment (9 May 2007), para 123.

[88]   *Krstić* Appeals Judgment, para 142.

[89]   Ibid.

– given the requirement as to specific intent – is one who does much more than merely offer assistance or carry out preparatory acts that facilitate the genocide; rather, his role is to implement or carry out the dictates or plans of the principals to such a degree that his contribution may be deemed significant.

The reader should consult the chapter on liability and modes of participation in crime in order to acquaint himself with these and other forms by which a person may commit genocide and international crimes more generally.

9.7   Incitement to Commit Genocide

We have already briefly explained that incitement to commit genocide is not a mere mode of participation in a genocidal campaign, but rather an inchoate crime in its own right. It commences as soon as the inciter utters or publishes the contested words and is continuous in nature until such time as those incited go on to commit genocide.[90] Given that it does not require consummation in order for liability to arise, it follows that unsuccessful incitement to commit genocide is also a punishable act. Before I set out to explain the mental and conduct elements of this offence it is crucial that some light is shed on two related issues; its relation to freedom of expression and its resemblance to hate crimes. As far as the former is concerned, if freedom of expression is subject to no limitations then there is no place in the criminal law for a crime such as incitement to genocide! Article 10(2) of the European Convention of Human Rights clearly limits the boundaries of this freedom in respect of situations that are 'necessary in a democratic society in the interests of national security or public safety, for the prevention of disorder or crime . . .'. Equally, the public is entitled to receive information through the press[91] and as such this entitlement can only be curtailed when it is used to spread propaganda,[92] or when the information under consideration is not in the interest of the public, in the sense that it is in no way informative (eg as would be the case with sensational news-reporting that moreover causes harm to certain people).[93] The spirit of Article 10(2) has even led the Court and several European legislatures to prohibit or criminalise speech whose purpose is to deny the WW II Holocaust.[94] On the other hand, the 1791 First Amendment to the US Constitution does not readily allow for any such limitations and is considered a paradigm of unlimited free speech that is antithetical in its philosophy to that of the European Convention system. Nonetheless, the US Supreme Court declared as unconstitutional any limitations on the freedom of

---

[90]   *Nahimana* Appeals Judgment (28 Nov 2007), para 1017.

[91]   *Gaskin v UK*, (1989) 12 EHRR 36 and *Sirbu and Others v Moldova*, Judgment (15 Jun 2004) [2004] EHRR 264.

[92]   *Yalçin Küçük v Turkey*, Judgment (22 Apr 2008), App No 71353/01.

[93]   See *Mamére v France*, Judgment (7 Nov 2006), App No 64772/01; *Hachette Filippachi Associés v France*, Judgment (14 Jun 2007), App No 71111/01, in which a domestic court order banning the reproduction of a picture depicting the murdered corpse of a public figure by the press was approved by the Eur Ct HR.

[94]   *Lehideux and Isorni v France*, 30 EHRR 665; see the 1947 Austrian Prohibition Act [Verbotsgesetz], whose 1992 amendment prohibited the outright denial or gross minimalisation of the Holocaust.

expression that 'forbid or proscribe advocacy of the use of force or of law violation except where such advocacy is directed *to inciting or producing imminent lawless action* and *is likely to incite* or produce such action'.[95] The two extremes therefore agree that incitement to criminal activity does not warrant protection. As a result, the crime of incitement to genocide is not at all inconsistent with the freedom of expression and its associated freedom of the press. As for hate crimes premised on the offender's particular bias, although their effect may be to instil in others the urge to commit widespread offences against members of a group or simply to accept the contours of this bias, a hate crime is radically different from incitement to genocide. Hate crimes, particularly those premised on propaganda or incitement to racial hatred that are based on ideas of racial superiority, are subject to mandatory criminal sanctions under Article 4 of the 1965 International Convention on the Elimination of All Forms of Racial Discrimination.[96] The principal in hate crimes may not even intend to incite others to attack members of the group, let alone possess the specific intent for genocide. As with ethnic cleansing, hate crimes can amount to genocide only if they satisfy the requisite subjective and objective elements.[97]

The Rwandan genocide exemplifies the role of incitement in societies that give eminence to their leaders and figureheads. This genocide was conceived at the highest level by Hutu officials and was executed by lower level individuals, including Hutu youth teams and private actors that had been incited through the mass media and public speeches. The seminal role of the media as a means of instigating hatred and calling for extermination of the Tutsi by falsifying or exaggerating events was made clear in the case of former Prime Minister Kambanda, but more so in the case of *Georges Ruggiu,* a Belgian national who was responsible for broadcasting these messages on Rwandan radio.[98] Public speeches given by influential individuals were found to have had the same effect, as was evident in the case of Akayesu's rallies with which he intended to directly create a particular state of mind in his audience that would lead to the destruction of the Tutsi. The ICTR defined the *actus reus* of incitement as 'encouraging, persuading or directly provoking another through speeches, shouts, threats or any other means of audiovisual communication to commit an offence'.[99] Incitement to commit genocide must further be committed in public (in the sense that the location must be a public place or through publicly accessible means of communication) and be direct as to what its author wants to achieve. However, the 'directness' element, as correctly propounded by the *Akayesu* Trial Chamber, should be assessed in light of its cultural and linguistic content and the particular perception of each individual audience.[100] This subjective approach takes into consideration not the understanding of the neutral observer, given that certain utterances may be disguised or may mean nothing to said observer. Rather, it

---

[95]   *Brandenburg v Ohio* (1969) 395 U.S. 444, at 447.
[96]   660 UNTS 195.
[97]   Under certain circumstances 'hate speech' can also amount to persecution as part of crimes against humanity. *ICTR Prosecutor v Nahimana*, Trial Chamber Judgment (3 Dec 2003), paras 1072–84.
[98]   *ICTR Prosecutor v Ruggiu*, Trial Chamber Judgment (1 Jun 2000), paras 17, 44, 50.
[99]   *Akayesu* Trial Judgment, para 555; *Nahimana* Trial Judgment, para 1011. This is known as the *Media* case, because the three accused were, among others, charged with using radio, television and the printed press for inciting the Hutu to destroy the Tutsi.
[100]   *Akayesu*, ibid, paras 557, 559.

is the understanding of the intended audience that is crucial. The *Akayesu* Trial Judgment defined the *mens rea* of incitement to commit genocide as existing:

> ... in the intent to directly prompt or provoke another to commit genocide. It implies a desire on the part of the perpetrator to create by his actions a particular state of mind necessary to commit such a crime in the minds of the person(s) he is so engaging. That is to say that the person who is inciting to commit genocide must have himself the specific intent to commit genocide.[101]

---

[101] Ibid, para 560.

10

Offences Against The Person

10.1 Introduction

This chapter examines offences against the person with an international or transnational element. Most of these, however, constitute *erga omnes* obligations, and as such the very act of perpetration even within a single State creates a legal interest for every country in the world, particularly in terms of legislative and judicial jurisdiction. Here we examine the following offences: slavery and related practices, torture, apartheid and enforced disappearances. Other offences against the person, such as grave breaches, war crimes, crimes against humanity and genocide are covered in other discrete chapters. The distinction is therefore artificial. Other international offences that offend the person, albeit where the effect on the person is incidental to the primary aim of the perpetrator, which is either financial or sociopolitical, such as piracy, terrorism and organised crime are also covered in distinct chapters. All of these offences against the person, by their very nature constitute serious human rights violations. Although reference is made to the various international human rights instruments these were not designed to deal with the individual responsibility of the perpetrators, at least in the sphere of international law; rather, their purpose was to implement legislation criminalising such conduct at the domestic level, enforcing the protection of would-be victims and deterring future perpetrators. This does not mean that human rights instruments are irrelevant in the international criminalisation process. Although they have a very important role to play, caution should be exercised when human rights notions are transplanted in the international criminal process, as will be evident throughout this chapter.

10.2 Slavery and Related Practices

A study conducted by the non-governmental organisation Anti-Slavery International revealed the conclusion of some three hundred international agreements concerning the suppression of slavery between 1815 and 1957. These were, however, largely ineffective as a result of the lack of national mechanisms by which to evaluate incidences of slavery between States parties.[1] Although by the late eighteenth century many States had formally abolished slavery[2] and considered such practice as being contrary to the law of nations they nonetheless tolerated the slave trade in countries where it was permitted by law and by nationals of such countries on the high seas.[3] In the dispute arising between the USA and Great Britain in the *Creole* cases the arbiter assigned to settle the ensuing claims held that in situations of *force majeure* forcing a slave vessel to seek refuge in the territorial waters of an abolitionist State the latter is obliged to respect the law of the Flag State.[4] Although this arbitral award was criticised on humanitarian grounds it does demonstrate slavery was considered an entitlement that any nation could exercise and permit under its own laws. The courts and legislatures of abolitionist States naturally sought legal avenues by which to curb this entitlement without offending international relations and at the same time releasing slaves from their servile status. One such avenue was to render the slave trade on the high seas tantamount to piracy *jure gentium*, thus providing a broad range of jurisdiction to all nations. As attractive as this option may have seem, most national courts refused to follow it because of the striking legal differences between the two types of conduct.[5] The status of slave vessels as private vessels flying the flag of a State could not be ignored. At the time, search and seizure of private vessels on the high seas was dependent on bilateral treaties granting reciprocal rights and so it is of no surprise that the first multilateral treaties of this kind, the 1885 General Act of the Conference of Berlin Concerning the Congo,[6] as well as the 1890 Brussels General Act Relative to the African Slave Trade[7] contained limited enforcement prerogatives to non-flag States. Despite the limitations in search and seizure arising from these instruments and the continuation of unrestricted engagement in the slave trade by certain countries, the above mentioned agreements and relevant State practice suggested in unequivocal terms that by the late nineteenth century the slave trade was an international offence that was treated as such by national criminal legislation.[8]

---

[1] Report of the Working Group on Contemporary Forms of Slavery, UN Doc E/CN4/Sub2/ 1999/17 (20 Jul 1999), para 41.

[2] See Abolition of Slavery Act 1833, which by abolishing slavery in the British colonies rendered the slaves apprentices and ordered their compensation by public funds paid by their owners.

[3] *The Fortuna* (1811) 165 ER 1240; *The Diana* (1813) 165 ER 1245; *San Juan Nepomuceno* (1824) 166 ER 94; *The Antelope* (1825) 23 US 66.

[4] *The Creole* (1853); JB Moore, *Moore's Digest of International Law*, (Washington DC, Government Printing Office, 1906), vol 2, at 352; see DP O'Connell, *The International Law of the Sea*, (Oxford, Clarendon Press, 1984) 854–55.

[5] *Le Louis* (1817) 2 Dods 213, at 218, *per* Scott J.

[6] Declaration Concerning the Slave Trade, Art 9, allowed interdiction on land and sea in the territories forming the conventional basin of the Congo. Reprinted in 82 BFSP 55.

[7] 1890 Brussels General Act Relative to the African Slave Trade, Art XXII, granted reciprocal rights of search and seizure to States parties, but only in the Persian Gulf and the Red Sea (Art XXI), over vessels of less than 500 tonnes (Art XXIII). Reprinted in 1 Bevans 134.

[8] Berlin Act, Art 9 and Brussels Act, Arts V and XIX.

As a matter of customary law it is now settled that all persons are entitled to be free from slavery or servitude,[9] as well as from forced or compulsory labour.[10] It is equally true that all persons have a right to be free from institutions and practices similar to slavery and that the enjoyment of these fundamental rights are subject to *erga omnes* obligations.[11] Article 1(1) of the 1927 Slavery Convention defines slavery as 'the status or condition of a person over whom any or all of the powers attaching to the right of ownership are attached'. The plethora of anti-slavery conventions and the detailed framework of rights contained in each obfuscates the distinction that should be drawn in every case between the granting of a right and the intentional promulgation of an offence, whether domestic or international in nature. In this book a particular conduct is deemed to possess a criminal character where this is explicit in a treaty, as a result of State practice, or by reason of the fact that the implementation of a specific right requires penalisation of the corresponding conduct that impedes it. What this means is that even if particular conduct has not been criminalised by a treaty it may still amount to an international crime if it has been widely penalised in domestic laws. Conversely, marginally ratified treaties that expressly criminalise particular conduct are not considered as evidence of State practice in respect of that crime. It is equally true that one cannot read too much into marginally ratified treaties that prohibit the lodging of reservations, because it is not always clear that non-ratifying States are opposed to the crime in question, as opposed to some of its procedural or other substantive qualities.[12]

10.2.1   The Slave Trade and Similar Institutions

Trading in slaves should be conceptually distinguished from an act of enslavement. Clearly, however, enslavement is a prerequisite for any conduct associated with the slave trade. Article 1(2) of the 1927 Slavery Convention defines the slave trade as including:

> ... all acts involved in the capture, acquisition or disposal of a person with intent to reduce him to slavery; all acts involved in the acquisition of a slave with a view to selling or exchanging him; all acts of disposal by sale or exchange of a slave acquired with a view to being sold or exchanged, and, in general, every act of trade or transport in slaves.

---

[9] 1927 Slavery Convention, Art 2(b), 60 UNTS 253, amended by 1953 Protocol Amending the 1927 Slavery Convention, 182 UNTS 51; Universal Declaration on Human Rights, Art 4, GA Res 217A (10 Dec 1948); 1966 International Covenant on Civil and Political Rights (ICCPR), Art 8(1) and (2), 999 UNTS 171.

[10] 1927 Slavery Convention, Art 5; 1966 ICCPR, Art 8(3); 1930 International Labour Organisation (ILO) Forced Labour Convention (No 29), Art 2(1).

[11] *Barcelona Traction Light and Power House Co Ltd* (Belgium v Spain), Second Phase Judgment (1970) ICJ Reports 3, at 32.

[12] eg the UK has refused to ratify the 1949 Convention for the Suppression of the Traffic in Persons and of the Exploitation of the Prostitution of Others, 96 UNTS 271, although it has passed legislation conforming to most provisions contained in this instrument. The reason for the UK's refusal is that the Convention penalises more acts than are penalised under UK law. See Report of the Working Group on Slavery, above n 1, para 37.

The slave trade as a commercial enterprise was effectively starved by the abolition of slavery and to the extent that it exists today it approximates the practice of trafficking. It is also well settled that conveying, attempting, or being an accessory to the conveyance of slaves from one country to another constitutes a serious offence under international law.[13] Although the definition of slave trade contained in Article 1(2) of the 1927 Slavery Convention seems to encompass a wide range of acts, the drafters of this instrument in fact excluded a range of similar practices that affected and still affect a substantial part of the population of developing countries. Extreme poverty compounded by the lack of social and administrative structures soon revealed a different facet of slavery; one where the individual was forced to submit to exploitation or risk extinction.

The 1956 Supplementary Convention on the Abolition of Slavery, the Slave Trade, and Institutions Similar to Slavery (Supplementary Slavery Convention) was purposely designed to address the gaps in the Slavery Convention. Article 1 prohibits the institutions of debt bondage, serfdom, bride-price and the illegal transfer of children. Debt bondage arises from a pledge by a debtor of his personal services or of persons under his or her control as security for a debt. This transaction becomes unlawful under Article 1(a) of the Supplementary Slavery Convention where the value of those services as reasonably assessed are not applied towards the liquidation of the debt, or the length and nature of those services are not respectively limited and defined. The Ad Hoc Committee established by the Economic and Social Council (ECOSOC) of the United Nations in 1949 to formulate this Convention was of the view that debt bondage was also constituted where the bondsman and the debtor submit to conditions not allowing the exercise of rights enjoyed by ordinary individuals within the framework of local social custom,[14] as would necessarily be the case with a contract of performance in which the nature of the servitude and its duration are undefined and potentially unlimited. Debt bondage is endemic in the majority of developing nations where due to the lack of access to cash personal labour becomes a tradable commodity. A study conducted in 1995 estimated the existence in India alone at least 15 million child labourers as a direct result of a debt incurred by a parent.[15] These debts are not susceptible to repayment because of the astronomical interest rates imposed by the lenders and low wages of the debtors. As a result, children may typically work throughout their youth without having managed to repay the loan, which could subsequently be inherited by another family member, most likely a younger child. This practice is so entrenched at the local level that any attempts to curtail it by the central government without strict local enforcement are doomed to fail. Thus, despite the passing of the 1976 Bonded Labour System (Abolition) Act (No 19), which obliges the governments of the various Indian States to release the bonded labourers and rehabilitate them[16] debt bondage continues with impunity. That debt bondage is a form of slavery that incurs the criminal liability of

---

[13] 1956 Supplementary Slavery Convention, Art 3(1), 266 UNTS 3.

[14] JAC Gutteridge, 'The Supplementary Slavery Convention 1956' (1957) 6 *International & Comparative Law Quarterly* 449, at 452.

[15] L Tucker, 'Child Slaves in Modern India: The Bonded Labour Problem' (1997) 19 *Human Rights Quarterly* 572, at 573.

[16] *Chaudhary v State of Madhya Pradesh* (1948) 3 SCC 243, at 255; see ibid, Tucker, at 622.

the perpetrator is evident by the provisions of the 1999 International Labour Organization (ILO) Convention for the Prohibition and Immediate Action for the Elimination of the Worst Forms of Child Labour (No 182).[17]

The prohibition of bride-price in Article 1(c) of the Supplementary Slavery Convention penalises the acquisition of girls by purchase disguised as payment of dowry for marriage. This institution becomes a criminal offence where the female is either denied the right to consent and is given to marriage on the basis of a financial transaction of any kind by familial or any other persons, or where upon the death of her husband her family or clan members transfer her to another person, thus reducing her to an object of inheritance. States are generally free to prescribe a minimum age of marriage and, although the 1962 Convention on Consent to Marriage, Minimum Age for Marriage and Registration of Marriages[18] is not widely ratified, the principle of full and free consent of both parties declared in Article 1 therein is undoubtedly a rule of customary international law on account of its presence in the widely ratified 1956 Supplementary Slavery Convention. Bride-price and indeed all the institutions and practices penalised in the 1956 Convention were so deeply rooted in traditional rural societies in the developing world that the western delegates agreed, despite the vehement opposition of many non-governmental organisations, to allow for progressive abolition of these practices rather than impose an immediate prohibition. Although the grace period in respect of these practices should be deemed to have expired, poverty and poor education has been the principal factor for the continuation of bride-price.

The practice of bride-price should be distinguished from that of 'bride-wealth'. The latter constitutes a substantial and obligatory payment from the groom's kin to the bride's family, not to the bride. Bride-wealth represented both marital cement and an assurance for both partners against the bad behaviour of the other and was to be returned if the marriage ended on account of the wife's 'fault'. Although the material elements of bride-wealth did not traditionally fit within supply/demand market notions, during the twentieth century this institution has been distorted as its ingredients have acquired national currency values. As the material gifts associated with bride-wealth acquired modern money value the prospect always loomed that bride-wealth would indeed become transformed into bride-price. For this reason many African countries have now regulated the cash value of bride-wealth. As the 1956 Supplementary Slavery Convention only intended to penalise and prevent the downgrading of marriage to a financial transaction lacking the consent of the bride traditional bride-wealth practices do not violate the Convention.

The transfer of children under the age of 18 by their natural parents or guardian to another person, whether for financial benefit or not, with a view to exploiting the child or its labour is an international offence under Article 1(d) of the 1956 Convention. A number of international instruments under the same terms expressly prohibit the trafficking, more specifically the sale or exploitation of children in any form, such as the 1989 Convention on the Rights of the Child,[19] the 2000 Optional

[17]   1999 ILO Convention, Arts 3(a) and 7, (1999) 38 ILM 1207.
[18]   521 UNTS 231; see also GA Res 2018(XX) (1 Nov 1965) endorsing this principle.
[19]   1989 Convention on the Rights of the Child, Arts 35 and 36, (1989) 28 ILM 1448.

Protocol II thereto on the Sale of Children, Child Prostitution and Child Pornography[20] and the 1999 ILO Worst Forms of Child Labour Convention.[21] These instruments do not intend to penalise those adoptions which the natural parents earnestly believe are in the best interest of their children and are moreover completed lawfully and without any personal benefit to the parents.[22] Interpol research suggests that illicit foreign adoptions are carried out through the falsification of birth certificates, followed by abductions or deceit of uneducated mothers by organised criminal rings.[23]

It is equally undisputed that the acts of procuring or offering of children in sexual activities for remuneration or any other form of consideration (child prostitution), or for representation of children engaged in real or simulated explicit sexual activities or any representation of the sexual parts of a child for sexual purposes (child pornography) constitute international offences.[24] This would include procurers and clients engaged in sex tourism, as well as distributors and possessors of pornography through postal services or the Internet.[25] It should be stressed that the Special Rapporteur on the Sale of Children, Child Prostitution and Child Pornography identified four causes related to the sexual exploitation of children; namely, ineffective justice systems, the role of the media, lack of education, but foremost she emphasised that, besides cases of kidnapping, it was the family of the children that was responsible for their eventual exploitation in the hands of others.[26]

Serfdom is also prohibited under Article 1(b) of the 1956 Supplementary Slavery Convention. This refers to the condition of a tenant who is bound to live and labour on land belonging to another person and provide determinate service to the landowner, whether for reward or not, and who is not free to change that condition. In *Van Droogenbroeck v Belgium* the European Commission of Human Rights observed, *obiter dictum*, that the notion of servitude embraces, in addition to the obligation to perform certain acts for others, 'the obligation for the serf to live on another person's property and the impossibility of altering his condition'.[27] Contemporary serfdom resembles the existence of the feudal system in medieval Europe, where in the absence of an industrial middle class and the accumulation of land in the hands of a small group of landlords two social classes were necessarily established: the dominant class (*domini, nobiles*) and the vassals. The vassals gradually became animate objects tied

---

[20] Contained in GA Res 54/263 (25 May 2000), Art 2(a).

[21] ILO Worst Forms of Child Labour Convention, Art 3(a).

[22] In accordance with Arts 1 and 21 of the 1993 Hague Convention on Protection of Children and Co-operation in Respect of Inter-Country Adoptions, (1993) 32 ILM 1134 and the 1989 Convention on the Rights of the Child, respectively.

[23] Y Bird, *The Trafficking of Children for Sexual Exploitation and Foreign Adoption: Background and Current Measures*, (The Hague, Interpol, 1999).

[24] 2000 Optional Protocol II to the Convention on the Rights of the Child, Arts 2(b), (c) and 3; 1999 ILO Worst Forms of Child Labour Convention, Art 3(a), (b); 1989 Convention on the Rights Of the Child, Art 34; ECOSOC Res 1996/26 (24 Jul 1996), entitled Measures to Prevent Illicit International Trafficking in Children and to Establish Penalties Appropriate to Such Offences.

[25] See LM Jones, 'Regulating Child Pornography on the Internet: The Implications of Article 34 of the United Nations Convention on the Rights of the Child' (1998) 6 *International Journal of Childrens' Rights* 55.

[26] UN Doc E/CN4/2000/73 (14 Jan 2000).

[27] *Van Droogenbroeck v Belgium* (1982) 4 EHRR 443.

to the land (*servi terrae*). The same medieval elements are present in cases of contemporary serfdom taking place in developing countries, whose eradication can only be premised on courageous land reform and industrial development. Since in the vast majority of contemporary cases the vassal will have consented to his or her status the institution of serfdom is illegal no matter how it has come about.

Traffic in persons, especially for purposes of sexual exploitation, is a specific form of slavery-related institution. One treaty has in the past penalised trafficking in persons without defining the term. Article 1 of the 1949 Convention for the Suppression of the Traffic in Persons and of the Exploitation of the Prostitution of Others (1949 Convention), which supersedes several previous instruments relating to the trafficking of women and children (so-called 'white slavery'), penalises any person who, in order to gratify the passions of another:

1. procures, entices or leads away, for purposes of prostitution, another person, even with the consent of that person;
2. exploits the prostitution of another person, even with the consent of that person.

The aim of this provision is to eradicate both the initial enticement into prostitution, which usually commences as a result of socio-financial hardships, as well as the eventual procuring of prostitution in urban or other centres. The relevant discussions in the various human rights bodies of the UN have revealed two schools of thought on this issue. One maintains that controlled and lawfully registered prostitution should be allowed and that only the initial trafficking should be punished, whereas the other argues for a total ban and penalisation of prostitution. This division among States, further reinforced with the penalisation of the financing or maintenance of brothels or places facilitating prostitution in Article 2 of the 1949 Convention, is manifested by the limited ratifications this instrument has received. This number should not mislead one to believe that prostitution in all its manifestations is lawful except where it is prohibited by States parties to the 1949 Convention. Rather, although exploitation of the prostitution of others not culminating to a condition of ownership over a person and performed with the prostitute's consent does not draw consensus to warrant its characterisation as an international offence, the procurement or enticement of a person for the purposes of prostitution does constitute a transnational offence.[28] This conclusion is derived from the fact that the latter facet of prostitution is a criminal offence in the vast majority of States and because the declarations of non-parties to the 1949 Convention clearly demonstrates that their decision not to ratify was premised on the fact that their domestic laws traditionally permits State-controlled prostitution.[29]

---

[28] See also Art 6 of the 1979 Convention on the Elimination of All Forms of Discrimination Against Women, (1980) 19 ILM 33, which requires States to suppress all forms of traffic in women and exploitation of the prostitution of others; ECOSOC Res 1999/40 (26 Apr 1999) urged States to criminalise traffic in women and girls, whether the offence was committed in their own or third countries; para 24 of the Organisation for Security and Co-operation in Europe Charter for European Security prescribes an undertaking by this organisation to eliminate all forms of trafficking and sexual exploitation of human beings, (2000) 39 ILM 255: strategic objective D3 of the Beijing Platform for Action of the Fourth World Conference on Women (Report of 15 Sep 1995), aiming to eliminate trafficking in women.

[29] Possible ratification of the 1949 Convention by retentionist States with the inclusion of relevant reservations would run counter to the purpose and object of the treaty and would be null, in accordance with the 1969 Vienna Convention on the Law of Treaties, Art 19(c), 1155 UNTS 331.

The ineffectiveness of the 1949 Convention necessitated the adoption of a specific instrument in November 2000, the UN Protocol to Prevent, Suppress and Punish Trafficking in Persons, Especially Women and Children.[30] The Protocol applies with respect to cases of trafficking involving force and a transnational aspect (movement of people across borders or exploitation within a country by a transnational organised crime group) and is intended to prevent and combat trafficking, facilitate international cooperation, as well as provide protection and assistance to victims. Article 3(a) defines 'trafficking in persons' as:

> The recruitment, transportation, transfer, harbouring or receipt of persons, by means of the threat or use of force or other forms of coercion, of abduction, of fraud, of deception, of the abuse of power or of a position of vulnerability or of the giving or receiving of payments or benefits to achieve the consent of a person having control over another person, for the purpose of exploitation.

The term 'exploitation' is further elaborated as exploitation of prostitution and other forms of sexual exploitation, forced labour, slavery and related practices, as well as the removal of organs. There is great expectation that the Protocol, as well as the 2000 UN Convention Against Transnational Organized Crime, will be effective in its preventive and punitive aspects and succeed where its predecessors failed.

There does exist one final form of slavery-related practice which is an offence only when committed by instrumentalities or agents of State entities: forced or compulsory labour. Article 2(1) of the 1930 ILO Forced Labour Convention (No 29) (1930 ILO Convention) defines forced labour as:

> All work or service which is exacted from any person under the menace of any penalty and for which the said person has not offered himself voluntarily.

This definition of forced labour excludes military service, civic duties, work arising from lawful conviction properly supervised, labour as a result of natural calamities or other emergencies and other cases of minor communal services.[31] All other forms of forced labour constitute penal offences under the 1930 ILO Convention[32] and wide ratification of this instrument has rendered the offence a rule of customary international law. In June 1999 the ILO decided to boycott commercial or other activities in Myanmar (Burma) for its 'grave and persistent' violation of the 1930 ILO Convention,[33] which eventually culminated in the expulsion of this country from the organisation itself.[34] Myanmar is of course a unique case and it is estimated that more than 800,000 civilians, particularly from ethnic minorities, have been forcibly recruited by the Myanmar government to work on public projects, resulting in the displacement of between 5 and 10 per cent of the Burmese population.[35]

---

[30] UN Doc A/55/383 (2 Nov 2000).

[31] 1930 ILO Convention, Art 2(2).

[32] Ibid, Art 25.

[33] ILO Resolution, The Widespread Use of Forced Labour in Myanmar of 14 June 1999, (1999) 38 ILM 1215.

[34] Report of the Commission of Inquiry Regarding the Observance by Myanmar of the 1930 Forced Labour Convention (2 Jul 1998).

[35] In *Doe v Unocal* (1997) 963 F Supp 880, a US District Court held that two American private corporations engaged in commercial activities involving the use of forced labour in Burma could be found liable under the 1789 Aliens Tort Claims Act, 18 USC § 1350.

The UN Working Group on Contemporary Forms of Slavery has stated that slavery in all its forms and manifestations is a crime against humanity.[36] This is certainly the case in respect of organised enslavement taking place either in armed conflict or as part of a systematised policy by States or sufficiently well organised non-State entities. In these situations the object of the perpetrators is usually to force the victims to flee or to destroy them in one way or another. The most prevalent form of contemporary slavery, however, takes place through the trafficking of persons by organised criminal groups. It is evident that its eradication is primarily dependent on the strengthening of civil society and public institutions, the imposition of severe criminal sanctions against organised crime and its offspring, particularly corruption.

10.3   Torture as a Crime under International Law

The prohibition of torture in international law is regulated by instruments whose primary purpose is the establishment of appropriate preventive and deterrent mechanisms. This forms part of a wider obligation undertaken by States in the context of human rights law.[37] Although these treaties envisage the application of criminal laws against the perpetrator their primary purpose is to form the platform for the adoption of implementing legislation and engage the responsibility of States parties. It should not, therefore, be assumed that these treaties apply *mutatis mutandis* to assess the criminal liability of perpetrators under international law. The prohibition of torture as laid down in human rights treaties entails a positive and negative right from which no derogation is permitted, reflecting also a solid *jus cogens* norm. This is confirmed by the fact that the prohibition against torture has been construed as such by domestic and international judicial bodies,[38] never having been officially denied by any country. Moreover, in Europe at least, States are not permitted to return or extradite to another country persons that are in danger of being subjected to torture, or practices that have the same effect as torture, incluing being placed on death row.[39] The ICTY in the *Furundžija* case logically therefore concluded that international law not only prohibits torture but also: '(i) the failure to adopt the national measures necessary for implementing the prohibition and (ii) the maintenance in force or passage of laws which are contrary to the prohibition'.[40]

---

[36] UN Doc E/CN4/Sub2/1997/13 (11 Jul 1997), para 80 and UN Doc E/CN4/Sub2/1999/17 (20 Jul 1999), para 103.

[37] ICCPR, Art 7.

[38] Human Rights Committee, General Comment No 24 (4 Nov 1994), para 10; *Siderman de Blake v Argentina* (1992) 965 F 2d 699, *cert denied; Argentina v De Blake* (1993) 507 US 1017; *Xuncax and Others v Gramajo* (1995) 886 F Supp 162; *ICTY Prosecutor v Furundžija*, Trial Chamber Judgment (10 Dec 1998), paras 153–57.

[39] 1984 UN Convention against Torture and Other Cruel, Inhuman or Degrading Treatment or Punishment, Art 3, 1465 UNTS 85; 1969 Inter-American Convention on Human Rights, Art 13(4); *Soering v UK* (1989) 11 EHRR 439, para 91; *Chahal v UK* (1996) 23 EHRR 413; *C v Australia*, Human Rights Committee, Com No 900/1999 (28 Oct 2002).

[40] *Furundžija* Trial Judgment, para 148.

10.3.1   Defining Torture

The definition of torture under customary international law remains ambiguous. It is of course contained in one universal and a number of regional treaties, yet the precise extra-conventional nature of these treaties and the crystallisation of a customary definition is itself doubtful. While the various instruments enjoy common elements there is divergence on two particular issues: (a) the range of conduct that constitutes torture; and (b) whether torture may be committed by persons other than State agents. These issues will be duly examined in the following sections. It is useful, first of all, to consider the definition of torture under the most widely ratified of the aforementioned instruments, the 1984 UN Convention Against Torture and Other Cruel, Inhuman or Degrading Treatment or Punishment (UN Torture Convention). Article 1(1) defines the offence to mean:

> Any act by which severe pain or suffering, whether physical or mental, is intentionally inflicted on a person for such purposes as obtaining from him or a third person information or a confession, punishing him for an act he or a third person has committed or is suspected of having committed, or intimidating or coercing him or a third person, or for any reason based on discrimination of any kind, when such pain or suffering is inflicted by or at the instigation of or with the consent or acquiescence of a public official or other person acting in an official capacity. It does not include pain or suffering arising only from, inherent in or incidental to lawful sanctions.

This definition coincides to a very large degree with the 1975 General Assembly Declaration on Torture that was adopted by consensus.[41] However, the definition contained in Article 3 of the 1985 Inter-American Torture Convention[42] is broader than that contained in the 1984 UN Torture Convention, in that it does not require any particular threshold of pain or other suffering for an act of ill-treatment to constitute torture. In actual fact, neither physical nor mental suffering is required if the intent of the perpetrator is 'to obliterate the personality of the victim or to diminish his physical or mental capacities'. This definition, moreover, does not encompass an exhaustive list of purposes that can be pursued by the perpetrator but instead provides indicative examples of such purposes. This is clearly reflected with the use of the disjunctive 'or any other purpose'. The European Court and Commission of Human Rights have construed torture as constituting an aggravated and deliberate form of inhuman treatment which is directed at obtaining information or confessions, or as a means of inflicting a punishment.[43] This definition echoes Article 1 of the aforementioned 1975 UN Declaration on Torture. ICTY jurisprudence has put forward the proposition that under customary international law there is no requirement that the conduct be solely perpetrated for one of the prohibited purposes.[44] Thus, in the *Furundžija* judgment the ICTY held that the intentional

---

[41]   GA Res 3452 (XXX) (9 Dec 1975), Declaration on the Protection of All Persons Being Subjected to Torture and Other Cruel, Inhuman or Degrading Treatment or Punishment.

[42]   (1986) 25 ILM 519.

[43]   *Ireland v UK* (1978) 2 EHRR 25, para 167; *Greek* case (1969) *Yearbook of the European Court of Human Rights* 134, at 186.

[44]   *ICTY Prosecutor v Delalić and Others* (*Čelebići* case), Trial Chamber Judgment (16 Nov 1998), para 470; *ICTY Prosecutor v Kunarac and Others*, Trial Chamber Judgment (22 Feb 2001), para 486.

humiliation of the victim is among the possible purposes of torture, since this would be justified by the general spirit of international humanitarian law whose primary purpose is to safeguard human dignity.[45] The Trial Chamber further justified this proposition by noting that 'the notion of humiliation is, in any event, close to the notion of intimidation, which is explicitly referred to in the [1984] Torture Convention's definition of torture'.[46] This statement should be approached with extreme caution, since if true it would render the offences of 'outrages upon personal dignity' and 'inhuman and degrading treatment' largely redundant in situations involving intentional humiliation. This is more so because Trial Chamber II in the *Krnojelac* case rejected the proposition espoused in the above mentioned judgments that intentional humiliation may constitute torture under customary law.[47] The common denominator of all the instruments to which reference was made points to the conclusion that the underlying act must be instrumental to achieve a particular purpose set out by the perpetrator. It is contentious whether customary law permits other forms of ill-treatment to constitute torture. Nonetheless, the use of rape, especially in the course of detention and interrogation as a means of intimidation, punishment, coercion or humiliation of the victim, or for the purpose of obtaining information or a confession, has increasingly been viewed as a definite form of torture, even though it is not strictly encompassed in the definition of the 1984 Torture Covention.[48] In the *Krnojelac* judgment the ICTY held that where confinement of the victim can be shown to pursue one of the prohibited purposes of torture and to have caused the victim severe pain or suffering, the act of putting or keeping someone in solitary confinement may amount to torture. The same result is true by reason of analogy in situations involing the deliberate deprivation of sufficient food for one's sustenance.[49]

The distinguishing characteristic between torture and other lesser forms of ill-treatment is the severity of the pain or suffering of the victim. A precise threshold would be impractical to delineate and thus the task of assessment is left to the discretion of the judge. ICTY and European Court of Human Rights (ECHR) jurisprudence does not clearly set out a single test, whether objective or subjective. Rather, they are in agreement that: (a) the severity of the harm rests on an objective test; whereas (b) the mental or physical suffering requires subjective assessment, involving consideration of factors such as the victim's age, health, sex and others.[50] The objective test regarding the severity of the harm may be triggered by beating,

---

[45] *Furundžija* Trial Judgment, para 162. The judgment in the same case recognised that being forced to watch serious sexual attacks inflicted on a female acquaintance amounted to torture for the forced observer. The same is true in respect of the person being raped where the event is watched in the presence of onlookers, especially if these are family members, para 267.

[46] Ibid, para 162.

[47] *ICTY Prosecutor v Krnojelac*, Trial Chamber Judgment (15 Mar 2002), para 186.

[48] *Aydin v Turkey* (1998) 25 EHRR 251, paras 82–84; *Fernando and Raquel Mejia v Peru*, Decision (1 Mar 1996), Report No 5/96, Case No 10,970, Annual Report of the IACHR (1995), Doc OEA/Ser L/V/II 91, pp 182–88; *Furundžija* Trial Judgment, para 163.

[49] *Krnojelac* Trial Judgment, para 183.

[50] *Ireland v UK* (1978) 2 EHRR 25, para 162; *ICTY Prosecutor v Kvočka and Others*, Trial Chamber Judgment (2 Nov 2001), para 143.

sexual violence, prolonged denial of sleep, food, hygiene, and medical assistance, as well as threats to torture, rape, or kill relatives, as well as mutilation of body parts.[51]

Despite this overwhelming body of evidence on the *actus reus* of torture it should not surprise the reader that in situations of national security emergencies the target States usually try to stretch the boundaries of the definition through the use of detention and interrogation techniques of doubtful legality. Following the 9/11 terrorist attacks against the USA the then US government embarked on its War against Terror. The Department of Justice's Office of Legal Counsel (OLC) was asked to provide advice on particular detention and interrogation policies and techniques against captured Al-Qaeda members. The OLC's first memo of 22 January 2002 argued that the US's treaty obligations towards Afghanistan had been effectively suspended because the latter was a failed State, thus negating the protections offered by the Geneva Conventions and the Torture Convention. This was followed by another memo of 1 August 2002 – now known as the Bybee Torture memo, after its author – in which its authors attempted to redefine torture and the obligations of the USA. The redefinition of torture was arbitrarily premised on an augmentation of the permissible thresholds of physical and mental pain. Thus, interrogators were advised that physical pain 'must be equivalent in intensity to the pain accompanying serious physical injury, such as organ failure, impairment of bodily function, or even death'. Equally, the threshold for mental pain was deemed to be severe and long-term psychological harm.[52] As a result, the memo approved otherwise prohibited conduct, including hooding, waterboarding, exploitation of phobias, the employment of stress positions, sleep deprivation and others.[53] The Obama administration swiftly rescinded those orders based on the Bybee Torture memos[54] and in conjunction with their secretive character the *jus cogens* nature of torture as this is encapsulated in the Torture Convention is strongly reaffirmed. Thus, in no way does the acceptance of the legal position stated in the memos by the Bush administration reflect a deviation from customary international law. Of equally doubtful legality is the exception to the infliction of torture based on the so-called ticking bomb scenario, which envisages that in situations of extreme urgency a confirmed offender may be tortured in order to reveal the whereabouts of a time-bomb, or operation that is in the process of execution. The Israeli Supreme Court, although ruling that brutal and inhuman interrogation techniques are prohibited at all times, did not rule out the defence of necessity against the ticking bomb scenario.[55]

Torture in the context of armed conflict is specifically prohibited by the 1949

---

[51] *Kvočka* Judgment, ibid, para 144; confirmed also in the views of the UN Human Rights Committee in *Grille Motta*, Com No 11/1977; *Miango Muiyo v Zaire*, Com No 194/85; *Kanana v Zaire*, Com No 366/89; *Herrera Rubio v Colombia*, Com No 161/1983.

[52] Memorandum from Jay Bybee to Alberto R Gonzales, Counsel to the President, Standards of Conduct for Interrogation under 18 USC §§ 2340–2340A, available at: <http://www.washingtonpost.com/wp-srv/nation/documents/dojinterrogationmemo20020801.pdf>.

[53] DA Wallace, 'Torture v The Basic Principles of the US Military' (2008) 6 *Journal of International Criminal Justice* 309.

[54] Executive Order, Ensuring Lawful Interrogations (22 Jan 2009).

[55] *Public Committee against Torture in Israel and Others v The State of Israel and Others*, Judgment (6 Sep 1999).

Geneva Conventions[56] and the two Additional Protocols of 1977.[57] As will become evident below the *Kunarac* judgment concluded that whether or not international human rights law generally recognises that only public offcials or State agents can commit the crime of torture, international humanitarian law makes no such distinction, thus rendering any individual culpable of the offence as long as the appropriate *mens rea* and *actus reus* have been satisfied.[58] The separate existence of torture as a war crime will be discussed separately and in more detail in the chapter dealing with war crimes.

10.3.2   The 'Public Official' Requirement of Torture

As already examined, the definition of torture in Article 1 of the 1984 UN Torture Convention requires that the offence be perpetrated at the instigation, consent, or acquiescence of a public official. Although this requirement is most probably outdated under customary law it remains the basis for prosecutions under domestic laws. As a notion it is problematic because if a particular act of torture is undertaken by a public official under orders from his government it constitutes an act attributable to the State and the perpetrator may be deemed immune from criminal prosecution. While it is true that most States do not recognise that torture can ever be attributable to a State, in practice courts have a hard time rejecting the immunity of the State and the official that committed torture. What is equally problematic in practice is that State officials under orders to employ interrogation techniques that amount to torture will without exception escape prosecution because it falls within the scope of their employment.[59] The public official requirement was historically retained because of the belief that negative human rights obligations, such as the duty to refrain from the infliction of torture, are addressed to States. Contemporary international law dictates that State officials are not free from criminal liability for acts of torture, whatever the immunity of the State itself may be before national courts.

It is equally clear that State officials are not the sole perpetrators of torture. If the public official requirement constitutes a generally mandatory requirement under treaty and customary law the ambit of the offence becomes very narrow and necessarily results in the exclusion of all cases of torture committed by non-State actors, such as guerrillas, paramilitaries and terrorists. In order to bring within the remit of torture the infliction of physical or mental harm by non-State actors one would need to look at possible developments in the extra-conventional life of the concept – particularly as this might have evolved under customary law – or otherwise attempt a purposive interpretation of the Torture Convention.

---

[56]   Common Art 3; Arts 12 and 50, Geneva Convention I; Arts 12 and 51, Geneva Convention II; Arts 13, 14 and 130, Geneva Convention III; Arts 27, 32 and 147, Geneva Convention IV.
[57]   Protocol I, Art 75; Protocol II, Art 4.
[58]   *Kunarac* Trial Judgment, paras 490–96.
[59]   *Rasul v Myers*, 512 F 3d 644, 661 (DC Cir, 2008); *In Re Iraq and Afghanistan Detainees Litigation*, 479 F Supp 2d 85 (DDC, 2007).

To be sure, two distinct torture regimes exist under international law; that subject to the Torture Convention and the other following the prescriptions of the *jus in bello*. As a result of the latter regime criminal liability is generally not dependent on the status of the perpetrator as a State official or other. Under the 1949 Geneva Conventions and the two 1977 Protocols the presence, involvement or acquiescence of a State official or any other authority-wielding person is not required for the relevant conduct to be characterised as torture. The same is true in respect of Articles 3 and 5 of the ICTY Statute, which was supposed to reflect the demands of customary law. This conclusion was correctly drawn by the *Kunarac* judgment, which examined in detail all the relevant provisions of humanitarian law.[60] Moreover, Article 7(2)(e) of the International Criminal Court (ICC) Statute, concerning torture as a crime against humanity, does not impose the State actor requirement.

The inclusion, on the other hand, of non-State actors outside the realm of humanitarian law is less clear. In a decision rendered by the UN Committee Against Torture (CAT) it was held that a civilian pogrom against Roma settlers in Yugoslavia, which was tolerated by the police, constituted a violation of Article 16 of the 1984 UN Torture Convention (inhuman and cruel treatment). In a common dissenting opinion two Committee members expressed the view that the acts could also be described as torture under Article 1.[61] The jurisprudence of the ECHR[62] and the UN Human Rights Committee[63] clearly articulates that Articles 3 and 7 of the European Convention on Human Rights and of the International Covenant on Civil and Political Rights (ICCPR) respectively may also apply in situations where organs or agents of the State are not involved in the violation of the rights protected under these provisions. Although both the European Convention on Human Rights and the ICCPR are primarily human rights instruments and the jurisprudence of their respective enforcement mechanisms does not directly involve reference to criminal liability it would be absurd to uphold one definition for human rights purposes and another with regard to international criminal law. The only doubtful issue in this scenario is whether the infliction of torture by non-State agents would entail the responsibility of the State in which the offence took place. This question, which is beyond the scope of this book, has been answered in the affimative by the UN Human Rights Committee in all cases where the State does not protect individuals from interference by private parties.[64]

10.4 Apartheid

The official policy of racial segregation and discrimination practised by the white minority regime of South Africa up until the early 1990s had sparked worldwide

---

[60] *Kunarac* Trial Judgment, paras 490–96.
[61] *Hajrizi and Others v Serbia and Montenegro*, Com No 161 /2000, CAT Doc CAT/C/29/D/161/2000 (21 Nov 2002).
[62] *HLR v France* (1997) 26 EHRR 29, para 40; *Costello-Roberts v UK* (1993) 19 EHRR 112, paras 27–28; *A v UK* (1998) 27 EHRR 611, para 22.
[63] General Comment No 7/16 (27 Jul 1982), para 2.
[64] General Comment No 20/44 (3 Apr 1992), para 2.

repugnancy and condemnation by both the UN General Assembly and the Security Council. Article 3 of the 1965 Convention on the Elimination of All Forms of Racial Discrimination (CERD)[65] first obliged parties to prevent, prohibit and eradicate racial segregation and apartheid, as well as all practices of that nature from territories under their jurisdiction. This general obligation was specifically articulated as entailing a duty to enact legislation criminalising all forms of advocacy of racial superiority or hatred, criminalise groups advocating the aforementioned, as well as personal participation therein and moreover prevent all public bodies from practising or promoting such forms of discrimination.[66] Reference in the CERD to apartheid and racial segregation was meant to emphasise them as particular manifestations of the wider offence of racial discrimination. Moreover, apartheid was practised officially in South Africa at the time and the CERD underlined its repugnant nature and the will of the international community to declare it illegal.

Notwithstanding the fact that all forms of racial discrimination constitute offences under international law the crime of apartheid has established a particular dynamic. The 1974 International Convention on the Suppression and Punishment of the Crime of Apartheid (Apartheid Convention)[67] recognised it as a crime against humanity.[68] This is natural given that the history of apartheid demonstrates that it is instituted as a policy against a targeted ethnic or racial group. Although the Convention possesses a universal character the historical context in which it was drafted meant that the principal and sole perpetrator was South Africa. The offence is completed, in accordance with Article II, by the commission of inhuman acts 'with the purpose of establishing and maintaining domination by one racial group of persons over any other racial group of persons and systematically oppressing them'. Although Article II contains a very broad and detailed list of underlying inhuman acts giving rise to the practice of apartheid this list is merely indicative and may indeed be augmented by other types of conduct. Both the CERD and the Apartheid Convention recognise that apartheid is an institutional policy that is borne by the State. This means that private individuals participating in the implementation of a policy of racial segregation – for example, a South African business conforming with domestic law in not recruiting black people or agreeing to use them under conditions of forced labour – do so because this policy has been formally established and institutionalised by State machinery. Article III suggests, however, that even under such circumstances, that is, of apartheid as binding domestic law, not only State agents but also private individuals incur international criminal responsibility. Since apartheid is a crime against humanity, the contours of which are not described in the Apartheid Convention, it must be assumed that the elements of crimes against humanity pertaining to apartheid will depend on the particular instrument under which a particular case is examined. Thus, the definition of crimes against humanity is different in the ICTY, International Criminal Tribunal for Rwanda (ICTR) (although neither of these makes reference to apartheid) and ICC Statutes, as well as in customary international

---

[65]   660 UNTS 195.
[66]   CERD, Art 4.
[67]   1015 UNTS 243.
[68]   Similarly, para 15 of the 2001 Durban Declaration Against Racism, Racial Discrimination, Xenophobia and Related Intolerance.

law and domestic laws. Depending on the forum before which a particular case is brought the determination of apartheid as a crime against humanity will necessarily vary. To illustrate its application to the South African experience under existing customary law the policy of segregation would constitute the 'attack' against the indigenous black population. Because of its proclaimed official status under the then laws of that country the 'systematic' element of crimes against humanity would be clearly established. Perpetrators include not only those persons in government that instituted and formulated the policy, but also all private individuals that implemented the policy to the detriment of the rights of the victims, with knowledge of the overall attack. The Apartheid Convention establishes broad jurisdictional competence, on the basis of an *erga omnes* obligation, the prevention and punishment of which the offence of apartheid necessarily entails. In any event, crimes against humanity are subject to universal jurisdiction under customary international law.

Apartheid is also recognised as a crime against humanity by Article 7(1)(j) of the ICC Statute. In accordance with para 2(h), it encompasses:

> Inhumane acts [intentionally causing great suffering, or serious injury to body or to mental health] committed in the context of an institutionalised regime of systematic oppression and domination by one racial group over any other racial group or groups and committed with the intention of maintaining that regime.

The definition is very similar to that contained in the Apartheid Convention, but the concept of crimes against humanity in the ICC context is narrower than that established under customary international law. In conclusion, apartheid constitutes a very specific crime against humanity, based solely on racial discrimination. It is relevant even after the collapse of the South African apartheid State and much will depend on the anthropological definition of 'race', in subsequent cases. The relevant jurisprudence on genocide which views the notion of a target group much broader than the Genocide Convention will prove influential in this regard.

10.5 Enforced or Involuntary Disappearances

The problem of enforced or involuntary disappearances first received international attention through the UN General Assembly Resolution 33/173 in 1978.[69] This particular practice was endemic and an integral part of the South American dictatorships in the 1970s and 1980s. Despite their demise, however, by at least the late 1980s the problem has not only persisted but has spread all over the world. As a result, the UN Human Rights Commission established in 1980 a Working Group on Enforced or Involuntary Disappearances. The mandate of the Working Group has been renewed ever since and in fact its reports clearly manifest an increase in individual communications with only few cases resolved.[70] Because of its prevalence in South America the Assembly and Commission of the Organisation of American States (OAS) have repeatedly referred to the practice of disappearances since 1978,

---

[69] GA Res 33/173 (20 Dec 1978); see also ECOSOC Res 1979/38 (10 May 1979).
[70] UN Human Rights Commission Res 2002/41 (23 Apr 2002).

urging that all cases be investigated and the practice stopped.[71] In the US, in two civil suits tried under the 1789 Aliens Tort Act, the courts ruled that the prohibition against enforced disappearances had assumed the status of *jus cogens*.[72]

The rationale underlying enforced disappearances explains why it is not simply a common crime. The immediate victims are numerous, yet they are not the sole targets. Rather, the disappearance aims to instill fear in the abductee's circle of family and friends. Because of the multiplicity of victims and its institutionalised nature its target audience is both broad and of a civilian character. No wonder therefore that in 1983 the OAS Assembly stated that the practice of enforced disappearances constituted a crime against humanity.[73] Without a legal instrument criminalising these type of disappearances or prohibiting them under the rubric of human rights law the Inter-American Court of Human Rights in the *Velásquez Rodríguez* case, although noting that its classification as a crime against humanity may be possible, held that the disappearance of 150 persons in Honduras between 1981 and 1984, and carried out as part of a systematic practice by that country's armed forces, amounted to a violation of three distinct human rights contained in the 1969 Inter-American Convention on Human Rights.[74] These were: Article 7 (right to personal liberty); Article 5 (right to humane treatment); Article 4 (right to life).[75] The most comprehensive international definition of the offence of enforced disappearance is that contained in the preamble to the UN General Assembly's 1972 Declaration on the Protection of All Persons from Enforced Disappearance.[76] Under this instrument such illegal disappearances occur when:

> Persons are arrested, detained or abducted against their will or otherwise deprived of their liberty by officials of different branches or levels of government, or by organised groups, or private individuals acting on behalf of, or with the support, direct or indirect, consent or acquiescence of the government, followed by a refusal to disclose the fate or whereabouts of the persons concerned, or a refusal to acknowledge the deprivation of the liberty, which places such persons outside the protection of the law.

This definition elaborates with more precision the elements of the offence found in Articles II and 7(2)(i) of the 1994 Inter-American Convention on the Forced Disappearance of Persons[77] and the ICC Statute respectively. However, although the 1994 Convention and the ICC Statute treat this practice as a crime against humanity, the 1992 Declaration makes no such statement, but instead provides that it shall be considered as an offence under domestic criminal law (Article 4), to which the defence of superior orders is not applicable (Article 6).

By its very nature, the practice of enforced disappearances is a serious and systematic attack against a dissenting civilian population within a State and as such qualifies as a crime against humanity. However, although the jurisprudence of the ad

---

[71] GA Res 443 (IX–0/79) (31 Oct 1979); Inter-American Commission on Human Rights, Annual Report (1978), 24–27.

[72] *Re Estate of Marcos* (9th Cir, 1994) 25 F 3d 1467, 1745; *Forti v Suarez-Mason* (1987) 672 F Supp 1531, 1542, *amended*, (1989) 694 F Supp 707, 710–11.

[73] GA Res 666 (18 Nov 1983).

[74] (1970) 9 ILM (1970).

[75] *Velásquez Rodríguez* case, Judgment on Merits (29 Jul 1988), 95 ILR 232.

[76] GA Res 47/133 (18 Dec 1992).

[77] (1994) 33 ILM 1259.

hoc tribunals and the ICC Statute clearly suggest that crimes against humanity can be committed by non-State agents enforced disappearances under some international instruments can only be committed by public officials or persons authorised by the State.[78] Abduction of persons by non-State actors would constitute the offence of kidnapping or hostage taking, depending on the facts of each case, but not the offence of involuntary disappearances. Thus, a divergence exists depending on the instrument under which the offence is assessed. In any event, were a particular case to be classified as a crime against humanity the status of the offender would be irrelevant under customary law.

The *actus reus* of the offence may commence lawfully, that is through the initial arrest of the victim by duly authorised government agents. The crime is not completed with the unlawful arrest or abduction of the victim by said agents but by the intentional and unlawful deprivation of the victim's liberty, coupled with a refusal to disclose his or her whereabouts to the victim's lawyer or family. The latter component of the crime (that is, non-disclosure) may take place while the victim is otherwise lawfully detained. In its General Comment No 20 the Human Rights Committee held that in order to guarantee the effective protection of detained persons provision should be made by States for detainees to be held in places officially recognised as places of detention, as well as for the names of persons responsible for their detention to be kept in registers made available to those concerned, including relatives and friends. Furthermore, the time, place and names of all present in the interrogation must be recorded.[79]

Besides qualifying as a crime against humanity the practice of enforced disappearances may well qualify as torture if the relevant criteria pertaining to the crime of torture are satisfied. As already noted, the crime of torture need not be committed only by State agents but also by private individuals. Although involuntary disappearances do not constitute a particular violation of the European Convention of Human Rights the European Court of Human Rights pointed out in the case of *Kurt v Turkey* that forced disappearance is a violation of Article 3 of the Convention, prohibiting torture, cruel and inhuman treatment, which as a result caused extreme suffering to the victim's mother.[80] Although all offences against the person have an emotional impact on the family or circle of friends of the victim this is usually incidental to the underlying crime. In the case of forced disappearances one of the aims of the perpetrators is to terrorise or otherwise intimidate those close to the victim but also, in a significant number of cases, a larger segment of the population. Thus, the practice of disappearance as torture could be substantiated not only vis-a-vis the victim, but also against his or her relatives or friends.

---

[78]   This is also the case with the 2006 International Convention for the Protection of all Persons against Enforced Disappearances.
[79]   General Comment No 20, UN Doc CCPR/C/21/Rev1/Add3 (7 Apr 1992), para 11; a similar provision is stipulated in Arts 8–12 of the 1992 Declaration.
[80]   *Kurt v Turkey* (1999) 27 EHRR 373, para 134.

11

Transnational Crimes

11.1 Introduction

The selection of offences in this chapter is based on their incorporation in multilateral treaties, although in most cases their effects will be of a transnational character. Moreover, it is assumed that the ultimate objective of the perpetrators of these crimes is a financial benefit and this element differentiates them from other crimes, such as torture, war crimes and others. This distinction of course is wholly artificial, given that trafficking of persons and slavery, both of which I have included in the chapter dealing with offences against the person, ultimately involve a pecuniary element. It would no doubt be beyond the scope of this book to analyse every transnational offence that was predicated on financial considerations. As a result, additional transnational financial offences, such as fraud, anti-competitive practices, tax evasion,[1] trafficking in obscene publications[2] and others are not covered. It should not be assumed, however, that these are outside the ambit of ICL. Rather, the prosecution of these offences is based either on domestic criminal law, bilateral treaties or the institutional law of international organisations, particularly the European Communities. The offences analysed herein are deemed to constitute transnational crimes in the sense described in chapter 1 and as such are distinguished from international crimes *stricto sensu*. The crimes examined in this chapter include the following: transnational organised crime, drug-trafficking, corruption, money laundering and postal offences – although the gravity of the latter is in most cases less significant than its other counterparts. The reader will come to appreciate the systemic risk in all of these crimes, in the sense that drug-trafficking requires the existence of organised crime and corruption, the proceeds of which further require money laundering. Equally, all of these types of criminal conduct have an impact not only on public health (eg through drug abuse), but also on the financial systems, levels of violence and general well-being.

---

[1] By way of illustration, tax evasion is the subject of cooperation in bilateral double taxation treaties, such as Article 27(1) of the US-UK Treaty, as well as in EC instruments, particularly Council Directive 2004/106/EC of 16 November 2004 amending Directives 77/799/EEC concerning mutual assistance by the competent authorities of the Member States in the field of direct taxation, certain excise duties and taxation of insurance premiums and 92/12/EEC on the general arrangements for products subject to excise duty and on the holding, movement and monitoring of such products, OJ L 359 (4 Dec 2004) which allows member States to exchange information on tax evasion with a view to national prosecution.

[2] 1910 Agreement for the Suppression of the Circulation of Obscene Publications, 1 Bevans 748; 1923 Convention for the Suppression of the Circulation of and Traffic in Obscene Publications.

11.2   Transnational Organised Crime

Until the collapse of the USSR and the subsequent cataclysmic effects of the new world order organised crime was essentially a domestic affair, even though transnational patterns were evident. Some States chose to see the phenomenon holistically,[3] while others preferred to view each underlying offence in isolation from the organised nature of the group. Similarly, requests for international cooperation such as extradition and mutual legal assistance were made on the basis of the underlying offence. The post-1990 era, with the advent of globalised trade and physical movement of persons, witnessed an increase in organised crime, originating especially from the former Eastern bloc, necessitating a different approach to the problem.[4] Two factors have generally contributed to the eruption of organised crime at the dawn of the twenty-first century: the emergence of 'weak' States and corruption.[5] The former refers to the institutional capacity of States to govern legitimately, effectively administer justice and demand obeisance from the entire population. This classification certainly applies to the majority of African, South American and former Soviet republics because of their failure to achieve these objectives. It is this very environment bred by the processes of weak States that provides the cauldron in which criminality multiplies. Corruption further exacerbates the situation,[6] as does the ability of criminal groups to launder their criminal proceeds in tax havens where banking regulations are relaxed.[7]

Since the early 1990s the United Nations General Assembly had detected the increase and expansion of organised criminal activity worldwide and made reference to the emergent links between organised crime and terrorism.[8] In 1994 the World Ministerial Conference on Organised Transnational Crime adopted the Naples Political Declaration and Global Action Plan against Organised Transnational Crime,[9] which *inter alia* addressed the issue of convening a conference for the negotiation of a convention on the matter. By Resolution 53/111 the General Assembly established an Ad Hoc Committee for the purpose of elaborating a convention and three additional protocols.[10] After a series of 11 sessions between 1999 and 2000 the UN Convention against Transnational Organized Crime

---

[3]   eg the 1951 US Racketeering Act, 18 USC § 1951ff.

[4]   N Passas, 'Globalisation and Transnational Crime: Effects of Criminogenic Asymmetries' (1998) 4 *Transnational Organized Crime* 2.

[5]   W Rensselaer, I Lee, 'Transnational Organised Crime: An Overview' in T Farer (ed), *Transnational Crime in the Americas* (London, Routledge, 1999) 4.

[6]   JM Waller, VJ Yasmann, 'Russia's Great Criminal Revolution: The Role of the Security Services' (1995) 11 *Journal of Contemporary Criminal Justice* 282.

[7]   RE Grosse, *Drugs and Money: Laundering Latin America's Cocaine Dollars*, (New York, Praeger, 2001); J Blum, 'Offshore Money' in T Farer, *Transnational Crime*, at 57.

[8]   GA Res 49/60 (9 Dec 1994), and 50/186 (20 Dec 1995). See E Mylonaki, 'The Manipulation of Organised Crime by Terrorists: Legal and Factual Perspectives' (2002) 2 *International Criminal Law Review* 213.

[9]   UN Doc A/49/748 (1994), approved by GA Res 49/159 (23 Dec1994). This was followed by the 1995 Buenos Aires Declaration on Prevention and Control of Organised Transnational Crime, UN Doc E/CN 15/1996/2/Add 1 (1996) and the 1997 Dakar Declaration on the Prevention and Control of Organised Transnational Crime and Corruption, UN Doc E/CN 15/1998/6/Add 1 (1998), and the 1998 Manila Declaration, UN Doc E/CN 15/1998/6/Add 2 (1998).

[10]   GA Res 53/111 (9 Dec 1998).

(CATOC)[11] and two Additional Protocols were adopted in late 2000, while another one on firearms was subsequently adopted on 31 May 2001.[12] CATOC establishes four distinct offences: (a) participation in organised criminal groups;[13] (b) money laundering;[14] (c) corruption,[15] and; (d) obstruction of justice.[16] Under Article 3 the Convention applies to the four aforementioned offences, as well as to any 'serious crime' as defined by Article 2(b),[17] if cumulatively the offence is 'transnational in nature' and 'involves an organised criminal group'. In accordance with Article 3(2), offences are transnational in nature if they are: committed in more than one State; committed in only one State, but are prepared, planned, directed, controlled or have substantial effects in other States; and committed in one State by an organised criminal group that engages in criminal activities in more than one State. It is evident that the relationship between the 2000 Convention and other sectoral agreements, especially those relating to narcotics and corruption,[18] is complementary but at the same time the convention is independent of those agreements. Because of its unique scope it finds application only where the underlying offence possesses a transnational element and involves an organised criminal group. The only other reference to organised crime in previous sectoral treaties is found in the 1988 UN Convention against Illicit Traffic in Narcotic Drugs and Psychotropic Substances. Article 3(1)(a)(v) of the latter instrument obliges States to 'criminalise the organisation, management or financing of the offences listed' therein, and relating to the various processes, from cultivation to final distribution.

Moreover, subsection (c)(iv) criminalises 'participation in, association or conspiracy to commit' any of the listed offences, while subsection (5)(a) and (b) of Article 3 requires that member States adopt legislation requiring courts to take into account the involvement of organised criminal groups and individual membership therein as rendering the offence 'serious' in nature. Not all of the offences established under CATOC, however, have in the past been subject to universal regulation, particularly, money laundering,[19] participation in organised criminal groups and obstruction of justice, and States parties are under an obligation to criminalise these activities in the context of their domestic penal laws. For the purposes of CATOC, an 'organised criminal group' is defined as:

---

[11] (2001) 40 ILM 335.

[12] Protocol to Prevent, Suppress and Punish Trafficking in Persons, especially Women and Children, (2001) 40 ILM 377; Protocol against the Smuggling of Migrants by Land, Sea and Air, (2001) 40 ILM 384; Protocol Against the Illicit Manufacturing of and Trafficking in Firearms, their Parts and Components, and Ammunition.

[13] CATOC, Art 5.

[14] Ibid, Art 6.

[15] Ibid, Art 8.

[16] Ibid, Art 23.

[17] This means any conduct constituting an offence punishable by at least a four-year incarceration term or a more serious penalty. The main criminal activities of criminal organisations are: racketeering, fraud, robberies, car theft, armed assault, drug trafficking, trafficking in arms and radioactive materials, trafficking in human beings, alien smuggling, smuggling of goods, extortion, gambling, embezzlement and control of black markets.

[18] 1988 UN Convention Against Illicit Traffic in Narcotic Drugs and Narcotic Substances, (1989) 28 ILM 497; 1997 OECD Convention on Combating Bribery of Foreign Officials in International Business Transactions, (1998) 37 ILM 1.

[19] See 1990 Council of Europe Convention on Laundering, Search, Seizure and Confiscation of the Proceeds from Crime, ETS 141.

A structured group of three or more persons, existing for a period of time and acting in concert with the aim of committing one or more serious crimes or offences established in accordance with this Convention, in order to obtain, directly or indirectly, a financial or other material benefit.[20]

The *travaux preparatoires* construe the term 'direct or indirect benefit' to be a broad one, encompassing, for example, crimes in which the predominant motivation may be sexual gratification, such as the receipt or trade of materials by members of child pornography rings, the trading of children by members of paedophile rings or cost sharing among ring members.[21] Although a group falls within the scope of CATOC if it is 'structured', this would exclude randomly formed groups, but would certainly encompass groups with a hierarchical or other structure, as well as non-hierarchical groups, where the roles of the members of the group need not be formally defined.

The offence of participating in an organised criminal group under Article 5 of CATOC is constituted by taking part in the activities of such a group, either with the knowledge of the group's aims, or in the knowledge that one's activities will somehow contribute to the achievement of those aims. Whether these mental elements require direct intent (*dolus directus* of the first and second degree) or also recklessness is a matter to be decided by each State in accordance with its criminal laws.[22] The offence requires also a distinct *dolus specialis* (specific intent) in that the perpetrator must have intended to commit a serious crime in order to obtain a benefit.

Moreover, a person is also culpable by means of organising, directing, aiding, abetting, facilitating or counselling the commission of serious crime involving an organised criminal group. These modes of participation in crime are also subject to domestic penal laws, although as has already been observed elsewhere there exists a growing body of jurisprudence that uniformly defines these legal concepts.[23] Under Article 23 of CATOC, parties are obliged to criminalise any form of obstruction of justice, including the use of corrupt or coercive methods in order to influence testimony, other evidence or the actions of any law enforcement or other justice official at both pre-trial and trial stage. This would not, however, cover those countries whose legislation grants natural persons the privilege not to give evidence.[24]

Besides criminalisation of the types of conduct analysed, the main purpose behind CATOC was the enhancement of cooperation and mutual legal assistance between States. Cooperation was central to the participation of developing countries who viewed organised crime as a serious destabilising threat.[25] As a result, it has assumed a twofold dimension in the Convention. First, law enforcement agencies are required to assist one another in general and specific terms, while the usual forms of cooperation are also provided, such as extradition and mutual legal assistance,[26] as

---

[20] CATOC, Art 2(a).

[21] Interpretative Notes, UN Doc A/55/383/Add 1 (2000) 2.

[22] See chapter 2.3.

[23] See generally chapter 3.

[24] Interpretative Notes (2000), at 9.

[25] *Report of the Ad Hoc Committee on the Work of its First to Eleventh Sessions*, UN Doc A/55/383 (2000) 18.

[26] CATOC, Arts 16 and 18; police cooperation in the context of the 1990 Schengen Agreement on the Gradual Abolition of Checks at Common Borders, (1991) 30 ILM 68; Member States have agreed to allow

well as more specialised measures, such as collection and exchange of information.[27] Secondly, since States are required to maintain adequate expertise in dealing with transnational organised crime it is only developed countries that can afford to efficiently comply. For that purpose, both CATOC and the Protocols envisage the creation of technical assistance projects, whereby developed nations must provide material and financial assistance to developing nations.[28] Moreover, States parties are obliged to adopt domestic laws and practices that would prevent organised crime-related activities. Some of these are already contained in other international instruments, and deal mainly with money laundering,[29] such as maintaining accurate bank records, lifting of bank secrecy with regard to organised crime investigations,[30] while under the 2001 Protocol Against the Smuggling of Migrants by Land, Sea and Air (Smuggling Protocol), minimum standards for the issuance and verification of passports and other travel documents are required.[31]

11.2.1 Additional CATOC Protocols: Migrant Smuggling and Illicit Traffic in Firearms

The three additional Protocols are supplementary and subordinate to CATOC. Under Article 37(2) of CATOC before a State can become a party to any of the Protocols it must first ratify CATOC itself. It is obvious and explicit that the offences stipulated in the Protocols are both transnational in nature and must be committed in the context of an organised criminal group or operation. The structure of CATOC is such that its provisions relating to cooperation and technical assistance are applicable to the Protocols; however, each Protocol establishes in addition specific provisions supplementing and adapting the general rules found in CATOC. Reference to the Trafficking Protocol is made elsewhere in this book.[32] The Smuggling Protocol obliges States to criminalise the smuggling of migrants, which includes the procurement of either illegal entry or illegal residence with the aim of financial benefit, as well as the procurement, provision, possession or production of a fraudulent travel document, where this was done for the purpose of smuggling migrants.[33] In addition to the cooperation procedures established under the Smuggling and Trafficking Protocols, both instruments require parties to take measures to protect trafficked and smuggled persons, whether by giving them access to medical, welfare, social and other

---

pursuit over national frontiers for, *inter alia*, breach of laws relating to explosives and arms, illicit traffic in narcotic drugs, traffic in human beings, and others, in accordance with Arts 40 and 41.

[27] CATOC, Arts 27 and 28.
[28] A special voluntary fund is to be set up for this purpose. See Art 30(2)(b) and (c) of CATOC.
[29] FATF 40 Recommendations; SC Res 1373 (29 Sep 2001); 1999 International Convention for the Suppression of the Financing of Terrorism, Art 18, (2000) 39 ILM 270.
[30] CATOC, Arts 7 and 12(6).
[31] 2001 Smuggling Protocol, Arts 12 and 13.
[32] See chapter 10.1.
[33] 2001 Smuggling Protocol, Art 2. The IMO Maritime Safety Committee's 2002 'Report on Unsafe Practices Associated with the Trafficking or Transport of Migrants by Sea' IMO Doc MSC 3/Circ 3 (30 Apr 2002), noted that by that date 276 incidents had been reported to the Organisation, involving 12,426 migrants.

facilities and programmes, or by entitling them to confidentiality and protection against offenders where they provide evidence to prosecutorial authorities.[34] Of particular importance is Pt II of the Smuggling Protocol, which refers to the taking of measures against vessels at sea. This was drafted in conformity with the 1982 UN Convention on the Law of the Sea (UNCLOS) and the 1988 UN Narcotics Convention, discussed below. The general rule is that no action can be taken in the territorial sea of a State without the coastal State's consent. Similarly, no action can be taken against a vessel at sea without the approval of the Flag State. However, the Protocol requires parties to 'co-operate to the fullest extent possible'. In cases where a State has credible evidence that a vessel registered in another State is involved in the smuggling of migrants it must acquire the permission of that Flag State in order to board, search and, if evidence of smuggling is found, to take other action with the consent always of the Flag State.[35] The Flag State must respond to such requests expeditiously and may impose conditions upon the requesting State. Although the conditions set by the Flag State must be respected, the requesting State may exceptionally take other remedial action where this is necessary in order to relieve imminent danger to the lives of persons, or where a bilateral agreement with the Flag State otherwise allows it to resort to such exceptional action.[36] It would not be inconsistent with the Protocol and UNCLOS to assimilate a smuggling vessel to a slave-carrying vessel, thereby granting the right to any other ship to liberate the migrants, even without the consent of the Flag State.[37]

In May 2001 the Protocol against the Illicit Manufacturing of Trafficking in Firearms, their Parts and Components and Ammunition (Firearms Protocol) was adopted. The origins of this instrument can be traced back to the 1997 Organisation of American States (OAS) Convention against the Illicit Manufacturing of and Trafficking in Firearms, Ammunition, Explosives and Other Related Materials. Article 5 of the Protocol criminalises illicit manufacturing and trafficking of firearms, components and ammunition, as well as falsification or illicit obliteration, removal or alteration of the marking on firearms. The Protocol sets out comprehensive procedures for the import, export and transit of firearms, their components and ammunition. It is a reciprocal agreement requiring States to provide authorisation to each other before permitting shipments of firearms to leave, arrive or transit across their territory and enables law enforcement authorities to track the movement of shipments through record-keeping and unique marking in order to prevent theft and diversion.[38] This is reminiscent of the post-1961 drugs conventions system, whereby a detailed import and export control mechanism was established with a view to identifying with precision those substances destined for medicinal purposes. The Firearms Protocol does not apply to inter-State transactions relating to the transfer of arms, nor does it prejudice or have any impact upon national security.[39]

---

[34] Trafficking Protocol, Arts 4–6; 2001 Smuggling Protocol, Arts 16 and 18. Art 5 of the Smuggling Convention further provides that migrants will not become subject to criminal prosecution.

[35] Smuggling Protocol, Art 8(2).

[36] Ibid, Art 8(5).

[37] UNCLOS, Art 99. However, only the Flag State may seize the slave vessel and arrest those engaged in slave trade. The arresting vessel may only intercept the slave vessel and free its victims.

[38] 2001 Firearms Protocol, Arts 7–12.

[39] Ibid, Art 2.

11.3 Money Laundering

One of the fundamental problems originally related to the practice of money laundering is whether it should be criminalised at all. Although it presupposes the evasion of the legitimate financial systems and as such the perpetrators seem at first glance to simply be avoiding the payment of some taxes, the evasion itself does not necessarily justify criminal sanctions. In reality, money laundering does not produce the same consequences as tax evasion. It is an offence that necessitates the existence of another predicate crime (eg sale of illicit drugs), in the absence of which the money laundering offence does not arise. It is only logical that a person will attempt to conceal funds that are derived from illicit conduct in order to avoid detection and prosecution, but will ultimately want to use them otherwise they are just paper in his hands. It was precisely these types of illicit conduct that the prohibition of money laundering was set up to counter, particularly drug-trafficking and organised crime. Drug-trafficking generates vast amounts of money which the perpetrators cannot openly use because of the source from which it is derived. Therefore, they must convert their proceeds and incorporate them into the legitimate economy without any trace of their illegality. It is evident that drug-trafficking and cash conversion are inextricably linked. If the authorities are able to stifle and prevent concealment and conversion of funds they can get to the perpetrators of the predicate offence. The first multilateral definition of money laundering was inserted in Article 3(1) of the 1988 UN Convention against Illicit Traffic in Narcotic Drugs and Psychotropic Substances. This is defined as:

(i)   The conversion or transfer of property, knowing that such property is derived from any of the drugs offences established by the Convention, or from an act of participation in such offences, for the purpose of concealing or distinguishing the illicit origin of the property or of assisting any person who is involved in the commission of such an offence to evade the legal consequences of his actions;

(ii) The concealment or disguise of the true nature, source, location, disposition, movement, rights with respect to, or ownership of property, knowing that such property is derived from any of the drugs offences established by the Convention or from an act of participation in such offences;

(iii) And, subject to the constitutional principles and the basic concepts of the Parties' legal systems, the acquisition, possession or use of property, knowing, at the time of receipt, that such property was derived from Convention drug offences or from an act of participation in them. Participation in, association or conspiracy to commit, and aiding, abetting, facilitating and counselling the commission of any of these offences are also criminalised.

It soon became clear that drug-trafficking was but one criminal activity that required conversion of its illicit proceeds. This acknowledgement is evident in Article 6 of CATOC, which iterates the money laundering definition in the 1988 Convention but significantly extends the range of available predicate crimes.[40] These not only encompass the substantive CATOC crimes, ie corruption, organised crime and

---

[40] In the *Yukos* case the Russian authorities charged its directors and shareholders with establishing a 'criminal corporate group' which operated a network of shell companies with the purpose of tax evasion

obstruction of justice, but also all other serious crimes punishable by a maximum deprivation of four years, as well as those extraterritorial offences subject to the dual criminality rule.[41] Article 23 of the 2003 UN Corruption Convention follows the same rationale, the *travaux* of which clearly demonstrate that there is no need to establish a conviction as to the predicate offence. With the advent of the global terrorist era following the 9/11 attacks, the processes associated with terrorist financing were linked to anti-money laundering law and policies. Whereas there is no reason why the measures adopted to deal with both of these may be similar or the same, in reality the two offences are wholly distinct. Terrorist financing is not a predicate crime for terrorism but an independent international offence. Moreover, the collection of funds with the intention that they be used to finance terrorism may be derived from legitimate sources (eg donations), in contrast to money laundering's predicate forms of conduct, which are always unlawful.[42] Money laundering is not specifically criminalised in the three relevant EC Directives, not because member States reject this notion generally, but rather because the first pillar in which Directives are adopted does not allow for criminalisation.[43]

The articulations of money laundering in the relevant multilateral conventions clearly stipulate that the knowledge of the accused is required as to the existence of the predicate offence. It is not, however, obvious whether the accused must have intended to convert the illicit funds, as opposed to simply being reckless about a subsequent conversion. It seems reasonable that both of these standards are applicable because the perpetrator is already aware of the illegal nature of the funds' origin and hence any attempt to introduce it in the legitimate economy will be done with some degree of foreseeability.[44] In the unlikely event that no conversion takes place the accused will be liable under the predicate offence only.

In practice, three stages are recognised in the money laundering process, namely placement, layering and integration. Placement involves inserting illicit proceeds in the legitimate economy without detection. This is achieved by purchasing otherwise legitimate businesses, shares, real estate, precious metals and others with a view to minimising the link between the dirty money and the proceeds under cleansing. This is insufficient, however, because the placement of large amounts of cash will give rise to suspicions from the authorities. In order to avoid detection the culprits must further dissipate their cash through multiple transactions in a variety of fields, all of

---

through optimisation schemes, which were thereafter laundered through the company's assets. See D Gololobov, 'The Yukos Money Laundering Case: A Never Ending Story' (2007) 29 *Michigan Journal of International Law* 711, at 725.

[41] Art 6(2)(b) and (c) CATOC; not every criminal act involving money gives rise to money laundering. In *Cuellar v USA* (2008) 128 S. Ct 1994, the accused was attempting to smuggle cash into Mexico by hiding it in his car and was arrested in the process. The US Supreme Court reversed the money laundering charge on the ground that this could not be sustained solely because the defendant concealed the funds during their transport.

[42] See chapter 12.3.4.

[43] Although this assumption is now in doubt following *Commission v Council*, Case C-176/03, ECR [2005] I-7879, in which the ECJ recognised the EC Commission's power to impose criminal sanctions in the field of ship-source pollution.

[44] This may be surmised also from Art 6(2)(f) of CATOC, although the language may at first sight seem confusing compared to other more elaborate *mens rea* formulations, such as Art 30 ICC Statute.

which involve relatively smaller sums of cash. For example, they may purchase shares in different industries in a variety of countries, as well as multiple real estates, or convert small amounts of cash into other currencies. Given the plethora of global daily transactions it is very difficult to identify these as suspicious, especially if the invested funds are moved around through subsequent transactions, wire and bank transfers in the course of several months or years and across different jurisdictions. When funds are no longer suspicious they have safely been integrated in the legitimate economy and the launderers can prove and verify their source of origin. Evidence demonstrates that money laundering is rendered an impossible exercise if the primary channels that are employed to insert money into the legitimate economy are free from corruption and perform strict customer due diligence checks; these primary channels are banks, accountants, lawyers, electronic remittance operators, casinos, exchange bureaus and others. In the *BCCI* case, a Pakistani bank was used by drug-traffickers and arms dealers to launder illicit proceeds although the bank was close to liquidation. Non-existent banking supervision by Pakistan and widespread corruption led to BCCI's constant investment expansion and the creation of seventy-six branches across the world, despite the bank's $12 billion deficit. The life-span of these operations lasted close to twenty years.[45]

Criminalisation is not the cornerstone of the international efforts to thwart money laundering; rather, the international community has focused on prevention and cooperation with respect to transnational illicit proceeds. Although it is beyond the scope of this chapter to discuss these measures in detail, a brief analysis is warranted because these measures form an inextricable part of the criminalisation of money laundering. Prevention has assumed a twofold approach. On the one hand, concerned financial institutions pre-empted governmental or inter-State rule making and adopted industry-wide preventive obligations as a matter of self-regulation. This is true for example of the Basle Committee on Banking Supervision,[46] which consists of 13 central banks, as well as other efforts by associations of private banks.[47] Inter-State regulation of the banking and financial sector has come about through the work of the Financial Action Task Force (FATF), located within the OECD. The FATF quickly identified the inefficiencies of the global financial system and issued its Forty Recommendations with a view to enhancing customer identification, record keeping and the reporting of suspicious transactions. With the advent of the Al-Qaeda era of terrorism the FATF further adapted its Recommendations to reflect the important role of so-called gatekeepers to the legal and financial systems (ie lawyers and accountants),[48] international payments systems (eg wire transfers) and the potential in the use of corporate vehicles by money launderers and terrorists.

---

[45] *Bank of Credit and Commerce International (BCCI) S.A v Aboody* [1990] 1 QB 923.

[46] See MS Barr, GP Miller, 'Global Administrative Law: The View from Basel' (2006) 17 *European Journal of International Law* 15.

[47] The so-called Wolfsberg Principles are one of the best examples of self-regulation undertaken by private banks. T Graham, 'What's Behind the Wolfsberg Principles?' (2001) 4 *Journal of Money Laundering Control* 348.

[48] In *Ordre des Barreaux Francophones et Germanophones & Others v Conseil des Ministres* (*Ordre des Barreaux*), Case C-305/05, Judgment (26 Jun 2007) [2007] ECR I-05305, the Grand Chamber of the ECJ emphasised the compatibility of the legal professional privilege with the obligation imposed on the legal profession under the EC Money Laundering Directives to disclose relevant information about their clients.

Although non-binding, these Recommendations have been the backbone of all subsequent instruments that specifically implemented them, particularly the three EC Directives,[49] the CATOC[50] and self-regulatory arrangements. The importance of the Recommendations is moreover reflected by the fact that they have expressly been endorsed by the Security Council.[51]

The other parallel component in the global preventive effort against money laundering concerns the detection, freezing and confiscation of assets even if the culprit has evaded arrest and prosecution. This approach has not only necessitated the lifting of bank secrecy but has also resulted in the opening of accounts through a direct injunction by the authorities, rather than waiting for the culprit to first be arrested before determining the fate of the funds.[52] As a result, more than $1 billion worth of funds siphoned by former Nigerian President Sani Abacha were recovered in the early 2000s from banks in Switzerland, Liechtenstein, England and Jersey either through mutual legal assistance requests by the Nigerian government or on the basis of independent investigations by the forum States.[53] In these cases it made no difference that the funds were in the hands of Abacha's son, who was not directly implicated in money laundering or other criminal acts; it was sufficient that the origin of the funds was illicit. For the purposes of confiscation some countries, such as the UK, have extended the range of predicate offences to any criminal conduct, and as a result the property or assets derived from such conduct is classified as 'criminal property' and is thus subject to seizure and confiscation.[54]

11.4 Drug-Trafficking as a Crime under International Law

Any serious assessment of conduct classified as drug-trafficking must be predicated on a definition encompassing substances that are expressly prohibited under international law.[55] This is not an easy exercise because the relevant conventions are unable to spell out every single substance from their inception, given that the manufacturers

---

See A Odby, 'The European Union and Money Laundering: The Preventive Responsibilities of the Private Sector' in I Bantekas (ed.), *International and EU Financial Criminal Law* (London, Butterworths, 2006) 305ff.

[49] Council Directive of 10 June 1991 on the Prevention of the Use of the Financial System for the purpose of Money Laundering, 91/308/EEC, OJ L 166 (28 Jun 1991); Council Directive 2001/97/EC of 4 December 2001, OJ L 344 (28 Dec 2001); Council Directive of 26 October 2005 on the Prevention of the Use of the Financial System for the Purpose of Money Laundering and Terrorist Financing, 2005/60/EC, OJ L 309/15 (25 Nov 2005),

[50] Art 7, CATOC.

[51] SC 1617 (29 Jul 2005), operative para 7.

[52] See M Levi, 'Criminal Asset-Stripping: Confiscating the Proceeds of Crime in England and Wales' in A Edwards, P Gill (eds.), *Transnational Organised Crime: Perspectives on Global Security* (London, Routledge, 2003) 212–15; Art 5(1) 1988 UN Convention; Arts 12–14, CATOC.

[53] See *Abacha and Nine Others v Office Fédéral de la Justice,* Judgment of the Swiss Federal Supreme Court, Judgment No 1A.215/2004 /col (7 Feb 2005), in which funds in the accounts of the dictator and his cronies that could not be traced to him were repatriated to Nigeria following an ad hoc mutual legal assistance request by the authorities of that country.

[54] Proceeds of Crime Act (POCA) 2002, ss 340(2) and 340(3)(a).

[55] See generally N Boister, *The Penal Aspects of the Drugs Conventions* (Leiden, Kluwer, 2001).

of drugs are proactive and always move faster than the authorities. It is evident that the implicit criminalisation of new substances on the basis of these multilateral treaties may be challenged by virtue of the legality principle, especially the prohibition of analogies, albeit there is a risk that such an argument may turn out to be absurd and unreasonable. As a result, Article 3(2)(iii) of the 1961 Single Convention on Narcotic Drugs[56] introduced the so-called 'similarity' concept, whereby if it is found that a 'substance is liable to similar abuse and productive of similar ill effects' as the drugs in the Schedules in the 1961 Convention it shall be added to said Schedules. This principle has not, however, been transplanted in subsequent narcotics treaties, particularly the 1971 Convention on Psychotropic Substances.[57] In practice, the respective boards of these conventions through the UN's Commission on Narcotic Drugs (CND) constantly update the list of substances prohibited in their Schedules, thus rendering any legality claim unjustifiable. The similarity concept in the 1961 Convention does not apply to every substance but only to the family of those narcotic substances encompassed in that convention (essentially those derived from the cultivation of particular plants).[58] This means that amphetamines, barbiturates and hallucinogens are outside the scope of the 1961 Convention, which it was felt should not accommodate them as this would have unnecessarily diluted that convention and would have moreover deterred prospective parties by adding a large number of substances to the list of controlled drugs.[59] These psychotropic substances are by their very nature almost exclusively synthetic drugs. As a result the 1971 Convention was promulgated in order to incorporate them therein as distinct controlled substances.[60] Besides narcotic and psychotropic substances the 1988 Convention further outlaws so-called precursors, which although not drugs themselves, are nonetheless chemical products that are essential in the manufacture of illicit narcotic substances.

A significant component to both the 1961 and 1971 conventions is their criminalisation provisions, which are quite detailed and extensive. Article 36(1)(a) of the 1961 Convention obliges parties to:

> adopt such measures as will ensure that cultivation, production, manufacture, extraction, preparation, possession, offering, offering for sale, distribution, purchase, sale, delivery on any terms whatsoever, brokerage, dispatch, dispatch in transit, transport, importation and exportation of drugs contrary to the provisions of this Convention, and any other action which in the opinion of such Party may be contrary to the provisions of this Convention.[61]

---

[56] 18 UST 1407, as amended by the 1972 Protocol Amending the Single Convention on Narcotic Drugs, 976 UNTS 3.

[57] 1019 UNTS 175.

[58] These consist of opium and its derivative morphine, cocaine as produced from the coca bush and cannabis or Indian hemp.

[59] International Narcotics Control Board (INCB) Report, UN Doc E/INCB/2008/1 (2008), para 9.

[60] The meaning of psychotropic substance in accordance with Art 2(4)(a) of the 1971 Convention includes any substance, natural or synthetic, that has the capacity to produce: a) a state of dependence; b) central nervous system stimulation or depression, resulting in hallucinations or disturbances in motor function or thinking or behaviour or perception or mood, and; c) similar abuse and similar ill effects as any other substance in the Schedules to the 1971 Convention.

[61] Art 22(1)(a) of the 1971 Convention is less elaborate, but equally effective in that it requires criminalisation 'of any action contrary to a law or regulation adopted in pursuance of its obligations under [the] Convention'.

Both instruments demand that parties render the relevant offences extraditable and subject to their criminal laws criminalise intentional participation, conspiracy or attempt.[62] This is recognition of the fact that drug-trafficking involves a complex operation in which many layers of organisation and activities are required, from the cultivators, to the traders and from there to the launderers of proceeds. The 1988 UN Drugs Convention whose money laundering provisions we have already examined not only consolidated the objectives of its two predecessors, but moreover acknowledged for the first time that drug trafficking is part of a wider criminal context associated with organised crime. Thus, the Convention is not so much concerned with specifying the prohibited substances, as it is with identifying the various contours of the offence and sets up enhanced mutual legal assistance, extradition, transfer of proceedings and confiscation mechanisms.[63]

The multilateral nature of these conventions and their inter-connectedness with organised crime, money laundering and corruption-related treaties renders the relevant conduct a transnational crime. Prosecution of drug-related offences naturally takes place before national courts, albeit given the organisation and membership of organised criminal groups certain small island States find it logistically impossible to tackle the trade of illicit substances. As a result, a group of Caribbean nations asked the United Nations in 1989 to assist in the arrest and prosecution of drug-traffickers and to establish an international criminal court with jurisdiction over drug-trafficking offences.[64] Eventually, although there was a glimmer of hope that treaty crimes, such as those related to illicit substances, would find a place in the ICC Statute they were ultimately left out.[65] During the reign of the Taliban in Afghanistan the UN Office for Drug Control and Crime Prevention pointed out that that regime had accumulated a large stock of illicit drugs, having made efforts to halt production in order to prevent a decrease in prices.[66] The Security Council took action regarding the Taliban's dealings with narco-terrorism by adopting Resolution 1214, demanding they cease such activities.[67] The link with terror was made more apparent in Resolution 1333, in which the Council determined that proceeds from narcotics strengthened the regime's capacity in harbouring terrorists.[68] Resolution 1333 provided for the creation of a Sanctions Committee, which in practical terms was able to

---

[62] Art 36(20)(a)(ii), 1961 Convention; Art 22(2)(a)(ii), 1971 Convention, which also criminalises preparatory acts.

[63] Art 17, moreover, iterates the customary rule that non-flag States may request the Flag State of a vessel suspected of transporting illicit substances to board and search it. See chapter 14.8.

[64] UN General Assembly, Letter dated 21 Aug 1989 from the Permanent Representative of Trinidad and Tobago to the UN Secretary-General, UN Doc A/44/195 (1989) and UN General Assembly, UN Doc A/44/49 (1989). See F Patel, 'Crime without Frontiers: A Proposal for an International Narcotics Court' (1989–90) 22 *New York University Journal of International Law & Politics* 709.

[65] N. Boister, 'The Exclusion of Treaty Crimes from the Jurisdiction of the proposed International Criminal Court: Law, Pragmatism, Politics' (1998) 3 *Journal of Armed Conflict Law* 27; P Robinson, 'The Missing Crimes' in A Cassese, P Gaeta and JRWD Jones, *The Rome Statute of the International Criminal Court: A Commentary* (Oxford, Oxford University Press, 2002) 497–98.

[66] Estimates of the income derived by the Taliban from taxes levied on opium production ranged during the relevant times from $15 to $27 million per annum. UN Doc S/2001/511 (22 May 2001), paras. 55–60.

[67] SC Res 1214 (8 Dec 1998).

[68] SC Res 1333 (19 Dec 2000).

regulate the freezing of incoming imports and outgoing exports, but could not oversee the circulation of products that only appear in illegal markets, such as narcotics.

Drug production, trafficking and consumption involve issues that go far beyond the current international legal framework. Three alternative theories have been propagated to counter the phenomenon at national and international level, all of which are related to our discussion of criminalisation. Those advocating in favour of the *supply reduction* theory claim that increased use is a direct result of abundance and availability and therefore all efforts should strive to minimise supply. This may be achieved through crop eradication, crop substitution and strict law enforcement operations. This theory reflects the current framework of narcotics control as explained above. Its antithetical counterpart, the *demand reduction* theory, is based on the assumption that drug production is driven exclusively by huge demand and as a result States must focus on education and rehabilitation so as to avert voluntary consumption. A third strand views the process of *decriminalisation* as central to this debate, albeit its adherents vary as to which drugs must be legalised.[69] In any event, this is an attractive proposition from the point of view that it has the potential to eradicate the evils accompanying drug-trafficking, particularly organised crime. It is evident that none of the three theories are wholly opposed to one another and each has a role to play in the global effort against drugs.

11.5   Bribery of Foreign Public Officials

Corruption and, in particular, bribery of foreign public officials was until recently considered merely a matter pertinent to each country's domestic laws and commercial practices. Another reason for industrialised States not extending extra-territorial jurisdiction against nationals or domestically registered corporations known to have bribed public officials of third nations was because the prospects of investments abroad were obviously perceived as boosting national economies, regardless of their unethical dimension. On a short-term scale this may be true for a local economy, but IMF studies have revealed that corruption is negatively linked to the level of investment and economic growth because it leads to resource misallocation in the sense that funds are not applied to their most efficient ends.[70] As a result, bribery may also constitute an act of unfair competition at both the domestic and global level[71] and can also have a serious impact on the enjoyment of fundamental human rights.[72]

---

[69]   See B Leroy, MC Bassiouni, JF Thony, 'The International Drug Control System' in MC Bassiouni, *International Criminal Law*, vol I (Dordrecht, Martinus Nijhoff, 2008) 855, 894–904.

[70]   V Tanzi and H Davaodi, 'Corruption, Public Investment and Growth' IMF Working Paper (1997) 97/139.

[71]   International Chamber of Commerce (ICC), 'Revisions to the International Chamber of Commerce Rules of Conduct on Extortion and Bribery in International Business Transactions' (1996) 35 ILM 1306, at 1307.

[72]   Report of the Working Group on Contemporary Forms of Slavery, UN Doc E/CN4/Sub2/1999/17 (20 Jul 1999), para 53, which describes corruption as an inescapable element in the struggle against contemporary forms of slavery.

The US was the first country to enact extra-territorial legislation prohibiting bribery of foreign public officials by US nationals or corporations of any type, which are either controlled by US nationals, or have their principal place of business in the US, or are organised under US laws.[73] The concept of bribery under the Foreign Corrupt Practices Act (FCPA) 1977 is defined as the offer of payment of money or anything of value to an official of a foreign government or a political party with corrupt intent for business purposes. This definition excludes so-called 'facilitating payments' intended to expedite otherwise lawful government action, as well as any payments permitted in accordance with the laws of the foreign State,[74] as long as, of course, it does not adversely disadvantage other competitors. The FCPA, although a bright light in the darkness of international business corruption, was rightly perceived by US corporations and their foreign subsidiaries as placing them at an onerous disadvantage against their international competitors who were not susceptible to such draconian laws.

US-led efforts to achieve global normative consensus on the international criminalisation of foreign bribery prompted various organisations to confront this issue for the first time. On 15 December 1975 the General Assembly of the UN adopted Resolution 3514, condemning bribery by transnational and multinational corporations and the United Nations Economic and Social Council (ECOSOC) was directed to formulate a code of conduct regarding payments in international trade. Although an ad hoc Working Group on Corrupt Practices was established and produced a draft Agreement on Corrupt Practices, lack of support from developed nations eventually shelved the project. At the same time the OECD established a Committee on International Investment and Multinational Enterprises (CIME) with the purpose of drafting a relevant code of conduct. On 21 June 1975 the OECD Ministerial Conference adopted a Declaration on International Investment that prohibited the solicitation and payment of bribes to foreign officials, as well as other unlawful political contributions.[75] However, it was not until 1994 with the adoption by the OECD Council of a Recommendation on Bribery in International Business Transactions[76] that mounting pressure had paved the way for establishing concrete normative guidelines on international corruption. This Recommendation called upon OECD Member States to deter bribery through their national legislation and practice, especially by amendment of any tax laws that permitted or favoured bribery and further urged them to facilitate international cooperation. On the instigation of the US the OECD Council adopted on 11 April 1996 a Recommendation calling upon States to re-examine their laws on tax deductibility concerning bribes paid to foreign public officials – preferably by treating such bribes as illegal – the majority of which

---

[73] 1977 FCPA, 15 USC, §§ 78a, 78dd-1, 78dd-2 (Supp 1997).

[74] See L H Brown, 'The Extra-Territorial Reach of the US Government's Campaign Against International Bribery' (1999) 22 *Hastings International & Comparative Law Review* 407, 410–16.

[75] Likewise, the International Chamber of Commerce issued a report in 1977 containing Rules of Conduct to Combat Extortion and Bribes, in connection with retaining or obtaining business, requiring the adoption of codes of conduct and rigorous accounting controls by participating States. These Rules were revised in 1996, reprinted in (1996) 35 ILM 1306.

[76] OECD Doc C(94)75/FINAL (27 May 1994), (1994) 33 ILM 1389.

were often listed as commissions or fees![77] In accordance with its mandate on 23 May 1997 CIME submitted a Revised Recommendation on Combating Bribery in International Business Transactions, which the OECD Council subsequently adopted.[78] This instrument recommended the adoption of specific legislative proposals in every field of national laws – criminalisation of bribery, non-recognition of tax deductibility, enforcement of adequate accounting, independent external audit, internal company controls, transparency in public procurement and international cooperation – and eventually formed the basis for the OECD's 1997 Convention on Combating Bribery of Foreign Officials in International Business Transactions (OECD Convention).[79] Article 1(1) of this Convention makes it a criminal offence for any person:

> intentionally to offer, promise or give any undue pecuniary or other advantage, whether directly or through intermediaries, to a foreign public official, for that public official or for a third party, in order that the official act or refrain from acting in relation to the performance of official duties, in order to obtain or retain business or other improper advantage in the conduct of international business.

It is also an offence under the Convention to commit bribery through complicit conduct, incitement, aiding or abetting, by means of attempts or on the basis of a conspiracy.[80] Article 1 also prohibits bribes paid for the benefit of third parties, lest one could avoid criminal liability by forwarding his benefit to a third entity, particularly legal persons such as political parties. This definition of bribery of foreign public officials is entirely consistent with similar international instruments, such as the 1996 Organisation of American States (OAS) Inter-American Convention Against Corruption,[81] the 1997 EU Convention on the Fight Against Corruption Involving Officials of the EC or Officials of Member States of the EU,[82] the 1999 Council of Europe Criminal Law Convention on Corruption,[83] and the 2000 CATOC.[84] Although illicit enrichment is an offence in two of the above instruments,[85] advantages collected by foreign public officials are generally recognised as not constituting bribery if they are permitted by statute or case law of the official's

---

[77] 1996 Recommendation on the Tax Deductibility of Bribes to Foreign Public Officials, OECD Doc C(96)27/FINAL (17 Apr 1996), (1996) 35 ILM 1311; following publication in May 1997 of the OECD's Committee on Fiscal Affairs (CFA) 'Report on the Recommendation on Tax Deductibility', which noted that in twelve member States bribes to foreign officials were in principle deductible tax credits. The majority of these States subsequently re-examined their tax legislation. See Brown, Extraterritorial Bribery, at 494.

[78] OECD Doc C(97) 123/FINAL (29 May 1997), (1997) 36 ILM 1016.

[79] (1998) 37 ILM 1; the most significant changes to the FCPA 1977 made by the International Anti-Bribery and Fair Competition Act 1998, which is intended to implement into US law the OECD Convention, are that it adds officials of public international organisations to the definition of 'foreign officials' and expands US jurisdiction both to acts committed by US nationals wholly abroad, without a nexus requirement to US inter-State commerce, and also to acts committed by non-US nationals while in the USA: Pub L No 105–366, 112 Stat 3302 (1998). See SD Murphy, 'Contemporary Practice of the US Relating to International Law', (1999) 93 *American Journal of International Law* 161.

[80] 1997 OECD Convention, Art 1(2).

[81] Art 4(1).

[82] Arts 2 and 3, distinguishing between passive and active corruption. 1997 OJ C195/1, (1998) 37 ILM 12.

[83] ETS 173.

[84] Art 8, UN Doc A/55/383 (2 Nov 2000).

[85] 1996 OAS Convention, Art 11; GA Res 51/191 (16 Dec 1996), containing the UN Declaration against Corruption and Bribery in International Commercial Transactions.

country, or are in fact 'facilitation payments'.[86] Nonetheless, these advantages must be deemed impermissible even when dictated by statute where the country in question is itself corrupt, authoritarian or simply failed. The FCPA provides an exception to the foreign bribery offence for any facilitating or expediting payment whose purpose is 'to expedite or to secure the performance of a routine governmental action'. A few countries, namely Italy and Hungary provide a statutory defence to the corruptor of a foreign official where said official has coerced the corruptor to provide the benefit.[87] Equally, the crime of corruption does not arise where a pecuniary advantage accrues to the State rather than to any particular individual or group, as would be the case with a highly preferential contract in favour of a foreign investor.

The 1997 OECD Convention renders legal persons responsible for acts of bribery and requires that member States subject them to financial and administrative sanctions.[88] The 1997 EU Convention makes explicit reference to the criminal liability of heads of businesses – defined as the people having power to exercise control or take decisions – where an act of bribery was performed by a person under their authority acting on behalf of the business.[89] Significantly, as of 2006, 12 parties to the 1997 OECD Convention had established the criminal responsibility of legal persons (Australia, Belgium, Canada, Finland, France, Iceland, Japan, Korea, Norway, Switzerland, UK and the USA), while six a non-criminal form of responsibility (Germany, Greece, Hungary, Mexico, Italy and Sweden). Of the latter six, Hungary, Mexico and Sweden provide for criminal sanctions but do not consider the liability as criminal *per se*.[90] The liability of the legal person is generally linked to the acts of management or someone in a senior position (the 'directing mind' principle), but a newer trend has emerged whereby the legal person will still incur liability where senior management has delegated decision-making authority to lower level employees, or where such employees are under the direction or supervision of senior management.[91] The offence contemplated is an extraditable one,[92] subject to the usual qualification of bilateral extradition treaties between the parties concerned.

The relevant anti-bribery conventions confer territorial jurisdiction on States parties where at least part of the offence takes place on their territory. The OECD has rightly criticised those States parties to the 1997 Convention whose legislation provides that prosecution can only commence where the victim or the government of the State in which corruption took place file a complaint.[93] In the majority of cases, if not all, the government is complicit in the corrupt act and the legal standing of a victim – other than the government – is uncertain, but may include a competing corporation and the rightful owners of their country's resources, its people. The application of the nationality principle of jurisdiction to legal persons is determined:

---

[86] Commentaries on the 1997 OECD Convention, (1998) 37 ILM 8, at 9.

[87] OECD Mid-Term Study on the 1999 Treaty, OECD Doc. DAF/INV/BR/WD(2005)19/REV5, paras 83–86.

[88] 1997 OECD Convention, Arts 2 and 3(2).

[89] 1997 EU Convention, Art 6. See *Acres International Ltd v The Crown*, Lesotho High Court of Appeals Judgment [*Lesotho Highlands Development Authority* cases] (15 Aug 2003), in which the legal person of the corruptor was held to be criminally liable.

[90] OECD Mid-Term Study, para 116.

[91] Ibid, paras 137–144. For an analysis of international corporate liability, see chapter 3.11.

[92] 1997 OECD Convention, Art 10; 1997 EU Convention, Art 8.

[93] OECD Mid-Term Study, para 237.

(a) in accordance with the law of the place where the legal person is incorporated (common law countries);

(b) the effective seat of the legal person (civil law countries); or

(c) on the basis of the nationality of particular individuals.

The responsibility of the parent company for the acts of the subsidiary is a complex issue which finds inconsistent regulation in the various States. Some countries require a sufficient connection between the subsidiary and the parent, whereas in others it would be necessary to demonstrate direction or authorisation by a directing mind.[94] Interestingly, although possibly restricted in practice, four parties to the OECD Convention, namely Belgium, Hungary, Iceland and Norway, apply universal jurisdiction to foreign bribery.[95]

Besides the stress on inter-State cooperation, treaties and non-binding instruments alike either urge or oblige parties to adopt sound economic regulatory and disclosure procedures, auditing, surveillance of public officials and to initiate prosecutions in cases of corruption.[96] The 1997 OECD Convention established a monitoring mechanism under the supervision of the Working Group on Bribery in International Business Transactions, incorporating both a reporting system and an examination procedure for each Member State.[97] In 1996, the IBRD's (World Bank) Board of Executive Directors revised the organisation's Guidelines for Loans and Credits by requiring that all parties to a transaction that is financed, or partly financed, by the Bank observe the highest standards of ethics and that where corrupt practices are found to have taken place the Bank is to reject financing proposals or discontinue existing ones.[98] The World Bank has taken concrete action regarding bribes allegedly paid to win contracts for the Lesotho Highlands Water Project, a dam construction venture partly funded by the Bank. It has provided financial assistance to the Lesotho Government's investigation into the corruption allegations, stating further that if a company were discovered to have paid bribes it could be excluded from participating in any World Bank projects elsewhere. Another possible deterrent for States seeking to attract investment is the annual publication by Transparency International – a private organisation – of its *Corruption Perception and Bribe Payers Indexes*. A country's poor performance on the Index may result additionally in heavier loan guarantees for prospective investors, which in itself may turn out to be a primary disincentive.

It is obvious that bribery of foreign public officials has been finally recognised as a contemporary scourge, a treaty-based transnational offence that is a threat to commerce, stability and the enjoyment of human rights. Whatever may be the domestic practice with regard to other international offences, the application of the 'act of State' and similar doctrines is incompatible with the purposes of the above anti-corruption treaties, as these instruments are by their nature intended to regulate

---

[94] Ibid, paras 247–48.

[95] Ibid, para 252. For an analysis of universal jurisdiction, see chapter 15.6.

[96] International Chamber of Commerce, 'Revisions to the Rules of Conduct on Extortion and Bribery in International Business Transactions' (1996) 35 *ILM* 1306; 1997 OECD Convention, Art 8; GA Res 51/191 (16 Dec 1996).

[97] 1997 OECD Convention, Art 12.

[98] The World Bank, 'Guidelines for Procurement under IBRD Loans and IDA Credits' (1996) 7.

acts of public officials.[99] It would thus be absurd to hold that solicitation and receipt of bribes constitutes a public act of a foreign State committed on its territory and hence not one that is susceptible to the criminal jurisdiction of other States. Such a conclusion would defeat the object and purpose of the relevant conventions.

Finally, it has been argued elsewhere that large scale and persistent acts of corruption that culminate into widespread famine of local populations may constitute crimes against humanity.[100] This is possible only where a significant link is established between the corrupt acts of a government and the deprivation of one's people from sustenance, or the means and resources of natural sustenance. Under Article 7(2)(b) of the ICC Statute, extermination as a crime against humanity may be perpetrated by the intentional deprivation of access to food that is calculated to bring about the destruction of part of a population. Article 30(2)(b) of the ICC Statute states that a person has intent 'in relation to a consequence, [where] that person means to cause that consequence or is aware that it will occur in the ordinary course of events'. This mental element in the ICC Statute refers to *dolus directus* of the first or second degree[101] and suffices to hold members of government responsible for crimes against humanity perpetrated against their own people in peacetime by placing them in conditions of life, which in the ordinary course of events would deprive them of access to sufficient food and medical care.

11.6 International Postal Offences

Although channels of postal communication had been established since at least 255 BC it was not until the seventeenth century that the first postal treaty was agreed, consisting of bilateral agreements governing the transit of mail within several European countries. The enormous growth in postal communications which subsequently expanded at a global level was later regulated on the basis of further bilateral arrangements that employed a multitude of postal rates, units of measurements and currencies and which by the mid-nineteenth century warranted a radical reform in order to ensure some uniformity. At a conference convened in Berne between September and October 1874 and attended by representatives from 22 nations an agreement establishing the General Postal Union was adopted. In 1878, and in reflection of growing membership, the organisation's name was changed to Universal Postal Union (UPU).

Although the aim of the UPU Conventions was to unify the regulation of postal activities, the 1878 Convention expressed the Union's concern over the unlawful use

---

[99] *Zambia v Meer Car and Desai and Others* [2007] EWHC 952 (Ch), para 198.

[100] For an elaboration of this possibility, see I Bantekas, 'Corruption as an International Crime and Crime against Humanity: An Outline of Supplementary Criminal Justice Policies' (2006) 4 *Journal of International Criminal Justice* 466.

[101] See chapter 2.3.

of the mail by private individuals.[102] Article 11 forbids the public to send by mail letters or packets containing gold or silver substances, pieces of money, jewellery, or precious articles, as well as any packets containing articles liable to customs duty. The successive UPU Conventions since 1878, each terminating its predecessor, clearly established two categories of offences: (a) the fraudulent use of counterfeit postage stamps or used stamps, as well as the fraudulent manufacture and distribution of forged or imitated stamps; and (b) the illegal use of the mail.[103] The list of objects falling in this latter category included, besides articles subject to customs duty and precious items, any other articles which by their nature would expose postal officials to danger, or otherwise damage the correspondence. It also prohibits the mailing of explosive, inflammable or other dangerous substances.[104] The list was later expanded to include narcotic drugs and obscene articles.[105] The wording of Articles 18(5) and 20 of the 1920 UPU Convention strongly suggests that only the acts of counterfeiting postage stamps and the insertion of narcotic drugs in the mail were recognised as constituting transnational offences, since with respect to all other unlawful usages there did not exist an express obligation to prevent and punish the offenders. This wording has been consistently applied in subsequent UPU Conventions[106] and the 1964 Final Protocol to the Universal Postal Union Constitution obliged Member States additionally to prevent and punish the insertion of explosives or other easily inflammable substances in postal articles.[107] With the adoption of the 1994 UPU Postal Parcels Agreement it is clearly discernable that under customary international law it is an offence to: (a) counterfeit stamps or international reply coupons, as well as to fraudulently manufacture or imitate such stamps and coupons;[108] (b) insert narcotic drugs and psychotropic substances in postal items;[109] and (c) insert explosive, flammable or other dangerous substances in postal items where their insertion has not been expressly authorised by UPU conventions.[110]

As regards all other objects that are prohibited from being placed in postal items, the penalisation of the act itself is not addressed in the UPU Conventions and Protocols and is therefore dependent on the regulations employed by each individual

---

[102] 1 Bevans 51; Art VIII of the 1885 Additional Act to the 1878 Convention elaborated that the sending by mail of precious articles was prohibited only in case the legislation of the countries concerned forbade their being placed in the mail or being forwarded. Reprinted in 1 Bevans 97.

[103] eg 1906 UPU Convention, Arts 16(3) and 18, 1 Bevans 492.

[104] 1906 UPU Convention, Art 16(3).

[105] 1920 UPU Convention, Art 18(1), 2 Bevans 282; Art 19 of the 1988 UN Convention against Illicit Traffic in Narcotic Drugs and Psychotropic Substances, to the same effect.

[106] 1924 UPU Convention, Arts 41 and 79, 2 Bevans 443; 1929 UPU Convention, Arts 45 and 80, 2 Bevans 873; 1939 UPU Convention, Arts 46 and 81, 3 Bevans 539; 1964 Final Protocol to UPU Constitution, Art 14, TIAS 5881.

[107] 1964 UPU Constitution Final Protocol, Art 14(e).

[108] 1994 UPU Postal Parcels Agreement, Art 58(1.1)–(1.3).

[109] Ibid, Art 58(1.4); this is confirmed in the 1988 UN Convention against Illicit Traffic in Narcotic Drugs and Psychotropic Substances, Art 19 of which obliges parties to adopt appropriate legislation in order to apply investigative and control techniques designed to detect illicit consignments of narcotic drugs in the mail.

[110] 1994 UPU Postal Parcels Agreement, Art 58(1.4).

country.[111] In any case, the sender of such objects incurs civil liability as a result of the UPU Conventions and Protocols, as long as the relevant instrument has been transposed into domestic law.

Although no relevant mention is made in the UPU conventions, jurisdiction over the aforementioned international postal offences is based primarily on the subjective territorial principle (that is, the place where the illegal postal item was mailed, or where the stamps were counterfeited), but also on objective territoriality (that is, the country of destination or the country of transit if the illegal item was discovered there, and the country where economic loss was suffered as a result of the counterfeiting). Other legitimate bases of jurisdiction cannot be excluded. In all cases of illegal use of the mail, it will hardly seem appropriate to national prosecutors to charge an accused with a postal offence usually carrying a lighter penalty, especially where other domestic provisions relating to drug offences or offences against the person can be applied instead.

Other postal offences such as mail fraud,[112] which in the US alone is responsible for defrauding private individuals of over US$100 million annually, constitute domestic crimes, albeit with a transnational character. The combating of this type of activity is at present pursued at an inter-State level through the cooperation of the afflicted States. The UPU, recognising the need for postal security, established the Postal Security Action Group in 1989 with the aim of developing worldwide security standards, promoting the creation of internal security units in national postal administrations and establishing cooperation with other international organisations. For this purpose, it has been working closely with Interpol, drawing special emphasis on illicit drug-trafficking, child pornography and paedophile networks, as well as mail fraud and money laundering. It is this potential that has necessitated the inclusion of postal offences in this chapter.

---

[111] US federal law, for example, penalises the mailing of obscene or crime inciting matter. See Obscenity Act 1948, 18 USC § 1461; similarly, UK Postal Services Act 2000, s 85(3)–(5).

[112] Mail Fraud Act 1948, 18 USC § 1341.

12

Terrorism

12.1 Introduction

The term terrorism is commonly and widely used in everyday parlance with varying
political and legal connotations,[1] yet at the same time it remains a designation which
is elusive and one that has never been singly defined under international law,[2] at least
at the global level. The first ever international attempt at codification was made in
1937 through the League of Nations by the adoption of a Convention for the
Prevention and Punishment of Terrorism.[3] Article 1(2) of that Convention, which
required merely three ratifications to come into force, but received only one and was
subsequently abandoned, defined:

> ... acts of terrorism [as] criminal acts directed against a State and intended or calculated to
> create a state of terror in the minds of particular persons, or groups of persons or the
> general public.[4]

Such a definition does not accurately describe a criminal act of terrorism as distinct
from a common crime and leaves a wide margin of discretion with respect to the
specific *mens rea* of a terrorist offence, that is, the creation of a state of terror. What
is further problematic, and more so in 1937, was determining when otherwise
unlawful conduct is deemed to have been committed for a political purpose and not
in the context of a purely criminal enterprise. Since, in many countries the characterisation of a criminal offence as a political one traditionally tended to remove personal
culpability, this so-called 'political offence exception' to terrorist offences may in fact
turn out to negate terrorist criminality altogether. With the emergence of the global
terrorist following the 9/11 attacks against the USA the political offence exception is
no longer valid in international affairs and no terrorist act is susceptible to this
defence. This conclusion stands in marked contrast to the situation in the 1970s and
80s.

Terrorism is comprised of conduct that is otherwise categorised as common crime;
ie murder, injury to person, intimidation, assault, criminal damage, endangerment
and others. What distinguishes terrorism from its constituent offences is that it is

---

[1] 'Tibetan Leader Accused of Terrorism' (23 Oct 1999) *The Times,* in which China accused the Dalai
Lama of masterminding several explosions and assassinations in Tibet.

[2] See MT Franck, BB Lockwood, 'Preliminary Thoughts Towards an International Convention on
Terrorism' (1974) 68 *American Journal of International Law* 69.

[3] (1938) 19 *LNOJ* 23.

[4] A Cassese, 'The International Community's Legal Response to Terrorism' (1989) 38 *International &
Comparative Law Quarterly* 589, at 591.

perpetrated through a structured group and on the basis of a very particular *mens rea*. Much like the crime of genocide, the aim of which is to highlight and underpin the heinous nature of the acts that underlie it, although these could just as well be charged as war crimes, crimes against humanity and others, the construction of terrorism under international law seeks to emphasise the destructive nature of terrorist offences for international society. The international community's response to terrorism has always been reactive, as opposed to pro-active, because the terrorist mind has traditionally always been one step ahead of the authorities, whose pre-occupation has largely been to suppress rather than think imaginatively about 'why' and 'how'. As a result, the international community's legal arsenal has been premised on a pattern of direct responses to poignant facets of terrorism. Attention was early centred on the alarming number of seizures and interference in the fledgling private aviation industry in the 1960s and 1970s by private individuals making financial as well as political demands. This led to the adoption of three distinct international treaties: the 1963 Tokyo Convention on Offences and Certain Other Acts Committed on Board Aircraft;[5] the 1970 Hague Convention for the Suppression of Unlawful Seizure of Aircraft;[6] and the 1971 Montreal Convention for the Suppression of Unlawful Acts Against the Safety of Civil Aviation.[7] The second terrorist phase, which occurred during the same time, encompassed political activists and national liberation movements with the employment of violence to further their aims, albeit generally seeking to enjoy popular support. The third and current phase, which started slightly prior to the crucial events of 9/11, is concerned with fundamentalist terrorism, which is predicated on mass violence, large numbers of members, cells and followers and which does not seek to engage the support of the victim populations.

One of the myths of international law is that there does not exist a definition of terrorism. While it is true that no multilateral treaty defines its constituent elements,[8]

[5] (1963) 2 ILM 1042.
[6] 860 UNTS 105.
[7] 974 UNTS 177.
[8] Shortly after 9/11, on 27 December 2001, the Council of the EU adopted Common Position 931, which obliged the EU and its member States to freeze the funds and financial assets of designated terrorists and organisations, as well as enhance police and judicial cooperation and afford each other the 'widest possible assistance in preventing and combating terrorist acts'. The definition of 'persons' and 'groups' involved in terrorism supplied in Art 1(2) of the Common Position was later supplemented by Council Framework Decision 202/475/JHA on Combating Terrorism (2002). Art 1 of the Framework Decision defines terrorist offences as intentional acts committed with the aim of:
− seriously intimidating a population, or;
− unduly compelling a government or international organisation to perform or abstain from performing any act, or;
− seriously destabilising or destroying the fundamental political, constitutional, economic or social structures of a country or an international organisation, [involving]
a) attacks upon a person's life which may cause death;
b) attacks upon the physical integrity of a person;
c) kidnapping or hostage taking;
d) causing extensive destruction to a government or public facility, a transport system, an infrastructure facility, including an information system, a fixed platform located on the continental shelf, a public place or private property likely to endanger human life or result in major economic loss;
e) seizure of aircraft, ships or other means of public or goods transport;
f) manufacture, possession, acquisition, transport, supply or use of weapons, explosives or of nuclear, biological or chemical weapons, as well as research into, and development of, biological and chemical weapons;

State practice, particularly in the form of domestic statutes and UN General Assembly resolutions, has tacitly manifested a concrete consensus of these elements. Yet, the distinction between the various forms of terrorism has proven much more expedient in the treaty-making practice of the community of nations. This has culminated in a so-called thematic consideration and codification of international terrorist conduct.[9] This is clearly exemplified by the various subject specific conventions relating to hijacking, hostage taking, bombings, financing of terrorist operations and others. This thematic approach is still the preferred route in concluding counter-terrorism treaties among States,[10] with organs of international organisations increasingly taking an active part in reinforcing and crystallising those rules that are common to all these treaties.[11]

The most pressing issue related to the international law of terrorism is currently the legality and legitimacy of responses against accused persons. Is it justified that they depart from human rights standards applicable to all persons or should terrorists not deserve the same treatment? Throughout this book I have taken the view that human rights considerations should permeate every area of international criminal law, if for no other reason because this serves to humanise the 'enemy' and avoid distinguishing between 'us' and 'them', from which there is no return. Equally, terrorism is more frequently viewed from the perspective of its direct or indirect sympathisers and sponsors. Thus, State-sponsored terrorism which has re-emerged in recent years has for some time provoked harsh extraterritorial legislation.[12] At the same time, it is generally acknowledged that most terrorist groups finance their activities through organised crime,[13] whereas fundamentalist terrorism relies in addition on the collection of funds from its sympathisers.

---

g) release of dangerous substances, or causing fires, floods or explosions the effect of which is to endanger human life;

h) interfering with or disrupting the supply of water, power or any other fundamental natural resource the effect of which is to endanger human life;

i) threatening to commit any of the acts listed.

Art 2 of the Framework Decision defines a 'terrorist group' as a structured group of more than two persons, with some degree of permanency, defined roles, continuity of membership and acting in concert to commit terrorist offences.

[9]   In *Tel-Oren v Libyan Arab Republic* (1984) 726 F 2d 795, where an action for tort against an alleged terrorist attack on a bus in Israel was dismissed, Edward J noted the lack of international consensus on terrorism and stated that besides those acts which are already prohibited by international conventions no other terrorist action can be regarded as a crime under international law.

[10]   1998 UN Convention for the Suppression of Terrorist Bombings, (1998) 37 ILM 249, and 2000 UN Convention for the Suppression of the Financing of Terrorism, (2000) 39 ILM 270.

[11]   See, eg GA Res 49/60 (1994).

[12]   US Anti-Terrorism and Effective Death Penalty Act (AEDPA) 1996, 28 USC § 1605(a)(7).

[13]   Resolution of the UN Commission for the Prevention of Crime and Criminal Justice, 9th Cairo Congress on the Prevention of Crime and Treatment of Offenders, UN Doc A/CONF 169/16 (12 May 1995) 17; see also 10th Vienna Congress, UN Doc A/CONF 187/4/Rev 3 (15 Apr 2000) 4, adopting the Vienna Declaration on Crime and Justice.

12.2 The Thematic Evolution of Terrorism in International Law

Following an attack against Israeli athletes during the 1972 Munich Olympic Games, the General Assembly of the UN commenced discussions on a US draft treaty proposal for the prevention and suppression of certain acts pertinent to international terrorism. This proposal was outvoted by developing and communist countries which, with the urging of Syria, desired to see the adoption of a convention containing a single definition of terrorism. Western States argued that a general definition would not only be impossible to achieve but would further serve the purposes of organisations such as the Palestine Liberation Organisation (PLO), whose aim was, it was contended, to distinguish between terrorism and national liberation movements in order to further their causes. There was a fear, thus, that sitting on the same table with non-like minded States risked legitimising the very conduct they had joined forces to combat. Moreover, it was feared by the West that a wide embracing definition would result in subsuming Israel under the rubric of State terrorism. The burgeoning non-aligned movement at the time had to a large degree succeeded in isolating Israel from a significant portion of international law-making by depicting it in the same light as the apartheid regime of South Africa. Nonetheless, a compromise was reached and an Ad Hoc Committee was established by the General Assembly under Resolution 3034 in 1972 to examine the matter fully. The Committee met three times between 1972 and 1979. During this time, developing nations argued that terrorism should be viewed from its root causes, such as racism, colonialism, occupation and apartheid and that it should not be differentiated from action undertaken by national liberation movements. Nothing concrete emerged from these discussions as Western States vociferously opposed the above proposals.

From 1979 onwards it was the Sixth (Legal) Committee of the General Assembly that became the forum for discussions on terrorism and since 1985 the Syrian proposal has either been raised in brief or abandoned from the Committee's agenda. It should be noted that between 1972 and 1989 the General Assembly, upon request of the then Secretary-General Kurt Waldheim, had been discussing the issue of terrorism on an annual basis under the unusually long title 'Measures to Prevent International Terrorism which Endangers or Takes Innocent Human Lives or Jeopardises Fundamental Freedoms, and Study of the Underlying Causes of Those Forms of Terrorism and Acts of Violence Which Lie in Misery, Frustration, Grievance and Despair and Which Cause Some People to Sacrifice Human Lives, Including their Own, in an Attempt to Effect Radical Changes'. The title of the series is significant because it underpins its Arab and developing world sponsorship and because moreover it places emphasis on the underlying causes of terrorism, which is currently a taboo subject in legal and political discourse. Although in recent years there has been renewed interest on the drafting of a comprehensive terrorist convention, to a very large degree this is no longer considered necessary. There exist more than twenty thematic conventions and the Security Council has played a very dynamic role that has even allowed it to authorise force against the culprits. Any talk of a comprehensive convention would certainly be perceived as undermining these developments to the detriment of the interests of the Security Council's permanent members, all of whom are subjected to home-grown or external terrorist threats. The combination of the thematic approach and the pioneering role of the Council have consolidated the legal position that any violence directed at civilians – or against combatants by non-combatants – whatever its cause or origin is not only criminal in nature but is subject to no excuses or justifications. Moreover, any conduct the purpose of which is to facilitate this violence, such as financing, is equally treated as a terrorist offence. As a result, international law quite clearly recognises an international offence of terrorism.

12.3   The Specialised Anti-Terrorist Conventions

12.3.1   Offences Against Civil Aviation

The first international agreement to emerge on the subject was the 1963 Tokyo Convention on Offences and Certain Other Acts Committed On board Aircraft (Tokyo Convention).[14] Its application extends to any conduct, whether a recognised offence or not, which jeopardises the safety of an aircraft or 'of persons or property therein or which jeopardise[s] good order and discipline on board'.[15] Such conduct is transformed into offences under the Tokyo Convention only if committed by a person on board an aircraft in flight or on the surface of the high seas.[16] An aircraft is considered to be 'in flight' for the purposes of the Tokyo Convention 'from the moment when the power is applied for the purpose of take-off until the moment when the landing run ends'.[17] Although it is not clear from its wording it must be presumed that conduct taking place solely on the territory of one State does not give rise to criminal liability, at least under the framework of the Tokyo Convention. This position contrasts with the contemporary understanding of terrorism, which is considered an international crime – sometimes subject to universal jurisdiction – irrespective if it arises and is committed locally. It should be noted that the Tokyo Convention does not apply to three types of public aircraft: military, custom and police.[18] Unlike later other anti-terrorist treaties the Tokyo Convention was not designed to address urgent problems and was generally viewed as reflecting customary law; yet, it was frugally ratified by signatory States.[19]

The plethora of attacks against aircraft in the 1960s and the inadequate hortatory anti-hijacking provision contained in Article 11 of the Tokyo Convention rendered imperative the adoption of a new instrument which would not only elaborate the

---

[14]   See M Mendelsohn, 'In-Flight Crime: The International and Domestic Picture Under the Tokyo Convention' (1967) 53 *Virginia Law Review* 509.

[15]   1963 Tokyo Convention, Art 1(1).

[16]   Ibid, Art 1(2). It is also required that the aircraft in question be registered in a contracting State.

[17]   Ibid, Art 1(3).

[18]   Ibid, Art 1(4).

[19]   E McWhinney, *Aerial Piracy and International Terrorism*, (Dordrecht, Martinus Nijhoff, 1987) 39–40.

elements of the offence but would moreover affirm and reinforce inter-State mechanisms with a view to effective suppression and eradication.[20] It soon became clear that any successful attempts to prevent and eradicate aerial hijacking by legal means required an overhaul of the airline and airport industries. The lack of surveillance equipment or security safeguards necessarily meant that the majority of attacks against civil aviation took place by persons embarking aircraft with weapons and seizing control when external doors had closed.[21] Moreover, it should be understood that at the time it was not obvious to every State that aerial hijacking should be a crime, let alone an international crime. Many countries openly or tacitly allowed hijacked aircraft to land on their territories and either gave refuge to the culprits or otherwise refrained from arresting them. This specific problem of aircraft hijacking was the focal point of the 1970 Hague Convention for the Suppression of Unlawful Seizure of Aircraft (Hague Convention). The 1970 Hague Convention deals exclusively with acts of international hijacking committed by persons on board an aircraft in flight.[22] The notion of an aircraft 'in flight' is wider in relation to the 1963 Tokyo Convention since its temporal application encompasses the period of time when all external doors are closed following embarkation until the moment any such door is opened for disembarkation.[23] The offence of aircraft hijacking under the 1970 Hague Convention is consummated by a person who:

(a) unlawfully, by force or threat thereof, or by any other form of intimidation, seizes, or exercises control of [an] aircraft, or attempts to perform any such act; or

(b) is an accomplice of a person who performs or attempts to perform any such act.

The phrase 'any other form of intimidation' seems to be superfluous, since there can be no other form of unlawfully taking over an aircraft without the use or threat of force,[24] so it seems as though the drafters intended to cover every possible future situation, even if it was unknown to them at the time. It is possible, nonetheless, that seizure could be perpetrated without use of force, particularly through an act of bribery or illicit collusion with the aircraft's pilots or cabin crew. An Australian proposal to include a more specific list of non-forceful seizure in the text of the Hague Convention was rejected by the Legal Committee of the International Civil Aviation Organisation (ICAO) by 25:7, under whose aegis the Convention was adopted and who by that time had become the key player in respect of aerial terrorism. Shubber argued in 1973 that a reasonable interpretation, compatible with the aim and purpose of the Convention requires a wide construction, particularly one

[20] Art 16(2) of the 1963 Tokyo Convention notes that nothing in the Convention 'shall be deemed to create an obligation to grant extradition'.

[21] See ICAO Resolutions A17–3 (1970), A17–4 (1970), A17–5 (1970) and A17–6 (1970), reprinted in OY Elagab, *International Law Documents Relating to Terrorism,* (London, Cavendish, 1997) 443–45.

[22] Art 1, 1970 Hague Convention; in *Public Prosecutor v SHT* (1987) 74 ILR 162, the accused was charged with hijacking a British aircraft in flight from Beirut to London, forcing it to land in Amsterdam. The Dutch court applied Art 385(a) of the 1971 Dutch Penal Code which implemented the 1971 Montreal Convention and provided for the punishment of persons 'who by force, threat thereof or intimidation seize or exercise control over an aircraft, and cause it to change course'.

[23] 1970 Hague Convention, Art 3(1).

[24] S Shubber, 'Aircraft Hijacking under the Hague Convention 1970 – A New Regime?' (1973) 22 *International & Comparative Law Quarterly* 687, at 691.

which would define non-forceful seizure as hijacking.[25] This inference seems to be arbitrary, especially in light of its previous rejection by the members of ICAO's legal committee and the highly specialised nature of the Convention. Nonetheless, I cannot exclude the possibility that through the passage of time since 1970 this interpretation has become valid by reason of international consensus.

For the purposes of the Hague Convention the seizure must originate and be perpetrated by the principal from within the aircraft. Likewise, an accomplice falls within the ambit of the Convention only if such person provides assistance while on board the aircraft in flight. Accomplices whose participation in the offence takes place outside the aircraft are subject only to local criminal jurisdiction.[26] To meet the growing refusal of certain recalcitrant States to counter the aforementioned terrorist offences the delegates to the 1978 Bonn Economic Summit issued a Joint Statement whereby they agreed to cease all incoming and outgoing flights to those countries that refused to extradite or prosecute hijackers and/or did not return illegally seized aircraft. It is worth noting that a joint US-Canadian draft sanctions treaty to the same effect was rejected by the Legal Committee of the ICAO in 1972.[27] The Bonn Declaration was subsequently enforced against Iran, Afghanistan and later Libya. This limitation against the airports of countries that do not meet international standards of security or which are indifferent to prevention and punishment is a logical corollary to contemporary terrorist problems.

A very specific form of unlawful aircraft seizure is that of aerial piracy, as defined under Article 15 of the 1958 Geneva Convention on the High Seas[28] and Article 101 of the 1982 UN Convention on the Law of the Sea (UNCLOS)[29] –although the term is also generally employed to describe offences under the three anti-terrorist civil aviation conventions. Unlike aerial hijacking under the Hague Convention, air piracy under UNCLOS involves an illegal act of violence, namely an unlawful diversion to a destination other than that envisaged in the target aircraft's original flight plan and originating from outside the attacked aircraft – thus requiring a distinct aircraft of assault – and occurring in a place outside the jurisdiction of any State. Although the Hague Convention obliges States parties to consider the offences described therein as extraditable offences,[30] in effect denying the culprits a political motive excuse, the application of this rule to aerial piracy under UNCLOS would be problematic because piracy *jure gentium* requires that the piratical conduct be undertaken for private ends, thus excluding conduct perpetrated on the basis of a political ground or motive. One is therefore presented with the regulation of aerial piracy by two distinct legal regimes: on the one hand, UNCLOS and on the other the anti-terrorist treaties. The former has traditionally allowed the invocation of a political motive whereas the latter does not. Clearly, the two regimes are contradictory and there do not exist any discernible guidelines as to which should prevail. However, in light of the by now

---

[25]   Ibid, 692–93.
[26]   Ibid, 704–05.
[27]   McWhinney, *Aerial Piracy*, 48–62.
[28]   450 UNTS 82.
[29]   Both UNCLOS and the 1958 Convention reflect well established customary law; S Shubber, 'Is Hijacking of Aircraft Piracy in International Law?' (1968–69) 43 *British Yearbook of International Law* 193.
[30]   1970 Hague Convention, Art 8(1).

customary prohibition of unlawful interference with civil aviation, it is uncertain whether the illegal diversion of a civil aircraft, even for political purposes, could merit some kind of defence under UNCLOS, unless it was credited to a universally recognised national liberation movement and then only exceptionally.

With the signing of the 1971 Montreal Convention for the Suppression of Unlawful Acts against the Safety of Civil Aviation (Montreal Convention), the international community supplemented the legislative framework initialled by its two precursor conventions.[31] The aim of the Montreal Convention was to combat the scourge of attacks and other forms of aerial sabotage endangering the safety of civil aviation. Under Article 1, an offence is committed where a person unlawfully and intentionally:

(a) performs an act of violence against a person on board an aircraft in flight if that act is likely to endanger the safety of that aircraft; or

(b) destroys an aircraft in service or causes damage to such an aircraft which renders it incapable of flight or which is likely to endanger its safety in flight; or

(c) places or causes to be placed on an aircraft in service, by any means whatsoever, a device or substance which is likely to destroy that aircraft, or to cause damage to it which is likely to endanger its safety in flight; or

(d) destroys or damages air navigation facilities or interferes with their operation, if any such act is likely to endanger the safety of an aircraft in flight; or

(e) communicates information which he knows to be false, thereby endangering the safety of an aircraft in flight.

The concept of an aircraft 'in flight' is identical to that contained in the Hague Convention,[32] while an aircraft is considered to be 'in service' from the beginning of its pre-flight preparation until twenty-four hours after landing; the duration of an aircraft 'in service' cannot be shorter than that 'in flight'.[33] Besides this latter innovation and the various offences it covers the Montreal Convention is similar to its Hague counterpart in all its other procedural provisions, that is, jurisdiction,[34] rendering proscribed offences extraditable, incorporation of the *aut dedere aut judicare* principle, mutual legal assistance and other forms of inter-State cooperation and the obligation to adopt implementing legislation. In fact, these early anti-terrorist treaties set out the legislative drafting blueprint for the majority of later instruments dealing with international crimes. Overall, it is fair to say that solely from the point of view of the offences stipulated by the Hague and Montreal Conventions combined, the Tokyo Convention has, in fact, but not in law, been superseded.

The enhancement of security services in airports worldwide since the early 1980s has made hijacking far less frequent than in previous decades.[35] This has resulted,

---

[31] CS Thomas, MI Kirby, 'Convention for the Suppression of Unlawful Acts against the Safety of Civil Aviation' (1973) 22 *International & Comparative Law Quarterly* 163.

[32] 1971 Montreal Convention, Art 2(a).

[33] Ibid, Art 2(b).

[34] For a discussion on jurisdiction see chapter 15.

[35] A supplementary Protocol to the Montreal Convention on the Suppression of Unlawful Acts of Violence at Airports Serving International Civil Aviation was also agreed in 1988, reprinted in (1988) 27 ILM 627. Art II(1) thereof criminalises unlawful and intentional acts of violence against persons at international airports which cause serious injury or death, as well as acts of destruction or serious damage to facilities of such airports, where such acts endanger or are likely to endanger airport safety.

however, in an increase in remotely controlled detonations using plastic explosives and has rendered the application of the Montreal Convention all the more relevant. Observation of the Montreal Convention without other combined efforts to prevent the production and distribution of plastic explosives would be futile. Hence, under the aegis of ICAO a Convention on the Marking of Plastic Explosives for the Purpose of Detection was adopted in 1991,[36] which obliges States parties to introduce detection agents into explosive products, whether manufactured in that State or simply imported therein, in order to render such explosives detectable. This process is termed 'marking' of explosives.[37]

During the 1980s the provisions of the Montreal Convention were frequently triggered by clandestine or confessed attacks against civil aircraft through the use of agents instructed by State entities. The most notorious attack of this kind, for which the culprit State, the USA, subsequently admitted responsibility, concerned the downing of Iranian Airbus Flight 655 on 3 July 1988 by two surface-to-air missiles launched from a warship. This caused the death of the 290 passengers and crew. Iran brought the case to the International Court of Justice (ICJ), claiming the US had violated the Montreal Convention by refusing to prosecute or extradite those responsible.[38] The US argued that the Convention was not applicable to acts committed by the armed forces of a State and the two parties finally resolved their dispute through a Settlement Agreement adopted on 9 February 1996.[39] In another incident, North Korea was implicated in the destruction of a South Korean airliner on 29 November 1987. Although there was sufficient evidence demonstrating that a North Korean female agent was responsible for the bombing,[40] that country did not assume responsibility for the incident, nor, of course, did it launch an investigation against the alleged offender. By that time it had become obvious that whereas the envisaged culprits of the aerial terrorism conventions had been private actors, no other legal arsenal existed in respect of terrorist activity instituted by States entities. This had the effect of putting an unnecessary strain on the Montreal Convention, as became evident in the *Lockerbie* case.

Prior to 9/11 the Lockerbie incident epitomised State-sponsored aerial terrorism. On 21 December 1988 Pan Am flight 103A with direction from London to New York exploded above Lockerbie in Scotland killing all its passengers and crew, as well as eleven unsuspecting Lockerbie residents from the raining debris. Three years later two Libyans were indicted in the US. Libya refused to extradite the accused, claiming it had investigated the case against them and had found no indication of criminal liability.[41] The case was, moreover, complicated by the fact that both the US and UK

[36] (1991) 30 ILM 721.

[37] Ibid, Arts II, III and IV. The terms of the Convention do not apply to authorities performing military or police functions, unless they are used for purposes inconsistent with objectives of the Convention (Arts III(2) and IV(1)).

[38] *Aerial Incident of 3 July 1988* (Islamic Republic of Iran v USA). Iran instituted proceedings on 17 May 1989. (1989) 28 ILM 843.

[39] Reprinted in (1996) 35 ILM 572. By an order of 22 February 1996 the ICJ struck the case off its docket: (1996) ICJ Reports 9.

[40] See European Parliament Resolution of 10 March 1988 on Terrorist Attacks on Civil Aviation, reprinted in Elagab, 440.

[41] See C Joyner, W Rothbaum, 'Libya and the Aerial Incident at Lockerbie: What Lessons for International Extradition Law' (1992–93) 14 *Michigan Journal of International Law* 643.

argued that the two men were Libyan agents ordered by the government of that country to sabotage the aircraft. From the point of view of its accusers this meant that any Libyan prosecution or, indeed, criminal investigation was, thereafter, an exercise in futility. Continued intransigence through Libya's refusal to extradite prompted the Security Council to pass Resolution 731 on 21 January 1992 by which it urged Libya to cooperate with the US and UK in establishing responsibility for the incident and its authors. Rather than comply with the Council's request, on 3 March 1992 Libya lodged two separate complaints against its two accusers by which it claimed a violation of Articles 5(2)–(3), 7 and 11(1) of the Montreal Convention and asked the Court to order provisional measures. Meanwhile, on 31 March 1992, in a move that pre-empted the World Court's decision, the Security Council acting under Chapter VII of the UN Charter adopted Resolution 748 with which it demanded that Libya extradite the two accused, denounce terrorism and, further, imposed a number of sanctions. On 14 April 1992 the ICJ ruled that under Articles 25 and 103 of the UN Charter Security Council resolutions take precedence over all other treaty commitments, including Libya's claim for refusal to extradite under the Montreal Convention, which, as most of the judges determined, would have probably been in the right had it not been for Resolution 748.[42] Despite an ICJ ruling on 27 February 1998 finding jurisdiction over the merits of the dispute,[43] for the purposes of international criminal law the above cases exemplify the inherent difficulties in the application of the Montreal Convention to situations of terrorist attacks involving States, which the treaty in question was not initially envisaged to cover. By 1998 the deadlock regarding the criminal prosecution of the two accused had been broken and an agreement was reached whereby a court established in The Netherlands and composed of Scottish judges applying Scottish law would sit in trial of the two Libyans.[44]

The conclusion of the Lockerbie process also marked the end of State-sponsored aerial terrorism. Its aftermath led to stringent security measures at airports and for a while made air travel safer. In fact, at the second meeting of its 156th Session on 22 February 1999 the ICAO Council reported a sharp decline in the number of incidents of unlawful interference with international civil aviation.[45] The events of 9/11 demonstrated that aerial terrorism is still attractive to fundamentalist groups that seek public exposure and the widespread infliction of terror through their conduct. The Hague and the Montreal conventions can once again be employed to counter terrorism originating from private actors.

---

[42] *Questions of Interpretation and Application of the 1971 Montreal Convention Arising from the Aerial Incident at Lockerbie* (Libya v UK, Libya v USA), Provisional Measures, Order (14 Apr 1992), (1992) ICJ Reports 3, at 114.

[43] *Lockerbie* case, Preliminary Objections Decision (27 Feb 1998), (1998) ICJ Reports 115; see V Debbas-Gowland, 'The Relationship between the International Court of Justice and the Security Council in the Light of the Lockerbie Case' (1994) 88 *American Journal of International Law* 643; K Kaikobad, 'The Court, the Council and Interim Protection: A Commentary on the Lockerbie Order of 19 April 1992' (1996) 17 *Australian Yearbook of International Law* 87.

[44] Agreement between the Government of the Kingdom of The Netherlands and the Government of the UK of Great Britain and Northern Ireland, Concerning a Scottish Trial in The Netherlands, 18 September 1998, reprinted in (1999) 38 ILM 926.

[45] Report of the UN Secretary-General, Measures to Eliminate International Terrorism, UN Doc A/54/301 (3 Sep 1999) 7.

12.3.2   Hostage Taking and Attacks Against Internationally Protected Persons

The practice of hostage taking for political ends, which was especially prevalent in the 1970s and 1980s among terrorist organisations active in the Middle East, Western Europe and South America,[46] has once again resurfaced in the territories of the former Soviet Union, countries under UN administration, particularly Iraq and Afghanistan, as well as in the various civil wars in South America. The context for such conduct varies from act to act and from country to country and is not infrequently linked to organised criminal activity. Under Article 1(1) of the 1979 International Convention against the Taking of Hostages the offence of taking hostages is committed by:

> ... any person who seizes or detains and threatens to kill, to injure or to continue to detain another person (hereinafter referred to as the 'hostage') in order to compel a third party, namely, a State, an international intergovernmental organisation, a natural or juridical person, or a group of persons, to do or abstain from doing any act as an explicit or implicit condition for the release of the hostage.

As is evident acts of hostage taking overlap with conduct that is otherwise criminalised in most counter-terrorist treaties. The provisions of the Convention are not applicable to purely internal situations of hostage taking, thus requiring at least one international element.[47] The Convention, like all its other anti-terrorist predecessors, recognises the grave nature of the offence[48] and obliges States parties to define it as an extraditable crime under their domestic laws.[49] The Convention is inapplicable to situations involving armed conflicts, albeit it is well established that acts of terrorism are prohibited as a means and method of warfare by both customary law and the *jus in bello*.[50]

Although the 1979 Convention makes no provision regarding the handling of hostage situations once these have occurred, it does require parties to take all appropriate measures with a view to 'eas[ing] the situation of the hostage, in particular, to secure their release'[51] and subsequently return to them any object which the offender has obtained as a result of the offence.[52] Naturally, this is not a license to employ unilateral extraterritorial enforcement jurisdiction. Most States have in

---

[46] SC Res 579 (18 Dec 1985), 618 (29 Jul 1988) and 638 (31 Jul 1989); Organisation of American States (OAS) GA Res 4 (I-E 170) (30 Jun 1970).

[47] Art 13, Hostage Taking Convention.

[48] Ibid, Art 2.

[49] Ibid, Art 10(1); likewise, all forms of unlawful detention constitute offences under Art 1(d) of the 1976 European Convention on the Suppression of Terrorism, which member States are obliged to regard as extraditable.

[50] 1949 Geneva Convention Relative to the Protection of Civilian Persons in Time of War, Arts 3(1)(b) and 34, 75 UNTS (1950) 287; *USA v List* (*Hostages* case), 8 Law Reports of Trials of War Criminals (LRTWC) 34; see also SC Res 674 (29 Oct 1990), demanding that Iraq release all hostages in occupied Kuwait. See chapter 7.5 for a discussion of the prohibition of terror during armed conflict.

[51] Art 3(1), Hostage Taking Convention.

[52] Ibid, Art 3(2).

theory adopted a policy of refusing to yield to terrorist demands,[53] a practice which is compatible with Article 3(1) of the Convention so as to discourage an endless chain of abductions. In practice, however, as is the case with Somali pirates, States are not averse to private efforts to secure the release of hostages through the payment of ransom by insurance companies; sometimes, they are also parties to relevant release agreements as was the case with the US hostages in Iran during the 1979 crisis.[54] Although States are obliged to do their best to secure the release of hostages international law does not impose on them a duty to yield to terrorist demands or to release hostages on their territory.

A more specialised international offence against the person is that formulated by the 1973 UN Convention on the Prevention and Punishment of Crimes against Internationally Protected Persons, Including Diplomatic Agents.[55] This Convention penalises what has been an ancient customary obligation to protect the person and property of diplomatic agents and other foreign public officials[56] as this was succinctly reaffirmed in the year-long hostage incident involving fifty-nine US diplomatic personnel in Iran.[57] Article 1 of the Convention distinguishes between two categories of internationally protected persons: first, Heads of State, Heads of Government or Foreign Affairs Ministers whenever these persons are in a foreign State, as well as accompanying family members.[58] This protection persists regardless of official capacity and extends under customary law only to immediate family members.[59] The second category includes representatives of States or intergovernmental organisations who are entitled to special protection under general international law; that is, diplomats, consuls, accredited officials of States and international organisations on official visits.[60] The offence is consummated through the intentional commission, threat, attempt, or complicity in the murder, kidnapping, attack upon the person or liberty thereof, or by means of a violent attack against the official premises, private accommodation or transportation of internationally protected

[53]   The participating nations in the G8/Russia 1995 Ottawa Anti-terrorist Summit agreed, *inter alia,* to deny demands from kidnappers.

[54]   The two countries negotiated an agreement whereby Iran was to release the hostages under the condition that the US unfreeze Iranian assets and an arbitral tribunal be established to settle individual claims for compensation arising from the 1979 coup. Elagab, 615–49.

[55]   (1974) 13 ILM 41.

[56]   Arts 29 and 30 of the 1961 Vienna Convention on Diplomatic Relations, 500 UNTS 95; Art 2 of the 1971 OAS Convention to Prevent and Punish the Acts of Terrorism Taking the Form of Crimes Against Persons and Related Extortion that are of International Significance, (1971) 10 ILM 255, renders kidnapping, murder and other assaults against the life or integrity of internationally protected persons 'common crimes of international significance'. Therefore, unlike the 1973 Convention, the relevant offences contained in the 1971 OAS Convention are not considered international offences.

[57]   *US Diplomatic and Consular Staff in Iran case* (USA v Iran), Judgment (24 May 1980), (1980) ICJ Reports 3.

[58]   Art 1(a) of the 1973 UN Convention on the Prevention and Punishment of Crimes against Internationally Protected Persons Including Diplomatic Agents.

[59]   CL Rozakis, 'Terrorism and the Internationally Protected Persons in the Light of the ILC's Draft Code' (1974) 23 *International & Comparative Law Quarterly* 32, at 43.

[60]   In *R v Donyadideh and Others,* 101 ILR 259, eleven persons were charged with offences against representatives of Iran in Australia. The Australian Supreme Court convicted the culprits under s 8(2) and (3) of that country's Internationally Protected Persons Act 1976, which incorporated the 1973 UN Convention and thus criminalised illicit conduct directed against the liberty of protected persons and damage to their property; see also UK Internationally Protected Persons Act 1978, s 1.

persons likely to endanger their person or liberty.[61] Additionally, the accused must be aware of the protected status of the person when perpetrating the *actus reus* of the offence. Therefore, the infliction of a fatal road traffic accident does not necessarily fall within the scope of Article 2.[62]

The rise in attacks against internationally protected persons accelerated concerted international efforts towards acknowledging the seriousness of the problem and the adoption of measures to give effect to the 1973 Convention. The Venice Economic Summit Conference of 1980 contained a Statement on the Taking of Diplomatic Hostages (the Venice Statement), noting the duty of States to adopt appropriate policies and criminal legislation and to refrain from taking a direct or indirect part in such acts. The Venice Statement was reaffirmed in the Ottawa Summit of 1981, which further addressed the resolve of participating States to take prompt action in cases of State support of related terrorist activities. Moreover, a reporting procedure was established by the General Assembly in 1980 urging member States to submit reports on offences against protected persons, as well as the application of domestic laws and measures taken to effectively implement them.[63] This procedure was supplemented in 1987 by a request for more detailed information to be supplied to the Secretary General with regard to his *Annual Report* on the subject.[64]

12.3.3   Terrorist Bombings and Nuclear Terrorism

By the mid-1990s the focus of the international community on terrorism had shifted to address the action of groups possessing strong religious or ethnical underpinnings and which found popular support among their kinsmen. By this time aerial hijacking and hostage taking had decreased dramatically as a result of technological and security developments and terrorists resorted to clandestine operations involving explosives and other incendiary materials. The Ad Hoc Committee on Terrorism established by the General Assembly in 1996[65] examined the drafting of three distinct treaties dealing with matters of increasing concern: terrorist bombings, terrorist financing and nuclear terrorism. Agreement on the first two was swift, but nuclear terrorism was of a far thornier nature and a treaty was only agreed in 2005. The issue of urban terrorist bombings was never placed on the international agenda before the end of the Cold War because the vast majority of such attacks were committed within a single State by persons or groups that were nationals of that State. Countries also felt that such incidents were of purely domestic concern for an additional reason. They did not wish to trigger debate over the possible application of the laws of armed conflict in their battle against terrorist organisations and as a negative result give rise to questions of self-determination. This was particularly the case with the provisional

    [61] 1973 Convention, Art 2; see also 1976 European Convention on the Suppression of Terrorism, Art 1(c).
    [62] Rozakis, 49–50.
    [63] GA Res 35/168 (15 Dec 1980).
    [64] GA Res 42/154 (7 Dec 1987), operative para 9.
    [65] GA Res 51/210 (17 Dec 1996), as affirmed by GA Res 53/108 (8 Dec 1998).

Irish Republican Army (IRA) in the UK and the Kurdistan Workers' Party (PKK) in Turkey. Incidents involving these groups assumed an international element either when governmental forces acted clandestinely abroad,[66] or where the afflicted States requested the extradition of alleged perpetrators apprehended elsewhere.[67] This practice of branding groups as terrorist organisations and refusing to recognise the existence of a non-international armed conflict and combatant status vis-a-vis enemy belligerents, particularly in situations where common Article 3 of the 1949 Geneva Conventions were satisfied,[68] resulted in appalling human rights abuses against belligerents and civilian populations.

With the demise of communism and the concentration of politics and commerce in supra-national institutions, terrorist organisations began conducting urban warfare across international frontiers as restrictions in cross-border crossings were gradually declining in many parts of the world. It soon became evident that the terror campaign of purely domestic groups was an international problem requiring global solutions. In 1998 the UN Convention for the Suppression of Terrorist Bombings (Terrorist Bombings Convention) was adopted by the General Assembly of the UN. This instrument made it an offence to unlawfully and intentionally deliver, place, discharge or detonate an explosive or other lethal device in, into or against a place of public use, a State facility, a public transportation system or infrastructure facility, with intent to cause death or bodily injury, or extensive destruction, resulting or likely to result in major economic loss.[69] In order to avoid the political shortcomings identified above, Article 3 of the Convention requires that the operation leading to a terrorist bombing involve at least one extraterritorial element, whether in terms of the locus or the nationality of the victim or perpetrator.

Both the terrorist bombings and financing conventions view terrorism as a series of pre-planned operations carried out by persons participating in multifaceted organisational webs and oblige member States to take specific measures to curb terrorism from its roots. Building on a growing de-politicisation of terrorist-related activities the Terrorist Bombings Convention makes it clear that no justification is to be provided under domestic law for the offences contemplated therein, regardless of political, philosophical, ideological, religious, or other motive which the perpetrators may invoke.[70]

Finally, with the growth of criminal organisations and the restructuring of some terrorist groups into such, the issue of nuclear terrorism has once again resurfaced. The 1979 Convention on the Physical Protection of Nuclear Material,[71] an instrument indirectly related to terrorism, was adopted with a twofold objective: to establish levels of physical protection of nuclear material used for peaceful purposes

---

[66] *McCann v UK* (1996) 21 EHRR 97.

[67] *Re Croissant* (1978) 74 ILR 505.

[68] The protection offered under common Art 3 is not dependent on unilateral recognition by States, but is instead applicable as a matter of its status as a norm of customary international law. See *Military and Paramilitary Activities in and against Nicaragua* (Nicaragua v USA), Merits, (1986) ICJ Reports, para 218.

[69] Art 2(1) of the 1998 Terrorist Bombings Convention. It is also an offence to attempt (Art 2(2)), participate (Art 2(3)(a)), organise or direct (Art 2(3)(b)), or act in a common purpose (Art 2(3)(c)) to commit any of the offences contained in Art 2(1).

[70] Art 5 of the 1998 Terrorist Bombings Convention.

[71] (1979) 18 ILM 1422.

while in international nuclear transport[72] and to provide for measures against unlawful acts (for example, the requirements that relate to making specified acts criminal offences under national law, to establish jurisdiction over those offences and prosecute or extradite alleged offenders) with respect to such material while in international transport, as well as in domestic use, storage and transport.[73] The adoption in 2005 of the UN Convention on the Suppression of Acts of Nuclear Terrorism was a response to the possibility that nuclear or radioactive material may fall in the hands of terrorists. Indeed, the gravity of illicit trafficking in nuclear material has alarmed the International Atomic Energy Agency (IAEA) since the early 1990s. To this end the IAEA's Illicit Trafficking Database (ITDB) programme for incidents involving nuclear materials and other radioactive sources dates from August 1995 when the IAEA Secretariat invited governments to participate in its database programme and to identify points of contact for that purpose. In its 2005 Report the IAEA confirmed 103 incidents of illicit trafficking and unauthorised activities concerning nuclear and radioactive material for that year alone. However, the Report stressed the fact that these incidents did not involve a terrorist element or threat thereof, not even criminal liability in the vast majority of cases, but highlighted security vulnerabilities in nuclear-handling facilities.[74]

A person commits an offence within the meaning of the Nuclear Terrorism Convention if that person unlawfully and intentionally:

(a) Possesses radioactive material or makes or possesses a device:

    (i) With the intent to cause death or serious bodily injury; or
    (ii) With the intent to cause substantial damage to property or to the environment;

(b) Uses in any way radioactive material or a device, or uses and damages a nuclear facility in a manner which releases or risks the release of radioactive material: [with intent to cause death, serious bodily injury, substantial damage to property or the environment]

    (iii) With the intent to compel a natural or legal person, an international organisation or a State to do or refrain from doing an act.[75]

A person commits an offence within the meaning of Article 2 if he or she threatens to employ nuclear or radioactive material, or unlawfully demand such material, device or nuclear facility under circumstances indicating the credibility of a threat. The offence may be consummated through an attempt, accomplice and common purpose liability,[76] as well as by ordering or organising others to do so.[77] In accordance with Articles 3 and 4 the Convention is inapplicable in respect of offences taking place on the territory of a single country, or where the offender and victims are nationals of the same country. It is equally inapplicable in situations concerning the activities of armed forces during an armed conflict, or in their exercise of official duties. This

---

[72] Arts 2 and 3 of the 1979 Convention on the Physical Protection of Nuclear Material.

[73] Ibid, Arts 7–11.

[74] IAEA, Illicit Trafficking and Other Unauthorised Activities Involving Nuclear and Radioactive Material (2005), available at: <http://www.iaea.org/NewsCenter/Features/RadSources/PDF/fact_figures2005.pdf>.

[75] Art 2(1), Nuclear Terrorism Convention.

[76] For an analysis of these types of liability, see chapter 3.

[77] Art 2(2)–(4), Nuclear Terrorism Convention.

provision was included to alleviate the concerns of nuclear powers over the workings of their military personnel, albeit it should not be read as condoning nuclear theft or threats to use nuclear or radioactive material by the intelligence services of States during peace-time.[78] In all other respects the Convention resembles the post-1998 generation of anti-terrorist treaties by granting wide territorial and extraterritorial jurisdiction[79] and rejecting all possible defences or justifications offered by the perpetrators. On the other hand, the provisions on cooperation are weak and subject to numerous exceptions.

12.3.4 Terrorist Financing and Security Council Resolution 1373 (2001)

Prior to the collapse of communism it was not uncommon for terrorist groups to be funded by particular States. This was achieved through direct funding or logistical support and by allowing or tolerating the use of their territory by such groups as a base for launching and planning illegal acts. The New World Order, following the end of the Cold War, created a financial vacuum because culprit States no longer saw the need for externally-funded terrorism and thus terrorist groups turned increasingly to other means of self-preservation. It is not surprising therefore that since the early 1990s the UN General Assembly had identified possible links between terrorism and organised crime.[80] The 2000 UN Convention against Transnational Organized Crime (CATOC)[81] acknowledges this connection, yet despite the manifest links between the two[82] the insertion of terrorist acts in the definition of organised crime was finally avoided. Nonetheless, some groups such as the Colombian FARC and the Taliban, who at the time sheltered Al-Qaeda in Afghanistan, were known to cultivate and traffic illicit narcotic substances.[83] In other instances, terrorists had formed alliances with organised criminal rings in order to conduct trafficking of arms, drugs and women, launder illicit proceeds and infiltrate legitimate banking and commercial markets. Security Council Resolution 1333 determined that proceeds from narcotics strengthened the Taliban's capacity in harbouring terrorists and imposed a sanctions regime.[84]

---

[78] Art 4(3), ibid.

[79] Art 9(2)(b) confers jurisdiction even to the State whose government facilities abroad, including embassies or consular premises, were the target of an offence.

[80] GA Res 49/60 (9 Dec 1994); the Vienna Declaration and Program of Action adopted at the World Conference on Human Rights emphasised that the linkage between terrorism and drug-trafficking aims at the 'destruction' of human rights and democracy by terrorists. UN Doc A/CONF 157/23 (14–25 June 1993). The term 'destruction' should be contrasted with the usual reference to human rights 'violations'. The distinction is deliberate and misguiding, aiming to demonstrate that States are not the only entities incumbent with human rights obligations.

[81] (2001) 40 ILM 335.

[82] Second session of the Ad Hoc Committee (8–12 Mar 1999), UN Doc A/AC 254/4 Rev 1 (10 Feb 1999).

[83] SC Res 1214 (8 Dec 1998).

[84] SC Res 1333 (19 Dec 2000).

In January 2000 the UN General Assembly opened for signature an International Convention for the Suppression of the Financing of Terrorism.[85] This Convention makes it an offence to directly or indirectly, unlawfully and wilfully: provide or collect funds with the intention or knowledge they are used, in full or in part, to carry out acts described in the various anti-terrorist conventions; commit other criminal acts with the aim of intimidating a population; or compel a government to do or abstain from a certain act.[86] The Convention establishes a distinct offence of terrorist financing, which is constituted by 'directly or indirectly, unlawfully and wilfully providing or collecting funds with the intention that they should be used or in the knowledge that they are to be used, in full or in part', in order to carry out an offence described in any one of the nine counter-terrorist treaties, or to commit any other violent act with the intent of intimidating a population or of compelling a government to act in a certain way.[87] While the criminalisation of funding of acts falling within the ambit of previous counter-terrorist treaties requires ratification of those treaties by the State concerned, no ratification is required in respect of 'other violent intimidating acts', as described in sub-paragraph 1(b). This wide definition may well encompass offences encountered in the nine counter-terrorist treaties. For example, the provision of financial assistance by an individual who is a national of country A with the aim of kidnapping a Head of State becomes an international offence only if country A has ratified both the 2000 Terrorist Financing Convention and the 1973 Convention on the Prevention and Punishment of Crimes against Internationally Protected Persons, Including Diplomatic Agents.[88] The effect of sub-paragraph (1)(b), however, is to criminalise this conduct under the 2000 Terrorist Financing Convention where the kidnapping in question was either intended to intimidate the civilian population or compel a government to do or abstain from doing a certain act.[89] As regards the definition of 'financing', it was pointed out during the deliberations in the Sixth Committee of the General Assembly that while the Convention focused on the financing of the most serious terrorist acts all means of financing were covered, including both unlawful means (such as racketeering) as well as lawful (such as private and public financing, charity collection and others).[90] The Convention obliges parties to take appropriate measures in order to identify, detect, freeze, or seize terrorist-related funds as well as the proceeds derived from such offences.[91] Because terrorists use the legitimate economy to channel funds across jurisdictions it is apparent that banks and other private financiers must partake in the processes envisaged by the Convention. Initially, the measures imposed on private

---

[85] GA Res 54/109 (25 Feb 2000); see V Morris, A Pronto, 'The Work of the Sixth Committee at the Fifty-Fourth Session of the UN General Assembly' (2000) 94 *American Journal of International Law* 582, at 585.

[86] Art 2(1), 2000 Terrorist Financing Convention.

[87] Art 2(1)(a) and (b); Art 2(d) of the 1999 Convention of the Organisation of the Islamic Conference (OIC) on Combating International Terrorism states, *inter alia,* that 'all forms of international crimes, including illegal trafficking in narcotics and human beings, money laundering, aimed at financing terrorist objectives shall be considered terrorist crimes'.

[88] (1979) 3 ILM 41.

[89] Report of the Ad Hoc Committee established by GA Res 51/210 (1996), GAOR 54th Session, UN Doc A/54/37/Supp No 37 (5 May 1999) 3.

[90] Ibid.

[91] Art 8(1), 2000 Terrorist Financing Convention.

institutions were based on anti-money laundering models with an emphasis on strict client identification. For example, the so-called 'Know Your Client' (KYC) principle requires that financial institutions verify in as much detail as possible the personal and financial details of all their clients, whether these are natural or legal persons.[92]

Following the 11 September 2001 terrorist attack against the USA the Security Council adopted Resolution 1373 on 28 September 2001. This seminal instrument establishes a general – that is, not specifically directed against Al-Qaeda and their associates – financial regime which: criminalises all activities falling within the remit of terrorist financing; obliges States to freeze all funds or financial assets of persons and entities that are directly or indirectly used to commit terrorist acts or that are owned and controlled by persons engaged in, or associated with, terrorism; obliges States to prevent their nationals (including private financial institutions) from making such funds available, thus imposing strict client detection measures, requires the filing of suspicious transactions reports (STRs) and imposes adherence to orders requiring the freezing of assets of persons listed by subsidiary organs of the Council, as and when these are circulated.[93] The resolution finally imposes substantive and procedural criminal law measures at the domestic level, including an obligation to cooperate in the acquisition of evidence for criminal proceedings.[94] In order to implement and monitor the terms of the Resolution the Council decided to establish a subsidiary organ, the Counter-Terrorism Committee.[95] Given the urgency of the situation, member States were originally obliged to report to the Committee within ninety days on the steps they had taken to implement the Resolution. In the vast exchange of communication that has transpired since early 2002 the process assisted many States in adapting their legislation to the prevailing exigencies.

The Security Council proceeded to impose so-called targeted sanctions against persons associated with terrorist-related funds, much in the same way it had done with other international crimes prior to 9/11. UN targeted sanctions operate through a subsidiary organ to the Council, a sanctions committee, which is authorised to draw up a list of targeted persons or organisations on the basis of information received from official sources. In practice, the sanctions committee receives its information through secret intelligence and although a recommendation to list a particular person/group must be accompanied by an account of some evidence the committee does not possess the technical capacity to assess the veracity of the submitted information.[96] Once the decision to list a particular person has been taken the Council or the organ itself may thereafter proceed to issue binding orders on States and private entities (eg banks) with a view to freezing or confiscating the relevant assets. Besides the UN list issued by the 1267 Committee various US government

---

[92] Ibid, Art 18(1)(b)(ii) requires, in respect of legal persons, the following: proof of incorporation, including information concerning the customer's name, legal form, address, directors and their powers within the company's structure. Sub-paragraph 1(b)(iv) further requires that 'financial institutions maintain, for at least five years, all necessary records on transactions, both domestic or international'.

[93] Operative para 1; although in practice this also includes national law enforcement authorities, such as the FBI, CIA and OFAC (Office of Foreign Assets Control).

[94] Operative para 2.

[95] Operative para 6.

[96] The Committee has set up Guidelines for assessing listing and de-listing. Available at: <http://www.un.org/Docs/sc/committees/1267/1267_guidelines.pdf>.

agencies, in particular OFAC, as well as the UK, EU[97] and others have produced distinct, yet complementary lists, which in some cases are more extensive than the UN list. Although these have no binding effect on other States, let alone private financial institutions, in practice the latter are obliged to conform because of their business relations with the issuing States and the possible consequences in cases of non-compliance. In the case of terrorist-related funds the sanctions committee established under Council Resolution 1267[98] – whose mandate originally encompassed the Taliban regime and which was later extended to cover Al-Qaeda terrorist financing blacklisting – imposed a number of obligations, including asset freezing, travel bans and others. This expansion of the 1267 Committee's work was achieved by Resolution 1390,[99] which does not impose a time limit or a link between the targeted individual/group and a State. The Security Council later also provided a definition of 'association with' Al-Qaeda, through Resolution 1526[100] because a number of States thought it wise to report political dissidents to the sanctions committee![101]

In practical terms both the 2000 Convention and Resolution 1373 must be construed in accordance with the findings and Recommendations of the OECD's Financial Action Task Force (FATF). The FATF had long warned the international community about the potentiality of the channelling of funds to terrorists from money laundering activities, underground remittance systems *(hawala)*, disguised charities and trusts. Most of these activities are difficult to detect and so it is the duty of financial or other institutions to implement appropriate monitoring mechanisms (such as KYC and the filing of STRs). At an extraordinary plenary on October 2001 the FATF expanded its mandate to encompass also terrorist financing and subsequently went ahead to issue its Special Recommendations on Terrorist Financing. These commit members to: ratify counter-terrorism treaties; criminalise terrorist financing; freeze and confiscate terrorist assets; report suspicious transactions; provide related assistance to other countries; impose anti-money laundering requirements on alternative remittance systems; strengthen customer identification measures in international and domestic wire transfers, and; ensure that non-profit organisations cannot be misused to finance terrorism.[102] The Special Recommendations are not binding but are of very high persuasive value and very few jurisdictions openly

---

[97] EU freezing measures are predicated on the Consolidated Targeted Financial Sanctions List (e-CTFSL) database, which represents a joint initiative between the EC Commission and European banks, containing all persons and entities subject to EU financial sanctions. See also Council Regulation 2580/2001 of 27 Dec 2001 on Specific Restrictive Measures directed against certain Persons and Entities with a view to Combating Terrorism (OJ L 344, 28 Nov 2001); see also Council Regulation 881/2002 of 27 May 2002, imposing certain specific Restrictive Measures directed against certain Persons and entities associated with Osama bin Laden, the Al-Qaeda network and the Taliban ... and extending the Freeze of Funds and other Financial Resources (OJ l 139, 29 May 2002). This Regulation authorises the EC Commission to supplement and amend the list on the basis of Security Council resolutions or the Sanction Committee's determinations through the adoption of subsequent EC Regulations.

[98] SC 1267 (15 Oct 1999).

[99] SC 1390 (16 Jan 2002).

[100] SC 1526 (30 Jan 2004).

[101] I Cameron, 'Terrorist Financing in International Law' in I Bantekas (ed), *International and European Financial Criminal Law* (London, Butterworths, 2006).

[102] FATF Special Recommendations on Terrorist Financing (31 Oct 2001); see I Bantekas, 'The International Law of Terrorist Financing' (2003) 97 *American Journal of International Law* 315.

refuse to follow them. In fact, they have been expressly adopted by associations of private financial institutions and as a form of self-regulation.

12.4   State-Sponsored Terrorism

Too many political intricacies have so far obstructed the attainment of a single definition of terrorism. It is of no wonder therefore that there is no hint in any of the aforementioned anti-terrorist treaties about the possibility of establishing any sort of criteria for terrorist conduct perpetrated by States and their instrumentalities. In theory, this is a contradiction of terms because the very object of terrorism is to spread terror to a civilian population and in this manner coerce its government to give in to the culprits' demands. Thus, State terrorism is only feasible if a government were to manipulate its own people by scaremongering techniques or by otherwise manipulating public opinion in third nations through the use of terror. Although both alternatives have been practiced by States, it is the latter that is of interest in the present discussion, given that the infliction of terror against one's own population has gradually given rise to distinct international offences, particularly enforced disappearances and torture.

Starting in the late 1960s the West was disinclined to accept claims made by developing and Arab countries that Israel was a 'terrorist State', believing that only individuals or groups could be characterised as terrorists. However, since the 1980s and with ample evidence that a handful of countries were behind terrorist activities this stance was altered and the term State sponsored terrorism was coined. The precise fault line for the attribution of liability to a State in respect of terrorist conduct is unclear and will not be attempted in the limited confines of this chapter. What is clear however is that liability arises where a State tolerates the use of its territory by terrorists, even if it is otherwise opposed or indifferent to their cause.[103] In the face of contemporary mass-victim terrorism the question is no longer whether the sponsoring State is liable, but rather whether the victim nation is entitled to treat the conduct (taken as a whole) as an armed attack that would entitle it to respond with armed force. Such an exceptional invocation of self-defence seems to have been justified in the text of Resolution 1368 which authorised the USA to employ armed force against the perpetrators of the 9/11 terrorist attacks as a matter of its inherent right to self-defence. This view is certainly shared by the USA and Israel, the former since the 1980s and the latter from the 1970s, arguing that terrorist attacks justify the use of force not only as an immediate response but also by reason of pre-emptive self-defence.[104]

On 7 August 1998 US embassies in Nairobi and Dar-es-Salaam were devastated by bomb blasts that killed approximately 300 people, including 12 American nationals. Investigations led US authorities to suspect the involvement of Al-Qaeda which was

---

[103]   See GA Res 49/60 (9 Dec 1994).

[104]   See Israeli claim of pre-emptive self-defence regarding the interception of a Libyan civil aircraft in 1986, UN Doc S/PV 2655/Corr 1 (18 Feb 1986); US Presidential Directives 62 (on combating terrorism), 22 May 1998, and 63 (on critical infrastructure protection), 22 May 1998.

at the time based in Afghanistan. In retaliation, on 20 August 1998, the US launched 79 Tomahawk Cruise missiles against paramilitary camps in Afghanistan and a Sudanese pharmaceutical plant in Sudan, claiming the latter produced chemical weapons. In his subsequent report President Clinton stated that the USA acted in the exercise of its right of self-defence under Article 51 of the UN Charter, pointing out that the strikes were necessary and proportionate to an imminent terrorist threat. He further argued that they were intended to prevent and deter future attacks.[105] Resolution 1368 further solidified this conclusion. Yet, even if one were to consider a more generalised application of this exceptional measure in practice it is difficult to employ armed force against States in which terrorist organisations have entrenched their presence through a plethora of clandestine cells. The position is far from clear.

The Security Council has in the past condemned the involvement of States in acts of violence associated with terrorism,[106] but even where, as in the Lockerbie incident, it acted under Chapter VII of the 1945 UN Charter, it has never used the term 'State sponsor' of terrorism, preferring instead to demand that culprit States desist from all forms of terrorist action and all assistance to terrorist groups.[107] The Council refrained from making any characterisations against Syria, despite the latter's apparent involvement in the assassination of Lebanese President Rafiq Hariri and the subsequent creation of the Special Tribunal for Lebanon. The inclusion of terrorism within the ambit of Chapter VII necessarily equates some forms of terrorist activity with either a threat to the peace, breach of the peace or an act of aggression, making them theoretically susceptible to collective enforcement action, as was the case with Resolution 1368. Some commentators have argued that terrorist action of this kind is tantamount to 'low intensity aggression'.[108]

In light of the controversies and ambiguities highlighted it is highly unlikely that cases involving direct or indirect State support of terrorism can or should be solved through the mechanisms envisaged in anti-terrorist treaties. Not only are these treaties predicated on mutual trust and recognition that terrorism is a crime of international concern perpetrated by non-State entities, but moreover they do not allow for prosecution of State officials sanctioning or authorising terrorist-related violence. Therefore, the most appropriate forum for the discussion of State-sponsored terrorism is the Security Council, which has dealt with Lockerbie, 9/11 and the Hariri assassination through the UN Charter and ad hoc mechanisms, some of which involved the use of armed force whereas others did not.

If the Council is unwilling or otherwise blocked from addressing State- sponsored terrorism, unilateral action by concerned countries should not be precluded. In its fight against State-sponsored terrorism the US Congress amended its Foreign Sovereign Immunities Act (FSIA) in 1996 through the adoption of the AEDPA, permitting civil suits for compensatory and punitive damages against a foreign State, State agency or instrumentality that either committed the terrorist act or provided aid to

---

[105] SD Murphy, 'Contemporary Practice of the US Relating to International Law' (1999) 93 *American Journal of International Law* 161.

[106]   eg SC Res 461 (31 Dec 1979); SC Res 731 (21 Jan 1992); SC Res 1044 (31 Jan 1996).

[107]   SC Res 748 (31 Mar 1992); SC Res 883 (11 Nov 1993); SC Res 1054 (26 Apr 1996).

[108]   See SS Evans, 'The Lockerbie Incident Cases: Libyan Sponsored Terrorism, Judicial Review and the Political Question Doctrine' (1994) 18 *Maryland Journal of International Law & Trade* 20, at 70.

the culprit group.[109] A terrorist act under the AEDPA includes torture, extra-judicial killing, aircraft sabotage and hostage taking, provided that the victim is a US national and the offence occurs outside the US. The terrorism exception to the FSIA applies only against States that are designated by the State Department as State sponsors of terrorism.[110] Significantly, the AEDPA 1996 permits the claimant to execute a judgment against State owned property that is used for a commercial activity in the USA even if the property cannot be connected to the terrorist act.[111] Successful suits have been brought against Cuba[112] and Iran.[113] Nonetheless, the State Department has objected to the passing of AEDPA by Congress, believing that the terrorism exception to immunity is incompatible with US treaty obligations and that it will negatively impact on the country's ability to use frozen assets to negotiate with recalcitrant States.[114]

12.5 Terrorism and National Liberation Movements

Contemporary terrorism has primarily manifested itself through ideological and revolutionary movements.[115] The earliest revolutionary movements appeared in the 1920s in South America following the establishment of autocratic regimes that were assisted by reason of external intervention. Contemporary urban movements are less inclined to remove anti-democratic governments as they are to bringing revolutionary terrorism to the masses,[116] which is also the cause for numerous illicit operations such as drug-trafficking. The erosion of the South American revolutionary movements began with the death of Ernesto 'Che' Guevara. Following his demise terrorist violence was brought from the countryside to the cities and its indiscriminate nature was justified by its adherents on the basis of the need to uproot political power.[117] These movements, detached from Che Guevara's idealist socialist society ultimately failed to sway public opinion in their favour and their successors gradually made use of their existing organisational structures to pursue other agendas. By the early 1990s the vast majority of these groups had significantly increased their recruits, effectively controlled parts of the territory in which they operated, participated in organised crime and were engaged in an armed conflict with their respective governments.

---

[109] AEPDA 1996, 28 USC §§ 1603(b) and 1605(a)(7).

[110] The Secretary of State is authorised to determine whether a foreign country has provided repeated support to international terrorism, on the basis of which he may thereafter designate the culprit as a State sponsor of terrorism. See the 1979 Export Administration Act, 50 USC § 2405(j); 1961 Foreign Assistance Act, 22 USC § 2371.

[111] 28 USC §§ 1610(a)(7) and (b)(2).

[112] *Alejandre v Republic of Cuba* (1997) 996 F Supp 1239.

[113] *Flatow v Islamic Republic of Iran,* (1998) 999 F Supp 1; *Cicippio v Islamic Republic of Iran,* (1998) 18 F Supp 2d 62.

[114] M Vadnais, 'The Terrorism Exception to the Foreign Sovereign Immunities Act: Forward Leaning Legislation or Just Bad Law?' (2000) 5 *University of California Los Angeles Journal of International Law & Foreign Affairs* 199, at 201.

[115] G Schwarzenberger, 'Terrorists, Hijackers, Guerillas and Mercenaries' (1971) 24 *Current Legal Problems* 257.

[116] See E Halperin, *Terrorism in Latin America,* (London, Sage, 1976).

[117] Ibid, 32–33.

Ideological movements in Europe had until very recently been inspired by Marxist and to a lesser degree by fascist theories. Other groups such as Baader Meinhof and the Red Brigades drew their motivation from the theories of anarcho-communism as formulated by Kropotkin and Bakunin, the latter especially advocating the abolition of capitalism and collectivisation of production and consumption.[118] The fine line it seems between terrorist and revolutionary ideology is the degree of violence permitted by domestic and international law to pursue such ideology. Human rights law is certainly an ally of groups advocating or disseminating their ideas without recourse to violence. The question then arises as to whether violence is always and at all times restricted to defensive action by States or whether it may also be employed by non-State entities under particular circumstances. The mere fact that violence has been used by a group does not automatically render it a terrorist organisation. Since the principle of self-determination of peoples is well established in international law[119] a certain degree of violence must necessarily be legitimised when all other peaceful means have failed to dissuade the oppressive State. Self-determination therefore gives rise to a right to revolt to a limited number of groups. This entitlement is well reflected in international humanitarian law. Article 1(4) of the 1977 Additional Protocol I to the Geneva Conventions of 1949 and Relating to the Protection of Victims of International Armed Conflicts (Protocol I) equates those struggles in which peoples are fighting against colonial domination, alien occupation and racist regimes in the exercise of their right to self-determination to international armed conflicts.[120] The three conditions contained in Article 1(4) are exhaustive, thus being applicable only to a limited number of groups. Article 1(4) was earlier preceded by the General Assembly Declaration on Principles of International Law Concerning Friendly Relations and Cooperation among States in Accordance with the Charter of the UN, which affirmed not only a duty to refrain from forcible action depriving peoples of their right to self-determination, but made it clear that in their actions against, and resistance to, such forcible action, peoples are entitled to seek and receive support in accordance with the UN Charter.[121] On the strength of these indisputable instruments one may safely draw the conclusion that organised groups and members thereof enjoy legitimate combatant status under international law, as long as their struggle falls within Article 1(4) of the 1977 Protocol I.[122] The level of violence that international law tolerates by these groups in their armed conflict against government forces is subject to the imperatives of humanitarian law. What this means is that the legality of armed violence employed by a group in its pursuit of self-determination will not be assessed on the basis of the various anti-terrorist conventions. If this conclusion is not sustained then one is effectively denying the right of self-determination altogether.

---

[118] Ibid, 35–39.

[119] Arts 1(2) and 55, UN Charter; Art 1, 1966 International Covenant on Civil and Political Rights, 999 UNTS 171.

[120] 1125 UNTS 3.

[121] GA Res 2625 (24 Oct 1970); similarly GA Res 3103 (12 Dec 1973) affirmed the legitimate character of self-determination struggles and the fact that ensuing armed conflicts are of an international nature that is covered by the protection offered by the 1949 Geneva Conventions.

[122] See C Pilloud *et al*, *Commentary on the Additional Protocols of 8 June 1977 to the Geneva Conventions of 12 August 1949*, (Geneva, Martinus Nijhoff, 1987) 41–56.

With the demise of the major racist, colonial and occupation regimes by the 1980s while the General Assembly Sixth Committee's resolutions on terrorism continued to affirm the legality of revolutionary action for all national liberation movements,[123] in practice the entitlement to violence had been effectively eroded. It had by this time become apparent to Western governments that home-grown ideological groups were keen to use the self-determination card in order to justify their own brand of violence. Because the rules of the game had changed to the detriment of State interests it is no wonder that terrorism was eliminated from the International Law Commission's final version of the Draft Code of Crimes.[124] Although it is not the place of this book to assess whether any particular group is of a terrorist nature, one should not naturally adopt the Statist approach that the infliction of indiscriminate violence by members of a group is sufficient to render it a terrorist organisation. Certainly, the culprits of indiscriminate violence incur criminal liability and their acts should not be tolerated even by subsequent amnesties. Nonetheless, the branding of groups such as the PKK and the PLO as terrorist groups fails to consider their place under Article 1(4) of Protocol I. Such a sweeping characterisation is aimed at negating their inherent right to self-determination. It should be noted that on the insistence of Turkey an Annex was attached to General Assembly Resolution 49/60 (1994) by which terrorism was identified as a factor endangering friendly relations and territorial integrity. This insistence on territorial integrity is an outright denial of Kurdish self-determination and is aptly achieved through the branding of Kurdish rebel groups as terrorists and the de-legitimisation of their armed struggle.[125]

In the case of the Taliban and Al-Qaeda no justification of violence could seriously be predicated on self-determination by the culprits of extremely heinous acts of indiscriminate violence. Yet, notwithstanding the similarities between the two entities they are different. Despite a series of confusing statements in early 2002 the US Government's position differentiated between Taliban and Al-Qaeda members, characterising the latter as unlawful combatants while recognising that the former belonged to the forces of a State that was a party to the Geneva Conventions.[126] Both the Military Order of 13 November 2001 and the US position in general make it clear that the protection and guarantees afforded under the Geneva Conventions are not applicable to Al-Qaeda members. Certainly, the characterisation of Al-Qaeda fighters as unlawful combatants may to a large degree be justified and as a result of the gravity of the situation and the potentiality of further attacks strict security measures are required. However, this does not mean that captured members are not entitled to fair trial guarantees under the Geneva Conventions and Protocol I of 1977, Article 75 of which obliges parties to grant fundamental guarantees to those combatants that

---

[123]   GA Res 36/109 (10 Dec 1981); GA Res 38/130 (19 Dec 1983); GA Res 40/61 (9 Dec 1985); GA Res 42/159 (7 Dec 1987); GA Res 44/29 (4 Dec 1989); GA Res 46/51 (9 Dec 1991); GA Res 49/60 (9 Dec 1994); GA Res 50/53 (11 Dec 1995); GA Res 51/210 (17 Dec 1996); GA Res 52/165 (15 Dec 1997).

[124]   International Law Commission, Report on the Work of Its 48th Session, UN Doc A/51/10, Supp No 10 (6 May–26 Jun 1996).

[125]   Even if the PKK is considered to fall outside the strict ambit of Art 1(4) of the 1977 Protocol I, the sheer scale of military operations between government and rebel forces is unquestionably within the boundaries of common Art 3 to the 1949 Geneva Conventions, as well as customary international law.

[126]   Both are to be tried by military commissions in accordance with the Military Order of 13 November 2001, on Detention, Treatment and Trial of Certain Non-Citizens in the War Against Terrorism, F Reg 57833, vol 66, No 222.

do not benefit from more favourable provisions. Similarly, the use of military commissions against individuals deemed to fall outside the ambit of armed conflict and humanitarian law presents a serious contradiction in criminal procedure terms.[127] That is, if one is classified as falling outside the scope of the laws of war then the alleged offences are common criminal offences, even if extremely serious, and must thus be subject to the jurisdiction of ordinary courts.

The US government attempted to sever the detainees from the reach of the US justice system by detaining them outside US territory and by characterising them as unlawful combatants. In a series of judgments the US Supreme Court held that US courts possess authority to decide the *habeas corpus* claims of unlawful combatants that are US nationals,[128] as well as of non-US nationals held in territory under the authority and control of the USA.[129] As a response to the *Hamdi* judgment the US Department of Defence instituted Combatant Status Review Tribunals (CSRT), which grossly lack the credentials of impartial tribunals mandated by Article 5 of Geneva Convention III (1949) and customary international law relating to due process rights.[130] Indeed, the US Supreme Court in *Hamdan v Rumsfeld* held that military commissions were neither authorised by federal law (including particularly the Uniform Code of Military Justice), nor military necessity, being moreover contrary to the Geneva Conventions.[131] In order for military commissions to conform to the rule of law, the Court continued, they must either operate by the rules of regular court-martial or the government should ask Congress for specific permission to proceed differently. The Supreme Court held that a military commission can be regularly constituted 'only if some practical need explains deviation from courts-martial practice'.[132]

12.6 Organised Crime and its Relation to Terrorism

In recent years concerns have been raised about the links between terrorism and organised crime. Narco-terrorism, unlawful arms trade, money laundering and smuggling of nuclear and other lethal material feature prominently among activities linked to terrorism in the Annex attached to General Assembly Resolution 49/60

---

[127] See generally DA Mundis, 'The Use of Military Commissions to Prosecute Individuals Accused of Terrorist Attacks' (2002) 96 *American Journal of International Law* 320; HH Koh, 'The Case against Military Commissions' (2002) 96 *American Journal of International Law* 337.

[128] *Hamdi v Rumsfeld* (2004) 542 US 507.

[129] *Rasul v Bush* (2004) 542 US 466. In *Gherebi v Rumsfeld*, 352 F 3d 1278 (9th Cir, 2003) the US Court of Appeals for the Ninth Circuit assessed the Treaty with Cuba over Guantanamo Bay holding that the US exercised complete jurisdiction and control over Guantanamo for over a century and as a result the US courts have *habeas corpus* jurisdiction and the detainees recourse to legal remedies accordingly, at 8, 17, 23.

[130] This was followed by the creation of a criminal tribunal to prosecute individuals designated as 'unlawful enemy combatants' under the 2006 Military Commissions Act, 10 USC § 948(a). The rationale for this Act was to cure the common Art 3 deficiencies of the military commissions.

[131] *Hamdan v Rumsfeld*, Judgment (29 Jun 2006), (2006) 548 US 62–68. Rather confusingly the Court relied on common Art 3 of the Geneva Conventions on the premise that Al-Qaeda was not a party to the Geneva Conventions, ignoring the fact that Afghanistan was.

[132] Ibid, *Hamdan* judgment, 69–70.

(1994).[133] In that year the World Ministerial Conference on Organised Transnational Crime adopted the Naples Political Declaration and Global Action Plan against Organised Transnational Crime, which, *inter alia,* recognised the existence of links between transnational organised crime and terrorist conduct.[134] A later General Assembly Resolution pointed out that organisations financing terrorists are usually also engaged in unlawful activities, such as the ones described in Resolution 49/60, for the purpose of funding terrorist operations.[135] These observations are not useful for ascertaining legal principles *per se* since despite the similarity in organisation and violence between terrorist organisations, organised crime terrorism involves a political element which is absent from organised crime, whose primary pursuit is a financial gain. Article 2(a) of the Transnational Organised Crime Convention (CATOC)[136] is instructive:

> Organised criminal group shall mean a structured group of three or more persons, existing for a period of time and acting in concert with the aim of committing one or more serious crimes or offences established in accordance with this convention, in order to obtain, directly or indirectly, a financial or other material benefit.

Some delegations participating in the preparatory working groups of CATOC, including those of Algeria, Egypt and Turkey, were of the view that the scope of the Convention should be widened to specifically include crimes committed in order to obtain, directly or indirectly, a moral benefit. Other delegations, however, were of the view that this concept was ambiguous. During the Eighth session the delegation of Algeria proposed the addition of the words 'or any other purpose', which was supported by Egypt, Morocco and Turkey. In the same Eighth session the Turkish representative stated that his country could not accept the proposed formulation on the ground that it excluded not only crimes committed for purposes other than financial or material benefit but also because it omitted any mention to the links between transnational organised crime and terrorist acts, as these had already been established in the 1994 Naples Political Declaration which Turkey strongly favoured annexing to the draft Convention.[137] Although this position was supported by some delegations at the Ninth session of the ad hoc Committee, including Algeria, Egypt and Mexico, the eventual definition of organised crime contains neither express nor tacit reference to terrorism.[138] This is not only reasonable, it also prevents unnecessary confusion because it would be inconsistent to designate a group involved in drug-trafficking or bribing for financial benefit a terrorist organisation under any of the anti-terrorist conventions. CATOC does not address the likelihood of a 'Robin Hood' scenario, whereby the proceeds of otherwise illicit activities are channelled to a

---

[133] Similarly GA Res 50/186 (22 Dec 1995).

[134] UN Doc A/49/748 (23 Nov 1994).

[135] GA Res 51/210 (17 Dec 1996).

[136] UN Doc A/55/383 (2 Nov 2000).

[137] Ad Hoc Committee on the Elaboration of a Convention against Transnational Organised Crime, Revised Draft United Nations Convention Against Transnational Organised Crime, 10th Session (Vienna, 17–28 Jul 2000), UN Doc A/AC 254/4/Rev 9 (29 Jun 2000) 3.

[138] The Ad Hoc Committee's interpretative notes on Art 3 (scope of application) emphasised 'with deep concern' the growing links between transnational organised crime and terrorist crimes, taking into account the 1945 UN Charter and relevant General Assembly resolutions; UN Doc A/55/383/ Add 1 (3 Nov 2000) 2.

charitable organisation. Under such circumstances one should not dismiss a quintessential ideological motivation of the culprits, which thereafter may be associated with terrorist violence.

Our previous analysis on national liberation movements helps us better comprehend the political benefits associated with the insistence of countries such as Turkey, Algeria and Egypt about the possible connections between terrorism and organised crime. Indeed, the branding of a national liberation movement either as a terrorist group, or as a collectivity involved in organised crime on the basis of its participation in offences aimed at financing its otherwise legitimate struggle, justifies political manoeuvres targeted to removing all legitimacy from the target group. On the one hand it is unarguable that terrorist groups engaged in prohibited conduct animated by a desire for financial benefit do in fact enter the sphere of organised crime. On the other hand prohibited acts attributed to national liberation movements with the aim of financing the movement's otherwise legitimate struggle – given the asymmetry in power and resources in comparison to its foe – do not reasonably de-legitimise the movement. This conclusion can only be sustained where the illicit conduct in question does not violate *jus cogens* and other fundamental human rights norms.

13

The Crime of Aggression

13.1 Introduction

The absence of an acceptable binding definition of crimes against peace since that offence first appeared as Article 6(a) of the Nuremberg Charter,[1] coupled with resistance from the permanent members of the Security Council over its definition and identification by another body, meant that the definition of aggression for the purposes of the ICC Statute had become too cumbersome to negotiate in time for its inclusion in the Statute in August 1998. As a result, although it was agreed that the crime of aggression would nonetheless be incorporated in the body of the ICC Statute, through Article 5(2) thereof, it was not endowed with a definition. Hence, it is inactive and cannot be employed by the Prosecutor to launch investigations and prosecutions. It is therefore an offence 'in waiting'. While Article 5(2) does not set out the subjective and objective elements of this crime it does establish one contextual element; that a future definition must be consistent with the UN Charter provisions relating to aggression and the use of force. Of course, this contextual element does little, if any, to explain the role of the Security Council in determining acts of aggression or of triggering the relevant investigations. Similarly, it says nothing about the precise relationship between aggression as a matter of State responsibility and aggression as an international crime giving rise to personal liability. From the perspective of this chapter, although it is true that any future consensus among ICC State parties – and non-parties – on a binding definition of aggression will be predicated on political considerations, it is equally unchallenged that the incorporation of an offence, even if undefined, in the statute of a global instrument, such as the ICC Statute, is a manifestation of its recognition as a living international crime by, at the very least, the parties to the Statute. It will be recalled that prior to the adoption of the ICC Statute the fate of crimes against humanity were strikingly similar to that of aggression, in that they had not since the Nuremberg Tribunal been defined in a multilateral treaty. There can be no contention, therefore, that the crime of aggression had gradually disappeared from international law simply because it had not been incorporated in a subsequent multilateral treaty following its birth in the aftermath of WW II.[2]

---

[1] The London Charter for the Nuremberg IMT (Nuremberg Charter), 5 UNTS 251.
[2] The House of Lords accepted in *R v Jones* [2007] 1 AC 136, that the core elements of the crime of aggression were uncontested under customary international law, albeit it held that the offence had not been

The following subsections deal with the crime of aggression as this has emerged in the two distinct phases of its development. The first examines its incorporation in the Nuremberg Charter and its subsequent passage in the realm of customary law, whereas the second looks at the current status of the offence in the context of the relevant discussions in the ICC Statute.

13.2   Aggression under Customary Law

A century apart, both Napoleon and Kaiser William II of Germany were arraigned for international offences akin to crimes against peace. In the case of the Kaiser, Article 227 of the 1919 Peace Treaty of Versailles[3] contemplated his arraignment under the charge that he initiated a war in violation of international morality and the sanctity of treaties. Whereas Napoleon was exiled twice the Kaiser fled prosecution by escaping to the Netherlands, which denied his surrender to the Allies. In our analysis of the legality of crimes against peace in the context of the Nuremberg Tribunal it will be explained that no international instrument between 1919 and 1939 provided that individuals are capable of incurring liability for acts of aggression.[4] Thus, the inclusion of crimes against peace in the Nuremberg Charter, and later in the International Military Tribunal for the Far East (IMTFE) Charter was criticised as violating the principle of legality. Article 6(a) of the Nuremberg Charter gave rise to individual criminal responsibility for crimes against peace, constituted of the following elements:

> Planning, preparation, initiation, or waging of a war of aggression, or a war in violation of international treaties, agreements, or assurances, or participation in a common plan or conspiracy for the accomplishment of any of the foregoing.

The Nuremberg Tribunal held that Germany had violated a number of bilateral anti--aggression pacts, as well as other multilateral agreements prohibiting the use of armed force, especially the 1928 Kellogg-Briand Pact.[5] From a legal point of view, of course, neither the bilateral agreements nor the Kellogg-Briand Pact stipulated any individual criminal responsibility, merely State responsibility. To a certain degree the determination as to the validity of crimes against peace flew in the face of the principle of legality, but as will be ascertained in the chapter dealing with the Nuremberg tribunal the illegality of aggression was clearly foreseeable to the accused,

---

incorporated as a crime in English law. In recent years there have been some other attempts to prosecute the crime of aggression, particularly as a result of the use of US military bases in Germany for the launching of the 2003 invasion of Iraq, but all have been unsuccessful. See C Kress, 'The German Chief Federal Prosecutor's Decision not to Investigate the Alleged Crime of Preparing Aggression against Iraq' (2004) 2 *Journal of International Criminal Justice* 245.

[3] 2 Bevans 43.
[4] See chapter 17.2, where I also discuss crimes against peace in the context of the Nuremberg Tribunal. However, for reasons of coherency I have decided to allow for some overlap.
[5] 94 LNTS 57.

as was the case with war crimes. Whether this foreseeability was sufficient to render the waging of an aggressive war an international crime at the time is a wholly different matter.

Be that as it may, Article 6(a) focuses on the objective elements (*actus reus*) of the offence, which it unconvincingly merges with the various modes of participation therein (ie planning, direct perpetration and conspiracy). The actual objective element is the partaking of a war of aggression or a war in violation of international treaties through any of the aforementioned modes. From this slim definition it is nonetheless evident that the offence encompasses only a small circle of culprits; ie those that have the power and capacity to plan, prepare, initiate and wage an aggressive war. If the offence was not confined to an elite number of individuals, but was open to anyone, then every German soldier and civilian who worked during the war may be deemed as having participated in the conspiracy or the execution (waging) of the aggressive war. Such a dilution of the offence, however, would fail to distinguish the clear responsibility of those persons that possessed life or death decision-making powers about going to war. Crimes against peace were clearly viewed as a leadership (political or military) crime.

Despite the glaring absence of a *mens rea* formulation it is rational to assume at the very least that the drafters of Article 6(a) required intent and knowledge on the part of the accused leaders that the war was an aggressive one and that it was not undertaken merely in self-defence. I cannot therefore accept the view that the early definition of the offence encompassed a specific intent (*dolus specialis*) dimension by which the perpetrators sought in addition territorial or financial gains or interference in the internal affairs of the target State.[6] Although in practice acts of aggression are not undertaken without an ulterior motive, they could just as well occur out of revenge or fear of an anticipated attack, neither of which gives rise to a specific intent. In the post-2000 era there are hardly any new annexations and none of the contemporary invasions (such as the 2003 coalition invasion of Iraq) are claimed by their authors as having been undertaken with a view to a regime change. This is a requirement that is not only very difficult to substantiate, but is also unnecessary as it was never expressly required by customary law.

Following the Nuremberg proceedings and despite the inclusion of crimes against peace in the Nuremberg Principles, adopted by the General Assembly in 1946,[7] the crime of aggression has not featured in any legally binding instrument since. The explanation is simple. A crime of aggression gives rise to criminal liability upon the commission of an *act of aggression*. If we are unsure what the fundamental elements of an act of aggression look like we cannot determine the existence of criminal liability in respect of the crime of aggression. This circular argument is, however, misconceived to some degree, principally because it is premised on the notion that the ascertainment of an act of aggression must be judged strictly in accordance with the rules pertinent to the regulation of the use of force. The two regimes (ie criminal

---

[6] S Glaser, 'Culpabilité en Droit International Pénal' (1960-I) 99 *Revue des Cours Academie de Droit International (RCADI)* 504.

[7] GA Res 95(1) (11 Dec 1946).

liability and State liability for aggression) are distinct.[8] If this were not so then the criminality of aggression would depend solely on the definition of armed force under international law, some facets of which are in any event controversial. In brief, Article 2(4) of the UN Charter prohibits all instances of armed force by one State against another (irrespective of gravity), save for two express exceptions. The first concerns force as a means of self-defence, in accordance with Article 51 of the Charter, whereas the second relates to armed force authorised by the Security Council under Article 42 of the Charter. Article 51 permits the use of armed force only where the target State is under an 'armed attack', clearly suggesting that an armed attack amounts to a very significant quantum of armed violence. The precise ambit of legitimate self-defence is obscured by claims that it applies not only to armed attacks that have occurred, but also to those that are imminent, to which I subscribe. Any other suggestions that that 'inherent' nature of self-defence extends to anticipatory force, reprisals and other forms of armed action are incompatible with the foundations of the UN Charter, although certain schools of thought accept them as valid.

Although this regime on the use of force as enshrined in the UN Charter and customary international law was designed with a view to regulating inter-State conduct and determining State responsibility, it cannot be completely discarded when elaborating the various elements of the crime of aggression. What I mean is that in order for the prohibition of force rule as a matter of State responsibility to give rise to criminal liability the contextual elements of the rule must be adapted accordingly and supplemented by an appropriate *actus reus* and *mens rea*. These must in turn be precise enough so as to be foreseeable to accused persons and thus satisfy the principle of legality. As a result, the General Assembly's Resolution on the Definition of Aggression cannot be considered as an instrument that criminalised aggression – even at the soft law level – because its definition was not exhaustive – thus leaving considerable latitude and discretion to the Security Council – and moreover failed to clearly specify that a war of aggression gave rise to criminal responsibility in the manner that is expected of a provision of criminal law.[9] It has correctly been pointed out that the 1974 Definition was intended to serve as a guide for the Security Council in determining acts of aggression and therefore did not precisely elaborate under what particular circumstances an individual would incur personal liability as a result. It did, however, strongly suggest that the criminality of aggression is to be sought at the level of State action.[10] This speaks volumes about the consensus which dictates that the crime of aggression must be linked to action attributed to the State. This approach has survived in the context of the ICC Statute and its ongoing deliberations on the definition of the offence.

---

[8] A Cassese, 'On Some Problematic Aspects of the Crime of Aggression' (2007) 20 *Leiden Journal of International Law* 841, 844–46.

[9] GA Res 3314(XXIX) (14 Dec 1974). Equally, Art 16 of the ILC's Draft Code of Crimes against the Peace and Security of Mankind failed to define an act of aggression. It read: 'An individual, who, as leader or organiser, actively participates in or orders the planning, preparation, initiation or waging of aggression committed by a State, shall be responsible for a crime of aggression'.

[10] C Antonopoulos, 'Whatever Happened to Crimes against Peace?' (2001) 6 *Journal of Conflict & Security Law* 33, at 39.

13.3 Aggression in the ICC Statute

Discussions on the crime of aggression in the context of the ICC Statute did not reveal the kind of uniformity one would otherwise expect of a customary rule. However, this variety of opinion is not necessarily attributable solely to the elements of the crime itself, but also to the potential gatekeeper role of the Security Council, the relevance of the UN Charter and the powers vested in the Prosecutor. As a result, one should view the early negative stance of countries such as the USA and UK with regard to the incorporation of the offence in the ICC Statute through the lens of the multiple layers – both political and legal – underlying the offence in its particular ICC context.[11] The Working Group on the Crime of Aggression has found sufficient agreement among State parties as to some of the constituent points underpinning the offence. Let me start with the possible culprits. I have already explained that following the Nuremberg tradition it is only persons in the highest echelons of political or military power that can wage an act of aggression. While the executioners and implementers of aggressive acts cannot incur liability for the crime of aggression, other modes of participation that are consistent with Article 25 of the ICC Statute are applicable to the offence. This means that co-perpetration, perpetration through another, aiding and abetting, instigation and common plan liability are acceptable modes by which a person may be found liable for the crime of aggression.[12] Exceptionally, an individual, no matter his or her position, cannot incur liability for aggression by reason of the doctrine of command responsibility because this contains elements of negligence and recklessness – which are inapplicable to aggression, being a direct intent crime – and moreover aggression requires active participation, whereas command responsibility is premised on a certain degree of passivity on the part of the superior.[13]

The Working Group seems to have reached significant consensus on the *actus reus* of the offence, that is the *act of aggression*. The problem lay in achieving a definition that would be consistent with the principle of legality. If the determination in each case rested on the authority of the Security Council it is evident that foreseeability would be absent. The Council is certainly unpredictable and its deliberations and resolutions are coloured primarily by politics. This cannot serve therefore as the basis for a sound criminal justice policy. The compromise solution consists of an indicative list of acts, as well as a more general category involving the use of armed force in violation of the UN Charter. It was deemed crucial by the participants to the Working Group that the *actus reus* be qualified further through the introduction of a threshold of *gravity*, other than the general gravity requirement contained in Article 17(1)(d) of the ICC Statute. This cautious approach is justified in order to avoid encompassing every violation involving the use of armed force, save for those that are

---

[11] N Weisbord, 'Prosecuting Aggression' (2008) 49 *Harvard International Law Journal* 161, 170–71.
[12] Report of the Special Working Group on the Crime of Aggression, ICC Doc ICC-ASP/6/20/Add. 1/Annex II (6 Jun 2008) 3. Of course, it will be recalled that Nazi leaders were charged with conspiracy at Nuremberg, but ultimately the conspiracy charged was only applied to aggression and even then it was merged with the mode of planning.
[13] Ibid, 3–4.

of particularly high gravity.[14] It is not evident whether this is a closed or an open list, albeit the truth most probably lies in the latter.

As for the *mens rea*, this clearly requires intent and knowledge. Under customary international law the accused must have not only been privy to such an inner circle that is capable of committing an act of aggression, but he must have known about this plan. Moreover, the accused must be shown to be aware that the act in question is aggressive and not simply a war of a general nature. Thus, evidence of ample knowledge but incapacity to partake in the decision-making echelons of an aggression does not give rise to culpability.[15] Besides one's influential position and knowledge the *mens rea* of the offence also requires that the accused acted with intent in the planning, preparation, initiation and waging of an aggressive war.[16] Exceptionally, the Nuremberg Tribunal concluded that where a person acts in a manner whereby he intends to wage or in any other way participate in an aggressive war even though he or she is unaware of the initial plan [or the conspiracy in the Nuremberg context] it is presumed that this person is acting intentionally and knowingly.[17] Contrary to a certain flow of scholarly opinion I do not subscribe to the notion that the offence requires specific intent (*dolus specialis*). Certainly, one may posit that a degree of specific intent must be demonstrated if an act of aggression is directed against the political independence or sovereignty of a nation, but this phraseology was adopted from the UN Charter and the 1974 Aggression Definition, none of which intended to set out a specific intent in respect of a crime of aggression. It is worth setting out in full this proposed Article 8*bis* to the ICC Statute as constructed by the Working Group:

1.   For the purpose of this Statute, 'crime of aggression' means the planning, preparation, initiation or execution, by a person in a position effectively to exercise control over or to direct the political or military action of a State, of an act of aggression which, by its character, gravity and scale, constitutes a manifest violation of the Charter of the United Nations.

2.   For the purpose of paragraph 1, 'act of aggression' means the use of armed force by a State against the sovereignty, territorial integrity or political independence of another State, or in any other manner inconsistent with the Charter of the United Nations.

Any of the following acts, regardless of a declaration of war, shall, in accordance with United Nations General Assembly resolution 3314 (XXIX) of 14 December 1974, qualify as an act of aggression:

---

[14]   Ibid, p 5.

[15]   In *USA v von Leeb and Others* [*High Command* case], 11 Trials of War Criminals before the Nuremberg Military Tribunals under Control Council Law No 10 [Trials] 462, at 468, the accused were high-ranking field officers arraigned for having partaken in the planning of a war of aggression. The military tribunal dismissed this charge, noting that not only must a person possess actual knowledge that an aggressive war will be launched, but that such person will be in a 'position to shape or influence the policy that brings about its initiation or its continuance after initiation, either by furthering, or by hindering or preventing it'.

[16]   *USA v Krupp and Others*, 9 Trials 1327, where the military tribunal emphasised that the accused, who were industrialists, were not influential enough to have a voice in the formulation of aggressive policies and by all accounts were not even privy to such policies.

[17]   IMT Judgment, The Trial of German Major War Criminals: Proceedings of the International Military Tribunal Sitting at Nuremberg, part XXII, 489–91.

(a) The invasion or attack by the armed forces of a State of the territory of another State, or any military occupation, however temporary, resulting from such invasion or attack, or any annexation by the use of force of the territory of another State or part thereof;

(b) Bombardment by the armed forces of a State against the territory of another State or the use of any weapons by a State against the territory of another State;

(c) The blockade of the ports or coasts of a State by the armed forces of another State;

(d) An attack by the armed forces of a State on the land, sea or air forces, or marine and air fleets of another State;

(e) The use of armed forces of one State which are within the territory of another State with the agreement of the receiving State, in contravention of the conditions provided for in the agreement or any extension of their presence in such territory beyond the termination of the agreement;

(f) The action of a State in allowing its territory, which it has placed at the disposal of another State, to be used by that other State for perpetrating an act of aggression against a third State;

(g) The sending by or on behalf of a State of armed bands, groups, irregulars or mercenaries, which carry out acts of armed force against another State of such gravity as to amount to the acts listed above, or its substantial involvement therein.

While it is clear that the crime of aggression is a leadership offence that is certainly applicable to persons within a State apparatus, it is not clear from customary law or the ICC deliberations whether non-State actors can commit aggressive acts. If at all, this may only be read in subparagraphs 2(f) and (g) of Article 8*bis*, which foresee the possibility that a State's territory may be willingly used by private actors or that such actors may be employed by States to carry out aggressive acts on their behalf. Nonetheless, this suggests that private actors cannot commit a crime of aggression directly, but only by reason of agency.[18] This makes sense from a fair labelling and criminalisation point of view since otherwise every significant act of terrorism may be classified as a crime of aggression, which was clearly reserved for a very particular class of perpetrators. It would degrade the liability of State and military chiefs if terrorists could also be charged with the crime of aggression, in addition to crimes against humanity – which we have already determined is applicable thereto.[19]

What remains to be seen is the role of the Security Council in the determination of an act of aggression. The discussions on this issue evince considerable strands of disagreement, although parties to the ASP were keen not to exclude the Council and thus alienate the Court's closest, yet unpredictable, ally. Some delegates are of the view that Article 39 of the UN Charter which grants the Council authority to

---

[18] For a contrary point of view, see Cassese, On Some Problematic Aspects, at 846.

[19] In fact, the 2008 Report of the Working Group on Aggression, at 14, has resolved to add the following paragraph in Art 25 of the Statute: 'In respect of the crime of aggression, the provisions of this article shall apply only to persons in a position effectively to exercise control over or to direct the political or military action of a State'. This should dispel any notions that in the ICC Statute, at least, aggression may be committed by private actors.

determine an act of aggression is exclusive, but this contention is not shared widely.[20] Although I take the position that the Council is not vested with exclusive authority to determine acts of aggression – particularly as the Charter was not geared towards the ascertainment of individual guilt, given that this pertains to a judicial function – one cannot, however, underestimate the potential for unnecessary fragmentation and its consequences for international relations. By reason of consistency and coherency the two systems must meet somewhere. From a political perspective it is evident that the Council cannot and will not succumb to the *proprio motu* powers of the Prosecutor in respect of aggressive acts. The range of alternative options in the Report of the ICC Working Group on Aggression, adopted as Article 15*bis* of the Statute, is indicative of the plethora of views and disagreements between delegates. There is some agreement that a Council determination is required before the Prosecutor can proceed with an investigation. However, this is not a *sine qua non* condition for an investigation since it is very likely that a politically divided Council may be unable to make a formal deliberation through the adoption of a resolution.[21] Under such circumstances a number of alternative options have been suggested; either the Prosecutor cannot commence the desired investigation, or where no such determination has been made by the Council within six months after the Prosecutor's date of notification the investigation may nonetheless proceed. In the absence of a Council resolution, the authority of the Prosecutor to proceed with the investigation may be sought from the UN General Assembly or the International Court of Justice.[22] This is logical as otherwise even though aggression may be defined it may never be employed in clear-cut cases because of Council intransigence. Whatever the final outcome to these discussions, it is now clear that the States parties to the ICC have resolved in their majority in favour of a dominant role for the Council. This role should not be confused with the authority to adjudicate criminal liability, which lies with the Court. Thus, even if in a particular case the Council conclusively determines the existence of an act of aggression the Court may validly acquit the accused of all aggression charges. The impartial and independent nature of the Court does not allow it to ratify the Council's referrals by convicting the accused in each case brought to it.

What is also significant is that a future agreement on the definition of aggression in the ICC Statute will pave the way for national legislators to either introduce or apply existing laws on aggression without the apprehension inherent in innovation. Equally, jurisdictions in which the judiciary is active will be prompted to assume bolder action and as a result take the crime of aggression out of its hibernation.

---

[20]   M Stein, 'The Security Council, the ICC and the Crime of Aggression: How Exclusive is the Security Council's Power to Determine Aggression?' (2005) 16 *Indiana International & Comparative Law Review* 1, 12–25.
[21]   It suffices to mention that while the Council has in the past made two determinations of aggressive acts (eg SC Res 573 (4 Oct 1985) and SC Res 577 (6 Dec 1985) it has failed to condemn others of a similar or higher gravity under the same terminology.
[22]   2008 Working Group on Aggression Report, 13–14.

14

International Criminal Law of the Sea

14.1 Brief Introduction to the Law of the Sea

Before we set out to explore maritime crime it is useful to recall the sources of the body of law known as the law of the sea, namely customary law and treaty law. Most of the former has been codified in the 1982 United Nations Convention on the Law of the Sea (UNCLOS), as well as its precursor, the three 1958 Geneva Conventions.[1] The regulation of maritime masses is not, however, restricted to these instruments. Other agreements, of a bilateral or multilateral nature, address issues such as ship-source pollution, marine conservation, enforcement action for the purposes of deterring crime and others. Moreover, it is doubtful that every aspect of the law of the sea has been codified by UNCLOS and therefore the importance of customary law and subsequent practice remains paramount. States have certain rights and duties with regard to the seas, depending on the maritime belt under consideration. The reader not familiar with this field of international law should be foretold that while UNCLOS clearly sets out the various maritime belts, some of these may well overlap with others or not be claimed by all coastal States – for example, not every coastal State claims a contiguous zone or a 200 mile EEZ.

The measurement of maritime belts seawards commences from what are known as baselines. UNCLOS provides for two types of baselines, normal and straight.[2] Where a coastline is not heavily indented, the officially recognised low water mark point represents the normal baseline and thus the starting point for measuring the breadth of the various maritime belts. In the case of indented coastlines, the method of drawing straight lines between points on the coast or at sea may be used. The territorial sea may extend *up to* 12 nautical miles seaward from the baselines,[3] whereas all waters landward from the baselines are considered internal waters.[4] States retain sovereignty in both internal waters and the territorial sea but there is an obligation to grant a right of 'innocent passage' in the latter, provided that such passage is not detrimental to the security of the coastal State.[5] UNCLOS also introduced a regime for archipelagic States, that is, States made up of a group of relatively closely spaced islands, such as Indonesia. For those States, the territorial sea is a 12 mile zone

---

[1] Convention on the Territorial Sea and Contiguous Zone, 516 UNTS 205; Convention on the High Seas, 450 UNTS 11; Convention on the Continental Shelf, 499 UNTS 311.

[2] Arts 5 and 7 UNCLOS.

[3] Art 3 UNCLOS.

[4] Art 8 UNCLOS. This may include rivers, river mouths, lagoons and others.

[5] Arts 17–19 UNCLOS.

extending from a line drawn joining the outermost points of the outermost islands of the group that are in close proximity to each other.[6] The waters between the islands are declared archipelagic waters, where ships of all States enjoy the right of innocent passage.[7] As regards international straits, the regime of 'transit passage' retains the international status of the straits and gives naval powers the right to unimpeded navigation and over-flight.[8] In all matters other than transient navigation, straits are considered territorial waters. Coastal States are also empowered, if they so wish, to implement certain rights in an area beyond the territorial sea, extending 24 nautical miles from their baselines for the purpose of preventing certain violations and enforcing police powers. This area, known as the contiguous zone, may be used to curtail offenders violating the laws of the coastal State within its territory or its territorial sea.[9] The exclusive economic zone (EEZ) extends *up to* 200 nautical miles from the baselines. The coastal State retains sovereign rights but not sovereignty in the EEZ,[10] and is moreover incumbent with several duties under international law, such as conservation. The continental shelf comprises the seabed and its subsoil that extend beyond the limits of the territorial sea throughout the natural prolongation of the coastal State's land territory to the outer edge of the continental margin, or to a distance of 200 miles from the baselines, where the outer edge of the continental margin does not extend up to that distance. In cases where the continental margin extends further than 200 miles, States may claim a continental shelf up to 350 miles from the baseline or 100 miles from the 2,500 metre depth isobath.[11] The coastal State possesses exclusive rights of exploration and exploitation of the continental shelf's natural resources. The rights of the coastal State over the continental shelf do not affect the legal status of the superjacent waters or of the air space above those waters.[12] Finally, the high seas are open to all States and for a number of purposes, such as navigation, over-flight, laying of submarine cables and fishing, subject to certain restrictions.[13] The international seabed, too, is not subject to the sovereignty of any State and is part of the 'common heritage of mankind', requiring special permission for its exploitation.

In this chapter we examine both substantive and procedural maritime criminal law. The first encompasses the crimes of piracy *jure gentium*, armed robbery at sea, mutiny-type offences, maritime terrorism, unlawful damage to submarine cables, unauthorised broadcasting, illicit fishing and ship-source pollution. The procedural part involves an examination of the general and special rules on enforcement against non-flag States on the high seas, as well as an analysis of the right of hot pursuit. Maritime crime is also explored in other chapters, especially those dealing with the territorial limits of jurisdiction, the transport of slaves, the smuggling of migrants on the high seas by organised criminal groups and the chapter dealing with the status of victims in international criminal law generally and criminal proceedings specifically.

---

[6] Arts 46–47 UNCLOS.
[7] Art 52 UNCLOS.
[8] Art 34 UNCLOS.
[9] Art 33 UNCLOS.
[10] Arts 55–57 UNCLOS.
[11] Arts 76–77 UNCLOS.
[12] Art 78 UNCLOS.
[13] Art 87 UNCLOS.

14.2 Piracy *Jure Gentium*

That piratical attacks have soared in the last decade, particularly since 2004, is now common knowledge. This has even led the UN Security Council to determine that piracy in some parts of the globe constitutes a scourge that is tantamount to a threat to international peace and security.[14] Prior to the piratical attacks by Somali pirates in the Gulf of Aden, the areas most affected included the Far East, in particular the South China Sea and the Malacca Strait;[15] South America and the Caribbean, and; the Indian Ocean. By comparison to the frequence of incidents off the coast of Somalia, these other hot spots now seem rather insignificant, with the exception of the seas of China. The increase in this international crime may be explained on several grounds, such as the need for small crews on large technologically advanced vessels, which renders them vulnerable, lack of adequate diplomatic representation where vessels fly flags of convenience and the existence of poor countries with large coastlines that are unable to afford adequate patrol of their territorial waters, let alone the adjacent high seas. In the case of Somali pirates the situation is structurally and substantially different, because the aim of the perpetrators is not to conceal the identity of the seized vessel, but rather to receive a ransom from the ship owner.

Contemporary pirates, other than the Somali-type, can be classified into two categories. First, there are those who operate on a small scale, interested either in the possessions of the crew (the captain usually keeps a good amount of money for payroll, maintenance and port fees), or various equipment on board the vessel. The majority of such pirates operate when ships are anchored in, or pass through, territorial waters. The second category involves well-organised groups whose operations go far beyond random attacks at sea. Organised piracy aims either at the cargo of merchant vessels or the vessel itself. When ships are stolen in this manner they are repainted, renamed and re-registered. Temporary registration certificates may be obtained through consulate offices, whether by bribery or presentation of false documents, or both. The pirates will then look for a shipping agent with a letter of credit that has almost expired and will offer the services of their ship, upon which the ship is loaded and the shipper receives the bill of lading. The pirates then sail to a different destination than the one specified on the bill of lading. There they may unload the cargo to an accomplice, or an unsuspecting buyer and change the temporary registration certificate again. This is tantamount to laundering. Low freight rates and financial recession has created an upsurge in organised piracy in South East Asia, not only in the form of attacks against merchant vessels, but also in defrauding insurance companies through acts of piracy against ships owned by criminal groups such as the Chinese Triads. Contemporary organised piracy is also believed to be heavily involved in the illicit traffic of narcotic drugs and arms, while

---

[14] SC Res 1816 (2 Jun 2008).
[15] T Arbuckle, 'Scourge of Piracy Returns to Southeast Asia' (1996) 29 *Jane's International Defence Review* 26.

reports indicate that corruption in a number of countries is responsible for both the lack of prosecutions and enforcement, as well as for facilitating the disposal of stolen vessels and cargo.[16]

14.2.1 Definition of Piracy under International Law and its Difference from Armed Robbery at Sea

Piracy under international law, otherwise known as piracy *jure gentium*, is the oldest international offence. Until the 1536 Statute of Henry VIII,[17] piracy was punished in England only when committed within the realm of the Admiralty of the Crown and then merely as a civil offence. The 1536 Statute changed the jurisdictional element of piracy but not the nature of the offence as robbery at sea. It was well recognised by the seventeenth century that the common law definition was in no essential respect different from that of the law of nations.[18] A major feature in the customary definition of piracy *jure gentium* was the distinction between acts undertaken for a public or private purpose (for 'private ends'). Piracy was punishable only when undertaken for a private purpose. This classification arose from the need to distinguish between privateering, which was lawful, from other acts against belligerents that had not however received governmental authorisation. Although privateering was formally abolished by a Paris Declaration of 1856 and effectively by the application of international humanitarian law later on, a private actor that received a letter of marque was permitted to attack and seize enemy ships on the high seas and was thereafter entitled to a portion of the prize.[19] Anyone who was found not to have acted under authority of a letter of marque or in violation of the terms of such a letter was deemed to have acted for private ends.

Although jurisdiction for piracy *jure gentium* under customary law was acknowledged as belonging to all States,[20] no authoritative definition existed as to its substantial elements.[21] Hence, until the adoption of an international definition in the 1958 Geneva Convention on the High Seas,[22] national statutes, the majority of which purported to incorporate therein the concept of piracy under customary international law,[23] were interpreted in accordance with each domestic judiciary's understanding of the prevailing elements of piracy. This has not always produced uniform and consistent results.

---

[16] J Hitt, 'Bandits in the Global Shipping Lines' (20 Aug 2000) *New York Times Magazine*, where the author furnishes information implicating Chinese authorities in the release of captured pirates.

[17] Offences at Sea Act 1536, ch 15.

[18] *USA v Smith* (1820) 18 US 153, at 159, *per* Story J.

[19] E Kontorovich, 'The Piracy Analogy: Modern Universal Jurisdiction's Hollow Foundation' (2004) 45 *Harvard International Law Journal* 183, 210–14.

[20] *Talbot v Jansen* (1795) 3 US 153; *Lotus* case (Turkey v France) (1927) Permanent Court of International Justice (PCIJ) Reports, Ser A, No 10, at 10, *per* Moore J.

[21] M Halberstam, 'Terrorism on the High Seas: The *Achille Lauro*, Piracy and the IMO Convention on Maritime Safety' (1988) 82 *American Journal of International* Law 269, at 272.

[22] 450 UNTS 82, Arts 13–22.

[23] This is true for the vast majority of contemporary statutes, if not all. See the US Piracy and Privateering Act 1948, 18 USC, § 1651.

The earliest element in the definition of piracy was that of *animus furandi*, ie the intention to rob a vessel on the high seas – or, as in the case at hand, in any waters within the jurisdiction of UK admiralty.[24] It was later held, in other plagued jurisdictions, that robbery or an intention thereof was not an essential element and that acts of revenge, hatred, or abuse of power against another ship were tantamount to piracy. In the *Malek Adhel* case, the rather mentally disturbed captain of a commercial ship made it a habit of aggressively forcing other merchant vessels on the high seas to halt their course, without however robbing or looting them, except only to claim the gunpowder used to force them to stop![25] The US Supreme Court stressed that a piratical act is an act of aggression unauthorised by the law of nations, being hostile and criminal in character and without sanction from public or sovereign authority. This was so irrespective of whether the aim of the perpetrator was plunder, hatred, revenge, or wanton abuse of power.[26] This signalled a clear move towards an *actus reus* of piracy that involved *any* criminal offence against another vessel.

Since the time of Grotius a pirate has been considered to be *hostis humanis generis*, an enemy of mankind. This is not a rhetorical statement, but rather carries legal substance; for, if a person commits otherwise unlawful acts against persons and property of one country on the high seas that person cannot readily be characterised as an enemy of mankind, only of that specific country and may only be apprehended by the authorities of the Flag State. Such a state of affairs was clearly found unacceptable four-hundred years ago by the community of nations. The internationalisation of piracy on the high seas was encountered when national courts determined cases involving interference with maritime commerce not for private ends but as part of political or ideological struggles. The law in the nineteenth century, as it also stands today, was that insurgents fighting for a political cause should not be treated as pirates as long as in their struggle against the target government they attack only vessels and persons of that State,[27] and they remain within the permitted limits of the law of warfare. This did not mean, of course, that the mere existence of political motives justified under any circumstances all acts of insurgency. It was clear that common crimes, regardless of their motive, would result in the liability of the perpetrator.[28] Although now obsolete with the advancement of international humanitarian law, especially common Article 3 of the 1949 Geneva Conventions, the recognition of insurgency or belligerency status was of seminal importance both for the relations between belligerents, but also for the law of neutrality. Insurgency referred to a state of conflict where the dissident group, even though of considerable strength, did not receive international recognition as a legal entity under international law. Belligerency, on the other hand, existed when an armed conflict was recognised as taking place between two legal entities.[29] Having established a set of criteria for its

---

[24] *Rex v Dawson* (1696) 13 St Tr 451.

[25] *USA v Cargo of the Brig Malek Adhel* (1844) 43 US 210.

[26] Ibid, at 230; in *Re Piracy Jure Gentium* [1934] AC 856, the Privy Council held that actual robbery was not an essential element, as a frustrated attempt to commit piratical robbery is equally piracy *jure gentium*.

[27] *Dole v New England Mutual Marine Insurance Co* (1864) 7 F Cas 838, at 847; *Republic of Bolivia v Indemnity Mutual Marine Assurance Co Ltd* [1909] 1 KB 785, at 795.

[28] *Magellan Pirates* (1853) 1 A&E 81.

[29] A Arend and R Beck, *International Law and the Use of Force*, (London, Routledge, 1993), 81–82.

recognition,[30] it was accepted by the end of the nineteenth century that belligerency was viewed as a question of fact rather than as one of law.[31] The relevant jurisprudence seems to suggest that the absence of belligerency did not render politically motivated acts by rebel groups piratical. In the *Ambrose Light*, the New York District Court held that unrecognised insurgents (that is, belligerents) were deemed to be pirates, even though in that case there was no proof of violence or depredation beyond that required for the group's political aims against the Venezuelan Government.[32] This judgment was vociferously rejected by the US executive and overturned by its judiciary shortly after it was issued, as having no standing in international law.[33] The Harvard Draft Convention on Piracy, which was relied upon heavily by the International Law Commission's (ILC) rapporteur for the 1958 Convention on the High Seas, found that under customary law an attack by an unrecognised group is not piratical if, had the group received recognition, the contested act would not have been one of piracy.[34]

The elements already described constitute the offence of piracy *jure gentium* under customary law and as such they were incorporated in the relevant definition in Articles 14 and 101 of the 1958 Geneva Convention on the High Seas and UNCLOS respectively. The latter provides that:

Piracy consists of any of the following acts:

(a) any illegal acts of violence or detention, or any act of depredation, committed for private ends by the crew or the passengers of a private ship or a private aircraft, and directed:

  (i) on the high seas, against another ship or aircraft, or against persons or property on board such ship or aircraft;
  (ii) against a ship, aircraft, persons or property in a place outside the jurisdiction of any State;

(b) any act of voluntary participation in the operation of a ship or of an aircraft with knowledge of facts making it a pirate ship or aircraft;[35]

(c) any act of inciting or of intentionally facilitating an act described in paragraphs (a) or (b).

---

[30] These consisted of a generalised armed conflict, effective occupation and administration of a substantial portion of the territory under consideration, the existence of organised armed forces under a responsible leader and circumstances justifying recognition. H Lauterpacht, *Recognition in International Law*, (Cambridge, Cambridge University Press, 1948) 176.

[31] L Moir, 'The Historical Development of the Application of Humanitarian Law in Non International Armed Conflicts to 1949' (1998) 47 *International & Comparative Law Quarterly* 347.

[32] *Ambrose Light, The* (1885) 25 Fed 408.

[33] See LC Green, 'The Santa Maria: Rebels or Pirates?' (1961) 37 *British Yearbook of International Law* 496, at 502; *Castle John and Nederlandse Stichting Sirius v Nv Marjlo and Nv Parfin* (1986) 77 ILR 537 and commentary in SP Menefee, 'The Case of the Castle John, or Green beard the Pirate?' (1993) 24 *California Western International Law Journal* 1; C Hyde, *International Law Chiefly as Interpreted and Applied by the United States* (Boston, Little Brown, 1945) 774.

[34] Harvard Research in International Law, Commentary to the Draft Convention on Piracy, (1932 Supp) 26 *American Journal of International Law* 749, at 857; see (1955) 1 *Yearbook of the International Law Commission* 41.

[35] *Talbot v Jansen* (1795) 3 US 153, at 156, *per* Paterson J.

This definition is in line with customary law as explained above. The *actus reus* of the offence is not dependent on factors such as gravity or an intention to act openly. Hence, in *Athens Maritime Enterprises Corp v Hellenic Mutual War Risks Association Ltd*, the court erred when it held that a clandestine attempt to rob a ship anchored three miles from the coast of Bangladesh did not constitute piracy simply because the culprits intended to steal without recourse to violence.[36] It is also clear that the offence requires two vessels or aircraft: the piratical and the victim vessel or aircraft. It is thus evident that piracy under international law cannot be born through an act of mutiny, unless the mutineers subsequently engage in acts of violence or depredation against other vessels or aircraft on the high seas. Likewise, the perpetration of piratical acts, as defined in Article 101 of UNCLOS, by a warship, government ship or government aircraft whose crew has mutinied and taken control of the ship or aircraft are assimilated to acts committed by a private ship or aircraft.[37]

Unlike the position accepted in the seventeenth to the nineteenth centuries, the contemporary interpretation of the 'private ends' proviso logically suggests that illegal violence, detention or depredation against another vessel or its passengers on the high seas, even for political ends of any kind, entails the criminal liability of the perpetrators if they violate any of the universal anti-terrorist conventions. However, a common act of violence on the high seas for political ends cannot be readily characterised as piratical, because it lacks the required private aim; it may, nonetheless, fall within the ambit of a specialised terrorist offence, as these treaties contain clauses specifically renouncing the political character of the crimes contained therein. The seizure of a vessel may also be deemed piratical where the perpetrators' conduct does not justify their claim to be acting under an otherwise legitimate political motive (eg by raping or unnecessarily killing passengers from the seized vessel).

The jurisdictional element of piracy *jure gentium* (ie that the *actus reus* be perpetrated on the high seas) is of paramount importance. It should be stressed that UNCLOS only addresses the repression of acts of piracy taking place on the high seas and, owing to the reference in Article 58(2) of UNCLOS, also those acts which are perpetrated in the EEZ. Therefore, any act of a similar nature landward from the beginning of the EEZ (essentially the contiguous zone and the territorial sea) would not constitute piracy under international law. What this means in practice is that any act otherwise amounting to piracy but perpetrated in a country's territorial sea is not an international crime and moreover does not attract universal jurisdiction. As a result, enforcement in the territorial sea of a State by third nations is prohibited. This represents a major obstacle in respect of those pirates that operate either in territorial waters or on the high seas (or in international maritime shipping lanes adjacent to the territorial sea) but with access to a coastal State that fits the criteria of weak or failed State. This is in fact a true reflection of the situation with pirates operating off the coast of Somalia. The IMO has traditionally distinguished between piracy on the high seas from similar acts perpetrated in territorial seas and contiguous zones and has termed the latter 'armed robbery against ships'. This offence is defined as:

---

[36] *Athens Maritime Enterprises Corp v Hellenic Mutual War Risks Association Ltd* [1983] 1 All ER 590. The court would have been right, however, had it stated that the incident did not constitute piracy *jure gentium* because it occurred in territorial waters.

[37] UNCLOS, Art 102.

any unlawful act of violence or detention or any act of depredation, or threat thereof, other than an act of piracy, committed for private ends and directed against a ship or against persons or property on board such a ship, within a State's internal waters, archipelagic waters and territorial sea.[38]

It is exactly because of this lack of enforcement jurisdiction in these maritime belts that a Security Council authorisation was required in order for multinational forces to chase Somali pirates into that country's territorial waters. The alarming rate of seizure of commercial vessels following their passage from the Suez Canal rendered piracy one of the most significant problems on the Council's agenda. The adoption of resolution 1816, following a request for assistance from the Somali Transitional Federal Government (TFG), urged States that are active in the region to cooperate and increase their efforts to deter both piracy and armed robbery. More significantly, the Council authorised all interested States to enter the territorial waters of Somalia and *use all necessary means* in order to repress these offences in a manner consistent with action permitted on the high seas with respect to piracy under international law.[39] A subsequent resolution, 1851, extended this authorisation and called all States to 'undertake all necessary means that are appropriate in Somalia', which is construed as permitting even the land pursuit of the pirates.[40] All relevant resolutions have strongly emphasised that the granting of authority to enter Somalia's territorial sea – let alone its land territory – is exceptional and that it should not be considered as reflecting a rule of customary international law.[41] This is a clear example of exceptionalism in international law, the aim of which is to achieve a particular goal without, however, extending the particular entitlement to all nations in the future.

14.2.2 Mutiny and other Violence against Ships not amounting to Piracy

As is evident from the definition of Article 101 of UNCLOS and, indeed, customary law, illegal acts of violence, detention or depredation originating from within a vessel, or other acts of interference with maritime commerce not involving an attacking ship, do not constitute piracy *jure gentium*.[42] The same is true with regard to acts of mutiny.[43] Such incidents, although of considerable concern to contemporary maritime commerce, have not traditionally attracted the attention of international institutions because they were perceived as existing on a small local scale, which did not pose too serious a threat to global maritime safety. This perception radically altered in October 1985 when the Italian cruise ship *Achille Lauro* was seized by members of

---

[38] IMO, Report on Piracy and Armed Robbery against Ships, IMO Doc MSC.1/Circ.1333 (26 Jun 2009) 1. This definition is consistent with the 2005 Regional Cooperation Agreement on Combating Piracy and Armed Robbery against Ships in Asia (ReCAAP).

[39] SC Res 1816 (2 Jun 2008), operative paras 7–8.

[40] SC 1851 (16 Dec 2008), para 6.

[41] D Guilfoyle, 'Piracy off Somalia: UN Security Council Resolution 1816 and IMO Regional Counter-Piracy Efforts' (2008) 57 *International & Comparative Law Quarterly* 690.

[42] See *USA v Palmer* (1818) 16 US 610, at 635.

[43] *The Creole* (1841); JB Moore, *Moore's Digest of International Law* (Washington DC, Government Printing Office, 1906), vol 2, at 352, 358.

a Palestinian militant organisation while the ship was en route from Alexandria to Port Said. The hijackers boarded the cruiser in Genoa and threatened to blow it up and kill the passengers unless the Government of Israel released fifty Palestinian prisoners. When their demands were not met they killed a disabled Jewish-American passenger and threw his body overboard.[44] Despite the branding of the whole incident as piratical by the then US President,[45] this was a case of vessel hijacking or 'boatjacking' that was not clearly regulated by international law. The offences committed could well have been punished on the basis of domestic statutes prohibiting interference with maritime safety or that of committing a homicide or other offences against the person, but terrorist acts on board private vessels did not constitute an international or transnational offence at the time.

In response to the *Achille Lauro* incident the IMO adopted in March 1988 a Convention on the Suppression of Unlawful Acts Against the Safety of Maritime Navigation (SUA Convention),[46] which covered offences against maritime safety not falling under the enforcement regimes of UNCLOS. Individuals are liable under the Convention if they unlawfully seize or exercise control over a ship or endanger its safe navigation by either violence against persons on board, destruction or damage to a ship or its cargo, destruction of its navigational facilities or interference with their operation, placing of a device likely to destroy a ship, or by communicating false information to a ship.[47] This wide-ranging international offence in fact resembles a combination of the 1970 Hague Convention for the Suppression of Unlawful Seizure of Aircraft[48] and the 1971 Montreal Convention for the Suppression of Unlawful Acts Against the Safety of Civil Aviation,[49] applicable to merchant vessels on the high seas. Article 11 of the SUA obliges member States to render the contemplated offences extraditable, thus removing any doubt that politically motivated acts of seizure and violence could be justified. Unfortunately, the SUA has not received wide ratification, despite calls to that effect from the IMO and the General Assembly,[50] albeit it was recently given some prominence through the relevant Security Council resolutions that called on States to engage with piratical vessels off the coast of Somalia.

14.2.3 Mechanisms for the Prevention and Eradication of Piracy

It cannot be overemphasised that piracy can only be combated by inter-State cooperation. Parties to UNCLOS, in particular, are under an express obligation to

---

[44] See Halberstam, 269–70.

[45] (1985) 24 ILM 1515.

[46] (1988) 27 ILM 668; see also Protocol for the Suppression of Unlawful Acts Against the Safety of Fixed Platforms Located on the Continental Shelf (SUA Protocol), (1988) 27 ILM 685.

[47] 1988 Convention on the Suppression of Unlawful Acts Against the Safety of Maritime Navigation, Art 3(1).

[48] 860 UNTS 105.

[49] 974 UNTS 177.

[50] See GA Res 53/32 (24 Nov 1998) and 54/31 (18 Jan 2000).

this effect.[51] On the high seas any State may assert a right of visit upon vessels suspected to be engaged in piracy[52] and where these suspicions prove well-founded to seize the pirate ship and prosecute its crew.[53] Both seizure and visit can be enforced solely by warships, or other governmental vessels that are authorised to act in this manner.[54] This is meant to dispel any fears of re-introducing the concept of privateering. In the case of piracy off the coast of Somalia the Security Council was aware of all relevant unilateral and multilateral efforts already under way by the European Union (operation Atalanta), NATO and the USA (eg the US-led Combined Task Force 151) and it was as a result of these that it was convinced of the necessity to extend their enforcement powers into Somalia's territorial sea. It is obvious that under the exigencies of the Somali paradigm the right to visit as a result of reasonable suspicions will almost certainly follow armed confrontation with the pirates. It is for this reason that relevant Council resolutions require that such use of armed force be consistent with general international law; this naturally refers to proportionality and compliance with IHL in the sense that an act of surrender must always be respected, or that no unnecessary suffering be imposed, among others, irrespective of the character of the incidents or the legal status of the pirates.

The application in practice of the principle of universal jurisdiction in the situation in Somalia has demonstrated its inherent problems. Many States involved in the multilateral operations were weary of sending the culprits to their national courts to face criminal proceedings out of fear that their laws may turn out to be inadequate or that their jurisdiction may be challenged, or that the accused may be inclined to invoke a number of defences (ie refugee status, political act defence, unlawful force, etc). On top of these considerations it becomes evident that the transfer of pirates for prosecution in Europe or America entails a significant amount of expenses.[55] The Security Council identified this reluctance following a number of successful seizures of pirates in which the culprits were subsequently released without any further action taken against them![56] In order to counter some of these concerns the patrolling States in the Gulf of Aden entered into agreements with the coastal States in the region with the purpose that the accused either stand trial there or that alternatively they can be transferred through their territory to that of the capturing State.[57] The surrender of the accused to a third State is inconsistent with the capturing State's obligation under Article 105 UNCLOS which clearly provides that prosecution must be carried out by 'the courts of the State which carried out the seizure'.

---

[51] UNCLOS, Art 100.

[52] Ibid, Art 110.

[53] Ibid, Art 105.

[54] Ibid, Art 107.

[55] Not least, the transfer of the culprit to the territory of the apprehending State, without the warship departing from the Gulf of Aden; the release of its own crew for the purposes of offering testimony before the court, and; all the expenses related to the prosecution and detention of the accused.

[56] SC Res 1851, preamble.

[57] See the so-called Djibouti Code of Conduct on Maritime Security, Piracy and Armed Robbery against Ships in the Western Indian Ocean and the Gulf of Aden, adopted as an Annex to IMO Resolution 1 (29 Jan 2009). Although this is not a binding instrument it involves a serious undertaking by these regional States to confront and prosecute pirates and to set up avenues for information sharing and cooperation.

Legal considerations aside, the sheer scale of the areas covered by seas render patrolling a difficult exercise, even in the modern satellite surveillance era. Unless a merchant vessel is escorted by a warship the ship owner cannot be certain that it will not come under piratical attack. Ship owners are therefore tempted to install arms or private military contingents on board vessels sailing through dangerous waters. The IMO has consistently warned against any defensive action by means of firearms under the rationale that this will only lead to further escalation of violence.[58] The incentive to install private security marksmen is further augmented by the decrease in insurance premiums.[59] The only problem with this measure is that, save for purposes of self-defence, the private vessel possesses no authority to make an arrest or seizure and of course it cannot deny even a pirate of his or her rights under international human rights law. In such cases it would be absurd to argue that the private vessel is not authorised to apprehend pirates when under an attack because this only provides an incentive to either kill or release the pirates at sea. As a result, the capturing vessel should be deemed as possessing the authority to surrender them not only to a warship of its own nationality, but also to a third State, without its crew or owner suffering civil or criminal liability.

14.3   Maritime Terrorism

Since the terrorist events of 11 September 2001 the USA had made it a priority to combat those terrorist operations on the high seas that were aimed at land-based targets, whether on US territory or elsewhere. At the time no international agreement existed on maritime terrorism and the provisions of the 1988 SUA were far too restrictive to serve this purpose. As a result, the US government embarked on a twofold objective: (a) to conclude bilateral ship-boarding agreements and; (b) to revise the terms of the SUA with a view to its encompassing terrorist operations. These bilateral agreements were modelled on existing bilateral treaties, particularly those encountered in the field of drug-trafficking and smuggling and generally provide for the automatic consent of the Flag State to a request from its other counterpart to board and search a vessel of concern flying its flag on the high seas. A presumption is often inserted in such bilateral agreements to the effect that if the requested State does not respond within a given time (typically anywhere between two to four hours), then consent is deemed to have been provided. Since 2001 the USA has concluded bilateral agreements of this type with the major convenience Flag States, such as Panama, Cyprus, Liberia, Marshall Islands and Belize, to name a few.

The other major development has been the expansion of the SUA through two distinct Protocols adopted in 2005; the Protocol for the Suppression of Unlawful

---

[58]   2009 IMO Report, 2–3.

[59]   The nature of most insurance contracts constitutes a significant factor in the under-reporting of piratical attacks, since they generally tend to exclude all instances of theft that do not involve actual force or threat of force, thus providing little incentive to ship owners to report incidents that do not entail substantial losses. See DR Thomas, 'Insuring the Risk of Maritime Piracy' (2004) 10 *Journal of International Maritime Law* 358, at 364.

Acts against the Safety of Maritime Navigation (Protocol I) and the Protocol for the Suppression of Unlawful Acts against the Safety of Fixed Platforms located on the Continental Shelf (Fixed Platforms Protocol). Although the title of Protocol I makes no claim to a terrorist connection, the body of the Protocol and Article 7 thereof – which refers to all existing relevant anti-terrorist treaties – makes it abundantly clear that the Protocol focuses on both terrorist and nuclear threats. Article 4(5) of Protocol I establishes a new Article 3*bis* offence to the SUA, as follows:

1. Any person commits an offence within the meaning of this Convention if that person unlawfully and intentionally:

(a) when the purpose of the act, by its nature or context, is to intimidate a population, or to compel a government or an international organisation to do or abstain from doing any act:

(i)   uses against or on a ship or discharges from a ship any explosive, radioactive material or BCN [biological, chemical, nuclear weapons or devices] weapon in a manner that causes or is likely to cause death or serious injury or damage; or

(ii) discharges, from a ship, oil, liquefied natural gas, or other hazardous or noxious substance, which is not covered by subparagraph (a)(i), in such quantity or concentration that causes or is likely to cause death or serious injury or damage; or

(iii) uses a ship in a manner that causes death or serious injury or damage; or

(iv) threatens, with or without a condition, as is provided for under national law, to commit an offence set forth in subparagraph (a)(i), (ii) or (iii); or

(b) transports on board a ship:

(i)   an explosive or radioactive material, knowing that it is intended to be used to cause, or in a threat to cause, with or without a condition, as is provided under national law, death or serious injury for the purpose of intimidating a population, or compelling a government or an international organisation to do or to abstain from doing any act; or

(ii) any BCN weapon, knowing it to be a BCN weapon as defined in Article 1; or

(iii) any source material, special fissionable material, or equipment or material especially designed or prepared for the processing, use or production of special fissionable material, knowing that it is intended to be used in a nuclear explosive activity or in any other nuclear activity not under safeguards pursuant to an IAEA comprehensive safeguards agreement; or

(iv) any equipment, materials or software or related technology that significantly contributes to the design, manufacture or delivery of a BCN weapon, with the intention that it will be used for such purpose.

The Protocol does not apply to the maritime operations of States parties to the 1968 Treaty on the Non-Proliferation of Nuclear Weapons, or to the activities of armed forces. Article 3*quater* introduced by the Protocol sets out in detail the various forms of criminal liability – instead of entrusting this task to national law – a trend which is apparent in recent anti-terrorist treaties. Of particular importance is the incorporation of common purpose or joint criminal enterprise liability, first introduced by the

ICTY in the 1999 *Tadić* Appeals Judgment[60] and later codified in Article 2(4)(c) of the 2005 UN Convention for the Suppression of Acts of Nuclear Terrorism.[61] This is further evidence that a corpus of general criminal international law – especially that related to forms of liability and defences – is perceived as applicable to all international and transnational crimes. The terrorist element of the offence in Article 3*bis* of the SUA Protocol is apparent in the specific intent (*dolus specialis*) requirement that the accused intended to intimidate or compel a specified body or entity to do or abstain from particular action.

Of particular importance in the SUA Protocol are its enforcement provisions. Article 8*bis* iterates the customary rule that the permission of the Flag State is imperative for the purposes of boarding and search. However, pursuant to the cooperation envisaged in the bilateral ship-boarding agreements mentioned in the start of this section, the USA was successful in incorporating a similar, albeit narrower, provision in the Protocol. Article 8*bis* 5(d) permits State parties, following ratification, to notify the IMO Secretary-General that a requesting State party may presume that Flag State consent to board, search and question persons on board has been given where there is no response from the Flag State within four hours of acknowledgment of receipt of a request to confirm nationality. Equally, under subparagraph 5(e) a notification may also be made whereby a requesting State party is permitted to board and search a foreign vessel under any circumstance within the scope of the Protocol. Such notifications may be withdrawn at any time. The Protocol obliges member States to cater for the liability of legal persons (although not necessarily criminal) and to provide for effective and dissuasive penalties.[62] The provisions on other forms of cooperation, including extradition and mutual legal assistance, although detailed, do not depart from relevant practice in international criminal law treaties. It is generally clear that the bulk of the efforts against maritime terrorism are not concerned with isolated incidents, but with the transport of weapons of mass destruction (WMD), or parts thereof, to rogue States or non-State actors engaged in terrorism.

In a following section of this chapter dealing with enforcement on the high seas reference is made to a particular regime regarding interdiction of vessels suspected of transporting WMD.

14.4 Offences Against Submarine Cables and Pipelines

The era of submarine transmission cables was launched in 1850 when the first telegraph cable was laid across the English Channel, connecting England with France. Within days, however, a French fisherman who had stumbled upon it proceeded to carve it, assuming he had discovered a peculiar seaweed! Although a boom in the laying of submarine cables followed, it was not until August 1858 that a

---

[60] *ICTY Prosecutor v Tadić*, Appeals Chamber Judgment (15 Jul 1999), paras 194 *et seq.* For an analysis of JCE liability see chapter 3.2.
[61] See chapter 12.3.3.
[62] Art 5*bis*.

third attempt to lay a trans-Atlantic cable was crowned with success. The cable was operational for only a month and it was in 1866 that the truly first enduring trans-Atlantic cable was finally laid. For a period of 30 years since the 1920s, radio carried the bulk of the globe's communications, but was unreliable in adverse weather conditions and had a limited capacity. The development in the 1950s of a lightweight co-axial cable, which was reinforced with a high-tensile steel core and a polythene outer skin meant that it did not require armouring in deep water. Since the first fibre optic submarine cable was laid in the 1980s, underwater cables have overtaken satellites as the leading means of overseas communication. Cables now carry more than two-thirds of all telephone, fax and data transmissions crossing oceans, with over 150,000 miles of fibre optic cable already laid on the seabed and rapidly increasing.[63]

The general freedom to lay submarine cables beneath the high seas and on the seabed thereof is expressly recognised under UNCLOS,[64] as well as its predecessor, the 1958 Geneva Convention on the High Seas[65] and was acknowledged as such under customary international law prior to the twentieth century. No such freedom exists with regard to another State's territorial sea and internal waters, or, indeed, in archipelagic waters in accordance with Article 51 of UNCLOS, except with the coastal State's consent. For the purposes of legal protection two types of submarine cable exist: 'trans-territorial' systems, which transcend the oceans and are therefore deployed on the high seas and 'festoon' systems, which are laid along several coastlines and are thus in large part contained in territorial or internal waters. The 1884 Convention for the Protection of Submarine Cables (1884 Convention),[66] which has not been superseded by other instruments and is still the basis for most national statutes, was adopted to suppress, punish and compensate breaking or injury to cables outside of territorial waters. Article 2(1) of the 1884 Convention made it a punishable offence to:

> … wilfully or through culpable negligence, [commit any act] resulting in the total or partial interruption or embarrassment of telegraphic communication.

In accordance with Article 2(2) of the 1884 Convention, any injuries to cables inflicted with the sole purpose of saving one's life or vessel, after all necessary precautions have been taken to avoid such occurrences, negate the criminal character of the act.[67] The application of Article 2(1) extends also to cable owners, presumably through the actions of their agents who wilfully or negligently break or injure another cable while laying or repairing their own.[68] Both the 1958 Geneva Convention on the High Seas[69] and

---

[63] See HM Field, *The Story of the Atlantic Telegraph* (New York, Scribner's, 1892); see International Cable Protection Committee website: <http://www.iscpc.org>.

[64] UNCLOS, Arts 87(1)(c) and 112. Art 58 further extends this freedom to the EEZ, although strictly speaking this does not form part of the high seas.

[65] 1958 Geneva Convention on the High Seas, Arts 2(3) and 26(1).

[66] 1 Bevans 89.

[67] Similarly, 1958 High Seas Convention, Art 27 and UNCLOS, Art 113.

[68] 1884 Convention, Art 4, 1958 High Seas Convention and UNCLOS, Arts 28 and 114 respectively, removed reference to criminal liability in such cases, but this should not be viewed as absolving them of such if they act wilfully or negligently.

[69] Ibid, High Seas Convention, Art 27.

UNCLOS[70] encapsulated the *actus reus* and *mens rea* contained in Article 2(1) of the 1884 Convention and extended it to cover also submarine pipelines and high-voltage power cables. Significantly, Article 113 of UNCLOS features an additional sentence, whereby it penalises not only wilful commission and negligence, but also 'conduct calculated or likely to result in such breaking or injury'.[71]

The breaking of submarine cables is by no means an international crime, but is rather a transnational offence. Unlike piracy *jure gentium*, which, too, is an offence committed on the high seas, judicial jurisdiction for injuries to submarine cables under Article 8 of the 1884 Convention and, indeed, customary law, is not universal but belongs to the Flag State, or that of the nationality of the offender, in cases where the Flag State is unable to act.[72] The same is true with respect to Article 113 of UNCLOS. Article 10(2) of the 1884 Convention makes a minor departure from the rule of exclusive enforcement jurisdiction of the Flag State on the high seas, by granting the limited right to other States parties to approach but not board suspected vessels in order to determine their nationality.[73] Both the British Submarine Telegraph Act 1885[74] and the US Submarine Cable Act 1888,[75] enacted to implement the 1884 Convention, reproduce almost verbatim the elements of the offence found in the 1884 Convention, including its jurisdictional clause. The light penalties provided in the British and US statutes, which have remained the same since their enactment, may well account for the lack of criminal prosecutions and reluctance to engage in costly litigation with little material benefit on the horizon.

In time of armed conflict, although it is permissible to sever the adversary's submarine cables,[76] it is prohibited to seize or destroy submarine cables connecting an occupied territory with a neutral State, except in situations of absolute necessity.[77] In a case tried by a British-American Claims Arbitral Tribunal in 1923 a British corporation claimed compensation for repairs incurred in repairing the Manila–Hong Kong and the Manila–Cadiz submarine telegraph cables cut by the US naval authorities during the Spanish–American War of 1898. The tribunal dismissed the claim by stating that not only was the cutting of cables not prohibited by the rules of international law applicable to warfare at sea, but 'such action may be said to be implicitly justified by that right of legitimate defence which forms the basis of the rights of any belligerent nation'.[78]

---

[70] UNCLOS, Art 113.

[71] In a Supplementary Declaration to the 1884 Convention, signed in 1886, the parties to the former construed the term 'wilfully' contained in Art 2(1) of the 1884 Convention as not imposing penal responsibility 'to cases of breaking or of injuries occasioned accidentally or necessarily in repairing a cable, when all precautions have been taken to avoid such breakings or damages'. Reprinted in 1 Bevans 112.

[72] MS McDougal and WT Burke, *The Public Order of the Oceans: A Contemporary Inter-national Law of the Sea*, (New Haven, Yale University Press, 1962) 1079.

[73] See RR Churchill and AV Lowe, *The Law of the Sea*, (Manchester, Manchester University Press, 1999) 175.

[74] Ch 49, ss 3, 6(5).

[75] 47 USC §§ 21, 22, 33.

[76] 1884 Convention, Art 15.

[77] 1907 Hague Regulations, Art 54.

[78] *Eastern Extension, Australasia and China Telegraph Co Ltd Claim* (1923–24) 2 AD 415, at 417; see also *Cuba Submarine Co Ltd Claim* (1923–24) 2 AD 419, at 419, whose facts and judgment were similar to the previous case.

Protection and prosecution of cases involving injury to submarine cables and pipelines is dependent on each individual State, by application and adaptation of domestic statutes to contemporary exigencies, as well as by international cooperation and rigid police enforcement action. State action has unfortunately proven inadequate. For this purpose an International Cable Protection Committee (ICPC) was established in 1958 by cable owners with the purpose of promoting the protection of submarine cables against natural and man-made hazards. Since the largest threat to cables is encountered from fisheries activities, especially trawl fishing, shellfish dredging, as well as negligent harbouring and towing, the ICPC has issued and distributed cable warning and cable awareness charts, as well as notices to mariners, and has developed standard procedures for activities such as cable routing and cable/pipeline crossing, in an effort to foster cable awareness in the fishing and offshore industries. In practice, legal action with respect to injury of submarine cables and pipelines is pursued through civil actions claiming pure or other economic loss, rather than simply damage.[79]

It is evident that the existing penal regime against the breaking of submarine cables is substantially insufficient to encompass would-be terrorists from intentionally severing these cables in order to bring about chaos in major urban centres. Such conduct is best covered by the existing anti-terrorism legal armoury, particularly the post-9/11 resolutions and sanctions adopted by the Security Council under the banner of threats to international peace and security.

14.5   Unauthorised Broadcasting from the High Seas

The rigid regulation of broadcasting in Western Europe in the early 1960s and the inability of private individuals to be granted broadcasting licences resulted in the establishment of so-called pirate radio stations outside the jurisdiction of coastal States, on the high seas. Because of the customary rule permitting only Flag State jurisdiction on the high seas for offences other than piracy *jure gentium*, member States of the Council of Europe adopted in record time in 1965 the European Agreement for the Prevention of Broadcasts Transmitted from Stations Outside National Territories (1965 Agreement).[80] Article 2 of the 1965 Agreement, which was widely ratified, criminalises the establishment or operation of broadcasting stations, as well as any acts of collaboration knowingly performed, such as the provision of services concerning advertising for the benefit of the stations.[81] The 1965 Agreement provided for jurisdiction based on the nationality and territoriality principles.[82] The

---

[79]   See *Qenos Pty Ltd v Ship APL Sydney* [2009] FCA 1090.
[80]   ETS 53.
[81]   1965 Agreement, Art 2(2)(e).
[82]   Ibid, Art 3.

entry into force of the 1965 Agreement and its enforcement by member States caused most stations to cease their operations.[83]

Article 109 of UNCLOS has a broader spectrum than the 1965 Agreement. It defines unauthorised broadcasting as:

> ... the transmission of sound, radio or television broadcasts from a ship or installation on the high seas intended for reception by the general public contrary to international regulations, but excluding the transmission of distress calls.

It provides for the following bases of judicial jurisdiction: (a) Flag State, depending on whether the broadcasting emanates from a vessel or a structure not amounting to a vessel; (b) nationality; (c) that which pertains to the State receiving the unauthorised transmissions, or whose authorised radio communications suffer as a result. States that enjoy judicial jurisdiction further enjoy enforcement jurisdiction, including a right of visit as well as a right to seize the offending vessel and crew. In accordance with Articles 109(4) and 110 of UNCLOS, only warships of the States having jurisdiction are permitted to visit and seize the offending vessels and crew members, but if it is proven that the vessel under suspicion was not in fact at fault it is entitled to compensation, as is the case generally under UNCLOS.

Although it is only the States listed in Article 109 that have jurisdiction over offending vessels, paragraph 1 of this provision obliges all States parties to UNCLOS to cooperate in the suppression of this particular offence. This would not, obviously, involve any enforcement action, but it would necessitate police cooperation, extradition procedures, etc. With the privatisation and private licensing of all types of telecommunications transmissions, pirate stations seem to have disappeared. However, as Churchill and Lowe correctly point out, UNCLOS retains its importance as it may be applicable to other forms of illegal broadcasting, such as unofficial propaganda broadcasts from the high seas the aim of which is to spread terror or hatred among ethnic, religious and racial groups.[84] Under these circumstances and depending on the severity of the underlying offence for which the broadcast is made, the obligation for all States to cooperate may involve the use of radio-jamming techniques that interfere with the illegal broadcasts and render the message inaudible.[85] In the extreme case where the broadcast is deemed to attempt to incite a group of people to commit genocide, it is possible for every State to seize the vessel and prosecute the offenders. This would not be premised on the 1948 Genocide Convention, which does not expressly provide for universal enforcement jurisdiction, but on the basis of customary law, to the extent that no significant objections to such jurisdiction are posited by interested States.[86] In a following section relating to enforcement on the

---

[83] See JC Woodliffe, 'The Demise of Unauthorised Broadcasting from Ships in International Waters' (1986) 1 *Journal of Estuarine and Coastal Law* 402; NM Hunnings, 'Pirate Broadcasting in European Waters' (1965) 14 *International & Comparative Law Quarterly* 410.

[84] Churchill and Lowe, *Law of the Sea*, at 212.

[85] The legal and factual premise of this possibility is eloquently explored by JF Meltz, 'Rwandan Genocide and the International Law of Radio Jamming' (1997) 91 *American Journal of International Law* 628, although radio jamming was not employed by third States during the Rwandan genocide.

[86] See I Bantekas, *Principles of Direct and Superior Responsibility in International Humanitarian Law*, (Manchester, Manchester University Press, 2002) 57–62.

high seas we shall explore a little further the possibility of arrest on the basis of the nationality principle, contrary to the Flag State principle.

14.6   Ship-Source Pollution

The inherent tension between ship owners and governments is well known, as is the fact that powerful shipping associations have resisted criminalisation of activities related to the industry. The criminalisation of ship-source pollution is a field of major contention because although it is reasonable and foreseeable to impose liability for the intentional discharging of polluting substances, it is a wholly different proposition to argue that criminal liability may also be incurred with respect to pollution resulting from accidents. In the latter case the only conceivable mental standard – absent reasonable foreseeability by the owner or master – is gross negligence and strict liability. The position is somewhat unclear in general international law.[87] Article 4(1) and (2) of the 1973 International Convention for the Prevention of Pollution from Ships, as amended in 1978 (MARPOL)[88] requires member States to prohibit and impose sanctions upon those discharging harmful substances or effluents containing such substances into the seas. Both the Flag State and the country in whose maritime belts the violation occurred may assume jurisdiction, with primacy afforded to the Flag State. Flag State primacy does not, however, prejudice the territorial or protective interests of the coastal State,[89] albeit the general rule is that the adoption of laws and enforcement of jurisdiction must not 'hamper innocent passage of ships' in the territorial sea.[90] Article 4 of MARPOL is silent as to whether the liability incurred may be of a criminal nature, in addition to its obvious civil character. In practice, industrialised States have enacted elaborate criminal legislation to transpose the MARPOL Convention into their domestic laws.[91] Article 4 of MARPOL mandates the Flag State to prosecute offenders even with respect to unlawful discharge that takes place on the high seas, otherwise the high seas would constitute an area that provides impunity to would-be polluters. I have already stated in my

---

[87]   Although Art 230 UNCLOS seems to suggest that criminal liability is indeed possible.

[88]   1340 UNTS 61.

[89]   The US Oil Pollution Act 1990 purports to bring within US jurisdiction all foreign vessels carrying certain oils or hazardous chemicals and sailing through its EEZ, even if they are not bound towards a US port. See EJ Molenaar, *Coastal State Jurisdiction over Vessel-Source Pollution* (Dordrecht, Martinus Nijhoff, 1998) 376. The jurisdiction of the coastal State over its EEZ vis-a-vis foreign polluting vessels is circumscribed by the general rule in Art 220(6) UNCLOS, arising where there has been 'a discharge causing major damage or threat of damage to the coastline or related interests of the coastal State or to any resources of its territorial sea or EEZ'. Mere suspicion therefore of a polluting incident is insufficient to ground physical inspection or seizure. M Gavouneli, *Functional Jurisdiction in the Law of the Sea* (Dordrecht, Martinus Nijhoff, 2007) p 86.

[90]   Art 211(4) UNCLOS.

[91]   Section 131 of the UK's Merchant Shipping Act 1995 makes it a criminal offence for the owner or master to discharge oil or oil mixtures in UK navigable waters. Moreover, in accordance with Regs 12, 13 and 36 of the Prevention of Oil Pollution Regulations, the applicable mental standard is one of strict liability. In the USA the MARPOL Convention was implemented by virtue of the Act to Prevent Pollution from Ships (APPS), 33 USC §§ 1901ff. APPS imposes criminal liability in respect of those who knowingly violate the Act and MARPOL, irrespective of the nationality of their flag, as long as the violation occurred within the US 12 mile jurisdictional limit.

analysis of the principle of legality in chapter 1 that one should not expect from treaties to spell out precisely the mental elements of the prohibited conduct. What is clear, however, is that in accordance with Regulation 11(b)(i) and (ii) of Annex I to MARPOL a discharge does not give rise to liability, including criminal as the case may be, where 'all reasonable precautions have been taken after the occurrence of the damage . . . or discharge . . . except if the owner or the master acted either with intent to cause damage, or recklessly and with knowledge that damage would probably result'. Thus, MARPOL establishes intent (*dolus* directus of the first and second degree) and recklessness as the appropriate mental standards for criminal liability, clearly excluding negligence-based or strict liability, which would place accidents outside its criminal law regime. In practice, some States have broadened the scope of criminal liability with a view to punishing ship owners who fail in their duty of care. In the USA ship owners and their operators have been held subject to vicarious corporate criminal liability in cases of prohibited discharges and in respect of any ships entering US waters with falsified entries in their Oil Record Book (ORB) designed to hide discharges.[92] This is tantamount to strict liability and the trend towards this type of liability seems to gradually constitute a common feature in the judicial practice of courts in Europe and North America.[93]

The European Communities have specifically dealt with this matter. On 2005 the European Union, acting under the Third Pillar, adopted a Framework Decision on ship-source pollution in which it established criminal liability where the relevant actors acted with intent, recklessness or serious negligence.[94] This Framework Decision caused a huge outcry within the shipping community and the traditional shipping powers, particularly Greece, Cyprus and Malta, and it was widely argued that criminalisation was not the optimum way forward.[95] It was not long before the

---

[92] *USA v Jho* (5th Cir, 2008) 534 F. 3d 398; *USA v Ionia Management S.A* (2nd Cir, 2009) 555 F. 3d 303.

[93] In the *Erika* case, the Paris Criminal Court, in its Judgment of 16 January 2008, upheld a charge of criminal liability for pollution and endangerment in respect of an accident in which a tanker split in half and released 30,000 tonnes of toxic fuel 30 miles from the coast of Brittany. Contrary to the MARPOL mental standards, Art L218–22 of the French Environmental Code requires negligence or recklessness. In addition, criminal liability attaches not only to the master, ship owner and operator, but also, in an echo of the doctrine of command responsibility, to 'any other person exercising a de facto power of control or direction over the management of the running of the ship, who by his fault involuntarily caused a marine accident which resulted in pollution or omitted to take the measures necessary to prevent the pollution'; in the *Grand Europa* case (unreported), the Piraeus District Court in a judgment of 28 January 2008 convicted the pilot and the master of the ship for infringing the Collision Regulations on the basis of negligence. Other courts are also following suite. In the *Hebei Spirit II* case, a vessel harboured in South Korea (SK) caused a huge oil spill after inappropriate towing. Despite their best efforts to contain the damage the master and his deputy were held guilty on account of negligence by a lower court and the Court of Appeals. In late 2009 the SK Supreme Court eventually rescinded the negligence-based liability.

[94] Council Framework Decision 2005/667/JHA of 12 July 2005 to Strengthen the Criminal-Law Framework for the Enforcement of the Law against Ship-source Pollution, OJ L 255 (30 Sep 2005), Art 4(4)–(7).

[95] In *International Association of Independent Tanker Owners (Intertanko) and Others v Secretary of State for Transport*, Case C-308/06, ECJ Judgment (3 Jun 2008), the plaintiffs argued that the *mens rea* in the Framework Decision was inconsistent with MARPOL and Art 230 UNCLOS and the vague language of 'serious negligence' gave rise to a violation of the legality principle. The ECJ argued that the *mens rea* standards in the MARPOL Annexes were not part of customary international law and given that the EU was not a party to that convention no incompatibility could be demonstrated. The same conclusion was evident in respect of UNCLOS because it was found not to confer rights on individuals and as a result the pertinent *mens rea* had to be provided by national law. Finally, although it agreed that intent, recklessness

Framework Decision was effectively annulled by the ECJ, not because the EC did not have the power to produce criminal law, but because the regulation of the environment fell within the First Pillar and not the Third. Thus, the EC Commission was found to possess competence to impose criminal legislation if by doing so this was essential for combating environmental crimes.[96] The Framework Decision eventually gave way under more or less the same terms to a Directive in late 2009.[97] The main issue, however, remained, in that not only the relevant conduct persisted as a criminal offence, but moreover the Directive retained serious negligence as an alternative *mens rea* standard.[98] In all other respects, where discharge or other pollution takes place the relevant actors possess the defences available under MARPOL and its Annexes (ie accidental and approved discharges).[99] Although this is a conduct crime and hence does not require that the discharge produce any particular environmental harm, it does not apply to minor infringements unless these are repeated and cumulatively result in deterioration in the quality of water.[100] Criminal corporate liability arises not only by reason of criminal penalties against the legal person, but more importantly against any physical person who has a leading position within its structure, based on: a) a power of representation of the legal person; b) authority to take decisions on behalf of the legal person, or; c) authority to exercise control within the legal person.[101] Finally, anyone found inciting, aiding or abetting a prohibited discharge with intent is equally liable for a criminal offence.[102] For a detailed analysis of corporate criminal liability and the concepts of inciting, aiding and abetting, see chapter 3.10 and 3.11.

14.7   Criminal Liability for Fisheries-related Violations on the High Seas

There are three types of prohibited fishing under international law; illegal, unreported and unregulated (IUU). Illegal fishing consists of fishing in violation of a multilateral fisheries regime or a regime established by a coastal State. Unreported fishing, on the other hand, concerns unreported or misreported fishing to the relevant authorities in contravention of applicable laws and regulations. Finally, unregulated

and serious negligence were not defined in the Framework Decision, they nonetheless: 'correspond to tests for incurring of liability which are to apply to an indeterminate number of situations that it is impossible to envisage in advance and not to specific conduct capable of being set out in detail in a legislative measure, of Community or of national law', para 73.

[96] *Commission v Council*, Case C-440/05, ECR [2007] I-9097; *Commission v Council*, Case C-176/03, ECR [2005] I-7879, paras 47–48. See V Mitsilegas, *EU Criminal Law* (Oxford, Hart Publishing, 2009) 70–84.
[97] Directive 2009/123/EC of 21 October 2009 on Ship-Source Pollution and on the Introduction of Penalties for Infringements.
[98] Ibid, Art 4(1).
[99] Ibid, Art 5.
[100] Ibid, Art 5(a)(3).
[101] Ibid, Art 8(b)(1). Additionally, a legal person incurs criminal liability where lack of supervision or control by a natural person has made the commission of a prohibited discharge possible for the benefit of that legal person by a natural person under its authority.
[102] Ibid, Art 5(b).

fishing involves either stateless vessels, or vessels whose Flag State is not a party to the regional organisation governing the particular fishing area or species. Unregulated fishing may also encompass areas or fish stocks in respect of which there does not exist a conservation regime. Besides the problem of depletion of fish stocks worldwide, which is detrimental to the feeding needs of millions of people, it is estimated that the global value of IUU fishing lies somewhere between US$ 4.2 billion and US$ 9.5 billion.[103]

Article 19(1)(a) of the 1995 UN Agreement for the Implementation of the Provision of UNCLOS relating to the Conservation and Management of Straddling Fish Stocks and Highly Migratory Fishstocks,[104] provides powers of enforcement to the Flag State irrespective of where the violations occur. Nonetheless, the sanctions which the Flag State must impose on the violator should be severe enough to render them 'effective in securing compliance and to discourage violations wherever they occur and shall deprive offenders of the benefits accruing from their illegal activities'.[105] In accordance with Article 20(6) of the Agreement, coastal States can only board and inspect a vessel on the high seas which they reasonably believe was undertaking unauthorised fishing in their maritime belts, but only with the consent of the Flag State. It should be noted that unlike UNCLOS the 1995 Agreement is not universally ratified.

Whereas the 1995 Agreement itself fails to provide enforcement rights (particularly visit and investigation) to countries other than the Flag State, it does provide for this eventuality in cases of regional fisheries agreements and organisations (RFOs). Article 21(1) of the 1994 Agreement stipulates that the right to visit and inspect is indeed available to non-flag States through specially authorised RFO inspectors. Even so, the Flag State must be notified, but if it declines to respond the inspectors may lead the vessel to the nearest port, albeit the port or coastal State does not possess the authority to prosecute the offenders.[106] The situation is much more straightforward in respect of the clear and unambiguous enforcement mechanisms found in RFOs, such as the 1999 Barents Sea Agreement, the Commission for the Conservation of Southern Bluefin Tuna, the International Whaling Committee, the Convention for the Conservation of Antarctic Marine Living Resources and many others.[107] Although the International Tribunal for the Law of the Sea (ITLOS) has not been called upon to rule on the legality of domestic criminal sanctions against illegal fishing by foreign vessels, it has confirmed this eventuality implicitly. Cases on illegal fishing before ITLOS have concerned the prompt release of the vessel and master following the posting of a reasonable bond, in accordance with Articles 73(2) and 292 UNCLOS. ITLOS has not challenged the coastal State's right of arrest in

---

[103] High Seas Task Force, *Closing the Net: Stopping Illegal Fishing on the High Seas* (IUU Fishing Coordination Unit, 2006) 18.
[104] (1995) 34 ILM 1542.
[105] Art 19(2), Straddling Fish Stocks Agreement.
[106] Ibid, Art 21.
[107] See RR Churchill, 'The Barents Sea Loophole Agreement: A Coastal State Solution to a Straddling Stock Problem' (1999) 14 *International Journal of Marine and Coastal Law* 467; RG Rayfuse, *Non-Flag State Enforcement in High Seas Fisheries* (Dordrecht, Martinus Nijhoff, 2004).

respect of illegal fishing in its EEZ, but only its subsequent wrongful detention of the master either because the bond is unreasonable or because after having been paid the master is not promptly released.[108]

Legal considerations aside, criminal enforcement on the high seas is highly impractical, even for developed nations. Inadequate national fisheries management and patrolling capacities are reasons that contribute to IUU, among others. The scourge of illegal fishing does not concern lone fishermen but most importantly organised crime groups that control the chain of supply that links producers, processors and retailers. In this manner the ultimate proceeds of illegal fishing are tantamount to money laundering on account of the criminal nature of the predicate conduct; ie illegal fishing.[109] The only feasible way of applying criminal law against illegal fishing is through strict trade, import and export checks and restrictions, but many coastal States are institutionally unable or disinclined to impose such measures, particularly on account of widespread corruption. It then befalls upon developed nations to institute appropriate import mechanisms. The leader in this field has been the USA through the adoption of the Lacey Act, which makes it a criminal and civil offence to unlawfully import, export, transport, sell, receive, acquire or purchase any fish or wildlife in violation of foreign or international laws.[110] It is obvious that such laws are effective if the penalties are severe and dissuasive and where the prosecuting State employs asset sharing schemes with the country where the ship is registered or in whose waters the offence took place.

14.8   Enforcement on the High Seas

The fundamental rule as to criminal enforcement on the high seas rests with the Flag State.[111] Typically, a ship can only be registered under a single State, otherwise it risks becoming stateless. This seems like a simple enough proposition but is in fact the starting point for all the problems associated with compliance and enforcement. The reason is that for obvious financial considerations ship owners choose to fly so-called flags of convenience, in respect of which the registering States are unable or unwilling to enforce the minimum requirements of seaworthiness, maritime labour standards, environmental safeguards and ultimately criminal legislation. The advantages for ship

---

[108] *Camouco* case (Panama v France), Judgment on Application for Prompt Release (7 Feb 2000), paras 61–72.

[109] High Seas Task Force, *Closing the Net*, 22–24. This is particularly prevalent where illegal catches are mingled with legitimate catches.

[110] Lacey Act, 16 USC § 3371 (as amended in 2009). In *USA v Arnold Bengis, David Bengis, Jeffrey Knoll, Hout Bay Fishing Industries, Icebrand Seafoods Inc et al* (unreported), cited in *Closing the Net*, ibid, p 35, the accused were charged with formulating a conspiracy spanning over fifteen years to illicitly fish South African rock lobster and Patagonian toothfish far in excess of their permitted quotas. They unreported their catch to RSA authorities and bribed a number of officials in order to rubber stamp false documentation showing that their catch was legitimate. They then proceeded to export their catch to the USA. The accused were convicted to a period of incarceration and handed a criminal fine of $US 5.9 million.

[111] Art 110(1) UNCLOS. See generally D Guilfoyle, *Shipping Interdiction and the Law of the Sea* (Cambridge, Cambridge University Press, 2009).

owners are not only the possibility of tax breaks but also the ability to engage in global maritime operations on the basis of a lax regime courtesy of the Flag State rule. This reality renders the Flag State rule a burden for international law and the obligations of Flag States to the international community a fiction. This fiction is moreover reinforced by the fact that a ship is no longer owned or run by the archetypal ship owner, but may be partly owned by a plethora of known or unknown persons in a holding company, while at the same time being chartered by an agent that is distinct from the 'owner'. That the Flag State should possess all powers of jurisdiction over a private vessel on the high seas is made even more incredible by virtue of the fact that none of the acts or omissions of the vessel are attributable to the State by reason of the law of State responsibility.[112]

The concept of enforcement entails a number of disjunctive actions, namely those of visit, inspection, seizure, confiscation and ultimately prosecution. In accordance with the basic rule none of these actions is permissible against a foreign registered vessel by a warship of another nation. The case is different in respect of stateless vessels, in which case the right to visit, at least, is sustained by practice.[113] The basic rule of Article 110(1) UNCLOS is subject to three exceptions. The first, as we have already examined, relates to acts of piracy *jure gentium*, but even so the intercepting State may not indefinitely seize or confiscate the piratical vessel. The second exception, as articulated in paragraphs 1 and 2 of Article 110 concerns those situations in which the foreign warship invokes a 'reasonable ground for suspecting' that any of the following acts have occurred on board a foreign vessel: slave trade, unauthorised broadcasting, the ship is without nationality, or though flying a foreign flag or refusing to show its flag is in reality of the same nationality as the warship. Even so, the warship is only entitled to visit the vessel and if suspicions persist it may thereafter proceed to a further examination of the ship. If said suspicions are well founded and the vessel is indeed found to have committed any of the above offences Article 110 does not, as one would assume, grant powers of arrest, seizure and prosecution to the State of the interdicting warship. Rather, these subsequent measures of enforcement are the prerogative of the Flag State, unless conferred elsewhere by express agreement, whether prior to the visit or following its interdiction. This result is confirmed not only by virtue of customary practice but also by reference to recent multilateral agreements, such as Article 8(2) of the 2000 Smuggling Protocol of CATOC,[114] which stipulates that 'a State Party that has reasonable grounds to suspect that a vessel ... of another State party is engaged in the smuggling of migrants by sea may so notify the Flag State, request confirmation of registry and, if confirmed, request authorization from the Flag State to take appropriate measures with regard to that vessel', including the right to board, search the vessel and if evidence is found that the vessel is indeed engaged in such activity, 'to take appropriate measures with respect to the vessel and persons and cargo on board, as

---

[112] Not that this eventuality is impossible, but is certainly rare. See Gavouneli, *Functional Jurisdiction*, 34–35.

[113] *Molvan v Attorney-General for Palestine* [1948] AC 351; *USA v Marino-Garcia* (1982) 679 F. 2d 1373, *cert*. denied (1983) 459 US 1114.

[114] Protocol against the Smuggling of Migrants by Land, Sea and Air, supplementing the UN Convention against Transnational Organized Crime. See chapter 11.2.1.

authorized by the Flag State'. This limitation on the power of non-flag States to suppress crimes, even by curtailment of the right to visitation, absent express authorisation from the Flag State is also evident in Article 17 of the 1988 UN Convention against Illicit Traffic in Narcotic Drugs and Psychotropic Substances, which concerns drug-trafficking.[115] Article 108 UNCLOS only demands that States parties strive to cooperate against drug-trafficking on the high seas, but does not grant any rights of enforcement against non-flag States.

The third exception to the general rule concerns those bilateral or multilateral agreements through which non-flag States are granted express enforcement powers.[116] In fact, a significant number of bilateral agreements have been agreed between adjacent nations or those sharing common seas or oceans. The basic feature of these agreements is that one of the parties is usually a developing State that lacks the material capacity to enforce its criminal laws against its own private vessels, while on the other hand the particular prohibited conduct harms the interests of the developed nation (as is the case with migrant smuggling or drug-trafficking). These agreements typically provide for a right to visit only and in their majority the instrument in which they are contained is of an informal nature; ie Memoranda of Understanding (MoU). In this manner, the agreement need not be made public and the developing State saves itself from the embarrassment of being seen to delegate its sovereign rights to third nations. The multilateral fisheries agreements analysed in a previous section of this chapter constitute examples in which rights of enforcement are conferred by reason of contract. In some cases, particularly those concerning illicit migrant smuggling, certain developing nations have conferred broad enforcement rights to individual States, or political and military alliances, such as NATO or the EU, with a view to 'intercepting' migrant smuggling in its early stages. Thus, interception rights are granted also in respect of operations pertaining to the conferring nation's territorial sea. The primary objective of this type of interception is to prevent the migrants reaching a maritime belt of the intercepting State, such that they could thereafter claim refugee status and thus render themselves insusceptible to refoulment.[117]

A recent radical approach to circumventing the general rule of Article 110 of UNCLOS is the so-called Proliferation Security Initiative (PSI), which consists of a limited number of powerful maritime nations – fifteen at the time of writing, including among others the USA, UK, Russia, Australia, France and Germany (so-called 'core group' nations). The aim of the PSI is to permit and facilitate the interdiction of shipments of Weapons of Mass Destruction (WMD) on sea, land and air.[118] Although the framers of the PSI claim that its application is to be consistent with international law, the PSI Interdiction Principles are in conflict with Article 110

---

[115] See chapter 11.4 for a discussion of trafficking in illicit substances.

[116] Security Council resolutions to this effect fall within this category because they are premised on a multilateral treaty, the UN Charter.

[117] Ibid, 80–82; see also P Mathew, 'Legal Issues Concerning Interception' (2003) 17 *Georgetown Immigration Law Journal* 221.

[118] DH Joyner, 'The Proliferation Security Initiative: Non-proliferation, Counter-proliferation and International Law' (2005) 30 *Yale Journal of International Law* 534.

in that they allow the boarding and seizure of non-flag State vessels upon suspicion that a particular vessel is carrying WMD. Article 4(d) of these Interdiction Principles allows member States:

> To take appropriate actions to (1) stop and/or search in their internal waters, territorial seas, or contiguous zones (when declared) vessels that are reasonably suspected of carrying such cargoes to or from States or non-State actors of proliferation concern and to seize such cargoes that are identified; and (2) to enforce conditions on vessels entering or leaving their ports, internal waters or territorial seas that are reasonably suspected of carrying such cargoes, such as requiring that such vessels be subject to boarding, search, and seizure of such cargoes prior to entry.[119]

This freedom to board, search and seize suspected vessels of non-flag States is more akin to the enforcement mechanism of piracy *jure gentium* and thus it purports to equate the interdiction of WMD on the seas with the regime of piracy, which is unacceptable under UNCLOS. Although the PSI Interdiction Principles do not extend these enforcement rights on the high seas, a State in whose EEZ a suspected vessel has passed may well deem it appropriate to activate a hot pursuit onto the high seas, albeit none of the relevant agreements make reference to such possibility. It is clear that the PSI is directed toward so-called rogue States that pose a threat to international peace and security, particularly North Korea, Yemen and Iran.[120] The PSI suffers from a number of obvious limitations. For one thing, its participation is very limited, although the Bush administration argued that it was 'supported' by eighty other nations, albeit without specifying these or the type of support offered, which in any event seems to be rather weak. Secondly, it establishes a legal regime that purports to bind third parties without even approval from the Security Council (since China is not a member of the core group of nations to the PSI).[121] Finally, it plainly overrides the clear demands of the UNCLOS enforcement regime, without any evidence at all that it gives rise to a rule of customary international law. Despite the above concerns, there is significant merit to this initiative and it will be interesting to see how it will be received globally. If so, it has the capacity to amend the limitation in Article 110 UNCLOS, at least as far as WMD shipments are concerned.

The fiction of absolute Flag State jurisdiction should be considered also from another angle; that of universal jurisdiction. Where civilians from group Y are taken on board a vessel on the high seas with a view to their execution or enslavement as part of an act or genocide or crimes against humanity why may a foreign warship not seize the vessel and prosecute the culprits when this assumption of powers would be perfectly permissible had the offence been perpetrated on land? While this proposition certainly does not apply to every international or transnational offence, it does encompass a good number. In my opinion, all international crimes (subject to

---

[119]   Adopted on 4 September 2003. Available at: <http://www.state.gov/t/isn/c27726.htm>.

[120]   See M Byers, 'Policing the High Seas: The Proliferation Security Initiative' (2004) 98 *American Journal of International Law* 526, who notes that the final straw for the adoption of the PSI was the inability of the international community to interdict a North Korean vessel transporting SCUD missiles to Yemen.

[121]   This interdiction entitlement is not supported, either expressly or implicitly, by SC 1540 (28 Apr 2004), which mandates States to cooperate, criminalise and punish non-State actor involvement in WMD proliferation.

universal jurisdiction and which are being perpetrated on the high seas) are subject to enforcement – including the employment of force – by warships other than those of the Flag State.

An issue associated with the exercise of universal jurisdiction, although not totally obvious, is whether the full gamut of the domestic law of the seizing State and its related regional or international human rights regime is applicable to the accused. If the seizing State was successful in arguing that its laws were inapplicable to the accused on the high seas, assuming that the culprit vessel was stateless, then the seizing State would in theory not be obliged to conform to any law at all. This is absurd as a result and inconsistent with international human rights standards. It should therefore come as no surprise that the European Court of Human Rights has accepted in a string of cases involving drug-trafficking and illegal smuggling on the high seas that they fall within the juridical space of the European Convention on Human Rights,[122] in much the same way as if the underlying events had taken place outside the territory of member States but under their effective control.

A legal question that has received little attention concerns those – rare it should be admitted – cases where the interdicting non-flag State violates the terms of Article 110 UNCLOS or its bilateral undertakings and yet brings the accused before its national courts. This issue has received differing interpretations in respect of illegal seizures on land, with the US Supreme Court arguing in favour of the *male captus bene detentus* rule,[123] while in the UK its courts have consistently rejected the validity of this maxim as constituting an abuse of process.[124] The position with respect to unlawful maritime seizures seems to be much more coherent and predictable because of the specificity of UNCLOS and customary law; ie that unlawful seizures do not give rise to legitimate criminal jurisdiction. This is confirmed by some case law[125] and State practice,[126] but we have no recent test cases. Thus, I am not certain that US courts seized with an otherwise unlawful interdiction of vessels carrying WMD or of crews committing other serious crimes on the high seas – particularly after the

---

[122] *Xhavara and Fifteen Others v Italy and Albania*, App No 39473/98, Admissibility Decision (11 Jan 2001), where the Eur Ct HR accepted, however, that Italy did have the right to impose a maritime blockade in order to restrict the entry of illegally smuggled migrants; *Rigopoulos v Spain*, App No 37388/97, Decision (12 Jan 1999), regarding drug-trafficking; *Medvedyev and Others v France*, App No 3394/03 Judgment (10 Jul 2008), where a French warship intercepted and arrested the crew of a Cambodian vessel transporting drugs following the consent of the Cambodian authorities. The Eur Ct HR simply chided France as to the length of temporary detention, not of its right to arrest under the circumstances. In fact, the Court even went so far as to misconstrue the ambit of Art 110 UNCLOS, by asserting that non-flag States do not require the consent of the Flag State in cases of piracy, slave-trade, unauthorised broadcasting and in respect of stateless ships (para 54).

[123] The real test case in favour of this maxim is *Attorney-General of Israel v Eichmann* 36 ILR 5 (District Court of Jerusalem, 1961), aff'd 36 ILR 277 (Supreme Court of Israel, 1962). The US Supreme Court followed suit in *USA v Alvarez-Machain* (1992) 112 S Ct 2188, albeit its conclusion was premised on the consideration that abduction was not outlawed by treaty and that a warrant had already been issued against the accused.

[124] *Bennett v Horseferry Road Magistrates Court*, [1993] 3 All ER 138; *Re Mullen* [1999] Cr App R 143.

[125] *Cook v USA* (1933) 288 US 102, *per* Brandeis J, which involved the arrest of an alcohol smuggling vessel outside the jurisdiction of the USA, as defined by the terms of a 1924 USA–UK Agreement for the Prevention of the Smuggling of Intoxicating Liquors into the USA.

[126] See F Morgenstern, 'Jurisdiction in Seizures Effected in Violation of International Law' (1952) 29 *British Yearbook of International Law* 265.

precedent of *Alvarez-Machain* and the Bush administration National Security Policy – would dismiss the case because of the unlawful nature of the interdiction.

14.9   The Right of Hot Pursuit

The right of hot pursuit is amply established under customary law, as well as the 1958 Geneva Convention on the High Seas and UNCLOS.[127] It gives coastal States the right to pursue and arrest foreign vessels that have committed an offence within their maritime zones onto the high seas. As a result, it constitutes an exceptional measure departing from the rule of exclusive Flag State jurisdiction on the high seas. Before considering the details of this entitlement of coastal States, it is useful to scrutinise its justificatory basis. Under the relevant treaties it is not only an exceptional measure; its exercise is also subject to certain limitations, such as that the pursuit must be continuous and uninterrupted. Moreover, other sea-trafficking treaties stress the primacy of Flag State jurisdiction, the security of the foreign vessel, safety of life at sea, as well as the commercial interests of the Flag State.[128] On the other hand, hot pursuit operates as a right of necessity for the enforcement of the laws and regulations of the coastal State, which would otherwise be unenforced if the general rule of Article 110 UNCLOS was strictly observed.[129] It would seem that, unless otherwise explicitly permitted by new rules of customary law or unilateral acquiescence, hot pursuit must be exercised only in accordance with the strict requirements of UNCLOS.

It is clear from the text of Article 111 of UNCLOS and the *travaux* of the 1958 Geneva Convention on the High Seas[130] that States are not restricted in terms of offences that are deemed susceptible to hot pursuit. This is a matter for the coastal State's domestic law and is in no way dictated by international law. This general freedom, however, is subject to two limitations. First, hot pursuit may be exercised in any one of the coastal State's areas of maritime jurisdiction – including the continental shelf – provided that the pursuit is in response to a violation for the protection of which the particular maritime belt was established. For example, since Article 33 of UNCLOS permits the establishment of a contiguous zone in order to prevent the infringement of the coastal State's customs, fiscal, immigration or sanitary laws, hot pursuit is available only if the foreign vessel has, while in the

---

[127] 1958 High Seas Convention, Art 23; Art 111 UNCLOS; see Churchill and Lowe, *Law of the Sea*, 214–16. States are increasingly concluding bilateral or regional multilateral treaties providing for cooperation in the exercise of the right of hot pursuit, such as the 1993 Conakry Convention on Sub-regional Cooperation in the Exercise of Hot Pursuit.

[128] 1988 UN Convention Against the Illicit Traffic in Narcotic Drugs and Psychotropic Substances, Art 17, (1989) 28 ILM 493; Council of Europe Agreement on Illicit Traffic by Sea, Implementing Art 17 of the UN Convention Against Illicit Traffic in Narcotic Drugs and Psychotropic Substances, ETS 156. For an analysis of the international legal regime against the cultivation and trafficking of narcotic and psychotropic substances, see chapter 11.4.

[129] RC Reuland, 'The Customary Right of Hot Pursuit Onto the High Seas: Annotations to Article 111 of the Law of the Sea Convention' (1993) 33 *Virginia Journal of International Law* 557, at 558.

[130] (1956) *Yearbook of the International Law Commission (YBILC)*, vol II, at 285.

contiguous zone, violated any such laws. Similarly, the non-prescribed but limited sovereign rights granted to coastal States under Article 56 of UNCLOS restrict hot pursuit to a small range of environmental, illegal fishing and similar offences. Secondly, while international comity suggests that hot pursuit should be avoided with regard to trivial infringements,[131] violation of less serious offences such as illegal fishing – although we have explained the significant repercussions of this conduct – has in the past given rise to legitimate pursuit.[132] Irrespective of whether a crime has in fact been committed by a foreign vessel in a maritime belt, hot pursuit is lawful only where the pursuing vessel 'has good reason to believe'[133] that the particular violation has taken place. What is thus required is either actual knowledge or reasonable suspicion, but mere suspicion would not suffice.[134] This proposition that mere suspicion is an insufficient basis for asserting a right of hot pursuit was reinforced by the judgment in the *M/V Saiga (No 2)* case, where the International Tribunal for the Law of the Sea (ITLOS) stated that when the Guinean pursuing ship made its 'initial decision to pursue, it had insufficient grounds for hot pursuit. Guinea could have had no more than a suspicion that the *Saiga* had violated its laws in the EEZ'.[135] The argument that the flight of a foreign vessel onto the high seas upon its visual or radar contact with a ship belonging to the authorities of the coastal State constitutes reasonable suspicion of committing a crime[136] is incompatible with the justificatory principle of hot pursuit enunciated above. In any event, the test of reasonable suspicion should be interpreted to encompass particular criminal activity, as opposed to suspicion about general criminal activity.

Hot pursuit represents enforcement action by the coastal State and as such the use of force is permissible in two cases: (a) for the purposes of self-defence; and (b) in order to effectively interdict the offending vessel and arrest those on board. Force, however, must conform to the principles of proportionality and reasonableness. In the *I'm Alone* case,[137] a Canadian ship was pursued by a US Customs vessel onto the high seas and upon refusing to surrender she was fired upon with more than 100 shots, resulting in her sinking and the death of one crew member. The Mixed Committee of Arbitration ruled that the sinking of the pursued vessel must be incidental to the exercise of necessary and reasonable force. Similarly, in the *M/V Saiga* case the ITLOS observed that considerations of humanity must apply in the law of the sea, pointing out that since the *Saiga* was fully laden and its maximum

---

[131]   Reuland, 'Customary Hot Pursuit', at 558.

[132]   *The North* case (1905, Canada) 11 Ex Rep 141.

[133]   UNCLOS, Art 111(1).

[134]   McDougal and Burke, *The Public Order of the Oceans*, at 896; NM Poulantzas, *The Right of Hot Pursuit in International Law* (Dordrecht, Martinus Nijhoff, 2002) 154–57; Reuland, 'Customary Hot Pursuit', at 569.

[135]   *Saint Vincent and the Grenadines v Guinea* (The *M/V Saiga*) *(No 2)*, Judgment on Merits (1 Jul 1999), (1999) 38 ILM 1323, para 147.

[136]   Reuland, 'Customary Hot Pursuit', at 570.

[137]   *I'm Alone* case (Canada v USA) (1935) III UN Reports of International Arbitral Awards (UNRIAA) 1609.

speed was 10 knots it could have easily been overrun and boarded by the Guinean warship, without excessive force.[138]

14.9.1 Commencement and Continuous Nature of Hot Pursuit

Under Articles 111 of UNCLOS and 23 of the 1958 Geneva Convention on the High Seas respectively, the right of hot pursuit commences where a foreign vessel has committed an offence in a maritime belt, is moreover present therein and the pursuing public ship has ordered the foreign vessel to stop at a distance which enables it to be seen or heard by the foreign vessel. Refusal to stop would give rise to pursuit onto the high seas. As Article 111 of UNCLOS speaks only in terms of 'ship' and not persons, hot pursuit would be available for offences committed by passengers on board a foreign ship only where they are acting under the authority of those in charge of the ship. The coastal State may thereafter lay claim for the offenders to be tried before its courts on the basis of the law of extradition.[139] Moreover, although the wording of both UNCLOS travaux to the 1958 Geneva Convention suggest that only a completed offence justifies pursuit, the *travaux* to the 1958 clearly illustrate that the special rapporteur perceived any reference to 'attempts' as superfluous, taking it for granted that they were implied in the text.[140]

Once the pursuit commences it must remain continuous and uninterrupted. A pursuit is deemed to have been interrupted in the following cases:

(a) where the pursued vessel has entered the territorial sea of a third State,[141] although other maritime belts are assimilated to high seas for the purposes of hot pursuit;[142]

(b) where the warship has abandoned pursuit, this cannot thereafter be resumed. Although UNCLOS is silent, case law suggests that only significant interruptions can invalidate a right of hot pursuit. Thus, if the warship momentarily stops to pick the mother ship's dories or in order to rescue persons at sea, this should not terminate pursuit;[143]

(c) finally, since UNCLOS requires that the foreign vessel be given an audible or visual signal to stop, it is necessary that the pursuing ship maintain some sort of visual observation of the foreign vessel. This requirement of visual observation would have to be fulfilled despite the existence of radars which make observation possible without the need for visual proximity.[144]

---

[138]   *M/V Saiga* Judgment on Merits, paras 153–57; see also *The Red Crusader* case (1962) 35 ILR 485, and 1995 Agreement for the Implementation of the Provisions of UNCLOS, Art 22(1)(f), Relating to the Conservation and Management of Straddling Fish Stocks and Highly Migratory Fish Stocks.

[139]   Reuland, 'Customary Hot Pursuit', at 570.

[140]   Poulantzas, *The Right of Hot Pursuit*, at 154.

[141]   In *R v Mills* (unreported), Croydon Crown Court adopted a more liberal view. See WC Gilmore, 'Hot Pursuit: The Case of *R v Mills and Others*' (1995) 44 *International & Comparative Law Quarterly* 949.

[142]   (1956) 84 YBILC, vol I, at 52. Poulantzas, *The Right of Hot Pursuit*, at 180 argues that a short stay of passage through a third State's territorial waters, with the aim of evading the law, does not preclude the resumption of hot pursuit. He notes, however, that in all other instances where the fleeing vessel has entered the territorial waters of a third State the jurisdictional link between the pursuing and pursued vessel has been broken.

[143]   *The North* case.

[144]   Poulantzas, *The Right of Hot Pursuit*, at 212.

Pursuit is possible by either a duly authorised warship or aircraft. UNCLOS permits a warship to take over the pursuit from an aircraft, but is silent as to whether an aircraft can continue the pursuit commenced by a warship. Juristic opinion generally takes the view that this is possible.[145] Furthermore, in accordance with UNCLOS, it is not necessary that at the time when the foreign ship within the territorial sea or the contiguous zone receives the order to stop, the warship or aircraft giving the order be within the territorial sea or the contiguous zone.

A pursuit is lawful only where, as already stated, the foreign vessel does not respond to a clearly audible or visual signal to stop. In *USA v Postal*,[146] the Fifth circuit court ruled that the arrest of a foreign vessel on the high seas was unlawful because, *inter alia*, the giving of visual or auditory signals to stop did not occur until after a second boarding of the fleeing vessel, by which time the foreign vessel was outside US territorial waters. It is argued that since the signal requirement is intended to give the foreign vessel time to heave and await inspection, it may be dispensed with where the foreign vessel attempts to flee upon sighting the intercepting warship or aircraft.[147] Although Article 111(4) of UNCLOS allows only visual or auditory signals, recent case law has accepted the use of signals given by radio.[148] This result is certainly mandated by practical and logical considerations.

14.9.2   The Doctrine of Constructive Presence

The practice of States has, at least since the latter part of the nineteenth century, accepted that the presence of a mother ship beyond the crucial maritime belt – or on the high seas – would still give rise to a right of hot pursuit against it where boats belonging to, or associated with, the mother ship commit offences in the coastal State's maritime zones of jurisdiction.[149] This is known as the doctrine of constructive presence, whereby for the purposes of hot pursuit the mother ship, otherwise not lawful prey, is deemed to be within the enforcement jurisdiction of the coastal State.[150] The doctrine has been codified in the 1958 Geneva Convention and Article 111(4) of UNCLOS provides that hot pursuit is not deemed to have commenced:

> ... unless the pursuing ship has satisfied itself ... that the ship pursued or one of its boats or other craft working as a team and using the ship pursued as a mother ship is within the limits of the territorial sea, or, as the case may be, within the contiguous zone or the exclusive economic zone or above the continental shelf.

---

[145]   Churchill and Lowe, *Law of the Sea*, at 215.
[146]   *USA v Postal* (1979) 589 F 2d 862.
[147]   *The Newton Bay* case (1929) 36 F 2d 729. The recent Judgment (Merits) in the *M/V Saiga* case, however, supports a stricter view, para 148.
[148]   *R v Mills*; *R v Sunila and Soleyman* (1986) 28 DLR 450.
[149]   *Araunah* (1888) Moore, *Int Arb* 824; *Grace and Ruby* (1922) 283 F 475.
[150]   See WC Gilmore, 'Hot Pursuit and Constructive Presence in Canadian Law Enforcement' (1988) 12 *Marine Policy* 105.

Although the doctrine of constructive presence was born to challenge situations involving a mother ship and smaller boats operating from the mother ship (eg the *Araunah* case involved canoes engaged in sealing within Russian territorial waters and operating from a British Columbian schooner on the high seas), in recent years it has become common practice for a number of large vessels to be cooperating in illegal activities (especially drug-trafficking and smuggling) without the existence of a mother ship in the traditional sense. Thus, in the case of *R v Mills*, a ship registered in St Vincent was smuggling cannabis into the UK by transferring the drugs through the high seas to Ireland and from there to a British trawler which subsequently sailed into British waters. Croydon Crown Court was not troubled by the fact that the British trawler was not one of the boats of the pursued St Vincent vessel. Although this case does not conform to the spirit of Article 111 of UNCLOS, its evolution will undoubtedly depend on relevant State protests and consensus emanating from recent international criminal cooperation initiatives in the spheres of organised crime, drug-trafficking and terrorism.

Part IV

Enforcement of International Criminal Law

15

The Exercise of Criminal Jurisdiction

15.1 International Law Principles on Criminal Jurisdiction

Jurisdiction refers to the power asserted by States by which they seek to prescribe and enforce their municipal laws over persons and property. This power is typically employed in three forms, which correspond to the three branches of government. Hence, legislative or prescriptive jurisdiction relates to the competence to prescribe the ambit of municipal laws, judicial jurisdiction relates to the competence of courts to apply national laws and enforcement jurisdiction refers to the ability of States to enforce the fruits of their legislative or judicial labour (for example, gathering of evidence, arrest and infliction of sanctions). In this manner jurisdiction may be both civil as well as criminal. Because the very concept of jurisdiction encompasses a claim, it is important to assess whether jurisdictional claims are predicated on an entitlement under domestic or international law. Whereas some treaties provide for the exercise of criminal jurisdiction by member States, most areas of criminal law, particularly those relating to common crimes, are not regulated by treaties. Moreover, even where some regulation is undertaken by means of a treaty this will not typically provide an elaborate hierarchy of jurisdictional claims.[1] Even if said treaties were to set out strict hierarchical rules they would be of little value to third States that may entertain a jurisdictional claim since they would be inapplicable to them. Thus, when States exercise prescriptive and judicial jurisdiction over common or international crimes they are seemingly relying on a unilateral act that is the direct product of domestic legislation. This is, nonetheless, only half the story. In actual fact, any exercise of jurisdiction on the basis of domestic law must ensure that no express rule or principle of international law is violated in the process. As a result, States generally refrain from prosecuting common crimes taking place in the territory of other nations, nor do they arrest persons on foreign territory without consent, because this would entail a violation of the non-intervention principle.[2] Equally, States cannot investigate or prosecute persons covered by an applicable immunity that is granted

---

[1] Art K3(d) of the 1998 Amsterdam Treaty Amending the Treaty on the European Union, reprinted in (1998) 37 ILM 56, provides that European Union (EU) States are to prevent conflicts of criminal jurisdiction arising among themselves; in similar fashion, and for the first time articulated in an anti-terrorist treaty, Art 7(5) of the 2000 United Nations (UN) Convention for the Suppression of the Financing of Terrorism, (2000) 39 ILM 270, obliges States parties, in cases of jurisdictional conflicts, to strive to co-ordinate their actions appropriately, 'in particular concerning the conditions for prosecution and modalities for mutual legal assistance'.

[2] Developed principally in the seminal UNGA Res 2625 (XXV) (24 Oct 1970). The US Supreme Court in *Hoffman-La Roche Ltd and Others v Empragan SA and Others* (2003) 124 S Ct 2359, 2366 held

under international law. Thus, international law is the acid test through which all claims of jurisdiction should be weighed, irrespective of their origin. Given that States enjoy almost unlimited authority over all conduct undertaken on their territory, the general abhorrence against extraterritorial enforcement jurisdiction,[3] particularly abductions and arrests, is self-evident.

The Permanent Court of International Justice (PCIJ) in the *Lotus* case held that in the absence of an international rule permitting jurisdiction in a particular case (permissive rule) States are free to exercise jurisdiction, as long as a prohibitive rule does not negate such a claim.[4] This *Lotus* principle gives rise to valid unilateral jurisdictional entitlements. It does not, however, explain the fate of such entitlements in situations where they are in conflict with counter-opposing claims asserted by other nations. For one thing, the *Lotus* principle was applied by the PCIJ only in respect of a State's extraterritorial prescriptive and judicial competence, not its enforcement competence abroad.[5] As a result, a State may unilaterally adopt legislation that allows its courts to investigate a particular criminal conduct without at the same time being entitled to arrest or subject the accused to its criminal justice system. Where two or more States assert a jurisdictional claim over conduct they describe as criminal, certain international rules have evolved with a view to alleviating – the rigid effects at least – of such conflicts. Firstly, a variety of cooperation mechanisms, such as extradition and mutual legal assistance, are designed to offer the conflicting parties the opportunity of mutual reconciliation. Ultimately, however, only one request among many must be satisfied, if at all. Secondly, States have the option of protesting against the exercise of jurisdiction by another nation where they perceive themselves as possessing a stronger link to the conduct or to the accused.[6] Of course, a protest can only prove successful if the claiming State yields enough power to convince its opposing counterpart; this is a salient feature of international life that cannot be ignored. Thirdly, prosecuting States will naturally endeavour to demonstrate that they enjoy a legitimate interest over the case, usually in the form of a genuine link[7] and

that on the basis of the non-interference principle it is assumed that Congress takes into consideration the legitimate interests of other nations when drafting extraterritorial legislation.

[3] Exceptionally, some common law countries do not object to foreign consuls serving writs to persons on their territory. Furthermore, visiting Heads of State have been permitted to perform their official functions while abroad, such as signing decrees. See M Akehurst, 'Jurisdiction in International Law' (1972–73) 45 *British Yearbook of International Law* 145, at 146, 150. Equally, the ICJ in *Certain Questions of Mutual Assistance* (Djibouti v France) Judgment (4 Jun 2008), held that the dispatch of a witness summons to a visiting Head of State that was, however, unaccompanied by threat of legal action did not violate international law.

[4] *Lotus* case (France v Turkey) (1927) PCIJ Reports, Ser A, No 10, 18–19; see W Estey, 'The Five Bases of Extra-Territorial Jurisdiction and the Failures of the Presumption against Extra-Territoriality' (1997) 21 *Hastings International & Comparative Law Review* 153; R Higgins, *Problems and Process: International Law and How We Use It,* (Oxford, Oxford University Press, 1994) 77, who takes the opposite view by contending that the *Lotus* presumption should not be relied on because it is based on a much dissented judgment.

[5] C Ryngaert, *Jurisdiction in International Law* (Oxford, Oxford University Press, 2008) 23–24.

[6] Akehurst, 'Jurisdiction', at 176.

[7] See FA Mann, 'The Doctrine of Jurisdiction in International Law' (1964) 111 *Recueils des Cours Academie Droit International (RCADI)* 44, at 82, who formulated the theory of 'reasonable link', according to which jurisdiction should be dependent upon the strongest possible connection between the conduct and the claimant forum; see I Brownlie, *Principles of Public International Law,* (Oxford, Oxford University Press, 1998) 313, who also adds the general principles of non-intervention and proportionality.

that through the exercise of jurisdiction they do not impose harm upon a third State that may entertain a much stronger interest in the particular case. The concept of harm under such circumstances is naturally quite subjective.[8] Why, for example, does a State on whose territory criminal conduct commenced incur harm simply because the country where the crime was consummated decides to exercise prescriptive and judicial jurisdiction? In situations, however, where the exercise of jurisdiction in State A relates wholly to the public finances of State B, the latter may validly claim some degree of harm, particularly where it considers the evidence confidential or prejudicial to its national interests. As a result, a particular exercise of jurisdiction will defeat competing claims of harm where it is demonstrated that said jurisdiction is reasonable and proportionate in comparison to the advantage asserted.[9] Finally, and as a matter of practical necessity, the apprehending State enjoys primacy as regards possible extradition requests. From a political point of view the apprehending State will be far less susceptible to accusations of bias if it decides to prosecute itself, rather than if it accepts one of many extradition requests which will undoubtedly disgruntle all the other suitors.

Domestic law has a significant role to play in the shaping and enforcement of criminal jurisdiction. In some sense, international law serves to prohibit particular – abusive, excessive and unreasonable – instances of criminal jurisdiction or provide rudimentary rules in cases of conflicts. Domestic law, on the other hand, provides the authorities within a State with the necessary tools by which to investigate crimes, seek the extradition of accused persons and ultimately undertake prosecutions. Depending on a country's resources, its legal tradition and relative power the jurisdictional reach of its laws may turn out to be significantly wide. From a practical perspective, if an accused person is within the authority of a country's courts these will not be concerned with other competing claims and will rely exclusively on the permissibility of domestic criminal law in exercising their jurisdiction. The resolution of any competing claims will be handled by the executive branch of government. In the course of the twentieth century five bases of criminal jurisdiction have been asserted by States: territorial, active personality, passive personality, universal and jurisdiction premised on the protective principle. Because these jurisdictional principles pertain to manifestations inherent in statehood – eg active personality jurisdiction requires the granting of nationality, which is a function attributable solely to States – they should be distinguished from the jurisdictional bases under which international criminal courts and tribunals operate. These principles will be examined in a distinct section in this chapter, but are also discussed more generally in the specific chapters dealing with the various international criminal judicial institutions.

Such a link is sometimes asserted even by the courts of States exercising the principle of universal jurisdiction, which does not require any connection between the offence and the prosecuting State. See the *Scilingo* case, Spanish Audencia Nacional Judgment No 16/2005 (19 Apr 2005), where it was held that a legitimate interest in the exercise of universal jurisdiction was warranted in respect of crimes that took place in Argentina. This interest was found to be the disappearance of 500 Spaniards during the reign of the accused.

[8] Ryngaert, *Jurisdiction*, 32–35.
[9] Ibid, 145–50.

15.2   Territorial Jurisdiction

It is uncritically noted that the territorial principle of jurisdiction represents the single most important rule when assessing competing claims, if for no other reason because its application does not give rise to external intervention and is the least harmful to a country's territorial integrity and political independence. The territorial principle is also taken for granted because it is the natural basis upon which national legislatures draft their criminal laws and through which the courts and law enforcement agencies apply them. Indeed, legislation encompassing extraterritorial conduct is the exception, rather than the norm to the prosecutorial practice and preference of States. Nonetheless, conduct that takes place on the territory of country A may well produce harmful consequences in country B, which the latter defines as criminal. This is true for example of anti-competitive practices, as well as in respect of trading with a third State in circumstances where that State is under sanctions from country B but not country A. Thus, if citizens of country A were to engage in trade relations with the sanctioned State they would only incur an offence under the laws of country B, although they owe no allegiance to it and may never set foot on its territory. Moreover, certain countries may decide to de-criminalise particular conduct or otherwise offer amnesties to the culprits, thus desisting from exercising territorial jurisdiction. The question that naturally arises is whether it is legitimate and reasonable for another nation to ignore the amnesties and de-criminalisation of the territorial State and prosecute the persons benefiting from them. State practice demonstrates a general reluctance to accept local amnesties that pertain to serious violations of human rights. The erosion of strict territorial jurisdiction has further been doubted in situations where elements of effective occupation and authority are exercised by one country over another. The emerging rule seems to suggest that the occupying force cannot exclude the applicability of its laws in occupied territory. Finally, the application of territorial jurisdiction over certain nationals of third States may be perceived as producing harm upon those States, particularly where the accused are members of its government or otherwise of high profile. These considerations are pertinent to the law of immunity which may bar the exercise of territorial jurisdiction in certain cases.

As a result of these considerations, territoriality is certainly less evident than originally assumed. Even in legal systems such as that of England, where territoriality is the cornerstone of criminal jurisdiction[10] – sometimes even to the detriment of justice – the historical reasons behind its primacy are generally unrelated to international relations or comity.[11] Rather, the persistence of strict rules of evidence, particularly the limitations in the admissibility of hearsay evidence and the requirement of cross-examination, necessarily meant that evidence collected abroad would be of little value before English courts; this situation is further compounded by the fact that neither the evidence nor the witnesses could be transferred there. Moreover,

---

[10]   *Madeod v AG for New South Wales* [1891] AC 455, at 458, *per* Lord Halsbury, who famously stated that because all crimes are local therefore jurisdiction is territorial; *Compania Naviera Vascongando v SS Cristina* [1938] AC 485, at 496, *per* Lord Macmillan.

[11]   Although exceptionally in *Treacy v DPP* [1971] AC 537, at 561, the Court of Appeals opined that the exercise of extraterritorial judicial jurisdiction would interfere with the sovereignty of other nations.

unlike other nations where the notion of criminal conduct is related to the victim or social order and justice, in the common law conduct is reprehensible only if it upsets the social order of that State (ie Queen's or King's peace).[12] Of course, at the present time England has significantly expanded the jurisdictional ambit of its laws, but these remain conservative in relation to the criminal laws of other nations.

Yet another significant factor that favours territorial jurisdiction is its relative advantage in terms of cost and time. National prosecutors are under constant financial constraints and are unable to over-stretch their budgets. This does not mean that financial considerations should override the dictates of justice, but they do certainly dictate prosecutorial priorities. Evidence and witnesses situated abroad are inaccessible and expensive to collect and utilise and there is little guarantee that a sufficiently strong case can be made back home. Moreover, investigations must by law be concluded within confined spatial boundaries, thus militating against lengthy extraterritorial expeditions. As a result, in some countries, such as the USA, the grounding of the presumption against extraterritoriality has been significantly influenced by domestic dictates – particularly Congressional intent – rather than international law considerations.[13]

The territoriality principle operates without problems and counter-claims where all the elements of criminal conduct have taken place on the territory of the prosecuting State. However, in the classic example of one person firing a shot across a frontier and subsequently causing the death of another on the other side, the principle of territoriality proper gives rise to questions of primacy between two competing jurisdictions. In such circumstances national criminal legislation in the concerned countries may classify the particular offence either as a conduct crime, a results crime or both. In this manner, the firing of the shot (conduct) may suffice to trigger the jurisdiction in country A whereas the country where the victim was killed (result) may equally assert the territoriality principle because the offence was consummated there. The latter is usually termed qualified territoriality and is widely recognised in State practice, although it is susceptible to abuse or expansive interpretation, most typically by powerful nations. This practice has given rise to two distinct but interrelated principles; that of objective and subjective territoriality.

15.2.1 Subjective Territoriality

States applying this principle generally claim that when an element of the conduct of a particular offence either commences or is otherwise physically perpetrated on their

---

[12] Ryngaert, *Jurisdiction*, at 57.
[13] See particularly *Foley Bros Inc v Filardo* (1949) 336 US 281, 285. Exceptionally, in cases of extraterritorial anti-trust (ie anti-competitive) behaviour strict territoriality was abandoned ever since *USA v Aluminium Company of America* (2nd Cir, 1945) 148 F 2d 416.

territory they may validly assert jurisdiction over the accused.[14] For the purposes of jurisdiction it is irrelevant that the result of the conduct does not take place in that country. This principle was recognised early on in two international treaties although it was not widely regarded as a general principle of national law.[15] These were the 1929 Convention for the Suppression of Counterfeiting Currency and the 1936 Convention for the Prevention of Illicit Drug Traffic, which bound the contracting parties to assume jurisdiction over the prescribed offences, irrespective of the *locus* where the offence materialised, as long as an attempt, commission or conspiracy was perpetrated on their territory.

While at the inter-State level subjective territoriality satisfies the pressing need to combat a range of transnational and international crimes in respect of which some countries may not otherwise have an interest to prosecute, its application to common crimes necessitates the existence of a nexus that is stronger than that claimed by other nations. This nexus may well be satisfied because the conduct was much more substantial in State A than in State B, albeit the litmus test is whether a 'real and substantial link' exists between the offence and the claiming State[16] and that jurisdiction under the circumstances was moreover reasonable. In *Libman,* the accused committed fraud in Canada by selling worthless shares over the telephone to buyers in the USA who, as directed, paid the accused in Central America. Subsequently, Libman retrieved the money in Canada. The Canadian Supreme Court exercised jurisdiction on the basis of the 'real and substantial link' theory, substantiated by the fact that the largest part of the criminal conduct had in fact taken place in Canada.[17] Naturally, the courts in the USA and the other affected nations could have equally laid claim to a valid jurisdictional entitlement.

The exercise of subjective territorial jurisdiction is not generally fraught with competing claims. On the contrary, its application is particularly welcome because it acts as a deterrent to aliens considering engaging in criminal activity in countries that possess weak criminal justice systems (eg transnational fraud and sex-related offences). If the territorial State did not prosecute them for these offences it is generally unlikely that their country of nationality would have eagerly undertaken an investigation of common crimes for which it has little or no information. As a result, subjective territorial jurisdiction constitutes a most useful supplement to criminal jurisdiction and crime prevention generally.

---

[14] See G Gilbert, 'Crimes sans Frontières: Jurisdictional Problems in English Law' (1992) *63 British Yearbook of International Law* 415, at 430, who makes reference to the 'doctrine of ubiquity', which allows States to assume jurisdiction over an offence, as well as any connected inchoate offences, if a part of the offence or its effects are felt in the prosecuting State.

[15] I Shearer, *Starke's International Law,* 11th edn (London, Butterworths, 1994) 186; as an example of municipal law, Gilbert, ibid, at 431, who cites s7 of the New Zealand Crimes Act 1961.

[16] *Libman v R* (1986) 21 DLR 174, at 200, *per* La Forest J.

[17] On the same basis, and without proof of damage to the interests of the prosecuting State, an Australian Criminal Appeals Court assumed jurisdiction over an offence of grievous bodily harm with intention, committed by the mailing of poisoned food from Australia to Germany: *R v Nekuda* (1989) 39A Crim R 5, (New South Wales); similarly, an act of murder committed in Mexico by a US citizen was held to fall within the jurisdiction of Arizona courts because the crime had been premeditated in Arizona, this being a substantial element of first degree murder: *State of Arizona v Willoughby* (1995) 114 ILR 586.

15.2.2   Objective Territoriality

The flip side of subjective territoriality gives rise to jurisdiction in those cases where conduct committed abroad produces effects in a third State, which thereafter seeks to prosecute on the basis of its criminal laws. The classic example associated with this principle involved the *Lotus* case, which we have already briefly touched upon. There, eight Turkish crewmen perished as a result of a collision on the high seas between a French and Turkish vessel. Upon arrival in Turkish territorial waters the captain of the French *Lotus* was apprehended and charged with the death of the Turkish crewmen. The French authorities subsequently appealed against this exercise of jurisdiction by Turkey and the case was brought before the PCIJ. The majority of the Court ruled that since the Turkish vessel was flying the flag of that country it was to be assimilated to Turkish territory. It was not a far leap thereafter to hold that the manslaughter of the Turkish nationals had occurred on Turkish soil, thus legitimating the exercise of criminal jurisdiction over the French captain. Although this particular aspect of the *Lotus* judgment (ie that jurisdiction for collisions on the high seas rests with the Flag State of the victim vessel) has been universally discredited,[18] objective territoriality itself has gained much prominence in the last thirty years, at least.

   Although the magnitude of harm that gives rise to objective territoriality in respect of conduct physically perpetrated abroad is circumscribed by domestic law, its exercise is necessarily conditioned by considerations pertinent to international law and rules of comity. Such a utilisation of objective territoriality is very much akin to the protective principle. We have already stated that federal US courts are mandated to construe statutes under a presumption of territoriality. The rise of transnational crime and anti-trust activities abroad, however, coupled with the economic prowess of the USA, dictated an expansive interpretation of territoriality. As a result, the so-called 'effects doctrine' was pioneered, which allows US courts to assume extraterritorial jurisdiction in cases where the economic or injurious consequences of an offence are directly felt in the United States.[19] Although it is not unusual or impermissible for States to institute jurisdictional mechanisms on the basis of harm originating from third nations,[20] these mechanisms may ultimately turn out to harm the interests of innocent nations and persons. The adoption of the Helms-Burton Act and the Iran-Libya Sanctions Act in 1996 (D'Amato-Kennedy Act) by the US

---

[18]   In his dissenting opinion in the *Lotus* judgment, at 53, Lord Finlay argued that criminal jurisdiction for negligence causing a collision belongs to the Flag State, unless the accused is of a different nationality, in which case it is his or her own country that may also assume jurisdiction. This is the rule adopted in Art 27 of the 1982 United Nations Law of the Sea Convention (UNCLOS), (1982) 21 ILM 1261.

[19]   See Sherman (Anti-Trust) Act 1890, 15 USC § 1; *USA v Aluminium Co of America* (1945) 148 F 2d 416; *Mannington Mills Inc v Congoleum Corp* (1979) 595 F 2d 1287; *Hartford Fire Insurance Co v California* (1993) 113 S Ct 2891; see also DHJ Hermann, 'Extra-Territorial Criminal Jurisdiction in Securities Laws Regulation' (1985–86) 16 *Cumberland Law Review* 207.

[20]   The EU generally assumes jurisdiction over anti-competitive activities performed outside its boundaries either on the basis of relevant subsidiaries situated in the EU or by finding that such activity was implemented in the EU, although originating outside it. See *ICI v Commission* (*Dyestuff* case) [1972] ECR 619; *Ahlstrom v Commission* (*Wood Pulp* case) [1988] 4 CMLR 901; DGF Lange and JB Sandage, 'The *Wood Pulp* Decision and its Implications for the Scope of EC Competition Law' (1989) 26 *Common Market Law Review* 137.

Congress imposed a number of sanctions on foreign nationals and foreign legal persons investing in Cuba, Iran and Libya, despite the fact that such investment activities were perfectly legal from the point of view of the investors' country of nationality.[21] Given the unreasonable nature of these measures and the abuse of the effects doctrine the EU adopted a set of instruments which instructed its member States and their nationals not to succumb to judgments or sanctions originating from US courts.[22] Moreover, it called on its member States to take appropriate measures to protect themselves.[23] Eventually, even federal US courts themselves determined that such a broad exercise of territorial jurisdiction was not appropriate in light of the economic interests of third nations and the international relations of the USA.[24] In the end the matter was settled by mutual agreement between the parties.

Another alternative form of the objective territoriality principle is the 'continuing act' doctrine. This stipulates that a State enjoys jurisdiction over an offence which, although committed abroad, is continuing to produce results within that State. In *DPP v Doot*[25] the accused were charged with conspiring to import cannabis into the UK. Although the conspiracy was fully carried out abroad and UK courts would not normally entertain jurisdiction in such a case the House of Lords rejected the defendants' plea by stating that the offence continued to occur in England since the result of the conspiracy was ongoing.

15.2.3   The Ambit of National Territory

The application of a country's criminal laws is not strictly restricted to that part of its territory that is circumscribed within its internationally recognised borders. It is now accepted that the reach of a country's human rights and criminal legislation extends also to territories, or parts thereof, over which it exercises elements of effective occupation.[26] This is justified by the fact that a different result would culminate in impunity for the crimes committed by members of the occupying power. Moreover, it

---

[21] US Cuban Liberty and Democratic Solidarity Act (Helms-Burton Act), 22 USC § 6021. Title III of the Act concerns nationals of third States 'trafficking' in nationalised US property by the Cuban authorities in 1959, imposing on such persons penalties such as treble damages and denial of entry to the US. See AV Lowe, 'US Extra-Territorial Jurisdiction: The Helms-Burton and D'Amato Acts' (1997) 46 *International & Comparative Law Quarterly* 378.

[22] Council Regulation No 2271/96 (22 Nov 1996) Protecting against the Effects of the Extraterritorial Application of Legislation adopted by a Third Country and Actions based Thereon or Resulting Therefrom, OJ L 309 (29 Nov 1996).

[23] Joint Action 96/668/CFSP, 1996 OJ L309, (29 Nov 1996) 7.

[24] *Timberlane Lumber Co v Bank of America* 66 ILR 270.

[25] *DPP v Doot* [1973] 1 All ER 940.

[26] *Banković v Belgium et al*, (2001) 11 BHRC 435 and *Secretary of State for Defence v Al-Skeini and Others* [2007] UKHL 26. Whereas the claim in *Banković* failed because during the bombing of Belgrade by NATO forces the latter were not in occupation of Yugoslavia, in *Al-Skeini* the House of Lords was prepared to accept that had British forces been in effective occupation of the town of Basra in Iraq, then the whole gamut of human rights law incumbent on Britain would have been applicable thereto. This rule seems well entrenched even where it is seemingly rejected, as was the case with *Amnesty International Canada and British Columbia Association for Liberties v Civil Chief of Defence Staff for the Canadian Forces et al*, Canadian Federal Court Judgment (12 Mar 2008), where the extraterritorial application of the Canadian Charter of Rights and Freedoms over Afghan detainees in Afghanistan was rejected because Canada was not considered an occupying power of that country.

is absurd and unjust for the occupying force to deny justice to victims of the local population, particularly in situations where local justice mechanisms are crippled and the offence is attributable to an agent of the occupier.

For the purposes of common territorial jurisdiction the application of domestic criminal law extends beyond a State's land territory until the outermost part of its contiguous zone at sea. Unlike the generally permissive international rules pertinent to territorial jurisdiction on land, jurisdiction on the various maritime belts under customary international law and the UN Convention on the Law of the Sea (UNCLOS) is generally premised on strict, non-negotiable, principles. Hence, the permissive *Lotus* principle is inapplicable to jurisdictional competences on the seas. The basic rule is that the Flag State enjoys criminal jurisdiction over offences perpetrated on vessels flying its flag. This rule is subject to very narrow and specific exceptions, namely: a) universal jurisdiction over acts of piracy on the high seas; b) non-flag State enforcement jurisdiction on the basis of bilateral or multilateral ship-boarding agreements; c) notwithstanding the principle of Flag State jurisdiction, exceptionally foreign merchant vessels are susceptible to the criminal jurisdiction of the coastal State, assuming its local laws so permit, in cases where conduct on board said vessel while situated in internal waters or the territorial sea is deemed injurious to the safety or welfare of the coastal State.[27] The reader should consult chapter 14 for a more detailed analysis of the regime of enforcement on the seas, as well as for an exposition of the general features of the law of the sea.

As regards offences committed in airspace, without prejudice to those multilateral aviation conventions and concurrent jurisdiction specified therein, the general rule is that primary criminal jurisdiction lies with the subjacent State.[28] Much like other treaties dealing with terrorism the subjacent country principle of jurisdiction is an extension of the territoriality principle. Nonetheless, the relevant treaties do not grant an exclusive entitlement to the subjacent State; rather, this is one among numerous jurisdictional avenues, given that terrorism of this nature takes place or produces effects in multiple nations. The subjacent nation principle was enforced in the case of the Pan Am flight bombing over Lockerbie, Scotland, through the establishment of a criminal tribunal in The Netherlands with the application of Scots substantive and procedural criminal law.[29] The application of this principle in the *Lockerbie* case, however, was more the result of a political compromise than an adherence to jurisdictional principles.

It must be assumed that State succession results in the wholesale transfer of jurisdictional competence to the new successor nation. As simple as this proposition sounds, it is not devoid of significant legal problems. Whereas the successor's jurisdiction encompasses the competences otherwise enjoyed by the succeeding

---

[27] In the *Wildenhus'* case (1887) 120 US 1, the murder of a Belgian crewman by his compatriot on board a Belgian merchant vessel in a US port was held by the US Supreme Court to be subject to local prosecution. In *R v Anderson* (1868) 11 Cox Crim Cases 198, the UK Court of Criminal Appeals upheld the jurisdiction of the courts of the Flag State for offences on board its merchant vessels in foreign territorial waters, but recognised that this jurisdiction was concurrent to that of the coastal State.

[28] See *Smith v Socialist People's Libyan Arab Jamahiriya* 113 ILR 534, at 541.

[29] See 1998 Agreement Between the Government of the Kingdom of The Netherlands and the Government of the United Kingdom of Great Britain and Northern Ireland Concerning a Scottish Trial in The Netherlands, (1999) 38 ILM 926.

nation both prior to the succession as well as after, the successor is not generally entitled to exercise jurisdiction in violation of fundamental human rights norms (particularly the non-retroactivity rule and *ne bis in idem*). In the *Former Syrian Ambassador to the German Democratic Republic* (GDR) case[30] the Syrian Ambassador to the GDR was charged with fostering and co-ordinating a terrorist bombing in the Federal Republic of Germany. The Federal Constitutional Court upheld the jurisdiction of German courts (following unification) on the basis that federal criminal law was applicable even prior to German reunification. This is nothing more than a purposive interpretation of a federal statute, but it also underpins the logical conclusion that all unpunished criminal conduct and jurisdictional competencies of the succeeding State are automatically inherited by the successor.

15.3   The Active Personality Principle

The active personality principle (or nationality) of jurisdiction is based on the nationality of accused persons.[31] It allows States to prescribe legislation regulating the conduct of their nationals abroad and in some cases it has also been applied to persons with residency rights.[32] The first point of departure is the legal nature of nationality. This may only be conferred by State entities and as a result only they are competent to set out the legal requirements for its conferral.[33] However, where the legal effects of the granting or withdrawal of nationality produce legal consequences in the relations between two or more States any assessment of nationality must be construed in accordance with international law.[34] If this were not so then any State could light-heartedly render stateless a large part of its population and as a result bring about a global refugee crisis.

The competence of a State to prosecute its nationals on the sole basis of their nationality – and regardless of the territorial State's competing claim – is based on the allegiance that is owed to one's country of nationality under domestic law.[35] Although traditionally the active personality principle has been mostly prevalent in civil law jurisdictions it is not unknown in common law States.[36] It has already been explained that common law nations generally disfavoured extraterritorial jurisdiction

---

[30] *Former Syrian Ambassador to the German Democratic Republic* (GDR) case, 115 ILR 597, 604–05.

[31] GR Watson, 'Offenders Abroad: The Case for Nationality-Based Criminal Jurisdiction' (1992) 17 *Yale Journal of International Law* 41.

[32] UK War Crimes Act 1991, s 1(2) brings within the jurisdiction of English courts persons who are accused of committing war crimes during the Second World War, if at the time of prosecution they are either residents or citizens of the UK. See *R v Sawoniuk* (2000) 2 CAR 220.

[33] 1930 Hague Convention on Certain Questions Relating to the Conflict of Nationality Laws, Art 1, 179 LNTS 89.

[34] In the *Nottebohm* case (Guatemala v Liechtenstein), (1955) ICJ Reports 4, Second Phase, the International Court of Justice (ICJ) pointed out that a State claiming protection on behalf of one of its naturalised nationals against a respondent State needed to establish an effective and genuine link.

[35] Harvard Research, Draft Convention on Jurisdiction with Respect to Crime, reprinted in (1935 Supp) 29 *American Journal of International Law* 480, at 519.

[36] *Blackmer v USA* (1932) 284 US 421, at 436; *USA v Columba-Colella* (1979) 604 F 2d 356, at 358.

because their evidentiary rules would hamper the work of the prosecution. Nonetheless, even the most conservative of common law nations, the UK, has applied the nationality principle to a limited number of offences, namely treason,[37] murder and manslaughter,[38] bigamy,[39] offences on board foreign merchant vessels[40] and, more recently, conspiring or inciting sexual offences against children.[41]

Traditionally, the nationality principle was employed with a view to countering extraterritorial offences that harmed the person of the State and its interests or in order to combat impunity. The primary example of the former is the offence of treason, which is recognised only under domestic law. As regards the combating of impunity, this is not straightforward. State A incurs no harm and has no immediate or direct interest in the sexual exploitation of women and children in distant State B, even if it considers this practice abhorrent. This result is further reinforced if said conduct does not constitute a punishable offence in country B, contrary to the situation in country A. If country A were to prosecute one of its nationals for committing this offence in country B it would have to do so under exceptional grounds because common crimes are normally subject to territorial jurisdiction; unless the criminal laws of country A expressly prescribe otherwise in respect of its nationals. In such cases the exercise of criminal jurisdiction on the basis of the principle of nationality is an exceptional ground because it is justified on account: a) of the maintenance and pursuit of justice; b) that human rights possess a universal character and entail an *erga omnes* obligation, and because; c) States refuse to portray themselves as facilitating safe havens for those nationals committing crimes abroad.[42]

There exists yet another reason, of a constitutional nature, that has necessitated the prosecution of nationals in respect of extraterritorial crimes, even in situations where prosecution may otherwise be deemed excessive. In *Public Prosecutor v Antoni* the Swedish Supreme Court found the criminal provisions of the Traffic Code of that country to be applicable against Swedish nationals abroad.[43] Had Sweden not opted for the prosecutorial avenue it would have been obliged to extradite the accused. Civil law nations have traditionally declined to extradite their nationals as a matter of constitutional imperative. As a result, in order to avoid impunity and to counter vexing extradition requests they have made extensive use of the nationality principle of jurisdiction. It should be emphasised that the adoption of the European Arrest Warrant (EAW) by member States of the European Union has effectively put an end to the invocation of nationality as a bar to extradition. This result did not, however, come about without fierce, yet highly flexible and adaptable, constitutional debates.

---

[37] Treason Act 1351 and Official Secrets Act 1989, s 15(1); see also *R v Casement* [1917] 1 KB 98; *Joyce v DPP* [1946] AC 347, where the offence of treason was sustained even though Joyce's allegiance to the UK was made possible through a fraudulently obtained passport.

[38] Offences Against the Person Act 1861, s 9.

[39] Ibid, s 57; *Trial of Earl Russell* [1901] AC 446.

[40] Merchant Shipping Act (MSA) 1995, s 281. In *R v Kelly* [1981] 2 All ER 1098, the House of Lords admitted charges under the Criminal Damage Act 1971 (then under MSA (1894), s 686(1)), against UK passengers for damage caused by them on board a Danish vessel.

[41] Sexual Offences Act 1956 and Sexual Offences (Conspiracy and Incitement) Act 1996. See P Alldridge, 'The Sexual Offences (Conspiracy and Incitement) Act 1996' [1997] *Criminal Law Review* 365.

[42] See *Re Gutierez* 24 ILR 265.

[43] *Public Prosecutor v Antoni* 32 ILR 140.

The Cypriot Supreme Court in *General Attorney of the Republic of Cyprus v Konstantinou*[44] held that the Cypriot EAW implementing legislation allowing for the surrender of nationals was unconstitutional. What was required was clearly an amendment to the Constitution, which the government proceeded to do following the Court's judgment.[45] The same conclusion was reached by the Polish Constitutional Court, which in accordance with the Constitution of the country proceeded to suspend judgment for a period of eighteen months in order to provide sufficient time for the legislature to either abrogate the implementing law or amend the Constitution.[46] On the contrary, the Areios Pagos (Hellenic Supreme Court of Cassation) held that there was nothing in the Hellenic Constitution that forbade the surrender of nationals, thus finding no constitutional impropriety.[47] Similarly, the French Conseil d'Etat ruled that the practice whereby French nationals were not extradited in the past was not founded on a constitutional principle and as a result there was need to amend the Constitution to accommodate the EAW.[48] The nationality principle of jurisdiction is firmly entrenched in the vast majority of treaties dealing with international and transnational crimes,[49] as well as in customary international law.

15.4 The Passive Personality Principle

Criminal jurisdiction under the passive personality principle is exercised by the State of the victim's nationality in situations where the crime takes place abroad.[50] It is highly doubtful whether the exercise of this type of jurisdiction satisfies the test of reasonableness, particularly where the territorial State is able and willing to prosecute the accused. The reasonableness of this jurisdictional link is further put into doubt by the abundance of mechanisms in most States that allow the victims and his or her representatives to participate as a civil or other party in the criminal proceedings.[51] There is little justification therefore for the country of the victim to bypass the territorial State. No wonder that passive personality jurisdiction was criticised in the early part of the twentieth century and was not included in the 1935 Harvard Research Draft on Jurisdiction. Even the USA, one of the most ardent contemporary supporters of the passive personality principle, was once its staunchest opponent. The leading case in support of the early negative stance of the USA is the *Cutting*

---

[44] *General Attorney of the Republic of Cyprus v Konstantinou*, Case No 294/2005, Judgment (7 Nov 2005).

[45] Communication from the Republic of Cyprus to the Council on the Decision of its Supreme Court concerning the EAW, 14281/05 (11 Nov 2005).

[46] Case No P1/05, Judgment (27 Apr 2005).

[47] Case No 591/2005, Judgment (8 Mar 2005).

[48] Case No 368–282, Judgment (26 Sep 2002); in Case No 4540, Judgment (5 Aug 2004), the Supreme Court of Appeal held that a chamber to which a preparatory inquiry had been assigned could not validly order the surrender of a French national who is the subject of an EAW for acts that do not constitute a violation of French criminal law.

[49] 1988 Convention for the Suppression of Unlawful Acts Against the Safety of Maritime Navigation, Art 6(1)(c), (1988) 27 ILM 668; 1984 Convention Against Torture and Other Cruel Inhuman or Degrading Treatment or Punishment (Torture Convention), Art 5(1)(b), 1465 UNTS 85.

[50] See GR Watson, 'The Passive Personality Principle' (1993) 28 *Texas International Law Journal* 1.

[51] See chapter 22.4.

case, where a US citizen was arrested in Mexico for a libel charge against a Mexican national.[52] The action for which the libel was charged had been committed whilst its author was in the US, but his arrest was effectuated much later during the author's subsequent trip to Mexico. The US Government vigorously opposed Mexico's claim of jurisdiction and the case was finally discontinued. State practice nonetheless reneged on its earlier position since the early 1980s with the steady rise of terrorist incidents, many of which went unpunished in the territorial or other States, whether because of the political offence exception or on account of political unwillingness.

Under these circumstances of inability or unwillingness to prosecute the passive personality principle may be deemed as a reasonable, yet auxiliary, form of criminal jurisdiction. Following the *Achille Lauro* incident which involved the unprovoked murder of a US citizen the US Congress enacted a number of statutes the effect of which was to expand the jurisdiction of its courts over persons charged with the extraterritorial murder of US nationals, where the intention of the perpetrator was to intimidate, coerce or retaliate against any government or its people.[53] Other nations followed suit and similar provisions included, among others, section 3(4) of the UK Taking of Hostages Act 1982.[54] In very little time the passive personality principle of jurisdiction became entrenched in the judicial practice of the USA, particularly following *USA v Yunis*.[55] In that case the accused had been responsible for hijacking a Jordanian airliner in Beirut with two US passengers on board. Although the exercise of prescriptive and judicial jurisdiction in that case was not in serious doubt, the fact that the accused was lured to international waters in order to be arrested may be deemed unreasonable. However, it will be recalled that Lebanon at the time was a failing State that was unable to prosecute people like Yunis, which to a large degree satisfies the *erga omnes* obligation incumbent on States to combat impunity in respect of serious international crimes.

Passive personality jurisdiction has found a solid place in multilateral treaties. It is generally provided for in two distinct forms: either by directly granting a concurrent right of jurisdiction based on the nationality of the victims,[56] or indirectly by not

---

[52] JB Moore, *Moore's Digest of International Law* (Washington DC, Government Printing Office, 1906), vol 2, at 228.

[53] Omnibus Diplomatic Security and Anti-Terrorism Act 1986, 18 USC § 2331. This particular *mens rea* component of the Act may, in fact, render such jurisdiction more akin to the protective, rather than the passive personality, principle.

[54] In *Rees v Secretary of State for the Home Department* [1986] 2 All ER 321, the House of Lords accepted the extradition to FRG of a British national accused of participating in the kidnapping of a German citizen in Bolivia.

[55] *USA v Yunis* (1991) 88 ILR 176. The prosecution of the accused was made possible on the basis of the Hostage Taking Act (HTA) 1984, 18 USC § 1203 and the Anti-Hijacking Act 1974, 49 USC App § 1472(n). Jurisdiction was predicated on the passive personality principle under § 1203(b)(1)(A); similarly, *In the Matter of Extradition of Atta* 104 ILR 52, the accused, a US national, was implicated by Israel in an attack against an Israeli bus in the West Bank resulting in the death of two civilians. The accused challenged an Israeli request for extradition but a US District Court recognised a claim under s 7(a) of the 1977 Israeli Penal Code, providing for passive personality jurisdiction.

[56] eg 1973 Convention on the Prevention and Punishment of Crimes Against Internationally Protected Persons, Including Diplomatic Agents, Art 3(1)(c), (1974) 13 ILM 42; 1984 UN Torture Convention, Art 5(1)(c); 1988 UN Convention for the Suppression of Unlawful Acts Against the Safety of Maritime Navigation, Art 6(2)(b).

excluding any criminal jurisdiction exercised in accordance with national law.[57] This latter form is necessarily secondary, as can be ascertained from its inclusion and purpose in the relevant treaties.

15.5   The Protective Principle

It is unequivocally accepted that every country is competent to take any measures that are compatible under international law in order to safeguard its national security interests. This implication of State sovereignty is the basis for the protective or security principle,[58] which to some degree overlaps with the effects doctrine that is employed to assess the reasonableness of territorial jurisdiction. The necessity for the protective principle may be justified by the lack of adequate measures in most municipal legal systems through which to criminalise harmful behaviour or prosecute persons for acts which, although committed abroad, are directed against the security of the target State.[59] The problem with this theoretical construct is that national parliaments enacting the protective principle may take a very expansive, or at least subjective, view of what is actually injurious to their national interests. For example, State A might consider that the avoidance of mandatory military service by any of its nationals residing abroad harms its national security because it decreases its defensive capacity. Would an extradition request under such circumstances and grounded on the protective principle be reasonable and consonant with human rights? A positive response is doubtful, although an extradition request on the basis of the territoriality principle would no doubt be meritorious. In contemporary international law the extent to which the *forum deprehensionis* can extradite a person on the basis of the protective principle is limited by the list of extraditable crimes in extradition treaties and fundamental human rights norms, especially the rule of non-extradition for political offences. If the accused is not in the custody of the prosecuting State, a request for extradition may be denied where no offence is deemed to have been committed in the *forum deprehensionis,* in order to safeguard its own national interests. As alliances come and go a similar situation may be accommodated through the rules of comity, by recognising the requesting State's protective jurisdictional competence.

Case law suggests that the executive and judiciary perceive the concept of 'national interests' quite broadly. Espionage and treason are classic examples of the application of the protective principle, both having traditionally been viewed as types of conduct endangering internal security. In *Re Urios,*[60] a Spanish national was convicted of espionage on account of his contacts against the security of France, albeit whilst in

---

[57] eg 1971 Montreal Convention for the Suppression of Unlawful Acts against the Safety of Civil Aviation, Art 5(3), (1971) 10 ILM 1151.

[58] See generally I Cameron, *The Protective Principle of International Criminal Jurisdiction* (Dartmouth, Ashgate, 1994).

[59] Harvard Research, Draft Convention on Jurisdiction, at 552.

[60] *Re Urios* (1920) 1 AD 107.

Spain, during the First World War. In *Joyce v DPP*[61] the House of Lords in a rather confusing judgment took the view that an alien with a fraudulently obtained British passport owed allegiance to the Crown and was liable for treason in respect of propaganda broadcasts during the Second World War, notwithstanding that nationality is irrelevant in the enforcement of the protective principle.[62] Relying on *Joyce*, the District Court of Jerusalem upheld, *inter alia,* the applicability of protective jurisdiction in the *Eichmann* case.[63] The accused was responsible for implementing Hitler's so-called Final Solution programme. After the war he fled to Argentina but was subsequently abducted by Israeli agents with a view to standing trial in Israel under the 1951 Nazi and Nazi Collaborators Law for war crimes, crimes against the Jewish people and crimes against humanity. The judgment of the District Court, which was subsequently affirmed by the Israeli Supreme Court,[64] held that a country whose 'vital interests' and ultimately its existence are threatened, such as in the case of the extermination of the Jewish people, has a right to assume jurisdiction to try the offenders.[65] The application of the protective principle in the *Eichmann* case is exceptional, given that the State of Israel did not exist at the time of the Jewish persecutions.

The protective principle was employed by western European States during the Cold War in cases involving enlistment or espionage which resulted in a threat to the interests of allied countries. In *Re van den Plas,*[66] for example, a Belgian national was held liable for acts of espionage against Belgium by a French tribunal on the basis that his conduct was injurious to the interests of both France and Belgium. US jurisprudence has perceived the ambit of 'national interests' under the protective principle as encompassing conduct that does not necessarily require a direct or actual effect within the territory of the USA.[67] This has had considerable impact on cases involving the breach of US immigration law in situations where the breach was perpetrated outside US territory.[68] This has been justified by the fact that US courts have approached the issue of immigration as vital to the homeland security of their nation.[69] Applying the protective principle in cases involving the extraterritorial

---

[61]   *Joyce v DPP* [1946] AC 347, at 372, *per* Lord Jowitt. Jurisdiction was also sustained on the basis of the active personality principle. See also H Lauterpacht, 'Allegiance, Diplomatic Protection and Criminal Jurisdiction over Aliens' (1947) 9 *Cambridge Law Journal* 330.

[62]   Nonetheless, in *R v Neumann* (1949) 3 SA 1238, a South African Special Court convicted a South African national of treason on account of his participation on the German side during the Second World War. The judgment of the court stated that jurisdiction was obtained due to the impairment of national security caused by the act of treason.

[63]   *AG of the Government of Israel v Eichmann* (1961) 36 ILR 5.

[64]   *Eichmann v Israel* (1962) 36 ILR 277.

[65]   See H Silving, 'In *re Eichmann:* A Dilemma of Law and Morality' (1961) 55 *American Journal of International Law* 307; JES Fawcett, 'The *Eichmann* Case' (1962) 38 *British Yearbook of International Law* 181.

[66]   *Re van den Plas* 22 ILR 205; Akehurst, Jurisdiction, at 158, argues that such decisions are defensible only where the accused are nationals of allied powers.

[67]   *USA v Pizzarusso* (1968) 388 F 2d 8, at 11; *USA v Keller* (1978) 451 F Supp 631, at 635.

[68]   *Rocha v USA* (1961) 288 F 2d 545; *USA v Pizzarusso* (1968) 388 F 2d 8, at 11; *Giles v Tumminello* 38 ILR 120.

[69]   See Restatement (Third) of the Foreign Relations Law of the USA 1986, § 402(3).

apprehension of drug-traffickers[70] or suspected terrorists[71] has proved less arduous, since a threat to security or other national interests can be easily discerned and proven. Certainly, the use of the protective principle to assume jurisdiction in respect of attacks against one's embassy buildings abroad is at the heart of its intended application.[72] It is generally agreed that in order to restrict possible abuse the use of statute-based protective jurisdiction should be limited to incidents where both significant national interests are at stake and, moreover, where its application in each particular case does not cause a third State to incur harm.

15.6 Universal Jurisdiction

The four forms of jurisdiction discussed above require some kind of link or connection with the prosecuting State, whether based on the territory where the offence took place, the nationality of the perpetrator or the victim, or the threat to the interests of the State concerned. The application of universal jurisdiction to a particular offence does not require any link whatsoever and all States are empowered to assert their authority over those offences that are subject to the universality principle.[73] Scholars generally distinguish between 'pure' or 'absolute' and 'conditional' universal jurisdiction. While neither requires a link with the prosecuting State the former does not necessitate the presence of the accused therein, where its conditional counterpart does.[74]

Due to the broad extraterritorial competence encompassed by the exercise of the principle of universal jurisdiction it is reasonable that it be applicable only to a limited number of offences. Besides the range of offences subject to universal jurisdiction this section examines also its legal bases and whether it is applicable where the accused is not in the hands of the prosecuting State (so-called universal jurisdiction *in absentia*). It should be stated from the outset that the exercise of universal jurisdiction has received strong condemnation from those States that perceive it as a direct attack on their political institutions. The African Union, for example, found it unacceptable that European prosecutors have engaged in a widespread campaign to indict African officials, while African nations have generally

---

[70] *Rivard v USA* (1967) 375 F 2d 882; *USA v Bright-Barker* (1986) 784 F 2d 161.

[71] *USA v Yunis* 88 ILR 176; Omnibus Diplomatic Security and Anti-Terrorism Act 1986, 18 USC § 2331.

[72] *USA v Bin Laden* [2000] 92 F Supp 2d 189, 197.

[73] See K Randal, 'Universal Jurisdiction under International Law' (1988) 66 *Texas Law Review* 785; ES Kobrick, 'The *Ex Post Facto* Prohibition and the Exercise of Universal Jurisdiction Over International Crimes' (1987) 87 *Columbia Law Review* 1515.

[74] Other more subtle categorisations have also been attempted in the scholarly literature. See L Reydams, *Universal Jurisdiction: International and Municipal Legal Perspectives* (Oxford, Oxford University Press, 2003) 28–42, who distinguishes between: a) general cooperative universality, which applies to all serious offences recognised by nations, whether domestic or international; b) limited cooperative universality, which applies only to international crimes, and; c) unilateral limited universality, which corresponds to the contemporary pure or conditional model.

stayed out of the universal jurisdiction game.[75] As a result, despite the generous jurisdictional laws of most European nations the politics of universal jurisdiction do not allow States to become arch-predators, because there may well be a price to pay somewhere down the international relations road. Prosecutorial and judicial practice thus tends to be inconsistent from case to case even within the same nation.

Crimes under international law have customarily attracted universal jurisdiction in two independent ways: (a) on the basis of the repugnant nature and scale of the conduct, as is the case with grave breaches of humanitarian law[76] and crimes against humanity;[77] or (b) as a result of the inadequacy of domestic law and enforcement in respect of unlawful conduct committed in locations not subject to the authority of any State, such as the high seas. The extension of universal jurisdiction over piracy under international law (piracy *jure gentium*) has substantially contributed to combating this scourge.[78] It cannot be overemphasised that these two bases for attracting universal jurisdiction are independent and conjunctive. The practical significance of this observation is that in order to discern whether or not an international crime is subject to universal jurisdiction one must first ascertain which of the two bases, nature and scale, or that of the *locus delicti commissi* is appropriate. It is not unusual for national courts to confuse or conflate the two legal bases. Thus, in *Re Röhrig*[79] a Dutch Special Cassation Court assimilated the legal basis for war crimes to that of piracy. The existence, however, of any of the two aforementioned legal bases does not automatically guarantee that the conduct in question is susceptible to universal jurisdiction. The missing ingredient is global consent in favour of this type of jurisdiction. Courts have made laudable efforts to hide the absence of express consent in respect of a number of international crimes and that is why the statements of national courts do not always constitute the most appropriate authority for ascertaining the precise state of universal jurisdiction at any given time. In *Re Pinochet (No 3)*[80] Lord Millet succinctly argued that international crimes attract universal jurisdiction where they violate a rule of *jus cogens*, are serious and perpetrated on such a large scale that they can be regarded as an attack against international legal order.[81] This statement, correct though it may be, lacks a most essential ingredient: the consent of States to subject an offence to universal jurisdiction through treaty or

---

[75] Decision of the Report of the Commission on the Abuse of the Principle of Universal Jurisdiction of 1 July 2008, AU Doc Assembly/AU/Dec.199 (XI). This culminated in an EU-AU ministerial meeting wherein it was agreed to set up a technical committee that would make recommendations about the principle and how best it can be used between the nations of the two continents. This led to the drafting of the AU-EU Expert Report on the Principle of Universal Jurisdiction, Doc 8672/1/09/REV 1 (16 April 2009).

[76] 1949 Geneva Conventions and both Additional Geneva Protocols 1977 to the 1949 Conventions. See also C Joyner, 'Arresting Impunity: The Case for Universal Jurisdiction in Bringing War Criminals to Accountability' (1996) 59 *Law and Contemporary Problems* 153.

[77] *Federation Nationale de Deportes et Internes Resistants et Patriotes and Others v Barbie* 78 ILR 125, at 130; see also *Re Pinochet* (1999) 93 *American Journal of International Law* 700, Brussels Tribunal of First Instance, 702–03.

[78] In *Re Piracy Jure Gentium* [1934] AC 586, Lord Macmillan confirmed the application of universal jurisdiction over piracy *jure gentium* and noted that a pirate 'is no longer a national, but *hostis humani generis* and as such he is justiciable by any State anywhere', at 589.

[79] *Re Röhrig* 17 ILR 393, at 395.

[80] *R v Bow Street Metropolitan Stipendiary Magistrate and Others ex p Pinochet Ugarte (No 3)* [1999] 2 All ER 97

[81] Ibid, *Pinochet* judgment, at 177.

custom. The vast majority of international crimes violate *jus cogens* norms on a large scale. Can it seriously be contended that all States parties to these international criminal law conventions intended to confer universal jurisdiction over the relevant crimes? Furthermore, the legal position of non-States parties to these conventions is unknown and cannot be assumed in the absence of sufficient evidence. This global consent must be expressly demonstrated in the relevant treaty or in the practice of States giving rise to a customary rule.

I will first deal with treaty-based universal jurisdiction by contrasting the language of the various provisions. Article 105 of UNCLOS sets out the jurisdictional competence of member States in relation to piracy as follows:

> On the high seas, or in any other place outside the jurisdiction of any State, *every State* may seize a pirate ship or aircraft, or a ship or aircraft taken by piracy and under the control of pirates, and arrest the persons and seize the property on board [emphasis added].

Notice now the difference in wording in Article 99 of the same Convention, which prohibits the transport of slaves on the high seas:

> Every State shall take effective measures to prevent and punish the transport of slaves in ships authorised to fly *its flag* and to prevent the unlawful use of *its flag* for that purpose [emphasis added].

Although it is obvious that Article 99 renders slave-trafficking on the seas an international crime, whether by criminalising it anew or by acknowledging its existence, it does not confer the right to employ universal jurisdiction, regardless of the undoubtedly repugnant character of slavery or its perpetration on the high seas. On the contrary, Article 105 clearly confers universal jurisdiction on States parties with regard to piracy *jure gentium*. Treaty-based universal jurisdiction materialises expressly only in respect of grave breaches of international humanitarian law and piracy *jure gentium*.[82] As for non-parties to UNCLOS and the 1949 Geneva Conventions, the *jus cogens* character of grave breaches and piracy precludes any persistent objection as to their criminal nature and conferral of universal jurisdiction.[83]

The fact that a particular crime, whether international or transnational in nature, does not attract express treaty-based universal jurisdiction need not necessarily mean that in the passage of time the international community cannot subject it to universality on the basis of customary law. Thus, despite the absence of universality in the relevant instruments, it is beyond doubt that war crimes other than grave

---

[82] I am, thus, in disagreement with the US Court of Appeals Judgment in *USA v Yunis (No 3)* 88 ILR 176, at 182, that hijacking is a clear case of an international crime endowed with universal jurisdiction; similarly, Principle 2(1) of the Princeton Principles of Universal Jurisdiction lists the following as serious international crimes subject to universal jurisdiction: piracy, slavery, war crimes, crimes against peace, crimes against humanity, genocide and torture, without necessarily excluding it with regard to other offences. The Princeton Principles, the final version of which was adopted in 2001, were formulated through a series of meetings by a group of experts claiming to represent current international law.

[83] 1969 Vienna Convention on the Law of Treaties, Art 53, 1155 UNTS 331; see also J Charney, 'The Persistent Objector Rule and the Development of Customary International Law' (1985) 56 *British Yearbook of International Law* 1.

breaches,[84] crimes against humanity,[85] genocide,[86] torture and the most serious forms of slavery are currently subject to universal jurisdiction.

Equally, in the absence of protests or an international prohibition to the contrary States may reasonably confer pure or conditional universal jurisdiction upon themselves under their domestic law. This is not always the direct result of a unilateral act. In fact, relevant international treaties encourage parties to assert expansive jurisdiction with respect to the offences contemplated therein, very much akin to universal jurisdiction. This is evident for example with Article 5(1) of the 1984 UN Torture Convention, which primarily establishes territorial,[87] nationality[88] and passive personality jurisdiction.[89] Article 5 further confers jurisdiction on:

> (2) Each State party [to] *take such measures as may be necessary to establish its jurisdiction* over such offences in cases where the alleged offender is present in any territory under its jurisdiction and it does not extradite him to any of the States mentioned in paragraph 1 of this Article.

> (3) This Convention *does not exclude any criminal jurisdiction exercised in accordance with internal law* [emphasis added].

Article 5(2) and (3) thus indirectly permits the exercise of universal jurisdiction with respect to the incorporated domestic offence of torture. It is not clear whether such universal jurisdiction is primary or secondary to those mentioned in Article 5(1). In terms of international comity and reasonableness, at least, the *locus delicti* State enjoys primary jurisdiction, unless it is genuinely unable or unwilling to prosecute. Even so, there is no obligation under treaty or customary law on the State with the weaker jurisdictional link to surrender an accused over whom it has no nexus to the State with the stronger nexus, particularly if by doing so it subjects the accused to potential human rights violations. As a result, some countries have exceptionally chosen to employ universal jurisdiction in respect of common crimes committed abroad. In the *Austrian Universal Jurisdiction* case[90] the accused had fled his native Yugoslavia and was convicted in Austria for offences committed there. While serving his sentence Yugoslavia requested his extradition for common crimes perpetrated while he was still a resident of that country, but Austria refused because the accused was in danger of being subjected to political persecution in Yugoslavia. Instead, the Supreme Court of Austria argued that its judicial authorities could exercise universal

---

[84] *Public Prosecutor v Djajic* (German) (1998) 92 *American Journal of International Law* 528; *Public Prosecutor v Grabec* (Swiss) (1998) 92 *American Journal of International Law* 78.

[85] *AG of Israel v Eichmann* (1961) 36 ILR 5; *In re Demjanjuk,* (1986) 457 US 1016.

[86] *Re Pinochet* (1999) 93 *American Journal of International Law* 690, Spanish National Court, Criminal Division (Audencia Nacional). Art 23(4) of the Spanish Judicial Branch Act of 1985 (Ley Orgánica del Poder Judicial) establishes universal jurisdiction of Spanish courts over genocide, terrorism, piracy, unlawful seizure of aircraft, as well as any other international crime which must be prosecuted in Spain. In *Re Munyeshyaka*, Cour de Cassation, Bull Crim (1998), 3–8, the French Court of Cassation upheld jurisdiction over genocide, not on the basis of universality but in accordance with its ICTR implementing statute. In essence, it seems to support the typolatrical view that since universal jurisdiction is not prescribed in the Genocide Convention it cannot be applied in the French legal system.

[87] 1984 Torture Convention, Art 5(1)(a).

[88] Ibid, Art 5(1)(b).

[89] Ibid, Art 5(1)(c).

[90] *Austrian Universal Jurisdiction* case 28 ILR 341.

jurisdiction over the alleged conduct of the accused in Yugoslavia on the basis that it would be punishable under Austrian law if committed in Austria. The exercise of such jurisdiction was predicated on then Article 40 of the Austrian Criminal Code, which provided that where competent foreign authorities refuse or are unable to prosecute this task is to be undertaken by Austrian courts in accordance with local criminal law.[91] In similar fashion, in the *Universal Jurisdiction over Drug Offences* case,[92] the FRG Federal Supreme Court upheld universal jurisdiction over drug-trafficking offences committed abroad on the basis of Article 6(5) of the 1998 Federal Criminal Code, which rendered the criminal law of that country applicable to drug-trafficking abroad regardless of the law of the *locus delicti commissi*. The Supreme Court found Article 6(5) compatible with international law in the absence of a contrary special treaty provision, particularly as it opined that it implemented Article 36 of the 1961 Single Convention on Narcotic Drugs, which calls on States parties to ensure that every relevant offence receives appropriate punishment.[93]

There is a further natural limitation to the universality espoused in Article 5(2) and (3) of the Torture Convention, which is not expressly encountered in piracy *jure gentium* or the grave breaches provisions. This is the requirement that the alleged offender actually be in the hands of the prosecuting State. The adherents to the conditional universality principle require the presence of the accused on the territory of the prosecuting country as a precondition for the exercise of universal jurisdiction.[94] A different conclusion, it is claimed, risks trials *in absentia* and violation of the double jeopardy principle. Yet, both the pure and conditional universality schools of thought converge in the belief that preliminary investigations *in absentia* are welcome because they allow the collection and preservation of crucial evidence with a view to future trials.[95] Where the alleged offender is apprehended in a State that is unwilling to prosecute that State must extradite the accused – subject to bilateral or multilateral extradition arrangements – to a country with a sufficiently close connection to the offence.[96] This should not be considered a strict rule, but rather the product of comity or good international relations. As long as an extradition is lawful under international law and takes into consideration the rights of the accused it is subject to no other limitation.

Finally, there is significant debate as to whether universal jurisdiction is an entitlement, an obligation, or both. State practice and the treaties within which it is

---

[91]   Ibid, 341–42.

[92]   *Universal Jurisdiction over Drug Offences* case 28 ILR 166.

[93]   In similar reasoning it was held in *USA v Marino-Garcia* (1982) 679 F 2d 1373 that USC § 955(a), s 21 gives the federal Government criminal jurisdiction over all stateless vessels on the high seas engaged in the distribution of controlled substances, noting that this exercise of jurisdiction is not contrary to international law.

[94]   See, for example, *H v Public Prosecutor* [*Afghan Asylum Seekers* case], Hague Court of Appeal Judgment (29 Jan 2007), holding that universal jurisdiction cannot be applied *in absentia*.

[95]   See A Poels, 'Universal Jurisdiction in Absentia' (2005) 23 *Netherlands Quarterly of Human Rights* 65. In the *Guatemalan Generals* case, the Spanish Constitutional Tribunal (Judgment of 26 Sep 2005) held that the Ley Orgánica del Poder Judicial (LOPJ), which provides the courts of that country with extraterritorial jurisdiction over crimes such as genocide, torture and terrorism should be construed as permitting unconditional universal jurisdiction. Although Spanish law does not permit trials *in absentia* the Tribunal did not find this to constitute a distinct ground of jurisdiction, thus paving the way for the permissibility of extradition requests in cases where the accused was not on Spanish territory.

[96]   Art 8(4), UN Torture Convention.

contained clearly demonstrate the existence of an entitlement, irrespective if it gives rise to a plethora of competing claims. In fact, the concurrence of multiple universal jurisdiction claims fulfils the very aim of the principle, which is to combat impunity and extinguish all safe havens. State practice, however, is divisive with regard to the obligatory nature of universal jurisdiction. My opinion is that no such obligation exists and this is principally justified by the cautious and conservative approach of the vast majority of States in prosecuting crimes with which they have no link. This conclusion may stand in contrast to the laudable writings of many jurists and the *erga omnes* nature of international crimes, but contemporary reality cannot be ignored. At the very least, however, the apprehending State is under an obligation to extradite persons accused of crimes subject to universal jurisdiction if it chooses not to institute criminal proceedings. This conservatism in the recognition of a right of universal jurisdiction has manifested itself in the course of several important judicial proceedings. A narrow view was confirmed, albeit *obiter dicta,* by the ICJ in the *Belgian Arrest Warrant* case. In that case a Belgian Investigating Judge issued in April 2000 an international arrest warrant against the then incumbent Congolese Foreign Minister, on the basis of the Belgian 1993 Law Relative to the Repression of Grave Breaches, charging him for grave breaches in violation of the 1949 Geneva Conventions, Protocols I and II of 1977, as well as crimes against humanity. The ICJ did not view universal jurisdiction as central to the issue, but in his Separate Opinion, Judge Guillaume took a narrow view of universal jurisdiction, finding it applicable in limited cases, and certainly not *in absentia.*[97] Equally, in *Jones and Others v Kingdom of Saudi Arabia* the House of Lords held that no evidence exists whereby States recognise an international obligation to exercise universal jurisdiction over claims arising from breaches of *jus cogens*, nor is there any compelling judicial opinion that they should.[98]

15.7   Jurisdiction with Respect to Crimes Against Civil Aviation

The widespread seizure and hijacking of civil aircraft in the 1960s, mainly for political purposes it has to be said, culminated in the adoption of several treaties regulating specific aspects of air terrorism. These agreements do not abandon the customary rule granting criminal jurisdiction to the subjacent State; they merely supplement it by conferring competence also to third countries that entertain a pertinent link with the incident. The first major attempt to combat aerial terrorism was undertaken by the 1963 Tokyo Convention on Offences and Certain Other Acts Committed on Board Aircraft.[99] Article 4 of this instrument endowed the country of registration of the aircraft with competence over the prescribed offences and further authorised the employment of jurisdiction under the nationality (including the State of the lessee where the aircraft was leased without a crew) and passive personality

---

[97]   *Arrest Warrant of 11 April 2000* case (DRC v Belgium), Judgment (14 Feb 2002), (2002) ICJ Reports 3, Separate Opinion of Judge Guillaume, para 9.
[98]   *Jones and Others v United Kingdom of Saudi Arabia* [2006] UKHL 26, *per* Lord Bingham, para 27.
[99]   704 UNTS 219.

principles. Moreover, jurisdiction was also granted to the country where the accused took refuge following the consummation of the offence. Similarly, Article 4(1) of the 1970 Hague Convention for the Suppression of Unlawful Seizure of Aircraft (1970 Hague Convention)[100] grants criminal jurisdiction over hijacking and associated acts of violence to the country of registration of the aircraft, the State of landing (when the accused is on board)[101] and the State of the lessee's nationality. Paragraph 2 of Article 4 permits the exercise of criminal jurisdiction by any State on whose territory the alleged offender is present, but only in respect of acts of hijacking, while paragraph 3 allows the exercise of criminal jurisdiction on any domestic legal basis. As a result of this broad provision many scholars contend that the Hague Convention confers a species of universal jurisdiction.

The 1971 Montreal Convention for the Suppression of Unlawful Acts against the Safety of Civil Aviation[102] adds two new jurisdictional elements in comparison to the 1970 Hague Convention. First, it covers relevant acts perpetrated not only 'in flight', but also 'in service'.[103] Secondly, because the objective of the 1971 Montreal Convention was to supplement the provisions of the 1970 Hague Convention in order to encompass beyond acts of hijacking also armed attacks, sabotage and other forms of violence and intimidation against civil aviation, Article 5(1)(a) thereof provides a further ground of jurisdiction when the offence is committed in the territory of a contracting State. Overall, the aerial terrorism conventions provide a wide array of jurisdictional and cooperation possibilities to States parties.

15.8   Foreign and Multinational Armed Forces Abroad

Since time immemorial foreign armed forces have been allowed to transit or station on the territory of allied or other States by reason of mutual agreement. Where a State allows a foreign military contingent passage or sojourn on its territory it does so, in the words of Justice Marshall in the *Schooner Exchange* case, under an implied waiver of criminal and other jurisdiction.[104] The rationale for such a waiver by the receiving State is justified for the maintenance of the efficiency and integrity of the foreign contingent.[105] In the absence of a specific agreement between the receiving and transiting/sending States it is fair to argue that immunity from the receiving State's criminal jurisdiction is not absolute – such immunity in any case being functional. Under customary international law the sending State typically exercises exclusive jurisdiction over internal disciplinary or other offences committed by its

---

[100] S Shubber, 'Aircraft Hijacking under the Hague Convention 1970 – A New Regime?' (1973) 22 *International & Comparative Law Quarterly* 687, at 714.

[101] This was the basis of jurisdiction asserted by a Dutch District Court regarding the hijacking of a British aircraft whose crew was forced to land in Amsterdam. *Public Prosecutor v SHT* (1987) 74 ILR 162.

[102] 974 UNTS 177.

[103] Under the 1971 Montreal Convention, Art 2(b), an aircraft is considered to be in service from the beginning of pre-flight preparation until 24 hours after landing.

[104] *Schooner Exchange v McFaddon* (1812) 7 Cranch 116. This case concerned the passage or transiting of foreign troops.

[105] *Wright v Cantrell* 12 AD 37; *Chow Hung Ching v R* (1948) 77 CLR 449.

forces when on duty, while the receiving State enjoys jurisdiction in respect of all other offences.[106] In cases where the distinction is not clear cut in respect of a particular out of duty incident, Brownlie suggests that jurisdiction should be assessed on the basis of the principles of interest or of substantial connection.[107]

Notwithstanding the above general considerations it is usual for States to regulate such matters through the conclusion of special agreements that make room for detailed arrangements. The 1951 NATO Status of Forces Agreement (NATO SOFA)[108] provides in general for the exercise of concurrent jurisdiction over the civilian and military personnel of a NATO visiting force. The sending State typically enjoys primary criminal jurisdiction over offences and persons falling within the ambit of its military law, as well as over any act or omission done in the performance of official duty, whereas the receiving State entertains jurisdiction with respect to persons and offences under its own municipal law, which in any event is construed in narrow terms. In *Public Prosecutor v Ashby* a US Army aeroplane, part of a NATO contingent in Italy, crashed in a residential area causing substantial material damage and killing several civilians.[109] The Italian court held that in cases where jurisdiction is concurrent priority goes to the sending State, especially in situations involving an offence that is directed solely against the interests of that State,[110] or committed in the performance of official duty.[111] In the case at hand, the offence in question, brought about by a flight in the course of a training mission was determined to have arisen in the performance of official duty under Article VII, § 3(b)(ii) of the 1951 NATO SOFA. In practice, it is unlikely that the host State will prosecute a member of a foreign military contingent even in respect of a common offence for which it would otherwise enjoy territorial jurisdiction. In all likelihood, and despite public local sentiment, it would surrender the accused to his national authorities to stand court martial.

As for UN peacekeeping forces, other than those constituted as a means of enforcement action, deployment is based only on the consent of the receiving State, unless there is an absence of government authority to grant such consent, as was the case with Somalia in 1993. In the post-1945 era peacekeeping agreements have secured broad terms of functional immunity for UN forces.[112] As a matter of internal organisation, with respect to UN and other multinational forces, jurisdiction over offences committed in the context of such operations remains with the State of the nationality of the accused. This represents well established customary law[113] and is recognised in section 4 of the UN Secretary General's Bulletin on Observance by

---

[106] Brownlie, *Principles*, at 374.

[107] Brownlie, ibid, at 374.

[108] (1954 Supp) 48 *American Journal of International Law* 83; H Rouse and GB Baldwin, 'The Exercise of Criminal Jurisdiction under the NATO Status of Forces Agreement' (1957) 51 *American Journal of International Law* 29; J Woodliffe, 'The Stationing of Foreign Armed Forces Abroad in Peacetime' (1994) 43 *International & Comparative Law Quarterly* 443. See also the UK Visiting Forces Act 1952.

[109] *Public Prosecutor v Ashby* (1999) 93 *American Journal of International Law* 219.

[110] Art VII, § 3(a)(i) of the 1951 NATO Agreement.

[111] Art VII, § 3(a)(ii), ibid.

[112] See DS Wijewardane, 'Criminal Jurisdiction over Visiting Forces with Special Reference to International Force' (1965–66) 41 *British Yearbook of International Law* 122.

[113] I Bantekas, 'The Contemporary Law of Superior Responsibility' (1999) 93 *American Journal of International Law* 573, at 579.

United Nations Forces of International Humanitarian Law, which subjects all infractions to domestic prosecution or courts martial.[114] This principle of exclusive nationality-based jurisdiction permeating UN military contingents does not necessarily apply to the territorial State, unless it has agreed to the contrary. As a result, it is in theory free to prosecute offences committed by UN personnel on its territory as well as surrender the accused persons to the ICC or third States. This was precisely why the USA sought to immunise its military personnel from possible, although in practice wholly unlikely, ICC referrals by agreeing so-called impunity agreements with ICC member States.[115]

15.9   International Criminal Jurisdiction

The five principles discussed above address the ambit of the prescriptive and judicial competence of States as this emanates from treaties, custom and national legislation. Such jurisdiction, especially when it is concurrent with that of other nations, is subject to a myriad of limitations. International criminal tribunals are not susceptible to all these limitations. Their competence is derived from their constitutive instrument and is not at all restricted by the jurisdictional principles and constraints applicable to municipal courts (ie the five bases of jurisdiction). This form of jurisdiction is termed 'international'. This is natural, given that international tribunals do not possess territory, cannot confer nationality or residency rights and do not have national security interests. Nonetheless, in a very broad, non-legal, sense they exercise the raison d'étre of universal jurisdiction; ie that international crimes should not go unpunished and that all States have a right to prosecute. Moreover, another seminal difference between common jurisdiction and the jurisdiction of international tribunals is that their mandate may authorise them to disregard fundamental principles of international law, which domestic courts and legislatures cannot. This is certainly true in respect of Head of State immunity.[116]

Both the International Criminal Tribunal for the Former Yugoslavia (ICTY) and Rwanda (ICTR) are products of Chapter VII Security Council resolutions. In theory the Security Council could have prescribed a very wide jurisdictional competence for these ad hoc tribunals, whether *ratione materia* or *ratione temporis,* which would otherwise have been *ultra vires* had it been prescribed by national courts. A similarly broad jurisdictional ambit was available to States parties to the International Criminal Court (ICC) if they had so chosen in their agreement on the Court's Statute; yet, its competences are much more restricted in comparison to the ad hoc tribunals. Since every international tribunal is a self-contained system its jurisdictional powers can only be limited by its constitutive instrument, but only to the extent

---

[114] Secretary General's Bulletin ST/SG-B/1999/13 (6 Aug 1999), reprinted in (1999) 836 *International Review of the Red Cross* 812.

[115] See chapter 19.7.

[116] *SCSL Prosecutor v Taylor*, Appeals Chamber Judgment (31 May 2004), para 51. I do not take the view, however, that the Special Court for Sierra Leone (SCSL) is an international tribunal, but a domestic tribunal with international elements. See also, *ICTY Prosecutor v Milošević*, Decision on the Preliminary Motions, Kosovo (8 Nov 2001), paras 26–34, rejecting the validity of Head of State immunity.

that such limitation does not endanger its judicial character.[117] Although the ICTY is a subsidiary organ of the Security Council the Appeals Chamber in the *Tadić Jurisdiction* case correctly pointed out that it is a special kind of subsidiary organ, a tribunal endowed with judicial functions.[118] By implication of its judicial nature a tribunal enjoys a certain degree of 'inherent' or 'incidental' jurisdiction. One element of this inherent jurisdiction, which is exercisable even if not mentioned in its Statute, relates to an international tribunal's competence to determine its own jurisdiction.[119] The ICTY has further held that it may, in the exercise of its incidental jurisdiction, examine the legality of its establishment by the Security Council, but only so far as this is needed to ascertain the scope of its 'primary' jurisdiction.[120]

It has already been pointed out that even where a treaty delimits the prescriptive competence of States there is no clear jurisdictional hierarchy when it comes to prioritising concurrent claims. International tribunals, with the exception of the ICC, do not face such conflicts. Article 9(1) of the ICTY Statute provides for concurrent jurisdiction with national criminal courts. However, paragraph 2 of Article 9 emphatically establishes primacy for the ICTY, by stating that:

> The International Tribunal shall have primacy over national courts. At any stage of the procedure, the International Tribunal may formally request national courts to defer to the competence of the International Tribunal in accordance with the present Statute and the Rules of Procedure and Evidence of the International Tribunal.

The ICC does not enjoy the primacy of the ad hoc tribunals. The ICC's jurisdiction is premised on the concept of complementarity with national courts, which means that it can only assume jurisdiction over a situation if it is referred to it by the relevant State. Exceptionally, it may override the primary authority of States parties where a State is shielding an accused,[121] or is otherwise genuinely unable to carry out an investigation or prosecution.[122] The Court is also competent to entertain a case where the Security Council refers that case to the Court, irrespective of the protestations of the territorial State. The ICC's jurisdiction is constrained even further by the operation of Article 124, according to which a State party may declare its non-acceptance of the Court's jurisdiction for a period of seven years after the entry into force of the Statute, with respect to war crimes alleged to have been committed by its nationals or on its territory.[123]

The difference in the powers vested in the ICTY and ICC can be explained by the fact that the former was the product of a Security Council resolution under Chapter VII of the UN Charter, whereas the ICC was established as a result of a multilateral

---

[117] *ICTY Prosecutor v Tadić*, Appeals Chamber Decision on the Defence Motion for Interlocutory Appeal on Jurisdiction (2 Oct 1995), para 11; see also *ICTR Prosecutor v Kanyabashi*, Trial Chamber Decision on the Defence Motion for Interlocutory Appeal on the Jurisdiction of Trial Chamber I (3 Jun 1999); I Bantekas, 'Head of State Immunity in the Light of Multiple Legal Regimes and Non-Self Contained System Theories: Theoretical Analysis of ICC Third Party Jurisdiction against the Background of the 2003 Iraq War' (2005) 10 *Journal of Conflict and Security Law* 21.

[118] Ibid, *Tadić* Appeals Decision on jurisdiction, para 15.

[119] *Advisory Opinion on the Effect of Awards of Compensation Made by the United Nations Administrative Tribunal* (1954) ICJ Reports 47, at 51. This power is termed 'Kompetenz Kompetenz'.

[120] *Tadić* Appeals Decision on jurisdiction, para 21.

[121] ICC Statute, Arts 17(1)(a), (b) and 2(a).

[122] Ibid, Art 17(1)(a), (b).

[123] For an analytical discussion on the jurisdiction of the ICC, see chapter 19.

treaty, which necessarily entailed a great deal of compromise. The enforcement jurisdiction of the ICTY under Article 29 of its Statute is thus significantly enhanced, since it has the power, *inter alia,* to order the arrest and surrender of persons and the production of documents irrespective of the nationality of persons or the location of documents or other evidentiary material.[124] Because international tribunals are limited by their Statute the application of the *Lotus* rule by national courts and legislatures, whereby national criminal jurisdiction under any basis is permissible subject only to a contrary binding rule of international law, does not apply to the subject matter jurisdiction of the ad hoc tribunals or of the ICC. The subject matter jurisdiction of these international tribunals cannot be extended through an expansive construction of their statutes under the jurisdictional principles applicable to municipal courts, nor as part of these courts' incidental jurisdiction.

International jurisdiction is enjoyed by tribunals established through inter-State agreements and Security Council resolutions. Unlike the International Military Tribunal at Nuremberg (IMT) the various subsequent tribunals established by the Allies in Germany after 1945 were not the product of treaty making. Despite the application of international law by some of them, their legal basis was domestic legislation, such as the Allied Control Council Law for Germany No 10, the British Royal Warrant and various US Theatre Regulations and Directives. These tribunals were, therefore, obliged to observe the internationally acceptable rules pertaining to the exercise of national judicial jurisdiction.

---

[124] *ICTY Prosecutor v Blaškić,* Appeals Chamber Judgment on the Request of the Republic of Croatia for Review of the Decision of Trial Chamber II (29 Oct 1997).

16

International Cooperation in Criminal Matters

16.1 Introduction

Cooperation in criminal matters is crucial not only to prosecuting authorities but also the accused. Lack of effective cooperation by one State may significantly hamper the defence of an accused where he or she is seeking exculpatory material that the requested State is not willing to hand over. This in turn precludes equality of arms between the prosecution and the accused. The globalisation of crime and movement of persons has given rise not only to transnational crime but has necessarily meant that important evidence required for an otherwise domestic offence may lie in a third State. It is for this purpose that a variety of international instruments have appeared through which the collection of evidence and surrender of accused persons can best be facilitated. This chapter examines mutual legal assistance *stricto sensu* (involving exchange of evidence and information), prisoner transfer agreements, extradition agreements and the various aberrations to these modes of cooperation.

16.2 Mutual Legal Assistance *Stricto Sensu*

In their conduct of criminal investigations judicial and prosecutorial authorities require a plethora of evidence and information. Some of this is directly relevant to an investigation, whereas other material may turn out to be inadmissible or simply irrelevant. Where the information and evidence sought is situated within a single State the authorities therein can employ the panoply of their criminal procedure laws and thus gain access to it, provided it conforms to this body of law. Where, however, a crime is of a transnational nature and the evidence is known to be in a different jurisdiction the prosecuting authorities must rely on their counterparts in that jurisdiction to secure it. There is no entitlement to such evidence and moreover States cannot conduct investigations on the territory of other nations, as this constitutes a violation of sovereignty that gives rise to State responsibility. As a result, access to information and evidence located in a foreign jurisdiction must be predicated on appropriate agreements of a general nature or ad hoc arrangements, both of which are binding. Whatever form these assume they are known as mutual legal assistance (MLA) agreements.

The most basic, yet ad hoc, MLA arrangement concerns the employment of letters rogatory. These do not constitute formal treaties, albeit they encompass both an offer and a consideration on the basis of two distinct acts and therefore possess the legal attributes of treaties, albeit only after the offer has been accepted. Prior to this, the decision as to whether to accept the request is predicated solely on considerations of comity. Letters rogatory are used in the absence of a standing MLA treaty between two nations, albeit the process itself may be stipulated in a MLA treaty;[1] this is exceptional in contemporary practice. They consist of a letter issued by a judge or other public authority (eg prosecutor or the police) and addressed to one's counterparts in a different nation with the aim of securing evidence or of imposing other measures required for an ongoing investigation in the requesting State. These are submitted to the requested State's intended addressees through diplomatic channels, but the request is open to refusal on a variety of grounds that pertain to the law of the requested country (eg bank secrecy, violation of public order, inconsistency with double criminality and others). Moreover, the entire process could be extremely lengthy, by which time the required evidence or information may be lost or otherwise become unavailable or unnecessary to the prosecuting authorities. It is evident therefore that a more predictable, stable and less cumbersome mechanism is required. Because a multilateral mechanism of this nature requires mutual trust between contracting States for a very long time the adoption of bilateral MLA treaties prevailed in international practice. Only member States to the Council of Europe had achieved in 1959 to negotiate and adopt a rudimentary multilateral MLA convention. Since then these types of agreements have not only flourished, but elaborate MLA provisions are consistently inserted in multilateral treaties dealing with transnational and international crimes; in fact, this is now the norm. MLA agreements should be distinguished from treaties dealing solely with matters of extradition, not only because the latter concern the surrender of persons with the purpose of criminal prosecution, but also because the legal principles emanating from MLA agreements are far more State oriented.

Given the vastness of this topic and the abundance of available agreements I have decided to focus on common principles and extrapolate any noteworthy deviations where appropriate. From a methodological point of view, since the negotiation of agreements between States yielding asymmetric power would lead to the wrong conclusions, my selection of agreements casts a wider net that encompasses both symmetrical and asymmetrical partners.

Let us first of all start off by explaining the range of assistance encompassed in MLA agreements. These may include: a) the taking of testimony or statements of persons; b) providing items; c) locating or identifying persons or items; d) notification of rulings and judgments; e) serving documents; f) examination of objects or places; g) transferring persons in custody for testimony or other purpose; h) executing requests for searches or seizures, or; i) immobilisation and sequestration of property, freezing of assets and assistance in procedures relating to seizures.[2] Increasingly,

---

[1] Art 3, 1959 Council of Europe Convention on Mutual Assistance in Criminal Matters, ETS No 30 (20 Apr 1959).
[2] Art 7 OAS Convention on Mutual Legal Assistance in Criminal Matters; Art 1(2), 2002 USA-Liechtenstein Treaty on Mutual Legal Assistance in Criminal Matters.

requests for forfeiture are inserted in more contemporary MLA agreements to which the USA is a party.[3] Between the symmetrical actors and alliances of the European Union (EU) requests for interception of telecommunications have additionally found their place in Article 18 of the 2000 MLA Convention between the member States of the EU.[4] In addition, subject specific treaties oblige parties to offer very particular forms of assistance, other than the general already identified, such as asset recovery and repatriation of embezzled funds to their countries of origin.[5] Besides the wide scope of MLA agreements, the reason why they are much more advantageous than letters rogatory lies in the fact that mutual assistance requests from one authority can be transmitted to their designated counterpart in another country (and from there to the competent organ) without the need for other executive intermediaries. If the request satisfies the enumerated criteria in the MLA agreement it must be duly acted upon subject to judicial approval.

One of the common features between MLA and extradition treaties is that the offence in respect of which the particular assistance is sought must have been expressly agreed in advance by the parties. Most treaties avoid appending a definitive list of offences as any future developments will necessitate renegotiation of a new amendment or treaty. As a result, limitations to assistance requests are usually framed either on the basis of the double criminality rule (ie that the offence in question must exist in both States),[6] or on the ground that certain types of crime fall outside the scope of the agreement (eg political, military or fiscal crimes, or where the request is likely to prejudice the sovereignty, security or public order of the requested State).[7] Whereas traditionally fiscal offences were purposely excluded from the ambit of MLA treaties, many post-9/11 agreements have reserved a special place for these,[8] principally because they give rise to terrorist financing and money laundering. The main problem in the negotiation of fiscal offences entails convincing the requested State to procure evidence for tax fraud to the requesting nation – which is generally of no concern to the requested State, particularly where the accused pays his or her taxes therein in accordance with the law of that country. Moreover, a natural consequence of such requests is the lifting of bank secrecy, which is crucial to the commercial functioning of the banking system of certain nations. It is evident that the conclusion of MLA arrangements in respect of fiscal offences, particularly tax evasion, is predicated on the relevant actors' politico-financial considerations.[9] In the case of the

---

[3] Art 1(1) US-Liechtenstein MLA Treaty.

[4] Convention established by the Council in accordance with Article 34 of the Treaty on European Union, on Mutual Legal Assistance in Criminal Matters between the Member States of the European Union, OJ C 197/3 (12 Jul 2000).

[5] See Art 61, 2003 UN Convention against Corruption, (2004) 43 ILM 37.

[6] Art 2(1), 1993 Central American Treaty on Mutual Legal Assistance in Criminal Matters, I-34455 UNTS 167; Art 3(1)(4), 2003 US-Japan Treaty on Mutual Legal Assistance in Criminal Matters; but see Art 5 of the OAS MLA Convention which does not require conformity to the double criminality rule, save where the request concerns immobilisation and sequestration of property, or searches and seizures.

[7] Art 2 Council of Europe MLA Convention.

[8] The First Protocol to the 1959 Council of Europe MLA Convention, signed in 1978, expressly included fiscal offences. ETS No 99 (17 Mar 1978).

[9] Information sharing in respect of tax fraud investigations is also catered in bilateral double taxation treaties, as well as multilateral tax instruments, such as the 2002 OECD Model Agreement on Exchange of Information in Tax Matters. See R Earle, 'Cross-Border Tax Fraud and Cross-Border Anti-Tax Fraud' in I Bantekas, *International and European Financial Criminal Law* (London, Butterworths, 2006) 244, at 263ff.

US-Liechtenstein MLA Treaty, US negotiators demanded the signing of the particular treaty otherwise they threatened to remove the Qualified Intermediary (QI) status of Liechtenstein banks in the USA, which allows banks to undertake unimpeded international flow of capital. Although tax fraud is defined in Article 1(4) of this treaty and in the Exchange of Notes between the two nations and is not made subject to double criminality, a request for assistance may nonetheless be refused where, because it does not constitute an offence in the requesting State, its courts are unable to adopt or execute a coercive measure.[10] Given that tax fraud – as well as money laundering and terrorist financing – was the prime reason behind this treaty, in order to avoid the possibility of inadmissible requests, the government of Liechtenstein is practically obliged to adapt its tax criminal law to that of the USA.

Every MLA agreement contains a provision according to which the processes of mutual assistance are not to be afforded to physical or legal persons, other than the designated public authorities of the contracting States.[11] Thus, in the course of a criminal investigation or trial only the State (essentially the Prosecutor) can request evidence situated abroad. The reason underlying such provisions is to avoid impeding the execution of requests by the accused the aim of which is to suppress and exclude evidence that is valuable in a particular investigation. These provisions therefore do not violate the principle of equality of arms because the authorities in both States must make available to the accused any evidence obtained as a result of the MLA process, even if of an exculpatory nature.

Equally noteworthy is the common principle found in all MLA agreements, according to which any requests for the provision of testimony or evidence by a witness or accused in the requesting State is by invitation only. This means that the witness or accused must personally consent to appear before the authorities of the requesting State.[12] This is a cardinal principle of general applicability that has been bypassed in, at least, one instrument. The phraseology of Article 9(3) of the 2000 EU MLA Convention makes it clear that the consent of the transferred person is only required where national legislation so demands. This is a unique exception that is justified by the high degree of integration and approximation of EU member States, since in every other case it would stretch the ambit of constitutional laws to compel a person that is not under investigation to be transferred to a foreign jurisdiction in order to produce evidence or offer testimony. In every other MLA treaty, besides the personal consent of the witness, where the requested person consents to appear before the requesting State's investigating authorities, he or she enjoys particular guarantees, such as the right not to be prosecuted there, the granting of safe passage back to the requested State and the restitution of the evidence.[13]

The desired effect of MLA agreements would be unachievable if the concerned national authorities were to undertake their obligations acting in bad faith and by religiously observing the letter of the treaty in order to impose limitations on

---

[10]   Art 1(3) US-Liechtenstein MLA Treaty.
[11]   Art 2(1) OAS MLA Convention; Art 1(5), US-Japan MLA Treaty.
[12]   Arts 8–9, Central American MLA Treaty; Art 14, US-Japan MLA Treaty; Art 11(1) Council of Europe MLA Convention; Art 20 OAS MLA Convention.
[13]   Art 22 OAS MLA Convention; Art 10(3)–(4) US-Liechtenstein MLA Treaty; Art 12 Council of Europe MLA Convention.

requests, particularly where no legal impediments otherwise arise in the requested State in respect of a specific request. As a result, unless otherwise indicated in the text of the agreement, the obligations arising for requested States under MLA treaties necessitate a construction that is tantamount to 'the widest possible measure of assistance'.[14] Whereas originally mutual assistance agreements were conceived for the benefit of judicial authorities in recent years the range of entities that are entitled to make requests relating to criminal investigations has widened to include also administrative authorities.[15] This is logical given the fact that non-judicial entities, such as national competition committees, financial services authorities, securities commissions and customs and excise authorities, among others, are increasingly assuming broad mandates that encompasses elements of criminal investigations. It is therefore necessary for these entities to want to benefit from the accessibility of evidence arising from MLA agreements with other States.

One of the problems inherent in mutual assistance is that on account of sovereignty considerations the requested State will undoubtedly demand that the type of assistance sought be implemented in accordance with its own laws. This demand is also consistent with the training of local investigating personnel and is therefore cost effective. Nonetheless, in the event that the techniques and methods used in the collection of evidence violate the criminal procedure law of the requesting State the evidence collected will be declared inadmissible therein, even if legitimate in the requested State. This is obviously a serious problem that cannot be ignored lightly. The most advanced MLA agreements in fact oblige the requested State to comply with the formalities and procedures expressly indicated by the requesting State, unless these are contrary to its fundamental principles of law.[16] This is not a uniform rule,[17] but it is the most sensible one and where a treaty provides that States are to offer the widest possible assistance the obligation to take action in accordance with the requesting State's laws is implicit, unless of course this culminates in the violation of local laws. The matter is of grave practical importance. MLA treaties do not generally make provision with respect to the admissibility of evidence in cases where this has been collected abroad in contravention of the treaty or the laws of the requested State. The question of admissibility is therefore left to the laws of the forum and the discretion of its courts. As a matter of practice the courts of the USA have demonstrated significant flexibility in cases involving evidence gathering in violation of the laws of a foreign State that would otherwise violate the Fourth Amendment to the US Constitution that prohibits unlawful search and seizure. Evidence collected

---

[14] Art 1, 1990 UN Model Treaty on Mutual Legal Assistance in Criminal Matters, (1991) 30 ILM 1419; in fact, the 1959 Council of Europe MLA Convention was supplemented in 2001 by a Second Additional Protocol, ETS No 182 (8 Nov 2001), whose Art 1(1) endorsed this wording and replaced the lukewarm provision in the 1959 Convention.

[15] Art 1(3) Council of Europe MLA Protocol; Art 3(1), 2000 EU MLA Convention.

[16] Art 4(1), 2000 EU MLA Convention; Art 7(1) Central American MLA Treaty; Art 4(1), Council Framework Decision 2003/577/JHA (22 Jul 2003) on the Execution in the EU of Orders Freezing Property or Evidence, OJ L 196/45 (2 Aug 2003); Art 8 of the Council of Europe Protocol states that the requested State is under an obligation to implement the request in accordance with the law of the requesting State, even if it is wholly unfamiliar with this law.

[17] See, for example, Art 13(1) of the OAS MLA Treaty, which states that in respect of requests for search, seizure, attachment and surrender of property the implementing action must be in accordance with the law of the requested State.

abroad in violation of the Fourth Amendment is insusceptible to the general exclusionary rule set out by the Amendment (so-called silver platter doctrine).[18] The silver platter doctrine is subject to two exceptions. If the conduct of the foreign officials in the conduct of the search or seizure is such as to 'shock the judicial conscience' the evidence will be rendered inadmissible. This arises, for example, where a confession was achieved by means of torture.[19] The second exception applies in those cases where the participation of US agents in the particular operation abroad was so substantial that it constituted a 'joint venture' between them and the local agents (joint venture doctrine).[20] In practice, United States courts have shown reluctance in recognising the existence of a joint venture. In Europe, although evidence collected abroad in violation of fundamental human rights would be excluded on the basis of the European Convention on Human Rights,[21] courts are generally reluctant to exclude evidence collected in breach of foreign law.[22] The same is true in situations where although the evidence was collected in conformity with foreign law it is found to be in breach of the rules of evidence of the prosecuting State.[23]

The more recent generation of MLA agreements, particularly those adopted among EU member States themselves and/or with the USA, have introduced some novel developments in the regimes of legal assistance. For one thing the parties have agreed to expedite the relevant procedures where an undue delay could harm the course of an investigation. These so-called expedited requests allow parties to communicate the request by fax or email without going through the formal channels.[24] Moreover, provision has been made for the setting up of joint investigative teams with the purpose of operating on the territories of the parties and with a view to facilitating criminal investigations and prosecutions involving one or more States.[25] The modalities relating to the operation, duration and powers of the foreign investigators on the territory of the receiving States is subject to further bilateral deliberation and agreement. The mandate of such investigators cannot under any circumstance violate the laws of the receiving State, even if in conformity with the law of the sending State, albeit there is no impediment to the granting of diplomatic immunities to seconded personnel participating in such teams. The main worry for civil liberties groups in respect of this new generation of mutual legal assistance relates to the access and use of personal data. The EU-US MLA Agreement, for example, provides not only that assistance may not be refused on grounds of bank

---

[18] *USA v Janis* (1976) 428 US 433, at 455; *USA v Mitro* (1st Cir, 1989) 880 F 2d 1480, at 1482; *USA v Barona* (9th Cir, 1995) 56 F 3d 1087, at 1091; *USA v Verdugo-Urquidez* (1990) 494 US 259.

[19] *Barona*, ibid, p 1091; *USA v Fernandez-Caro* (SD Texas, 1987) 667 F Supp 893.

[20] *USA v Peterson* (9th Cir, 1987) 812 F 2d 486, at 490; *USA v Behety* (11th Cir, 1994) 32 F 3d 503, at 510.

[21] See *A and Others v Secretary of State for the Home Dept* [2005] 3 WLR 1249.

[22] *Governor of Pentonville Prison, ex p Chinoy* [1992] 1 All ER 317.

[23] *R v Quinn* [1990] Crim LR 581.

[24] Art 7, EU-USA Mutual Legal Assistance Agreement, OJ L181/34 (19 Jul 2003).

[25] Art 5, ibid.

secrecy,[26] but that no generic restrictions on the processing of personal data may be imposed by the requested State on any evidence or information collected as a result of a request.[27]

16.3   Informal Assistance Arrangements

Formal MLA agreements are significant tools for investigative authorities because they can become the cornerstone for the production of valuable evidence situated abroad. Nonetheless, these agreements can only produce the desired effect if the signatories are committed to the stated aim. Thus, the existence of mutual confidence between two nations lacking a formal MLA relationship can lead to the rendering of significant assistance on the basis of an informal, ad hoc, arrangement. By way of example, the Swiss authorities cooperated in full with Nigeria in order to investigate the embezzled funds of the former President of Nigeria, Sani Abacha, and thus complete the process of asset recovery, despite the fact that no MLA agreement was in existence between the two nations. The Swiss authorities employed their Federal Act on MLA in Criminal Matters and in 2005 the Swiss Federal Supreme Court ruled that since Abacha could not establish the source of the contested funds and his lawful entitlement thereupon the funds could be returned to Nigeria in the absence of a formal agreement or a confiscation order by a Swiss court.[28]

Whereas the repatriation of Abacha's assets to Nigeria took place on the basis of the Swiss MLA Act, other instances of mutual assistance can proceed on the basis of memoranda of understanding (MoU), which are not meant by the parties to be binding. The advantage of MoU over treaties is that they are simpler, cheaper and time-efficient to negotiate and most importantly do not require parliamentary scrutiny and approval. Given their secretive nature, particularly in the wider spectrum of criminal law enforcement, it is impossible to predict the areas encompassed by MoU and their scope. Nonetheless, some information clearly demonstrates that the use of informal arrangements is quite prevalent, for example, in respect of ship-boarding operations by non-flag States on the high seas.[29] These allow non-flag States not only to board suspected vessels, but also to seize evidence found therein.

---

[26]   Art 4(5), ibid.
[27]   Art 9(2)(b), ibid.
[28]   *Abacha and Nine Others v Office Fédéral de la Justice*, Judgment No 1A.215/2004 /col (7 Feb 2005).
[29]   See E Papastavridis, 'Fortress Europe and FRONTEX: Within or Without International Law?' (2010) 79 *Nordic Journal of International Law* 75, 87–92.

16.4   Recognition of Foreign Penal Judgments: The Principle of Mutual Recognition

The penal judgments of one nation are not generally enforceable in the territory of other States;[30] no treaties to this effect actually exist. Although mutual recognition of judgments is now commonplace in respect of private law and foreign arbitral awards, its application to the sphere of criminal law is far more problematic because it is tied to civil liberties and sovereignty considerations. The enforcement of foreign penal judgments should be distinguished from assistance in the collection of evidence or requests for extradition and surrender, all of which are clearly stipulated in bilateral and multilateral treaties. Exceptionally, the countries of the European Union have gradually developed a system of cooperation whereby certain penal judgments are directly enforceable among themselves. This process is known as mutual recognition.[31]

The principle of mutual recognition of final judicial decisions and pre-trial orders necessitates that the authorities of one State will recognise and give direct effect to the judgments and orders of another State without further examination of the substantive or procedural aspects of the case. Given its aforementioned ramifications it is evident that mutual recognition cannot simply be achieved by the mere signing of an agreement. This is because it may turn out that the contracting criminal justice systems are inadequately equipped or otherwise legally incapacitated – from the point of view of both constitutional and criminal law – from carrying out the terms of such agreements. Whereas the principle of reciprocity is a suitable legal basis for transposing the obligations contained in international agreements into the domestic sphere (ie that the two parties will simultaneously fulfil their obligations in a similar or the same manner), this is not the case with mutual recognition because in order to achieve any meaningful transposition of foreign legal elements in the criminal justice field these elements must conform with the substantive and procedural criminal legal framework of the recipient State. The same state of affairs is also true with regard to the requesting State, since its request for evidence to another State is only of value if its criminal procedure allows such evidence to be admissible. Thus, it is evident that the two legal systems (both that of the issuing State and that of enforcement) must somehow adapt their procedural and substantive criminal laws in such a way as to facilitate the transmission and completion of all relevant procedures without legal impediments. With regard to the substantive criminal law front, this objective can be achieved in two ways: a) either in relation to a limited number of offences whose definition the parties must necessarily agree to in advance, or; b) in the absence of agreement on definitions, the parties must seek consensus in relation not to specified offences but to a mutually agreed minimum penalty threshold that is further subject

---

[30]   This obvious rule was expressed as far back as *Huntington v Attrill* [1893] AC 150, *per* Lord Watson. In *USA v Inkley* [1988] 3 WLR 302, *per* Purchas LJ, p 310, the English Court of Appeal held that an award for the payment of a default appearance bond issued in civil proceedings in a US court, but in respect of fraud charges, was not capable of enforcement in England because the purpose of the action (ie the criminal fraud) was the execution of a penal judgment.

[31]   I Bantekas, 'The Principle of Mutual Recognition in EU Criminal Law' (2007) 37 *European Law Review* 365.

to other limitations. As regards procedural criminal law the parties must come to agreement as to minimum standards concerning the nature and scope of judicial orders (eg freezing, confiscation, search, etc), the application of *ne bis in idem* and fundamental guarantees, the role of double criminality and the modalities for admissibility of evidence. The EC Commission has proceeded to untangle the web of mutual recognition of penal judgments by giving emphasis to the strengthening of trust among EU nations[32] and by advancing a gradual process of approximation, rather than harmonisation, of their national criminal laws. Approximation involves a process whereby diverse legal elements retain their individuality, but adapt forming a coherent whole in order to accommodate a particular objective.[33]

The EU has implemented the principle of mutual recognition in a number of areas, principally in the execution of foreign surrender warrants through the European Arrest Warrant, which abolishes the cumbersome process of extradition between member States. The same results have been achieved in respect of freezing orders issued in any member State and relating to assets and evidence,[34] as well as in the fields of financial penalties[35] and confiscation orders.[36]

16.5 International Prisoner Transfers

The idea that persons serving a sentence for a criminal offence can be transferred from the sentencing country to their country of nationality is not new. This process should be distinguished from extradition in that the process of prisoner transfer does not entail a new investigation or trial against the transferred person; rather, it is meant to allow the prisoner to serve his or her sentence elsewhere. Its implementation is aimed towards facilitating the rehabilitation of the offender and the interests of justice, rather than for logistical or financial reasons.[37] This process, however, is not self-evident. For one thing, it necessitates a certain degree of trust between the sentencing and the receiving (or administering) States in that the offender will not be released but will carry out the remainder of his or her sentence. Moreover, the transferring State may be disinclined to allow the transfer of particular prisoners whose crimes have made a lasting impact on the local communities; the effects of public opinion should not be underestimated. Finally, given that national criminal

---

[32] See Communication from the Commission to the Council and the European Parliament on the Mutual Recognition of Judicial Decisions in Criminal Matters and the Strengthening of Mutual Trust between Member States, COM (2005) 195 Final (19 May 2005).

[33] A Weyembergh, 'Approximation of Criminal Laws, the Constitutional Treaty and the Hague Programme' (2005) 42 *Common Market Law Review* 1567.

[34] Council Framework Decision 2003/557/JHA (22 July 2003) on the Execution in the EU of Orders Freezing Assets and Evidence, OJ L 196/45 (2 Aug 2003).

[35] Council Framework Decision 2005/214/JHA (24 Feb 2005) on the Application of the Principle of Mutual Recognition to Financial Penalties, OJ L 76/16 (22 Mar 2005).

[36] Framework Decision 2006/783/JHA (6 Oct 2006) on the Application of the Principle of Mutual Recognition to Confiscation Orders, OJ L 328/59 (24 Nov 2006).

[37] This is not to say that financial considerations play no part at all. Prisoner transfers generally require that the offender has at least six months left to serve, thus making it a worthwhile exercise. Art 3(1)(c) Council of Europe Convention.

justice systems do not neatly correspond in terms of their substantive and sentencing laws, the initial sentence may be insusceptible to identical enforcement in the receiving State. These problems have generally been overcome through a series of compromises with the adoption of bilateral[38] and multilateral transfer treaties that are now common among nations.

These treaties give rise to a number of immutable principles that underpin this area of inter-State cooperation. The most significant instrument in this regard is the 1983 Council of Europe's Convention on the Transfer of Sentenced Persons.[39] Membership to this agreement is universal, unlike the 1993 Inter-American (OAS) Convention on Serving Criminal Sentences Abroad.[40] The first principle underlying these agreements is the requirement of consent to the transfer by the two interested States. Secondly, the consent of the offender is a *sine qua non* condition of the transfer, as it is in his or her interests that this is undertaken.[41] In fact, a formal verification procedure is warranted in order to record the consent of the offender.[42] This approach is consistent with the practice in MLA treaties where requests for witness testimony before the authorities of the requesting State is only possible upon consent of the witness, victim or accused. Despite these considerations, exceptional situations have arisen where the consent of the prisoner was excluded from the ambit of a transfer agreement. This was the case with Article 3 of the 2008 UK-Libya Prisoner Transfer Treaty[43] which specifically concerned the repatriation to Libya of the sentenced Lockerbie bomber, although its remit was framed in more general terms. The absence of the prisoner's consent in such an agreement, despite the fact that it does not violate any international rule, is contrary to the general principle as to the requirement of consent that has evolved through the practice of States. The UK government has wrongly justified the absence of the prisoner's consent in its agreement with Libya on the alleged emerging rule found in the 1997 Additional Protocol to the 1983 Council of Europe Convention.[44] Although it is true that the Protocol renders the prisoner's consent irrelevant, this is applicable only where a sentenced person has fled from the sentencing State to his country of nationality before serving out the sentence, or where he or she is subject to deportation or expulsion as a result of the imposed sentence. It is rational in such cases to exclude the consent of the sentenced person under Article 2(3) of the Protocol. This particular provision of the Protocol, however, finds no application to the Convention, which deals with conventional prisoner transfers.

---

[38] The USA is a signatory to twelve bilateral prisoner transfer agreements, but has made it clear that it no longer wants to negotiate at the bilateral level and thus urges other nations to accede to relevant multilateral treaties.

[39] ETS No 112 (21 Mar 1983).

[40] OAS TS No 76.

[41] Art 3(1)(d) Council of Europe Convention. The offender may exceptionally be transferred in the absence of consent if this is justified by his age, physical or mental condition and confirmed by that person's legal representative.

[42] Art 7, ibid; 18 USC § 4100(b).

[43] CM 7540 (17 Nov 2008). The 2006 Police and Justice Act had already removed the requirement of consent that existed in the 1984 Repatriation of Prisoners Act.

[44] ETS No 167 (18 Dec 1997).

The third fundamental principle underpinning prisoner transfer agreements is that a person can only be transferred to the country of his or her nationality,[45] although in exceptional cases, as is the practice of Australia, this may extend to a country where the offender has community ties.[46]

Fourthly, in order for a request of transfer to be considered the sentence must not be subject to further appeal or similar measures in the sentencing State; it must therefore be final according to its laws.[47] Finally, there usually arises a requirement of double criminality, otherwise the receiving State may validly release the offender given that his or her continuing incarceration would be in respect of conduct that is not criminal according to its laws.[48] Thus, prisoner transfer agreements do not give rise to an obligation for mutual recognition of penal sentences between the contracting States.[49] Once these five conditions have been satisfied the requirements for the process of transfer are deemed to have been fulfilled.

Upon transfer to the receiving State the next and final phase of the international legal regime of transfer commences; the offender must serve the remainder of the sentence. The primary effect of the transfer is to suspend the enforcement of the sentence in the sentencing State.[50] The receiving State is under no circumstances entitled to revisit the merits of the case against the offender or commence new proceedings. It can, however, convert the sentence so as to adapt it to its own laws and procedures, even if this means substituting the foreign sentencing judgment with a local one.[51] If it decides to persist with the foreign sentence it is bound by the duration of that sentence and its legal nature. Where, however, such nature or duration is incompatible with its laws it may adapt the sanction to the punishment or measure prescribed by its own law for a similar offence, which must in any event correspond with the sentence to be enforced.[52] It is implicit in all transfer agreements that the receiving State is not entitled to further transfer the prisoner to a third State without the consent of the transferring State and the prisoner.

Prisoner transfers by international criminal tribunals to State entities is natural, given that these institutions have no capacity to enforce prison sentences other than through States. The ICTY and ICTR entered into numerous formal agreements with willing countries in this regard, all of which were generally predicated on the general principles identified above *mutatis mutandis*, subject to a single implicit exception, whereby the consent of the prisoner is not required. This is not surprising, considering that the ad hoc tribunals exercise international jurisdiction and in any event the

---

[45]   Art 3(1)(a) Council of Europe Convention.

[46]   International Transfer of Prisoners Act 1997 (as amended by Act 19 of 2004), s 3(a).

[47]   Art 3(1)(b),Council of Europe Convention.

[48]   Art 3(1)(e), ibid.

[49]   Art IX of the OAS Convention contains an exceptional mechanism, whereby on the basis of an: 'agreement between the parties, [the Convention] may be applied to persons whom the competent authority has pronounced un-indictable, for purposes of treatment of such persons in the receiving State. The parties shall, in accordance with their laws, agree on the type of treatment to be accorded such individuals upon transfer. For the transfer, consent must be obtained from a person legally authorized to grant it'.

[50]   Art 8(1), Council of Europe Convention. This should not be confused with the issue of criminal liability, which continues to persist.

[51]   Art 9, ibid.

[52]   Arts 10 and 11, ibid. The granting of a pardon, amnesty or commutation in accordance with the receiving State's laws is compatible with the terms of the Convention (Art 12).

detention at the UN's headquarters in The Hague is of a temporary nature.[53] In the context of the ICC the possibility of prisoner transfer – in the sense of transferring a person to serve his sentence – is regulated in the Statute itself and the process does not generally require implementing bilateral agreements, unless the receiving State desires to append particular conditions.[54] Despite the contractual obligation to undertake prisoner transfers the parties cannot be ordered to take on prisoners, since the process is meant to be consensual.[55] The sentences are to be served in accordance with the laws of the receiving State,[56] albeit the ICC retains a supervisory role over the process[57] and has the power at any time to transfer a person to another State.[58] Just like the practice of the ad hoc tribunals the consent of the sentenced person is not required, albeit it is to be taken into account by the Court, along with his or her nationality, for the determination of the most appropriate country.[59]

Besides the transfer of a sentenced person to serve the remainder of his sentence in his country of nationality there exist at least two further situations under which a prisoner transfer can take place. The first concerns the transfer of a person that is either detained or subject to a final judgment for the purpose of identification, testimony or otherwise providing assistance in obtaining evidence for the investigation or prosecution of particular offences. Such transfers require the prisoner's consent and assurances that he or she will be duly returned to the transferring State once the relevant process is complete. As a result, no prosecution can take place by the requesting State.[60] The second situation pertains to cases where a State consents to extradite a person in its custody to a third State under the explicit understanding that the imposed sentence, if any, is to be served in the transferring State.[61] The modalities of this procedure are subject to the constitutional law of the transferring State, particularly if the accused is a national thereof because it gives rise to numerous human rights considerations.

16.6   Horizontal and Vertical Cooperation between States and International Organisations

In the chapters relating to the ad hoc tribunals for Yugoslavia and Rwanda and the permanent International Criminal Court (ICC) the reader will become familiarised with the institutional modalities of cooperation. An examination of these issues will therefore be avoided in this chapter in order to avoid any replication. Nonetheless, reference to the pertinent fundamental rules will be made where necessary in order to

---

[53]   See A Tolbert, 'Case Analysis: The International Criminal Tribunal for the former Yugoslavia and the Enforcement of Sentences' (1998) 11 *Leiden Journal of International Law* 655.

[54]   Art 103(1)(b) ICC Statute.

[55]   Art 103(1)(a), ibid.

[56]   Art 106(2), ibid.

[57]   Art 106(1), ibid.

[58]   Art 104(1), ibid.

[59]   Art 103(3), ibid.

[60]   Art 16, 1999 International Convention for the Suppression of the Financing of Terrorism, (2009) 39 ILM 270.

[61]   Art 10(2), ibid.

elucidate the current discussion. To start off with, the characterisation of a particular form of cooperation as either horizontal or vertical necessarily stems from the instrument upon which the cooperation is predicated. Therefore, one would naturally assume that the contractual nature of the ICC Statute and the principle of complementarity stipulated therein suffice to render the relationship between that institution and its member States horizontal. Similarly, the overriding authority of the Security Council under the UN Charter would obviously subject the ICTY and ICTR cooperation mechanisms to vertical relationships of power. These natural assumptions, although correct in theory, have not always materialised with the expected degree of consistency and may, in fact, be doubted in practice.

16.6.1 Cooperation under the ICTY/ICTR Regime

Article 29 of the ICTY Statute employs binding terminology ('shall') in obliging UN member States to cooperate with the tribunal in its investigations and prosecutions, as well as in respect of requests or orders for assistance. These requests and orders may turn out to be wide-ranging, so long as they are directly pertinent to the tribunals' mandate, and may encompass the identification of persons, their arrest, surrender and detention, the taking of testimony, production of evidence and the service of documents. This provision seems to imply that UN member States are under a strict obligation at all times to adhere to any and all requests addressed to them by the ad hoc tribunals. Reality suggests that States cannot automatically comply with such requests. To do so they must ensure that they do not violate their domestic legal order, particularly their constitutional order. For example, an ICTY order mandating that State X must surrender its national may be contrary to the constitutional principle in State X whereby it is forbidden from surrendering or extraditing its nationals. Similarly, if State X has already acquitted the accused of the crime charged by the tribunal it would deem itself as violating the principle of double jeopardy (*ne bis in idem*) were it to surrender that person to the tribunal. The question then is deciding the most appropriate course of action for the requested State; should it violate its international obligations or its domestic ones? Given that the two options are mutually exclusive the requested State will base its decision on the option that gives rise to the least possible harm, or in respect of which it will suffer the least amount of legal and political repercussions.

It is no wonder therefore that may States have shown an express reluctance to cooperate with the ad hoc tribunals, particularly where by doing so they would have to violate their own laws. For example, Article 17 of the Swiss Federal Order on Cooperation with the ICTY[62] provides that assistance shall be granted to the tribunal only if the conduct charged is punishable under Swiss law. The same is true with regard to Article 7(2)(b) of the Italian Decree on Cooperation with the ICTY.[63] Article 7(2)(c) of this Decree purports not to recognise an ICTY order for surrender

---

[62] Adopted on 21 December 1995.
[63] Decree No 544 (28 Dec 1993).

in situations where a final judgment has already been rendered in respect of the same criminal conduct. Other statutes go even further. Sections 56 and 57 of the New Zealand International War Crimes Tribunals Act provides a number of circumstances under which the Attorney-General may decline to comply with requests for assistance by the ICTY and ICTR.[64] This involves requests for which compliance would prejudice the sovereignty, security and national interests of the country, or in respect of which the assistance sought would require implementing measures that are unlawful under the laws of New Zealand. In fact, few enactments posit no obstacles at all to the otherwise vertical cooperation between the ad hoc tribunals and UN member States. Article 10(3) of the Romanian Law on Cooperation with the ICTY provides that the surrender of a person in custody is to be undertaken without consideration of the country's extradition procedure and shall prevail over any other conflicting procedure in Romanian law or treaties to which Romania is a party.[65] Some national courts have also exhibited hostility to the promulgation of cooperation legislation by their countries' executives. In *re Surrender of Ntakirutimana*, a US District court in Laredo, Texas, refused to surrender the accused to the jurisdiction of the ICTR, despite the existence of an executive agreement between the US and the ICTR that had already found its place in the US domestic legal order. In the District court's view, the executive agreement was deemed unconstitutional because it had not been approved by Congress[66] and in this manner the judge demonstrated his dismay that US law could be subordinated to the United Nations. The constitutionality of the executive agreement was later confirmed by the US Supreme Court,[67] albeit the case provides an illustration of the hostility of some local courts to the primacy of Security Council-based tribunals.[68]

It is evident, therefore, that many States do not necessarily view their relationship with the ICTY and ICTR through the lens of a vertical cooperation, as should otherwise be the case. Rather, they take the view that they possess a legitimate interest to impose a number of conditions, both procedural and substantive, to any requests for assistance. These conditions are clearly not consonant with the obligations of States under the UN Charter and general international law. States cannot rely on domestic law to escape their obligations under international law and this certainly applies to the Security Council mandate articulated in Article 29 of the ICTY Statute. The ICTY chambers did not have to construct elaborate arguments to emphasise this point. The *Kordić* Appeals Chamber pointed out that when a State is seized with an order for the production of documents it does not possess *locus standi* to challenge their relevance.[69] In line with this reasoning the Appeals Chamber has also held that the requested State is not entitled to narrow a request for documents to those it deems

---

[64]   International War Crimes Tribunals Act (9 Jun 1995).

[65]   Law No 159/28 (28 Jul 1998).

[66]   In *re Surrender of Ntakirutimana* (SD Texas, 1997) 988 F Supp 1038.

[67]   *Ntakirutimana v Reno* (5th Cir, 1999) 184 F 3d 419, *cert denied*, (2000) 120 S Ct 977.

[68]   See R Kushen, KJ Harris, 'Surrender of Fugitives by the United States to the War Crimes Tribunals for Yugoslavia and Rwanda' (1996) 90 *American Journal of International Law* 510, who discuss the executive agreements.

[69]   *ICTY Prosecutor v Kordić and Čerkez*, Appeals Chamber Decision on the Request of the Republic of Croatia for Review of a Binding Order (9 Sep 1999), para 40.

exculpatory for the accused.[70] The ICTY Appeals Chamber made a tremendous effort in its early years of operation to augment and solidify the vertical cooperation mechanism of Article 29 of its Statute, in defiance of the various implementing statutes, albeit without being confrontational. As it turned out the most sensitive issue for States was not the surrender of accused persons, at least as far as countries that were not members of the former Yugoslavia were concerned. Rather, the most contentious matter was the production of material deemed to be strictly confidential and prejudicial to national security. The Appeals Chamber set out the fundamental rule according to which four criteria are required for issuing a binding order to a State for the production of documents: a) it should identify specific documents, as opposed to broad categories; b) it should highlight their relevance for trial; c) avoid being unduly onerous, and; d) provide the requested State sufficient compliance time.[71] The Appeals Chamber distinguished between a binding order addressed to a State to produce documents from a subpoena addressed to an individual, in the sense of a command to appear before the tribunal and bring along written evidence (*subpoena duces tecum*). It was held that subpoenas may be issued only against private individuals, whereas States and State officials can only be subject to binding orders.[72] The practical difference between the two is that failure to comply with a subpoena request gives rise to contempt proceedings, whereas non-adherence to an order may bring about a notification to the Security Council for the adoption of further measures, or even sanctions. The ICTY itself is not endowed with any powers of countermeasures in cases of non-compliance.

The critical question, however, remains whether requested States are obliged to adhere to requests that are prejudicial to their national security interests. The vertical nature of Article 29 of the ICTY Statute would certainly demand as much. States are of course free to argue differently, and although the tribunals' power to order disclosure of sensitive and confidential information is subject to significant limitations the ultimate power to decide on the actual disclosure rests with the tribunals.[73] Where the tribunals reach a judicial determination that the requested State's national security claim is unfounded they may make an order for production, albeit they will choose not to violate the confidentiality of the disclosed documents.[74] To be sure, the potential harm to national security interests generally binds the ICTY chambers to clad relevant information with protective measures, such as limited disclosure, *in camera* proceedings and others.[75] This means, however, that said material can be made available for trial by order of the tribunals.

---

[70] *ICTY Prosecutor v Milutinović*, Appeals Chamber Decision on Request of the USA for Review [*Milutinović USA Request* Decision] (12 May 2006), para 27.

[71] *ICTY Prosecutor v Blaškić*, Appeals Chamber Judgment on the Request of Croatia for Review of the Decision on Trial Chamber II of 18 July 1997 (29 Oct 1997), para 32.

[72] Ibid, paras 38–39.

[73] Ibid, paras 61–69.

[74] The accused himself must demonstrate that he has exercised due diligence in obtaining the requested material elsewhere but failed. *Milutinović USA Request* Decision, para 25. In the case at hand the accused succeeded in arguing that some of his contested conversations, which formed part of the charges against him, had been recorded by NATO personnel that had kept them on file. These conversations had not been recorded elsewhere.

[75] Ibid, paras 31–38.

Other horizontal forms of cooperation between the ad hoc tribunals and national authorities are not uncommon. Rule 11*bis* of the ICTR Rules of Procedure stipulates the possibility of transfer of proceedings to the courts of a willing country, provided that said courts are adequately prepared to accept such a case. This procedure has been activated on at least two occasions by the ICTR by means of agreement and subsequent referral to the jurisdiction of the national court, namely the courts of France.[76]

16.6.2   The Vertical Regime of the ICC

The cooperation mechanism envisaged in the ICC Statute is generally viewed from a horizontal angle on the ground that the relationship between the Court and the international community is predicated on an agreement. This result is further reinforced by the complementarity mechanism. In my opinion the presumed horizontal nature of the ICC cooperation procedure is not altogether true. Although the assumption of primary jurisdiction over a situation by ICC member States is horizontal (primary) vis-a-vis the Court, the obligation to offer assistance to the Court when declining the right to exercise jurisdiction is subject to a vertical authority. This is clearly enshrined in Article 86 of the ICC Statute, which obliges parties to fully cooperate with the Court in its investigation and prosecution of offences. This obligation is subject to some notable exceptions that have spurred some commentators to characterise them as having the same effect as treaty reservations and of rendering Part 9 of the Statute akin to a mutual legal assistance regime.[77] The core exceptions to the general obligation enshrined under Article 86 concern: a) the entitlement to surrender an accused person to a third State on the basis of a pre-existing bilateral or multilateral extradition treaty,[78] and; b) the denial to comply with a request for assistance – other than surrender of an accused – where the request concerns the production of any documents or disclosure of evidence which relates to a member's national security.[79] Whereas the exception enunciated in (a) is absolute, the invocation of national security interests does not necessarily deny the Court access to such materials. This is evident from Article 72 of the ICC Statute, which renders the Court the final arbiter as to the admissibility of material evidence that is otherwise deemed to prejudice a party's national security interests. Indeed, following an unsuccessful attempt at non-confrontational cooperation the Court may, if it still determines the evidence necessary for the establishment of the guilt or innocence of the accused, order disclosure through *in camera* or *ex parte* hearings. Of course, it may well determine that on a balance of interests there is no reason to order

---

[76] *ICTR Prosecutor v Bucyibaruta*, Office of the President, Designation of a Trial Chamber for the Referral of the Case to a State (11 Jul 2007); *ICTR Prosecutor v Munyeshyaka*, Office of the President, Decision on the Prosecutor's Request for the Referral of Munyeshyaka's Indictment to France (20 Nov 2007).

[77] R Rastan, 'Testing Cooperation: The International Criminal Court and National Authorities' (2008) 21 *Leiden Journal of International Law* 431, at 433.

[78] Arts 90(4) and 98 ICC Statute.

[79] Art 93(4), ibid.

disclosure, especially where it can otherwise make an inference as to the existence or not of a particular fact which the requested evidence may have helped elucidate. The bottom line is that the ICC operates on much the same vertical cooperation regime – at least as far as the production of documentary evidence is concerned – as the ad hoc tribunals.

The fact that ICC member States are under an obligation to adhere to the requests of the Court is distinct from the question as to whom the authority is vested to carry out the practicalities of a particular investigation. Is this the territorial State or the ICC Prosecutor? This issue is not expressly addressed in the Statute, albeit given that the execution of the parties' cooperation obligations are to be undertaken in accordance with implementing national legislation[80] it is the territorial State that is presumed to carry out the tasks stipulated in a request by the Court.[81] This is expedient and cost-effective from a logistical point of view, provided that the requested State is acting in good faith and with the requisite diligence. Certain legislative acts that facilitate cooperation with the ICC demonstrate a willingness to limit the sovereignty of the respective nations; this possibility is also hinted in Article 99(4) of the ICC Statute but it is unlikely that this limitation is couched in binding terms upon the requested State. Article 15 of the Serbian Law on Cooperation with the ICC[82] allows the ICC Prosecutor's representatives not only to witness the requested measures taken by the local authorities but also to 'ask questions and make proposals and may be granted video or sound recording of the action upon request'. Exceptionally, under Article 16 of the Law the ICC Prosecutor's representatives may be allowed to undertake independent investigative action in the territory of Serbia, although in every case this must be done in the presence of a local authority, judicial or otherwise. A similar provision is inserted in Article 38(1) of the Swiss Federal Law of 22 June 2001 on Cooperation with the ICC, according to which the Swiss Central Authority may authorise the ICC Prosecutor, upon request, to conduct investigative measures on Swiss territory. There is an emerging trend whereby the cooperation procedures set up under national law to facilitate the investigative work of the ICC are far more vertical and intrusive than their ICTY/ICTR counterparts. Germany, for example, has not only adopted a constitutional amendment to Article 16(2) of its Basic Law that allows the surrender of German nationals to international tribunals, but has moreover promulgated a Law on Cooperation with the ICC through which it has effectively conferred sovereign rights to the Court.[83]

---

[80] Art 99(1) ICC Statute.

[81] G-JA Knoops, RR Amsterdam, 'The Duality of State Cooperation within International and National Criminal Cases' (2007) 30 *Fordham International Law Journal* 260, at 276.

[82] Published in the RS Official Gazette No 72/09 (2009).

[83] This does not mean, however, that the law rejects double jeopardy claims or the validity of pre-existing extradition agreements, or that among competing requests the German authorities must surrender the accused to the ICC.

16.6.3   Cooperation under the Statutes of Hybrid Tribunals

The mandate of hybrid tribunals is limited from the outset by reason of the bilateral agreements upon which they are predicated between the host State and the United Nations. As a result, they possess no power to address binding orders or subpoenas to third nations or nationals thereof in the absence of a subsequent cooperation agreement. Nonetheless, hybrid tribunals may issue binding orders for assistance (including identification and location of persons, service of documents, arrest or detention and transfer of indictees) to the host State, which is under a strict obligation to comply. This is reflected clearly, for example, in Article 17 of the UN-Sierra Leone Agreement on the Establishment of the Special Court,[84] as well as Article 15 of the UN-Lebanon Agreement on the Establishment of a Special Tribunal. It should be reminded that the host State under the circumstances is also the country where the crimes took place.

16.7   International Tribunal Requests to International Organisations and Preservation of Confidentiality

Requests for assistance to international organisations vary significantly in scope. On the one extreme there are those that seek from military organisations – or the military contingents of international organisations – the apprehension and detention of accused persons and their surrender to the tribunal. This was the case with ICTY confidential agreements with SFOR that was set up and operated by NATO on the territory of the former Yugoslavia.[85] Such requests are unusual and are in any event predicated on agreement, either formal or informal (such as MoU). The vast majority of assistance requests concern the production of material evidence. The assistance of organisations such as NATO is crucial for the investigative function of international tribunals since it is well known that military or quasi-military contingents operated by international organisations undertake thorough accounts of events in conflict zones and in many cases even possess extensive audiovisual documentation.

   In the absence of an agreement with the requested organisation it is doubtful whether a subpoena may be issued to any one of its employees. This should certainly be seen as the guiding rule in relation to requests made by the ICC under Article 87(6) of its Statute. Besides its Agreement with the United Nations, the ICC has also entered into other bilateral agreements with international organisations with a view to accessing relevant documents held by them, among others. The ICC-EU Agreement on Cooperation and Assistance obliges both parties to ensure 'to the fullest extent possible' the exchange of information and documents of mutual interest.[86] However, by far the most contentious issue in this and similar agreements is the

---

[84]   Confirmed in *SLSC Prosecutor v Kanu*, Trial Chamber Decision on Defence Motion in respect of Santigie Borbor Kanu for an Order under Rule 54 with respect to Release of Exculpatory Evidence (1 Jun 2004), para 27.
[85]   See chapter 18.2.
[86]   ICC-PRES/01–01–6 (10 April 2006), Art 7(1).

preservation of the confidential and classified nature of the requested documents. The ICC-EU Agreement devotes an entire annex to confidentiality by requiring that the Court undertake all necessary steps to ensure that the content of submitted documents be authorised only to individuals who have a 'need to know' and that sufficient security arrangements be made available to physically preserve them out of public reach. What happens, however, in situations where material is in the hands of the ICC Prosecutor but cannot be disclosed to the accused because of a prior agreement with the information provider that demands strict confidentiality? The ICC Appeals Chamber has held that under similar circumstances it cannot override the Prosecutor's agreement with the provider, which is any way consistent with Article 54(3)(e) of the ICC Statute,[87] albeit it cannot disregard the right of the accused to a fair trial. As a result, if the information provider does not consent to a disclosure to the defence other counter-balancing measures will be adopted by the chambers to ensure that the trial remains fair.[88] In any event, this type of information cannot be admitted as primary evidence against the accused in accordance with Article 54(3)(e) of the ICC Statute.

The ICTY has adopted a much different approach. Although initially cautious about its relationship with NGOs and international organisations,[89] it subsequently took the position that Article 29 of the ICTY Statute is addressed to States acting both individually as well as collectively and therefore applies 'to collective enterprises undertaken by States, in the framework of international organisations and, in particular, their competent organs'.[90] Despite the adherence of the requested international organisations this position is clearly ill-founded. The legal person of international organisations under international law is wholly distinct from that of member States and it is on the basis of this understanding that member States are not liable for liabilities incurred by the legal person of the organisation.

16.8 Extradition

Extradition is a process whereby a person is surrendered to another State to undergo a criminal trial or investigation. Traditionally, it constitutes part of the wider ambit of MLA, albeit the process of extradition is distinguishable because it concerns the

---

[87] Material collected under Art 54(3)(e) ICC Statute cannot be used in trial proceedings without having been made available to the accused. They can only be employed in order to generate new evidence.

[88] *ICC Prosecutor v Lubanga*, Appeals Chamber Decision on the Appeal of the Prosecutor against the Decision of Trial Chamber I entitled 'Decision on the Consequences of Non-Disclosure of Exculpatory Materials covered by Article 54(3)(e) Agreements and the Application to Stay the Prosecution of the Accused' (21 Oct 2008), para 48.

[89] *ICTY Prosecutor v Kovačević*, Trial Chamber Decision Refusing Defence Motion for Subpoena (23 Jun 1998), arguing that binding orders to the OSCE were outside the ambit of Art 29 ICTY Statute.

[90] *ICTY Prosecutor v Simić and Others*, Trial Chamber Decision on Motion for Judicial Assistance to be Provided by SFOR and Others (18 Oct 2000), para 46; confirmed by *ICTY Prosecutor v Milutinović and Others*, Appeals Chamber Decision on Request of the North Atlantic Treaty Organisation for Review (15 May 2006), para 8; see also *ICTY Prosecutor v Kordić and Others*, Trial Chamber Order for the Production of Documents by the European Community Monitoring Mission and its Member States (4 Aug 2000), through which the ICTY ordered individual EC member States to produce documents held by the EC Monitoring Mission (ECMM) to Bosnia.

transfer of persons to stand trial rather than the transfer of evidence that is otherwise returnable to its source. Extradition must moreover be distinguished from the 'surrender' of accused persons to international criminal tribunals. International tribunals do not exercise jurisdiction similar to that of States (eg territorial, nationality-based, passive personality etc) and hence it is logical that any requests for surrender have to be predicated on a distinct legal basis. This legal basis is substantiated by their founding instruments and the obligation, if any, of States to surrender persons thereto is similarly stipulated in said instruments. It is reasonable therefore to treat surrenders to international tribunals differently from the process of extradition both in terms of substance and procedure.

It should be stated from the outset that in the absence of a Security Council resolution to the contrary there is no general obligation under international law on States to extradite. This is consistent with the notions of sovereignty and consent. An obligation to extradite arises only by reason of a treaty obligation or any other ad hoc arrangement with a requesting State that has the attribute of a treaty.[91] It is clear therefore that, unlike the transfer of prisoners where the consent of the offender is required, extradition is principally an inter-State affair. Obviously, the procedure is subject to a variety of human rights considerations, but these cannot be used to challenge the legitimacy of the process of surrender; in other words, the consent of the accused is irrelevant where his or her fundamental rights are not jeopardised. Traditionally, given the limited trust between nations and the sensitivity surrounding the surrender of nationals or other persons to a third State, extradition was premised on bilateral agreements between friendly States. This practice is sustained to the present day, despite the incorporation of elaborate extradition clauses in contemporary multilateral treaties. These extradition clauses are in no case a substitute for bilateral agreements[92] – unless parties so designate – but impose an obligation on participating States to render the offences stipulated therein extraditable in their bilateral relations.[93] Bilateral treaties do not constitute the sole source of extradition law and practice. National legislatures enact statutes to give effect to treaty obligations and in order to guide the courts and the executive. This is logical, given that many bilateral treaties are either outdated or of a general nature and in any event are silent on the procedure under which an extradition request will be handled and executed by the requested State. This procedure must certainly conform to the constitutional and other laws of the requested State and should be clear and unambiguous from the outset to the accused. In practice, extradition requests are subject to a two-tier process: a judicial determination through which the courts assess

---

[91] Under s 194 of the UK Extradition Act 2003 the Secretary of State is authorised to enter into special ad hoc arrangements with States that do not have an extradition treaty with the UK. This power was exercised in respect of a Rwandan request for persons living in the UK and suspected of participation in the 1994 genocide. The Secretary firstly enquired into the capacity of Rwanda to hold the trials through on-site visits and upon being satisfied entered into an MoU with the authorities of that nation. See *Rwanda v Bajinya and Others*, City of Westminster Magistrates Court (6 Jun 2008), which affirmed the legality of this arrangement.

[92] Art 8(2) of the 1984 UN Convention against Torture, for example, admonishes parties that do not have bilateral treaties to employ this provision as a legal basis for extradition. Belgium relied on Art 8(2) in requesting the extradition of former dictator Hissène Habré from Senegal in the absence of a bilateral treaty.

[93] Art 16(3), 2000 Convention against Transnational Organised Crime, (2001) 40 ILM 237.

the legality of the request, followed by an executive approval or rejection, most typically by the incumbent Minister of Justice.

On the basis of the domestic and international practice of States certain principles have arisen through which new bilateral treaties are drafted or older ones interpreted. Paramount among these is the principle of *double criminality*, which necessitates that a particular conduct is generally extraditable if it constitutes an offence in both States and is moreover incorporated in their mutual bilateral extradition treaty.[94] The requirement of double criminality is satisfied in two ways: firstly, the parties may insert into their treaty, by name, each and every crime they deem as extraditable among themselves (listing method), or; secondly, they can choose to allow extradition in respect of offences subject to a specified degree of severity or a period of incarceration. The latter method has the advantage of being flexible enough not to require constant amendments and moreover ensures that a particular offence is not similar only in name between the two nations, but also in the prescribed punishment. In this manner, in the event the two States ratify in the future a multilateral treaty such as the Transnational Organised Crime Convention, the relevant offences will be subject to extradition on the basis of their legislation implementing the Convention. As will be demonstrated later in this section, the double criminality rule has been eliminated in the context of the European Arrest Warrant in respect of a number of listed offences.

Another cardinal rule is that the offence for which the accused is sought must not already have been the subject of a final criminal investigation elsewhere (double jeopardy or *ne bis in idem*). This principle prohibits prosecution for the same set of facts, irrespective if the crime charged is different in the second investigation – unless of course the aim of the first prosecution was to shield the accused and thus abuse the double jeopardy principle for future purposes. Although double jeopardy also constitutes a fundamental human right principle[95] its application is not always straightforward. This was clearly highlighted by a referral to the ECJ by the Belgian Court of Cassation with a view to evaluating the status of Article 54 of the 1990 Convention Implementing the Schengen Agreement (CISA) on the Gradual Abolition of Checks at Common Borders.[96] The request related to a Belgian national who was convicted in Norway for importing narcotic drugs and later charged by Belgian authorities for exporting said drugs. Was this really the same offence? The ECJ refused to accept that a different classification of the act (ie import in one case and export in the other) would not give rise to double jeopardy, since the reality of divergent classification is counter-balanced by mutual trust between EC member States.[97] The removal of *ne bis in idem* under such circumstances would moreover severely hamper the objective of the right of freedom of movement.[98]

---

[94] See G Mullan, 'The Concept of Double Criminality in the Context of Extra-Territorial Crimes' [1997] *Criminal Law Review* 17.

[95] In Case C-254/99, *Limburgse Vinyl Maatschappij and Others v Commission* [2002] ECR I-8375, para 59, the ECJ held that protection offered under the double jeopardy rule constitutes a fundamental principle of EC law.

[96] OJ L 239/19 (22 Sep 2000).

[97] Case C-436/04, *Van Esbroeck*, [2006] ECR I-2333, Judgment (9 Mar 2006), paras 30–32, 42.

[98] Ibid, para 33; see also Case C-469/03, *Miraglia*, [2005] ECR I-2009, Judgment (10 Mar 2005), para 32.

Equally important is the principle of speciality, according to which the requesting State agrees to prosecute the accused only in respect of the particular offences to which the requested State has accepted.[99] As a result, even if the requesting State would otherwise possess jurisdiction to prosecute the accused for other crimes, it cannot prosecute the accused during his or her presence following the extradition. Upon completion of the investigation or trial for which the accused was extradited, assuming the accused is not convicted, he or she must be granted sufficient time to leave the country before extradition or arrest efforts are once again made. Given that the purpose underlying the rule of speciality is to shield the sovereignty of the requested State, the latter may validly decide to relax it in a particular case.[100]

16.8.1   Human Rights and Diplomatic Assurances

Besides the double jeopardy principle a number of other guarantees have been established in order to protect the rights of the accused person in the course of extradition proceedings. Traditionally, where the requesting State satisfied all the requirements of a bilateral extradition treaty it was considered that no judicial or executive scrutiny could be further undertaken to assess whether it was either hiding its true intentions with regard to the extradition or was acting in bad faith in its collection of evidence against the accused (rule of non-inquiry). The gradual imposition of human rights in every area of international life, including extradition treaties, has necessarily eroded the non-enquiry rule. For one thing, member States of the Council of Europe are no longer permitted to extradite a person to a country where there is a chance that the death penalty be imposed.[101] Equally, a person may not be extradited to a country where he or she faces the prospect of fundamental human rights violations, such as torture, illegal detention and others.[102] This means that the extradition court of the requested State must hear and evaluate any claims of potential abuse and refuse to extradite where it is demonstrated that this result is imminent either in respect of the particular accused, or a specified class of persons of which the accused is one. These processes are further enhanced by the demand for diplomatic assurances by the requested State, the effect of which is a solemn undertaking by the requesting country that it will abstain from any violations upon the physical or mental well-being of the extradited person. Recent jurisprudence has unfortunately exposed the manipulation of these assurances and has demonstrated that State officials of the requested State were not only aware but implicitly consented to the infliction of torture upon the accused.[103]

---

[99]   Art 18, 2003 US-UK Extradition Treaty, Cm 5821 (31 Mar 2003).

[100]   See Art 101(2) ICC Statute.

[101]   *Soering v UK* (1989) 11 EHRR 439.

[102]   See *Kalashnikov v Russia* (2003) 36 EHRR 34, paras 95–102, in which it was held that where poor prison conditions in the requesting State do not satisfy the 'minimum threshold of severity' extradition will be refused.

[103]   See *Agiza v Sweden*, CAT Doc CAT/C/34/D/233/2003 (20 May 2005), and *Youssef v Home Office* [2004] EWHC 1884, both of which concerned the abuse by Egypt of diplomatic assurances in respect of

The European Court of Human Rights has reaffirmed that persons should not be exposed to the risk of torture or ill-treatment by means of extradition or transfer to other States, refusing to entertain any counterbalance arguments predicated on threats to national security by that person or the seriousness of the crime.[104] In its particular examination of the practice of diplomatic assurances the Court held that it had found these to be wholly insufficient with respect to countries where ill-treatment was 'endemic and persistent'.[105] What is even more significant is that the Court has employed Rule 39 of its Rules of Court in order to adopt interim measures with regard to US extradition requests that would render extradited persons to US military commissions, despite any diplomatic assurances provided by the government of that country.[106] This practice is not, however, without its exceptions. The Canadian Supreme Court in *Suresh v Canada*, where a Sri-Lankan refugee argued that his deportation to that country risked a substantial likelihood of torture, held that although torture is strictly prohibited under international law there do exist exceptional circumstances where the infliction of torture as a result of deportation is justified on the basis of balance of competing interests. In the case at hand, such interests include the combating of terrorism and Canadian safety.[107]

The post 9/11 era has brought about a certain change of perceptions with regard to particular aspects of extradition law and practice. It should first of all be clarified that Security Council resolution 1373[108] has not imposed a general obligation on States to extradite, given that not only paragraph 3 of the resolution is clearly not couched in binding terms, but such a result would have the effect of re-writing the international law of extradition. Nonetheless, resolution 1373 has necessitated the abolition of the political offence exception to terrorist-related offences, at least, which is otherwise applicable to all extradition requests. Given, however, that the collection of terrorist funds may come about as a result of any criminal offence, a number of States have left open the possibility that no crime indirectly associated with terrorism is susceptible to the political offence exception.[109] It is also evident that the recent model of bilateral extradition treaties in which the USA is a (requesting) party places few constraints on the requested State, unlike their predecessors, such as the recent trend that renders the nationality of the accused no longer a bar to extradition.[110] Nonetheless, resolution 1373 cannot in any way be read as subordinating human rights concerns over the global fight against terrorism. This is evident in a follow-up

persons extradited under charges of terrorism. In the first case, the UN Committee against Torture found the Swedish government to have breached its international obligations by illicitly colluding with CIA agents to surrender Agiza and another person to Egypt.

[104] *Saadi v Italy*, ECHR Judgment (28 Feb 2008). The true test is whether the risk of torture is 'more likely than not', para 122.
[105] *Ismoilov v Russia and Others*, Judgment (24 Apr 2008).
[106] *Mustafa Kamal Mustafa (Abu Hamza) v UK*, App No 36742/08, rule 39 Order (4 Aug 2008).
[107] *Suresh v Canada (Minister of Citizenship and Immigration)* (2003) 1 SCR 3.
[108] SC 1373 (28 Sep 2001).
[109] Art 4(2) of the 2003 US-UK Extradition Treaty comes close to complete de-politicisation.
[110] Art 3, ibid.

resolution, 1456, to which a declaration is attached and according to which States are reminded that anti-terrorist action must be consistent with obligations under international human rights law.[111]

16.8.2   The Principle of 'Either Prosecute or Extradite'

The vast majority of multilateral conventions dealing with international crimes contain a special clause through which the apprehending State (*forum deprehensionis*) is under an obligation to either prosecute or extradite those persons who are suspected of having committed the prescribed offence. This is also known as *aut dedere aut judicare* and is itself subject to the conventional and customary limitations attached to extradition.[112] Although this principle, which is established only by treaty,[113] clearly seems to establish an affirmative obligation on parties to multilateral criminal law conventions to prosecute or extradite, in reality this assumption is misleading. The treaties in which this principle is contained do not *per se* constitute an independent and sufficient legal basis for extradition, unless of course otherwise stated. The ultimate act of extradition is dependent on the existence of specific bilateral treaties. Naturally, a State cannot be coerced into an extradition, particularly when it receives numerous legitimate requests, in which case it has a discretion which of these to satisfy if it chooses not to prosecute.

A State is obliged to extradite when it chooses not to prosecute. In order to avoid extradition of their agents States that support a particular criminal conduct typically assert that their criminal investigations revealed no wrongdoing on the part of the accused. As the *Lockerbie* case has demonstrated the *aut dedere* component of the principle requires that prosecution be carried out independently of the executive and in accordance with international standards. In that case, Libya refused to extradite two of its nationals accused by the US and UK of detonating an explosive device on a Pan Am flight over Lockerbie, Scotland. It argued that it had discharged its obligation under Article 7 of the 1971 Montreal Convention for the Suppression of Unlawful Acts Against the Safety of Civil Aviation (Montreal Convention), having already investigated the possible involvement of the accused. Although the subsequent Libyan investigation acquitted the two accused, there was ample evidence to

---

[111]   SC Res 1456 (20 Jan 2003).

[112]   CM Bassiouni, EM Wise, *Aut Dedere Aut Judicare: The Duty to Extradite or Prosecute in International Law*, (The Hague, Martinus Nijhoff, 1995). The earliest multilateral treaty to encourage the prosecution of non-extradited nationals was the 1929 Convention for the Suppression of Counterfeiting Currency, 112 LNTS 371.

[113]   The House of Lords in *T v Secretary of State for the Home Department* 107 ILR 552, at 564, noted that the *aut dedere* principle was to a limited extent a feature of the 1937 League of Nations Convention for the Prevention and Suppression of Terrorism (Arts 9 and 10); surprisingly, the Australian Federal Court in *Nulyarimma v Thompson* (2000) 39 ILM 20, at 23, stated that the *aut dedere aut judicare* principle was imposed by customary law on Australia in connection with the crime of genocide.

suggest that both were agents of the Libyan Government, which as it turned out was the orchestrator of that terrorist attack.[114]

The application of the *aut dedere aut judicare* principle is in all likelihood of a customary nature in relation to the core international crimes, particularly grave breaches, crimes against humanity and genocide. As a result, the obligation to prosecute the offenders (whether directly or through their extradition to a State that is willing to prosecute) constitutes an obligation owed to the entire international community.[115]

16.8.3   The European Arrest Warrant

The European Arrest Warrant (EAW)[116] is not a warrant for arrest issued by a central authority. Rather, it refers to judicial decisions issued by EU member States with a view to the arrest and surrender by another member State of a requested person, whether for the purposes of initiating a prosecution or for the execution of a custodial sentence or detention order.[117] It is therefore a request for extradition in the manner described above. However, the EAW is a very advanced form of extradition in which many of the usual limitations to executing such a request have been abolished; particularly the non-surrender of nationals, double criminality, the political offence exception, as well as the two-tier procedure of approval involving the courts and the executive branch of government. The ECJ has pointed out that the abolition of double criminality is not inconsistent with the principle of legality, equality and non-discrimination.[118] Evidently, the EAW replaces all other extradition procedures between EU States and the achievement behind its adoption is premised on the principle of mutual recognition, which we have already explained.

The general rule is that an EAW may be issued for acts punishable by the law of the issuing State where these are subject to a custodial sentence or a detention order for a maximum period of at least 12 months or, where a sentence has been passed or a detention order has been made, for sentences of at least four months.[119] For these non-listed offences the double criminality requirement remains in force.[120] In respect of a positive list of 32 offences, however, for which only the *ne bis in idem* limitation is applicable,[121] the obligation to surrender is mandatory if they are punishable in the

---

[114]   *Questions of interpretation and application of the 1971 Montreal Convention arising from the aerial incident at Lockerbie* [Libya v USA, Libya v UK], Interim Measures Decision, (1992) ICJ Reports 3.

[115]   CM Bassiouni, 'International Crimes: *Jus Cogens* and *Obligatio Erga Omnes*' (1996) 59 *Law & Contemporary Problems* 63.

[116]   Council Framework Decision 2002/584/JHA on the European Arrest Warrant and the Surrender Procedures between Member States (13 June 2002), OJ L 190 (18 Jul 2002).

[117]   Art 1(1), ibid.

[118]   *Advocaten voor de Wereld VZW v Leden van de Ministerraad*, Case C-303/05, Judgment (3 May 2007), paras 48–54.

[119]   Art 2(1), EAW.

[120]   Art 2(4), ibid.

[121]   Under Art 3, ibid, three mandatory reasons for the non-execution of an EAW are stipulated, of which double jeopardy is the most important. The other two are amnesties, or the age of the accused which precludes his or her liability in accordance with the law of the executing State.

issuing Member State by a custodial sentence or a detention order for a maximum period of at least three years.[122] Hence, it is taken for granted that all of these 32 offences are criminalised in all EU member States. These offences are: participation in a criminal organisation; terrorism; human trafficking; sexual exploitation of children and child pornography; illicit trafficking in narcotic drugs and psychotropic substances; illicit trafficking in weapons; corruption; fraud against EC financial interests; money laundering; counterfeiting; computer-related crime; environmental crime; facilitation of unauthorised entry and residence; murder, grievous bodily injury; illicit trade in human organs and tissue; kidnapping and hostage taking; racism and xenophobia; organised or armed robbery; illicit traffic in cultural goods; swindling; racketeering and extortion; counterfeiting and piracy of products; forgery of administrative documents; forgery of means of payment; illicit trafficking in hormonal substances and other growth promoters; illicit trafficking in nuclear or radioactive materials; trafficking in stolen vehicles; rape; arson; crimes within the jurisdiction of the ICC;[123] unlawful seizure of aircraft/ships; sabotage.

Clearly, the EAW constitutes a most radical departure from the prevailing extradition law and practice. Although it too was not without its share of constitutional problems among the participating EU member States, it is now firmly established and functioning smoothly without any of the problems initially anticipated.[124] Given that approximation of criminal and other laws gradually paved the way for the wider application of mutual recognition, it is doubtful that an extradition model predicated on the EAW can be set up outside the European Union.

16.9   The Effects of Extraterritorial Abduction and Illegal Rendition on Criminal Proceedings

Extradition treaties make no reference to the legality of abductions by the agents of their counterparts. It is implicit that such actions are prohibited under general international law because they entail the violation of sovereignty of the territorial State. Of course, it is highly unfortunate that certain States intentionally choose not to prosecute or extradite persons on their territory responsible for serious and large scale offences. Frustrated by the failure to effectuate a mutually agreed extradition arrangement some countries resort to extraterritorial abductions without the consent of the territorial State. In such cases the act of abduction gives rise to State responsibility, irrespective of who actually carries it out; ie direct employees of the sending State or persons acting on their behalf. Thus, in the abduction of Adolf Eichmann by Israeli secret agents the Security Council expressed its condemnation of Argentina's territorial sovereignty and set out the terms of a later compensation

---

[122] Art 2(2), ibid.

[123] See L Vierucci, 'The European Arrest Warrant: An Additional Tool for Prosecuting ICC Crimes' (2004) 2 *Journal of International Criminal Justice* 275.

[124] H Satzger, T Pohl, 'The German Constitution Court and the European Arrest Warrant: Cryptic Signals from Karlsruhe' (2006) 4 *Journal of International Criminal Justice* 686.

settlement.[125] Nonetheless, the Security Council stressed that its condemnation of Israel 'should in no way be interpreted as condoning the odious crimes of which Eichmann is accused'. There is clearly an obvious tension between the need to uphold international criminal justice and the maintenance of peace and security among nations. This issue has been addressed by national courts in a pragmatic manner.

The illegality of abductions under international law is distinct from the issue as to whether the accused can enjoy a fair trial in the courts of the apprehending State. The District Court of Jerusalem and the Israeli Supreme Court were adamant that their power to prosecute the accused was in no way contingent on the legality of arrest.[126] It would have been irrational to release Eichmann on these grounds given his role in the Holocaust and the campaign to trace him following the end of WW II. As a result, the international community was keen to allow justice to prevail over sovereignty. Clearly, the *Eichmann* case is exceptional and should not be employed as the benchmark for assessing whether the subsequent prosecution of an abducted accused violates the right to a fair trial. Two distinct schools of thought exist on the subject. The US approach, particularly as exemplified by the *Alvarez-Machain* case where the defendant was abducted in Mexico by US drugs enforcement agents, is that unless the accused is brought before a US court in violation of an extradition treaty – the violation being the abduction – he or she may lawfully be tried.[127] Given that no treaty explicitly prohibits abductions it is unlikely that this position will be reversed. In any event, the position of the US Supreme Court in *Alvarez-Machain* is not of recent vintage and is supported by long-standing jurisprudence and has come to be known as *male captus bene detentus* (ie illegally apprehended, but legally held for trial).[128] The opposing approach is that adopted by the courts of the United Kingdom, and generally accepted in European practice and in most other jurisdictions,[129] which posits that where the presence of the accused is secured by resort to a serious abuse of power by the prosecuting authorities the courts may refuse to sit in judgment.[130] In my opinion this is the most prudent position because it fosters and incentivises healthy inter-State cooperation, which is also crucial in collecting the appropriate evidence in each case. The presence of the accused before the courts of the prosecuting State is of little value if crucial evidence is unavailable and the country from where he or she was abducted refuses to hand it over as a reaction to the violation of its sovereignty. The abuse of process doctrine moreover strikes the correct balance between the omnipotence of prosecutors and the limited defence powers of the accused, particularly when the latter is suddenly brought to a new, foreign, environment.

---

[125]   SC Res 138 (23 Jun 1960).

[126]   *Attorney-General of Israel v Eichmann*, 36 ILR 5 (District Court of Jerusalem, 1961), aff'd 36 ILR 277 (Supreme Court of Israel, 1962).

[127]   *US v Alvarez-Machain* (1992) 112 S Ct 2188.

[128]   This is the so-called *Ker-Frisbie* doctrine. This stems from the following cases: *Ker v Illinois* (1886) 119 US 436 and *Frisbie v Collins* (1952) 342 US 519.

[129]   See *Levinge v Director of Custodial Services, Department of Corrective Services and Others* (1987) 9 NSWLR 546.

[130]   *Bennett v Horseferry Road Magistrates' Court* [1993] 3 All ER 138, at 150. See A Choo, 'Halting Criminal Proceedings: The Abuse of Process Revisited' [1995] *Criminal Law Review* 846.

Besides outright abductions a person may be brought to the jurisdiction of a court or an interrogator through an illicit agreement between the authorities of two or more nations. Unlike extradition which falls within the ambit of activities subject to sovereign will, but is otherwise constrained by numerous human rights considerations, the secretive rendition of persons without any judicial or other approval constitutes a flagrant violation of human rights, particularly the right to liberty of person. In the aftermath of the 9/11 terrorist attack the US secret services entered into clandestine agreements with other nations with a view to kidnapping suspected terrorists for significantly long durations and surrendering them to secret locations worldwide, whether for the purpose of interrogation or imprisonment.[131] Almost each one of these detainees was subjected to torture and held incommunicado for long periods of time. From a human rights point of view the UN Special Rapporteur on the Promotion and Protection of Human Rights and Fundamental Freedoms while Countering Terrorism emphasised that the extraordinary rendition of a person to another State for the purpose of interrogation or detention without charge is impermissible under international law.[132] It is clear that illegal rendition is inextricably connected with the illicit surrender of persons under the guise of extradition, particularly on the basis of false diplomatic assurances as already explained.

In closing, it should be pointed out that irrespective of the position adopted with respect to abductions and illegal renditions as constituting an abuse of process, national courts are generally reluctant to compel disclosure in cases brought by abductees whose effect would be to stifle information-sharing between allied nations, or which may be deemed prejudicial to national security, even if the evidence sought was obtained by torture or other illegal means. This conclusion has not only been reached by US courts,[133] but has reluctantly been accepted by courts in the UK in their examination of allegations of torture against British nationals held at Guantanamo Bay.[134] A necessary by-product of this limitation has been the inability to claim compensation through the judiciary because a proper case cannot be made

---

[131]   Council of Europe Parliamentary Assembly, Secret Detentions and Illegal Transfers of Detainees Involving Council of Europe Member States: Second Report, Doc 11302 Rev (11 Jun 2007).

[132]   UN Doc A/HRC/6/17/Add3 (22 Nov 2007), para 36.

[133]   *El Masri v Tenet* (4th Cir, 2007) 479 F 3d 296; *Mohamed v Jeppesen Dataplan Inc.* (ND Cal, 2008) 539 F. Supp. 2d 1128, at 1134. It should be mentioned that in subsequent phases of the latter case the Ninth Circuit took the view that an outright dismissal of a case on State secrets grounds should be disfavoured. See *Mohamed v Jeppesen Dataplan Inc* (9th Cir, 2009) 563 F 3d 992, at 1006. Eventually, sensitive information was not admitted at trial.

[134]   In re *Binyam Mohammed* [2008] EWHC 2048 (Admin), para 105, where the Queen's Bench Division of the Divisional Court held that the Foreign Office was under a duty to disclose classified information that was not only necessary but essential for the applicant's defence. It did however grant the government time to file a public interest immunity certificate, which it did, arguing that possible disclosure would hamper critical information-sharing with the USA and that such matters are best left to private discussions. The High Court eventually held that under the circumstances it would not compel disclosure. Judgment of 4 February 2009, [2009] EWHC 152 (Admin).

against the State for lack of evidence. Nonetheless, judges even in the USA who have turned down similar applications deplore this failure of the legal system, which offers no protection to victims of illegal rendition.[135]

---

[135] In *Arar v Ashcroft and Others*, Second Circuit Judgment (2 Nov 2009), the Court of Appeals held that as unfortunate as the situation was for the plaintiff, who had been rendered to Syria and tortured on the basis of a collusion between US and Canadian secret services, the US Constitution did not offer an appropriate remedy. An exceptional remedy such as that created by the US Supreme Court in *Bivens v Six Unknown Named Agents of the Federal Bureaux of Narcotics* (1971) 403 US 388, in which a direct cause of action was allowed against the offending individuals (so-called *Bivens* action), was not possible under the circumstances.

17

The Nuremberg and Tokyo Tribunals and the Origins of International Criminal Justice

17.1   The Historical Origins of International Criminality

By the late thirteenth century a code of behaviour between knights of all European nations had been established, the violation of which brought the culprit before special courts of chivalry. The chivalric code permitted only single combat between nobles and specified the conditions of ransom for captured knights, as well as the divisions of booty. The courts of chivalry applied the code only when the alleged infractions were perpetrated during a just war, frequently sentencing those found guilty to dishonour or death.[1] The nature of these trials was not criminal in the contemporary sense. The first recorded international trial for what today would be equivalent to war crimes is that of Peter von Hagenbach in 1474 at Breisach in Austria. Hagenbach was charged with instructing his troops to commit atrocities against civilians and combatants in his attempt to subjugate the city of Breisach. The accused was arraigned and tried by a multinational tribunal[2] and convicted of crimes such as rape and murder against the 'laws of God', but since at the time a state of war did not exist the crimes committed cannot be said to constitute war crimes, at least in the contemporary sense.[3] Schwarzenberger argued, nonetheless, that the occupation itself was a military one, recognising thus the existence of a state of war.[4] Both in the *Hagenbach* and a handful of other subsequent trials concerning offences perpetrated during armed conflict, prosecutorial authorities arraigned the accused under provisions of ordinary criminal law, in the same way they would with other domestic offences. However, it was evident that a corpus of law common to most nations had emerged since

---

[1]   MH Keen, *The Laws of War in the Late Middle Ages* (Oxford, Routledge, 1965) 50; see GIAD Draper, 'The Interaction of Christianity and Chivalry in the Historical Development of the Law of War' (1965) 3 *International Review of the Red Cross* 19. The *Hagenbach* case was the first international war crimes trial. Prior to this, in Naples in 1268, Conradin von Hohenstaufen, Duke of Swabia, was tried, convicted and executed for initiating an unjust war.

[2]   Whereas an ordinary trial would have taken place before a local court the Allies agreed on an *ad hoc* tribunal consisting of twenty-eight judges from all Allied towns, particularly Alsace, Germany and Switzerland. Notwithstanding its composition, Schwarzenberger doubted whether that tribunal was an international one, since this would have depended on the date the Swiss Confederation seceded from the Holy Roman Empire. G Schwarzenberger, *International Law as Applied in Courts and Tribunals: Armed Conflicts* (London, Stevens and Sons, 1968) 463.

[3]   Ibid, at 465.

[4]   Ibid, at 466. This would be the case if one were to apply retrospectively the rule found in common Art 2(1) of the 1949 Geneva Conventions.

antiquity which, although not international *per se*, transcended national borders establishing a set of minimum binding limitations in warfare.

Based on the normative nature of these chivalrous and natural law notions, European nations promulgated codes delineating one's conduct in armed conflict and imposed punishment by exercising a species of rudimentary universal jurisdiction. Of these, most prominent were King Ferdinand's Hungarian codes of 1526, King Maximilian's code of 1570 (Articles 8 and 9), the Dutch Articles of War of 1590 and the Swedish Articles of 'Military Lawwes' of 1621.[5] The latter formed the basis for the Articles of War adopted by both parties during the English Civil War.[6]

By the mid-eighteenth century states recognised personal criminal liability for a specific portion of *jus in bello* violations, attributable not only to the actual perpetrator but also to the superior of the culprit. It was by then well recognised that military commanders had a positive duty to restrain their troops from excesses in battle. Article 46 of the Swedish 'Articles of Military Lawwes', for example, established that a superior who ordered or commanded his troops to excesses would be criminally responsible for their actions, although not equally responsible.

The question then turned to the duties pertaining to military command. For, if nations truly opposed the infliction of cruelty as a means of warfare they had to adopt and ensure the effectiveness of both preventive and punitive mechanisms. It was believed that the cornerstone of military doctrine, obedience, should be deployed as a deterrent against war crimes. Article 11 of the Massachusetts Articles of War, adopted by the provisional Congress of Massachusetts in 1775, is viewed as the first authoritative expression of the doctrine of command responsibility.[7] This provides that persons in superior authority maintain a duty to prevent and punish the crimes of their subordinates. The doctrine was further developed and applied inconsistently under political pressure in a number of cases during the nineteenth century. A detailed exposition of this doctrine has already been undertaken in chapter 4.

The first attempt to draw up a modern code was undertaken by Professor Francis Lieber, under the instructions of Abraham Lincoln for the purposes of the US Civil War. What became known as the Lieber Code,[8] binding only on US Government forces, was based on the generally agreed laws of war at the time and envisaged by Lieber to act as an impetus for similar legislation in other countries. Between 1870 and 1904 a substantial number of countries promulgated analogous codes and as Green points out they constitute evidence of customary international law, especially since they were not overruled by treaty or expressly rejected by any State.[9]

---

[5] See K Ogren, 'Humanitarian Law in the Articles of War Decreed in 1621 by King Gustavus II Adolphus of Sweden' (1996) 313 *International Review of the Red Cross* 438.

[6] 'Laws and Ordinances of Warre' (1639), in TLH. McCormack, GJ Simpson (eds.), *The Law of War Crimes: National and International Approaches* (Leiden, Sijthoff, 1997) 39.

[7] WH Parks, 'Command Responsibility for War Crimes' (1973) 62 *Military Law Review* 1, at 5. This provision was retained and strengthened in the Articles of War of 1806.

[8] Instructions for the Government of Armies of the US in the Field, General Orders No. 100, 24 April 1863. See RR Baxter, 'The First Modern Codification of the Law of Armed Conflict' (1963) 29 *International Review of the Red Cross* 171.

[9] LC Green, *The Contemporary Law of Armed Conflict* (Manchester, Manchester University Press, 2000) 30. One should also point out that calls were made for the King of England to account for 'war against the natural rights of all mankind' following the US revolutionary war. See JJ Paust, 'Aggression

One may thus confirm the existence of a primitive body of norms regulating personal conduct in warfare as established through the customary practice of States by at least the middle of the eighteenth century. It should be made clear that until the first multilateral humanitarian law conventions (1864 onwards) this customary body of norms was defined, structured and enforced exclusively under domestic law.[10] This consideration should not urge the reader to dismiss its customary nature because as has already been elaborated the same criminalisation principles apply today with respect to transnational crimes. Up until 1907 it was understood that the concept of 'reprisal' was the legal foundation of war crimes jurisdiction.[11] Moreover, under customary international law of that time the exercise of jurisdiction over war criminals was optional, in the sense that international law did not postulate punishment but merely provided for 'an extraordinary type of jurisdiction which belligerents [could] exercise at their discretion'.[12]

The International Committee of the Red Cross (ICRC) which was established in the early second part of the nineteenth century set out a twofold objective; to assist the victims of war and develop the law by means of inter-State cooperation. This second objective did not take long to materialise and the ICRC was successful in garnering support for the conclusion of the 1864 Geneva Convention[13] as well as the 1868 Declaration of St. Petersburg.[14] While neither of these instruments provided for penal sanctions the Brussels Conference of 1874 and the Oxford Manual of 1880 – and later that of 1913 – put forward the proposition that the offences recognised under international law should be repressed and penalised under domestic criminal law.[15] The keen reader will once again discern the similarities with the contemporary criminalisation of transnational offences.

The Hague Peace Conferences of 1899 and 1907 culminated in the adoption of a substantial number of conventions regulating, *inter alia*, military conduct in land and sea warfare. Despite the detailing of prohibitions and acceptable practices, especially in the 1907 Hague Convention IV[16] and the Regulations annexed thereto, no sanctions were expressly prescribed and it was by no means evident that these

---

Against Authority: The Crime of Oppression, Politicide and Other Crimes Against Human Rights' (1986) 18 *Case Western Reserve Journal of International Law* 283, 283–84.

[10] G Manner, 'The Legal Nature and Punishment of Criminal Acts of Violence Contrary to the Laws of War' (1943) 37 *American Journal of International Law* 414. Manner noted that the US delegates to the 1919 Commission argued that the applicable law with regard to suspected German war criminals was the military legislation of the country against whose nationals the violations were committed. This view, according to USA and Japan, was justified in the absence of an international penal law upon which a criminal indictment of offenders against the rules of warfare could be predicated.

[11] Schwarzenberger, *International Law*, at 454.

[12] Ibid.

[13] 1864 Convention for the Amelioration of the Condition of the Wounded in Armies in the Field, 18 *Martens Nouveau Recueil General de Traites* (NRGT), at 607; the 1868 Additional Articles Relating to the Condition of the Wounded in War extended the humanitarian principles enunciated in the 1864 Convention to warfare at sea.

[14] 1868 St. Petersburg Declaration Renouncing the Use, in Time of War, of Explosive Projectiles under 400 Grammes Weight, 18 Martens NRGT 477.

[15] The 1874 Brussels Conference led to the adoption of the 1874 International Declaration Concerning the Laws and Customs of War, which was never considered binding. 4 (2nd) Martens NRGT 219; Oxford session of 1880, 'The Laws of War on Land', and Oxford session of 1913, 'The Laws of Naval War Governing the Relations Between Belligerents'.

[16] 1907 Convention Respecting the Laws and Customs of War on Land, 1 Bevans 631.

conventions established the international criminal liability of perpetrators.[17] A number of international agreements enacted in the next two decades failed to circumscribe appropriate penal mechanisms. They obliged, instead, States parties to adopt implementing criminal legislation.[18]

At the close of World War I, the Preliminary Peace Conference of Paris created the Commission on the Responsibility of the Authors of the War and on Enforcement of Penalties. It was entrusted, among others, with the incorporation of appropriate punitive mechanisms in the peace treaty between the Allies and Germany. The majority of the Commission supported the establishment of a tribunal with criminal jurisdiction over all persons belonging to enemy countries that were found to have violated the laws of war or the laws of humanity.[19] Despite reservations by the USA and Japan, the Commission's Report was unanimously accepted, further endorsed by the 1919 Paris Peace Treaty, eventually forming the basis for a number of criminal provisions in subsequent treaties; Articles 228–230 of the Treaty of Versailles of 28 June 1919,[20] Article 173 of the Treaty of St. Germain of 10 September 1919,[21] and Article 157 of the Treaty of Trianon of 4 June 1920.[22] These agreements recognised the personal liability of offenders and the right of the Allies to try them before military tribunals.[23] That part, however, of the Commission's report that endorsed the legality of setting up an international tribunal found very little support among the Allies and was not taken up any further. It was also proposed that the German Kaiser be tried before an international tribunal under the terms of the 1919 Peace Treaty of Versailles (Versailles Treaty), whereas other cases involving infractions of the laws of war could be tried by Allied military courts. Eventually, the Kaiser fled to the Netherlands and his extradition was sought by the Allied powers; however, the Netherlands refused the request on the grounds that Dutch law only provided for extradition to a sovereign State, not a coalition of States as was the case with the Allies. Moreover, he was deemed by the Dutch Government at the time to be a political fugitive. No further serious attempts were made to secure his presence for trial and the Kaiser remained in the Netherlands until his death. Also, under the terms of the Versailles Treaty, Germany had agreed to surrender suspected war criminals to the Allies for trial by specially established tribunals. However, since German capitulation was not unconditional the German Government in essence possessed an effective veto vis-a-vis the demands of the Allies. As a result, when the

---

[17] The 1906 Convention for the Amelioration of the Condition of the Wounded and Sick in Armies in the Field provided for the repression of the Convention's infractions and abuses regarding the Red Cross emblem in the form of injunctions in order that member States adopt appropriate legislation. 2 (3rd) Martens NRTG 620.

[18] Art 29, 1929 Geneva Convention for the Amelioration of the Condition of the Wounded and Sick in Armies in the Field, 118 LNTS 303.

[19] 'All persons belonging to enemy countries, however high their position may have been, without distinction or rank, including Chiefs of Staff, who have been guilty of offences against the laws and customs of war or the laws of humanity, are liable to criminal prosecution' (1920) 14 *American Journal of International Law* 95, 117, 123.

[20] TS No. 4 (1919).

[21] TS No. 11 (1919).

[22] TS No. 10 (1920).

[23] See 15 Law Reports of Trials of War Criminals (LRTWC) 23; E Colby, 'War Crimes' (1925) 23 *Michigan Law Review* 482, 496–97, argued that the agreement ending hostilities in the Boer War granted the right to try enemy combatants who violated the laws of war.

Allies demanded, during the Paris Peace Conference of 1920, the extradition of 896 Germans that were accused of violating the laws of war Germany refused to comply. As a compromise, the Allies agreed that some individuals would be tried before the Criminal senate of the Imperial Court of Justice in Leipzig. Only 12 accused were actually brought to trial and the Leipzig trials were hugely unpopular with the German press and public. The trials that took place dealt mainly with the treatment of survivors of torpedoed ships and prisoners of war and not with the actual conduct of hostilities.[24] The hearings fizzled out after a small number of cases had been considered. Some of these cases do, however, remain of value for the law set down, especially as regards the defence of superior orders.[25]

17.2 The Background to the Establishment of the International Military Tribunals

The beginning of the Second World War is generally thought to coincide with the German invasion of Poland in September 1939, although as will be demonstrated the Nazi government had since the early 1930s planned aggressive wars against numerous countries. During this time it had also proceeded to invade and annex Czechoslovakia and Austria. Early on in the course of the war news reached Western Europe of the atrocities committed by German forces and their allies against Jews in Germany and other occupied territories, gypsies, Catholic priests and other minority groups. As early in the war as 1941 Winston Churchill and Theodore Roosevelt, heads of Britain and USA respectively, made statements expressing their intention to seek retribution in respect of these offences. Subsequent discussions amongst the Allied powers and governments-in-exile developed the policy that war criminals would face prosecution after the war. In a Note sent by the British Government to the other Allied Governments on 6 August 1942 it was suggested that agreement should be reached on the appropriate basis for criminal trials in order to ensure rapid justice, prevent individuals and groups exacting their own revenge, all with a view to facilitating Europe's return to a peaceful and productive political atmosphere. Significantly, it was also proposed that in dealing with war criminals, whatever the court, the Allies should apply the existing laws of war and no specific *ad hoc* law should be enacted. By this time the extent of the atrocities against civilian populations was unclear not only to the Allies, but also to the average German citizen. As a result, when the situation was starting to become more clear the views of Roosevelt, Stalin and Churchill began to change and this is well reflected when the three leaders came to sign the Moscow Declaration on 30 October 1943. The Declaration stated that German war criminals would be returned to the countries in which their offences had taken place, and 'that they [would] be brought back to the scene of their crimes and

---

[24] See IF Willis, *Prologue to Nuremberg: The Politics and Diplomacy of Punishing War Criminals of the First World War*, (Westport, Greenwood Press, 1982).

[25] *Dover Castle* case (1922) 16 *American Journal of International Law* 704; *Llandovery Castle* case (1922) 16 *American Journal of International Law* 708; *Trial of Emil Mueller* (1922) 16 *American Journal of International Law* 684.

judged on the spot by the peoples whom they have outraged'. Shortly after this meeting Churchill proposed that the major war criminals should be declared as 'world outlaws' and be shot without trial. This may seem like an extreme and untenable view judged by contemporary standards, but it would not have upset public opinion at the time had it been carried through. Ultimately, this proposal would have deprived the Allies of any legitimacy and would have failed to set out a historic record of events.

The International Military Tribunal (IMT) at Nuremberg was formally established by the London Agreement of 8 August 1945 between the Governments of Great Britain, the US, France and the Union of Soviet Socialist Republics.[26] The Charter of the IMT was annexed to the London Agreement of which it is an integral part. The Charter provided for the prosecution of 'major war criminals of the European Axis'.[27] Other war criminals were to be tried by the authorities of all those Allied powers responsible for the administration of occupied Germany, in accordance with Allied Control Council Law No 10, while other countries were permitted to prosecute individuals on the basis of the territorial principle of jurisdiction, that is, with regard to offences perpetrated on their respective territories. The birth of the IMT certainly precipitated and contributed to the establishment of the International Military Tribunal for the Far East (IMTFE) sitting in Tokyo. Their primary difference rests in the fact that whereas the legal basis of the IMT was a treaty, the IMTFE was premised on a decree by one or more occupying powers.

17.2.1 The Law and Jurisdiction of the International Military Tribunal (IMT) at Nuremberg

The London Charter for the Nuremberg IMT (Nuremberg Charter)[28] is brief but is of enormous significance for the development of international criminal law. The Charter defines offences and sets out the parameters for individual criminal responsibility with regard to these offences. Both the Charter and the judgment of the IMT have been extremely influential on the evolution of the law and procedure of more contemporary institutions, namely the International Tribunals for the Former Yugoslavia and Rwanda (ICTY and ICTR, respectively), as well as the newly established International Criminal Court (ICC). The subject matter jurisdiction of the IMT was set out under Article 6 of the Tribunal's Charter, which provided:

> The tribunal established by the agreement referred to in Article 1 hereof for the trial and punishment of the major war criminals of the European Axis countries shall have the power to try and punish persons who, acting in the interests of the European Axis countries, whether as individuals or as members of organisations, committed any of the following crimes.

---

[26] See generally T Taylor, *The Anatomy of the Nuremberg Trials: A Personal Memoire*, (London, Bloomsbury, 1993); A Tusa, J Tusa, *The Nuremberg Trial* (London, Macmillan, 1983).
[27] Charter of the International Military Tribunal at Nuremberg (IMT Charter), Art 1.
[28] 5 UNTS 251.

The following acts, or any of them, are crimes coming within the jurisdiction of the tribunal for which there shall be individual responsibility:

(a) Crimes Against Peace: namely, planning, preparation, initiation or waging of a war of aggression, or a war in violation of international treaties, agreements, or assurances, or participation in a common plan or conspiracy for the accomplishment of any of the foregoing.

(b) War Crimes: namely, violations of the laws or customs of war. Such violations shall include, but not be limited to, murder, ill treatment or deportation to slave labour or for any other purpose of civilian populations of or in occupied territory, murder or ill treatment of prisoners of war or persons on the seas, killing of hostages, plunder of public or private property, wanton destruction of cities, towns or villages, or devastation not justified by military necessity.

(c) Crimes Against Humanity: namely, murder, extermination, enslavement, deportation, and other inhumane acts committed against any civilian population, before or during the war, or persecutions on political, racial, or religious grounds in execution of or in connection with any crime within the jurisdiction of the tribunal whether or not in violation of the domestic law of the country where perpetrated.

Leaders, organisers, instigators, and accomplices, participating in the formulation or execution of a common plan or conspiracy to commit any of the foregoing crimes are responsible for all acts performed by any persons in execution of such plan.

Although the crimes encompassed in Article 6 certainly fitted like a glove the types of conduct committed by senior members of the Nazi apparatus, they had never before appeared in a treaty or even domestic criminal law, with the exception of war crimes. Mindful that these offences had not been set out in this manner before, the IMT in its judgment set out the legal basis behind the offences. The Tribunal approached the question as to the legality of the crimes in a crude manner but did not refuse to examine the merits of the challenge, stating that:

The Charter makes the planning or waging of a war of aggression or a war in violation of international treaties a crime; and it is therefore not strictly necessary to consider whether and to what extent aggressive war was a crime before the execution of the London Agreement. But in view of the great importance of the questions of law involved, the tribunal has heard full argument from the prosecution and the defence, and will express its view on the matter.[29]

The IMT rejected the argument presented by the defence that the Charter breached the principle that there can be no crime or punishment without law, *nullum crimen sine lege, nulla poena sine lege*, by arguing that this maxim was a principle of justice and not a limitation of sovereignty. Its rationale was that if a war of aggression is illegal in international law then it necessarily follows that those who plan and wage such a war are committing a crime.[30] This reasoning is reasonable by contemporary standards but defied international law at the time which rejected the proposition that natural persons may incur international criminal liability by means of a treaty, without a specific and express undertaking by the States parties to that treaty. As to

---

[29] IMT Judgment, reprinted in (1947) 41 *American Journal of International Law* 172, at 217.
[30] Ibid, at 218.

whether the criminalisation of particular conduct requires foreseeability and how this is to be ascertained by the relevant actors,[31] the IMT had this to say:

> Occupying the positions they did in the Government of Germany, the defendants or at least some of them must have known of the treaties signed by Germany, outlawing recourse to war for the settlement of international disputes, they must have known that they were acting in defiance of all international law when in complete deliberation they carried out their designs of invasion and aggression. On this view of the case alone, it would appear that the maxim has no application to the present facts.[32]

The inherent problem with formulating the offence of crimes against peace lies with the fact that even if aggression could be deemed to have been illegal by 1939, this would at best be considered an act entailing State responsibility rather than personal criminal responsibility. The League of Nations Covenant had by no means prohibited recourse to armed force for the settlement of international disputes, although it had established a complex conciliatory mechanism that was aimed at delaying recourse to violence rather than prohibiting it altogether.[33] New attempts to define aggression as an international crime took place with the 1923 Draft Treaty on Mutual Assistance and the 1924 Protocol for the Pacific Settlement of International Disputes. Article I of the 1923 Draft Treaty declared that aggressive war was an international crime, as did the 1924 Protocol. Although the Protocol did not enter into force, forty-eight States recommended its ratification in the League Assembly, thereby indicating a willingness to outlaw such behaviour.[34] Where prior attempts to prohibit war had formally failed the 1928 General Treaty for the Renunciation of War as an Instrument of National Policy, also known as the Kellogg-Briand Treaty or Pact of Paris,[35] outlawed recourse to war entirely. However, not even the Pact of Paris specifically penalised aggression and, hence, it can hardly be asserted that as a matter of positive international law the perpetration of aggression entailed with certainty the personal liability of the culprit.

The IMT in its judgment made reference to the aforementioned instruments, to which Germany was a party. Whereas the objective of these instruments was clearly only the denunciation of aggressive war the Tribunal held that the crime of aggression had in fact been established under customary law. Interestingly, the Tribunal attempted an analogy with the Hague Convention IV of 1907 and its annexed Regulations, stating that neither had the Hague Regulations expressly penalised the breaches contained therein – that is, much like the Pact of Paris – but went on to say that breaches of this nature had long been prosecuted by national courts.[36] This analogy hardly supported the Tribunal's argument, since it is an example of a legal instrument having attained the status of customary law through consistent and

---

[31] See chapter 2.

[32] IMT Judgment, at 217.

[33] See I Brownlie, *International Law and the Use of Force by States*, (Oxford, Oxford University Press, 1963) 62.

[34] On 24 September 1927 the Assembly of the League of Nations unanimously adopted a resolution regarding wars of aggression, the preamble of which expressly stated that such wars constituted international crimes. See IMT Judgment, at 220.

[35] 94 LNTS 57.

[36] IMT Judgment, at 218.

continuous State practice, whereas the same cannot be said of the crime of aggression. A number of scholars, such as Finch, rejected the argument that the crime of aggression could have been established by reference to non-ratified treaties and resolutions of international conferences that were not sanctioned by subsequent national or international action. He argued, moreover, that if aggressive war in violation of international treaties was a crime entailing individual responsibility, then such responsibility should also encompass those in the UK and France that compelled Czechoslovakia to consent to German aggression, as well as those Soviet officials that were responsible for the invasion of Poland in violation of their non-aggression pact with Germany of 23 August 1939 – although Germany had herself invaded Poland 16 days earlier.[37] Other jurists, nonetheless, were of the view that the waging of an aggressive war was indeed an international crime.[38]

Since a war of aggression could only be committed by persons in the highest echelons of authority and after formulating a plan to that effect, the Tribunal set out the parameters of criminal participation in crimes against peace. First, it held that the conspiracy charge could only apply to the crime of aggressive war, although the indictment had applied it to all the offences in the Charter. It rejected the prosecution's argument that any significant participation in the workings of the Nazi Party since its inception in 1919 was evidence of involvement in a conspiracy to commit the offences that were within the Tribunal's jurisdiction, holding that the conspiracy must not have been too far removed from the time of decision and of action.[39] The IMT found that plans to wage aggressive war had been revealed as early as 5 November 1937, if not earlier, but this involved many separate plans rather than a single conspiracy embracing them all. The Tribunal was of the opinion that a crime against peace required not mere participation in the Nazi conspiracy, but also an intention to commit aggressive war. Thus, the accused Schacht was acquitted of this charge because he terminated his financial and armament building activity in 1937, after discovering Hitler's intention to invade other nations.[40] The IMT held that even though the plan or conspiracy may have been conceived by only one person its status as a conspiracy remains unaltered where other persons participate in its execution. Indeed, as the Tribunal pointed out, since Hitler could not have waged aggressive war on his own, it was evident that those executing the plan did not avoid responsibility 'by showing that they acted under the directions of the man who conceived it'.[41] The unsatisfactory, from a legal point of view, formulation of the crime against peace in Article 6(a) of the IMT Charter did not readily evolve as a principle of treaty law in the post-Nuremberg era. It was not until the 1998 ICC Statute that it was reinvigorated, albeit in dormant form until such time as an appropriate definition is agreed upon by participating States.

---

[37]   G Finch, 'The Nuremberg Trial and International Law' (1947) 41 *American Journal of International Law* 20, 26–28.

[38]   S Glueck, 'The Nuremberg Trial and Aggressive War' (1946) 59 *Harvard Law Review* 396; Lord Wright, 'War Crimes under International Law' (1946) 62 *Law Quarterly Review* 40.

[39]   IMT Judgment, at 222.

[40]   Q Wright, 'The Law of the Nuremberg Trial' (1947) 41 *American Journal of International Law* 38, at 67.

[41]   IMT Judgment, at 223.

An embarrassing factor was also the fact that the USSR had itself waged a war of aggression by the signing of a non-aggression pact with Germany on 23 August 1939, just prior to the latter's invasion of Poland. That pact contained a secrete protocol in which Germany 'ceded' the Baltic countries to the USSR in exchange of its non-participation in the ensuing war. A few weeks later Stalin marched into Eastern Poland as did the Germans under the protection of the secret protocol.[42] This event and the illegal occupation of the Baltics remained for obvious reasons outside the scope of the IMT. For a more comprehensive analysis of developments on the crime of aggression in the post-Nuremberg era see chapter 13.

The IMT adopted a more vague approach when it came to justifying the existence of crimes against humanity. It had been common knowledge that atrocities against German Jews and minority groups had been carried out by the Nazi regime, as well as similar offences against other civilians in countries occupied by Germany. Whilst the brutality against civilians of other countries during the course of fighting or occupation might have been covered by established international law on war crimes and aggression, it was inconceivable at the time that atrocities against a State's own citizens could be deemed to have taken place in armed conflict (or war). In fact, they could hardly be described as crimes at all given that German Jews did not even wage an armed insurrection against the Nazi regime. Article 6(c) of the Charter, concerning crimes against humanity, was drafted so as to encompass these crimes, which had occurred on such a massive scale that they could not be ignored. Article 6(c) of the Charter covered all crimes against *any* civilian population.[43] However, the IMT sidestepped any discussion of precedents for crimes against humanity in international law. Instead, it took the approach of delineating its own jurisdiction over such offences, in particular whether they were undertaken as part of other offences within its ambit:

> The tribunal is of the opinion that revolting and horrible as many of these crimes were, it has not been satisfactorily proved that they were done in execution of, or in connection with, any such crime.[44]

As a result, although it had found that the Jewish minority in Germany, as well as other minority groups, had been subjected to acute discrimination and extermination policies long before the outbreak of the Second World War, in order to describe these pre-war acts as crimes against humanity it had to establish that they were committed in 'execution of, or in connection with, any crime within the jurisdiction of the tribunal'. Evidently, the Tribunal was not prepared to go that far, possibly because of the evidentiary difficulties this exercise would entail, taking account of the limited resources and time it was allocated in carrying out its task. Alternatively, it could be said that because there was more than ample evidence of large scale atrocities perpetrated against civilians and other minority groups in the course of the war there was no need to indulge, at least for the purposes of that particular prosecution, in other events that were harder to establish in legal terms. The Tribunal did not, however, exclude the possibility that crimes against humanity might have been

---

[42] G Ginsburgs, *Moscow's Road to Nuremberg* (The Hague, Kluwer, 1996) 129, 142.
[43] Art 6(b) dealt with acts committed against the 'civilian population of, or in, occupied territory'.
[44] IMT Judgment, at 249.

committed also before a war. As a matter of fact, we now know that this was indeed the case through acts of persecution that did not entail murder or extermination.

Although Article 6(c) of the Charter required a link between crimes against humanity and crimes against peace or war crimes, it was not entirely clear whether international law required an additional nexus between crimes against humanity and the existence of an armed conflict. Control Council Law No 10 later provided for the prosecution of crimes against humanity, without requiring a nexus to other crimes in the IMT Charter, or other crimes in general. In fact, prosecutions under this law by US military courts resulted in the conviction of hundreds of Nazi soldiers and officers and, significantly, these courts were not limited to the examination of post-1939 events, but looked into crimes perpetrated before the outbreak of the war. Article 6(c) of the Charter distinguished between two categories of punishable acts: first, murder, extermination, enslavement, deportation and other inhuman acts committed against any civilian population, before or during the war; and second, persecution on political, racial or religious grounds.[45] For a more comprehensive analysis of the contemporary formulation of crimes against humanity, see chapter 8.

The legality of the concept of war crimes was unquestionable, although the defence counsel argued that the Tribunal did not enjoy jurisdiction for violation of the laws or customs of war. This argument was correctly rejected on the basis that war crimes prosecutions against aliens had a long history in the law of nations.[46] Since any nation could initiate criminal proceedings in respect of war crimes committed against its population it was therefore possible for a group of nations, in this case the Allies, to do so in concert. As far as the law of nations was concerned, the concept of war crimes was precisely delineated under treaty and customary law. Efforts to codify and enforce this law had begun as early as 1864 with the adoption of the Geneva Convention for the Amelioration of the Condition of the Wounded in Armies in the Field.[47] The most significant codification of the *jus in bello* principles was that undertaken in the context of the 1899 and 1907 Hague Peace Conferences, where a number of conventions regulating conduct in warfare were adopted. Most important among these was, undoubtedly, the 1907 Hague Convention IV on Respecting the Laws and Customs of War on Land and the Regulations annexed thereto. The IMT found that the evidence furnished by the prosecution demonstrated beyond doubt the perpetration of pre-planned war crimes that were to be committed whenever the Führer and his close associates thought them to be advantageous. This was done, for example, in relation to the plunder and ill-treatment of Soviet civilians and their property, the exploitation of slave labour of other occupied territories, as well as the murder of captured enemy commandos and Soviet Commissars.[48] The existence of these policies was revealed by reference to orders that were issued and circulated by some of the accused, such as the 1941 '"Night and Fog" decree' that was issued by Hitler and signed by Keitel, under which persons who committed offences against the

---

[45] See E Schwelb, 'Crimes against Humanity' (1946) 23 *British Yearbook of International Law* 178.

[46] *Ex p Quirin* (1942) 317 US 27 and *Re Yamashita* (1946) 327 US 1. This prerogative was also recognised in post-WW II criminal trials, such as the 1950 case of *Röhrig, Brunner and Heinze* 7 ILR 393.

[47] 18 Martens NRGT 607. The 1868 Additional Articles Relating to the Condition of the Wounded in War extended the humanitarian principles enunciated in the 1864 Convention to Warfare at Sea.

[48] IMT Judgment, at 224.

Reich or the German forces in occupied territories, except where the death sentence was certain, were to be taken secretly to Germany and handed over to criminal organisations for trial or punishment.[49] As is evident, the IMT dealt with war crimes as far as this concept encompassed a policy. Subsequent military tribunals had ample opportunity to prosecute individuals who had willingly implemented and executed such policies during the war.

Significantly, the Charter provided for the determination by the Tribunal of the criminal character of indicted German organisations whose purpose was to serve as a precedent in cases before subsequent military courts in occupied Germany.[50] This type of liability was inserted at the insistence of the USSR, whose diplomats argued that this would eliminate the need to prove the criminality of organisations in each case for which a member is tried.[51] The Tribunal declared that the Wafen SS and its subsidiary the SD, the Gestapo and the Leadership Corps of the Nazi Party were criminal. The SA (storm troopers), the Reich Cabinet and the High Command were acquitted without prejudice to the individual liability of their members. In exercising its power to declare organisations criminal, the Tribunal pointed out that membership of such organisations did not necessarily entail the liability of each member. Rather:

> A criminal organisation is analogous to a criminal conspiracy in that the essence of both is co-operation for criminal purposes. There must be a group bound together and organised for a common purpose. The group must be formed or used in connection with the commission of crimes denounced by the Charter. Since the declaration with respect to the organisations and groups will, as has been pointed out, fix the criminality of its members, that definition should exclude persons who had no knowledge of the criminal purposes or acts of the organisation and those who were drafted by the State for membership, unless they were personally implicated in the commission of acts declared criminal by Article 6 of the Charter as members of the organisation. Membership alone is not enough to come within the scope of these declarations.[52]

Criminal responsibility under the charter continued irrespective of an individual's official position or whether an individual was acting under orders from a superior.[53] The IMT did not deal in any great detail with the defence of superior orders for two reasons. First, as it was dealing with the most senior Axis officials it had already found that in their majority they were co-conspirators in the waging of aggressive wars and each according to his position had planned the commission of offences against the occupied civilian populations. Secondly, the orders circulated to the respective High Commands and Hitlerite groups were either issued by Hitler, but in the acquiescence and prompting of the accused, or were alternatively authored by them. The Tribunal held that the defence of superior orders could be urged in mitigation of punishment in cases where 'moral choice was in fact possible'. Hence, even in the extreme event that any one of the accused was under a direct order from

---

[49] Ibid, at 229. Similarly, Keitel was found to have issued the 'Commissar Order' in 1941 and the 'Commando Order' in 1942.

[50] For an analysis of group or corporate criminality, see chapter 3.11.

[51] Ginsburgs, *Moscow's Road to Nuremberg*, at 98.

[52] IMT Judgment, at 251. For an analysis of the defence of superior orders, see chapter 5.3.

[53] IMT Charter, Arts 7–8.

Hitler, his position in the Reich structure would, in fact, be so high that a moral choice should have been possible. The same is not always true of the soldier on the battlefield where the order and its consequences are not directly or immediately clear, whereas the threat of punishment for disobedience is always certain.[54]

The judgment of the IMT at Nuremberg was delivered on 30 September 1946 and sentences were pronounced on 1 October 1946. Of the twenty-two persons indicted – the accused Bormann was not found, while Goering had succeeded in committing suicide before the judgment was rendered – three were acquitted. The remainder were convicted of one or more of the crimes set down in Article 6 of the IMT Charter. Twelve of the accused were sentenced to death, while seven were sentenced to imprisonment for terms ranging from 10 years to life (three were actually sentenced to life imprisonment). As already observed, of the six accused organisations only three were found to be criminal. Judge Nikitchenko from the USSR dissented from all the aforementioned acquittals, but this is hardly surprising given his predisposition in favour of Soviet show trials.[55] The details of punishment, which in the case of the death penalty was hanging, as well as any appeals against the sentences passed upon the accused, were handled by the Allied Control Council.

The IMT is commonly regarded as the first 'international' criminal tribunal of its type. However, it can be argued that the Tribunal was not so much an international institution but rather an Allied Forces tribunal. In outlining the legal basis under which the Allied powers had established the Tribunal, the judgment of the IMT held that:

> The making of the Charter was the exercise of the sovereign legislative power by countries to which the German Reich unconditionally surrendered; and the undoubted right of these countries to legislate for the occupied territories has been recognised by the civilised world.[56]

This suggests that the nature of the IMT was more akin to that of a municipal court established by the Allied Governments exercising sovereign power in Germany after the war. This conclusion is also borne out from the fact that the Allies had effectively occupied Germany, without however intending its annexation. As for the recognition of the IMT by the international community, despite the fact that no State objected to its establishment, the Allied powers received only twenty-two statements of support.

Although the IMT Charter should be regarded as a landmark in international criminal law, the rules relating to evidence and procedure during trial seem simplistic in the light of modern day developments. Conduct of the trials at Nuremberg operated under the rules set out in Articles 17 to 25 of the IMT Charter. The rules of evidence and procedure seem hopelessly inadequate when one considers the complexity of the rules and procedure that apply in respect of the ICTY and ICTR. Whilst

---

[54] See ICC Statute, Art 33; see also MJ Osiel, 'Obeying Orders: Atrocity, Military Discipline, and the Law of War' (1998) 86 *California Law Review* 939.

[55] He famously stated that if a judge sitting at Nuremberg: 'is supposed to be impartial, [this] would only lead to unnecessary delays'. RE Conot, *Justice and Nuremberg* (New York, Harper & Row, 1994) 18.

[56] IMT Judgment, at 216.

Article 16(d) of the Nuremberg Charter gave the accused the right to legal representation the accused did not actually meet their counsel until immediately before, or
even on the first day of trial.[57] All this suggests that the IMT is an easy target for
criticism. Allegations that the law of the IMT was *ex post facto*, that there were
insufficient procedural safeguards for the accused, that the trials were victor's justice
have all been levelled at the Tribunal. A number of commentators criticised the way
in which the IMT supported the law of the Charter, especially with regard to the
crimes contained in Article 6.[58] Further criticisms were made regarding the delinea-
tion of crimes against humanity, which it has been suggested, because of the IMT's
decision to restrict its jurisdiction to events occurring only during the war, effectively
rendered the offence almost synonymous with war crimes.[59] On the other hand, had
the principal Axis officials not been held accountable for their atrocious deeds, justice
would have been sacrificed and their impunity would have adversely affected future
generations. Prosecution under the terms of German law was inappropriate because
the Reich Government had decriminalised all the crimes committed in Germany and
abroad. It was exactly for this reason that Art 6(c) upheld liability for crimes against
humanity, even if the said offence did not violate the domestic law of the country
where it was perpetrated. A final criticism concerns the lack of prosecutions for
crimes committed by the Allies, but this is hardly surprising. Even at trial, the USSR
had attempted to implicate the Germans for the Katyn massacre in which 15,000
Polish officers were summarily executed by USSR forces under the orders of Stalin.
The US and British prosecutors refused to support the charge and the Soviets decided
to finally drop it after the accumulation of evidence started to demonstrate that it was
in fact of their own doing.[60] Perhaps, therefore, the creation of the IMT with the
jurisdictional competence granted to it under Article 6 represented the most appropriate solution as far as the meting out of justice was concerned, regardless of the
legal sensitivities this exercise necessarily entailed. Let us now examine the other
international tribunal of WW II.

17.3   The International Military Tribunal for the Far East (IMTFE)

Imperial Japan had waged wars of aggression in the vicinity of South East Asia since
1928, in an effort to subjugate and control the Korean peninsula, east and central
China, which it later annexed and declared independent under the name Manchukuo.
Japanese expansionism into mainland Asia was vigorously opposed by Russia, USA
and the UK and none of its new territories were recognised as legitimate. In fact, it
was these condemnations that convinced Japan to withdraw its membership from the
League of Nations in 1933. On 27 September 1940 Japan entered into a pact with

---

[57]   By way of comparison, the accused Tojo who was arraigned before the IMTFE was interrogated for
a total of 124 hours in the absence of counsel, twenty hours of which was used in the trial against him. N
Boister, R Cryer, *The Tokyo International Military Tribunal: A Reappraisal* (Oxford, Oxford University
Press, 2008) 75.
[58]   Finch, 'The Nuremberg Trial and International Law', at 334.
[59]   F Biddle, 'The Nuremberg Trial' (1947) 33 *Virginia Law Review* 679.
[60]   Conot, *Justice and Nuremberg*, at 452.

Italy and Germany through which it sought to legitimise its new conquests and establish a mutual military alliance against external foes.[61] During their campaign on mainland Asia since 1931 Japanese forces were gradually responsible for an enormous amount of violations against mainly the local civilian populations, culminating in the so-called Rape of the Chinese city of Nanking in respect of which historic accounts detail widespread acts of unspeakable barbarity. Japanese aggression entered the greater theatre of the Second World War from the moment it attacked the US naval forces at Pearl Harbor, Hawaii, on 8 December 1941, albeit prior to this date it was also at war with Britain following its invasion of commonwealth territories under the sovereignty of the Crown.

On 1 December 1943 the Cairo Declaration on World War II was made by the Presidents of the US and Nationalist China and the Prime Minister of Great Britain. It read, in relevant part, that:

> The Three Great Allies are fighting this war to restrain and punish the aggression of Japan. They covet no gain for themselves and have no thought of territorial expansion.

Prior to the signing of the Instrument of Japanese Surrender on 2 September 1945 the Allied Forces adopted the Declaration of Potsdam on 26 July 1945, later acceded to also by the USSR. They reiterated what was said in the Cairo Declaration, but added that:

> We do not intend that the Japanese people shall be enslaved as a race or destroyed as a nation, but stern justice shall be meted out to all war criminals including those who have visited cruelties upon our prisoners.

Following Japan's surrender it was natural that the deliberations of the Potsdam Declaration would be taken forward. The USA did not want to appear the sole power behind any trials, despite its occupation of Japan, and hence during the Moscow Conference of 26 December 1945, which included the participation of all key Allied foreign ministers, it was agreed by all powers present that the US Supreme Commander of Allied Powers (SCAP) shall issue all orders for effectuating the terms of the surrender and the occupation and control of Japan. The Conference also established a Far Eastern Commission (FEC) that was composed of the Allies and all independent regional powers.[62] In reality the FEC was endowed with supervisory functions and the SCAP could act on his own initiative without requiring FEC approval.[63] This in turn demonstrated that the effective occupation of Japan was not a multilateral enterprise.

It was thus within the unilateral prerogative of SCAP, ie General Douglas McArthur, to set up a special tribunal in compliance with the commitments undertaken under the Potsdam Declaration. Unlike the Nuremberg Tribunal, however, the IMTFE[64] was established not by treaty but on the basis of a Special Proclamation adopted on 19 January 1946 by McArthur but without receiving any prior direction

---

[61] Boister and Cryer, 14–15.
[62] Ibid, p 24.
[63] Ibid.
[64] 4 Bevans 20 (as amended on 26 Apr 1946).

from the FEC.[65] His authority to establish the IMTFE in this manner and promulgate its Charter was exacted from his mandate, through which he possessed the competence to create military commissions and tribunals.[66] Many such commissions were subsequently established by all the Allied Forces involved in the war. In fact, the conviction of General Yamashita, Governor and Supreme Military Commander of the Japanese Army in the Philippines prior to the emancipation of the islands by the Allies, emanated from such a commission. This much is not in doubt and is consistent with the right of the occupying power to administer criminal justice in an occupied territory. What is of interest is the perceived status of the Tokyo Tribunal as of international import, rather than as a legislative act of the occupying power. Following the conclusion of judicial proceedings before the Tokyo Tribunal seven of the accused filed *habeas corpus* petitions with the US Supreme Court under the jurisdictional premise that the IMTFE was a US military tribunal which had been set up by the executive rather than the legislative branch of government. The Supreme Court dismissed its jurisdiction over the case, arguing that the Tokyo Tribunal was an international judicial institution set up by occupying forces and by virtue of the fact that the SCAP was an agent of said forces operating under the FEC and the Postdam Declaration.[67] The same conclusion was reached by the IMTFE, which viewed itself as the implementation of the relevant Allied declarations.[68]

The indictment included 55 counts, charging twenty-eight accused with crimes against peace, war crimes and crimes against humanity during the period from 1 January 1928 to 2 September 1945. Of the 28 accused, three were acquitted. Although the IMTFE was established with the aim of prosecuting the most senior Japanese officials holding both political as well as military positions, this did not affect Emperor Hirohito who was not arraigned, principally because of the vociferous position of the USA, despite the majority of the Allies' contention to the contrary. As a result, it became very challenging to draft an aggressive war conspiracy charge without implicating the constitutional leader of the country.[69]

The substantive and procedural law of the IMTFE was essentially the same as that of the Nuremberg Tribunal Charter. This is natural given the consensus as to the offences in the Nuremberg Charter; moreover, its jurisprudence served as a safe basis for any challenges to the legality of the Tokyo Tribunal, all of which were rejected on same or similar grounds. Unlike the IMT, the IMTFE addressed the issue of superior

---

[65] Boister and Cryer, at 25.

[66] The USA has a long tradition of setting up military commissions to try captured enemy personnel accused of violations of the laws and customs of war. Her right to institute these commissions was confirmed by the Supreme Court in *ex p Vallandigham* (1864) 68 US 243 and subsequently in *ex p Quirin* (1942) 317 US 1.

[67] *Hirota v McArthur* (1948) 338 US 197, 198. In similar fashion, the US Supreme Court in *Johnson v Eisentrager* 339 US 763 (1950), rejected the premise of a habeas corpus plea by German nationals convicted of espionage in favour of the Japanese, immediately following the surrender of Germany. Their trial had been entertained by a US military commission sitting in China and the accused had never set foot on US soil. This position is no longer tenable, following judgments in *Rasul v Bush* (2004) 542 US 466, 478–79 and *Loizidou v Turkey*, Preliminary Objections, Eur Ct HR (23 Mar 1995), para 62, which confirmed the extraterritorial reach of the ECHR in cases where a member State exercises effective control over a territory or if its acts produce effects therein.

[68] Boister and Cryer, 31, 36–37.

[69] Ibid, 65–67.

responsibility in count 55 of the indictment, holding, especially as this relates to the maintenance of prisoner of war camps, that all those involved with captured enemy personnel, from the incumbent Minister to the last camp commander, have a duty to initiate a system of protection and thereafter to ensure its effective functioning. While some judges dissented as to the Tokyo Tribunal's legality and their inability to assess whether the crimes within its Statute were justified under international law, principal among these Justice Pal from India, one should not exaggerate relevant criticisms. For one thing, save some procedural and evidentiary irregularities, the accused were given a fair trial. Moreover, the Tokyo judgment affirmed in the best possible manner the legality of the new international crimes that first appeared in the Nuremberg Charter. Finally, like all international criminal trials it helped instil the rule of law in occupied Japan and dismissed any further nationalistic hopes for expansion and domination in Asia, further contributing to the enhancement of the relationship between the occupier and his subjects.

17.4   The International Law Commission's Role in the Post-Nuremberg Era

Perhaps the crucial point which has given the judgment of the IMT its place as the starting point for contemporary international criminal law was the fact that one of the first acts of the newly created United Nations was the General Assembly's affirmation of the Principles of International Law recognised by the Charter of the Nuremberg Tribunal and the Judgment of the Tribunal.[70] In the following year, the Assembly requested the International Law Commission (ILC) to formulate the Nuremberg judgment and Charter provisions into a set of principles. The ILC considered this request during its first session in 1949 and concluded that since these principles had already been affirmed by the General Assembly its task should not be to express its appreciation on their content, but rather to formulate them as substantive principles of international law.[71] The report of special rapporteur Jean Spiropoulos was adopted by the Commission, which subsequently forwarded its formulation of the seven principles,[72] together with their commentaries to the

---

[70]   GA Res 95(1) (11 Dec 1946). Significantly, in 1963, the Lord Chancellor remarked before the UK Parliament that the Nuremberg Principles were 'generally accepted among States and [had] the status of customary international law'. Hansard, HL, vol 253, col 831 (2 Dec 1963).

[71]   Yearbook of the International Law Commission [YBILC] (First Session, 1949) 282.

[72]   Principle I, Any person who commits an act which constitutes a crime under international law is responsible therefore and liable to punishment; Principle II, The fact that internal law does not impose a penalty for an act which constitutes a crime under international law does not relieve the person who committed the act from responsibility under international law; Principle III, The fact that a person who committed an act which constitutes a crime under international law acted as a Head of State or responsible government official does not relieve him from responsibility under international law; Principle IV, The fact that a person acted pursuant to order of his government or of a superior does not relieve him from responsibility under international law, provided a moral choice was in fact possible to him; Principle V, Any person charged with a crime under international law has the right to a fair trial on the facts and law; Principle VI, Crimes against Peace, War Crimes and Crimes against Humanity are punishable as crimes under international law; Principle VII, Complicity in the commission of a crime against peace, a war crime, or a crime against humanity as set forth in Principle VI is a crime under international law.

General Assembly.[73] The Assembly asked member States for their comments and requested the ILC to prepare a Draft Code of Offences Against the Peace and Security of Mankind.[74]

The Commission's work in preparing the Draft Code of Offences was undertaken in two distinct phases, from 1947 to 1954, and the second from 1982 to 1996. Although it was successful in formulating and convincing States to adopt the ICC Statute in 1998, completion of the Draft Code was never achieved. The ILC had made such progress by 1951 that it submitted the Draft Code to the General Assembly, but in light of the comments received it resubmitted its final version in 1954.[75] The Assembly felt, however, that the definition of aggression raised unsurpassed problems and decided to postpone consideration of the Code until further work was done on this legal matter.[76] A definition on aggression was adopted with consensus some twenty years later in 1974[77] and the Commission once again suggested that it might resume examination of the Code. This was done in 1981 when the Assembly invited the Commission to examine the Code as a matter of priority, taking into account 'the results achieved by the process of the progressive development of international law'.[78] The Commission resumed its work in 1982 and by 1996 it had adopted a final set of 20 draft Articles constituting the Code of Crimes Against the Peace and Security of Mankind,[79] a number which constituted a substantial reduction from the initial proposals and drafts that had been presented since 1982. The Commission, however, made it clear that the inclusion of certain crimes in the Code did not affect the status of other crimes under international law, nor did the adoption of the Code preclude the further development of this area of law. As to the implementation of the statute, the Assembly was presented with two options: adoption of an international convention, or incorporation into the statute of an international criminal court. Since the Preparatory Committee for the establishment of the ICC had already commenced its work the Assembly drew the attention of the participating States to the relevance of the Draft Code.[80]

On 17 July 1998 the Statute of the ICC was adopted without the Code having ever entered into force. It is more than evident however that one of the significant catalysts for the adoption of the ICC Statute as well as the establishment of the ad hoc tribunals for Yugoslavia and Rwanda was the work of the ILC on the Draft Code. From a legal point of view, the possible adoption of the Code in light of the ICC would be relevant only for those countries that had not ratified the ICC Statute, while it would also reaffirm the substantive law of that statute and other international conventions. Its application might even instigate the extension of the ICC's jurisdiction to encompass other international crimes, or bind those States that are not parties to particular multilateral criminal conventions. Overall, the Draft Code represents an

---

[73] YBILC (Second Session, 1950), vol II, at 374.
[74] GA Res 488(V) (12 Dec 1950).
[75] YBILC (Sixth Session, 1954), vol II, at 149.
[76] GA Res 897(IX) (4 Dec 1954).
[77] GA Res 3314(XXIX) (14 Dec 1974).
[78] GA Res 36/106 (10 Dec 1981).
[79] See ILC Draft Code Commentary, UN Doc A/51/10 (1996), reprinted in (1997) 18 *Human Rights Law Journal* 96.
[80] GA Res 51/160 (16 Dec 1996).

example of the variety of processes that exist within the science of international law. The ILC worked diligently on a 'difficult' set of rules on the basis of State consent, waiting patiently for the time they matured into solid concepts, but did not insist on their adoption in the form contemplated in its reports. Instead, it proposed that they be accepted in any form the international community could reach agreement on. This turned out to be the ICC, but it could very well have been the Code.

In closing, the reader should not forget that the Nuremberg legacy is not confined to the Tribunal *per se*. Rather, this legacy encompasses moreover the plethora of cases heard before military tribunals (so-called subsequent trials) in the few years following the conclusion of the IMT proceedings. The jurisprudence of these trials was used extensively not only during the Cold War but also as part of the jurisprudence of the ICTY and ICTR. It should not be thought that every war crimes trial of that era possesses jurisprudential value. Trials held in the USSR and in other countries that failed to provide judicial guarantees and in which the guilt of the accused was a foregone conclusion, despite the abhorrent nature of the crimes charged, have not occupied any part in the corpus of international criminal law.[81]

---

[81] By a decree issued on 2 November 1942, the Presidium of the Supreme Soviet of the USSR established an 'Extraordinary State Commission for ascertaining and investigating crimes perpetrated by the German-Fascist invaders and their accomplices, and the damage inflicted by them on citizens, collective farms, social organizations, State enterprises and institutions of the USSR'. The first trial of Nazi members was held in Kharkov (now in Ukraine) from 15 to 18 December 1943. They were accused of a series of crimes: the gassing of thousands of people from Kharkov and the surrounding area, the ill-treatment and torture of prisoners of war and civilians, the destruction of villages and the execution – in some instances by burning alive – of women, children, the elderly, the wounded and prisoners of war. These have become known as the Krasnodar and Kharkov Trials. See I Bourtman, 'Blood for Blood, Death for Death: The Soviet Military Tribunal in Krasnodar, 1943' (2008) 22 *Holocaust and Genocide Studies* 246.

18

The International Criminal Tribunals for Yugoslavia and Rwanda

18.1 Introduction

Reports since 1991 of widespread and gross human rights violations as a result of the armed conflicts raging between rival ethnic groups in the territory of the former Yugoslavia prompted the Security Council to express its deep concern and describe the situation as a threat to international peace and security.[1] This determination was premised in large part on a series of detailed interim reports that were submitted to the Council by a United Nations (UN) Commission of Experts established under Security Council Resolution 780 in 1992. Security Council Resolution 808 instructed the Secretary-General to examine whether the establishment of a criminal tribunal would have a basis in law, and if so, to formulate an appropriate statute. The Secretary General promptly replied in the affirmative and duly formulated a statute on the basis that it would apply only to those portions of international law which were beyond any doubt part of customary international law.[2] Based on the Secretary General's report, to which a statute was annexed, the Security Council adopted Resolution 827 on 25 May 1993 and established the International Tribunal for the Prosecution of Persons Responsible for Serious Violations of International Humanitarian Law Committed in the Territory of the Former Yugoslavia (ICTY).[3]

Both the establishment of the Commission of Experts and, more so, the ICTY itself, constitute a historic breakthrough for the UN and the role of the Security Council. The Commission was created as an international fact-finding body as envisaged under Article 90 of the 1977 Protocol I Additional to the 1949 Geneva Conventions (Protocol I).[4] Although such commissions require the explicit consent of the States involved, the Council departed from this rule in Resolution 780 given that it was acting under Chapter VII of the UN Charter.[5] The establishment of the ICTY on the basis of a Security Council Resolution under Chapter VII merits closer consideration. It was preferred to a treaty because it was speedier and did not require

---

[1]   SC Res 808 (22 Feb 1993).

[2]   Report of the Secretary General pursuant to Security Council Resolution 808 (1993), UN Doc S/25704 (1993), para 2, reprinted in (1993) 32 ILM 1159.

[3]   See JC O'Brien, 'The International Tribunal for Violations of International Humanitarian Law in the Former Yugoslavia' (1993) 87 *American Journal of International Law* 639.

[4]   1125 UNTS 3.

[5]   See CM Bassiouni, 'The United Nations Commission of Experts Pursuant to Security Council Resolution 780 (1992)' (1994) 88 *American Journal of International Law* 784.

the consent of the, by then, crumbling Yugoslavia. Obviously, the reinvigoration of the Council after the end of the Cold War meant that it could far more easily than in the past reach consensus and take concerted action with regard to situations jeopardising international peace and security. The establishment of the ICTY under Chapter VII was a measure not involving the use of force and, thus, fell squarely within the ambit of Article 41 of the UN Charter. It makes no difference that the indicative list of measures envisaged in that provision make no reference to the setting up of judicial bodies. Its relation to the Security Council is that of a subsidiary organ under Article 29 of the UN Charter.[6] As the product of a Security Council resolution the Statute of the ICTY is binding upon every member of the UN in accordance with Article 25 of the Charter. There is no doubt that such a result would never have been achieved through the negotiation of a treaty, as few States would have seen any benefit in partaking of an enterprise of this magnitude, especially since the protagonist countries would, themselves, have refused to participate. From its very nature, therefore, the ICTY could not take the form of a permanent judicial institution but an ad hoc one, whose jurisdiction is limited in time, place and subject matter and whose mandate may theoretically be terminated or altered by its creator at any time.

In 1994, atrocities of a scale many times over those perpetrated in the former Yugoslavia were reported taking place in Rwanda in the form of genocide against the Tutsi minority by extremist Hutu elements. The estimated number of dead as a result of this genocide is estimated to be anywhere between 500,000 and one million. The Security Council instructed a Commission of Experts to investigate the situation in Rwanda in the same manner in which it had acted in the case of Yugoslavia and, on the basis of the Commission's reports, it determined that there was a threat to international peace and security. It subsequently ordered the establishment of an International Criminal Tribunal for the Prosecution of Persons Responsible for Genocide and Other Serious Violations of International Humanitarian Law Committed in the Territory of Rwanda and Rwandan Citizens Responsible for Genocide and Other Such Violations Committed in the Territory of Neighbouring States between 1 January 1994 and 31 December 1994 (ICTR).[7] By Resolution 977 the Security Council decided that the seat of the Tribunal would be located in Arusha, United Republic of Tanzania, instead of Rwanda.[8] Initial suggestions for expanding ICTY jurisdiction to incorporate crimes under Rwandan law failed because a number of States feared this would lead to a permanent international criminal court. Instead, the Council expedited matters further by establishing the ICTR, without demanding a prior report from the Secretary-General as in the case of the ICTY.[9] Both institutions are, nonetheless, interrelated not only because they are subsidiary organs of the Security Council, but also because they share a common Appeals Chamber[10]

---

[6] See D Sarooshi, 'The Legal Framework Governing United Nations Subsidiary Organs' (1996) 67 *British Yearbook of International Law* 413, 428–31.

[7] SC Res 955 (8 Nov 1994).

[8] SC Res 977 (22 Feb 1995).

[9] P Akhavan, 'The International Criminal Tribunal for Rwanda: The Politics and Pragmatics of Punishment' (1996) 90 *American Journal of International Law* 501, at 502.

[10] ICTR Statute, Art 12(2).

and prosecutor.[11] The intention behind these common institutions was the development of a balanced and coherent jurisprudence, which has evidently been achieved. It should be noted that although the ruling Rwandan Government that overthrew the Hutu extremists responsible for the genocide in that country had, itself, proposed the creation of the ICTR, it finally voted against Resolution 955 because, *inter alia,* it had envisaged both control over the Tribunal as well as wide temporal jurisdiction, well before the January 1994 boundary fixed by the Security Council.[12] The Security Council rejected both of these contentions and hence the ICTR was developed and functioned without the blessing of the post-genocide Rwandan government.

With the judicial activity of the ICTY being scarce to start off with, the legal world was necessarily eager for a first test case. In 1995 the Appeals Chamber of the ICTY was seized by a motion against a Trial Chamber decision regarding, amongst other issues, the legality of its establishment by the Security Council and its authority, as a subsidiary organ thereto, vis-a-vis the Council to determine the legality of its mandate. The Appeals Chamber, presided by Antonio Cassese, in a cornerstone decision for the development of international law ruled that in the case of the ICTY the Security Council intended to establish not just any subsidiary organ, but a special organ with judicial functions; a tribunal.[13] It further affirmed that international law at the time – as indeed now – dictated that each tribunal be set up as a self-contained system, whose jurisdictional powers may be limited by its constitutive instrument, although this does not mean that in the process the judicial character of these tribunals may be jeopardised.[14] More importantly, the Appeals Chamber expressly confirmed the inherent or incidental jurisdiction of any judicial body to determine its own competence, whether this is provided for in its constitutive instrument or not (that is, the so-called doctrine of Kompetenz-Kompetenz).[15]

Before we proceed to examine the substantive provisions and rich jurisprudence that has emanated from both Tribunals, it is useful to investigate the possible interpretative means by which to construe their Statutes. Although these are not *stricto sensu* international agreements, it is reasonable to subject them to the rules of interpretation available for treaties,[16] since they constitute legal instruments with the attributes of international agreements as defined by Article 2(a) of the 1969 Vienna Convention on the Law of Treaties (Vienna Convention).[17] The applicability of the interpretative rules of the Vienna Convention is further supported by the status of the ICTY and ICTR as subsidiary organs of the Security Council and, thus, directly

---

[11]   Ibid, Art 15(3).

[12]   Akhavan, 'The International Criminal Tribunal for Rwanda', 504–05.

[13]   *ICTY Prosecutor v Tadić,* Appeals Chamber Decision on the Defence Motion for Interlocutory Appeal on Jurisdiction (2 Oct 1995), para 15.

[14]   Ibid, para 11.

[15]   Ibid, para 18. Reference was made to Cordova J's dissenting opinion in the International Court of Justice (ICJ)'s Advisory Opinion on *Judgments of the Administrative Tribunal of the ILO,* (1956) ICJ Reports 77, at 163 (dissenting opinion of Judge Cordova).

[16]   *Tadić* case, Trial Chamber Decision on Protective Measures for Victims and Witnesses (10 Aug 1995), para 18.

[17]   1155 UNTS 331. Art 2(a) provides that the term treaty means 'an international agreement concluded between States in written form and governed by international law, whether embodied in a single instrument or in two or more related instruments and whatever its particular designation'; the Chinese representative to the Security Council made a statement to this effect during the deliberations of Resolution 808 (1993). See UN Doc S/PV3217 (1993) 33.

linked to the constituent instrument of the UN, its Charter. Therefore, since Article 5 of the 1969 Vienna Convention applies to treaties which are the constituent instruments of an international organisation and treaties adopted within an international organisation, it would seem appropriate that, by extension of the powers vested in the Security Council by the UN Charter, the rules of treaty interpretation apply also to the ICTY and ICTR Statutes.[18]

Thus, the ICTY Chambers' primary reliance on a 'literal' construction of their Statute, followed by 'teleological', 'logical' and 'systematic' methods of interpretation as secondary means,[19] is consonant with Article 31(1) of the 1969 Vienna Convention, according to which, treaties are to be interpreted in accordance with their ordinary meaning and in the light of their object and purpose, as well as Article 32 which allows for supplementary means when literal interpretation does not clarify the meaning of a provision. It should be stated that although humanitarian and human rights instruments warrant an interpretation which ensures their widest possible effectiveness in accordance with their object and purpose[20] the so-called 'evolutionary' method of interpretation,[21] according to which contemporary developments in international law are to be incorporated into the relevant provisions of humanitarian treaties, should not generally apply to the ICTY or ICTR because of their ad hoc character, their specific mandate to apply customary law and the violation of the principle of certainty belying criminal proceedings. The only possible exception could perhaps lie in those rules of procedure that are more favourable to the accused. Finally, although the issue of intra-ICTY precedent has been a problematic one, especially as regards the classification of armed conflicts by the various Chambers, it now seems settled that decisions of the Appeals Chambers should be followed, except where cogent reasons in the interests of justice require a departure. Such a departure is justified where the previous decision was decided on the basis of a wrong legal principle or wrongly decided on account of the judges' misconstruction of the relevant law.[22]

18.2 Formative Years of the Ad Hoc Tribunals

Unlike the ICTR, where a large number of accused were already apprehended by the new government or third States, the ICTY did not in its early years enjoy the cooperation of States on whose territory the alleged offenders had taken refuge.

---

[18] In accordance with the Latin maxim *delegatus non potest delegare*, a delegate cannot delegate his authority to a third entity and this is also true with respect to the powers conferred to subsidiary organs of the Council. Subsidiary organs can, however, delegate functions (as opposed to powers) which they themselves cannot fulfil. See D Sarooshi, The United Nations and the Development of Collective Security: The Delegation by the UN Security Council of its VII Powers (Oxford, Oxford University Press, 1999) 20ff.

[19] *Tadić* Appeals Jurisdiction Decision, paras 71–72, 79.

[20] Advisory Opinion *Concerning Reservations to the Genocide Convention* (1951) ICJ Reports 23; *Ireland v UK* (1978) Eur Ct HR, Ser A, No 25, para 239.

[21] Advisory Opinion *Concerning Legal Consequences for States of the Continued Presence of South Africa in Namibia* (1971) ICJ Reports 3, para 53; *Tyrer v UK* (1978) 2 EHRR 1, para 31.

[22] *ICTY Prosecutor v Aleksovski*, Appeals Chamber Judgment (24 Mar 2000), paras 101–15; *ICTY Prosecutor v Kordić and Čerkez*, Trial Chamber Judgment (26 Feb 2001), para 148.

This was due to a large degree to the fact that the various conflicts in the Republic of Bosnia and Herzegovina officially terminated as late as 14 December 1995, with the conclusion of the General Framework Agreement for Peace (GFAP, otherwise known as Dayton Peace Agreement).[23] Although the signatory former Yugoslav republics undertook an obligation after 1995 in accordance with the Dayton Agreement to cooperate with the Tribunal, such cooperation was not generally forthcoming, especially from Croatia[24] but more so from the Federal Republic of Yugoslavia (now Serbia).[25] Another complicating factor was the division of the Republic of Bosnia and Herzegovina into two autonomous entities, an ethnic Serbian (Republika Srpska) and a Moslem one (Federation of Bosnia and Herzegovina), governed however by a common presidency.[26] Republika Srpska has refused to render much assistance to the Tribunal on account of its leaders' alliance to a number of those indicted by the ICTY.

With an empty docket the ICTY faced an imminent danger of redundancy and oblivion by the very international community that created it, since it was no secret that by early 1995 a substantial number of States were growing weary of funding a judicial institution which had no accused to try.[27] During this time the Prosecutor was busy establishing liaisons and investigative teams in order to collect evidence and identify potential witnesses not only in the former Yugoslavia but across the globe, since a large number of witnesses and victims had subsequently sought refuge abroad. Endowed with the authority to formulate their own Rules of Procedure,[28] the ICTY judges adopted the first ever comprehensive code of international criminal procedure, adapted to the special needs of the Tribunal and based on a combination of both common law and civil law elements. For example, as regards examination of individuals, the adversarial system was preferred, while the introduction of almost unlimited admission of evidence, including hearsay, as long as it is deemed to have probative value,[29] reflects rather civil law criminal practice.

Rule 61 is of particular relevance to the present discussion. This rule permits the Prosecutor to submit his or her evidence against an accused to a Trial Chamber in order for the latter to review the indictment in cases where a warrant of arrest has not been executed and personal service of the indictment has not been given effect, despite sincere efforts by the Prosecutor. If, thereafter, the Trial Chamber ascertains that there are reasonable grounds for believing that the accused committed any or all of the crimes charged, it is empowered to make a formal declaration to that effect[30] and issue an international arrest warrant, which is then transmitted to all UN

---

[23] (1996) 35 ILM 75. Although the GFAP was signed in Paris, the Agreement itself was concluded in a US Air Force base in Dayton, Ohio, on 21 November 1995.

[24] Request by the Prosecutor under r 7*bis* (B) that the President Notify the Security Council of the Failure of the Republic of Croatia to Comply with its Obligations under Art 29 (28 Jul 1999).

[25] 'President Cassese reports to the Security Council on the continuing violation of the FRY of its obligation to co-operate with ICTY', ICTY Doc CC/PIO/075-E (23 May 1996).

[26] GFAP, Art 3.

[27] 'The judges of the ICTY express their concern regarding the substance of their programme of judicial work for 1995', ICTY Doc CC/PIO/OO3-E (1 Feb 1995).

[28] ICTY Statute, Art 15. The first version of the rules is reprinted in (1994) 33 ILM 484.

[29] ICTY Rules, R 89(C).

[30] Ibid, R 61(C).

Member States.[31] If any State fails to execute the contents of the warrant the ICTY President may notify the Security Council.[32] Five cases were brought before a Trial Chamber by the Prosecutor under r 61 proceedings, the most prominent of which was that against the political leader of the Bosnian Serbs, Radovan Karadžić and the Chief of Staff of the Bosnian Serb Army, Radko Mladić,[33] where an abundance of testimony and other documentation evinced the existence of a policy of 'ethnic cleansing' against non-Serbs. In the same course of proceedings it was discovered that the planning of these policies could be attributed to the two accused. In each of these cases, the judgment stressed that r 61 proceedings were intended to serve as public reviews of indictments and did not constitute trials *in absentia,* a guarantee pre-scribed under Article 21(d) of the ICTY Statute. They did not culminate in a verdict, nor deprive the accused of their right to contest the charges in person. Furthermore, it was pointed out that such proceedings provided an opportunity for victims to be heard in a public hearing and become part of history.[34] Indeed, the publicity that followed these proceedings and especially the detailing of the horrific crimes that were found to have been perpetrated sustained the impetus for international justice and instigated efforts for effective enforcement.

Despite the clear obligation under Article 29(2) of the ICTY Statute to arrest, detain or surrender accused persons to the Tribunal, Trial Chamber orders or requests to this effect were largely disobeyed by the independent former Yugoslav republics and all the Prosecutor and judges could do was inform the Security Council on an *ad hoc* basis, as well as make public declarations through the ICTY President's Annual Report to the Council. This stalemate was ultimately resolved on account of two factors: a) international pressure was placed on recalcitrant States,[35] coupled with an amelioration of the Tribunal's image, which subsequently led to the voluntary surrender of a significant number of accused persons, and; b) increased willingness on the part of the North Atlantic Treaty Organisation (NATO)-led Stabilisation Force (SFOR) – legal successor to IFOR under a Security Council mandate – to cooperate in the arrest of accused persons residing on the territory of Bosnia. As will be demonstrated later on in this chapter, the ICTY chambers unanimously held that abductions and forced arrests of suspects under sealed indictments did not give rise to an abuse of process. At the same time, some central European States had begun exercising universal criminal jurisdiction over persons accused of having violated the laws or customs of war in the course of the Yugoslav armed conflicts.[36] One such criminal proceeding that was initiated in the Federal Republic of Germany against one Duško Tadić was deferred to the jurisdiction of the ICTY after an official

---

[31]   Ibid, R 61(D).

[32]   Ibid, R 61(E).

[33]   *ICTY Prosecutor v Karadžić and Mladić* r 61 Decision (11 Jul 1996).

[34]   See *ICTY Prosecutor v Nikolić* r 61 Decision (20 Oct 1995).

[35]   It is instructive that one of the most significant reasons for Croatia's failed attempts thus far to enter the European Union has been its slack and failed cooperation with the ICTY.

[36]   *Prosecutor v Saric* (1995) unreported (Denmark); *Public Prosecutor v Djajic,* (1998) 92 *American Journal of International Law* 528, (FRG); *Public Prosecutor v Grabec* (Re G) (Swiss) (1998) 92 *American Journal of International Law* 78.

request, despite the accused's pleas to the contrary.[37] Tadić, although only a guard at the Bosnian Serb Omarska prisoner and detention facility was the first person physically brought before the jurisdiction of the ICTY and was 'utilised' as a vehicle for initiating prosecutions and developing a coherent jurisprudence, upon which both the ICTY and ICTR relied and further elaborated in future cases.

The obligation to cooperate with the Tribunal under Article 29 of its Statute is addressed only to States, not to international organisations or peacekeeping and peace enforcement entities. Accordingly, the ICTY having no enforcement mechanisms of its own was forced to rely on the cooperation of individual States and the goodwill of peacekeeping forces. In a meeting on 19 January 1996 between the ICTY President and the Secretary-General of NATO, it was agreed that within the limits of its resources and mandate, SFOR would not only assist in ICTY investigations but would also detain any indicted persons whom it came across in the ordinary conduct of its duties.[38] This led to the conclusion of a confidential MoU between NATO and the ICTY (the so-called SHAPE Agreement of May 1996), albeit an informal collaborative process of this nature had already been in place since December 1995. NATO made it clear that it bore no responsibility from this MoU, whether in terms of actual arrests or the manner in which they were effectuated.[39] Although it was initially doubted that NATO forces entertained the political or military will to make any arrests, such clouds soon dissipated as SFOR has since proceeded to detain a substantial number of accused in Bosnia.[40] This task has been considerably facilitated by the fact that since 1997 the ICTY Prosecutor has pursued only high-ranking officials and has applied a sealed indictment policy, thereby allowing for the element of surprise and relative safety of NATO operations in their pursuit of indicted persons.

There has also been much speculation over the existence, during the ICTY's early years, of a secret bargain between the leaders of the warring factions and the third party instigators and brokers of the Dayton Agreement to the effect that the former would be excluded from the prosecutorial ambit of the ICTY. It is alleged that this was the price for achieving peace and ending the war.[41] Even if this allegation contains some truth vis-a-vis the drafters and sponsors of the Dayton Agreement, it certainly carries no weight as far as the Office of the Prosecutor is concerned. In fact, not only has the prosecutor carried out a meticulous investigation against former Bosnian Serb leaders Karadžić and Mladić, which culminated in a detailed indictment, an r 61 review and an international arrest warrant; the Office of the Prosecutor went as far as charging an acting Head of State, President Slobodan Milošević of the

---

[37] Decision of the Trial Chamber on the Application of the Prosecutor for a Formal Request for Deferral to the Competence of the International Criminal Tribunal for the Former Yugoslavia in the Matter of Dusko Tadić (8 Nov 1994); see C Warbrick, 'International Criminal Law' (1995) 44 *International & Comparative Law Quarterly* 465, at 471.

[38] See 'The Parties, IFOR and ICTY' (1996) 2 *ICTY Bulletin*.

[39] *ICTY Prosecutor v Simić and Others*, Trial Chamber Decision on Motion for Judicial Assistance to be provided by SFOR and Others (18 Oct 2000), paras 43–45.

[40] See ICTY Doc JL/PIS/475-e (6 Mar 2000) and JL/PIS/513-e (26 Jun 2000), regarding the arrest by SFOR of the accused Prcać and Sikirica, respectively. From July 1997 until July 2000, SFOR had detained and transferred to the ICTY 15 suspected war criminals.

[41] A D'Amato, 'Peace vs Accountability in Bosnia' (1994) 88 *American Journal of International Law* 500.

Federal Republic of Yugoslavia (FRY) for a number of offences allegedly ordered or tolerated by him during the civil unrest in Kosovo in 1999.[42] At the same time that the indictment against Milošević was confirmed by a Trial Chamber, the prosecutor requested the freezing of all assets of the accused, whereby a subsequent order to all UN Members was duly issued by the Tribunal.[43] The accused was later transferred to the jurisdiction of the ICTY and the indictment was amended to encompass crimes committed during the civil war in Bosnia and Croatia. However, Milošević passed away before the tribunal had the chance to deliver its final judgment.

When Radovan Karadžić was eventually arrested in 2008 one of the first arguments he put forward was that he was entitled to immunity from prosecution by the ICTY because he had concluded a secret agreement on 18 and 19 July 1996 to that effect with US negotiator Richard Holbrooke following the Dayton Accords. This alleged agreement envisaged the accused's perpetual immunity if he agreed to disappear from public life from 1996 onwards. Karadžić further argued that Holbrooke brokered the agreement under actual or apparent authority from the Security Council and its result and legal effect was directly applicable to the Tribunal.[44] The ICTY rightly admitted that the Security Council, as its creator, is solely competent to limit or expand its jurisdictional ambit (whether *ratione loci* or *personae*)[45] and in fact in a subsequent resolution it had instructed it to focus its prosecutions on the highest figures of authority,[46] to which it would naturally obey. Thus, the ICTY cannot be presumed to possess inherent powers to override a Council resolution that limits its jurisdictional powers, even if this entails a natural curtailment to its fundamental purpose which is to uphold and serve international criminal justice. In the case at hand, the Tribunal was not convinced that such an immunity agreement existed and even if it did exist the Security Council would have had to ratify it by adopting a resolution ordering the ICTY to abstain from prosecuting the accused;[47] contrary to this, the Council never made any such declaration. Moreover, the ICTY underlined that even assuming the agreement did take place, there is no proof that Holbrooke acted under actual or apparent authority from the Council, but at best acted only under instructions from the government of the USA.[48] The Trial Chamber refused to consider *obiter dictum* what legal outcome may have resulted were the negotiator to be found acting under the authority of the Security Council and if in that case as an agent he would have bound his principal (ie the Council). The Appeals Chamber, without offering a convincing justification, held that even if the negotiator was acting

---

[42] See 'President Milošević and Four Other Senior FRY Officials Indicted for Murder, Persecution and Deportation in Kosovo' ICTY Doc JL/PIU/403-E (27 May 1999).

[43] *ICTY Prosecutor v Slobodan Milošević and Others*, Decision on Review of Indictment and Application for Consequential Orders (24 May 1999), para 29.

[44] *ICTY Prosecutor v Karadžić*, Trial Chamber Decision on the Accused's Holbrooke Agreement Motion (8 Jul 2009), paras 1–19, 33–37.

[45] Ibid, para 57; *Karadžić* Appeals Decision on Karadžić's Appeal of Trial Chamber's Decision on Alleged Holbrooke Agreement (12 Oct 2009), para 36.

[46] SC 1534 (26 Mar 2004).

[47] *Karadžić* Appeals Holbrooke Decision, paras 36–37.

[48] *Karadžić* Trial Decision on Holbrooke Agreement, paras 59ff.

under authority of the Council the alleged agreement would not bind the ICTY.[49] It is the suggestion of this author that in such eventuality the Council, represented under the legal person of the UN, could not renege on its agreement with a private entity,[50] save only through an express invalidation of said agreement by means of a subsequent Council resolution. In such eventuality, it does not mean that the accused would become immune from prosecution generally, but only in respect of those organs and institutions established by the United Nations.

As for the Prosecutorial discretionary practice of 'plea bargaining', which is common to many legal systems, it generally should not be applied to the ad hoc tribunals where the granting of immunity is specifically prohibited. However, neither of the two Statutes nor the Rules of Procedure deny the authority to engage in plea-bargaining, which as an implied power may be 'necessary for completing the investigation and the preparation and conduct of the prosecution'.[51] In order to balance, on the one hand, the interests of justice by avoiding impunity and the enhancement of its resources on the other, the Office of the Prosecutor has restricted its plea negotiations to lower level officials.[52]

The Rwanda Tribunal, as already explained, was not seriously plagued by problems relating to the absence of accused or lack of State cooperation, since most of the accused were already in Rwanda and, in any event, with the exception of the Republics of Congo and Burundi, no other States had or have any national or other substantial interest in shielding persons in their territory or withholding evidentiary material. Nonetheless, lack of support by the Rwandan Government as well as the Organisation for African Unity (OAU, subsequently renamed African Union (AU)),[53] serious delays in prosecution and poor trial management, coupled with financial and administrative mismanagement, resulted in the resignation of the first ICTR deputy Prosecutor, Honore Rakotomanana and plunged the by-then beleaguered Tribunal into chaos and uncertainty. The ICTR, moreover, was faced with overcoming a further obstacle directly related to its previously elaborated misfortunes. Although its judicial focus was on the highest ranking Hutu officials who had allegedly planned, instigated, incited and executed genocide, more than 75,000 accused were detained since the change of rule in July 1994 under extremely poor conditions in Rwandan prisons, the vast majority of which without having been formally indicted. The devastated infrastructure of the country and the absence of a criminal justice system

---

[49] *Karadžić* Appeals Holbrooke Decision, para 38. By implication, even if it were true that the alleged agreement was offered by the ICTY Prosecutor it would not bind the Tribunal because its powers and jurisdiction are circumscribed only by its Statute and Rules, ibid, para 41.

[50] Arts 3 and 4 of the ILC's Draft Articles on the Responsibility of International Organisations stipulate that an organisation commits an internationally wrongful offence where an act or omission is in violation of an international obligation and is attributable to it. This liability may arise from an act or omission of one of its organs or agents, irrespective of their position therein. UNGAOR 58th Session, Supp No 10, UN Doc A/58/10, 45–49; UNGAOR 59th Session, Supp No 10, UN Doc A/59/10, 104–09.

[51] ICTY Rules, r 39(ii).

[52] JE Alvarez, 'Crimes of States, Crimes of Hate: Lessons from Rwanda' (1999) 24 *Yale Journal of International Law* 365, 377–78.

[53] The OAU initially criticised the establishment of the ICTR under a Chapter VII resolution instead of through a treaty, but by 1997 its prior hesitation had given way to full cooperation. See D Wembou, 'The International Criminal Tribunal for Rwanda: Its Role in the African Context' (1997) 321 *International Review of the Red Cross* 685.

as a result of the genocide and the subsequent departure abroad of many educated Hutus, including lawyers, meant that not only were there insufficient local trial chambers to guarantee speedy trials for the multitudes of accused, but that there did not exist a single Rwandan lawyer who would be willing to defend them.[54] This problem was alleviated in large part through so-called *gacaca* courts, which are transitional justice mechanisms that operate at cellule (village) level in Rwanda and which co-exist in parallel with domestic Rwandan courts. Although this mechanism was traditionally established to deal with minor offences and family disputes at the community level on the basis of African customary law, the current *gacaca* courts were constituted under Rwandan law to prosecute the culprits of the lesser categories of the genocide.[55]

Moreover, the retention of the death penalty under Rwandan law, in contrast to its rejection in the ICTR, led to an absurd result whereby the planners and instigators of genocide would, at most, receive life imprisonment sentences by the ICTR, whereas minor executioners were to suffer capital punishment under Rwandan criminal law.[56] The Rwanda Tribunal could do nothing regarding the discrepancy in sentencing, but it has played a seminal role in raising awareness over the need to enhance the Rwandan criminal justice system through international financing and training so that at least accused persons would not suffer lengthy detention periods. The ICTR has since overcome its initial problems and has concluded a significant number of cases, including one against the former Prime Minister of the Interim Rwandan Government, Jean Kambanda and other protagonists of the genocide.[57] It has, moreover, made a substantial contribution to the development of international humanitarian law and restoration of peace in Rwanda.

18.3 Jurisdiction of the ICTY and ICTR

Although both the ICTY and ICTR enjoy concurrent jurisdiction with other national courts they are endowed with primacy over all national courts in relation to offences falling within the ambit of their respective Statutes.[58] However, since the ad hoc tribunals were established with the aim of prosecuting the most serious offences, it is natural that a large number of prosecutions dealing with minor offenders be undertaken by national authorities, especially from the countries in the former Yugoslavia. In order to better monitor these prosecutions and assess their relevance to ICTY proceedings a particular clause was inserted in an agreement signed in Rome

---

[54] Akhavan, The International Criminal Tribunal for Rwanda, at 49. This problem was resolved to a large degree by the Ministry of Justice's authorisation to foreign lawyers working for Lawyers Without Borders to plead on behalf of accused persons. O Dubois, 'Rwanda's National Criminal Courts and the International Tribunal' (1997) 321 *International Review of the Red Cross* 717.

[55] Rwandan Organic Law No 40/2000 (26 Jan 2001), as revised by Organic Laws No 16/2004 (19 Jun 2004) and 28/2006 (27 Jun 2006).

[56] From July 1996 until April 2000 more than 2,500 persons have been sentenced by Rwandan courts, 300 of them to death. The first executions took place on 24 April 1998, when 22 people were put to death publicly. There have been no executions since, although the Government has not ruled them out.

[57] *ICTR Prosecutor v Kambanda*, Judgment (4 Sep 1998).

[58] ICTY Statute, Art 9; ICTR Statute, Art 8.

on 18 February 1996 between the Presidents of FRY, Croatia and the Republic of Bosnia and Herzegovina. Paragraph 5 of the Rome Agreement requires review by the ICTY before the national authorities of the aforementioned States can arrest individuals suspected of having committed any offences related to the Yugoslav wars. To this end, a set of Procedures and Guidelines for Parties for the Submission of Cases to the ICTY under the Agreed Measures of 18 February 1996 was developed.[59] This procedure simply facilitates the ICTY's work and promotes justice and is in no way a substitute to the international Tribunal's primacy over any national proceedings. In fact, the rationale behind this arrangement was to enhance co-ordination and empower the residual jurisdiction of these national courts. This outcome is also strongly reflected in the Tribunals' completion strategy, as described at the close of this chapter.

The subject matter jurisdiction of the Yugoslav Tribunal consists of four core offences: grave breaches of the 1949 Geneva Conventions,[60] violations of the laws or customs of war,[61] genocide[62] and crimes against humanity.[63] A detailed analysis of these offences, as well as the significance of the ICTY/ICTR jurisprudence in their development is given in other chapters of this book. Although the majority of crimes charged took place in Bosnia the Tribunal enjoys under Article 1 of its Statute jurisdiction over the entirety of the territory of the former Yugoslavia, as long as the crimes charged took place after 1991. This wide jurisdiction both in time[64] and place has enabled the ICTY Prosecutor to investigate and indict persons for offences committed in Kosovo by FRY forces and by members of the Kosovo Liberation Army (KLA) in 1999,[65] as well as by Croat military and police personnel for crimes committed during, and in the aftermath of, operations 'Flash' and 'Storm' in the retaking of Serb-held Krajina. Equally, the ICTY has expanded its jurisdiction to cover events that took place in the Former Yugoslav Republic of Macedonia (FYROM), despite the fact that they were completely unrelated to the main conflicts for which it was originally set up.

In the case of the ICTR, the Security Council was conscious, on the one hand, that there were no international elements to the armed conflict between the Hutu Government and the Rwandan Patriotic Front (RPF) and, on the other, it wished it to be globally recognised that a well planned campaign of genocide had taken place.

---

[59]   These procedures have become known as the 'Rules of the Road'.

[60]   Convention for the Amelioration of the Condition of the Wounded and Sick in Armed Forces in the Field (No I), 75 UNTS 31; Convention for the Amelioration of the Condition of the Wounded, Sick, and Ship-wrecked Members of Armed Forces at Sea (No II), 75 UNTS 85; Convention Relative to the Treatment of Prisoners of War (No III), 75 UNTS 135; Convention Relative to the Protection of Civilian Persons in Time of War (No IV), 75 UNTS 287, Art 2.

[61]   ICTY Statute, Art 3.

[62]   Ibid, Art 4.

[63]   Ibid, Art 5.

[64]   In *ICTY Prosecutor v Boškovski*, Appeal Chamber Decision on Interlocutory Jurisdiction (22 Jul 2005), para 10 and *ICTY Prosecutor v Đorđevic*, Trial Chamber Decision on Preliminary Motion on Jurisdiction (6 Dec 2007), paras 11ff the ICTY rejected the view that its temporal jurisdiction was limited to events that took place between 1991–1995.

[65]   *ICTY Prosecutor v Slobodan Milošević*, Trial Chamber Decision on Prosecutor's Motion under Rule 73(A) for a Ruling on the Competence of the Amici Curiae to Present a Motion for Judgment of Acquittal under Rule 98*bis* (5 Feb 2004), paras 14–40, where the tribunal found that the intensity of the conflict between the KLA and Serbian armed forces satisfied the intensity required for an armed conflict.

This intention is clearly reflected in the Rwanda Tribunal's Statute, whose jurisdiction consists of the crimes of genocide,[66] crimes against humanity[67] and violations of Article 3 common to the 1949 Geneva Conventions and the 1977 Additional Protocol II to these Conventions.[68] Although one may presume that the temporal jurisdiction of the ICTR, spanning from 1 January until 31 December 1994, is wider than the actual duration of hostilities, since the mass killings commenced on 14 June 1994 and lasted approximately three months, evidence shows that plans to commit genocide existed at least as far back as 1992.

Both statutes penalise participation in the preparatory and execution stages of the prescribed offences, that is, planning, instigation, ordering, or aiding and abetting in the planning, preparation or execution.[69] However, an accused can only be found guilty if the offence charged was actually completed. This rule does not apply with regard to genocide which, taken verbatim from the 1948 Convention on the Prevention and Punishment of the Crime of Genocide (Genocide Convention), does not require the commission of acts of genocide in order to hold the accused liable. Furthermore, following established principles of customary law, persons incur criminal liability where they fail to either prevent or punish crimes committed by their subordinates in cases they know or had reason to know that subordinates were about to commit such acts or had already done so.[70] This latter form of criminal participation, initially borne for the exigencies of military authorities, is known as the doctrine of command or superior responsibility. The various forms of participation in crime and the different types of liability recognised by the ad hoc tribunals and generally in international law are examined in chapter 3 which discusses the various forms of liability and chapter 4 which deals exclusively with command responsibility.

18.4   Enforcement Capacity of the Tribunals

Article 29 of the ICTY Statute obliges Member States of the UN to cooperate and offer judicial assistance to the Yugoslav Tribunal without undue delay. Such calls for cooperation are to be addressed in the form of binding orders or requests, including, but not limited to:

    (a)   the identification and location of persons;
    (b)   the taking of testimony and the production of evidence;
    (c)   the service of documents;
    (d)   the arrest or detention of persons;
    (e)   the surrender or the transfer of the accused to the International Tribunal.

Since the ICTY Statute constitutes a Security Council enforcement measure, any order or request by a Trial or Appeals Chamber for the surrender and transfer of

---

[66]   ICTR Statute, Art 2.
[67]   Ibid, Art 3.
[68]   Ibid, Art 4. Geneva Protocol II Additional to the Geneva Conventions of 12 August 1949, and Relating to the Protection of Victims of Non-International Armed Conflicts, 1125 UNTS 609.
[69]   ICTY Statute, Art 7(1); ICTR Statute, Art 6(1).
[70]   ICTY Statute, Art 7(3); ICTR Statute, Art 6(3).

documents or persons is *ipso facto* binding on its addressee.[71] A large number of States have enacted implementing legislation in order to harmonise their obligations under Article 29 and so as to prepare their national mechanisms in coping with the legal intricacies of possible future requests.[72] Some of these domestic laws have been criticised for failing to offer adequate safeguards and for permitting extradition in respect of offences prescribed in the ICTY Statute that are not, however, contained in the substantive criminal law of the extraditing State.[73] These criticisms have no legal basis since as Warbrick correctly points out the obligation of States to surrender accused persons found on their territory does not amount to extradition in the traditional sense.[74] This is true given that it is not premised on bilateral or multilateral reciprocal relations of the nature encountered in extradition agreements.

In response to an ICTY subpoena for the production of documents addressed to Croatia, the latter challenged the Tribunal's authority by which it can order sovereign States and argued that, in any event, requests of this nature must adhere to national channels of communication and should not jeopardise national security. On appeal, the Appeals Chamber in the *Blaškić* case admitted that the ICTY possesses enforcement measures neither under its Statute, nor inherently by its nature as a judicial institution.[75] It pointed out that, as a general rule, States cannot be 'ordered' by other States or international organisations. The power to 'order' under Article 29 of the ICTY Statute, however, derives its binding force from Chapter VII and Article 25 of the UN Charter, both of which lay down an *erga omnes* obligation which every member of the UN has a legal interest in fulfilling.[76]

After deciding on the legitimacy of addressing binding orders, the Appeals Chamber next examined those requirements[77] that such subpoena *duces tecum* orders (that is, for the production of documentary evidence) must satisfy. These were held to include: (a) the identification of specific documents, rather than categories of documents; (b) justification of the relevance of requested documents to each trial; (c) avoidance of unduly onerous requests; and (d) allowance of sufficient time for compliance. Where a State persists in defying compliance, the Tribunal is endowed under its inherent and delegated power to make a judicial determination regarding a State's failure to observe the court's Statute or Rules. This power also includes formal

---

[71] Report of the Secretary General pursuant to Security Council Resolution 808 (1993), UN Doc S/25704 (1993), paras 125–26.

[72] United Kingdom UN ICTY Order 1996 SI 1996/716; Australian International War Crimes Tribunals Act No 18 (1995).

[73] H Fox, 'The Objections to Transfer of Criminal Jurisdiction to the UN Tribunal' (1997) 46 *International & Comparative Law Quarterly* 434, regarding the UK's 1996 SI.

[74] C Warbrick, 'Co-operation with the International Criminal Tribunal for Yugoslavia' (1996) 45 *International & Comparative Law Quarterly* 945, at 950; see R Kushen and KJ Harris, 'Surrender of Fugitives by the United States to the War Crimes Tribunals for Yugoslavia and Rwanda' (1996) 90 *American Journal of International Law* 510.

[75] *ICTY Prosecutor v Blaškić*, Appeals Judgment on the Request of the Republic of Croatia for Review of the Decision of Trial Chamber I of 11 July 1997 (29 Oct 1997), para 25.

[76] Ibid, para 26; the ad hoc tribunals have at times found it necessary to go beyond the indicative list of orders and requests identified in their respective Statutes, such as in the case of ordering all UN members to freeze former FRY President Milošević and co-accuseds' assets abroad. *ICTY Prosecutor v Milošević and Others*, Decision on Review of Indictment and Application for Consequential Orders (24 May 1999).

[77] *Blaškić* Appeals Subpoena Decision (29 Oct 1997), para 32.

notification to the Security Council.[78] The fact that Article 29 constitutes an *erga omnes* obligation empowers all UN Members to request termination of the breach once a relevant judicial determination has been made.[79]

Binding orders in the form of subpoenas cannot be addressed to State officials acting in their official capacity. It is the prerogative of each State to determine the internal organs competent to receive and carry out the order.[80] The Appeals Chamber found that it possessed unlimited authority, on the basis of its incidental jurisdiction, to issue orders to private individuals within the framework of domestic channelling procedures, unless otherwise permitted by national law or when State authorities refuse to comply by hindering this process.[81] The concept of private individuals for the purposes of Article 29 also includes State agents possessing information or material obtained before they accepted office, members of peacekeeping forces, because their mandate stems from the same source as the Tribunal and State agents who refuse to obey national authorities.[82] As for possible national security concerns, although every possible protective measure should be observed, the Appeals Chamber emphasised the exceptional departure from Article 2(7) of the UN Charter relating to the Security Council's authority acting under Chapter VII to interfere in the domestic affairs of States, the establishment of the ICTY being one such specific application.[83]

In a related case in 1999 the ICTY chambers were seized with a request by the prosecutor to order the International Committee of the Red Cross (ICRC) to disclose information that its employees had collected in the course of their field duties. The Chamber held that admissibility of evidence may be limited not only by the ICTY Statute and Rules, but also by customary international law.[84] The ICRC was found to be an independent humanitarian organisation organised under Swiss law, generally acknowledged as enjoying a certain degree of international legal personality and whose functions and tasks were directly derived from international law, that is, the 1949 Geneva Conventions and subsequent Protocols thereto.[85] Based on the object and purpose of the Geneva Conventions, the ICRC was found to be recognised by States parties as enjoying impartiality, neutrality and confidentiality, all of which are necessary in order to carry out its mandate. The ICTY noted that widespread ratification of these treaties, taken together with relevant State acceptance, reflected a customary international law privilege against mandatory disclosure by the ICRC, lest it jeopardise its humanitarian dimension.[86] In any event, the Trial Chamber held that Article 29 of the ICTY Statute does not apply vis-a-vis international organisations.[87]

---

[78] Ibid, para 33.

[79] Ibid, para 36.

[80] Ibid, paras 38, 43.

[81] Ibid, para 55.

[82] Ibid, paras 49–51.

[83] Ibid, para 64.

[84] *ICTY Prosecutor v Simić and Others*, Decision on the Prosecution Motion under r 73 for a Ruling Concerning the Testimony of a Witness (27 Jul 1999), paras 41–42.

[85] Ibid, para 46.

[86] Ibid, paras 72–74.

[87] Ibid, para 78. See S Jeannet, 'Recognition of the ICRC's Long Standing Rule of Confidentiality' (2000) 838 *International Review of the Red Cross* 403.

A final word should be devoted to the ad hoc tribunals' inherent power to impose criminal and civil sanctions upon persons found to be in contempt of its proceedings. This concept originates in the common law and encompasses conduct which obstructs, prejudices or abuses the administration of justice and in respect of which punishment is justified in order to ensure that the tribunals' exercise of jurisdiction is not frustrated and that the integrity of its proceedings and basic judicial function is safeguarded.[88] The ICTY has held various persons in contempt, including defence counsel that coerce witnesses to falsely testify,[89] witnesses that refuse to respond to questioning[90] and former employees that went on to publish confidential information despite an order by the Tribunal to the contrary.[91] The importance of these proceedings should not be underestimated or considered a mere manifestation of the ad hoc tribunals' institutional law. Rather, where a confidentiality order is not obeyed the harm caused may relate to the frustration of an investigation or the intimidation of potential or existing witnesses in a post-conflict society. Such an eventuality may frustrate judicial proceedings altogether in respect of a particular accused or situation.

18.5 Rights of the Accused and Abuse of Process

Despite the fact that the ICTY is obliged to employ only those portions of international law that are beyond any doubt part of customary international law, which includes obviously human rights law, it is implicitly accepted that it is not bound to apply every human right, no matter how fundamental this may otherwise be. This conclusion is inferred from its very mandate, which is to conduct criminal trials, without however jeopardising the national security interests of UN member States. Thus, where the press threatens to expose an event that otherwise constitutes a topic of public interest (to use the terminology of the European Court of Human Rights) but which may damage the national security of a State the ICTY may well restrict the freedom of expression. The same is true even where the event in question did not pose a threat to national security, because exposing a topic of public interest does not fall within the mandate of ICTY, unless this may be deemed as being encompassed within its secondary objective of truth-telling and reconciliation. Where

---

[88] ICTY Rule 77(A) contains a list of non-exhaustive acts that constitute contempt. See also *ICTY Prosecutor v Tadić* Appeals Chamber Judgment on Allegations of Contempt against Prior Counsel, Milan Vujin (27 Feb 2001), paras 13, 18.

[89] *ICTY Prosecutor v Aleksovski*, Judgment on Appeal by Anto Nobilo against Finding of Contempt (30 May 2001).

[90] *ICTY Prosecutor v Milošević*, Decision on Contempt Proceedings against Kosta Bulatović (13 May 2005), which found a defence witness guilty of contempt for failing to respond to questions posed by the tribunal.

[91] *ICTY Prosecutor v Hartmann*, Judgment on Allegation of Contempt (14 Sep 2009). In the latter type of case the ICTY rightly confirmed the essence of the jurisprudence of the Eur Ct HR that the restrictions on free speech are justified where the hearings or investigation are under way (*sub judice*), in which case any exposure does not only prejudice the right to a fair trial but may also put the safety of witnesses and victims in jeopardy. See particularly *Sunday Times v UK* [1979] 2 EHRR 245 and *Dupuis v France* [2008] 47 EHRR 52, in which the Eur Ct HR made it clear that the freedom of expression and that of the press may legitimately be curtailed in respect of sensitive information and ongoing confidential judicial proceedings.

the contested event was crucial for the defence of the accused it could be admitted, but if it constituted sensitive information, the Tribunal could restrict its import through *in camera* proceedings.

Other than these considerations, which are exceptional, the drafters of the ad hoc tribunals have paid heed to accusations of unfair proceedings that have in the past been levelled against the framers of the Nuremberg Tribunal, ensuring that not only customary international law would constitute applicable law,[92] but that fair trial guarantees would permeate trial and pre-trial proceedings. Articles 20 and 21 of the ICTY Statute guarantee such fair and expeditious proceedings to all accused. Established in accordance with appropriate procedures under the UN Charter, providing all necessary safeguards for a fair trial, both ad hoc tribunals are properly considered as being established by law, rather by an arbitrary unilateral act.[93] Their creation, the ICTY itself claims, does not violate the right to be tried by one's national courts, or by one's natural judge (known also as *jus de non evocando*), since transfer to the jurisdiction of the ICTY does not infringe or threaten the procedural rights of the accused.[94]

Although the principle of equality of arms underlies ICTY judicial proceedings[95] it is also true that the accused cannot compete with the Prosecutor's resources, despite being entitled to receive both legal and financial assistance to defend themselves.[96] In the later stages of the *Tadić* case the accused claimed violation of the principle of equality of arms on account of the Republika Srpska's failure to cooperate with the ICTY, thus depriving him of adequate facilities for the preparation of his defence. The Appeals Chamber interpreted the principle of equality of arms as obligating a judicial body to ensure that neither party is put at a disadvantage when presenting its case, so far as this applies to situations which are within the control of the court.[97] Other than that, several additional safeguards exist in order to protect an accused from prosecutorial abuse of authority and to remedy the imbalance in resources. Most importantly, the 'presumption of innocence' principle constitutes a fundamental right under Article 21(2) of the ICTY Statute, as is also the right against self-incrimination.[98] The Trial Chambers ensure that these rights are observed even in cases where the accused seems to have waived them. The Appeals Chamber in the *Erdemović* case did not hesitate to overturn a Trial judgment which accepted a guilty plea that did not, however, satisfy the criteria for its admission. The accused was a soldier in the Bosnian Serb Army and had taken part in the execution of civilians during the Srebrenica massacres, albeit under severe duress. Although he pleaded

---

[92] In this regard, cautious use of domestic legal concepts and precedent has been made. The *Aleksovski* Appeals Judgment (25 Jun 1999), paras 107–08, categorically stated that ICTY Chambers should observe precedent 'in the interests of certainty and predictability', but be free to depart from previous decisions for cogent reasons in the interests of justice, such as in the case of a legally incorrect decision.

[93] *Tadić* Appeals Jurisdiction Decision, para 47.

[94] Ibid, para 62.

[95] ICTY Statute, Art 21(1).This principle is also satisfied through the right to adequate time and facilities for preparation of one's defence, as well as to examine witnesses under the same conditions as the prosecutor, in accordance with Art 21(4)(b) and (e) respectively.

[96] Ibid, Art 21(4)(d).

[97] *Tadić* Appeals Judgment (15 Jul 1999), paras 44, 48–52.

[98] ICTY Statute, Art 21 (4)(g).

guilty to crimes against humanity he also invoked the said duress as a defence. The majority of the Appeals Chamber held that duress does not afford a complete defence and consequently found the appellant's guilty plea to have been equivocal.[99] In his dissenting opinion Judge Cassese correctly argued that a guilty plea must satisfy the following requirements under international law: it must be voluntary, that is, not obtained by threats, inducements or promises; the accused must be in good mental health; the plea must be entered knowingly, that is, the accused must be fully aware of its legal implications; and the plea must not be ambiguous or equivocal, that is to say the accused cannot be allowed on the one hand to admit his or her guilt and at the same time claim to be acting under some exculpatory reason.[100] The criteria established by Cassese J's dissenting opinion have subsequently been upheld by ICTY and ICTR Chambers as good law.[101]

The *Barayagwiza* case is perhaps highly instructive of the prosecutor's strict duty to adhere to all aspects of the 'fair trial' principle, or face possible dismissal of the charges. The accused was detained in Cameroon for nineteen months at the request of the Prosecutor without an indictment having been drawn against him before being transferred to the ICTR. He endured three further months of detention from the moment of transfer until his initial appearance before an ICTR Trial Chamber. On the basis of this lengthy delay the Tribunal held that although the prosecution may request other countries in cases of urgency to arrest and detain suspects[102] it certainly does not enjoy unlimited power to keep a suspect under indefinite provisional detention.[103] The remedy for failure to issue a prompt indictment is the release of the suspect.[104] Likewise, the Appeals Chamber held that when one State applies to another for a 'detainer', that is, a special type of warrant filed against a person already in custody so as to ensure his or her availability upon completion of present confinement, the accused is in 'constructive custody' of the requesting State while the detaining State acts as an agent of the requesting State for all purposes related to *habeas corpus* challenges.[105] Thus, despite lack of physical control the appellant was in ICTR custody because his detention in Cameroon was instigated upon request of the Prosecutor. Even if not deemed to be in custody on behest of the ICTR, the appellant's detention was impermissibly lengthy.[106] The right to be tried without undue delay was found to have been violated by the 96-day interval between the accused's transfer and his initial appearance before a Trial Chamber.[107]

---

[99] *ICTY Prosecutor v Erdemović*, Appeals Chamber Judgment (7 Oct 1997), para 19.

[100] *Erdemović* Appeals Judgment, Separate and dissenting opinion of Judge Cassese, para 10. Cassese J convincingly argued that in exceptional circumstances duress can be urged in defence to crimes against humanity or war crimes, paras 11–49.

[101] *ICTR Prosecutor v Serushago*, Judgment (5 Feb 1999).

[102] ICTY Rules, r 40.

[103] *ICTR Prosecutor v Barayagwiza* Appeals Chamber Decision (3 Nov 1999), para 46.

[104] Ibid.

[105] Ibid, paras 56–57; lack of an arrest warrant or evidence demonstrating the accused's responsibility over an offence is not required at the pre-trial stage of requesting States to detain a suspect, since the prosecutor's request will be determined in accordance with the requested State's domestic law. *ICTR Prosecutor v Kajelijeli*, Decision on the Defence Motion Concerning the Arbitrary Arrest and Illegal Detention of the Accused and on the Defence Notice of Urgent Motion to Expand and Supplement the Record (8 May 2000), para 34.

[106] *Barayagwiza* Appeals Decision, paras 58, 61, 67, 100.

[107] Ibid, para 71.

The Appeals Chamber classified this case of prosecutorial incompetence, resulting in a lengthy detention and delay in trial, as an 'abuse of process'.[108] This concept comprises proceedings which although lawfully initiated are thereafter continued improperly or illegally in pursuance of an otherwise lawful process, such as resort to kidnapping. Under such circumstances, courts or tribunals enjoy judicial discretion to terminate proceedings where it is felt that further exercise of jurisdiction in light of serious violations of the accused's rights would prove detrimental to the court's integrity.[109] Such discretion, the Tribunal remarked, may be relied upon where the delay has made a fair trial impossible, or in the particular circumstances of a case proceeding to the merits contravening the court's sense of justice due to pre-trial impropriety.[110] Barayagwiza's release understandably sparked vehement Rwandan condemnation, but it must be acknowledged that the initial decision on his release was fully justified, reflecting the will of an international tribunal that respects fundamental rights and the rule of law. The Appeals Chamber subsequently reconvened in order to examine the prosecutor's request for reconsideration of the release order on the basis of new information that was unavailable in 1999. In its Decision of 31 March 2000 the Appeals Chamber admitted the Prosecutor's evidence as 'new' and held that these new facts diminished the role played by the failings of the Prosecutor, as well as the intensity of the violation of the accused's rights. It, thus, revoked its earlier release and reparation order on the basis that this was disproportionate in relation to the Prosecutor's role in the continued detention of the accused.[111] Understandably, the independence of the tribunals and that of the judges was called into question and three of the judges entered separate opinions denying that their independence had been impaired as a result of coercion.

In the *Todorović* case the accused challenged his arrest by SFOR and requested to see certain SFOR documents and question SFOR officials. The ICTY agreed with this motion and issued a relevant subpoena,[112] deeming it consistent with fair trial guarantees, despite the fact that it was unlikely that its Security Council mandate stretched as far as enforcing an order of that nature upon SFOR. The US government, NATO and individual member States intervened and filed motions for judicial review against the subpoena issued by the Trial Chamber. Perhaps on account of these interventions Todorović eventually entered into a plea bargain and withdrew his motion, but as a result of admitting his motion for subpoena a decline in arrests by SFOR was thereafter apparent.

The ICTY has had on a number of occasions the opportunity to assess the legal effects of abductions and enforcement of sealed arrest warrants and their impact on the fairness of proceedings. The jurisprudence of the Tribunal clearly suggests that an otherwise involuntary arrest on the basis of a sealed indictment and in a clandestine manner will not give rise to an abuse of process. This was the case with the accused

---

[108] For an analysis of this concept with particular reference to extraterritorial abductions see chapter 16.9.

[109] *Barayagwiza* Trial Decision, para 74.

[110] Ibid, paras 77, 101.

[111] *ICTY Prosecutor v Barayagwiza*, Appeals Chamber Decision on Request for Review or Reconsideration (31 Mar 2000).

[112] *ICTY Prosecutor v Todorović*, Trial Chamber Decision (18 Oct. 2000) on the Motion for Judicial Assistance.

Nikolić who was allegedly illegally arrested and abducted from the territory of Serbia by unknown persons (not members of SFOR or the Prosecution) and transferred to Bosnia and from there to the Tribunal. The Appeals Chamber held that unless the rights of the accused have been egregiously violated the Tribunal will not generally set aside its jurisdiction, emphasising that 'a correct balance must be maintained between the fundamental rights of the accused and the essential interests of the international community in the prosecution of persons charged with [serious international crimes]'.[113] The Tribunal went on to note that even had Nikolic's abduction been attributed to SFOR and the Prosecutor its jurisdiction would still not have been set aside.[114]

Equally, the aforementioned alleged offer of immunity (essentially impunity) to Karadžić by Richard Holbrooke, even if proven, would not amount to any sort of duplicitous offer on the basis of which the Tribunal would be obliged to stay proceedings as a matter of abuse of process.[115]

The protection of the rights of the accused has not caused neglect for safeguarding victims and witnesses. This has been made possible by a variety of measures, such as the non-disclosure of identities,[116] assignment of pseudonyms,[117] ordering of closed sessions,[118] or the giving of testimony through image or voice altering devices and closed circuit television,[119] as well as through video conference link.[120] Furthermore, a Code of Professional Conduct for Defence Counsel was adopted by the ICTY Registrar on 12 June 1997 in an attempt to limit harassment and intimidation of victims and witnesses.[121] A more detailed exposition of ICTY/ICTR procedural law and the rights of victims and witnesses is provided in chapter 21 dealing with the submission and appraisal of evidence before international criminal tribunals.

18.6   Dissolution of the Tribunals and their Completion Strategy

Not all good things must come to an end, but the mandate of the ad hoc tribunals was limited from the outset by several factors. Firstly, evidence would necessarily be difficult to come by through the passage of time; secondly, given the exceptional nature of the ICTY and ICTR as a result of the breakdown of the legal systems of Bosnia and Rwanda, one should not forget that in due course the capacities of these

---

[113]   *ICTY Prosecutor v Nikolić*, Appeals Chamber Interlocutory Decision Concerning Legality of Arrest (5 Jun 2003), para 30.

[114]   Ibid, paras 18, 33.

[115]   *Karadžić* Appeals Holbrooke Decision, paras 51–53.

[116]   ICTY Rules, rr 69(A) and 75(B)(i)(a) and (b).

[117]   Ibid, r 75(B)(i)(d).

[118]   Ibid, rr 75(B)(ii) and 79.

[119]   Ibid, r 75(B)(i)(c). This is not a novel conception, as some States in the US allow it. The US Supreme Court held in *Maryland v Craig* (1990) 497 US 836 that closed circuit television depositions do not violate the sixth amendment right to confrontation where a court finds it necessary to protect a child witness from psychological harm.

[120]   Ibid, r 71(D).

[121]   See I Bantekas, 'Study on the Minimum Rules of Conduct in Cross-Examination to be Applied by the International Criminal Tribunal for the Former Yugoslavia' (1997) 50 *Hellenic Review of International Law* 205.

nations to hold trials would once again flourish and thus jurisdiction should be ceded back to them; thirdly, international funds, as well as the willingness to finance these projects indefinitely, had for some time been running short. Much of this may be attributed to so-called 'donor fatigue' and the expenses incurred through the proliferation of other international criminal tribunals. The Security Council envisaged an exit strategy (ie Completion Strategy), which it framed along two corresponding axes: a) completion of existing ICTY cases and prosecution of major fugitives at large; b) referral of minor cases to national courts.[122]

The Security Council set out the tribunals' completion strategies through a series of resolutions. Resolution 1503 initially called on the ICTY and ICTR to take all possible steps to complete investigations by 2004, all trial activities at first instance by 2008 and all work by 2010.[123] This was not entirely realistic, given that by that time the major culprits had not yet been arrested. As a result, a year later the Council adopted resolution 1534 which proceeded to request greater cooperation by States and ordered the tribunals to focus only on the most senior offenders in their respective jurisdictions.[124] In his latest Completion Strategy report the ICTY President noted that on account of the lengthy trial and appeals processes it was unrealistic to expect conclusion of all proceedings before 2013.[125] In the meantime the ICTY had already referred a number of cases to criminal courts in the various republics of the former Yugoslavia.[126]

Several important issues arise from the tribunals' completion strategy. To be sure, good personnel are hard to recruit or retain under circumstances of employment insecurity,[127] which in turn gives rise to concerns with regard to the administration of criminal justice. Equally, it may be deemed that the financiers of the tribunals have the upper hand in deciding when and how long international criminal justice is administered.[128] International lawyers tend not to observe the impact of financing on the dependence of international tribunals, but it is a reality of international life. This does not, however, imply that in the present case the neutrality of the ad hoc tribunals has been jeopardised as a result of their financing strategy. Finally, cases that would ordinarily fall within the jurisdiction of the ICTY and the ICTR after their dissolution will be filtered through to specific courts, such as the War Crimes Chamber of the courts of Bosnia, the Kosovo Special Courts, as well as other courts generally under the principle of universal jurisdiction.

---

[122] See D Raab, 'Evaluating the ICTY and its Completion Strategy' (2005) 3 *Journal of International Criminal Justice* 82.

[123] SC 1503 (28 Aug 2003), para 7.

[124] SC Res 1534 (26 Mar 2004).

[125] Letter Dated 14 May 2009 of the ICTY President Addressed to the President of the Security Council, UN Doc S/2009/252 (18 May 2009), para 4.

[126] Ibid, para 44.

[127] Ibid, para 43.

[128] See SD Roper, 'Donor Motivations and Contributions to War Crimes Tribunals' (2007) 51 *Journal of Conflict Resolution* 285, who views such financing as a form of foreign assistance.

19

The Permanent International Criminal Court

19.1 Introduction

Following the adoption of the 1948 United Nations Convention on the Prevention and Punishment of the Crime of Genocide (Genocide Convention)[1] the General Assembly invited the International Law Commission (ILC) 'to study the desirability and possibility of establishing an international judicial organ for the trial of persons charged with genocide'.[2] The ILC studied this question at its 1949 and 1950 sessions and concluded that a court of that nature was both desirable and possible.[3] Subsequent to the ILC's report the General Assembly established a committee to prepare proposals relating to the establishment of a permanent international criminal court. The committee first prepared a draft statute in 1951[4] and a revised draft statute in 1953,[5] but the Assembly decided to postpone consideration of the matter pending the adoption of a definition on aggression. Despite periodical consideration of the issue since 1953 it was in December 1989, in response to a letter addressed to the UN Secretary General by Trinidad and Tobago regarding the establishment of an international court with jurisdiction over the illicit trafficking in drugs, that the General Assembly once more requested the ILC to resume work on the creation of an international criminal court.[6] Following the shocking first reports from the armed conflicts in the former Yugoslavia and the establishment of the International Criminal Tribunal for the Former Yugoslavia (ICTY), the General Assembly urged the ILC to elaborate a viable statute as a matter of priority. This culminated in the production of a draft statute in 1994.[7] In order to consider major substantive issues arising from the draft statute the General Assembly created an Ad Hoc Committee on the

---

[1] GA Res 260(III) (9 Dec 1948), as an annex to which the Genocide Convention was appended. Reprinted in 78 UNTS 277.

[2] The impetus for this request was without doubt the Art VI of the Genocide Convention, which provided for the establishment of an international penal tribunal, alongside national courts, as an alternative judicial forum for the prosecution of genocide.

[3] Report of the ILC on the Work of its Second Session (5 Jun–29 Jul 1950) UN GAOR, Fifth Session, Supp No 12, UN Doc A/1316 (1950), para 140.

[4] UN GAOR, Seventh Session, Supp No 11, UN Doc A/2136 (1952).

[5] UN GAOR, Ninth Session, Supp No 12, UN Doc A/2625 (1954).

[6] GA Res 44/39 (4 Dec 1989).

[7] J Crawford, 'The ILC Adopts a Statute for an International Criminal Court' (1995) 89 *American Journal of International Law* 404.

Establishment of an International Criminal Court, which met twice in 1995.[8] After consideration of the Ad Hoc Committee's work the General Assembly established the Preparatory Committee (Prep Com) on the Establishment of an International Criminal Court.[9] The task of the Prep Com, unlike its predecessor, was to formulate a generally acceptable instrument and not simply to assess the viability and preliminary concerns regarding such a project, with a view towards submitting an instrument for submission to a diplomatic conference. Upon concluding its work the Prep Com, having met six times since 1996, asked the General Assembly to convene a diplomatic conference for the purposes of finalising the statute in treaty form and its adoption by the international community. A heavily bracketed draft treaty – the brackets indicating unresolved issues and details – was laid before a conference of plenipotentiaries for negotiation in July 1998 in Rome, where after extremely intense negotiations and compromises on all sides the International Criminal Court (ICC) Statute was adopted on 17 July 1998.[10] One hundred and twenty States voted in favour of the treaty, seven voted against (US, China, Libya, Iraq, Israel, Qatar and Yemen) and twenty-one abstained.

Following the Rome Conference in the summer of 1998 the US proclaimed that it would not sign the Statute. However, after fears that as a result of this stance the country would isolate itself from the proceedings of the ICC Preparatory Commission and create a negative international image[11] the US finally signed the text of the Statute on 31 December 2000. It subsequently withdrew its signature on 6 May 2002, making it clear that it had no intention of ratifying this instrument – later followed by Israel and Sudan. This was not a symbolic act, since it connoted that the US was no longer bound to respect the object and purpose of the treaty and as will become clear below in this chapter from that moment onwards it openly adopted a hostile attitude towards it. Following the required sixtieth ratification the ICC Statute finally entered into force on 1 July 2002. Of course, it should be emphasised that the final adoption of the Statute was much augmented by a parallel development, the ILC's Draft Code of Crimes against the Peace and Security of Mankind, which was under construction since the early 1950s. Although the project was finally discontinued and the final draft appeared in 1996, the Draft Code was a very influential document that fed into many of the provisions of the ICC Statute.

Unlike the two *ad hoc* Tribunals for Yugoslavia and Rwanda the ICC is a permanent international criminal court established by its founding treaty.[12] It currently sits in The Hague, but it possesses the ability to sit abroad depending on the exigencies at hand. It has been endowed with international legal personality[13] and although it is an independent judicial institution the drafters of the ICC Statute

---

[8] See Report of the Ad Hoc Committee on the Establishment of an International Criminal Court, UN GAOR, 50th Session, Supp No 22, UN Doc A/50/22 (1995); see V Morris and CM Bourloyannis-Vrailas, 'The Work of the Sixth Committee at the Fiftieth Session of the UN General Assembly' (1996) 90 *American Journal of International Law* 491.

[9] GA Res 50/46 (11 Dec 1995).

[10] (1998) 37 ILM 999.

[11] DJ Scheffer, 'Staying the Course with the International Criminal Court' (2002) 35 *Cornell Journal of International Law* 47.

[12] Art 1 ICC Statute.

[13] Art 4(1), ibid.

wished it to be related through an agreement with the UN.[14] The Preparatory Commission, established as a result of the 1998 Rome Conference worked, *inter alia,* on a relationship agreement between the ICC and the UN. This provides for mutual respect and recognition by the UN of the ICC's international legal personality and accordingly respect by the ICC of the UN's role in the maintenance of international peace and security, envisaging close cooperation between the two institutions. Thus, the Negotiated Relationship Agreement between the ICC and the UN was approved and came into being in 2004 in the form of a treaty between two international organisations. From the point of view of criminal law, Articles 15–18 of the Agreement provide for the types of judicial cooperation which the UN is to offer, including testimonial or written evidence held by itself or its employees. The need for a binding relationship between the Court and the Security Council is not only desirable, but crucial for two very specific reasons. Firstly, under the ICC Statute the Council can refer cases to the Court. Secondly, a number of countries emphasised the pressing need to assert the Council's absolute authority over issues concerned with international peace and security and in this manner maintain coherency in the corpus of international law related to the use or threat of the use of armed force.

There is no financial relationship between the ICC and the UN, except in cases where the Court's expenses have been incurred as a result of Security Council referrals.[15] All other expenses are to be borne from assessed contributions made by States parties, or otherwise by means of voluntary contributions.[16]

The Court, as is typical of international criminal tribunals, consists of a judicial, prosecutorial and administrative (registry) branch. The judicial section comprises eighteen full time judges, which are to be elected for a non-renewable nine-year term by the Assembly of States Parties (ASP).[17] Unlike the ad hoc tribunals, there is a requirement that at least nine judges possess competency in criminal proceedings while a minimum of five judges must be experts in relevant areas of international law, such as international humanitarian law and human rights. Moreover, both the pre-trial and trial chambers are to be composed predominately of judges with criminal law experience.[18] Under Article 43(4) the judges are also empowered to elect the registrar for a five-year term, whose office is open to re-election only once. The Prosecutor is an independent organ of the Court. He or she may designate appropriate deputy prosecutors whose candidacy must be approved by the ASP. Prosecutors are to serve on a full time basis.[19]

The ICC enjoys subject matter jurisdiction over four core crimes: genocide, crimes against humanity, war crimes and aggression.[20] No consensus was reached during the

---

[14] Art 2, ibid.

[15] Art 115(b), ibid. Nonetheless, in its referral to the ICC of the Darfur (Sudan) situation, the Security Council made it clear in Resolution 1593 (2005) that all expenses associated with the referral, including investigations and prosecution, were to be borne by ICC-State parties, as well as by voluntary contributions, if any.

[16] Arts 115(a) and 116 ICC Statute.

[17] Art 35, ibid. If the workload of the Court, however, does not justify the full time engagement of all 18 judges, the Presidency of the Court may decide from time to time to what extent the remaining judges shall be required to serve on a full time basis.

[18] Art 36, ibid.

[19] Art 42, ibid.

[20] Art 5, ibid.

Rome diplomatic conference on a definition for the crime of aggression, which will remain dormant until such time as the ASP approves a definition that is consistent with the Charter of the UN. All these crimes are analysed in detail in distinct chapters and the reader should turn to these for further reading. Many other matters pertinent to the ICC are not included in this chapter but are otherwise discussed elsewhere. Of particular significance is the victim's right to reparation and participation in criminal proceedings,[21] although in this chapter we go on to discuss the trust fund set up to facilitate this purpose; the various modes of liability and participation in crime;[22] the range of applicable defences[23] and; the mental element of the crimes within the Court's jurisdiction.[24] The following sections deal with the Court's substantive rules on jurisdiction and admissibility.

19.2   Jurisdiction and the ICC Triggering Mechanism

Under Article 12 of its Statute the ICC's jurisdiction over a crime or 'situation'[25] may be triggered in any of the following cases: where a situation or offence takes place in the territory of, or by a national of a State party,[26] in which case either the territorial State or the State of the nationality of the accused must be parties to the Statute and choose to refer the situation to the Court, and;[27] where the Security Council acting under Chapter VII of the UN Charter refers a situation.[28] A referral is also possible by a non-State party for a particular crime or situation, provided that such non-State party enters into a declaration under Article 13(2) of the Statute by which it accepts the jurisdiction of the Court and promises to offer full cooperation.[29] Finally, under certain circumstances the ICC Prosecutor may initiate a case *proprio motu* on the basis of information relating to crimes within the Court's jurisdiction, in accordance with Articles 15 and 17 of the Statute. The scope of this power is rather limited, however, since although the Prosecutor may seek approval for an investigation by an ICC Pre-Trial Chamber, ultimately the country in question must grant its approval before the case becomes admissible. Exceptionally, where a State party refuses to cede jurisdiction to the Court, the latter may yet entertain the case, provided that the particular State party is either unable or unwilling to institute criminal proceedings. This latter mode of referral should be viewed as rather exceptional.

---

[21]   See chapter 22.

[22]   See chapter 3.

[23]   See chapter 5.

[24]   See chapter 2.

[25]   The term 'situation' is obviously broader than conduct encompassed under a 'crime', typically consisting of a plurality of crimes committed over time or location. It does not feature in Art 12, but rather in Arts 13 and 14 of the ICC Statute.

[26]   Arts 12(1) and 14(1), ICC Statute.

[27]   Art 12(2), ibid.

[28]   Art 13(b), ibid.

[29]   A recent example is the Art 12(3) declaration lodged by the Justice Minister of the Palestinian Authority on 21 January 2009 in respect of conduct amounting to war crimes by Israeli agents on Palestinian territory since 2002. This was duly acknowledged by the Registrar and filed as ICC Doc 2009/404/SA/LASS (23 Jan 2009). See C Stahn, MM El Zeidy, H Olásolo, 'The International Criminal Court's Ad Hoc Jurisdiction Revisited' (2005) 99 *American Journal of International Law* 421.

The United States vehemently opposed the type of jurisdiction envisaged under Article 12(2) because in the opinion of its government this provision violates the rule that treaties can only bind contracting parties.[30] This is a valid legal argument, since Article 12(2) purports to establish ICC jurisdiction in situations where either the territorial State *or* the State of nationality of the accused is a party to the Court's Statute – or has made a declaration under Article 12(3) – although its other counterpart may not be a party to the ICC Statute and thus be adversely affected by the referral. A relevant example would arise where a US national – the US not being a party to the Court's Statute – is accused of having committed an offence in State B, which is either a party to the Statute or has lodged a relevant declaration accepting the Court's jurisdiction. Were the government of country B to surrender the accused to the jurisdiction of the Court, the ICC Statute would implicitly impose an obligation on a country that is not a party thereto, ie the USA. This mechanism cannot be justified by reference to the principles of territorial or active personality (nationality) jurisdiction, in the sense that States competent to exercise these types of jurisdiction may otherwise validly transfer their competence thereto to an international criminal tribunal. It is not that States cannot generally transfer their enforcement competence to other States or international judicial entities; rather, such transfer is naturally limited by reason of contractual or other normative interests of third countries. Thus, if third States do not possess an overriding entitlement the transfer of a particular type of jurisdiction to the ICC would be legitimate. In the case at hand, non-ICC member States have made it abundantly clear by their refusal to ratify the Statute that they do not wish the Court to adjudicate crimes or situations committed on their territory or involving their nationals. They therefore possess an overriding normative entitlement.

The inability of the Court to entertain referrals by parties acting under any of the acknowledged jurisdictional principles where such referral adversely affects the interests of third parties is also true in respect of universal jurisdiction. Although this type of jurisdiction is typically associated with national enforcement mechanisms – not international criminal tribunals whose jurisdiction is only derived from their statutes – it is worth mentioning a joint South Korean and German proposal put forward during the ICC's preparatory conferences that the Court be entitled to try anyone surrendered to it by reason of the fact that the surrendering State was entitled to exercise universal jurisdiction.[31] This proposal was ultimately rejected, thus demonstrating that the ICC is not entitled to receive by means of cession the jurisdictional competences of its member States, save for the limited competences stipulated in its Statute.[32] This restriction applies also to the apprehending State, which does not possess an unqualified right as to the choice of further surrender,

---

[30] DJ Scheffer, 'The United States and the International Criminal Court' (1999) 93 *American Journal of International Law* 12, at 18.

[31] Certainly, where conferral takes place by the custodial State many of the political problems related to the relationship between complementarity and universal jurisdiction are somewhat defused. This is also evident by the application of Art 90 ICC Statute, which is discussed below. See O Bekou, R Cryer, 'The International Criminal Court and Universal Jurisdiction: A Close Encounter?' (2007) 56 *International & Comparative Law Quarterly* 49, at 58.

[32] For a contrary view, see D Akande, 'The Jurisdiction of the International Criminal Court over Nationals of Non-Parties: Legal Basis and Limits' (2003) 1 *Journal of International Criminal Justice* 618.

particularly where this concerns a tribunal founded under contractual terms and whose jurisdiction has been explicitly rejected by interested States.[33] Exceptionally, the custodial member State is under an obligation to offer a primary choice of surrender to the ICC, if requested to do so, assuming it does not want to exercise jurisdiction over the accused, in accordance with Article 90 of the Statute. Of course, if the custodial State is under a treaty or customary obligation to surrender to a third State, such agreement or custom overrides the relevant ICC Statute obligation. It must equally be recognised that non-custodial member States cannot refer a situation to the ICC under the premise that they would otherwise be entitled in theory to exercise universal jurisdiction over that situation.

Let us determine, at least, how compatible the mechanism envisaged under Article 12(2) is in accordance with treaty law. Article 34 of the 1969 Vienna Convention on the Law of Treaties[34] clearly stipulates that international agreements are capable of producing binding legal effects only in respect of their contracting parties. They do not bind third States without their consent. It has been suggested that multilateral treaty arrangements may on the basis of considerations common to the interests of the community of nations impose certain constraints on the behaviour of third States. These constraints may not always originate from formal legal obligations – although in their majority they do – but in any event are the direct result of a broad international consensus stemming from multilateral agreements that possess a 'constitutional' nature.[35] Although this is true in the case of the UN Charter and its use of force, human rights, self-determination and other provisions, it is unlikely that the same result can be confirmed in respect of the jurisdictional mechanisms of the ICC Statute, in contrast to the *jus cogens* nature of the crimes contained therein; these jurisdictional mechanisms are clearly not of a constitutional nature. Moreover, international organisations cannot override their founding treaty and the treaty itself cannot depart from general principles of treaty law, save where a rule is of a *jus cogens* nature. In the discussion at hand, whereas the particular offences under the ambit of the ICC Statute undoubtedly possess this nature – and any objection by a non-State would be futile – the jurisdiction of the Court itself is premised on a contractual undertaking alone and as a result a constitutionality argument cannot be sustained. Were the accused to enjoy impunity, however, as a result of the absence of any jurisdictional venue to investigate his or her crimes, a strong case could be made to the effect that international law views prosecution of serious international crimes as a prerequisite to its coherence and legitimacy, which in turn may establish a constitutional rule in favour of the Court or other judicial authority that overrides the will of the State that declines, or is unable or unwilling to prosecute.[36] As a result,

---

[33] For a contrary view, see C Ryngaert, 'The International Criminal Court and Universal Jurisdiction: A Fraught Relationship?' (2009) 12 *New Criminal Law Review* 498, 502–03, who also points out that even if the conferral of universal jurisdiction was possible by the operation of law it would be highly impractical as the Court would be inundated with referrals.

[34] 1155 UNTS 331.

[35] GM Danilenko, 'The Statute of the International Criminal Court and Third States' (2000) 21 *Michigan Journal of International Law* 444, at 448.

[36] I am in favour of the US position on this matter, despite my earlier inhibitions. See I Bantekas, 'The Need to Amend Article 12 of the ICC Statute: Remedying the Effects of Multilateral Treaties upon Third Parties' (2009) 12 *New Criminal Law Review* 485.

the ICC's jurisdiction can only attain an international constitutional nature where no national court is willing to exercise jurisdiction in a particular case, or where other courts are unable or unwilling.

Having examined the legal requirements for member State referrals the following section will examine more closely the position in respect of referrals made by the Security Council. This task will be undertaken after an analysis of the principle of complementarity, whose role is to alleviate some or many of the concerns of parties and non-parties alike with regard to the exercise of the Court's jurisdiction.

19.3   The Principle of Complementarity and Security Council Referrals

The principle of complementarity, which is found in the Statute's tenth preambular paragraph as well as in Articles 1 and 17 thereto, stipulates that the Court's jurisdiction may be seized only in those situations in which State parties choose not to prosecute themselves, or are otherwise unable or unwilling. The Court's jurisdiction is therefore secondary (or complementary) to that of national courts and a case before it is inadmissible if it is being investigated or prosecuted by the courts of a State exercising its habitual jurisdiction.[37] In order for national authorities to invoke their primacy entitlement it is imperative that they adopt legislation that transposes all the offences in the ICC Statute – although they are not under an obligation to do so – otherwise their courts will not be able to assert jurisdiction over the relevant offences. While this means that the ICC will receive fewer referrals from States parties, it nonetheless entails the strengthening of all domestic criminal laws and enforcement mechanisms, thus rendering the ICC a court of last resort. The process of complementarity is unlike the mechanism adopted in relation to the ICTY and ICTR statutes where the ad hoc tribunals enjoy concurrent, yet primary, jurisdiction vis-a-vis other national courts.

This does not, however, mean that the jurisdiction of the ICC is always subject to the wishes of States parties. Exceptionally, given that those national authorities wishing to shield a particular accused may investigate a situation, yet not the conduct of the accused, or vice versa, it is imperative that national prosecutions 'encompass both the person and the conduct which is the subject of the case before the Court',[38] otherwise the ICC may validly declare a case under these circumstances as being admissible.[39] Equally, a national investigation in pursuit of the relevant situation and the accused, but only in respect of conduct X, will be deemed by the ICC as allowing the Prosecutor to investigate conduct Y by that accused under the same set of facts.

That complementarity must be read narrowly, therefore, is confirmed also by reference to Article 17(1) of the ICC Statute which makes it clear that in those cases

---

[37] Art 17(1) and (2) ICC Statute.

[38] *ICC Prosecutor v Lubanga*, Decision concerning Pre-Trial Chamber I's Decision of 10 February and the Incorporation of Documents into the Record of the Case against Lubanga (24 Feb 2006), para 31.

[39] In the Darfur situation, a pre-Trial Chamber accepted that although an accused was under investigation in Sudan, his investigation before the courts of Sudan did not encompass the same conduct which was the subject of the application before the Court. *ICC Prosecutor v Harun and Kushayb*, Decision on the Prosecution Application under Article 58(7) of the Statute (27 Apr 2007), paras 20–24.

where national legal systems are genuinely unable or unwilling to prosecute or investigate a particular situation the ICC Prosecutor may validly initiate criminal proceedings. The same is also true in respect of cases where although the accused has already been the subject of a criminal investigation or trial by national authorities, his subsequent prosecution by the ICC would not offend the principle of double jeopardy (*ne bis in idem*, meaning that an accused cannot be tried twice for the same conduct) because the national proceedings would have been undertaken in such a manner as to shield the accused. The shielding of the accused is also presumed in cases where the independence and impartiality of the national court or of the national prosecutor is manifestly lacking.[40] Although the inability of a State to conduct criminal proceedings is generally straight forward and is self-evident in post-conflict situations where the capacity of the State to manage its daily affairs is untenable (as was the case with post-genocide Rwanda or Sierra Leone), the ascertainment of unwillingness is not always clear-cut. With the exception of cases such as those of the Lockerbie bombing or the bogus investigation of high government officials in Sudan in respect of the Darfur massacres, it is unclear whether the establishment of alternative justice mechanisms can prevent the ICC Prosecutor from arguing that a State is unwilling to prosecute. In my opinion, truth commissions whose purpose or ultimate effect – even if unintended – is to avoid prosecutions in respect of the offences within the Court's jurisdiction are generally incompatible with a party's obligation to diligently prosecute under the ICC Statute. Each truth commission and its work should be assessed on its own merits. Equally, the granting of amnesties in accordance with national law does not release a person from criminal responsibility under international law.[41] A determination by the Court that a State party intended to shield an accused through impartial criminal proceedings is open to challenge either by the State that commenced or completed investigation of the case, or the State from which acceptance of jurisdiction was required under Article 12(2) of the Statute.[42]

What happens, however, in situations where the custodial State party, which possesses either territorial or nationality jurisdiction, is seized with competing requests for surrender, one of which is from the ICC Prosecutor? In such cases involving competing requests and where both requests relate to the same offence the custodial State shall give priority to the Court's request, if it has already determined that the case is admissible, in accordance with Article 90 of the ICC Statute. The same applies where the competing requests are for the same person, but not for the same crime. If, however, the requesting State is not a party to the ICC Statute then the requested State is not under a strict obligation to surrender the accused to the Court. Rather, the requested State may, under such circumstances, especially if it is

---

[40]   Art 17(1)(b) and (2) ICC Statute.
[41]   For a more comprehensive analysis on the status of amnesties under international law, see chapter 20.8.
[42]   Art 19(2) ICC Statute.

incumbent under a pre-existing extradition arrangement with the requesting State, surrender the accused under the terms of that arrangement and disregard the request of the ICC.[43]

We have already referred to the right granted to the Security Council to refer situations to the Court, following a resolution adopted under Chapter VII of its Charter. It may seem rational and a statement of the obvious that the Council may exercise a right of referral (and deferral), but this entitlement is not a necessary consequence under Article 103 of the UN Charter. Indeed, although Article 25 of the UN Charter expressly stipulates that Council resolutions are binding this quality pertaining to resolutions applies in respect of States parties and not international organisations to which such parties are members, as would be the case with the legal person of the ICC. As a result, without a relevant provision in the ICC Statute the Security Council would have had no authority to make binding referrals. This power was granted in order to sustain coherence between the UN as a whole – but specifically the Council's seminal role with regard to the maintenance of international peace and security – and the work of the Court.

Prior to the *Darfur* referral by the Security Council it was debated whether Council referrals were subject to the regime of complementarity in equal measure to other referrals by the Prosecutor. The answer to this question must clearly be answered in the negative. Where the Council adopts a resolution, such as that relating to Darfur,[44] it is addressed to two particular audiences: UN member States and the ICC. Whereas UN members are obliged to accept the terms of the referral and surrender of the accused, the Prosecutor and the Court are under a duty to investigate the referred situation. Yet, the language of resolution 1593, by which the Darfur situation was referred to the Court, is not all-embracing. The obligation to surrender is only implicitly addressed to all States and then only in theory because it is unlikely that the accused will leave the territory of Sudan. Moreover, the Council is careful to emphasise that UN member States, particularly non-ICC parties, have no obligation under the ICC Statute. This is not to say that the Council cannot engage the cooperation of all States on the basis of a binding resolution. Nonetheless, it will not lightly resort to such a measure in the future given the fact that two Council members, USA and China, are not parties to the ICC Statute. The early jurisprudence of the ICC chambers clearly demonstrates that Council referrals entail the exercise of primary and exclusive jurisdiction by the ICC over crimes committed in the territory of parties and non-parties and by nationals of all States.[45] Complentarity therefore is inapplicable in respect of Council referrals.[46]

---

[43] Art 98, ibid. In any event, the custodial State should take account of a number of factors in making its final determination, particularly the dates of the requests, the interests of the relevant States and the possibility of a subsequent surrender between the Court and the other State, in accordance with Art 90(6) of the ICC Statute.

[44] SC 1593 (31 Mar 2005).

[45] *ICC Prosecutor v Harun and Kushayb*, Decision on the Prosecution Application under Article 58(7) of the Statute (27 Apr 2007), para 16; *ICC Prosecutor v Al-Bashir*, Decision on the Prosecution's Application for a Warrant of Arrest against Al-Bashir (4 Mar 2009), paras 35–36, 40.

[46] See in support, D Akande, 'The Legal Nature of Security Council Referrals to the ICC and its Impact on Al-Bashir's Immunities' (2009) 7 *Journal of International Criminal Justice* 333.

It should be pointed out that following the adoption of the ICC Statute commentators feared the Court would be rendered a redundant institution because the operation of the complementarity mechanism would prevent the Prosecutor from investigating cases. This apprehension was naturally based on the assumption that no State would be willing to confer situations to the Court. Moreover, even if referrals were to take place there was always the danger of the Security Council stepping in to defer the case. In fact, not only did this doomsday scenario never materialise, but by mid-2006 the Prosecutor had already received 1,700 communications. These were submitted to his office from affected citizens or groupings of individuals and concerned countries where sustained violence was taking place. The Prosecutor declined to take any action given that a State party had not made the necessary referral.[47] At the time of writing the investigations and prosecutions had commenced on the basis of referrals from the Democratic Republic of Congo (DRC), Uganda and the Central African Republic. As already stated the Security Council has referred the Darfur situation in Sudan. An authorisation from a pre-Trial Chamber is pending in order for the Prosecutor to exercise his *proprio motu* powers in respect of the post-election eruption of violence in Kenya between 28 December 2007 and 28 February 2008.[48] Thus, far from being a redundant and peripheral judicial forum the ICC has already established itself as a serious and respected contender for the championing of international criminal justice.

19.4   Deferrals by the Security Council and Deferrals in 'the Interests of Justice'

We have already alluded to the fact that the Court's jurisdiction can be triggered by referral from a State party[49] or the Security Council[50] and exceptionally also *proprio motu* by the Prosecutor.[51] To alleviate the concerns of many States regarding potential abuse by the Prosecutor of his independent right of referral, or in order to avoid referrals of politically sensitive situations which powerful States may wish to keep out of the Court's portfolio, a variety of mechanisms serve as adequate counterbalance. Article 15(1) demands that the Prosecutor submit a case to a pre-Trial Chamber for authorisation of an investigation only if there exists a 'reasonable basis' to proceed with the investigation. Nonetheless, whether a case is deferred to national authorities or pending a ruling by the pre-Trial Chamber on the Court's jurisdiction, the Prosecutor is not prevented from seeking authority to take

---

[47]   See Office of the Prosecutor Response to Communications received concerning Iraq, (9 Feb 2006), available at: <http://www.icc-cpi.int/NR/rdonlyres/04D143C8–19FB-466C-AB77–4CDB2FDEBEF7/143682/OTP_letter_to_senders_re_Iraq_9_February_2006.pdf>. It should be stated that at the time of writing Iraq was not a party to the Statute. The majority of private communications received concerned Venezuela, Palestine, Guinea, Kenya and Iraq.

[48]   *Situation in the Republic of Kenya*, Request for Authorisation of an Investigation pursuant to Article 15 (26 Nov 2009).

[49]   Arts 13(a) and 14(1) ICC Statute.

[50]   Art 13(b), ibid.

[51]   Art 15(1), ibid.

necessary measures for preserving both material and oral evidence which could subsequently be impaired or lost.[52] In the event that a situation is deferred to the jurisdiction of a national court, the Prosecutor retains authority to request periodical progress reports of investigations and judicial proceedings, as well as review national investigations at any time a significant change of circumstances has occurred, which may subsequently signal a State's unwillingness or inability to proceed.[53]

What happens with situations in respect of which no State party has seemingly exercised its right of primary jurisdiction? Article 18(1)–(2) of the ICC Statute stipulates that when the Prosecutor has determined a reasonable basis to commence an investigation he must first notify all States parties and those States which, taking into account the information available, would normally exercise jurisdiction over the crimes concerned. This is meant to provide States with a first (last minute) pick, albeit this entitlement is only open for a month following the Prosecutor's notification and provided that within this space of time the country wishing to exercise this entitlement has commenced its investigation. Even so, the Prosecutor's deferral is open to review six months after the deferral, or at any time when it becomes obvious that the investigating State is unable or unwilling to carry out the investigation or prosecution.[54]

The Security Council acting under Chapter VII of the UN Charter may defer the investigation or prosecution of a situation for a period of twelve months, which is renewable under the same procedure in accordance with Article 16 of the Statute. Indeed, Article 16 could work against Chinese and US desire to dominate ICC referrals,[55] as the other permanent members of the Security Council can effectively use their veto power against such resolutions.[56] This type of deferral was put into practice in the early years of the Court's operation as a political tool by the then US government, following the adoption of resolution 1422.[57] The short history of this resolution can be traced to 19 June 2002 when the United States threatened to veto the continuation of the mandate of the UN Mission in Bosnia and Herzegovina (UNMIBH) under the pretence that US troops could potentially be prosecuted by the ICC in accordance with Article 12(2) of its Statute.[58] Following several Council meetings concerning the future of UNMIBH the Council members were convinced to adopt resolution 1422 under Chapter VII of the UN Charter, paragraph 1 of which requested that in accordance with Article 16 of the ICC Statute:

> If a case arises involving current or former officials or personnel from a contributing State not a party to the Rome Statute over acts or omissions relating to a United Nations established or authorized operation, [then the ICC] shall for a twelve-month period starting 1 July 2002 not commence or proceed with investigation or prosecution of any such case, unless the Security Council decides otherwise.

---

[52] Arts 17(6) and 19(8), ibid.
[53] Art 18(5), ibid.
[54] Art 18(3), ibid.
[55] Scheffer, 'The United States and the International Criminal Court', at 13.
[56] Equally, in the same manner the veto power may be exercised in order to block referrals to the Court.
[57] SC Res 1422 (12 Jul 2004).
[58] UN Press Release SC/7430 (21 Jun 2002).

The Resolution went on to say that such a deferral may be extended by subsequent twelve-month periods by the Council and that UN member States must take no action inconsistent with paragraph 1 and their international obligations. This resolution is worrying in the sense that, besides the impunity it grants, it implies that the application of criminal justice constituted under the Rome Statute represents a threat to international peace and security![59] Clearly, this is a step too far and it is unlikely that the USA will pursue efforts to adopt unnecessary resolutions like this in the future. Strong calls for deferrals on clear political grounds were also addressed in late 2009 by the African Union – albeit most African countries are supportive of the Court generally – to the Security Council in respect of the investigation of the Sudanese President's role in the Darfur situation. As a result, the AU has even vowed not to cooperate with the ICC in ongoing and future investigations concerning Africa.

Deferrals in the interests of justice are an important part of the ICC Statute, yet the pertinent provision is veiled under inconspicuous terms. Article 53(2)(c) of the ICC Statute calls upon the Prosecutor to consider prior to the initiation of an investigation whether a sufficient basis for prosecution does not in fact exist because it:

> is not *in the interests of justice*, taking into account all the circumstances, including the gravity of the crime, the interests of victims and the age or infirmity of the alleged perpetrator, and his or her role in the alleged crime.

The impact of this provision is not immediately obvious. In the Darfur situation the Court was seized by a motion of two pro-government Sudanese NGOs claiming that the prosecution of the Sudanese President and his co-accused was not in the interests of justice because it would have significant ramifications for the country's peace building efforts and national security and would entrench negative public sentiment in respect of the ICC in Sudan. The Court missed a golden opportunity to elaborate on this principle, but did emphasise that the enumerated circumstances in Article 53(2)(c) are indicative and not exhaustive[60] and that the ascertainment of a situation as being detrimental to the interests of justice is entrusted to the Prosecutor.[61] The 'interests of justice' proviso should not be used to compare dissimilar qualities. For example, the aforementioned claims by the Sudanese NGOs are political in nature and hence cannot be employed against arguments relating to the pursuit of international criminal justice, such as the imperative to prevent, investigate and punish persons responsible for international crimes. Throughout this book I have maintained that not only States have the duty to punish international crimes, but that international institutions are under an obligation to refuse to accept the validity of amnesties and sweeping immunities for such crimes. It is only natural therefore that

---

[59] The mandate of SC Res 1422 was renewed once under SC Res 1487 (12 Jun 2003). Equally, SC 1497 (1 Aug 2003) and relating to the deployment of a multinational stabilisation force to Liberia at the insistence of the USA, exempted non-ICC member State nationals from the Court's jurisdiction. It is no wonder, therefore, that the legality of these resolutions has been called into question. See S Zappala 'The Reaction of the US to the Entry into Force of the ICC Statute: Comments on UN SC 1422 (2002) and Article 98 Agreements' (2003) 1 *Journal of International Criminal Justice* 114.

[60] *Re Situation in Darfur*, Decision on Application under Rule 103 (4 Feb 2009), para 18.

[61] Ibid, para 22.

the ICC Prosecutor construe Article 53(2)(c) narrowly and apply it only for circumstances that pertain to the subject matter of criminal justice.[62] The ICC Office of the Prosecutor is of the opinion that besides the grounds mentioned in Article 53 it may decline to entertain a case where an investigation may exacerbate or otherwise destabilise a conflict situation or seriously endanger the successful completion of a reconciliation effort.[63] While the first of the two is debatable, albeit not a matter subject to conclusive and definitive determinations, the latter is clearly unacceptable as it suggests that international criminal justice may be an impediment to peace.

Another limitation that is akin to the effects of a deferral is found in Article 98 of the Statute, which recognises that where there are multiple competing requests for the surrender of an accused person under the custody of an ICC member State compliance with an ICC order for surrender should not violate the custodial State's obligations with third States under international law. Paragraph 1 of Article 98 requires the third State's express waiver of State or diplomatic immunity over persons and property situated in a country that has accepted the Court's jurisdiction.[64] Similarly, paragraph 2 requires the consent of the sending State in all cases of ICC surrender orders with regard to accused persons forming part of status-of-forces agreement contingents, and stationed at the time of the order in the receiving State. It also excludes the surrender of persons to the Court that are otherwise covered by pre-existing extradition treaties.[65]

19.5   Subject Matter Jurisdiction

As already explained, the ICC enjoys subject matter jurisdiction over genocide, crimes against humanity, war crimes (both international and internal) and the crime of aggression. Although the inclusion of other treaty crimes, especially drug-trafficking, and terrorism, was contemplated both before and during the Rome conference they were finally excluded since it was felt that investigation of drug-trafficking and terrorism involved sensitive and long-term planning operations best suited for domestic authorities. Equally, the delegates questioned the appropriateness of encompassing terrorism in the Statute in the absence of a universally accepted definition. Therefore, in order to salvage the Statute and avoid time consuming revisions detracting from more serious issues, only the four aforementioned core crimes were included. There is provision in Articles 121 and 123 for a future review of the list of crimes contained in Article 5, which may encompass possible amendment to the existing offences or the addition of new ones. In respect of the review conference scheduled to take place in 2010 Mexico has proposed the criminalisation

---

[62]   See HB Jallow, 'Prosecutorial Discretion and International Criminal Justice' (2005) 3 *Journal of International Criminal Justice* 145.

[63]   Draft ICC Regulations of the Office of the Prosecutor (3 Jun 2003), footnote 79.

[64]   Presumably, State officials who cannot claim immunity *ratione personae* must try to prove that they enjoy immunity *ratione materiae* under customary international law. Danilenko, 'The Statute of the ICC', at 472.

[65]   See below the discussion on Article 98 agreements between the USA and ICC member States.

of the use of nuclear weapons, Trinidad and Tobago has once again proposed the criminalisation of drug-trafficking, while the Netherlands have suggested the incorporation of the crime of terrorism.

In order to avoid any future arguments as to the precise definition and content of the crimes within the jurisdiction of the Court, proposals had been tabled prior to the adoption of the Statute regarding a detailed set of elements that would be annexed thereto. The objective of this instrument was to ensure compliance with the principle of legality. As a result, a preparatory commission charged with the drafting of these elements was appointed following the 1998 Rome conference, which succeeded in finalising the so-called Elements of Crimes, which were adopted by consensus in December 2002. These spell out the subjective, objective and contextual elements of each crime in detail. The Elements are clearly subordinate to the Statute, since in accordance with Article 9(1) of the Statute their purpose is to assist the Court in the interpretation of Articles 6–8. In this guiding and interpretative capacity their application is mandatory on the Court, since along with the Statute and the Rules of Procedure and Evidence they constitute the primary legal instruments for the Court, under Article 21(1)(a) of the Statute. The clear hierarchy established by Article 21 even places the Elements above relevant treaties and principles and rules of international law – such as the *jus in bello* conventions – as well as above general principles of laws. As a result, the chambers of the Court cannot disregard the Elements. Logic dictates, however, that when an Element is found to be in contravention of fundamental human rights or the rights of the accused it must be abandoned in favour of a more appropriate rule.

The Statute is applicable only to natural persons, and then only if they were 18 years of age at the time of the alleged offence.[66] The gravity of the four offences has further necessitated their exclusion from any statute of limitations.[67]

19.6   International Cooperation and Judicial Assistance

Parties to the Statute are under a general obligation to cooperate with the Court in accordance with Article 86. The Court enjoys broad authority to make requests of a varying nature where these are relevant for the investigation and prosecution of crimes within its jurisdiction, including the surrender of accused persons as well as material that may have evidentiary value. In the execution of any requests States are permitted to comply with their national procedural law.[68] Non-parties to the Statute are not obliged to cooperate with the Court, but may choose to do so on the basis of an ad hoc arrangement.[69] Under Article 87(4) of the Statute binding requests may demand that measures be taken for the protection of evidence or the physical and

---

[66]   Art 26 ICC Statute.

[67]   Art 29, ibid. This is in accordance with the 1968 Convention on Non-Applicability of Statutory Limitations to War Crimes and Crimes Against Humanity, Art 1, 754 UNTS 73. See chapter 8 for a more detailed analysis of this concept.

[68]   Art 88 ICC Statute.

[69]   Art 87(5), ibid.

psychological well being of victims, witnesses and their families. The Court may also ask any intergovernmental organisation to provide information or documents, in accordance with Article 87(4), but, since such entities are not parties to the Rome Statute, they are not bound to adhere.[70] Exceptionally, the UN must cooperate with the ICC on the basis of their bilateral agreement and the ICC will do well to enter into similar agreements with regional organisations.

In relation to the Congo investigation we are faced with conflicting statements. On the one hand, paragraph 5(g) of Security Council resolution 1565 of 1 October 2004 authorises the UN Mission in Congo (MONUC) to 'continue to cooperate with efforts to ensure that those responsible for serious violations of human rights and international humanitarian law are brought to justice, while working closely with the relevant agencies of the United Nations'. This could suggest an authorisation to cooperate with the ICC in the arrest of indicted persons, a position which would seem to coincide with the perception of the UN Secretary-General.[71] Such an authorisation, however, must be rejected because of a statement by the UN Ambassador to the UN, according to which the US supports Resolution 1565 with the 'understanding that it does not direct MONUC to cooperate with the ICC'.

Equally, the ICC cannot direct binding orders and requests to non-governmental organisations (NGOs) and the International Committee of the Red Cross. In practice, however, NGOs will provide substantial assistance, as has been the case with assistance rendered to the ICTY, where organisations of this kind actively supported many crucial areas of the Tribunal's work, such as the taking of depositions, affidavits and the collection of other forms of evidence.[72] Unlike the ad hoc Tribunals, Article 15(2) of the ICC Statute actually empowers the Prosecutor to seek additional information from a variety of sources, including NGOs. With regard to its investigations in Uganda, Darfur and the Congo, the ICC has directly requested the surrender of persons, evidentiary material and permission to conduct investigations from the referring States, but with regard to non-parties it has entered into cooperation agreements.[73]

Besides material evidence, the Court has the authority to request the arrest and surrender of persons from the custodial State.[74] While this process would normally be defined as extradition, in the context of inter-State criminal cooperation the terminology applied in the Statute, as indeed in the context of the ICTY and ICTR, refers to it as 'surrender' of persons. The accused may challenge the ICC request for surrender as being contrary to the principle of double jeopardy and, once surrendered, the Court must respect the principle of specialty, unless the requested State waives it.[75] Obviously, the primary obligation of the custodial State under Article 59

[70] For example, in order to receive logistical assistance and judicial support from the UN Mission in the Congo (MONUC), the ICC concluded a Memorandum of Understanding on 8 November 2005 with MONUC. See Report of the ICC, UN Doc A/61/217 (3 Aug 2006), para 47.

[71] Cited in Status of Cooperation with the ICC, Doc ICC-02/04–01/05 (6 Oct 2006), para 19.

[72] 'The ICTY and NGOs' (1996) 4 *ICTY Bulletin,* at 4.

[73] Cooperation Agreement of 2 October 2005 with Sudan, in relation to the investigation in Uganda. Equally, a General Framework Cooperation was concluded between the ICC and Chad on 18 August 2005 for the purposes of investigation and interviewing witnesses on the territory of the latter through an exchange of letters. See ICC Report, Doc ICC-02/04–01/05 (6 Oct 2006), paras 22, 24.

[74] Art 59 ICC Statute.

[75] Art 101, ibid.

of the Statute is to arrest the accused; thereafter, it is under an obligation to surrender him to the Court only where it decides not to prosecute him or her.

A party may deny a request for assistance, in whole or in part, only where the request concerns the production of any documents or disclosure of evidence that relates to its national security.[76] In such cases, Article 72(5) envisages a cooperative procedure whereby conciliatory attempts are to be made to modify the request, determine the relevance of the contested evidence or seek an alternative source, or otherwise convince that State to provide the information in terms that do not prejudice its national security, particularly through *in camera* or *ex parte* proceedings.[77] If, following this procedure, the dispute has not been resolved and the Court determines that the evidence is relevant and necessary for the establishment of the guilt or innocence of the accused, it may either request further consultations, inform the Assembly of States Parties or the Security Council of that State's refusal to comply, or make an inference as to the existence or not of a fact at trial.[78] The right to confidentiality afforded to States parties under Article 93(4) is not absolute, as sub-paragraph (7)(b)(i) of Article 72 empowers the Court to order the disclosure of evidence in all other circumstances. Sub-paragraph (b)(i) seems to adhere to the ICTY Appeals Chamber decision in the *Blaškić* appeals subpoena case, where it was held that although all possible modalities accommodating national security concerns must be provided States cannot invoke such concerns where a binding obligation for disclosure has been issued.[79]

In practical terms, however, refusal to comply with an order for disclosure of sensitive national information will be dealt with in the same way as all other instances of failure to comply with the Court's binding requests. In general, the Court will make a finding of non-compliance and thereafter refer the matter to the Assembly of States Parties, or, where the Security Council referred the matter to the Court, to the Council itself.[80] The experience of the Yugoslav Tribunal demonstrates that State co-operation and Security Council support are inextricably linked and are themselves dependent on the Court's image as a powerful institution. If the ICC manages to attain this status, as did the ICTY after 1996, it, too, will receive obeisance not only from parties to its Statute, who are under an express obligation to do so, but also from intergovernmental organisations, especially in the form of arrests and detention of suspects by peacekeeping missions, an aspect which has proved seminal to the ICTY's judicial and investigative function.

A more detailed discussion of the cooperative schemes and national laws by which ICC member States are to offer assistance (mutual legal assistance, surrender of persons and others) to the Court and its Prosecutor is offered in chapter 16.6.2.

---

[76] Art 93(4), ibid.

[77] The ICTY made use of *in camera* proceedings in relation to sensitive information, such as satellite photographs of the Srebrenica mass grave sites, which were utilised to compare the ground before and after its excavation. While this type of evidence may be excluded following official requests, States may allow for it to be made available. See 'Special: exhumations' (19 July 1996) *ICTY Bulletin,* at 8. Rules 72 and 73 of the ICC Rules of Procedure and Evidence permit *in camera* proceedings.

[78] Art 72(7)(a)(i)–(iii) ICC Statute.

[79] *ICTY Prosecutor v Blaškić,* Appeals Judgment on the Request of the Republic of Croatia for Review of the Decision of Trial Chamber I of 11 July 1997 (29 Oct 1997), paras 61–69.

[80] Art 87(5)(b) and (7) ICC Statute.

19.7 Impunity Agreements in Contravention of Article 98 ICC Statute

We have already analysed the opposition of the United States government to the jurisdictional mechanism of Article 12(2) of the ICC Statute. The apprehension of the US government was not wholly unreasonable. It feared that given its participation in the vast majority of peacekeeping, peace enforcement and other military missions around the globe that possible capture of US personnel by States opposed to its hegemony and international policies may result in a referral for political purposes.

As a result, following the adoption of the ICC Statute the US concluded a number of bilateral treaties with ICC States parties and non-parties with the aim of precluding investigation and prosecution of US nationals accused of offences falling within the jurisdiction of the Court. These so-called 'impunity agreements' (or Article 98 Agreements) were signed in the majority by countries that had some form of economic dependency on the USA and could thus not resist turning down such a request.[81] From the point of view of ICC member States the justificatory basis of these bilateral agreements rests in Article 98 of the ICC Statute. This constitutes an exception to the general obligation under Article 90, which requires ICC member States to surrender to the Court persons in their custody they do not wish to prosecute when faced with multiple and competing requests for surrender. The exception envisaged under Article 98 of the ICC Statute permits member States to depart from the obligation to surrender to the Court, in situations of multiple requests, only where a competing request is premised on a treaty or customary obligation with a third party. These treaty or customary obligations concern two types of issues. The first paragraph of Article 98 relates to diplomatic or other immunities established by treaty or customary law, whereas the second paragraph concerns extradition treaties. Bilateral impunity agreements are therefore allegedly predicated on the second paragraph of Article 98. The problem is that Article 98(2) does not specify whether the competing treaty must pre-exist the adoption of the ICC Statute by the member State thereto and thus it is no wonder that the adherents of these bilateral impunity agreements have found fertile ground upon which to claim their legitimacy.[82]

This argument, however, is wholly fallacious as far as ICC member States are concerned. Given that these bilateral agreements are clearly meant by the US government to frustrate the object and purpose of ICC referrals and surrenders, any post-Statute agreements will have the effect of violating the member State's obligations. Any other result is absurd since under general international law a State may not absolve its existing treaty obligations by entering into a new competing treaty, save if the prior treaty has been terminated by mutual consent either for all or some of the parties. By all accounts, the rationale belying the adoption of Article 98(2) was to

---

[81] Amnesty International (AI), 'International Criminal Court: US Efforts to Obtain Impunity for Genocide, Crimes Against Humanity and War Crimes' AI Doc IOR/40/025/2002 (2 Sep 2002). By mid-2005 the US had concluded 100 such agreements with both ICC and non-ICC member States.

[82] See M Benzing, 'US Bilateral Non-Surrender Agreements and Article 98 of the Statute of the International Criminal Court: An Exercise in the Law of Treaties' (2004) 8 *Max Planck Yearbook of United Nations Law* 181.

cater for existing Status of Forces Agreements (SOFAs), ensuring that they will not be nullified. It was never envisaged to apply in the manner contemplated under the bilateral impunity agreements.

19.8   Reservations and Amendments to the Statute

Article 120 does not permit reservations to the Statute. This prohibition must also include all interpretative declarations whose effect is that of reservations, except in cases where parties are expressly afforded discretion under the Statute. An example of an acceptable interpretative declaration would be that describing the national procedures required for cooperation with the Court, under Article 88 of the Statute. The prohibition of reservations in the Statute follows similar practice adopted with regard to contemporary human rights and humanitarian law treaties, even though such practice results, or is perceived to result, in smaller treaty participation.[83] Although less so in the case of the ICC, most provisions contained in human rights and humanitarian law treaties constitute miniature treaties in their own right, rendering thus any possible reservations, by and large, contrary to the purpose and object of these instruments. While it is true that the obligations incorporated in the ICC Statute are not reciprocal, in practice States find that to accept the unconditional nature of such obligations impairs their strategic or other interests. The adoption of the ICC Statute is no less of a bargain than is, say, the negotiation of other permanent international judicial organs, such as ITLOS or the dispute settlement panels of the World Trade Organisation. Despite early ominous predictions, by late 2009 a total number of 110 countries had ratified the Statute.

The body responsible for the functioning of the Court and the highest authority regarding all its substantive and procedural aspects is the ASP, established under Article 112 of the Statute. The ASP is composed of all States parties to the Statute, every one of which is represented by one official, accompanied by alternatives and advisers, holding a single vote. Decisions in the Assembly should be reached by consensus. If this proves untenable, decisions on matters of substance must be approved by a two-thirds majority of those present and voting, provided that an absolute majority of States parties constitutes the quorum for voting. Decisions on matters of procedure are taken by a simple majority of States parties present and voting.[84] The Assembly consists of a bureau encompassing a president, two vice

---

[83]   1993 Chemical Weapons Convention, Art 22; 1997 Convention on the Prohibition of the Use, Stockpiling, Production and Transfer of Anti-Personnel Mines and on Their Destruction, Art 19; the Human Rights Committee stated in its General Comment No 24, entitled 'General Comment on issues relating to reservations made upon ratification or accession to the Covenant or the Optional Protocols thereto, or in relation to declarations under Art 41 of the Covenant', that because human rights treaties are not a web of interstate exchanges of mutual State obligations, reservations should not lead to 'a perpetual non-attainment of international human rights standards', UN Doc CCPR/C/21/Rev 1/Add 6 (2 Nov 1994), paras 17, 19, reprinted in 107 ILR 64. This *erga omnes* character of human rights and humanitarian treaties was early recognised by the ICJ in its *Advisory Opinion in the Genocide* case (1951) ICJ Reports 15.

[84]   Art 112(7) ICC Statute.

presidents and 18 members elected by the Assembly for three-year terms and its purpose is to assist the Assembly in the discharge of its responsibilities.[85]

Amendments to the Statute can be proposed and considered only seven years after the Statute has entered into force. If the States parties cannot reach consensus on the amendment, a two-thirds majority is required to adopt it. This amendment would enter into force for all parties after its ratification by seven-eighths of them. This amendment procedure applies also with respect to a proposed amendment to Articles 5–8, which contain the four core crimes comprising the jurisdiction of the ICC. In this case, however, the Court cannot exercise its jurisdiction regarding a crime covered by the amendment where the party on whose territory or whose national committed the offence has not accepted the said amendment.[86] A practical implication of this latter procedure could arise with regard to a possible future prohibition of nuclear weapons, in which case, nuclear powers would remain parties to the Statute, but be excluded from the application of the nuclear weapons prohibition.[87] It has already been pointed out that the first review conference is to take place in mid-2010 and it is now certain that it will have to examine numerous proposals for amendments to the Statute, which may include expanding upon the list of crimes that are currently contained in Article 5.

The Court is to be funded not from the regular budget of the UN, as was proposed by some States, but from assessed contributions of States parties, adjusted in accordance with the principles on which the scale adopted by the UN for its regular budget rests.[88] In cases where a situation is referred to the Court by the Security Council the UN will cover any expenses incurred,[89] although as has already been explained the Security Council ordered otherwise in its referral of the Darfur situation to the Court. During the first meeting of the ASP in September 2002, a set of financial regulations and rules was adopted. It was decided that assessments would be determined based on membership of the ASP at the date of the adoption of that decision (that is, 3 September 2002), and that assessments after this date would be treated as miscellaneous income.[90] Article 116 of the Statute permits the Court to receive and utilise voluntary contributions from governments, international organisations, individuals and other entities, in accordance with criteria to be established by the ASP.[91]

19.9   Reparation of Victims and the ICC Trust Fund

Unlike the ICTY and ICTR, the Permanent International Court has been empowered to offer reparation to the victims of crimes, including restitution, compensation

---

[85]   Art 112(3), ibid.
[86]   Art 121, ibid.
[87]   D McGoldrick, *The Human Rights Committee: Its Role in the Development of the International Covenant on Civil and Political Rights* (Oxford, Oxford University Press, 1994) 631.
[88]   Arts 115(1) and 117 ICC Statute.
[89]   Art 115(2), ibid.
[90]   ICC Doc ICC-ASP/1/3 (3–10 Sep 2002), Resolution 14.
[91]   Resolution 6, ibid.

and rehabilitation.[92] Although a substantial number of arbitral tribunals have adjudicated tort claims in the past, this is the first time an international judicial organ whose mandate is to render criminal justice faces this dual task. Hence, the court is legally required to establish principles relating to reparations. This is a particularly sensitive issue, since there are no clear guidelines on whether monetary reparation need be made from the property, assets or instrumentalities of crimes as suggested by Articles 75(4) and 93(1)(k), or whether every asset belonging to the convicted person's estate is liable to forfeiture. The Statute merely subjects any measures which the Court might order to possible rights of *bona fide* third parties.[93]

In order to facilitate the purpose of such reparations, Article 79 provides for the creation of a trust fund for the benefit of victims and their families. When the ICC Statute received the requisite sixty ratifications and came into existence the ASP speedily adopted a resolution giving life to the Trust Fund.[94] This was followed in 2005 by a resolution on the Fund's Regulations.[95] The Fund is managed by a Board of Trustees whose members participate in an individual capacity and serve on a *pro bono* basis. The Fund is generally financed through voluntary donations by States and non-State entities, but does not accept voluntary contributions that create a manifest inequality between the recipient victims.[96] Besides voluntary contributions the ICC Fund may be financed by 'money and other property collected through fines or forfeiture transferred to the Fund if ordered by the Court pursuant to Article 79(2) of the ICC Statute', as well as from 'resources collected through awards for reparation if ordered by the Court'.[97] This is an exceptional measure, since trust funds under international law do not generally possess the authority to solicit compulsory contributions from State or non-State entities that are not members thereof, unless instructed to do so by the UN Security Council.[98] Hence, the legality of transferring to the ICC Trust Fund forfeited and seized assets must be based on the Court's authority, through the ICC Statute, to subject such assets to itself following a judicial determination to that effect. Because reparations can only be awarded by the Court's order 'through', instead of 'into' the Trust Fund, in accordance with Article 75(2) of the Statute, the Fund is merely an intermediary of the Court and does not possess an independent right to compensate.[99] Had this authority not been predicated in the ICC Statute[100] it is doubtful whether the Court may be deemed to possess inherent judicial powers to coerce the confiscation and seizure of the assets of convicted

---

[92]   Art 75 ICC Statute; in their plenary meeting in July 2000 the judges of the ICTY considered the issue of the right of victims to seek compensation. Upon completion of a report containing compensatory methods and practical recommendations in September of that year they invited the UN to consider its application. ICTY Doc JL/PIS/528-e (14 Sep 2000). The reader should refer to chapter 22 for a more thorough review of the ICC reparation regime.

[93]   Art 93(1)(k), ibid.

[94]   Res ICC/ASP/1/Res 6 (9 Sep 2002).

[95]   Res ICC-ASP/4/Res 3 (3 Dec 2005), Regulations of the Trust Fund for Victims.

[96]   ICC Doc ICC-ASP/1/3 (3–10 Sep 2002), Resolution 6.

[97]   Ibid, Regulations, Art 21(b) and (c).

[98]   See I Bantekas, *Trust Funds under International Law: Trustee Obligations of the United Nations and International Development Banks* (The Hague, TMC Asser Press, 2009).

[99]   T Ingadottir, 'The International Criminal Court: The Trust Fund for Victims, A Discussion Paper' (ICC Discussion Paper No 3, Feb 2001) 15.

[100]   Arts 75, 77(2)(b), 93(1)(k) ICC Statute.

persons. This power was purposefully excluded from the ambit of the ad hoc tribunals for Yugoslavia and Rwanda by its creating body, the Security Council, and thus there is no compelling reason suggesting that the international community regards confiscations and reparations as an inherent judicial prerogative.

The principle of complementarity necessarily entails that the relevant compensatory mechanisms are also subject to this principle. Although there is no requirement for member States to implement the ICC Statute in their domestic legislation in order to enjoy the privilege of primacy over the Court, it is wise for States parties to do so. In the present context the process of incorporation need not only encompass the Statute's provisions on substantive and procedural criminal law, but also those relating to the trust fund. Some countries have, as a result, set up trust funds under their domestic law with the purpose of channelling thereto money obtained through the enforcement of ICC orders for reparation, forfeitures, etc, donations and others.[101] These domestic trust funds, to the extent that they are set up to complement the work of the ICC and are indeed expressly mandated to receive orders from the Court are in some sense an extension of Articles 75 and 79 of the ICC Statute and possess therefore an international dimension. They do not, however, enjoy the privileges and immunities of the ICC Trust Fund, nor are they subject to regulation by the ASP.

---

[101] C Ferstman, 'The Reparation Regime of the International Criminal Court: Practical Considerations' (2002) 15 *Leiden Journal of International Law* 667, at 685.

20

Internationalised Domestic Criminal Tribunals, Truth Commissions and Amnesties

20.1 Introduction

In previous chapters we examined two types of tribunals: those established under Security Council resolutions as ad hoc tribunals, such as the International Criminal Tribunal for the Former Yugoslavia (ICTY) and International Criminal Tribunal for Rwanda (ICTR), and a permanent institution that was created through a treaty; ie the ICC. The Nuremberg Tribunal before these was premised on a treaty between the victorious allies of the Second World War. The judicial institutions examined in this chapter have all been established under different legal bases. Their common feature is that they can validly be considered domestic tribunals, albeit with international elements. In that sense they can be considered as mixed, or otherwise international-ised domestic criminal tribunals. They are also defined as 'hybrid' because they are unique in relation to their predecessors. The Sierra Leone Special Court, for example, is an extension of the Sierra Leonean judicial system, established by treaty between the government of that country and the United Nations (UN); the East Timor Special Panels are similarly an extension of the local judiciary, established by law under UN Transitional Administration in East Timor (UNTAET)'s mandate, as is the case with the jurisdiction of Kosovo courts under the UN Interim Administration Mission in Kosovo (UNMIK). The Extraordinary Chambers of Cambodia are premised *in toto* on Cambodian law, although the relevant law envisages the partici-pation of international judges from a list proposed by the UN Secretary General.[1] Equally, the Lebanon Special Tribunal is based on an agreement between the UN and Lebanon and ratified by a Security Council resolution and applies solely Lebanese criminal law. Finally, the Lockerbie Tribunal is a Scottish court that operated on neutral territory, in The Netherlands, applying Scottish law.

Such internationalised domestic tribunals attempt to balance their obligations between domestic and international law, and this is not always easy. Moreover, in the majority of the cases, the countries in which they operate have recently surfaced from devastation, or are otherwise in some political turmoil. These courts must, further-more, function in a legal environment where amnesties have been granted and while

---

[1] Although the War Crimes Chamber (WCC) in Bosnia and Herzegovina is also a hybrid internation-alised criminal tribunal, it is not examined in this book. For more information on the WCC, see Human Rights Watch, 'Looking for Justice: The War Crimes Chamber in Bosnia and Herzegovina' available at <http://hrw.org/reports/2006/ij0206/>.

these may not always be valid under international law, especially where they serve to preserve impunity for serious violations, they may well be deemed to be valid under domestic law. The fact that such tribunals continue to be established, despite the existence of the ICC, is not surprising. The victim States may invariably seek to assert some control over the proceedings, apply their own domestic law, secure some or all related funding, or legitimise such proceedings through the United Nations, without however ceding full control to an external institution, as would be the case with the ICC. They are thus to a certain degree creatures of political considerations, but this is hardly the feature that defines their entire existence. The employment of a penal mechanism in each case involving an international or transnational crime is subject to multiple considerations, political, legal and otherwise and the rich variety of precedent makes this discussion all the more colourful.[2] I have classified these hybrid tribunals as pertaining to offences perpetrated in the course of international or domestic armed conflict and those whose mandate emanates from terrorist-related offences. This is done for purely pedagogical purposes.

20.2 The Sierra Leone Special Court

Since 23 March 1991 the West African country of Sierra Leone had been the battleground of fierce fighting, initially between the Revolutionary United Front (RUF) led by Foday Sankoh and the one party military regime of the All People's Congress (APC).[3] Hostilities continued relentlessly since then but ceased for a short interlude with the signing of the Abidjan Peace Agreement on 30 November 1996 between a newly elected democratic government and the RUF. No sooner had the ink dried on the Peace Agreement than fighting on an even larger scale broke out again. The new circle of violence culminated in a *coup d'etat* orchestrated by the Armed Forces Revolutionary Council (AFRC), an ally of the RUF, which seized power over the greater part of Sierra Leone on 25 May 1997.[4] In an attempt to take control of the capital Freetown a combined force of AFRC/RUF forces launched a military

---

[2] In 1985 French secret agents sank a Greenpeace vessel, the Rainbow Warrior, that was at port in New Zealand in which one person was killed. The two agents were arrested by the local authorities and pled guilty to charges of manslaughter and criminal damage and were subsequently sentenced to a lengthy term of imprisonment. France protested and a dispute arose between the two nations, which culminated in an agreement to seek a binding ruling by the UN Secretary-General. The latter ordered a compensatory lump sum, in addition to a term of isolation for the two agents in a French military base in the Pacific. This was confirmed in a subsequent Exchange of Letters of 9 July 1986 and the culprits were taken to Hao island. See *R v Mafart and Prieur* 74 ILR 241. The case is better known for the flight of the two agents under the guise of medical necessity, which gave rise to arbitral proceedings between New Zealand and France (*Rainbow Warrior* case), (1990) XX UN Reports of International Arbitral Awards (UNRIAA) 215.

[3] Soon after Sankoh's arrest on 27 May 2000 by Sierra Leonean (SR) forces his wife applied for *habeas corpus* relief before the High Court in London, on the grounds that at the request of SR forces British troops provided assistance in transporting Sankoh and as a result he was under British custody and control. Both the High Court and Court of Appeal rejected these arguments. *In the Matter of Sankoh* (2000) 119 ILR 386.

[4] Acting under Chapter VII of the UN Charter the Security Council adopted Resolution 1132 on 8 October 1997, demanding that the RUF relinquish power and cease acts of violence, further imposing a general embargo.

operation which was marked by widespread atrocities against the civilian population, although serious violations of international humanitarian law had already been committed since the 1997 coup, especially in the form of mass rape, abduction of women, forced recruitment of children, mutilations and summary executions.[5] Likewise, during their retreat in February 1999, RUF forces abducted hundreds of people, particularly young women who they then proceeded to use as forced labourers, fighting forces, human shields and sexual slaves.[6] The Lomè Peace Agreement, signed on 7 July 1999 by the democratically elected government of President Ahmed Kabbah, the RUF and the Special Representative of the UN Secretary General, granted amnesty to RUF members – although the UN Special Representative expressly rejected the validity of any amnesties in respect of international crimes – and set up a truth commission to investigate and document violations in lieu of prosecutions. In further disregard to its commitments and the rule of law the RUF resumed attacks against government troops and the civilian population and, despite being quickly defeated and its leader captured, RUF forces had found time to commit yet more widespread atrocities against civilians.[7]

Following a relative period of stability, the government of Sierra Leone asked the UN to establish an international tribunal to prosecute those responsible for serious violations of international humanitarian law during the civil war. On 14 August 2000 the Security Council adopted Resolution 1315 wherein it instructed the Secretary-General to negotiate with Sierra Leone on the establishment of an independent special court, recommending that its subject matter jurisdiction include crimes against humanity, war crimes and other serious violations of international law, as well as crimes under Sierra Leonian law committed by 'persons who bear the greatest responsibility for [these] crimes'. The resolution requested the production of a detailed statute. After two rounds of successful negotiations the Secretary-General presented the Security Council with a report on the creation of a Special Court, to which both the Agreement[8] and the Statute were annexed.

Unlike the ICTY and ICTR the Special Court was established through a bilateral treaty between the UN and the Government of Sierra Leone of 16 January 2002 and not on the basis of a Security Council resolution. This means that the Special Court lacks primacy over other national courts and the public authorities of third countries, whether this involves requests for surrender of evidence or of accused persons. In examining measures to enhance the deterrent powers of the Special Court, the Secretary-General invited the Security Council to consider endowing it with Chapter VII powers for the specific purpose of requesting the surrender of an accused from outside its particular jurisdiction.[9] The Security Council never responded to that

---

[5] See SC Res 1181 (13 Jul 1998).

[6] Report of the UN Secretary-General on the Establishment of a Special Court for Sierra Leone, UN Doc S/2000/915 (4 Oct 2000), paras 25–26.

[7] Following international concern at the role played by the illicit diamond trade in fuelling the conflict in Sierra Leone, the Security Council adopted Resolution 1306 (5 Jul 2000) imposing a ban on the direct or indirect import of rough diamonds from areas not controlled by the government through the establishment of a certificate of origin regime.

[8] 2002 Agreement between the UN and the Government of Sierra Leone on the Establishment of a Special Court for Sierra Leone.

[9] 2000 Report of the Secretary-General, para 10.

request and in the absence of a relevant resolution the Special Court's powers are determined under its domestic law and the Agreement. The Agreement and the Statute should be read together as a single instrument, rather than two separate ones, in light of the fact that there is considerable overlap between them.[10] Under Article 8 of its Statute the Special Court possesses concurrent jurisdiction with Sierra Leone courts but enjoys primacy over them. The Special Court is composed of two Trial Chambers, each consisting of three judges and an Appeals Chamber consisting of five judges. Sierra Leone was to appoint one of the three trial judges in each chamber, as well as two of the judges that serve in the Appeals Chamber, with the remaining judicial vacancies to be filled by the UN.[11] Similarly, the Secretary-General was to appoint the Special Court's Registrar[12] and Prosecutor, who is assisted by a Sierra Leone deputy Prosecutor.[13] In accordance with Article 2 of the 2002 Agreement, from the three judges serving in the Trial Chamber, one is appointed by Sierra Leone, whereas the remaining two by the UN Secretary-General, upon nominations forwarded by Member States of the Economic Community of West African States (ECOWAS) and the Commonwealth. Under Article 3 of the 2002 Agreement the Prosecutor is appointed on the basis of a consultation between the Government of Sierra Leone and the Secretary-General.

The subject matter jurisdiction of the Special Court comprises crimes under international humanitarian law and Sierra Leone criminal law. The first category includes crimes against humanity,[14] violations of common Article 3 to the Geneva Conventions and of Additional Protocol II,[15] as well as 'other violations of international humanitarian law'.[16] Article 4 includes the intentional targeting of civilians, *hors de combat* and peacekeeping personnel, along with their installations, material, units or vehicles (as long as they do not take a direct part in hostilities on the side of either party), as well as abduction and forced recruitment of children under the age of 15 for the purpose of using them to participate actively in hostilities. Despite the Secretary-General's comment that the Special Court's list of acts that constitute crimes against humanity follows the enumeration included in the ICTY and ICTR Statutes, one readily observes that Article 2(g) contains 'sexual slavery, enforced prostitution, forced pregnancy and any other form of sexual violence', whereas the two *ad hoc* Tribunals make reference only to 'rape'. It must be presumed, however, that in every other respect Article 4 of the Statute of the Special Court for Sierra Leone follows the ICTY Statute and not that of the ICC. Recourse to SR law has been provided in cases where a specific situation was considered either unregulated or inadequately regulated under international law.[17] The crimes considered to be relevant for this purpose and included in the Statute[18] are: offences relating to the

---

[10]   A McDonald, 'Sierra Leone's Shoestring Special Court' (2002) 84 *International Review of the Red Cross* 121, at 126.

[11]   SLSC Statute, Art 12(1).

[12]   Ibid, Art 16.

[13]   Ibid, Art 15(3) and (4).

[14]   Ibid, Art 2.

[15]   Ibid, Art 3.

[16]   Ibid, Art 4.

[17]   2000 Report of the Secretary-General, para 19.

[18]   SLSC Statute, Art 5.

abuse of girls under the SR 1926 Prevention of Cruelty to Children Act (ss 6, 7 and 12) and offences relative to wanton destruction of property and in particular arson, in accordance with the SR 1861 Malicious Damage Act (ss 2, 5 and 6). Genocide was not included because the Security Council was not furnished with evidence of intent to annihilate an identified group as such.

Finally, the Special Court has no legal links with the ICTR and ICTY, except in so far as it is bound to apply the Rwanda Tribunal's Rules of Procedure[19] and its Appeals Chamber is to be guided by the decisions of the ad hoc Tribunals' common Appeals Chamber,[20] in order to produce a coherent body of jurisprudence. The Special Court has made it clear that it is not bound by the jurisprudence of the ad hoc tribunals and will only follow this where it finds its application appropriate.[21] As to its financing, the Secretary General had initially suggested this should take place through assessed contributions, rather than by voluntary emoluments.[22] Article 6 of the 2002 Agreement provided that the Special Court's expenses be borne by voluntary contributions from the international community, the Court becoming operational when sufficient funds had been gathered. Article 6 further provided that should voluntary contributions prove insufficient for the Court to implement its mandate, the Secretary-General and the Security Council would explore alternate means of financing. After agreement with the Sierra Leone Government it was decided that the temporal jurisdiction of the Special Court would commence from 30 November 1996.

20.2.1   The Fate of Amnesties and Immunities

Two important issues arise in connection with the existence of the Special Court; whether amnesties granted prior to its establishment continue to have binding force and whether the immunities generally afforded to foreign dignitaries constitute a bar to prosecution before the Court. As regards the non-applicability of immunities this would depend on whether the Special Court possesses international jurisdiction, much in the same way as the ICTY, ICTR and the ICC. Although there is no reason why international jurisdiction cannot be conferred by means of a bilateral treaty, the effect of such a treaty would be to limit that court's international jurisdiction to the particular contracting parties. It is nonsense to assume that a bilateral treaty can produce legal effects upon third countries, particularly where a customary rule to the contrary is in operation (ie the prevalence of sovereign immunity for the public acts of States before domestic courts), without moreover any Security Council authorisation. It is to be noted once again that the Security Council has given no authority to the Special Court whatsoever and where it discussed the Special Court's jurisdiction it simply 'recommended' the boundaries of its jurisdiction, but in no way normatively

---

[19] Ibid, Art 14(1). In accordance with Art 14(2) the judges may amend or adopt additional rules where the applicable rules do not adequately provide for a specific situation.

[20] Ibid, Art 20(3).

[21] *SLSC Prosecutor v Norman et al*, Appeals Chamber Decision on Interlocutory Appeals against Trial Chamber Decision Refusing to Subpoena the President of Sierra Leone (11 Sep 2006), para 13.

[22] 2000 Report of the Secretary-General, para 71.

defined it or imposed it on third States. In a decision defeating legal reasoning, the Special Court astonishingly emphasised that:

> The Agreement between the United Nations and Sierra Leone is thus an agreement between all members of the United Nations and Sierra Leone. This fact makes the Agreement an expression of the will of the international community. The Special Court established in such circumstances is truly international.[23]

On the basis of this remarkable legal conclusion the Special Court arbitrarily equated its jurisdiction and powers with those of the ad hoc tribunals and the ICC and thus held that the former Head of State of Liberia, Charles Taylor, did not enjoy even immunity *ratione personae* when indicted while still an acting Head of State.[24] Eventually the matter was resolved in practice. The successor President of Liberia not only accepted the Special Court's jurisdiction but requested Taylor's transfer to it (at which time the accused was no longer a serving Head of State and therefore susceptible to prosecution) and moreover the Security Council expressly recognised the Special Court's jurisdiction vis-a-vis all UN member States.[25] The chamber's proceedings against Taylor were eventually moved to The Hague following the Council's determination that his presence in Sierra Leone threatened international peace and security.[26]

With regard to the normative value of pre-existing amnesties the Special Court has done a much better job. Article 10 of the Statute does not consider amnesties granted with respect to offences included in Articles 2–4 of the Statute of the Special Court for Sierra Leone as posing a bar to prosecution. This provision necessarily refers to, and essentially purports to invalidate, Article IX of the 1999 Lomè Peace Agreement which indeed granted amnesties to all combatants as long as the terms of that Agreement were adhered to, but to which the Special Representative of the UN Secretary-General appended a reservation to the effect that amnesties under Article IX shall not apply to international crimes.[27] The Special Court did not hold that local amnesties are always invalid under international law, but that under the particular circumstances the terms of the Lomè Agreement had been breached. Robertson J correctly observed that although it may seem harsh to deprive combatants of an amnesty because their leaders reneged on the agreement, this is an inevitable occurrence to what is ultimately an enormous indulgence to persons that have committed serious offences.[28] Another reason for rejecting the Lomè amnesties was because of the status of the Special Court's Statute as an international agreement. Equally, it was held that a rule had emerged under customary international law that 'nullifies amnesties given to persons accused of bearing great responsibility for

---

[23] *SLSC Prosecutor v Taylor*, Appeals Chamber Decision on Immunity from Jurisdiction (31 May 2004), para 38.

[24] Ibid, paras 53–54.

[25] SC Res 1688 (16 Jun 2006), especially para 7.

[26] Ibid. The proceedings are to be held in the premises of the ICC, following the conclusion of a MoU between the two institutions.

[27] 2000 Report of the Secretary-General, para 22. This UN understanding on the status of the particular amnesties was reiterated in the preamble to SC Res 1315.

[28] *SLSC Prosecutor v Kondewa*, Appeals Chamber Decision on Lack of Jurisdiction/Abuse of Process: Amnesty Provided by the Lomè Accord (25 May 2004), Separate Opinion of Robertson J, para 28.

serious breaches of international law'.[29] Despite some of its original shortcomings the Special Court certainly broke new ground by refining particular offences, especially enlistment and conscription of children, collective punishments[30] and demonstrated the complexities of working alongside a truth commission.

20.3   The East Timor Special Panels

East Timor had been a Portuguese colony. During the post-Second World War decolonisation period Portugal was unwilling to forgo its power completely on the half-island entity. In 1960 the UN General Assembly declared East Timor to be a non-self-governing territory, administered by Portugal,[31] and this state of affairs persisted as East Timor was looking towards complete independence. This process was abruptly interrupted, however, when on 7 December 1975 the territory was invaded and subsequently occupied by Indonesian armed forces. During the twenty-four year occupation of East Timor there were frequent reports of extreme brutality and genocide, but the Indonesian government remained in power essentially because its purchase of military material from western States helped to silence its critics before international fora. After conclusion of a 'General Agreement' between Indonesia and Portugal on 5 May 1999 on the question of East Timor, a referendum was held on 30 August 1999 which was meant to determine its status.[32] This referendum, although supervised by a UN body, UNAMET, was conducted in the midst of intimidation and violence by East Timorese militias with the full support of the Indonesian Armed Forces. Nonetheless, 78.5 per cent of the population voted in favour of independence. The widespread violence sparked by the election result prompted the Security Council to adopt Resolution 1264 by which it mandated an international force (INTERFET) to restore peace and security in East Timor, facilitate humanitarian assistance and protect and support UNAMET in the fulfil-ment of its duties.[33] The presence of INTERFET secured significant stability on the island and paved the way for the Council to establish the UN Transitional Adminis-tration in East Timor (UNTAET), through Resolution 1272.[34] UNTAET was headed by a Special Representative of the Secretary-General who acted as Transitional Administrator of the Territory, until complete devolution to the people of East Timor was secured.

A significant function of UNTAET's mandate was the establishment of an effective judicial system, which included the administration of criminal justice. This was no easy task, as prior to 1999 the East Timorese as a general rule were excluded from public office or the civil service. Further compounded by the fact that 500,000 civilians became internally displaced as a result of the 1999 events, there was no

---

[29] Ibid Separate Opinion, para 57; see also, *SLSC Prosecutor v Kallon et al*, Appeals Chamber Decision on Challenge to Jurisdiction: Lomè Amnesty Accord (13 Mar 2004).

[30] See chapter 7.7.2

[31] GA Res 1542(XV) (15 Dec 1960).

[32] UN Doc S/1999/513 (1999), Annex I.

[33] SC Res 1264 (15 Sep 1999), operative para 3.

[34] SC Res 1272 (25 Oct 1999).

effective local judiciary on the island.[35] Moreover, under such circumstances, it would have been logistically impossible to prosecute offences that occurred during the twenty-four year Indonesian occupation, even if an ad hoc tribunal of the ICTY type was to be set up. A UN Commission of Inquiry specifically established for this purpose, concluded that an international tribunal should be instituted, comprising both Indonesian and East Timorese judges. It, nonetheless, opined that the examination of cases referring to the period of Indonesian occupation be excluded from its subject matter jurisdiction.[36] Ultimately, UNTAET, urged in part by Indonesian promises that they would investigate and prosecute alleged offenders decided to enhance the local judicial system, albeit augmented with an international presence. This development was not wholly welcomed by the East Timorese because they allege that for the largest part they were not sufficiently consulted on this issue.[37]

Finally, UNTAET established the Serious Crimes Project for the prosecution of serious criminal cases perpetrated in the period between 1 January and 25 October 1999, which was to operate through the District Court of Dili, East Timor's capital. On the basis of its authority to adopt legislation UNTAET promulgated Regulation 2000/11,[38] s 10.1 of which gave the District Court exclusive jurisdiction over the following offences: genocide, war crimes, crimes against humanity, murder, sexual offences and torture. Section 10.3 further envisaged the creation of Special Panels composed of East Timorese and international judges. The final composition of the Panels was elaborated through Regulation 2000/15,[39] s 22.2 of which required that they be composed of two international and one East Timorese judge, whereas in cases of special gravity or importance they were to be composed of three international and two local judges. The judgments of the Panels can be appealed to the Court of Appeal. Interestingly, s 10.4 of Regulation 2000/11 did not rule out the creation of a possible ad hoc or other tribunal with jurisdiction over the same offences.

Section 2.1 of Regulation 2000/15 specifically endowed the Special Panels with universal jurisdiction over the listed international offences, which as the term suggests is applicable irrespective of whether the offences were perpetrated in East Timor and irrespective of the nationality of the victim or the perpetrator. In accordance with s 2.4, the Panels additionally possess jurisdiction over offences that occurred in East Timor prior to 25 October 1999, which essentially covers the period during the Indonesian occupation. However, the applicable law for that period would encompass whatever Indonesian criminal law existed during the relevant time, so as not to offend the principle of retroactivity, but only so long as such laws comply with international human rights standards.[40] This is consistent with the principle of inter-temporal law, which may in fact turn out to demonstrate that the concept of grave breaches and the

---

[35] For an overview of the problems facing UNTAET, see H Strohmeyer, 'Collapse and Reconstruction of a Judicial System: The United Nations Missions in Kosovo and East Timor' (2001) 95 *American Journal of International Law* 46.

[36] Report of the International Commission of Inquiry on East Timor to the Secretary General, UN Doc A/54/ 726, S/2000/59 (2000), para 153.

[37] S Linton, 'New Approaches to International Justice in Cambodia and East Timor' (2002) 84 *International Review of the Red Cross* 93, at 106

[38] UNTAET/REG/2000/11 (6 Mar 2000), on the Organisation of Courts in East Timor.

[39] UNTAET/REG/2000/15 (6 Jun 2000), on the Establishment of Panels with Exclusive Jurisdiction over Serious Criminal Offences.

[40] UNTAET/REG/1999/1 (27 Nov 1999), s 3.1.

prohibition of genocide and crimes against humanity were binding upon Indonesia during relevant parts of its occupation of the island. The definition of the listed offences is almost identical to those encountered in other international legal texts. Hence, s 4 of Regulation 2000/15 adopts the customary definition of genocide as this is codified by the 1948 Convention on the Prevention and Punishment of the Crime of Genocide (Genocide Convention) and the ICC Statute. Equally s 5.1 reproduces the detailed definition of crimes against humanity found in the ICC Statute. Section 6.1 on war crimes once again mirrors Article 8 of the ICC Statute. The fact that no distinction is made with regard to the international or non-international character of the conflict implies either that the matter was left to be decided by the Panels, or that the formulation of Article 8 of the ICC Statute represents generally accepted law on war crimes.[41] The definition of the crime of torture in s 7.1 is wider than that found in the 1984 UN Convention Against Torture and Other Cruel, Inhuman or Degrading Treatment or Punishment, since it does not limit the commission of the offence to public officials or other persons acting in an official capacity. This may be due to the fact that many of the offences charged were committed by militias whose links with the Indonesian State authorities were not sufficiently clear for the purposes of attributing them to the Jakarta regime.[42] As for murder[43] and sexual offences,[44] Regulation 2000/15 states that the 'provisions of the applicable Penal Code in East Timor' will apply.[45]

As expected, the functioning of the Panels has generated significant problems. First, despite the existence of a Memorandum of Understanding between UNTAET and Indonesia, signed on 5 April 2000, by which the latter agreed to provide, *inter alia,* transfer of accused to the Special Panels, such cooperation has not materialised. The second point of frustration relates to the perceived impartiality of the Panels. In one of the first judgments rendered by them, the *Los Palos* case,[46] it was accepted that the existence of an extensive attack by 'pro-autonomy armed groups supported by Indonesian authorities targeting the civilian population in the area...had been proven beyond reasonable doubt'.[47] The Panel's reasoning was based on the report of the UN Commission of Inquiry, as well as certain witness testimonies and physical evidence supported by the Commission's findings. However, before reaching this conclusion the Panel examined the possible existence of an armed conflict in East Timor during 1999, wrongly assuming the requirement of a nexus between the crimes against humanity under consideration and an armed conflict.[48] No such nexus is required in Regulation 2000/15, or international law in general, apart from the ICTY Statute, which in any event is irrelevant for the purposes of the Special Panels,

---

[41]   See D Turns, 'Internationalised or Ad Hoc Justice for International Criminal Law in a Time of Transition: The Cases of East Timor, Kosovo, Sierra Leone and Cambodia' (2002) 7 *Austrian Review of International and European Law* 123.

[42]   Ibid.

[43]   s 8.

[44]   s 9.

[45]   UNTAET/REG/1999/1, s 3 provides that the applicable law in East Timor is that in force before 25 October 1999 (ie Indonesian law), as long as such law does not conflict with international human rights law, the mandate or other UNTAET Regulations.

[46]   *Prosecutor v Joni Marques and Others* (*Los Palos* case), Judgment (11 Dec 2001), Case No 09/ 2000.

[47]   Ibid, para 686.

[48]   Ibid, para 684.

because Regulation 2000/15 is premised on the ICC Statute formulation, which is more consistent with the dictates of customary international law. The judgment was flawed in some other respects, such as the omission of the fact that East Timor was occupied by Indonesia, and that alone is enough under common Article 2 of the 1949 Geneva Conventions to substantiate the existence of an armed conflict. Moreover, in the *Leki* case, which did not involve crimes against humanity, the Panel made findings about Indonesia's role in the 1999 events, without any evidence submitted by the parties and without the issues having been argued by the parties. The Panel relied on a test of 'what even the humblest and most candid man in the world can assess'.[49]

It should be noted that following international pressure the Indonesian authorities set up an independent commission of inquiry (KPP Ham) in order to investigate gross violations of human rights since January 1999 and to assess the involvement of State apparatus therein. Following KPP Ham's report an Ad Hoc Human Rights Court for East Timor was established. Although its mandate was understandably narrowed down by the Attorney-General's Office in Jakarta and the sentences handed out to most accused were substantially decreased, in the *Damiri* case, the Court found sufficient evidence of the Indonesian National Army's policy of attacks against the civilian population in East Timor.[50] Finally, in parallel with the Special Panels, UNTAET established a Commission for Reception, Truth and Reconciliation whose mandate covered the entirety of Indonesian occupation up until 25 October 1999.[51]

20.4   UNMIK and the Kosovar Judicial System

Until 21 March 1989 Kosovo was an autonomous region within the Socialist Federal Republic of Yugoslavia (SFRY). In order to appease Serbian nationalism, in part as a result of his own making, the then SFRY President Milosevic removed Kosovar autonomy, in violation of the SFRY Constitution. This was the starting point of mounting ethnic tension, which culminated in the establishment of ethnic Albanian pro-independence military movements, particularly the Kosovo Liberation Army (KLA), which clashed with FRY – the SFRY had by then disintegrated – security and armed forces. Clashes of this sort, as well as mounting military activity from both sides had been reported since 1997, with evidence suggesting that both sides were responsible for serious atrocities. By 1999 and with Milosevic having lost all international credibility NATO commenced a bombing campaign of dubious legality – if not complete illegality – against FRY on 24 March 1999. By early summer of that year, with FRY having sustained severe blows to its infrastructure and economy, it

---

[49]   *Prosecutor v Joseph Leki,* Judgment (11 Jun 2001), Case No 5/2000, reported in Linton, at 111.
[50]   *Damiri*, Judgment No 09/PID.HAM/AD.HOC/2002/PH.JKT/PST (5 Aug 2003).
[51]   UNTAET/REG/2001/10 (13 Jul 2001), particularly s 13. The Commission delivered its Final Report on 30 January 2006, in which it emphasised the brutality of the occupying power and the perpetration of a significant number of international crimes and human rights violations. In the meantime, East Timor and Indonesia concluded an agreement in 2005 in an attempt to improve their bilateral relations and in the course of which they set up a joint Commission of Truth and Friendship. Although this has no power to prosecute or compel persons to testify, the UN feared that it was a conduit to offer amnesties, a development to which it was ardently opposed.

concluded an agreement with NATO member States on 9 June, whereby it agreed to remove its security forces from Kosovo while retaining its sovereignty over the territory. This agreement is reflected in Security Council Resolution 1244 which was adopted on the following day. Operative paragraph 10 of the Resolution authorised the UN Secretary-General to establish an interim administration in Kosovo,[52] including, as provided in operative paragraph 11, the maintenance of civil law and order. This task was part of the UN Interim Administration Mission in Kosovo's (UNMIK) mission.

Although not on top of UNMIK's agenda, it had to decide how it would administer criminal justice in Kosovo; this mandate necessarily concerned issues of applicable criminal law, organisation of courts and possible establishment of special panels for serious violations of humanitarian law. In its first Regulation, 1999/1,[53] s 3 provided that the laws applicable in the territory of Kosovo prior to 24 March 1999 were to apply again so long as they did not conflict with international legal standards, UNMIK's mandate, or any subsequent UNMIK regulation. Since, however, pre-1999 law was FRY Milosevic-inflicted law, the Albanian judges either resigned from their posts or refused to enforce it, applying instead pre-1989 Kosovar criminal law, which in any event did not differ much from FRY criminal law. As a result of this intransigence, and in the face of a judicial vacuum, Regulation 1999/1 was amended by Regulation 1999/24,[54] which held as applicable law all primary and secondary UNMIK instruments, as well as the law in force in Kosovo on 22 March 1989. In case of conflict between the two, the former takes precedence and where a matter is not covered by the laws set out in a regulation but is instead covered by another law in force in Kosovo after 22 March 1989, which is not discriminatory and complies with international legal standards, that law is, as an exceptional measure, applicable. Moreover, s 3 of Regulation 1999/24 rendered this amendment retroactive as of 10 June 1999. However, between 10 June and 12 December 1999, at which time the amendment was adopted, some Kosovar courts had already convicted a number of defendants on the basis of the pre-1989 Kosovar criminal law, which had the effect of retrospectively validating convictions that had been handed down under a non-operative law. The saving grace in all this confusion, as far as the rights of the accused are concerned, is the fact that defendants are to benefit from the most favourable provision in the criminal laws which were in force in Kosovo between 22 March 1989 and 10 June 1999, in accordance with Regulation 1999/24.[55]

Unlike UNTAET, UNMIK did not introduce a regulation establishing special panels, nor international offences for adjudication before Kosovar courts. Nonetheless, on 13 December 1999 an UNMIK Commission recommended the creation of the Kosovo War and Ethnic Crimes Court (KWECC) with jurisdiction over war crimes, crimes against humanity and other serious offences on the grounds of ethnicity. The KWECC was supposed to function within the Kosovo legal system, albeit staffed also by international judges. Although the project was endorsed by all

---

[52] R Wilde, 'From Danzig to East Timor and Beyond: The Role of International Territorial Administration' (2001) 95 *American Journal of International Law* 583.
[53] UNMIK/REG/1999/1 (25 Jul 1999), on the Authority of the Interim Administration in Kosovo.
[54] UNMIK/REG/1999/24 (12 Dec 1999), on the Law Applicable in Kosovo.
[55] Regulation 1999/24, s 1.

relevant parties, it was eventually abandoned.[56] Instead of a discrete war crimes tribunal, in the manner of the East Timor Special Panels or its counterparts in Cambodia and Sierra Leone, a middle ground was deemed to be more appropriate. The promulgation of an UNMIK Regulation 2000/64[57] allowed the Prosecutors and defendants to petition the UNMIK Department of Judicial Affairs for the substitution of international judges where the impartiality of a local judge was in doubt; it also included petitions for the change of venue. This created a mixed judicial system which initially allowed for the appointment of international judges and prosecutors in the Mitrovica District Court, which was later extended to other regional district courts. The petition is of no avail once trial or appeal proceedings have commenced, hence the petitioner is required to institute proceedings in advance of such judicial proceedings.

20.5   The Cambodian Extraordinary Chambers

The Khmer Rouge seized power in Cambodia on 17 April 1975. By all accounts, although during the reign of the Khmer Rouge information from the country was extremely difficult to obtain, the Pol Pot regime eliminated their so-called internal enemies, which included Buddhist monks, the Muslim Cham, Chinese and Vietnamese communities, as well as anyone who was or even resembled an intellectual. Those urban dwellers that survived the genocide which ensued were sent to rural camps as part of the regime's peasant revolution, purging the country of all foreign elements as well as of economic, scientific or cultural institutions.[58] Following an invasion by the Vietnamese armed forces on 6 January 1979 Cambodia was liberated from Pol Pot – who regrouped and launched a guerrilla war – but the latter's legacy resulted in the extermination of at least 1.7 million people, amounting to 20 per cent of the country's entire population.

Despite the aforementioned atrocities, Cold War politics, which viewed the post-1979 Government of Heng Samrin as an instrumentality of the Vietnamese 'communists', were responsible for retaining for some time the Khmer seat at the United Nations. Following the Vietnamese withdrawal in 1989 and the subsequent Paris Conferences on Cambodia which resulted in the signing of a Comprehensive

---

[56] For an excellent overview of the post-1999 Kosovo legal system, see M Bohlander, 'Kosovo: The Legal Framework of the Prosecution and the Courts' in K Ambos and M Othman (eds), *New Approaches in International Criminal Justice: Kosovo, East Timor, Sierra Leone and Cambodia*, (Freiburg, Freiburg Br, 2003).

[57] UNMIK/REG/2000/6 (15 Feb 2000), on the Appointment and Removal from Office of International Judges and International Prosecutors, as later amended by UNMIK/REG/2000/64 (15 Dec 2000), on Assignment of International Judges/Prosecutors and/or Change of Venue, as also later amended by UNMIK/REG/2001/34 (15 Dec 2001).

[58] See B Kierman, *The Pol Pot Regime: Race, Power and Genocide in Cambodia under the Khmer Rouge, 1975–79* (New Haven, Yale University Press, 2002).

Settlement Agreement on 23 October 1991, the UN installed an interim administration, the Transitional Authority in Cambodia (UNTAC).[59] It was only after the departure of UNTAC that any attempted prosecution of Khmer Rouge members could take place. In 1997 the Cambodian government requested UN assistance. Thereafter, a Group of Experts was appointed with the task of evaluating the feasibility of trials, ascertaining an appropriate legal basis and court structure and assessing the viability of apprehensions.[60] Among five possible types of tribunals the Group of Experts recommended the establishment of an ad hoc international tribunal under the aegis of the UN, partly due to well documented and widespread corruption within the Cambodian judiciary.[61] By March 1999, however, when the report was circulated to the General Assembly and the Security Council the Cambodian government had rejected the option of an ad hoc tribunal. The UN eventually agreed on a compromise position, whereby jurisdiction would be vested in a tribunal situated within the Cambodian legal system and composed of both national and international judges. The UN pledged its cooperation in the process only if the Cambodians agreed to incorporate in their implementing law the modalities set out in a draft Memorandum of Understanding. Their failure to do so was explained as the most serious reason for the UN's first withdrawal from the negotiations. The truth remains that the UN was not prepared to support a corrupt judicial system over which it had no effective control.

This UN withdrawal did not deter the Cambodian government. Following a second approval by the Cambodian Senate on 23 July 2001 the Law on the Establishment of Extraordinary Chambers in the Courts of Cambodia for the Prosecution of Crimes Committed during the Period of Democratic Cambodia was adopted.[62] The 2001 Law establishes distinct chambers within the Cambodian legal system, albeit with a number of international elements. First, it includes international as well as domestic judges; secondly, all international judges and prosecutors, although appointed by Cambodia's Supreme Council of Magistracy, are selected from a list prepared by the UN Secretary-General.[63] Moreover, the UN contributes to the financing of the Chambers through the creation of a special fund that solicits voluntary contributions.[64] Thirdly, some of the listed offences have drawn heavily on definitions found in international instruments, as is natural given that their respective definitions are universal and customary in nature. In a surprising move, the UN brokered an agreement with the Cambodian government in mid-March 2003 allowing for UN participation in this project. This development was premised on earlier efforts to revive negotiations, especially General Assembly resolution 57/228, adopted in December 2002, which urged the Secretary-General to make the UN an active participant in the trials.

[59] R Ratner, 'The Cambodian Settlement Accords' (1993) 87 *American Journal of International Law* 1, 3–5; SC Res 717 (16 Oct 1991).

[60] GA Res 52/135 (12 Dec 1997), para 16.

[61] Report of the Group of Experts for Cambodia, UN Doc A/53/850-S/1999/231 (1999), para 129; see R Ratner, 'The United Nations Group of Experts for Cambodia' (1999) 93 *American Journal of International Law* 948.

[62] Translation reprinted in (2002) 34 *Critical Asian Studies* 611.

[63] 2001 Law on the Establishment of Extraordinary Chambers, Art 11(2) and (3); Linton, at 99.

[64] Linton, ibid, at 103.

The Extraordinary Chambers possess jurisdiction over offences under the 2001 Law, as well as offences under international law. As far as the former is concerned, Article 3 of the Law includes homicide, torture and religious persecution under the 1956 Cambodian Penal Code. Article 4, on the other hand, relating to genocide, is similar to that found in the 1948 Genocide Convention, while Article 5, on crimes against humanity, has been taken from the Statute of the ICTR – that is, including the requirement that they be committed on national, political, ethnic, racial or religious grounds – which does not conform with customary international law, in which this particular requirement is absent. Article 6 provides jurisdiction over grave breaches of the 1949 Geneva Conventions, Article 7 over destruction of cultural property during armed conflict, in accordance with the 1954 Convention for the Protection of Cultural Property in the Event of Armed Conflict[65] and Article 8 relates to crimes against internationally protected persons, in accordance with the 1973 Convention on the Prevention and Punishment of Crimes against Internationally Protected Persons, Including Diplomatic Agents[66] – although the relevant provision refers to the 1961 Vienna Convention on Diplomatic Relations.[67] An unsatisfactory aspect of the 2001 Law is the fact that it omits references to defences, except for superior orders,[68] which may constitute an excuse only if they are derived from a legitimate authority. Other than that the accused will have to rely on the 1956 Penal Code and the 1992 UNTAC Supreme National Council Decree on Criminal Law and Procedure, because the status of the relevant international criminal defences – which themselves are ambiguous – is uncertain, as they are not mentioned in the 2001 Law.[69]

As we have already mentioned, the Chambers also include international judges. The Chambers, based on the existing Cambodian court structure, comprise a trial court, consisting of three Cambodian and two international judges and a Supreme Court composed of five Cambodian and four international judges. Decisions are to be reached by unanimity and where this is not possible qualified majority voting will apply.[70] This formula, known as the super-majority rule, represents a compromise between the UN and the Cambodian government. Essentially, it requires that even if the Cambodian judges are unanimous among themselves they would still need the favourable vote of at least one international judge. Article 46 of the 2001 Law allows the Supreme Council of Magistracy to appoint judges, co-prosecutors and investigating judges where the foreign candidates do not assume their posts.

It is also difficult to assess the future of the Extraordinary Chambers in relation to the regime of amnesties, especially those granted to senior Khmer leaders, such as Ieng Sary, Pol Pot's second in command. In any event, Article 40 of the 2001 Law, rather confusingly, does not render amnesties a bar to prosecutions. The 2003

---

[65] 249 UNTS 240.
[66] (1974) 13 ILM 41; see chapter 12.3.2.
[67] 500 UNTS 95.
[68] 2001 Law on the Establishment of Extraordinary Chambers, Art 29(4).
[69] Linton, 100–02.
[70] 2001 Law on the Establishment of Extraordinary Chambers, Art 14.

UN-Cambodia Agreement clearly states that the Agreement is the principal instrument for the trials. Hence, any conflicting provision in the 2001 Law would be devoid
of legal force and the Chambers would be compelled to apply the law stipulated
under the Agreement.

20.6   The Iraqi Special Tribunal for Crimes Against Humanity

The Special Tribunal must be examined in light of Iraq's occupation by the USA and
coalition forces following an armed conflict in 2003.[71] The recognition of such de
facto status was conferred on the Coalition Provisional Authority (CPA), in essence
the occupying force's political wing in Iraq, by Security Council Resolution 1483, as
well as by the CPA itself through the promulgation of CPA Regulation No. 1.[72] Both
of these instruments acknowledged the exercise of temporary governmental powers
by the CPA. The exercise of judicial criminal jurisdiction by the occupying power is
within its prerogative, but Article 66 of the 1949 Geneva Convention IV requires that
accused persons subject to post-occupation penal legislation be tried before military
tribunals sitting in occupied territory.

Following the cessation of major military operations in May 1, 2003, the USA
appointed 25 Iraqis to the so-called Iraq Governing Council (IGC) on 13 July 2003.[73]
Although the IGC was proclaimed as assuming a transitional parliamentary role the
Coalition Provisional Authority (CPA) was in fact the real bearer of authority in the
country, having the power to veto all the decisions of the IGC, leaving it with
practically no law-making powers.[74] Exceptionally, however, the CPA granted temporary legislative authority to the IGC with the intent of formulating a law
establishing a tribunal for the most serious crimes perpetrated by the regime of
Saddam Hussein since its ascent to power in 1968.[75] However, by the time CPA Order
No. 48 was enacted in December 2003 the Statute had already been drafted and was
annexed to Order No. 48. Thus, approval by the IGC was in effect an act of
administrative assent, particularly since under Order No. 48 the promulgation of
subsequent Elements of Crimes and Rules of Procedure by the IGC was required to
meet with the approval of the CPA.[76] Unsurprisingly, the Statute was approved by the
IGC and thus the Iraqi Special Tribunal for Crimes against Humanity (Iraqi Special
Tribunal) was formally established on 10 December 2003. Following the entry into
force of the Iraqi Special Tribunal the IGC adopted on 8 March 2004 the Transitional Administrative Law (TAL).[77] The TAL was hailed as an interim constitution

---

[71]   See I Bantekas, 'The Iraqi Special Tribunal for Crimes against Humanity' (2005) 54 *International &
Comparative Law Quarterly* 237, from which this section has been excerpted.

[72]   CPA/REG/16 May 2003/01.

[73]   CPA Regulation No. 6, CPA/REG/13 July 2003/06.

[74]   See eg SC Res 1511 (16 Oct 2003) and 1500 (14 Aug 2003), which proclaim the IGC as being the
principal body of Iraqi interim administration, but make no reference to the fact that it has practically no
exclusive law or decision-making capacity.

[75]   CPA Order No 48, CPA/0RD/9 Dec 2003/48.

[76]   Arts 1 and 2, ibid.

[77]   Available at: <http://www.cpa-iraq.org/government/TAL.html>.

whose aim was to act as an instrument for governing Iraq upon restoration of sovereignty on 30 June 2004, until such time as a permanent constitution was adopted. A simple reading of the TAL clearly demonstrates that it was in conflict with the Special Tribunal Statute in respect of jurisdictional matters. For one thing, Article 48(A) of the TAL stated that: 'the [Iraqi Special] Statute exclusively defines its jurisdiction and procedures, notwithstanding the provisions of this Law'. Moreover, Article 15(I) of the TAL was unequivocal in that 'special or exceptional courts may not be established'. Despite the conflict between the TAL and the Special Statute the latter retained primary jurisdiction over its subject matter. Nonetheless, Article 48(A) of the TAL contradicts its own Article 15(I) in as much as the Special Tribunal is not merely exceptional but outside the 'Constitution'.

As regards the Tribunal's relationship with the national courts of Iraq, it is expressly stated in the Tribunal's Statute and reiterated in the TAL that jurisdiction is concurrent, albeit the Tribunal retains primacy in relation to war crimes, crimes against humanity and genocide.[78] However, in the case of offences lifted from Iraqi law and enumerated in Article 14 of the Tribunal's Statute no primacy is afforded to the Tribunal under Article 29(a) of its Statute, with the matter left unresolved also in Article 48(B) of the TAL, which refers back to the Tribunal's Statute.

The Tribunal's temporal jurisdiction spans from 17 July 1968, the date of the coup that brought the Ba'athists to power, to 1 May 2004, at which time an end to major hostilities was declared by US President Bush.[79] This expansive temporal jurisdiction aims to target crimes allegedly perpetrated in three significant military campaigns, ie the 1980–88 Iran-Iraq conflict, the 1990–91 Gulf War and the occupation of Kuwait, as well as the 2003 Iraq-US/Coalition war. It is also aimed at encompassing all cases of internal campaigns of repression and extermination against the Kurds, Shi'ites and Marsh Arabs – without excluding crimes against Sunnis disloyal to the regime.

As regards the Tribunal's jurisdiction *ratione loci*, this is not confined only to Iraqi territory, but extends to all other territories where Iraqi nationals or residents committed crimes falling within the Tribunal's Statute, 'including crimes committed in connection with Iraq's wars against Iran and Kuwait'.[80]

The Special Tribunal possesses subject matter jurisdiction over genocide,[81] crimes against humanity,[82] war crimes[83] and violations of stipulated Iraqi laws.[84] The formulation of the crime of genocide has been taken verbatim from the 1948 Genocide Convention[85] – and Article 6 of the ICC Statute where appropriate – whereas crimes against humanity have similarly been lifted verbatim from Article 7 of the ICC Statute with the omission of enforced sterilisation and apartheid as acts constituting an attack. The situation is no different with regard to war crimes, with slight differences in wording and order of listed offences in comparison to Article 8 of the ICC Statute. In accordance with Article 17(b) of the Special Tribunal Statute,

---

[78] Art 29(b), Special Tribunal Statute.
[79] Art 1(b), ibid.
[80] Art 1(b), ibid.
[81] Art 11, ibid.
[82] Art 12, ibid.
[83] Art 13, ibid.
[84] Art 14, ibid.
[85] Convention on the Prevention and Punishment of the Crime of Genocide, 78 UNTS 277.

when interpreting these international offences: 'the Trial and Appellate chambers may resort to the relevant decisions of international courts or tribunals as persuasive authority for their decisions'. The offences under Iraqi law are comprised of the following: a) manipulation of the judiciary; b) wasting national resources or squandering of public assets and funds, and;[86] c) abuse of position and the pursuit of policies that may lead to the threat of war or the use of the armed forces of Iraq against an Arab country.[87]

The incorporation of international offences taken verbatim from multilateral treaties or from the statutes of other international tribunals is not necessarily a wise option in every instance. It is doubtful, for example, whether international criminal liability existed prior to 1993 for offences taking place in non-international armed conflicts.[88] Equally, there is a need for an exceptional Tribunal of this nature to adapt itself to its particular contextual exigencies. One of the major factors contributing to violent repression in all fields of society and government during the reign of Saddam Hussein was the Ba'athification of all aspects of Iraqi life. Efforts to rid post-war Iraq of such elements are evident in the TAL, as well as the Special Tribunal Statute.[89] One, therefore, would have expected a provision similar to Articles 9 and 10 of the Charter of the International Military Tribunal (IMT) at Nuremberg,[90] which criminalised participation in designated criminal organisations. The object of those provisions was not the criminalisation of the organisation as a legal entity, but personal participation and involvement in its activities. Most possibly the drafters of the Special Tribunal Statute found no equivalent in Iraqi criminal law,[91] or adequate justification in customary international law and ultimately decided to exclude this concept from its ambit. Although the use of analogies in criminal law is wholly undesirable and prohibited,[92] 'common plan' liability is identical to that described under Articles 9 and 10 of the Nuremberg Charter. Its construction for present purposes would have added a historical and symbolic element to the trials – and would have probably been a good supplement for a truth and reconciliation commission – without jeopardising procedural or substantive fairness.

On the whole, the Special Tribunal is a domestic judicial institution, albeit with international elements. These are: a) occupation of Iraq by foreign State entities

---

[86]   In accordance with Art 2(g) of Law No 7 (1958), as amended.

[87]   In accordance with Art 1, ibid.

[88]   See eg. a Letter dated 24 May 1994, addressed to the President of the Security Council by the UN Secretary-General, which reads in relevant part: 'It must be observed that the violations of the law or customs of war... are offences when committed in international, but not in internal armed conflicts'. UN Doc S/1994/674 (1994), para. 52. This was at pace with scholarly writings at the time.

[89]   See Art 33 of the Special Tribunal Statute, which states that none of the Tribunal's judicial or other personnel must have been a member of the Ba'ath party; Art 31, TAL, which provides the criteria for election to the National Assembly. Similarly, the CPA adopted Order No 1, which is entitled 'De-Ba'athification of Iraqi Society', CPA/0RD/16 May 2003/01.

[90]   London Agreement for the Prosecution and Punishment of the Major War Criminals of the European Axis, 82 UNTS 280.

[91]   Iraqi Law No. 111 (15 Dec 1969, without regard to amendments made thereafter) [1969 Iraqi Criminal Code], and a limited number of sources of law for the Special Tribunal contains in Arts 55–59 the offence/liability form of 'criminal conspiracy', where participation or membership in the conspiracy even without an attempt to commit an offence renders the person liable as a conspirator.

[92]   Art 22(2), ICC Statute.

which internationalises the legal context, particularly through the automatic application of Geneva Convention IV; b) jurisdiction *ratione loci* extends beyond the borders of Iraq;[93] c) appointment of non-Iraqi judges[94] and advisors;[95] d) limited, yet direct application of international law[96] and; e) a limited role for the UN, with a potentially significant role for the Security Council. Although these elements purport to equate the Iraqi Tribunal with the hybrid, internationalised tribunals of Sierra Leone and Cambodia, this could not be further from the truth. Whereas the authority of the Sierra Leone and Cambodia Tribunals, as well as the insertion of international elements therein, is determined by their respective UN Agreements, the introduction of international elements in the Iraqi Special Tribunal is exclusively voluntary and may be removed at any point, subject to the rights of the accused. The judgments of the Special Tribunal and their operations have proven problematic in practice and are not recognised as reliable by the international community of jurists.[97]

20.7 Terrorist-related Tribunals

We shall now examine the two international tribunals that were set up to deal with two distinct terrorist incidents; the Lockerbie tribunal and the Special Tribunal for Lebanon. For a discussion of the concept of terrorism the reader can consult the relevant chapter in this book, although from a legal point of view none of the anti-terrorist conventions were invoked in respect of these proceedings. The chapter will conclude with an examination of truth commissions and the legal status of amnesties under international law.

20.7.1 The Lockerbie Tribunal

On 22 December 1988 Pan Am flight 103 exploded above the village of Lockerbie in Scotland, having taken off from London, killing all of its 259 passengers and crew as well as 11 Lockerbie residents killed by the aircraft's debris. Investigations immediately commenced in the UK and US, involving also law enforcement authorities around the world. All relevant investigations implicated two Libyan agents,

---

[93] Art 10, Special Tribunal Statute.
[94] Art 4(d), ibid.
[95] Arts 6(b), 7(n), 8(j), ibid.
[96] Arts 17(b) and 24(e), ibid; see also, Art. 2(1)–(2), CPA Order No 48, which states that the elements of crimes promulgated by the IGC should be consistent with international law and that the Tribunal must meet, at a minimum, international standards of justice.
[97] In the case against Saddam Hussein, for example, the Trial Chamber imputed knowledge of the conduct of subordinates to the accused based solely on their official position, seriously misapplied the JCE principle of liability and imputed knowledge of crimes to lower-ranking persons mainly on account of their membership in the Ba'ath party. *Dujail*, Case No 1/C1/2005, Trial Chamber Judgment (5 Nov 2006). The Appeals Chamber then issued a mere 17-page decision 45 days later, essentially iterating the legal reasoning of the Trial chamber. See A Cassese (ed), *The Oxford Companion to International Criminal Justice* (Oxford, Oxford University Press, 2009) 649–50.

Al-Megrahi and Fhimah, with evidence pointing to the two accused as having concealed plastic explosives in a suitcase on an Air Malta flight KM180 to Frankfurt, from which the suitcases were rerouted from there to London and subsequently transferred onto the tragic 103 flight bound for JFK airport at New York City. The explosives were detonated by an electronic timer, with the then alleged perpetrators managing not to board flight 103 and the luggage being stored on the aircraft without being counted or x-rayed.[98]

While ongoing investigations had been conducted in secrecy, on 27 November 1991 the Lord Advocate obtained an arrest warrant for the two Libyans, on charges of conspiracy to murder, murder and breaches of the 1982 Aviation Security Act. Thereupon, the US and UK governments demanded through the UN Security Council that Libya surrender the accused so that they could stand trial in either of the two countries. At the behest of the two governments Resolution 731 was initially adopted,[99] requesting Libyan condemnation of terrorism and severely criticising its lack of cooperation. The Libyan government protested that it was fulfilling its obligations under Article 7 of the 1971 Convention for the Suppression of Unlawful Acts Against the Safety of Civil Aviation (Montreal Convention), which imposes an obligation to either prosecute or extradite. The Libyans sued the US and UK before the International Court of Justice (ICJ), arguing that since they had submitted the case to a competent judicial authority they had fulfilled their obligations under the Montreal Convention. Before the ICJ could reach a judgment on the merits of its jurisdiction the Security Council proceeded to adopt Resolution 748,[100] acting under chapter VII of the UN Charter, demanding that within two weeks Libya establish its responsibility over the acts and essentially surrender the accused for trial; otherwise it threatened that a range of sanctions would have to be imposed.[101] The ICJ, somewhat crippled by Resolution 748, held that on the basis of Article 103 of the UN Charter, according to which obligations under the Charter supersede all other obligations of Member States, the Council's authority to adopt binding resolutions prevailed over the terms of the 1971 Montreal Convention. The majority of the judges noted, however, that had it not been for Resolution 748, Libya would not have been at fault.[102] During this time, and until 1998, Libya maintained that not only was it precluded by constitutional constraints from surrendering its own nationals, but because of the inevitable media coverage in the US and UK, the accused would not receive a fair trial had they been tried in any of the two nations. Nonetheless, Libya offered to surrender the accused for trial in a neutral country, but this proposal was initially resisted.

The impasse was finally resolved in 1998 when the UK agreed to a proposal envisaging the organisation of a trial in a neutral country and heard by a Scottish court. The Netherlands concurred to host it on its territory and an agreement was

[98] See A Klip and M Mackarel, 'The Lockerbie Trial – A Scottish Court in The Netherlands' (1999) 70 *Revue Internationale de Droit Pénal* 777.

[99] SC Res 731 (21 Jan 1992).

[100] SC Res 748 (31 Mar 1992).

[101] Further sanctions were imposed more than a year later through SC Res 883 (11 Nov 1993).

[102] *Questions of Interpretation and Application of the 1971 Montreal Convention Arising from the Aerial Incident at Lockerbie* (Libya v UK, Libya v USA), Order of 14 April 1992, (1992) ICJ Reports 3.

signed between the two countries on 18 September 1998.[103] Subsequently, Council Resolution 1192 welcomed the end to the stalemate, asking all States to cooperate, further designating The Netherlands as the detaining power once the accused had been surrendered for trial.[104] The Agreement between the UK and The Netherlands entered into force on 8 January 1999. Unlike the two ad hoc tribunals (that is, the ICTY and ICTR) and other internationalised domestic tribunals (that is, the Sierra Leone Special Court and the East Timor Special Panels), the court (the Scottish High Court of Justiciary) specified in the 1998 Agreement did not have a Security Council mandate and did not sit in the territory of the country exercising territorial jurisdiction. In that sense, it is a unique creature, adapted to the particular exigencies of the case, demonstrating a flexibility that is rare for international criminal justice. Under the Agreement, Scots law was applicable only in relation to the accused and the offences, whereas Dutch law was generally applicable in every other respect. Thus the jurisdiction of the Scottish court was limited to the trial, which included all investigative and pre-trial phases in accordance with Scots law and practice.[105] Thus, the Agreement was ultimately an instrument for delineating sensitive matters of sovereignty. Besides the particular details agreed to between the parties the Agreement fell within the category of host country treaties and the international law applicable with regard to official foreign premises. Under the terms of the Agreement the Lockerbie court was, *inter alia,* empowered to issue regulations concerning its day-to-day affairs,[106] exchange Letters of Understanding with the Dutch Ministry of Justice,[107] while The Netherlands was obliged to allow the entry and protection of witnesses[108] and international observers,[109] among others.

Although the matter of jurisdiction and the seat of the court were resolved in terms of international law, this was not self-evident as a matter of UK law. Council Resolution 1192, which had called on the UK to facilitate the arrangements for establishing the court, would have had to be implemented through the adoption of an Order in Council, approved by Parliament and given royal assent by the Queen, in accordance with the requisite procedure under the 1946 UN Act. Thus, the High Court of Justiciary (Proceedings in The Netherlands) Order 1998 (1998 Order) was adopted,[110] giving authority to the Scottish High Court to hear the case against the two accused, who were specifically named in the 1998 Order.[111] Contrary to Scots criminal procedure law, the case was not heard by a jury, although this need not have been so had the accused consented to a trial by jury in Scotland.[112]

Finally, the two accused, apparently with their consent, were handed to a UN official in Libya and were flown to The Netherlands to stand trial. The trial began on 3 May 2000 and on 31 January 2001 the High Court handed down its judgment,

---

[103] Agreement between The Netherlands and UK Concerning a Scottish Trial in The Netherlands, (1999) 38 ILM 926.
[104] SC Res 1192 (27 Aug 1998).
[105] 1998 Agreement, Art 1(I).
[106] Ibid, Art 6.
[107] Ibid, Art 27.
[108] Ibid, Art 17.
[109] Ibid, Art 18.
[110] SI 1998/2251 (16 Sep 1998), entering into force two days later.
[111] 1998 Order, s 3(1).
[112] Ibid, s 16(2)(a).

finding only one of the accused, Al-Megrahi, guilty of murder in respect of the bombing of PanAm flight 103 and the ensuing deaths caused both in mid-air and on the ground at the village of Lockerbie. The lengthy judgment did not analyse points of law in any great detail, but instead focused on the examination of evidence and fact. Although the evidence that was accumulated was circumstantial, it was such that it established Al-Megrahi's guilt beyond a reasonable doubt. He was handed a life sentence, which he appealed not on grounds of the sufficiency of evidence, but on its treatment by the trial court and the submissions made by the defence. By its judgment of 14 March 2002, the Appeal Court of the High Court of Justiciary rejected the appeal and the case was officially closed.[113] Al-Meghrahi was released in 2009 on compassionate grounds. His release caused a political furore in the UK and the USA because upon his return to Libya he received a hero's welcome, a result that infuriated the families of the victims.

20.7.2   The Special Tribunal for Lebanon

The creation of all the ad hoc and hybrid tribunals was prompted by particular criminal events; some of these events occurred on a large scale, such as mass extermination in Cambodia, whereas others concerned a particular incident, such as the Lockerbie case. The driving force behind the Security Council's interest in Lebanon was the assassination of former Lebanese President Rafiq Hariri in Beirut on 14 February 2005. Soon after the UN Secretary-General, following authorisation by the Security Council, mandated the dispatch of a fact-finding mission to Lebanon in order to investigate the causes and circumstances of the incident. This mission duly confirmed what was already widely speculated in the press and within political circles; that Syrian elements were most likely implicated, alongside Lebanese supporters of the Syrian government, both of which were antithetical to Hariri's political vision. It should be emphasised that Syrian involvement in Lebanese politics was not a new phenomenon. Moreover, the fact-finding mission reported that the infiltration of pro-Syrian supporters into the official Lebanese criminal investigation was such that evidence was being fabricated and cooperation was nowhere forthcoming. As a result, it was implicit that a fair investigation and prosecution was highly unlikely, unless this was undertaken through an international independent body.[114] The Council took note of the Report and particularly the inadequacy of the Lebanese investigation processes and set up, following an agreement with the Lebanese government, an International Independent Investigation Commission, whose work was to assist the local authorities with their investigation.[115] Given, however, the Commission's power to compel the collaboration of Lebanese authorities, this was more than a mere

---

[113] *Al-Megrahi v HM Advocate,* Opinion in Appeal against Conviction, Appeal No C104/01 (14 Mar 2002).

[114] Report of the Fact-Finding Mission to Lebanon, Inquiring into the Causes, Circumstances and Consequences of the Assassination of former Prime Minister Rafiq Hariri (24 March 2005), UN Doc S/2005/203 (2005).

[115] SC Res 1595 (7 Apr 2005).

assistant function.[116] Within three months the Independent Commission concluded its work and reported that there was indeed evidence of Syrian and Lebanese involvement and that a full trial was necessary in order to determine individual criminal responsibility.[117] The Council not only explicitly acknowledged the assassination to be a terrorist act, but it moreover brought into play resolution 1373 (2001)[118] and implicitly accepted that the offence entailed State-sponsored terrorism.[119] As a result, the matter was no longer strictly internal to Lebanon, but was deemed to have wider ramifications and the Council ordered each UN member State to cooperate with the investigations, arrest the accused, where possible, and freeze relevant assets.[120]

It was evident that the next step would be the creation of a hybrid judicial institution, such that would prove acceptable to both the Council and the government of Lebanon. The UN Secretariat, by that time highly experienced in such matters, went about the task of formulating the legal and logistical bases for setting up such a tribunal, alongside the Lebanese legal system. One of the key issues in the Report was the tribunal's temporal jurisdiction. It was acknowledged that the Hariri assassination was merely part of a wider terrorist campaign with the intention of intimidating Lebanon's free press, its political structures and ultimately its people. As a result, focusing solely on the Hariri incident would fail to serve the dictates of justice and hence a wider degree of temporal jurisdiction was warranted.[121] This is duly reflected in Article 1 of the Tribunal's Statute, which reads that besides the Hariri assassination the Tribunal shall have jurisdiction over:

> other attacks that occurred in Lebanon between 1 October 2004 and 12 December 2005, or any later date decided by the parties and with the consent of the Security Council, are connected in accordance with the principles of criminal justice and are of a nature and gravity similar to the attack of 14 February 2005 . . . This connection includes but is not limited to a combination of the following elements: criminal intent (motive), the purpose behind the attacks, the nature of the victims targeted, the pattern of the attacks (modus operandi) and the perpetrators.

The Secretary-General's report was fully endorsed by the Council and following the conclusion of an agreement between the UN and Lebanon on the establishment of a Special Tribunal in early 2007, the Council established it through resolution 1757, to which its Statute was annexed.[122] Despite the fact that the Special Tribunal was instigated at the insistence of the Lebanese government, the Council has been accused on this occasion that the rhetoric of international peace and security was an excuse for overriding what it conceived as a dysfunctional democracy.[123]

---

[116] Ibid, paras 2–3.
[117] UN Doc S/2005/662 (2005).
[118] For the significance of this resolution, see chapter 12.3.4.
[119] SC Res 1636 (31 Oct 2005).
[120] Ibid, para 1(a).
[121] Report of the Secretary-General on the Establishment of a Special Tribunal for Lebanon, UN Doc S/2006/893 (15 Nov 2006), paras 11–17.
[122] SC 1757 (30 May 2007).
[123] F Mègret, 'A Special Tribunal for Lebanon: The UN Security Council and the Emancipation of International Criminal Justice' (2008) 21 *Leiden Journal of International Law* 485, 492–93.

Unlike other international criminal tribunals whose applicable law is predicated either on international crimes, or a combination of international and domestic crimes, the Lebanon Special Tribunal is empowered to apply only the relevant portions of the criminal law of Lebanon.[124] This is limited to the crime of terrorism,[125] offences against life and personal integrity, illicit associations and failure to report crimes, including the rules regarding the material elements of a crime, criminal participation and conspiracy. Given the understanding within the Council that the attack against Hariri was part of an overall scheme to intimidate Lebanese political and civilian life, it is evident that crimes against humanity would be wholly relevant. The report of the Secretary-General opined that all the elements of this crime had been fulfilled, albeit certain members of the Security Council did not support the inclusion of crimes against humanity as a possible charge.[126] Although the Statute seems to exclude the application of any other law, the practice of international tribunals suggests that the judges will readily resort to substantive principles of international law, as much of this will be considered part of customary international law that is binding anyway on Lebanon. This result is moreover probable because a number of the modes of liability are predicated on international law, such as command responsibility and therefore would not raise obvious problems of legality.[127]

The Special Tribunal enjoys concurrent jurisdiction with the ordinary courts of Lebanon, but shall have primacy over them. In fact, the judicial authorities of Lebanon are under an obligation to defer all their investigations, accused persons and materials therefore, to the Special Tribunal.[128] This includes all evidence collected with regard to cases prior to the establishment of the Special Tribunal.[129] A special feature of the Statute that is not encountered elsewhere is the right to hold trials *in absentia*. This is permissible where the accused has expressly waived his right to be present, has not been handed over to the Tribunal, or where he has absconded or cannot be found after exhausting all reasonable steps to secure his presence.[130] The Statute, however, provides that in case of a conviction *in absentia*, the accused, if he or she had not designated a defence counsel of his or her choosing, shall have the right to be retried in his or her own presence before the Tribunal, unless he or she accepts the judgment.[131]

---

[124]   Art 2, Lebanon Special Tribunal Statute.

[125]   Art 314 of the Lebanese Criminal Code defines acts of terrorism 'as all acts that are intended to cause a state of alarm and have been committed by means such as explosive devices, inflammable substances, toxic or corrosive products or infectious or microbial agents that are liable to pose a public threat'.

[126]   Report of the Secretary-General (2006), paras 23–25.

[127]   Art 3, Lebanon Special Tribunal Statute.

[128]   Ibid, Art 4. A Pre-Trial Judge has already issued an Order regarding the Detention of Persons Detained in Lebanon in connection with the case of the *Attack against Hariri and Others*, Case No CH/PTJ/2009/06 (29 Apr 2009), through which it ordered Lebanese courts to defer some accused to the Tribunal.

[129]   Ibid Statute, Art 19.

[130]   Ibid, Art 22(1). National courts are generally extremely reluctant to undertake trials *in absentia*. See *Bouterse*, Netherlands Supreme Court Judgment (18 Sep 2001), (2002) Nederj No 559. In *Prosecutor v Engel*, Turin Military Tribunal Decision (15 Nov 1999), the accused, a WW II German commander, was tried *in absentia* for murder and violence against Italian civilians.

[131]   Ibid, Special Tribunal Statute, Art 22(3).

20.8   National Truth Commissions and Amnesties

While many view the processes of criminal accountability as among the only viable and reliable mechanisms for the reconstruction and reconciliation of devastated societies, some States have come to the conclusion that the same purpose may alternatively be served through truth commissions.[132] The purpose of these commissions is to administer restorative rather than retributive justice and their operation may be complementary to criminal proceedings, as in the case of South Africa, or the sole mechanism of accountability, as was the case with El Salvador. Such commissions are mechanisms used to investigate and accurately record human rights violations in a particular country, but very often result in sweeping amnesties.[133] Investigatory commissions of this type have been established at transitional phases in the democratic process of various States, in which civilian governments had recently replaced repressive regimes, with the aim of either investigating human rights abuses of prior regimes, as was the case with the panels created in Argentina and Chile, or as a means of resolving a civil war through a political agreement, as in El Salvador. In one instance, however, it was the Security Council that established an international commission of inquiry in order to investigate the violence that resulted from the 1993 coup in Burundi.[134]

Although most of these commissions were established and functioned at a purely domestic level, in every case it was evident that the involvement of international personnel would potentially lift suspicions of impartiality. Hence, the personnel serving on the El-Salvador commission were entirely foreign, as were those in Burundi, having been assigned and sponsored by the UN.[135] The purposes of investigative or truth commissions can vary, but in general their objectives include the creation of an authoritative record of events, provide redress for the victims, make recommendations for reform and establish accountability of perpetrators.[136] However, the primary purpose of most commissions is not to identify perpetrators, but to document repression and crime. This is best achieved only by permitting victims and culprits to come forward and recount their personal testimony as regards their participation in particular events. To secure such testimony, commissions are generally empowered, depending on their mandate, to grant amnesties to those who confess their past crimes and otherwise illegal behaviour.

Let us examine the most significant truth commission of the last decade, the South African Truth and Reconciliation Commission (TRC).[137] It was set up in 1993 on the

---

[132]   P Hayner, 'Fifteen Truth Commissions 1974 to 1994: A Comparative Study' (1994) 16 Human Rights Quarterly 597.

[133]   See M Scharf, 'The Case for a Permanent International Truth Commission' (1997) 8 *Duke Journal of International & Comparative Law* 1; T Klosterman, 'The Feasibility and Propriety of a Truth Commission in Cambodia: Too Little? Too Late?' (1998) 15 *Arizona Journal of International & Comparative Law* 2.

[134]   SC Res 1012 (25 Aug 1995).

[135]   See T Buergenthal, 'The United Nations Truth Commission for El-Salvador' (1994) 27 *Vanderbilt Journal of Transnational Law* 498.

[136]   M Ratner and J Abrams, *Accountability for Human Rights Atrocities in International Law* (Oxford, Oxford University Press, 1997) 196.

[137]   See generally P Parker, 'The Politics of Indemnities: Truth Telling and Reconciliation in South Africa' (1996) 17 *Human Rights Law Journal* 1.

basis of the 1993 interim Constitution and the Promotion of National Unity and Reconciliation Act, No 34 of 1995 and was comprised of three branches: a Committee on Human Rights Violations (HRV), a Committee on Amnesty and a Committee on Reparation and Rehabilitation (R & R). The mandate of the HRV Committee has been to investigate human rights abuses that took place between 1960 and 1994, based on statements made to the TRC. Its aim is to establish the identity and fate of victims, the nature of the crimes suffered and whether the violations were the result of deliberate planning by the prior regimes or any other organisation, group or individual. Victims are then referred to the R&R Committee, which considers requests for reparation only in regard to those formally declared victims by the TRC or their relatives and dependants. The primary purpose of the Amnesty Committee is to ascertain whether or not applications for amnesty concern human rights violations that were committed within the ambit prescribed by the 1995 Act, that is, whether they relate to omissions or offences associated with political objectives and committed between 1960 and 1994, in the course of the struggle for internal self-determination. An amnesty is granted only in those cases where the culprit makes a full disclosure of all the relevant facts. Therefore, in cases where an offence was committed for purely private motives, no amnesty is granted.

The majority of the internationalised domestic tribunals examined in the present chapter have been established alongside truth commissions. Their operation is problematic because: (a) the boundaries between the two institutions are not clearly delineated; (b) similarly problematic and ambiguous is the application of the rule *ne bis in idem* (that is, that one cannot be tried twice for the same offence) in both domestic and international law; and (c) where truth commissions grant blanket amnesties, or amnesties excusing serious international offences, neither the UN nor most individuals[138] will be inclined to recognise or respect them in their respective legal or institutional systems. Where the UN is involved in the interim administration of a war-torn nation, the truth commission established as a result does not supersede the jurisdiction of criminal tribunals, but supplements them.[139] The same is not true for Cambodia, however, where the status of amnesties granted prior to the creation of the Extraordinary Chambers remains uncertain. As even the most conciliatory commissions involve some kind of punitive judicial mechanisms, truth commissions are generally able to serve the purposes of both restorative and retributive criminal justice. To the extent they are not used as platforms for granting sweeping amnesties they are a welcome supplement to the emerging international criminal justice system. It should be remembered that in every case truth commissions are never a sole sufficient alternative to prosecution with respect to serious international offences.[140]

In the Sierra Leone context, a significant effort was made by the Special Court to accommodate the work of the Truth and Reconciliation Commission (TRC), although the Special Court is empowered with primacy. In 2003 a senior indictee,

---

[138] As far as subsequent claims in tort are concerned.

[139] UNTAET/REG/2001/10 (13 Jul 2001), on the establishment of a Commission for Reception, Truth and Reconciliation in East Timor.

[140] Inter-American Commission on Human Rights (IACHR), Report No 36/96, Case 10,843 (Chile), (15 Oct 1996), para 77; IACHR Report No 136/99, Case 10,488 *Ignacio Ellacuría S.J. and Others* (El Salvador), (22 Dec 1999), para 230.

Chief Norman, after having heard other high-ranking officials provide public testimonies before the TRC, and while awaiting for his trial to commence, requested the Special Court along with the TRC itself to be given permission to hold a public hearing. The request was refused twice on the grounds that there was a grave danger that such a public hearing would prejudice the defendant's position and that of his co-defendants, as well as influence witness testimonies, at trial. The Special Court did, however, authorise the use of an affidavit instead 'on condition that it gives an undertaking not to bring or assist any other person or agency to bring a prosecution for perjury'.[141]

We have already examined the practice of the Sierra Leone Special Court, which did not rule out the normative validity of local amnesties. Rather, the Special Court emphasised generally that: a) the terms of an amnesty are automatically invalidated where said terms are breached, even if the breach arose out of action undertaken by the leaders of an amnestied group and not as a result of acts undertaken by all of its members; b) amnesties are inapplicable before criminal tribunals exercising international jurisdiction; c) persons bearing great responsibility for serious international crimes are not exonerated by an amnesty, and; d) that a local amnesty can be invalidated by a subsequent treaty – apart from the conditions contemplated in (a)–(c) – is valid under international law but contrary to domestic law and would nonetheless create a bad precedent for the credibility of a particular government internally. In much the same manner, Article 6 of the Statute of the Lebanon Special Tribunal provides that an amnesty granted to any persons within the jurisdiction of the Tribunal shall not constitute a bar to prosecution.

Both the UN[142] and various multilateral treaties have advocated in favour of granting general amnesties, such as Article 6(5) of the 1977 Protocol II to the 1949 Geneva Conventions [and relating to non-international armed conflicts], which requires parties to grant 'the broadest possible amnesty to persons who have participated in the armed conflict'. However, none of these instruments and statements of support with regard to broad amnesties have ever been interpreted to encompass serious violations of international law, particularly grave breaches, crimes against humanity and genocide.[143] Given that these are international crimes carrying universal jurisdiction (at least under customary law for the latter two), it would be inconceivable that a domestic amnesty law could bar the exercise of jurisdiction by other courts or limit the liability of the perpetrators. Moreover, the granting of amnesties has been held by international human rights bodies to have violated many of the victims' (and that of family members) rights, particularly the right to life,

---

[141] *SLSC Prosecutor v Norman*, Decision on Appeal by the TRC and Chief Norman against the Decision of Bankole J delivered on 30 October 2003 to Deny the TRC's Request to Hold a Public Hearing with Chief Norman (28 Nov 2003), para 41.

[142] See Art 34 of the 2003 Accra Peace Agreement between the Government of Liberia and the Political Parties, LURD and MODEL, which drew UN support.

[143] See specifically, IACHR Report No 1/99, Case 10,480, *Lucio Parada Cea and Others* (El Salvador) (27 Jan 1999), para 116; *ICTY Prosecutor v Furundžija*, Trial Chamber Judgment (10 Dec 1998), para 155.

access to justice, security of person and others.[144] On the other hand, it is understandable that for those States that have granted general amnesties in respect of serious international crimes in order to bring about peace, such a ban on the legal effects of amnesties is unacceptable.[145]

The granting of amnesties for serious international crimes thus comes into conflict with particular State obligations such as the duty to prosecute or extradite those responsible for international offences. This has been the adamant position of the UN, so irrespective of the process utilised to grant amnesties for serious international offences such amnesties cannot constitute a bar to subsequent prosecution by other national or international judicial bodies.[146] Criminal trials will generally be required where the offence is a serious one, otherwise international law would be taken to imply that all amnesties are null *ab initio*.[147] Even if this was a valid statement in law – which it is not – it would, as Robertson J has noted in his Separate Opinion in the *Lomè Amnesty* case, create a significant logistical problem because the incumbent government would be pressed to hold tens of thousands of trials for all those accused of war crimes following the termination of an internal armed conflict.[148] It will be recalled that the UN Special Representative to the signing of the 1999 Lomè Agreement objected to immunity for the most serious offences, not all. Equally, it should not be forgotten that the Security Council approved the Governors' Island Agreement in Haiti, which provided a broad amnesty to all those implicated in the relevant events.[149]

---

[144] UN Human Rights Committee (HRC) General Comment No 20 (44) on Art 7 of ICCPR, UN Doc A/47/40, Supp No 40, Appendix VI.A (1992); *Sepulveda and Others* (*Sandoval* case), Supreme Court of Chile Judgment, 517/2004, Resolución 22267 (17 Nov 2004), in which the Supreme Court of Chile ruled against the applicability of Chile's amnesty laws at the sentencing level.

[145] *MRAP v Aussaresses*, French of Cassation Judgment (2003) Bull Crim Cour de Cassation 122, 465–69, which held that the granting of amnesties and pardons for all crimes committed during the Algerian war was valid and barred further prosecutions; equally, *Azanian Peoples Organisation v President of South Africa and Others* (1996) 4 SA 672.

[146] D Orentlicher, 'Settling Accounts: The Duty to Prosecute Human Rights Violations of a Prior Regime' (1991) 100 *Yale Law Journal* 2537; M Scharf, 'Swapping Amnesty for Peace: Was There a Duty to Prosecute International Crimes in Haiti?' (1996) 31 *Texas International Law Journal* 1.

[147] J Gavron, 'Amnesties in the Light of Development in International Law and the Establishment of the International Criminal Court' (2002) 51 *International & Comparative Law Quarterly* 91, 94–99.

[148] *Lomè Amnesty* Decision, Separate Opinion, para 25.

[149] Gavron, at 131.

Part V

Evidence and International Criminal
Procedure

21

Evidence before International Criminal Courts and Tribunals

21.1 Introduction

By virtue of Article 15 of the International Criminal Tribunal for the Former Yugoslavia (ICTY) Statute and Article 14 of the International Criminal Tribunal for Rwanda (ICTR) Statute their Rules of Procedure and Evidence were adopted on 11 February 1994 and 29 June 1995 respectively. The principal drafters of the Rules of Procedure and Evidence of the ICTY were the Trial Chamber judges and Appeals Chamber judges, in cooperation with States and organisations. Proposals were submitted by Argentina, Australia, Canada, France, Norway, Sweden, the United Kingdom, the United States, the American Bar Association, Helsinki Watch, the Lawyers Committee for Human Rights, the International Women's Human Rights Law Clinic and the judges themselves.[1] The purpose of this inclusionary approach was to ensure that different domestic legal systems would be considered and incorporated.[2] More particularly, common law and civil law systems, the most influential systems in the development of international criminal law and procedure, differ significantly from each other and have far-remote historical roots.

In civil law systems, which are considered to be inquisitorial, professional judges play an active role in ascertaining the truth. Most civil law systems have incorporated the concept of an investigative judge whose task is to ensure that the investigation is fair and efficient. In discharging this task the investigative judge reviews the actions of the investigators. In addition, the investigative judge may hear witnesses and assess their credibility. Most civil law systems apply the principle of immediacy, pursuant to which witnesses should be heard by the judges at trial in the presence of the accused. It is, however, not always considered necessary to hear witnesses again if they have been heard by an investigative judge.

At the end of the investigative stage, the Prosecution compiles a 'dossier', containing all incriminating and exonerating evidence obtained during the investigation, as well as other detailed information about the pre-trial stage. This dossier is then submitted for pre-trial review by the judges and the Defence before the commencement of trial. The core stage of a criminal proceeding in civil law systems is the pre-trial stage, rather than the trial stage. The trial is more adversarial in that the

---

[1] V Morris and MP Scharf, *The International Criminal Tribunal for Rwanda* (New York, Transnational Publishers, 1998) 414.

[2] Ibid, 413–14.

Prosecution and Defence play a leading role in the presentation of evidence. The trial is nonetheless controlled by one or more active judges. Judges control the questioning of witnesses and the accused and mostly ask questions before the parties are offered an opportunity to posit questions themselves. Where judges consider that the investigation is incomplete, they can order that further investigations be conducted at any time before, during or at the end of trial. Judges can also call witnesses in addition to those called by the parties, or ask that additional witnesses be called. The determination of guilt is a task incumbent on the judges, with or without the assistance of lay members who are trained and experienced in assessing the weight of evidence. Therefore, save for irregularly obtained evidence, evidence is more likely than not admitted at trial.

Common law systems are party-based. Judges have a more passive role to play. They respond to the submissions of the parties, but will rarely act *proprio motu*. Generally, the onus to object to the admission of evidence rests on the counsel. Judges may exclude that evidence which is deemed unreliable, irrespective of the charges, or that whose prejudicial effect outweighs its probative value. Such evidence will then not be presented to the twelve jury members charged with the determination of the guilt of the accused.

The Prosecution first presents its case and calls incriminating witnesses. If, at the close of the Prosecution's case there is a case to answer the Defence will be offered an opportunity to present its case and call defence witnesses. If the Prosecution, however, fails to establish a *prima facie* case, then the jury should not be invited to pass judgment on the guilt of the accused but the judge must instead enter an acquittal at the end of the prosecution case.

When a witness appears the party having called the witness will question him or her first. Subsequently, the opposing party may cross-examine the witness. Where new matters have arisen from the cross-examination the party having called the witness may re-examine him or her on those issues. Questioning of witnesses is subject to a regulatory process. A fundamental principle is that the examining party is not allowed to ask leading questions, whereas the cross-examining party is. The judge and jury do not ask any questions. At the end of the presentation of the evidence by the parties the jury will render a verdict relying solely on the evidence that is produced by the parties at trial.[3]

From these brief and simplified descriptions of common law and civil law systems it appears that they are fundamentally different, which explains the difficulties in finding consensus on the core issues of procedure and evidence.[4]

Representatives of common law systems, particularly the USA, played a more influential role in the drafting process of the ICTY Rules. Consequently, its Rules of Procedure and Evidence are predominantly rooted in common law, albeit mixed with

---

[3] For further reading about the differences between domestic systems, see R Haveman *et al* (eds), *Supranational Criminal Law: a System Sui Generis* (Antwerp, Intersentia, 2003); A West, Y Desdevises, A Fenet, D Gaurier, MC Heussaff, B Lévy, *The French Legal System*, 2nd edn (London, Butterworths, 1998); M Delmas-Marty and JR Spencer, *European Criminal Procedures* (Cambridge, Cambridge University Press, 2002).

[4] For similar arguments see C Buisman, 'Defence and Fair Trial' in R Haveman *et al*, *Supranational Criminal Law*, ch VI. See also H Friman, 'Inspiration from the International Criminal Tribunals when Developing Law on Evidence for the International Criminal Court' (2003) 3 *The Law and Practice of International Courts and Tribunals* 373, 373–77.

some civil law elements. Under influence of common law the proceedings adopted were of an adversarial nature, but without the use of a jury. The leading role is played by the parties which are responsible for presenting their evidence before a panel of three professional judges. Witnesses are examined by the parties in front of the judges who make all legal and factual findings throughout the entire proceedings. A body similar to an investigative judge has not been incorporated. The Office of the Prosecutor is solely in charge of investigating crimes and charging alleged perpetrators and of presenting evidence in support of all allegations, which the Defence can challenge. Where the Prosecutor has established a *prima facie* case the Defence may then decide to present a defence. The burden to prove the guilt of the perpetrator rests entirely with the Prosecutor.

The civil law influence is particularly apparent in two areas: (1) the role of the professional judge as the finder of law, fact and truth; (2) admissibility of evidence. This has led to greater flexibility in applying the rules, in particular as regards the admission of evidence. As Antonio Cassese J, first President of the ICTY, pointed out:

> ... there are two important adaptations to the general adversarial system. The first is that, as at Nuremberg and Tokyo, we have not laid down technical rules for the admissibility of evidence ... [T]his Tribunal does not need to shackle itself to restrictive rules which have developed out of the ancient trial by jury system. All relevant evidence may be admitted to this Tribunal unless its probative value is substantially outweighed by the need to ensure a fair and expeditious trial. An example of this would be where the evidence was obtained by a serious violation of human rights. Secondly, the Tribunal may order the production of additional or new evidence *proprio motu*. This will enable us to ensure that we are fully satisfied with the evidence on which we base our final decisions and to ensure that the charge has been proved beyond reasonable doubt. It will also minimise the possibility of a charge being dismissed on technical grounds for lack of evidence. We feel that, in the international sphere, the interests of justice are best served by such a provision and that the diminution, if any, of the accused's rights is minimal by comparison.[5]

These arguments, particularly that trials are conducted by professional judges, rather than juries, have often been repeated in the ad hoc tribunals.[6]

---

[5] Statement by the President of the International Tribunal, UN Doc IT/29 (1994), reprinted in Morris and Scharf, *International Criminal Tribunal for Rwanda*, 649, 651.

[6] See, *inter alia*, *ICTY Prosecutor v Tadić*, Decision on Defence Motion on Hearsay (*Tadić* Decision on Hearsay) (5 Aug 1996), paras 14 and 17. In this case the Trial Chamber held that one of the reasons the drafters of the Rules opted for a civil law approach towards the admission of evidence is because 'the trials are conducted by judges who are able, by virtue of their training and experience, to hear the evidence in the context in which it was obtained and accord it appropriate weight. Thereafter, they may make a determination as to the relevancy and the probative value of the evidence'. See also *ICTY Prosecutor v Brđanin and Talić*, Order on the Standards governing the admission of evidence (*Brđanin and Talić* Admission of Evidence Order) (15 Feb 2002), para 14; and *ICTY Prosecutor v Delalić et al* [*Čelebići* case], Decision on the Motion of the Prosecution for the Admissibility of Evidence (19 Jan 1998), para 20; SCSL *Prosecutor v Brima et al*, Decision on the Prosecution Motion for Concurrent Hearing of Evidence Common to Cases SCSL-2004–15-PT and SCSL-2004–16-PT (*Brima* Decision on Prosecution Motion), (11 May 2004), para 38; ICTR *Prosecutor v Ntakirutimana et al*, Decision on the Prosecutor's Motion to Join the Indictments ICTR 96–10-I and ICTR 96–17-T (*Ntakirutimana* Decision on Prosecutor's Motion), (22 Feb 2001), para 26.

The ICTY Rules of Procedure and Evidence served as a model for the ICTR Rules of Procedure and Evidence.[7] This was the intention of the Security Council as similar rules of procedure in the two tribunals would ensure consistency in the development of international criminal procedural rules. This also ensured a quick adoption of the Rules of Procedure and Evidence at the ICTR without having to elaborate on issues that were already discussed in detail in relation to the ICTY Rules.

Pursuant to Article 14 of the Statute of the Special Court for Sierra Leone (SCSL), which was created in 2002, the ICTR Rules would apply *mutatis mutandis* to proceedings before the SCSL.[8] As a result, the Rules of Evidence of the ICTY, ICTR and SCSL were identical, save for minor differences. Over the years the Rules have, however, evolved, resulting in a great number of amendments.[9] These amendments have widened the gaps between the Rules of Evidence of the three ad hoc tribunals. This is particularly apparent in relation to the admissibility of paper evidence in lieu of oral testimony.[10] The fundamental principles of the ICTY, ICTR and SCSL Rules of Evidence nevertheless remained similar, albeit clearly not identical.

In 2002 the International Criminal Court adopted its own Rules of Procedure and Evidence. The Rules were created by a preparatory committee consisting of representatives of States Parties to the Rome Statute and NGOs that were subsequently approved and adopted by the Assembly of States Parties.[11] Unlike the ad hoc international criminal tribunals, both the Rome Statute and the ICC Rules were the product of years of negotiations between representatives from different legal cultures, many of which represented a species of civil law. The ICC rules are, therefore, from the outset more heavily influenced by principles derived from civil law. For instance, a Pre-Trial Chamber has been adopted to enable greater judicial review of the investigation (Article 56 of the Rome Statute). There is also a public and adversarial confirmation hearing during which the Defence may challenge the charges laid against the accused and the Pre-Trial Chamber will determine whether the charges

---

[7] This is in compliance with Art 14 ICTR Statute, which provides that '[t]he judges shall adopt ... the Rules of Procedure and Evidence ... of the International Criminal Tribunal for the Former Yugoslavia with such changes as they deem necessary'.

[8] Art 14(1) of the SCSL Statute provides that '[t]he Rules of Procedure and Evidence of the International Criminal Tribunal for Rwanda obtaining at the time of the establishment of the Special Court shall be applicable *mutatis mutandis* to the conduct of the legal proceedings before the Special Court'.

[9] The main purpose of these amendments was to better guarantee fairness and efficiency. It should be noted that amendments are introduced by the judges after consulting proposals by the Prosecutor and the Registrar (ICTY, ICTR and SCSL Rules, r 6). Initially, defence counsel were excluded from this process, but could submit their proposals to the Registrar who would consider whether or not they were relevant for discussion in the Plenary Session. Recently, greater participation of defence counsel has been permitted. They are also invited to the discussions of the Plenary Session. The reason for choosing a system whose Rules are susceptible to amendment by the judges, whose authority also exceeds to applying and interpreting them, is to ensure flexibility and adaptability vis international criminal law exigencies. Although there may have been good reasons to choose a system where the legislative and legal tasks are carried out by the same body, this is incompatible with the principle of separation of powers. See ST Johnson, 'On the Road to Disaster: The Rights of the Accused and the International Criminal Tribunal for the Former Yugoslavia' (1998) 10 *International Legal Perspective* 111, 116–17, 166–71. In SCSL, the Principal Defender fulfils the role of representing the Defence.

[10] See, in particular, sections 21.4.1–21.4.5.

[11] SA Ferandez de Gurmendi, 'Elaboration of the Rules of Procedure and Evidence' in O Triffterer, *Commentary on the Rome Statute of the International Criminal Court, Observers' Notes, Article by Article*, 2nd edn (Oxford, Hart Publishing, 2008) 235–257.

should be confirmed (Article 61 of the Rome Statute). The Prosecutor has the same mandate and functions as at the *ad hoc* Tribunals with a number of important additional objectives set out in the Rome Statute. Pursuant to Article 54(1)(a) of the Rome Statute the Prosecutor shall, '[i]n order to establish the truth, extend the investigation to cover all facts and evidence relevant to an assessment of whether there is criminal responsibility under this Statute, and, in doing so, investigate incriminating and exonerating circumstances equally'. The judges moreover possess an explicit mandate to establish the truth. Pursuant to Article 69(3) of the ICC Statute the Court 'shall have the authority to request the submission of all evidence that it considers necessary for the determination of the truth'.

The proceedings remain largely adversarial and it is mainly the parties that present the evidence and examine the witnesses. The new feature is the participation of victims, who can ask questions and present evidence with leave of the Court.[12] In reality, however, their role is limited. Apart from rules addressing those new concepts, the ICC Rules are, in essence and nature, similar to the ICTY/ICTR/SCSL Rules and are clearly influenced by them.[13]

In this chapter an analysis is provided of the core rules and principles of evidence as developed and applied by the ICTY, ICTR, SCSL and the ICC. The focus is on principles of admissibility and weight for the assessment of evidence. Attention will be paid to the differences between the Rules and principles of the ad hoc tribunals and the ICC. In addition, this chapter will examine to what degree common law and civil law systems have influenced the Rules of Evidence and their application.

21.2 General Evidentiary Principles

Principles of evidence applied in the international system have not been regulated in any rigid format, unlike in domestic systems. The evidentiary rules and principles that have been incorporated in the international sphere are to be found throughout the Rules of Procedure and Evidence but primarily in sections 3 of the ICTY, ICTR and SCSL Rules. The lack of rigidity in the rules is no coincidence but a matter of choice. Flexibility in adopting and applying evidentiary principles was aimed at quickly responding to the complex and yet unforeseen circumstances of international criminal justice.[14] Given that the concept of an international system was new and was supposed to reflect a great variety of different legal cultures, it was believed that Trial

---

[12] See, in particular, *ICC Prosecutor v Lubanga*, Decision on Victims' Participation (18 Jan 2008); *Lubanga* Judgment on the Appeal of The Prosecutor and The Defence against Trial Chamber I's Decision on Victims' Participation of 18 January 2008 (11 Jul 2008); *ICC Prosecutor v Katanga & Ngudjolo*, Decision on the Set of Procedural Rights Attached to Procedural Status of Victim at the Pre-Trial Stage of the Case (13 May 2008); *Katanga & Ngudjolo*, Decision on Limitations of Set of Procedural Rights for Non-Anonymous Victims (30 May 2008); *Katanga & Ngudjolo*, Decision on the Modalities of Victim Participation at Trial (22 Jan 2010). This issue is discussed in more detail in chapter 22.4.1.

[13] DK Piragoff, 'Article 69' in Triffterer, *Commentary on the Rome Statute*, 1318; Friman, 'Inspiration from the International Criminal Tribunals', 377–379.

[14] G Boas, 'Creating Laws of Evidence for International Criminal Law: The ICTY and the Principle of Flexibility' (2001) 12 *Criminal Law Forum* 41, 81–82, 90; K Khan and R Dixon, *Archbold International Criminal Court: Practice, Procedure and Evidence* (London, Sweet & Maxwell, 2009) 680–681.

Chambers 'should not be hindered by technical rules in their search for the truth, apart from those listed in Section 3 of the Rules'.[15]

It was further pointed out that '[t]he purpose of the Rules is to promote a fair and expeditious trial, and Trial Chambers must have the flexibility to achieve this goal'.[16] This is also the essence of r 89(B) of the ICTY, ICTR and SCSL Rules pursuant to which the rules and principles of evidence applied by the Trial Chambers 'must be those which best favour a fair determination of the matter before the Chamber and which are consonant with the Tribunal's Statute and the general principles of law'.[17]

Thus, flexible rules have been adopted, which must be interpreted in accordance with overriding due process principles set out in the applicable Statute and Rules, as well as international human rights treaties, including the European Convention on Human Rights (ECHR) and the International Covenant on Civil and Political Rights (ICCPR). The various international criminal courts and tribunals often cite jurisprudence derived from these treaty bodies.[18] In this respect, it has further been held that the decisions of the ECHR are 'authoritative and applicable'.[19]

Article 21 of the Statute of the ICTY, in similar manner to Article 20 of the Statute of the ICTR and Article 17 of the Statute of the SCSL, has incorporated fair trial provisions resembling those covered by Article 6 of the ECHR and Article 14 of the ICCPR.[20] The rights set out in Article 21(4) of the ICTY Statute, Article 20(4) ICTR

---

[15] *Brđanin and Talić*, Admission of Evidence Order, para 10.

[16] *ICTY Prosecutor v Aleksovski*, Appeals Chamber Decision on Prosecutor's Appeal on Admissibility of Evidence (*Aleksovski* appeals decision on admissibility) (16 Feb 1999), para 19. As quoted in *ICTY Prosecutor v Kordić and Čerkez*, Decision on the Prosecution Application to Admit the Tulica Report and Dossier into Evidence (*Kordić and Čerkez* decision on the Tulica Report) (29 Jul 1999), para 11.

[17] *ICTY Prosecutor v Milošević*, Decision on Admissibility of Prosecution Investigator's Evidence, (30 Sep 2002), para 18.

[18] See for instance *ICC Prosecutor v Bemba Gombo*, Decision on the Prosecutor's Application for Leave to Appeal the Decision Pursuant to Article 61(7)(a) and (b) of the Rome Statute on the Charges of the Prosecutor Against Jean-Pierre Bemba Gombo, (18 Sep 2009), para 18; *ICTY Prosecutor v Tadić*, Appeals Chamber Judgement (15 Jul 1999), paras. 44, 48–51; *SCSL Prosecutor v Brima et al*, Decision on Brima-Kamara Defence Appeal Motion Against Trial Chamber II Majority Decision on Extremely Urgent Confidential Joint Motion for the Reappointment of Kevin Metzger and Wilbert Harris as Lead Counsel for Alex Tamba Brima and Brima Bazzy Kamara, (8 Dec 2005), para 89. See also Boas, 'Creating Laws of Evidence', 42–48.

[19] *Delalić* Decision on the Motion by the Prosecutor for Protective Measures for the Prosecution Witnesses Pseudonymed 'B' through 'M', Preliminary Judgment, (28 Apr 1997), para 27; *ICTY Prosecutor v Martić*, Decision on Appeal Against the Trial Chamber Decision on the Evidence of Witness Milan Babić (14 Sep 2006).

[20] Art 21 of the ICTY Statute provides (Art 20 ICTR Statute and Art 17 SCSL Statute are almost identical):

All persons shall be equal before the International Tribunal.

In the determination of charges against him, the accused shall be entitled to a fair and public hearing, subject to Article 22 of the Statute.

The accused shall be presumed innocent until proved guilty according to the provisions of the present Statute.

In the determination of any charge against the accused pursuant to the present Statute, the accused shall be entitled to the following minimum guarantees, in full equality:

(a) to be informed promptly and in detail in a language which he understands of the nature and cause of the charge against him;

(b) to have adequate time and facilities for the preparation of his defence and to communicate with counsel of his own choosing;

(c) to be tried without undue delay;

(d) to be tried in his presence, and to defend himself in person or through legal assistance of his own choosing; to be informed, if he does not have legal assistance, of this right; and to have legal assistance

Statute and 17(4) SCSL Statute constitute minimum statutory guarantees that must at all times be respected and considered in rendering evidentiary decisions. A dissenting ICTR judge held that '[t]he minimal guarantees under Article 21(4) are non-negotiable and cannot be balanced against other interests. The use of the word minimum demonstrates that these enumerated rights are an essential component of every trial'.[21]

Article 20 of the ICTY Statute, which is identical to Article 19 of the ICTR Statute, is also relevant to evidentiary determinations. It provides that '[t]he Trial Chambers shall ensure that a trial is fair and expeditious and that proceedings are conducted in accordance with the rules of procedure and evidence, with full respect for the rights of the accused and due regard for the protection of victims and witnesses'.[22] Thus, in addition to the rights of the accused the interests of witnesses have to be duly considered in applying evidentiary rules. Some Trial Chambers have held that the rights of the accused, on the one hand, and those of victims and witnesses, on the other, need to be balanced;[23] while at least one Trial Chamber held that 'the need to carry any balancing exercise which limits the rights of the accused necessarily results in a less than perfect trial'.[24]

Similarly, the ICC takes human rights very seriously in any interpretation of its legal provisions. Pursuant to Article 21(3) of the Rome Statute the application and interpretation of the ICC's institutional rules 'must be consistent with internationally recognised human rights, and be without any adverse distinction founded on grounds such as gender as defined in Article 7, paragraph 3, age, race, colour, language, religion or belief, political or other opinion, national, ethnic or social origin, wealth, birth or other status'. Further, in accordance with Article 69(7) of the ICC Statute, evidence must be obtained in compliance with internationally recognised human rights.[25]

In addition, the ICTY, ICTR and SCSL Rules explicitly state that national rules of evidence have no binding effect (r 89(A)).[26] The Rules themselves, as well as their

---

assigned to him, in any case where the interests of justice so require, and without payment by him in any such case if he does not have sufficient means to pay for it;

(e) to examine, or have examined, the witnesses against him and to obtain the attendance and examination of witnesses on his behalf under the same conditions as witnesses against him;

(f) to have the free assistance of an interpreter if he cannot understand or speak the language used in the International Tribunal;

(g) not to be compelled to testify against himself or to confess guilt.

[21] *ICTR Prosecutor v Bagosora et al*, Separate and Dissenting Opinion of Judge Pavel Dolenc on the Decision and Scheduling Order on the Prosecution Motion for Harmonisation and Modification of Protective Measures for Witnesses (5 Dec 2001), paras 11 and 14.

[22] The SCSL has not adopted a similar provision in its Statute.

[23] *ICTR Prosecutor v Musema*, Appeals Chamber Judgment (16 Nov 2001), paras 68–69; *ICTY Prosecutor v Haradinaj et al*, Decision on Prosecution's Application for Pre-Trial Protective Measures for Witnesses (20 May 2005) 4.

[24] *ICTY Prosecutor v Brđanin and Talić*, Decision on Motion by Prosecution for Protected Measures (3 Jul 2000), para 31.

[25] *Katanga & Ngudjolo* Decision on the Confirmation of Charges (30 Sep 2008), para. 92; see also Khan and Dixon, *Archbold*, 683–684.

[26] This has been confirmed by the case law of the ad hoc tribunals. See, eg, *Tadić*, Decision on Hearsay (5 Aug 1996), para 7; *Akayesu,* Trial Chamber Judgment (2 Sep 1998), para 131, where the Chamber noted that it is not restricted from applying any particular legal system and is not bound by any national rules of evidence. In accordance with r 89 of its Rules of Procedure and Evidence, the Chamber has applied the

interpretation, are nonetheless influenced by domestic legal systems.[27] Similarly, Rule 63(5) of the ICC Rules provides that the Chambers 'shall not apply national laws governing evidence, other than in accordance with Article 21'. In accordance with Article 21 of the Rome Statute, the Court shall first of all apply its own legal provisions and as a second resort principles and rules of international law. Failing that, the Court shall apply 'general principles of law derived by the Court from national laws of legal systems of the world including, as appropriate, the national laws of States that would normally exercise jurisdiction over the crime, provided that those principles are not inconsistent with this Statute and with international law and internationally recognized norms and standards' (Art 21(1)(c)). In considering the application of Article 21(1)(c) of the ICC Statute the Pre-Trial Chamber in *Lubanga* held that this provision does not suggest that the Court is 'bound by the decisions of national courts on evidentiary matters. [. . .] This is clear from Article 69(8) which states that "[w]hen deciding on the relevance or admissibility of evidence collected by a State, the Court shall not rule on the application of the State's national law"'.[28]

21.3   Admissibility

21.3.1   Rules and Principles of Admissibility

Rule 89(C) of the ICTY, ICTR and SCSL Rules represents the core provision dealing with the admissibility of any oral and written testimonial evidence or documentary evidence. The minimum conditions for admissibility under r 89(C) apply to any evidence that is sought to be admitted and cannot be circumvented by reliance on any other Rule. Pursuant to r 89(C) of the ICTY and ICTR Rules a Chamber 'may admit any relevant evidence which it deems to have probative value'. SCSL Rule 89(C), on the other hand, provides that a Chamber 'may admit any relevant evidence'.[29] Accordingly, as regards the SCSL, matters concerning the probative value of evidence are ascribed to weight, rather than admissibility.[30]

---

rules of evidence which in its view best favour a fair determination of the matter before it and are consonant with the spirit of the Statute and general principles of law. Further confirmed in *ICTR Prosecutor v Rutaganda*, Judgment (6 Dec 1999), paras 16–17 and *ICTR Prosecutor v Musema*, Trial Chamber Judgment (27 Jan 2000), para 33; *Brđanin and Talić*, Admission of Evidence Order, para 5.

[27] Although less so now than initially, the Chambers examine domestic systems, mainly those belonging to the civil and common law families when required to determine a particular issue. See *Tadić*, Decision on Hearsay (5 Aug 1996), para 7.

[28] *Lubanga* Decision on the Confirmation of Charges (31 Jan 2007), para 70; reiterated in *Prosecutor v Katanga* Confirmation Decision, para 91. Indeed, in line with Art 69(8) of the ICC Statute the Court will be bound by its own Statute, Rules and case law in determining issues of admissibility; not by those of any particular State. The same position was adopted by the ICTY in *Delalić*, Decision on Zdravko Mucic's Motion for the Exclusion of Evidence, (2 Sep 1997), paras 47–55; Khan and Dixon, *Archbold*, 682–683.

[29] SCSL Rule 89(C) in its original form read as ICTY and ICTR Rule 89(C). By an amendment of 7 March 2003, the reference to probative value has been deleted.

[30] *SCSL Prosecutor v Brima et al*, Decision on Joint Defence Motion to Exclude all Evidence from Witness TF1–277 pursuant to Rule 89(C) and/or Rule 95 (24 May 2005), para 13.

Directly interwoven with probative value is the issue of reliability. Although not explicitly stated, reliability has been considered a prerequisite to a showing of probative value necessary for admission of evidence.[31] At the SCSL reliability is not a condition for admission.[32]

In addition, r 89(D) of the ICTY Rules provides that a Chamber 'may exclude evidence if its probative value is substantially outweighed by the need to ensure a fair trial'. The ICTR and SCSL Rules do not refer to an explicit judicial discretion to exclude evidence to safeguard the fairness of the trial, save for r 95,[33] but in the context of the ICTR judges may exclude such evidence under the general rule, r 89(C). In the case of *Akayesu* the Trial Chamber determined that in accordance with r 89 any relevant evidence having probative value may be admitted into evidence, provided it conforms with the requirements of a fair trial.[34] That r 89(C) of the ICTR Rules gives power to a Trial Chamber to exclude evidence in order to safeguard fair trial principles is also apparent from r 70(F) of the ICTR Rules stating: 'Nothing in Sub-Rule (C) or (D) above shall affect a Trial Chamber's power under Rule 89(C) to exclude evidence if its probative value is substantially outweighed by the need to ensure a fair trial'.[35]

At the SCSL the discretion to exclude 'evidence whose probative value is manifestly outweighed by its prejudicial effect' has been acknowledged pursuant to r 95 and the Chamber's inherent jurisdiction.[36]

Rule 89(C) provides 'a preliminary threshold for the exclusion of irrelevant, unreliable or otherwise improper information'.[37] In line with r 89(C), Chambers have 'an obligation to refuse evidence which is not relevant, or does not have probative value'.[38] In circumstances other than where this is clearly the case the determination as to the admissibility of evidence is entirely a discretionary matter. Rule 89(C) has a wide scope for evidence to be admitted.[39] The preferable approach is to admit rather than exclude evidence, provided it is relevant and has probative value pursuant to r 89(C), and to assess the appropriate weight 'when all the evidence is being considered by the Trial Chamber in reaching its judgment'.[40]

The SCSL Appeals Chamber described the purpose of r 89(C) as follows:

---

[31] *ICTY Prosecutor v Milutinović et al*, Decision on Evidence Tendered Through Sandra Mitchell and Frederick Abrahams (1 Sep 2006), para 9.

[32] *SCSL Prosecutor v Norman et al*, Fofana – Appeal Against Decision Refusing Bail (11 Mar 2005), para 24; *SCSL Prosecutor v Taylor*, Decision on Prosecution Notice of Appeal and Submissions Concerning the Decision Regarding the Tender of Documents (6 Feb 2009), para 37.

[33] See section 21.10.

[34] *Akayesu* Trial Judgment para 136.

[35] SCSL Rule 70(F) is similar to ICTR Rule 70(F), with the difference that it refers to Rule 95, not Rule 89(C), which suggests that the Trial Chamber should exercise its discretion to exclude only if the evidence is obtained in violation of Rule 95, which requires a greater irregularity than Rule 89(C).

[36] *SCSL Prosecutor v Sesay et al*, Decision on Defence Motion to Request the Trial Chamber to Rule that the Prosecution Moulding of Evidence is Impermissible, para 12.

[37] *Bagosora* Decision on Admission of Statements of Deceased Witnesses, para 17.

[38] *Bagosora* Decision on Admissibility of Evidence of Witness DBQ, para 8.

[39] eg *Rutaganda* Trial Judgment, para 18. See also *Aleksovski* Appeal Judgment (24 Mar 2000), para 60, where the Appeals Chamber held that '[u]nless the Rules or general international law provides otherwise, Trial Chambers are free to admit various types of evidence to determine whether or not a particular fact has been established beyond reasonable doubt'.

[40] *Rutaganda* Trial Judgment, para 13; see also *Blaškić*, Trial Chamber Judgment (3 Mar 2000), para 34 and *Musema* Trial Judgment, para 41.

Rule 89(C) ensures that the administration of justice will not be brought into disrepute by artificial or technical rules, often devised for jury trial, which prevent judges from having access to information which is relevant. Judges sitting alone can be trusted to give second hand evidence appropriate weight, in the context of the evidence as a whole and according to well-understood forensic standards. The Rule is designed to avoid sterile legal debate over admissibility so the Court can concentrate on the pragmatic issue.[41]

Pursuant to Articles 64(9) and 69(4) of the ICC Statute the Court may consider the probative value and prejudice of proposed evidence when ruling on its relevance or admissibility. In accordance with Rule 63(2), a Chamber is authorised to 'assess freely all evidence in order to determine its relevance and admissibility in accordance with Article 69'.

The Chamber in *Lubanga* set out a number of principles in relation to its powers to consider the admissibility of evidence pursuant to Article 69 of the ICC Statute. First, pursuant to Article 69(3), the Chamber is allowed to request the submission of all evidence considered to be necessary to establish the truth. Second, pursuant to Article 64(2), the Chamber must ensure the fairness and expeditiousness of the trial. Thirdly, Article 69(2) authorises the admission of a wide range of evidentiary materials other than oral testimony. Fourthly, Article 69(4) confers on the Chamber a broad power to render evidentiary decisions.[42] The Chamber concluded:

[T]he drafters of the Statute framework have clearly and deliberately avoided proscribing certain categories or types of evidence, a step which would have limited – at the outset – the ability of the Chamber to assess evidence 'freely'. Instead, the Chamber is authorised by statute to request any evidence that is necessary to determine the truth, subject always to such decisions on relevance and admissibility as are necessary, bearing in mind the dictates of fairness. In ruling on admissibility the Chamber will frequently need to weigh the competing prejudicial and probative potential of the evidence in question. It is of particular note that Rule 63(5) mandates the Chamber not to 'apply national laws governing evidence'. For these reasons, the Chamber has concluded that it enjoys a significant degree of discretion in considering all types of evidence. This is particularly necessary given the nature of the cases that will come before the ICC: there will be infinitely variable circumstances in which the court will be asked to consider evidence, which will not infrequently have come into existence, or have been compiled or retrieved, in difficult circumstances, such as during particularly egregious instances of armed conflict, when those involved will have been killed or wounded, and the survivors or those affected may be untraceable or unwilling – for credible reasons – to give evidence.[43]

Following this approach, Article 64(9) has been interpreted as granting Chambers 'a seemingly unqualified and unfettered power to rule on admissibility or relevance of evidence'.[44] They must thereby take into account 'inter alia, the probative value of the evidence and any prejudice that such evidence may cause to a fair trial or to a trial

---

[41] *Norman* Fofana-Appeals Against Decision Refusing Bail, (11 Mar 2005), para 26; *Brima* Decision on Joint Defence Motion to Exclude all Evidence from Witness TF1–277 pursuant to Rule 89(C) and/or Rule 95, para 14.

[42] *Lubanga* Decision on the Admissibility of Four Documents (13 Jun 2008), paras 20–23.

[43] Ibid, para 24.

[44] *Lubanga* Decision on the Status before the Trial Chamber of the Evidence Heard by the Pre-Trial Chamber and the Decisions of the Pre-Trial Chamber in Trial Proceedings, and the manner in which Evidence shall be Submitted (13 Dec 2007), para 4; *Lubanga* Decision on the Admission of Material from the Bar Table, para 33.

evaluation of the testimony of a witness, in accordance with the Rules of Evidence and Procedure'.[45] Chambers must be careful 'not to impose artificial limits on their ability to consider any piece of evidence freely, subject to the requirements of fairness'.[46]

The threshold of admissibility of evidence for the purpose of the confirmation of charges is lower than that required for the purposes of trial. At the confirmation stage, considerations of probative value and prejudice mostly go to the weight rather than the admissibility of the evidence.[47] Any evidentiary ruling made by the Pre-Trial Chamber for the purpose of confirming the charges can be re-litigated at trial before the Trial Chamber.[48]

21.3.2   Relevant Definitions of Rule 89(C) Terminology

It has been held that

> [r]elevance, probative value and even prejudice are all relational concepts. The content of the putative facts must be defined and then evaluated in relation to their possible value as proof of the existence of a crime as described in the indictment. The nature of this evaluation explains the discretion conferred on the Trial Chamber by Rule 89(C).[49]

21.3.2.1   Relevance

The ICTY defined relevance as requiring that in relation to two facts there needs to be 'a connection or nexus between the two which makes it possible to infer the existence of one from the other',[50] thereby referring to the *Cloutier* case, determined by the Canadian Supreme Court.[51] This confirms that facts which are not related, whether directly or indirectly to the criminal responsibility of the accused are not

---

[45]   *Katanga* Confirmation Decision, paras 120, 150; *Lubanga* Confirmation Decision, paras 100 and 137.

[46]   *Lubanga*, Decision on Admissibility, para 29.

[47]   See in particular *Katanga* Confirmation Decision, para 70.

[48]   See *Katanga* Confirmation Decision, para 189, confirming the single Judge's expressed view that the Pre-Trial Chamber is not competent to decide on the admissibility of evidence at trial and that the confirmation hearing was not the appropriate stage for debate on the admissibility at trial of the evidence on which the parties intended to rely at the confirmation hearing. See also paras 71, 193 and footnotes 257, 258 thereto, confirming that 'the admission of evidence [at the pre-trial stage] is without prejudice to the Trial Chamber's exercise of its functions and powers to make a final determination as to the admissibility and probative value'.

[49]   *Bagosora* Decision on Admissibility of Proposed Testimony of Witness DBY, (18 Sep 2003), para 18.

[50]   *Delalić* Decision on the Prosecutor's Oral Request for the Admission of Exhibit 155 into Evidence and for an order to Compel the Accused, Zdravko Mucic, To Provide a Handwriting Sample (19 Jan 1998), para 29 (*Delalić* Decision on Admission of Evidence); relying on *R v Cloutier* [1979] 2 SCR 709; 99 DLR (3d) 577, *per* Pratte J. For a similar definition see *ICTR Prosecutor v Karemera et al*, Interim Order for the Prosecution to Identify Relevant and Probative Passages of Certain Materials it Intends to Tender into Evidence Under Rule 89(C) of the Rules of Procedure and Evidence (8 Aug 2007), para 7.

[51]   *R v Cloutier* [1979] 2 SCR 709, *per* Pratte J.

relevant to the issues to be adjudicated at trial.[52] For instance, evidence addressing matters that fall outside the scope of the indictment may be considered irrelevant to the charges.[53]

The SCSL Appeals Chamber held that

> [i]nsofar as the Trial Chamber is ascertaining the relevance of a particular document, it is within its discretion to make further inquiries of the party wishing to tender the document. It will wish to satisfy itself as to the relevance of the document to the case before it, and – as part of the relevance test – the document's relation to the witness at hand, where applicable.[54]

At the ICC, relevance has been defined as relating to 'the matters that are properly to be considered by the Chamber in its investigation of the charges against the accused and its consideration of the views and concerns of participating victims'.[55]

21.3.2.2 Probative Value

The probative value of evidence pertains to whether it tends to prove an issue that is relevant to the proceedings.[56] Dissenting Stephen J in the *Tadić* case defined probative value as a 'quality of necessarily very variable content and much will depend on the character of the evidence in question'.[57] Probative value is interwoven with the credibility and reliability of the evidence and its relevance to the charges.[58]

At the ICC it was held that in assessing the admissibility of evidence the Chamber 'must look at the intrinsic coherence of any item of evidence, and to declare inadmissible those items of evidence of which probative value is deemed prima facie absent after such an analysis. Any other assessment of the probative value of any given item of evidence will be made in light of the whole body of evidence introduced at the confirmation hearing'.[59] There are innumerable factors that are relevant to determining the probative value of evidence, including indicia of reliability. It has been emphasised that 'there is no finite list of possible criteria that are to be applied'. The lack of adequate and available means to test the reliability of evidence is a factor which may affect its probative value to such an extent that it should not be

---

[52] *Karemera* Decision on Prosecutor's Interlocutory Appeal of Decision on Judicial Notice (16 Jun 2006), para 48.

[53] *Bagosora* Decision on Ntabakuze Motion to Deposit Certain United Nations Documents (19 Mar 2007), paras 7, 9.

[54] *Taylor* Decision on Prosecution Notice of Appeal and Submissions Concerning the Decision Regarding the Tender of Documents (6 Feb 2009), para 38.

[55] *Lubanga* Decision on Admissibility, para 27.

[56] *Delalić* Decision on Admission of Evidence, para 29; *Karemera* Interim Order for the Prosecution to Identify Relevant and Probative Passages of Certain Materials it Intends to Tender into Evidence Under Rule 89(C) of the Rules of Procedure and Evidence, para 7; *Karemera* Decision on the Prosecutor's Motion for Admission of Certain Exhibits Into Evidence (25 Jan 2008), para 6.

[57] *Tadić* Decision on Hearsay, Separate Opinion of Judge Stephen, at 3. See also *Aleksovski* Appeals Chamber Decision on Admissibility, para 15, where reference is made to the content and character of the evidence in question in connection to relevance.

[58] *Musema* Trial Chamber Judgment, paras 39–40.

[59] *Katanga* Confirmation Decision, para 77.

admitted.[60] At the confirmation stage the inability to adequately test the evidence also affects its probative value, but goes to its weight rather than admissibility.[61]

21.3.2.3 *Probative Value Versus Prejudice*

Even if particular evidence is both relevant and probative a Trial Chamber may still exclude it, in accordance with its statutory obligation to safeguard the fairness and expeditiousness of the trial 'where its prejudicial effect will adversely affect the fairness or expeditiousness of the proceedings'. As aforementioned, r 89(D) of the ICTY provides an explicit basis for this.[62] In the ICTR and SCSL such a discretion follows from r 89(C) in combination with the Chamber's statutory duty to ensure the fairness of the proceedings. Prejudice may therefore be a ground for exclusion where it outweighs probative value. As the ICTR Appeals Chamber held, it has 'a broad discretion to direct the course of the proceedings in accordance with its fundamental duty to ensure a fair and expeditious trial pursuant to Article 19(1) of the Statute. In pursuit of these goals, the Trial Chamber may choose to exclude otherwise relevant and probative evidence where its prejudicial effect will adversely affect the fairness or expeditiousness of the proceedings'.[63]

The right to cross-examine is not absolute and deprivation thereof on its own is insufficient to exclude evidence.[64] Where evidence goes directly to the acts and conduct of the accused or is pivotal to the Prosecution case, such evidence may, under certain circumstances, be admitted without being subjected to the test of cross-examination, although it would require corroboration if relied upon for a conviction.[65]

---

[60] *Prosecutor v Lubanga*, Decision on the Admissibility of Four Documents (13 Jun 2008), para 29.

[61] *Katanga* Confirmation Decision, paras 109, 194. The probative value of such evidence will be particularly affected if it is not corroborated, ibid, para 70.

[62] *Tadić* Decision on Hearsay, para 18; *Milutinović* Decision on Interlocutory Appeal Against Second Decision Precluding the Prosecution from Adding General Wesley Clark to its 65*ter* List (20 Apr 2007).

[63] *Bagosora* Decision on Prosecutor's Interlocutory Appeals regarding Exclusion of Evidence (19 Dec 2003), para 16. See also *ICTR Prosecutor v Nahimana et al*, Decision on Interlocutory Appeal, Separate Opinion of Judge Shahabuddeen, (15 Sep 2003), para 90; *ICTR Prosecutor v Muvunyi*, Decision on the Prosecutor's Motion Pursuant to Trial Chamber's Directives of 7 December 2005 for the Verification of the Authenticity of Evidence Obtained Out of Court Pursuant to Rules 89(C) and (D) (26 Apr 2006), para 15; *Karemera* Decision on the Prosecutor's Motion for Admission of Certain Exhibits Into Evidence (25 Jan 2008), para 9.

[64] *Martić* Decision on Defence Motion to Exclude the Testimony of Milan Babić, Together with Associated Exhibits, from Evidence, (9 Jun 2006), para 56; *Martić* Decision on Appeal Against the Trial Chamber Decision on the Evidence of Witness Milan Babić, paras 12 and 20; *ICTY Prosecutor v Prlić*, Decision on Request for Admission of the Statement of Jadranko Prlič (22 Aug 2007), para 17.

[65] *Martić* Trial Decision to Exclude the Testimony of Milan Babić, Together with Associated Exhibits, from Evidence (9 Jun 2006), paras 67, 69, 77. In this case the testimony of a witness who died during his cross-examination was admitted on the grounds that the Defence had had an adequate opportunity to cross-examine him (10,5 hours to 15 hours examination-in-chief, para 57). The witness's death could not reasonably have been foreseen or avoided (para 58). Moreover, the evidence was sufficiently corroborated (par. 69) and the completed cross-examination was sufficiently advanced for the Chamber to fairly judge the credibility and reliability of the witness who had appeared before them and the Defence and had testified under oath (para 70). Finally, the Defence was allowed to tender further evidence to challenge the parts of the testimony that had not been tested in cross-examination (paras 79–83). This Decision was confirmed on appeal and reconfirmed by the Appeals Chamber in *Martić* Decision on the Evidence of Witness Milan Babić.

At the ICC, prejudice is one of the factors which Chambers must consider in exercising their discretion to admit or exclude evidence pursuant to Article 69(4) of the ICC Statute. A Chamber 'must, where relevant, weigh the probative value of the evidence against its prejudicial effect and be careful to ensure that it is not unfair to admit the disputed material, for instance because evidence of slight or minimal probative value has the capacity to prejudice the Chamber's fair assessment of the issues in the case'.[66]

21.3.2.4   Reliability

Reliability is not a separate condition for admission,[67] but an inherent and implicit component of relevance and probative value under r 89.[68] Reliability is the invisible golden thread that runs through all components of admissibility.[69] Complete lack of reliability, such that it is not probative, should therefore result in exclusion of the evidence.[70] Further, '[e]vidence whose reliability cannot adequately be tested by the Defence cannot have probative value'.[71]

At the admission stage it is sufficient to demonstrate *indicia* of reliability.[72] The assessment of reliability is predicated on a case-to-case determination and requires consideration for the circumstances under which the evidence arose, the content of the evidence, whether and how the evidence is corroborated, as well as its truthfulness, voluntariness and trustworthiness.[73] Matters concerning the credibility of a witness go to the weight of the testimony, rather than its admissibility.[74]

At the ICC, it has equally been held that in order to assess probative value the evidence must possess *indicia* of reliability.[75] However, reliability is considered to go to the weight, rather than the admissibility of the evidence.[76]

---

[66] *Lubanga* Decision on Admissibility, para 31.

[67] *Musema* Trial Judgment, para 38.

[68] *Tadić* Decision on Hearsay, para 15; confirmed in the *Musema* Trial Judgment, paras 35–36.

[69] *Delalic* Decision on Admission of Evidence (19 Jan 1998), para 32; *Musema* Trial Judgment, para 37.

[70] *Tadić* Decision on Hearsay, para 15; *Nyiramasuhuko v ICTR Prosecutor*, Decision on Pauline Nyiramasuhuko's Appeal on the Admissibility of Evidence (4 Oct 2004), para 7; *ICTR Prosecutor v Simba*, Decision on the Admission of Prosecution Exhibits 27 and 28 (31 Jan 2005), para 10; *ICTR Prosecutor v Rutaganda*, Appeals Chamber Judgement (26 May 2003) para 33; *Muvunyi* Decision on the Prosecutor's Motion to Admit Documents Tendered During the Cross Examination of Defence Witness Augustin Ndindliyimana (28 Feb 2006) para 12; *Bagosora* Decision on Admissibility of Evidence of Witness DBQ, para 8.

[71] *Bagosora* Decision on Admissibility of Evidence, ibid, para 8.

[72] *Nyiramasuhuko v ICTR Prosecutor*, Decision on Pauline Nyiramasuhuko's Appeal on the Admissibility of Evidence, para. 7; *ICTR Prosecutor v Ntagerura et al*, Appeals Chamber Judgement (7 Jul 2006), para 273

[73] *Musema* Trial Judgment, para 42; *Tadić* Decision on Hearsay, para 19; *ICTR Prosecutor v Kajelijeli*, Decision on Motion to Limit the Admissibility of Evidence (2 Jun 2001).

[74] *Bagosora* Decision on Ntabakuze Request for Exclusion of Testimony of Witness Jean Kambanda (6 Jul 2006), para 3.

[75] *Lubanga* Decision on Admissibility, para 28.

[76] *Katanga* Confirmation Decision, paras 78 and 116.

21.4 Principle of Orality

This right to an adversarial process is a common law principle. It means that witnesses are examined by the parties directly before the fact-finders with little intervention from the judge.[77] A written statement cannot be admitted unless the accused is given the opportunity to cross-examine the maker of the statement.[78] An increasing number of exceptions are applied to this principle. For example, hearsay is banned in common law jurisdictions but there are circumstances in which this ban may be circumvented.[79] There is also the best evidence rule pursuant to which the evidence that is being relied upon to prove an aspect of the case should be the best available evidence. This means that the original document, if available, rather than a copy must be produced. The best evidence rule is a rule of admissibility but is applied with increasing flexibility and is not absolute.[80]

Moreover, in civil law systems direct oral testimony is, in principle, preferred over other types of evidence. All European civil law jurisdictions are also bound by the European Convention on Human Rights which imposes adversarial hearings. The preference for oral testimony is referred to as the principle of orality, or immediacy.[81] In accordance with this principle witnesses have to be heard directly by the fact-finders and should testify exclusively in respect of what they have personally observed. In accordance with this principle direct evidence is preferred over hearsay evidence. In most civil law systems this principle merely expresses a preference of one over the other but does not have the effect of rendering inadmissible the least preferred evidence. The principle is therefore more comparable with the common law best evidence rule than with the exclusionary rule against hearsay. Within the boundaries set by the European Court of Human Rights, clearly preferring oral examination of witnesses before the finders of fact,[82] it is quite common for courts in civil law jurisdictions to rely heavily on paper evidence.[83]

In the case of international criminal tribunals there is a clear preference for oral in-court testimony in lieu of paper evidence. This preference follows from the statutory right of the accused 'to examine, or have examined, the witness against him', as set out in Article 21(4)(e) ICTY Statute, Article 20(4)(e) ICTR Statute and Article 17(4)(e) of the SCSL Statute. Pursuant to this right in conjunction with the

---

[77] *Turner* v *Louisiana* (1965) 379 US 466; P Murphy, *Murphy on Evidence*, 11th edn (Oxford, Oxford University Press, 2009).

[78] *Crawford* v *Washington* (2004) 124 S Ct 1354, 1370, *per* Scalia J.

[79] For example, where the maker of the statement has since died. See *Murphy on Evidence*, ch 8.

[80] See eg *Springsteen* v *Flute International Ltd* [2001] EMLR 654.

[81] See eg § 250 (1) of the German Code of Criminal Proceedings (Strafprozess Ordnung (StPO)); E Löwe, W Rosenberg, *Die Strafprozessordnung und das Gerichtverfassungsgezetz § 250 StPO, 24–26* (24th edn 1987); JF *Nijboer, Strafrechtelijk Bewijsrecht*, 3rd edn (Nijmegen, Ars Aequi Libri, 1997) 110, 139–141; Minkenhof and Reijntjens, *De Nederlandse Strafvordering* (Arnhem, 1993) 284–286.

[82] Such boundaries include giving an opportunity to the parties to examine the witness at an earlier time or the principle that untested indirect evidence can only be relied upon if corroborated. See, *inter alia, Delta v France* (1990) 16 EHRR 574; *Lüdi v Switzerland* (1992) 15 EHRR 172; *Unterpertinger v Austria* (1986) 13 EHRR 175; *Kostovski v The Netherlands* (1989) 12 EHRR 434.

[83] See, *inter alia*, JW Fokkens, 'Getuigen tussen Straatsburg en Den Haag' in PD Duys, PDJ van Zeben, *Via Straatsburg, Liber Amicorum Egbert Myjer* (Nijmegen, Wolf Legal Publishers, 2004) 150ff.

general right to a fair trial an accused is entitled to have an adversarial process where his accusers appear in court for testimony and cross-examination.

The Appeals Chamber has acknowledged that there is 'a general principle that witnesses before the Tribunal should give their evidence orally rather than have their statement entered into the record. . . . The principle of orality, and its complement, the principle of immediacy, act as analogues to common law hearsay rules and are meant to ensure the adversarial nature of criminal trials, and the right of the accused to confront witnesses against him'.[84]

Initially, r 90(A) of the ICTY, ICTR and SCSL Rules reflected this principle of orality, stipulating that: 'Witnesses shall, in principle, be heard directly by the Chambers unless a Chamber has ordered that the witness be heard by means of a deposition as provided for in r 71'. Whilst ICTR r 90(A) still reads the same, ICTY and SCSL r 90(A) have been adjusted in a manner undermining the preference for oral testimony. ICTY r 89(F), which has replaced the original r 90(A), reads: 'A Chamber may receive the evidence of a witness orally or, where the interests of justice allow, in written form'.[85]

Rule 89(F) of the ICTY Rules permits the admission of evidence in written form provided that its admission is in the interests of justice, in compliance with r 89(C) and does not moreover contravene r 92*bis*, r 92*ter*, r 92*quater* and r 92*quinquies*, as discussed below.[86] In which circumstances the receipt of written evidence is in the interests of justice pursuant to r 89(F) and is premised on a case-by-case determination, depends, *inter alia*, on the nature of the evidence[87] and the extent to which the opportunity to assess the credibility of the witness has been infringed.[88] SCSL r 90(A) reads: 'Witnesses may give evidence directly or as described in Rules 71 and 85(D)'.[89]

Initially, the only recognised exception to in-court testimony was deposition evidence taken pursuant to r 71 of the ICTY, ICTR and SCSL Rules. Where evidence is given by deposition the witness gives out-of-court evidence before a Legal Officer in

---

[84] *ICTY Prosecutor v Halilović*, Decision on Interlocutory Appeal Concerning Admission of Record of Interview of the Accused from the Bar Table (19 Aug 2005), para 16.

[85] ICTY r 90(A) was first amended on 25 July 1997 to include the possibility of receiving a testimony via video-conference link in exceptional circumstances and in the interests of justice. By the amendments of 1 and 13 December 2000, at the same time that r 92*bis* was introduced, ICTY r 90(A) became what is today r 89(F). The amendments aimed at facilitating the admission of written evidence. With reference to r 89(F), the Appeals Chamber held that the principle of orality is not absolute and that this rule merely states a preference for oral testimony. Ibid, para. 17.

[86] *ICTY Prosecutor v Milošević*, Decision on Admissibility of Prosecution Investigator's Evidence (30 Sep 2002), para 18.

[87] In *Martić* Decision on Prosecution's Motion for Admission of Statement of Witness Milan Babic Pursuant to Rule 89(F), a written statement and related exhibits were admitted pursuant to Rule 89(F) where the witness's statement did not directly relate to the accused, but contained information on the political developments in the territory.

[88] *Milošević* Decision on Interlocutory Appeal on the Admissibility of Evidence-in-Chief in the Form of Written Statements (30 Sep 2003), paras 20–21.

[89] It has, however, been held that the SCSL Rules clearly express preference for live testimony, given that this manner of evidence is the only kind for which no specific court order is required. See *Taylor* Decision on Prosecution Motion to Allow Witnesses to give testimony by Video-Link (30 Mar 2007), paras 22–24.

the presence of the parties and is subjected to cross-examination.[90] The Chamber does not hear the witness directly but must instead rely on the record made in the deposition. Given that a deposition deprives the Chamber of an opportunity to assess the demeanour of the witness this is allowed only if it is deemed in 'the interests of justice'. Whether a deposition is in the interests of justice depends on several factors, including the importance of the testimony; the unwillingness or unavailability of the witness to appear at trial and; the prejudice it causes to the right of the accused to confront the witness.[91]

Depositions must be treated as a last recourse. Important witnesses should appear in person for testimony in order to allow the judges to directly observe the witness's demeanour and to test his or her credibility. On the other hand, witnesses who do not directly implicate the accused in the crimes charged, or whose testimony is of a repetitive nature to other available evidence, may give evidence by means of deposition.[92]

At the ICTR and SCSL the deposition must further be justified by reason of 'exceptional circumstances'.[93] The witness's age or poor mental or physical condition may amount to exceptional circumstances.[94] Moreover, the refusal of the government of the country where the witness is residing to allow his or her transfer to the Tribunal may constitute an exceptional circumstance.[95]

[90] See JW Strong (ed), *McCormick on Evidence* (St Paul, West Publishing, 1999) 391–92. If the tribunals allow evidence to be given by deposition the accused has a right to attend (*Muvunyi* Decision on the Request of the Accused for Certification to Appeal Against the Decision Authorising the Deposition of Prosecution Witness QX (27 Nov 2003), para 7).

[91] *Delalić* Decision on the Motion to Allow Witnesses K, L, and M to Give Their Testimony by Means of Video-Link Conference (28 May 1997). In the ICTR, a fourth factor has been referred to, namely, 'the practical considerations (including logistical difficulties, expenses and security risks) of holding a deposition in the proposed location [should] not outweigh the potential benefits to be gained by doing so'. See *Bagosora* Decision on Deposition of Witness OW, paras 13–14; *Bagosora* Decision on Prosecutor's Motion to Allow Witness DBO to Give Testimony by Means of Deposition (25 Aug 2004), para 8.

[92] *ICTY Prosecutor v Naletilić and Martinović*, Decision on Prosecutor's Motion to Take Depositions for Use at Trial (Rule 71) (10 Nov 2000) 4; *ICTR Prosecutor v Niyitegeka*, Decision on the Prosecutor's Amended Extremely Urgent Motion for the Deposition of a Detained Witness pursuant to Rule 71, (4 Oct 2002), para 3.

[93] In its original version, ICTY r 71 also required exceptional circumstances. By an amendment of 7 Dec 1999 the ICTY deleted the requirement of 'exceptional circumstances' to make its use more flexible; thus, the party seeking to produce deposition evidence only needs to demonstrate that such is required in the interests of justice. The ICTY amendment gave effect to what had already become a reality, namely that exceptional circumstances were accepted very easily. For instance, the unavailability of one of the judges could have amounted to exceptional circumstances. See *Kordić and Čerkez* Decision on the Prosecutor's Request to Proceed by Deposition (13 Apr 1999); *ICTY Prosecutor v Kupreškić and Others*, Decision on Prosecutor's Request to Proceed by Deposition (25 Feb 1999). Thus, the deletion of 'exceptional circumstances' has not made a significant difference, as most requests are assessed on their impact on interests of justice.

[94] *Bagosora* Decision on Prosecutor's Motion for Deposition of Witness OW, para 12; *Muvunyi* Decision on Prosecutor's Extremely Urgent Motion for the Deposition of Witness QX (11 Nov 2003); *Simba* Decision on the Defence's Extremely Urgent Motion for a Deposition (11 Mar 2004), para 7. The fact that a witness is protected, indigent, or fearful does not amount to an exceptional circumstance justifying deposition. These are issues that can be dealt with by the Tribunal's Witness and Victim Support Unit and hence a deposition is not necessary. See *Semanza* Decision on Semanza's Motion for Subpoenas, Depositions, and Disclosure (20 Oct 2000), para 27.

[95] *Niyitegeka* Decision on the Prosecutor's Amended Extremely Urgent Motion for the Deposition of a Detained Witness Pursuant to Rule 71 (4 Oct 2002), para 5.

In 1997, a second alternative to in-court testimony was created, that is, testimony given by video-link by which the witness testifies and is being cross-examined from a different location via a direct video-link to the courtroom. A new legal provision was incorporated in the ICTY and later also in the SCSL Rules to explicitly permit the admissibility of video-link testimony if in the interests of justice.[96] The ICTR has not incorporated an explicit legal basis for video-link testimony but nonetheless allows such testimony pursuant to r 54 if once again they are found to be in the interests of justice.[97]

This alternative to the witness's in-court appearance is preferred over a deposition because it allows the Chamber to observe the witness's demeanour.[98] Indeed, the hearing of evidence via a video-link is not considered incompatible with the '[d]irect observation of the witness's demeanour'.[99] However, whilst the hearing by the judges and the accused of a witness via video-link is not considered problematic, this is different where the judges move to the location of the witness to be in a better position to assess the witness's demeanour but the accused stays behind and can follow the testimony through a video-link only.[100]

The criteria to assess whether video-link testimony is in the interests of justice are similar to those in relation to deposition evidence. The testimony of the witness in question must be shown 'to be sufficiently important to make it unfair to proceed without it'; the witness must be unable or unwilling to appear at trial,[101] and there is

---

[96] In 1997, r 90(A) was amended to include testimony via video-link as an alternative to oral testimony. Then, in 1999, r 71*bis* was introduced, which became r 81*bis* in 2007, with the additional condition that testimony can only be given via video-link 'in the interests of justice'. SCSL r 85(D) is wider in that it allows evidence to be given 'directly in court, or via such communications media, including video, closed-circuit television, as the Trial Chamber may order'. SCSL r 85(D) does not make reference to 'interests of justice'. However, it has been held that this rule only authorises testimony to be given by video-link where this is in the interests of justice, even if not explicitly stated because the Chamber 'is not entitled to ignore such a fundamental principle'. *Taylor* Decision on Prosecution Motion to Allow Witnesses to give testimony by Video-Link (30 Mar 2007), para 25.

[97] Rule 54 permits the Trial Chamber to 'issue such orders, summonses, subpoenas, warrants and transfer orders as may be necessary for the purposes of an investigation or for the preparation or conduct of the trial'. The first decision where the 'interests of justice' requirement was explicitly recognised was *ICTR Prosecutor v Nahimana et al*, Decision on the Prosecutor's Application to Add Witness X to Its List of Witnesses and for Protective Measures, (14 Sep 2001), para 35. Alternatively, Trial Chambers may hear testimony via video-link as a witness protection measure pursuant to Rule 75, where this is necessary to safeguard the witness's security, *Bagosora* Decision on Video-Conference Testimony of Kabiligi Witnesses KX-38 and KVB-46 (5 Oct 2006), para 2; *Bagosora* Decision on Prosecution Request for Testimony of Witness BT Via Video-Link (8 Oct 2004), paras 5–8; *Nahimana* Decision, ibid.

[98] The availability of the video-link option may constitute a ground for the rejection of requests for depositions. See *Simba* Decision on the Defence Request for Taking the Evidence of Witness FMP1 by Deposition (9 Feb 2005), para 4; *Bagosora* Decision on Prosecution Request for Deposition of Witness BT (4 Oct 2004).

[99] *Bagosora* Decision, ibid, para 12.

[100] *ICTR Prosecutor v Zigiranyirazo*, Decision on Defence and Prosecution Motions Related to Witness ADE, (31 Jan 2006), paras 28–34; *Zigiranyirazo* Decision on Interlocutory Appeal (30 Oct 2006).

[101] *Tadić* Decision on the Defence Motions to Summon and Protect Defence Witnesses, and on the Giving of Evidence by Video-Link, (25 Jun 1996), para 19. Additional factors to be considered include the persuasion of the reasons adduced for the inability or unwillingness to attend, and whether there is a fair opportunity to confront the witness and for the judges to assess the demeanour and credibility of the witness. See *Simba* Decision Authorising the Taking of Evidence of Witnesses IMG, ISG, and BJK1 by Video-Link (4 Feb 2005); *Bagosora* Decision on Testimony by Video Conference (20 Dec 2004); *Zigiranyirazo* Decision on Defence and Prosecution Motions Related to Witness ADE, para 31; *Muvunyi* Decision on Muvunyi's Amended Motion to Have Defence Witnesses M005, M015, M036, M046, and M073 Testify by Closed Video-Link Pursuant to Rules 54 and 71(D)of the Rules of Procedure and Evidence (7 Feb 2006), para 18; *Muvunyi* Decision on Muvunyi's Supplemental Motion to Have Defence

no efficient alternative.[102] It is not necessary that the witness's refusal to attend be objectively justified.[103]

21.4.1 Admissibility of Written Statements in lieu of Oral Testimony

In 1998, a new r 94*ter*, superseded in 2000 by r 92*bis*, was adopted by the ICTY, allowing witness statements to be admitted in lieu of oral testimony in certain circumstances. The ICTR and SCSL have also adopted r 92*bis*.

In accordance with r 92*bis*(A) statements containing witness testimonial evidence can only be admitted if they are not intended to prove the acts and conduct of the accused.[104] Evidence which is intended as proof of the acts and conduct of the accused under r 92*bis*(A) includes evidence relating to conduct of an indirect nature, such as the planning, instigation or ordering of the crimes charged, the accused's participation in a joint criminal enterprise, his shared requisite intent with the actual perpetrator(s) of the crimes charged or his role and knowledge as a superior to those who committed the alleged crimes.[105] The accused's conduct under r 92*bis*(A) may also refer to his omission to act.[106] The extent to which 'acts and conduct of the accused' also include the 'acts and conduct of subordinates or co-perpetrators' is dependent on the proximity of those acts and conduct to the charges laid against the

Witness MO72 Testify by Closed Video-Link Pursuant to Rules 54 and 71(D) of the Rules of Procedure and Evidence (21 Feb 2006), para 6; *Muvunyi*, Decision on Prosecution Motion to Have Prosecution's Witnesses QCM and NN Testify by Closed Video-Link Pursuant to rr 54 and 71(D) of the Rules of Procedure and Evidence (23 May 2005), para 20; *ICTR Prosecutor v Rwamakuba*, Decision on Confidential Motion for the Testimony of Defence Witness 1.15 to be Taken by Video-Link (8 Dec 2005), para 3; *Karemera* Decision on Prosecutor's Confidential Motion for Special Protective Measures for Witness ADE, paras 4 and 5; *Taylor* Decision on Prosecution Motion to Allow Witnesses to give Testimony by Video-Link (30 Mar 2007), para 26.

[102] *ICTY Prosecutor v Haradinaj et al*, Decision on Motion for Video-Link (Witness 30) (14 Sep 2007), paras 1, 2, 6.
[103] *Bagosora* Decision on Video-Conference Testimony of Kabiligi Witnesses KX-38 and KVB-46 (5 Oct 2006), paras 3, 6; *Bagosora* Decision on Testimony by Video-Conference (20 Dec 2004), paras 4–6; *Bagosora* Decision on Prosecution Request for Testimony of Witness BT Via Video-Link (8 Oct 2004), paras 6, 13; *Bagosora* Decision on Testimony of Witness Amadou Deme by Video-Link (29 Aug 2006), para 3; *Simba* Decision Authorising the Taking of the Evidence of Witnesses IMG, ISG, and BJK1 by Video-Link (4 Feb 2005), para 4.
[104] The term 'acts and conduct of the accused' means 'deeds and behaviour of the accused', as per the *Milošević* Decision on Prosecution's Request to have Written Statements Admitted under Rule 92*bis* (21 Mar 2002), para 22. It is not necessary that the statement refer to the accused by name in order to constitute his acts and conduct of the accused; it is sufficient that it is implied that the statement refers to the accused (*Karemera* Decision on Prosecution Motion to Admit Witness Statement from Joseph Serugendo (15 Dec 2006), para 9).
[105] *ICTY Prosecutor v Galić*, Decision on Interlocutory Appeal Concerning Rule 92*bis*(C), para 10(b)(d)(e)(g)(h)) (7 Jun 2002); *ICTY Prosecutor v Blagoević and Jokić*, First Decision on Prosecutor's Motion for Admission of Witness Statements and Prior Testimony Pursuant to Rule 92*bis* (12 Jun 2003), para17; *ICTY Prosecutor v Orić*, Decision on Defence Motion for the Admission of the Witness Statement of Avdo Husejnovic Pursuant to Rule 92*bis* (15 Sep 2005); *Bagosora* Decision on Prosecutor's Motion for the Admission of Written Witness Statements Under Rule 92*bis* (9 Mar 2004), para 13; *Karemera* Decision on Prosecution Motion for Admission of Evidence of Rape and Sexual Assault Pursuant to Rule 92*bis* of the Rules and Order for Reduction of Prosecution Witness List (11 Dec 2006), paras 11–13.
[106] *Galić* Decision on Interlocutory Appeal Concerning Rule 92*bis*(C), para 11.

accused. The Appeals Chamber in *Galić* held that '[w]here the evidence is so pivotal to the prosecution case and where the person whose acts and conduct the written statement describes is so proximate to the accused, the Trial Chamber may decide that it would not be fair to the accused to permit the evidence to be given in written form'.[107]

Under ICTR and ICTY r 92*bis*[108] evidence which is not excluded on the ground that it goes to the acts and conduct of the accused under r 92*bis*(A) must still meet the formal requirements under r 92*bis*(B) in order for it to be admissible. Pursuant to r 92*bis*(B) the statement must be supplemented by a declaration of the person providing it, stating that the contents are true and correct to the best of his or her knowledge and belief. This declaration has to be witnessed by a person authorised to do so on the basis of domestic law and procedure (r 92*bis*(B)(i)(a)), or by 'a Presiding Officer appointed by the Registrar of the Tribunal for that purpose' (r 92*bis*(B)(i)(b)). The witness attaches a dated note, mentioning the place of the declaration (r 92*bis*(B)(ii)(d)), identifying the person making the declaration as the person in the written statement (r 92*bis*(B)(ii)(a)), verifying that the person in question indeed stated that the contents are true and correct to the best of his knowledge and belief (r 92*bis*(B)(ii)(b)) and making note that the person knew that he may be prosecuted for false testimony if the content of the written statement was found not to be true ((B)(ii)(c)).

Provided the formal requirements under r 92*bis*(B) are met, and the evidence does not directly address the conduct of the accused as charged in the indictment, but is nonetheless relevant, reliable and probative to the case pursuant to r 89(C),[109] it is

---

[107] Ibid, *Galić*, para 13; see also, *Karemera* Decision on Prosecution Motion for Admission of Evidence of Rape and Sexual Assault Pursuant to Rule 92*bis* of the Rules and Order for Reduction of Prosecution Witness List, para 12; *Sesay* Decision on Defence Application for the Admission of the Witness Statement of DIS-129 Under Rule 92*bis* or, in the Alternative, Rule 92*ter* (12 Mar 2008); *Taylor* Decision on Prosecution Notice Under Rule 92*bis* for the Admission of Evidence Related to *Inter Alia* Kenema District and on Prosecution Notice under Rule 92*bis* for the Admission of the Prior Testimony of TF1–036 into Evidence (15 Jul 2008) 4–5. Most Chambers are, however, reluctant to exclude evidence which addresses the acts and conduct of co-perpetrators or subordinates pursuant to r 92*bis*(A), deeming this as going to proof of the acts and conduct of the accused. See eg *Milošević* Decision on Prosecution's Request to have Written Statements Admitted under Rule 92*bis*, para 22; *Orić* Decision on Defence Motion to Admit the Evidence of a Witness in the Form of a Written Statement Pursuant to Rule 92*bis* (6 Dec 2005); *Sesay* Decision on Defence Motion and Three Sesay Defence Applications to Admit 23 Witness Statements Under Rule 92*bis* (15 May 2008), para 34. However, in *Bagosora*, Decision on Prosecutor's Motion for the Admission of Written Witness Statements Under Rule 92*bis* (9 Mar 2004), a statement addressing the conduct of persons under the accused's command was excluded unless an opportunity to cross-examine the witness could be offered to the Defence.

[108] SCSL r 92*bis* was adopted in 2004 and has been amended to the effect that the requirements under r 92*bis*(B), as well as the factors to be considered in weighing the admissibility of a written statement under r 92*bis*(A) have been deleted. SCSL r 92*bis* possesses, however, a wider scope than ICTY and ICTR r 92*bis*. The Appeals Chamber in the SCSL case against *Taylor* has confirmed that any written evidence that is sought to be admitted in lieu of oral testimony and which is not introduced through a witness can be admitted only if the requirements of r 92*bis* have been met. Accordingly, written evidence which is not introduced through a witness is admissible only where such evidence does not go to the acts and conduct of the accused. See *Taylor* Decision on Prosecution Notice of Appeal and Submissions Concerning the Decision Regarding the Tender of Documents (6 Feb 2009), para 34.

[109] *ICTR Prosecutor v André Ntagerura and Others*, Decision on the Defence Motion for Leave to Present Evidence in the Form of a Written Statement under r 92*bis* (13 Mar 2003), para 14, where it was held that the evidence 'needs to bear some evidentiary value related to the issues at stake'; and *Ntagerura* Decision, ibid, para 16, where the Trial Chamber stated that statements cannot be admitted pursuant to

within the Trial Chamber's discretion to admit such evidence, giving due consideration to the factors in favour and against admission of evidence under r 92*bis*(A).[110]

The Chamber may condition its admission on the availability of the witness for cross-examination pursuant to r 92*bis*(E), particularly where the evidence, although not directly addressing the acts and conduct of the accused, is nonetheless pivotal to the Prosecution's case. In such a situation or other situations where the fair trial rights of the accused are at issue, the invitation of the witness for cross-examination may be necessary to ensure proceedings are fair.[111]

Under the original r 92*bis*, where a Chamber was satisfied on a balance of probabilities that a witness had died after providing a statement, could no longer with reasonable diligence be traced, or was by reason of bodily or mental condition unable

r 92*bis* if they have not passed the relevance test under r 89(C). See further, *ICTR Prosecutor v Zigiranyirazo*, Decision on Motions to Admit Witness Statements of Witnesses Joshua Abdul Ruzibiza, RW2 and RW3 (22 Nov 2007), para 3. See for similar reasoning the SCSL cases of *Sesay*, Decision on the Prosecution Request for Leave to Call an Additional Witness and Notice to Admit Witness's Solemn Declaration Pursuant to Rule 73*bis*(E) and 92*bis* (5 Apr 2006) 4; *Norman* Decision on Prosecution's Request to Admit Into Evidence Certain Documents Pursuant to Rule 92 bis and 89(C) (14 Jul 2005); *Sesay* Decision on Prosecutor's Notice Under Rule 92*bis* to Admit the Transcripts of Witness TF1–334 (23 May 2006) 3; *Sesay* Decision on Prosecution Notice Under Rule 92*bis* and 89 to Admit the Statement of Witness TF1–150 (20 Jul 2006), para 17. A defendant may be unfairly prejudiced if evidence is admitted without giving the Defence an opportunity to cross-examine (*Sesay* Decision on the Prosecution Request for Leave to Call an Additional Witness and Notice to Admit a Witness's Solemn Declaration Pursuant to Rule 73*bis*(E) and 92*bis* (5 Apr 2006) 4).

[110] Factors in favour of admitting such evidence include its cumulative nature ((A)(i)(a)); its relationship with relevant historical, political or military backgrounds ((A)(i)(b)); whether the evidence consists of a general or statistical analysis of the ethnic composition of the population in respect of localities related to the indictment ((A)(i)(c)); whether it concerns the impact of crimes upon victims ((A)(i)(d)); its relationship with the character of the accused ((A)(i)(e)); or its relationship with factors to be taken into account in determining sentence ((A)(i)(f)). Factors against admitting such evidence include: an overriding public interest as to the evidence in question being heard orally ((A)(ii)(a)); a demonstration by an objecting party that its nature and source renders the evidence unreliable, or that its prejudicial effect outweighs its probative value ((A)(ii)(b)); any other factors which make it preferable that the witness gives evidence in court ((A)(ii)(c)). See *Bagosora* Decision on Prosecutor's Motion for the Admission of Written Witness Statements Under Rule 92*bis* (9 Mar 2004), para 16; *Brđanin and Talić* Decision on Objection and/or Consent to Rule 92*bis* Admission of Witness Statements Number One (30 Jan 2002), paras 4–5, 17–18, 30; *Naletilić and Martinović* Decision regarding Prosecutor's Notice of Intent to Offer Transcripts under Rule 92*bis*(D) (9 Jul 2001).

[111] *Karemera* Decision on Prosecution Motion for Admission of Evidence of Rape and Sexual Assault Pursuant to Rule 92*bis* of the Rules and Order for Reduction of Prosecution Witness List, para 8, 14–16, 19–20; *Bizimungu* Decision on Casimir Bizimungu's Motion to Vary Witness List; and to Admit Evidence of Witness in Written Form in Lieu of Oral Testimony (1 May 2008), para 19; *Karemera* Decision on Joseph Nzirorera's Motion to Admit Statements of Augustin Karara (9 Jul 2008), para 4; *Milošević* Decision on Prosecution's Request to have Written Statements Admitted under Rule 92*bis* (21 Mar 2002), paras 24, 26; *Bagosora* Decision on Prosecutor's Motion for the Admission of Written Witness Statements Under Rule 92*bis* (9 Mar 2004); see also *ICTY Prosecutor v Prlić et al*, Decision on the Prosecution Motion for Admission of Transcript of Evidence Pursuant to Rule 92*bis* of the Rules (28 Sep 2006), para 23; *Galić*, Decision on Interlocutory Appeal Concerning Rule 92*bis*(C) (7 Jun 2002), para 13; *ICTY Prosecutor v Limaj et al*, Decision on Prosecution's Motion to Admit Rebuttal Statements Via Rule 92*bis* (7 Jul 2005), para 5; *Sesay* Decision on Defence Application for the Admission of the Witness Statement of DIS-129 Under Rule 92*bis* or, in the Alternative, Rule 92*ter* (12 Mar 2008); *Taylor*, Decision on Prosecution Notice Under Rule 92*bis* for the Admission of Evidence Related to *Inter Alia* Kenema District and on Prosecution Notice under Rule 92*bis* for the Admission of the Prior Testimony of TF1–036 into Evidence (15 Jul 2008) 4–5; *Taylor* Decision on public with confidential annexes A to D & F to G Prosecution notice under Rule 92*bis* for the admission of evidence related to *inter alia* Freetown & Western Area – TF1–098, TF1–104 and TF1–227 (21 Oct 2008) 4; *Sesay* Decision on Defence Motion and Three Sesay Defence Applications to Admit 23 Witness Statements Under Rule 92*bis*, para 40.

to testify orally, the witness's statement could be admitted under r 92*bis*(C) in conjunction with r 92*bis*(A), even where the conditions under r 92*bis*(B) had not been met, provided that the Chamber surmised from the circumstances in which the statement was taken that there were satisfactory *indicia* in respect of its reliability.[112]

ICTR r 92*bis* still reads the same as when it was originally adopted. Accordingly, until today, oral testimony is preferred and can only be replaced by written testimony if the above criteria are complied with. The main principle is that statements that go to proof of the acts and conduct of the accused are not admissible, irrespective of whether the witnesses are deceased, untraceable, or unavailable for testimony[113] and independent of any evaluation of the admissibility of hearsay evidence under the more general provisions of r 89(C).[114] Whilst the conditions of r 89(C) must be met in order to admit evidence under r 92*bis*, the requirements under r 92*bis* cannot be circumvented by relying on r 89(C). This is so given that 'the general requirement under r 89 that admissible evidence be relevant and probative applies in addition to, and not in lieu of, the more specific provisions of r 92*bis*'.[115] Rule 92*bis* in conjunction with r 90(A) provides the only basis for the admission of testimonial evidence in written form, which is done by following the procedure set out in r 92*bis*.[116]

21.4.2   Further Steps to Admit Written Statements in lieu of Oral Testimony

Contrary to ICTR r 92*bis*, ICTY and SCSL r 92*bis* have been significantly amended and expanded. By amendments adopted on 13 September 2006 Rule 92*bis* was amended to include transcripts of evidence given by a witness in proceedings before the Tribunal, which do not need to meet the criteria under r 92*bis*(B) as described above. Two new Rules were adopted: r 92*ter* and r 92*quater*.

---

[112] See *Bagosora* Decision on Admission of Statements of Deceased Witnesses (19 Jan 2005), para 15; *Muhimana* Decision on the Prosecution Motion for Admission of Witness Statements (Rule 89 (C) and 92*bis*) (20 May 2004), para 26.

[113] *ICTR Prosecutor v Nyiramasuhuko et al*, Decision on the Prosecutor's Motion to Remove From Her Witness List Five Deceased Witnesses and to Admit Into Evidence the Witness Statements of Four of the Said Witnesses (22 Jan 2003), para 21.

[114] *Muhimana* Decision on Prosecution Motion for Admission of Witness Statements (20 May 2004); *Nyiramasuhuko* Decision on the Prosecutor's Motion to Remove from her Witness List Five Deceased Witnesses and to Admit Into Evidence the Witness Statements of Four of Said Witnesses (22 Jan 2003), para 21.

[115] See *ICTR Prosecutor v Kanyabashi and Others*, Decision on the Prosecutor's Motion to Remove from her Witness List Five Deceased Witnesses and to Admit into Evidence the Witness Statements of Four of Said Witnesses (22 Jan 2003), para 20, thereby following the approach adopted in the *Galić* Appeal Judgment (7 Jun 2002), para 31; see also *Nyiramasuhuko* Decision on Prosecution Motion for Verification of the Authenticity of Evidence Obtained Out of Court, Namely the Alleged Diary of Pauline Nyira-Masuhuko (1 Oct 2004), para 26.

[116] *Bagosora* Decision on Admission of Statements of Deceased witnesses (19 Jan 2005), para 15; *Muhimana* Decision on Prosecution Motion for Admission of Witness Statements (rr 89(C) and 92*bis*) (20 May 2004), paras 23–28; *Nyiramasuhuko* Decision on Prosecutor's Motion to Remove from Her Witness List Five Deceased Witnesses, and to Admit into Evidence the Witness Statements of Four of the Said Witnesses (22 Jan 2003), para 20; *Bagosora* Decision on Admission of Statement of Kabiligi Witness Under Rule 89(C) (14 Feb 2007), paras 3–5.

Pursuant to r 92*ter*, a written statement or a transcript containing a witness's testimony can be admitted in lieu of oral testimony, even where it goes to proof of the acts and conduct of the accused as charged in the indictment (r 92*ter*(B)), provided that the witness is present in court (r 92*ter*(i)), available for cross-examination and questioning by the judges (r 92*ter*(ii)) and attests that the statement or transcript accurately reflects the witness's declaration and what the witness would say if examined (r 92*ter*(iii)). Thus, r 92*ter* facilitates the admission of written statements and transcripts, provided that the witnesses are available for cross-examination. Prior to the amendments this was not an explicit possibility for statements directly addressing the acts and conduct of the accused. The purpose of introducing r 92*ter* was 'to facilitate the admission of evidence from previous proceedings without going through a process of examination-in-chief. It's not a new procedure; it's ... [Rule] 89(F) codified. [T]he purpose of the procedure ... is to expedite the proceedings. ... The procedure is designed to avoid examination-in-chief'.[117]

Pursuant to r 92*quater*, which has replaced former r 92*bis*(C) as described above, a written statement or transcript may be admitted in lieu of oral testimony if the Chamber is satisfied that the witness has subsequently died, can no longer with reasonable diligence be traced, or is by reason of bodily or mental condition unable to testify orally (r 92*quater*(A)(i)). In addition, the Chamber must find from the circumstances in which the statement was made and recorded that it is reliable (r 92*quater*(A)(ii)). A written statement admitted under this rule does not need to meet the requirements under r 92*bis* and may go to proof of acts and conduct of the accused as charged in the indictment, although that is a factor which may weigh against admission of the evidence, or that part of it (r 92*quater*(B)).[118] The fact that a statement under r 92*quater* is not necessarily excluded if it goes to the acts and conduct of the accused is the main difference as compared to former r 92*bis*(C). Another difference is that the standard of reliability required for admission has gone up from *indicia* of reliability to reliability proper. However, the jurisprudence on this rule has indicated that the applicable test of reliability is equal to the test applicable to former r 92*bis*(C).[119]

The general requirements under r 89(C) apply to evidence admitted under r 92*bis*, r 92*ter* or r 92*quater*.[120] Rule 92*quater* has a much wider ambit than r 92*ter*, allowing

---

[117] *ICTY Prosecutor v Dragomir Milošević*, Transcript (15 Jan 2007) at 354.

[118] Evidence that is pivotal to the prosecution's case is more likely than not admitted under r 92*quater* where it is corroborative and cumulative to other evidence. See *Haradinaj* Decision on Prosecution's Motion for Admission of Evidence Pursuant to Rule 92*quarter* and 13th Motion for Trial-Related Protective Measures (7 Sep 2007), paras 7, 10, 12; *Prlič* Decision on the Prosecution Motion for Admission of a Written Statement Pursuant to Rule 92*quarter* of the Rules (Hasan Rizvic) (14 Jan 2008), paras 13, 16 and 22.

[119] *Milutinović* Decision on Prosecution Motion for Admission of Evidence Pursuant to Rule 92*quater* (16 Feb 2007), paras 4, 7; *Prlič* Decision on the Prosecution Motion for Admission of Evidence pursuant to Rules 92*bis* and *quater* of the Rules (27 Oct 2006), para 8; *Prlič* Decision on Hasan Rizvic, ibid, para 11; *ICTY Prosecutor v Delić*, Decision on Prosecution Motion for Admission of Evidence Pursuant to Rule 92*quarter* (9 Jul 2007) 4; *Haradinaj* Decision on Prosecution's Motion for Admission of Evidence Pursuant to Rule 92*quarter* and 13th Motion for Trial-Related Protective Measures (7 Sep 2007), para 8.

[120] *Milutinović* Decision, ibid, paras 5–6; *Delić* Decision, ibid, 4. It has, however, been held that once the reliability test under Rule 92*quater*(A)(ii) has been met, there is no additional reliability test under r 89(C). See *Haradinaj* Decision, ibid, para 11; *Prlič* Decision, ibid, para 12.

statements and transcripts of witnesses whose demeanour cannot be tested by the Chamber and whose credibility cannot be tested through cross-examination. These amendments, therefore, greatly undermine the principle of orality. The amendments were considered necessary to accelerate the proceedings in light of the tribunals' completion strategy.[121] The SCSL has adopted similar rules. However, the ICTR which has a similar completion strategy did not consider it necessary to incorporate the changes. It is, therefore, questionable whether these curtailments of the principle of orality were truly necessary and whether they have assisted in accelerating the proceedings.

On 10 December 2009 the ICTY adopted another new rule, r 92*quinquies* to allow the admission of testimonial evidence by written statement in lieu of oral testimony. Pursuant to r 92*quinquies*, statements or transcripts containing testimony may be admitted if the maker of the statement was scheduled to testify but failed to attend as a result of improper interference arising from threats, intimidation, injury, bribes or coercion (r 92*quinquies*(A)(i) and (ii)). Such a statement is admissible even if it goes to proof of the acts and conduct of the accused (r 92*quinquies*(B)(iii)), provided that reasonable efforts have been made to secure the attendance of the maker of the statement as a witness (r 92*quinquies*(A)(iii)) and that it is in the interests of justice to admit the statement (r 92*quinquies*(A)(iv)).

This rule appears to have been introduced as a reaction to a number of situations where witnesses were interfered with and refused to testify subsequently, as is alleged to have occurred in the ICTY cases of *Haradinaj* and *Seselj*. It is yet another curtailment of the principle of orality. This increasing trend to resort to paper evidence in lieu of oral testimony without the judges being able to assess the demeanour of the witness and the parties to cross-examine him or her, is at odds with the statutory right to a fair trial.

This trend is not universally supported. Former ICTY Judge Hunt expressed his clear dissent to the supplanting of oral testimony by written statements, holding that this new approach went further than common law or civil law fact-finding method-ologies. Judge Hunt correctly pointed out that there is a fundamental difference with the civil law approach, namely that the dossier relied upon in civil law systems is 'prepared by a judicial officer, who is required to seek out exculpatory and inculpa-tory evidence with equal determination, and who is expected not to favour either the prosecution or the defence'.[122] International criminal tribunals are hybrids between civil law and common law[123] and do not employ an independent judicial officer to take statements, but rather rely on the parties for doing so. The result is that international criminal tribunals, whilst readily accepting the use of out-of-court evidence, have not incorporated the safeguards inherent in domestic systems which have a tendency to rely on paper evidence.[124]

---

[121] SC Resolution 1503 (28 Aug 2003). See also G Boas, 'Developments in the Law of Procedure and Evidence at the International Criminal Tribunal for the Former Yugoslavia and the International Criminal Court' (2001) 12 *Criminal Law Forum* 167, 168–170.

[122] *Milošević* Dissenting Opinion of Judge David Hunt on Admissibility of Evidence-in-Chief in the Form of Written Statement (Majority Decision given 30 Sep 2003) (21 Oct 2003), para 6.

[123] On this, see generally Haveman *et al*, *Supranational Criminal Law*.

[124] PL Robinson, 'Rough Edges in the Alignment of Legal Systems in the Proceedings of the ICTY' (2005) 3 *Journal of International Criminal Justice* 1037, at 1046.

The ICC legal provisions dealing with testimonial evidence do not differ significantly from those originally adopted by the ad hoc international criminal tribunals. Article 69(2) of the ICC Statute clearly states a preference for oral testimony, by providing that:

> The testimony of a witness at trial shall be given in person, except to the extent provided by the measures set forth in Article 68 or in the Rules of Procedure and Evidence. The Court may also permit the giving of viva voce (oral) or recorded testimony of a witness by means of video or audio technology, as well as the introduction of documents or written transcripts, subject to this Statute and in accordance with the Rules of Procedure and Evidence. These measures shall not be prejudicial to or inconsistent with the rights of the accused.

Accordingly, testimonial evidence must be given in person, subject to any exceptions that may be set out in Article 69(2) itself, or elsewhere in the Statute and Rules.[125] Rule 67 authorises the use of audio or video-link technology in hearing *viva voce* witnesses. Pursuant to Rule 68, previously recorded audio or video testimony of a witness, or the transcript or other documented evidence of such testimony, may be admitted in two situations:

(a) If the witness who gave the previously recorded testimony is not present before the Trial Chamber, both the Prosecutor and the defence had the opportunity to examine the witness during the recording; or

(b) If the witness who gave the previously recorded testimony is present before the Trial Chamber, he or she does not object to the submission of the previously recorded testimony and the Prosecutor, the defence and the Chamber have the opportunity to examine the witness during the proceedings.[126]

In *Lubanga*, the written statements of two prosecution witnesses who were available for cross-examination were admitted under r 68(b) in lieu of their examination-in-chief. The Chamber nonetheless recognised that 'there can be material advantages in testimony being given in its entirety viva voce before the Court, particularly when evidence of significance is challenged or requires comprehensive investigation. The live questioning of a witness in open court on all aspects of his or her evidence can have a material impact on the Chamber's overall assessment of the evidence, since oral testimony is, for obvious reasons, of a different nature to a written statement: most importantly the evidence can be fully investigated and tested by questioning, and the Court is able to assess its accuracy, reliability and honesty, in part by observing the conduct and demeanour of the witness'.[127] In this particular situation the Chamber allowed the admission of the statements because they provided background evidence not central to the core issues of the case and there was no indication that the evidence was materially in dispute.[128]

---

[125] Triffterer, *Commentary on the Rome Statute*, 1312–3.

[126] See also *Lubanga* Decision on the Prosecution's Application for the Admission of the Prior Recorded Statements of Two Witnesses (15 Jan 2009), para 19.

[127] Ibid, para 21.

[128] Ibid, para 24.

In another situation the prosecution sought to admit a prior statement of a *viva voce* witness at the close of his testimony. The Chamber dismissed the application because it considered that r 68(b) could not be implemented at the end of the testimony of a witness.[129]

The exact scope of, in particular, r 68(a) has still to be determined. A number of scholars hold the view that Rule 68 is the exclusive avenue on the basis of which testimonial evidence may be admitted in written form.[130] On this issue, there is a pending motion in the *Katanga* case to exclude testimony of a dead witness because this is not covered by r 68, given that the Defence did not have the opportunity to examine the witness during the recording.[131] The testimony of that dead witness was admitted for the purpose of the confirmation hearing. In admitting the statement the single Judge highlighted the difference between the trial and confirmation hearing, which is limited in scope in that it only determines whether a case should proceed to trial. In addition, she pointed out that Article 61(5) of the ICC Statute expressly states that for the purposes of the confirmation hearing 'the Prosecutor may rely on documentary or summary evidence and need not call the witnesses expected to testify at trial'.[132]

The ICC did not adopt any of the above rules, eg r 92*bis*, r 92*ter*, r 92*quater*, or r 92*quinquies*, although r 68(b) is similar to r 92*ter*. Nonetheless, the ICC Rules on admissibility may be flexible enough to allow the admission of statements in lieu of oral testimony over and above the situations explicitly provided for in r 68. Only time will tell what direction the ICC will take in respect of admitting written statements instead of oral testimony.

21.4.3   Prior Inconsistent Statements

In the ICTY case of *Simic et al*, the Chamber denied the prosecution the right to put prior inconsistent statements to the witness, either for the purpose of impeachment or in order to refresh his memory.[133] The Chamber held that the objective of r 92*bis* was to limit the admissibility of this 'very special type of hearsay evidence'. It further held that 'Rule 92*bis* allows the Trial Chamber to admit, in whole or in part, the written evidence of a witness and that portions of the witness statement that are struck out by the Trial Chamber for non-compliance with Rule 92*bis* may not be resurrected by parties for the purpose of cross-examination of the credibility of the witness, and may not be treated as a prior representation for cross-examination purposes as they

---

[129]   *Katanga and Ngudjolo*, Transcripts (23 Feb 2010), 48.

[130]   Triffterer, *Commentary on the Rome Statute*, 1317–18.

[131]   *Katanga and Ngudjolo* Defence Objections to Admissibility in Principal and in Substance (23 Oct 2009).

[132]   *Katanga and Ngudjolo* Decision on the Admissibility for the Confirmation Hearing of the Transcripts of Interview of Deceased Witness 12 (18 Apr 2008).

[133]   ICTY *Prosecutor v Simić et al*, Trial Transcript of 2 Apr 2003, at 17931; Trial Transcript of 15 Apr, 2003, at 16480.

exist only for the purpose of the Rule 92*bis* procedure and do not stand alone'.[134] This decision was found to be in error. The Appeals Chamber held that a witness's prior inconsistent statement could be used in cross-examination for the purpose both of questioning him on contradictions, and for refreshing the witness's memory.[135] Such statements cannot, however, normally be admitted for ascertaining the truth, but merely as a tool to test the witness's credibility or to refresh his or her memory.[136] Some Chambers have held that prior inconsistent statements may be admitted even if the requirements of r 90(A) and r 92*bis* are not complied with, as long as it is clear that the only purpose of their admission is to assess the credibility of *viva voce* witnesses and not to prove the truth of their content.[137]

In the ICTY case of *Limaj*, prior inconsistent statements were admitted as evidence of the truth of their content under Rule 89(C). The case concerned video-recorded statements of two witnesses who had been declared hostile in light of their significant departure in oral testimony from what they had narrated in their previous statements. Given that the statements were video-recorded, shown and discussed at length at trial, the Chamber considered that the statements were sufficiently reliable to be admitted under Rule 89(C).[138]

Similarly at the ICC, prior statements made by the testifying witness may be put to him or her to refresh his or her memory. In one case, it was, however, emphasised that this is the exception to the principle that a witness should testify to what he or she remembers having observed. In order to determine whether such an exception should be made consideration must be given to the person of the witness, including the witness's profile, mastery, facility of expression and ability to remember what was seen or heard, as well as to add nuance to his or her remarks.[139]

If a witness is reluctant to provide precise answers, not because he or she is suffering from memory gaps, but rather because of a personal interest, the witness's prior statement cannot be shown to him or her to refresh his or her memory.[140] In such a case, the prior statement can only be shown to the witness in examination-in-chief if he she is adverse to the case of the party having called him or her. In order to declare a witness adverse or hostile, he or she must give answers in a way that is directly opposed to what he or she affirmed in a previous statement made to the investigators.[141] If not, such a statement may only be put to him in cross-examination

---

[134] *ICTY Prosecutor v Simić et al*, Decision on Prosecutors Motion for Trial Chambers Redetermination of its Decision of 2 Apr 2003 Relating to Cross-Examination of Defence Rule 92*bis* Witnesses or Alternatively Certification under Rule 73(B) of the Rules of Procedure and Evidence (28 Apr 2003) 2–3; relying on *Milošević* Decision on Admissibility of Prosecuting Investigator's Evidence (30 Sep 2002) 11.

[135] *Simić* Decision on Prosecution Interlocutory Appeals on the Use of Statements not Admitted into Evidence Pursuant to Rule 92*bis* as a Basis to Challenge Credibility and to Refresh Memory (23 May 2003), paras 19–20. See also *ICTR Prosecutor v Niyitegeka*, Appeals Chamber Judgment (9 Jul 2004), para 33; *Norman* Oral Decision (16 Jul 2004) 8–9.

[136] *Bagosora* Decision on Nsengiyumva Motion to Admit Documents as Exhibits (26 Feb 2007), paras 6–7.

[137] *Simba* Decision on the Admission of Certain Exhibits, (23 Jun 2005), para. 7; *Simba* Appeal Judgement (28 Nov 2007), para 20; *Norman* Oral Decision (16 Jul 2004) 7–8.

[138] *Limaj* Decision on the Prosecution's Motions to Admit Prior Statements as Substantive Evidence (25 Apr 2005), paras 16, 17, 22, 23, 25, 33, 34.

[139] *Katanga and Ngudjolo*, Transcripts (30 Nov 2009), at 26.

[140] *Katanga & Ngudjolo*, Transcripts (8 Feb 2010), 63–64.

[141] Ibid, 64–69.

to contradict his or her in-court testimony and to test his or her credibility in cross-examination. As such, the statement or at least parts thereof may be admitted into the record. No prior inconsistent statement has yet been admitted before the ICC. The prosecution sought to do so under r 68, but the request was made too late and, therefore, not considered on its merits.[142]

21.4.4   Admissibility of Suspect Interviews

The statement of an accused made prior to trial to the prosecution's investigators can be admitted as evidence in the trial against him, provided it has probative value, reliability, relevance and all procedural guarantees under the rules were respected during the interview.[143] If all conditions for admission are met, the statement of an accused is admissible against the accused even if he decides not to take the stand.[144] The rights of the suspect and accused that need to be respected during the interview are set out in Rules 42–43 and 63 of the ICTY, ICTR and SCSL Rules. The accused is entitled to be represented by counsel at the interview and to be informed of this right. Unless he explicitly and unambiguously waives his right to legal representation the investigators should not interview him unless counsel is by his side. The interview must be voluntary without incentives.[145] The suspect or accused should be made aware of his right not to incriminate himself and the possible consequences of giving an interview.[146] The interview should further be recorded. A statement taken from the accused under circumstances where these rights are respected will normally be admissible under r 89(C) unless that would cause prejudice to the accused.[147]

21.4.5   Admissibility of Suspect Interviews Against a Co-Accused

The admission of suspect interviews is more problematic when this is done with the purpose of using them as evidence against an alleged co-perpetrator. If they are not

---

[142] *Katanga and Ngudjolo*, Transcripts (23 Feb 2010), 48.

[143] *Prlić* Decision on Request for Admission of the Statement of Jadranko Prlić (22 Aug 2007), para 12.

[144] *Halilović* Decision on Interlocutory Appeal Concerning Admission of Record of Interview of the Accused from the Bar Table (19 Aug 2005), para 14.

[145] *Sesay* Written Reasons – Decision on the Admissibility of Certain Prior Statements of the Accused Given to the Prosecution (30 Jun 2008), paras 49–52, 68; *Halilović* Decision, ibid, paras 14–15.

[146] *Prlić* Decision on the Prosecution Motion for the Admission into Evidence of the Testimony of Milivoj Petkovic Given in the Other Cases before the Tribunal (17 Oct 2007), paras 15, 20; *Prlić* Decision on the Admission into Evidence of Slobodan Praljak's Evidence in the Case of Naletilić and Martinović (5 Sep 2007), para 21.

[147] *Prlić* Decision on the Admission into Evidence of Slobodan Praljak's Evidence in the Case of Naletilić and Martinović, ibid, paras 14–15; *Prlić* Decision on the Request for Admission of the Statement of Jadranko Prlić, para 12; *ICTY Prosecutor v Kvočka et al*, Appeals Chamber Judgment (25 Feb 2005), para 128; *Milutinović* Decision on Prosecution Motion to Admit Documentary Evidence (10 Oct 2006), paras 43–44; *ICTY Prosecutor v Popović et al*, Decision on Appeals Against Decision Admitting Material Related to Borovcanin's Questioning (14 Dec 2007), para 32; *Karemera* Decision on Prosecutor's Motion to Admit Prior Sworn Trial Testimony of the Accused Persons (6 Dec 2006). See further section 21.10.

jointly tried, the prosecution should call the maker of the statement in order to use it against another accused. If, however, the alleged co-perpetrators are jointly tried, the prosecution cannot call the maker of the statement as a witness against his alleged co-perpetrator and cannot force him to testify in his own case. The accused who conducted the interview has a right to silence. Accordingly, if he declines to testify, his co-accused is deprived of an opportunity to cross-examine him on the statement he made to the investigators. This is particularly problematic if the accused who gave the interview puts the blame on his co-accused.

The testimony of an alleged perpetrator against his alleged co-perpetrator should be treated with caution, given the significant incentive to shift the blame to the co-perpetrator in order to avoid culpability.[148] Indeed, Chambers have been reluctant to admit such statements, given that this constitutes untested hearsay from an unreliable source. Admission of such a statement would, therefore, be unfair to the co-accused.[149] The ICTY Appeals Chamber, on the other hand, has held that 'it would be wrong to exclude evidence solely because of the intrinsic lack of reliability of the contest of a suspect's questioning in relation to persons who later became that suspect's co-accused'.[150]

The Appeals Chamber's view is related to the fact that interviews from suspects or accused conducted in accordance with Rules 42, 43 and 63, have, in general, sufficient *indicia* of reliability under r 89(C). The circumstances in which such an interview was taken – the suspect having been informed of his right to silence and to legal representation, as well as the audio and video recording of the entirety of the interview including all questions and answers – render said interview sufficiently reliable to be admissible. Accordingly, in the ICTY it has now become common practice to admit statements made by one accused as evidence against a co-accused even if the statement goes to the heart of the case and directly incriminates the co-accused who has no opportunity to examine him on the statement. This is a further curtailment of the principle of orality. Notwithstanding that such statements are a form of testimonial evidence they can be admitted under r 89(C), even if they are not admissible under the applicable rules for the admission of written witness statements, notably r 92*bis*, r 92*ter*, r 92*quater* or r 92*quinquies*.

This development is a step further than in some civil law countries where a statement from one accused cannot be used against his co-accused.[151] In common law this is a type of hearsay evidence, which is inadmissible unless the accused testifies *viva voce* and is subjected to cross-examination by his co-accused.[152]

---

[148] *Popović* Decision on the Admissibility of the Borovcanin Interview and the Amendment of the 65*ter* exhibit list (25 Oct 2007), para 65; see also *ICTY Prosecutor v Blagoević and Jokić*, Decision on Prosecution's Motion for Clarification of Oral Decision Regarding Admissibility of Accused's Statement (18 Sep 2003), para 24; *Prlič* Decision on Request for Admission of the Statement of Jadranko Prlič, paras 22, 25–27.

[149] See *Popović* Decision, ibid, and *Blagoević and Jokić* Decision, ibid.

[150] *Popović* Decision On Appeal Against Decision Admitting Material Related to Borovcanin's Questioning (14 Dec 2007), para 49.

[151] See, for instance Arts 210, 500, 511, 513 and 514 of the Italian Code of Criminal Procedure and its Dutch counterpart (HR 27 mei 1929, NJ 1929, 1329; HR 15 December 1953, NJ 1954, 71).

[152] See *Lee v Illinois* (1986) 476 US 530, 541, where the United States Supreme Court held 'that when one person accuses another of a crime under circumstances in which the declarant stands to gain by

In approving the admissibility of statements from a co-accused the Appeals Chamber of the ICTY considered the position in domestic law but, with regard to civil law jurisdictions, concluded that 'no discernable general principle may be inferred from domestic practice in this area'.[153] Yet, the Appeals Chamber acknowledged that the practice of admitting statements from a co-accused is inconsistent with common law principles. The Appeals Chamber, however, distinguished the international tribunals from common law systems by the fact that international trials are conducted by professional judges, as opposed to a lay jury. According to the Appeals Chamber, 'professional judges are better able to weigh evidence and consider it in its proper context than members of a jury. Furthermore, as opposed to a jury's verdict, professional judges have to write a reasoned decision, which is subject to appeal'.[154]

On this basis the Appeals Chamber allowed the admission of statements of a co-accused under the general provision of r 89(C). The concerns relating to the lack of opportunity to cross-examine the accuser if he decides not to testify and the incentive such accuser has to shift the blame upon others are matters of weight and do not concern admissibility. The Appeals Chamber, however, clearly cautioned for vigilance.

> One of the central tenets of the procedure before the Tribunal is the right of all accused to a fair and public hearing. While such a hearing generally entails the examination of evidence against the accused, this principle is not absolute. In fact, there are various provisions that, by balancing the rights of the accused against other relevant interests, safeguard the overall fairness of the proceedings. The Appeals Chamber recalls that this is a complex feat, since under the cloak of 'fairness' a court may be led to construe troublesome curtailments of the rights of the accused in specific instances, which in turn might impact on fundamental rights of the accused. Trial Chambers are called to be vigilant and effective in protecting those rights.[155]

At the very least, such evidence must be sufficiently corroborated by other evidence.[156]

The admission of statements from one accused as evidence against a co-accused has been an ICTY initiative. At the ICTR this doctrine is less developed and less far-reaching. In one case it was held that it would be antithetical to the integrity of the proceedings to admit those parts of the interview of an accused that concern the co-accused before the accused decides whether to testify.[157] In another case the admission of a statement from another accused was accepted because the accused

---

inculpating another, the accusation is presumptively suspect and must be subjected to the scrutiny of cross-examination'. See further *Cruz v New York* (1987) 481 US 186, 189–190; *Lilly v Virginia* (1999) 527 US 116, 139; *Lobban v R* [1995] 2 All ER 602.

[153] *Prlić* Decision on Appeals against Decision Admitting Transcript of Jadranko Prlić's Questioning into Evidence, para 50

[154] Ibid, para 57.

[155] Ibid, para 41.

[156] Ibid, para 33; *Blagoević and Jokić* Decision on Prosecution's Motion for Clarification of Oral Decision Regarding Admissibility of Accused's Statement (18 Sep 2003), para 26; *Prlić* Decision on Request for Admission of the Statement of Jadranko Prlič (22 Aug 2007), paras 17, 27–28, 33. See further section 21.11.2.

[157] *Karemera* Decision on the Prosecution Motion for Admission into Evidence of Post-Arrest Interviews with Joseph Nzirorera and Mathieu Ngirumpatse (2 Nov 2007), para 46.

was offered an opportunity to cross-examine the other accused.[158] Thus, until now, the ICTR has not gone as far as the ICTY in allowing the admission of incriminating statements made by one accused against another accused. This has not occurred in the context of the SCSL.

At the ICC, there is a pending motion on the admissibility of the transcripts of a recorded interview of an alleged co-perpetrator who has since died. The Defence has challenged the admissibility of the statement made by his co-perpetrator.[159] At the confirmation hearing this statement was admitted, but for the purpose of the confirmation only. The Pre-Trial Chamber held that any dispute regarding the credibility of a witness who may have reasons to distort facts to disguise his own responsibility is not a matter for admissibility, but rather concerns the appropriate weight to be given to the evidence.[160] It remains to be seen whether the Trial Chamber will adopt the same approach.

21.5 Documentary Evidence

Documentary evidence consists of:

> ... documents, produced as evidence for evaluation by the Tribunal. For the purposes of this case, the term document is interpreted broadly, being understood to mean anything in which information of any description is recorded. This interpretation is wide enough to cover not only documents in writing, but also maps, sketches, plans, calendars, graphs, drawings, computerised records, mechanical records, photographs, slides and negatives.[161]

There is no provision regulating the admission of documentary evidence. The general scheme for admissibility of evidence pursuant to r 89(C) has been equally applied to the tendering of documents. In the *Brđanin and Talić* case[162] the ICTY Trial Chamber set out some general principles relating to the admission and weight of documentary evidence. In brief, these principles are as follows:

1   A distinction should be made between legal admissibility of documentary evidence and the weight given to it.[163]

---

[158] *Nyiramasuhuko* Decision on Arlene Shalom Ntahobali's Motion to Exclude Certain Evidence from the Expected Testimony of Kanyibashi's Witness D-2–13-O (29 Jun 2007).

[159] *Katanga and Ngudjolo, Defence Objections to Admissibility in Principal and in Substance* (23 Oct 2009).

[160] *Katanga and Ngudjolo* Decision on the Admissibility for the Confirmation Hearing of the Transcripts of Interview of Deceased Witness (18 Apr 2008), para 12.

[161] *Musema,* Trial Chamber Judgment (27 Jan 2000), para 53; *Karemera* Decision on the Prosecutor's Motion for Admission of Certain Exhibits Into Evidence (25 Jan 2008), para 5.

[162] *Brđanin and Talić* Admission of Evidence Order (15 Feb 2002).

[163] Ibid, para 16. See also *ICTY Prosecutor v Martić*, Decision Adopting Guidelines on the Standards Governing the Admission of Evidence, Annex A Guidelines on the Standards Governing the Admission of Evidence (19 Jan 2006) (*Martić* Guidelines Admission of Evidence), para 2: 'Parties should always bear in mind the basic distinction that exists between the admissibility of documentary evidence and the weight that documentary evidence is given under the principle of free evaluation of evidence. The practice will be, therefore, in favour of admissibility'.

2   Judges are entitled to reverse a decision to exclude evidence if at a later stage 'further evidence emerges that is relevant, has persuasive value and hence justifies the admission of the evidence in question'.[164]

3   The 'mere' admission of a document into evidence does not indicate that the contents will be considered to be 'an accurate portrayal of the facts'. *Inter alia*, authenticity and proof of authorship are important factors, not so much in relation to the admission of documents, but rather in relation to the assessment of the weight of a particular piece of evidence.[165] As already mentioned, 'the threshold standard for the admission of evidence ... should not be set excessively high, as often documents are sought to be admitted into evidence, not as ultimate proof of guilt or innocence, but to provide a context and complete the picture presented by the evidence in general'.[166] At the stage of admission of evidence, 'the implicit requirement of reliability means no more than that there must be sufficient indicia of reliability to make out a *prima facie* case for the admission of that document'.[167]

4   Authenticity is a matter of weight, rather than admissibility.[168]

5   There is 'no blanket prohibition on the admission of documents simply on the grounds that their purported author has not been called to testify'. Also, absence of a signature or a stamp does not necessarily mean it lacks authenticity.[169]

6   Hearsay evidence is admissible if relevant and has probative value.[170]

7   The Tribunal applies the 'best evidence rule', a common law concept.[171] In determining what is the best evidence, whilst exercising its discretion, the Tribunal will take account of the 'particular circumstances attached to each document and to the complexity of [the case in question] and the investigations that preceded it'.[172]

8   Statements that were made involuntary as a result of oppression will be excluded on the basis of r 95. The Trial Chamber held that it is up to the prosecutor to 'prove beyond reasonable doubt that the statement was voluntary and not made under oppression'.[173]

9   'Reliability is an inherent and implicit component of each element of admissibility ... However, in respect to other documentary evidence, the Trial Chamber does not agree that the determination of the issue of reliability, when it arises, should be seen as a separate, first step in assessing a piece of evidence offered for admission'.[174]

10   The Trial Chamber imposes on itself 'an inherent right and duty' to secure the

---

[164] *Brđanin and Talić*, Admission of Evidence Order, para 17; *Martić* Guidelines Admission of Evidence, para 4.

[165] *Brđanin and Talić* Admission of Evidence Order, para 18. See also *Martić* Guidelines Admission of Evidence, para 3.

[166] *Brđanin and Talić*, ibid, para 18. See also *Martić* Guidelines Admission of Evidence, para 3; *Tadić* Judgment on Allegations of Contempt (31 Jan 2000), para 94, where the Appeals Chamber held that a document may be admitted, not so much to prove the guilt of the accused, but to 'demonstrate a particular course of conduct or to explain the events in issue which took place within that period'.

[167] *Brđanin and Talić*, ibid, para 18.

[168] Ibid, para 19. See also *Blagoević and Jokić*, Trial Chamber Judgment (17 Jan 2005), para 29; *Blaškić*, Trial Chamber Judgment (3 Mar 2000), para 36; see Principle 4 enunciated in *Brđanin and Talić*, ibid, para 19. At common law, authenticity, which needs to be proven through direct or circumstantial evidence, is a requirement for the admission of a document.

[169] *Brđanin and Talić*, Admission of Evidence Order (15 Feb 2002), para 20. See also *Martić* Guidelines Admission of Evidence, para. 5.

[170] *Brđanin and Talić*, ibid, para 21. See also *Martić* Guidelines Admission of Evidence, para 8.

[171] For an analysis of the common law concept of the '"best evidence rule" as applied in the UK, see C Allen, *Practical Guide to Evidence*, 2nd edn (London, Cavendish Publishing, 2001) 22.

[172] *Brđanin and Talić*, Admission of Evidence Order, para 22. See also *Martić* Guidelines Admission of Evidence, para 7, where the Chamber held that applying the best evidence rule means that 'the Trial Chamber will rely on the best evidence available in the circumstances of the case and parties are directed to keep in mind this rule when submitting evidence to the Trial Chamber'.

[173] *Brđanin and Talić*, ibid, para 23. See also *Martić* Guidelines Admission of Evidence, para 9.

[174] *Brđanin and Talić*, ibid, para 24.

admission of each piece of evidence that so qualifies. At the same time, the Trial Chamber will go out of its way, *ex officio* where needed, to ensure that pieces of evidence that do not so qualify on the basis of the Rules are not admitted.[175]

Accordingly, there is a tendency to admit documentary evidence provided that the minimum requirements of *indicia* of relevance, probative value and reliability under r 89(C) are met. These requirements have been further defined in the jurisprudence of the ad hoc tribunals. Some Chambers are more inclined to admit evidence than others. A uniform approach does not exist, particularly in respect of the requisite *indicia* of reliability.

One Chamber has held that the fact that the author is unknown, his signature illegible and the seizure disputed constitute matters which will affect the weight to be given to the evidence so long as there is a minimum showing of *indicia* of reliability.[176] This confirms the general approach that only where the evidence is 'so lacking in terms of the indicia of reliability as to be devoid of any probative value', would documents be excluded.[177] Another Chamber, on the other hand, has held that *indicia* of reliability need be demonstrated by giving some explanation of what the document is and whether it is authentic: 'Authenticity and reliability are overlapping concepts: the fact that the document is what it purports to be enhances the likely truth of the contents thereof'.[178] *Indicia* of reliability include:

1. the place where the document was seized;
2. the chain of custody after seizure of the document;
3. corroboration of the contents of the document with other evidence;
4. the nature of the document itself such as signature, stamps, handwriting.[179]

---

[175] Ibid, para 25. See also *Martić* Guidelines Admission of Evidence, para 11, where the Chamber adopted this same principle but went further in explaining why, where necessary, it would intervene *ex officio* to exclude evidence. 'The Trial Chamber emphasises what it considers to be an over-riding principle in matters of admissibility of evidence. The Trial Chamber is, pursuant to the Statute of the Tribunal, the guardian and guarantor of the procedural and substantive rights of the accused. In addition, it has the obligation to strike a balance in seeking to protect the rights of victims and witnesses. As a trial is an often complex journey in search for the truth in relation to the alleged individual criminal responsibility of the Accused, bearing in mind that the truth can never be fully satisfied, the Trial Chamber considers that questions of admissibility of evidence do not arise only when one of the parties raises an objection to a piece of evidence sought to be brought forward by the other party. This Trial Chamber has an inherent right and duty to ensure that only evidence which qualifies for admission under the Rules will be admitted. For this purpose, as may turn out to be necessary from time to time, the Trial Chamber will intervene *ex officio* to exclude from these proceedings those pieces of evidence which, in its opinion, for one or more of the reasons laid down in the Rules, ought not to be admitted in evidence'.

[176] *Simba* Decision on the Admission of Prosecution Exhibits 27 and 28 (31 Jan 2005), para 10.

[177] *ICTR Prosecutor v Rutaganda*, Appeals Chamber Judgment (26 May 2004), para 216.

[178] *Bagosora* Decision on Admission of Tab 19 of Binder Produced in Connection with the Appearance of Witness Maxwell and Nkole (13 Sep 2004), para 8. In this case the Trial Chamber excluded 22 handwritten documents attached to an FBI report because the prosecution, who sought their admission, failed to provide any explanation as to where those documents came from, thus undermining their reliability and authenticity (para 10).

[179] *Bagosora* Decision on Request to Admit United Nations Documents Into Evidence Under Rule 89(C) (25 May 2006), para 4; *Bagosora* Decision on the Prosecutor's Motion for the Admission of Certain Materials Under Rule 89(C) (14 Oct 2004), para 22; *Bagosora* Decision on Admission of Tab 19, ibid, para 8; *Bagosora* Decision on Ntabakuze Motion to Deposit Certain United Nations Documents (19 Mar 2007), para 3; *Karemera* Decision on Joseph Nzirorera's Motion for Admission of UNAMIR Related Documents (28 Nov 2007), para 4; *Prosecutor v Delalićet al*, Appeals Chamber Decision on Application of Defendant Zejnil Delalić for Leave to Appeal Against the Decision of the Trial Chamber of 19 January

None of these requirements are absolute. For instance, a document may be admitted even if there is no proof of the chain of custody, particularly in light of the difficulty of maintaining the chain of custody in armed conflicts.[180]

It should be noted that Chambers are inclined to admit a document without any further debate in situations where the opposite party does not dispute the relevance, probative value and reliability of the document. Documents in general are mostly admitted as evidence, even if their source is dubious, the justification being that they do not usually directly address the issue of guilt, but are of a more general nature.[181]

If a copy of a document is sought to be admitted there should be some explanation about the non-availability of the original, or some confirmation that the copy sought to be tendered genuinely emanates from the original.[182]

When objections are raised on grounds of authenticity or reliability the Chamber may, under r 89(E) of the ICTY Rules and under r 89(D) of the ICTR Rules,[183] request the tendering party to provide it with a verification of the authenticity of evidence obtained out of court. In addition, the Chamber may require the tendering party to 'produce sufficient indicia of reliability to make a *prima facie* case for the admission of the document, audio tape or video in question. On the request of a party or *proprio motu* the Trial Chamber may order the party tendering copies of evidence to present the original or the best legible, audible or visible copy available'.[184]

The party which seeks the admission of a document needs to prove that it meets the criteria necessary for admission.[185] The standard of proof is on the balance of probabilities. This means that the party seeking to tender a document has to show some relevance, probative value and reliability.[186] This must be done for each document. The wholesale admission of lengthy documents on the basis of general submissions regarding their relevance is generally not acceptable because it impedes the expeditiousness of the proceedings and imposes a heavy burden on the Chamber and opposing parties.[187]

1998 for the Admissibility of Evidence (4 Mar 1998), para 18; *Kordić and Čerkez* Decision on Prosecutor's Submissions Concerning 'Zagreb Exhibits' and Presidential Transcripts (1 Dec 2000), paras 43–44.

[180]   *Orić* Trial Chamber Judgement (30 Jun 2006), para 27.

[181]   *Delalić et al* Decision on Admissibility (21 Jun 1998); *Brđanin and Talić* Order on the Standards Governing the Admission of Evidence, (15 Feb 2002), para 18; *Tadić* Appeal Judgment on Allegations of Contempt against Prior Counsel, Milan Vujin, (31 Jan 2000), para 94.

[182]   *Muvunyi* Decision on the Prosecutor's Motion to Admit Documents Tendered during the Cross-Examination of Defence Witness Augustin Ndindliyimana (28 Feb 2006), para 13.

[183]   SCSL Rule 89(D) has been deleted from the SCSL Rules.

[184]   *Martić* Guidelines Admission of Evidence, para 6.

[185]   *Musema* Trial Judgment, para 55. On appeal, Musema claimed that it was not fair to place a burden of proof on the defence to demonstrate that the documents he wished to tender were reliable. Musema alleged that the only burden that was placed upon the defence was the burden to cast reasonable doubt on the prosecution's case. His arguments were rejected. See *Musema* Appeal Judgment (16 Nov 2001), para 39.

[186]   *Musema* Trial Chamber Judgment, para 56; see also Principle 3 enunciated in *Brđanin and Talić* Admission of Evidence Order, para 18; *Bagosora* Decision on Admission of Tab 19, para 7; *ICTY Prosecutor v Hadžihasanović & Kubura*, Decision on the Admissibility of Documents of the Defence of Enver Hadžihasanović (22 June 2005), para 21.

[187]   *Karemera* Interim Order for the Prosecution to Identify Relevant and Probative Passages of Certain Materials it Intends to Tender into Evidence Under Rule 89(C) of the Rules of Procedure and Evidence (8 Aug 2007), para 12.

When the rights of the accused are at stake, it may be more appropriate to apply the burden of proof beyond reasonable doubt to demonstrate reliability.[188]

Unlike common law jurisdictions, these documents do not necessarily need to be presented by a witness.[189] In certain circumstances it may nonetheless be necessary to call a witness to authenticate the document even for the purpose of admission. For instance, it has been held that an audio-taped interview was not admissible without the journalist testifying to the authenticity of the tape.[190] Similarly, the admission of a diary without calling the purported author may be unfair to the accused.[191]

In the SCSL, unlike the ICTY and ICTR, it has been held that a document must be tendered through a witness and a foundation must be established.[192] The Appeals Chamber held as follows:

> Undoubtedly, the Trial Chamber in exercising its unfettered discretion under Rule 89(C) ('may admit any relevant evidence') as to whether or not the proposed evidence is relevant, cannot properly do so in thin air. When determining the relevance of a document, the Trial Chamber must require the tendering party to lay a foundation of the witness's competence to give evidence in relation to that document. ... Without a connection to the document, the witness is only capable of offering opinion evidence ... It is imperative on the Prosecution to lay sufficient foundation to enable the Trial Chamber, in properly exercising its discretion, to come to a conclusion that, *prima facie*, the proposed evidence is relevant.[193]

When *indicia* of relevance, probative value and reliability have been established the document can be admitted pursuant to r 89(C). Unless the admission is reconsidered at a later stage upon showing that these *indicia* were based on a false premise,[194] the question whether the relevance, probative value and reliability are sufficient for judges to rely on the document is a question of weight, not of admissibility. Credibility is not yet an issue at the admission stage.[195]

The result of maintaining such a low threshold for admissibility of documentary evidence is that thousands of lengthy documents are being admitted in the course of each trial. According to a distinct scholar,[196] it is not helpful to the judges to admit massive amounts of evidence that are of mere peripheral significance. In such a labyrinth of papers, judges easily lose track of the pivotal issues in 'a cloud of

---

[188] *Musema* Trial Chamber Judgment, para 58, thereby relying on the arguments in *Delalić* Decision on Zdravko Mucic's Motion for the Exclusion of Evidence (2 Sept 1997).

[189] *Blaškić* Trial Chamber Judgment, para 35; *Blagoević and Jokić* Trial Chamber Judgement (17 Jan 2005), para 29.

[190] *ICTY Prosecutor v Mrkšić et al*, Decision on Motion to Reopen Prosecution Case (23 Feb 2007).

[191] *Delić* Decision on Prosecution Submission on the Admission of Documentary Evidence (16 Jan 2008), para 14.

[192] *Taylor* Trial Transcript, (21 Aug 2008) 14253; confirmed in *Taylor* Decision on Prosecution Notice of Appeal and Submissions Concerning the Decision Regarding the Tender of Documents, (6 Feb 2009), para 35.

[193] *Taylor* Decision, ibid, paras 40–42.

[194] *Muvunyi* Decision on Motion to Strike or Exclude Portions of Prosecutor's Exhibit #34, Alternatively Defence Objections to Prosecutor's Exhibit #34 (30 May 2006).

[195] *Musema* Judgment, ibid, para 57; *Delalić and Others* Decision on the Motion of the Prosecution for the Admissibility of Evidence (*Delalić* decision on admissibility) (21 Jun 1998); *Rutaganda* Appeal Judgment, para 216: reliability and credibility are not synonymous.

[196] Professor P Murphy, Circuit Judge, 'Excluding Justice or Facilitating Justice? International Criminal Law would Benefit from Rules of Evidence' (2008) 12 *International Journal of Evidence and Proof* 1.

irritating and useless collateral issues'.[197] Having to search through so many documents for matters that are probative, reliable and relevant to the charges does not facilitate the judges' important and difficult task of ascertaining the truth. In addition, allowing the admission of unnecessarily large amounts of evidence, whose relevance to the charges is minimal, is a waste of the Court's time and resources. This is the case not only because the judges will have to spend much time assessing the relevance of the material, but also because it misdirects the efforts of other parties to the case and requires the Defence to meet issues only remotely relevant. It is not suggested that judges should favour wholesale exclusion, but it is regrettable that they have opted for practically a wholesale admission.

It seems that the ICC is going in the same direction. Until now, and particularly for the purpose of the confirmation hearing, the tendency is to admit practically all evidence. The conditions for admission of documentary evidence at the ICC are similar to those at the ad hoc tribunals. In order to admit a document several *indicia* of reliability, relevance and probative value must be met. Reliability is interwoven with authenticity. The fact that a document is not signed or dated does not necessarily deprive it of authenticity.[198] It has further been held that the admission of documents does not prejudice the fairness of the trial provided there are sufficient means to test and evaluate the reliability of those documents.[199] Equally, 'photographic evidence will be admissible for the purposes for which it is submitted and will be accorded probative value in proportion to (i) the level of authentication provided by the witness who introduces the evidence, and (ii) the reliability of the accompanying witness statement'.[200]

21.6   Hearsay Evidence

Hearsay has been described as 'the statement of a person made otherwise than in the proceedings in which it is being tendered, but nevertheless being tendered in those proceedings in order to establish the truth of what that person says'.[201] On the basis of this definition hearsay evidence may cover 'any written document, including expert reports and official documents, which is not adduced by its author while testifying, as well as any behaviour carried out and words uttered by a person other than the witness who reports them in court to establish the truth of the matter'.[202] Common law and civil law systems have adopted different positions in relation to hearsay evidence although traditionally more so than now. While the civil law traditions have

---

[197]   See Murphy, ibid, at 25, citing the address of Sir James Fitzjames Stephen, a distinguished advocate and judge, to the Council of the Governor-General of India of 31 March 1871 (reprinted in P Murphy (ed.), *Evidence, Proof and Facts: A Book of Sources* (Oxford, Oxford University Press, 2003) 65 *et seq*). See also Murphy, ibid, at 22, where he expresses the need to protect fact-finders, even where professionally trained, against misleading evidence and to promote efficient trials.

[198]   *Katanga* Confirmation Decision, para.112.

[199]   *Lubanga* Decision on Admissibility, para 41; *Katanga* Confirmation Decision, para 165.

[200]   *Katanga* Confirmation Decision, para 165.

[201]   *Aleksovski* Appeals Decision on Admissibility (16 Feb 1999), para 14.

[202]   A Rodrigues and C Tounaye, 'Hearsay Evidence' in R May *et al, Essays on* ICTY *Procedure and Evidence in Honour of Gabrielle Kirk McDonald* (The Hague, Kluwer, 2001) 291.

no specific ground on which to exclude hearsay evidence,[203] at common law hearsay evidence is inadmissible save a number of limited exceptions.[204]

The ad hoc tribunals do not evaluate the admissibility of hearsay evidence in the same way as common law courts. Their view is that, provided that the minimum requirements under r 89(C) are met, hearsay evidence is admissible, given that the trials are conducted by professional judges who seek to avoid being hampered by technicalities.[205] Accordingly, statements made out of court are admissible in order to prove the veracity of their content, rather than merely the fact that they were made. Hearsay evidence 'may be oral, as where a witness relates what a third person confided to him out of court, or written, as when (for example) an official report written by someone who is not called as a witness is tendered in evidence. Rule 89(C) clearly encompasses both these forms of hearsay evidence'.[206]

In principle, witnesses must provide oral testimony in the presence of the accused (r 89(F) of the ICTY Rules and r 90(A) of the ICTR/SCSL Rules in combination with Article 21(4)(e) of the ICTY Statute, Article 20(4)(e) of the ICTR Statute and Article 17(4)(e) of the SCSL Statute).[207] However, it has been underscored that the principle set out in r 90(A) of the ICTR Rules, which is currently set out in different terms in r 89(F) of the ICTY Rules, does not necessarily indicate that priority is given to direct and oral evidence. Instead, this rule deals with technicalities in relation to the reception of testimony. Following that approach, irrespective of the availability of the actual witness, both parties can produce hearsay evidence instead.[208] To avoid a violation of the Trial Chamber's statutory obligation to safeguard the fairness of the trial, which includes the right to cross-examination pursuant to Article 21(4)(e) ICTY

---

[203] The European Convention on Human Rights, of which a large number of European civil law jurisdictions are members, may constitute a possible ground for excluding hearsay evidence. Although the European Court of Human Rights does not prohibit the use of hearsay evidence *per se*, it has imposed restrictions on States in its application. Assessing evidence is primarily a matter for domestic courts. See, eg *Delta v France* (1990) 16 EHRR 574, para 35, and *Van Mechelen and Others v The Netherlands* (1997) 25 EHRR 647, para 50. However, where the right to a fair trial is affected it will nevertheless intervene, such as in *Lüdi v Switzerland* (1992) 15 EHRR 172, para 49. Hearsay evidence should not be the most substantial evidence (*Unterpertinger v Austria* (1986) 13 EHRR 175, para 33), otherwise, its admission violates the right to question the witness (Art 6(3)(d)). Reading out statements rather than hearing the witness is itself not inconsistent with Art 6, 'but the use made of the statements as evidence must nevertheless comply with the rights of the defence'. (*Unterpertinger v Austria*, para 31).

[204] The necessity for the exclusionary rule of hearsay evidence is explained in the case of *Teper v R* [1952] AC 480. The truthfulness and accuracy of the person whose words are spoken by another witness cannot be tested by cross-examination and the light which his demeanour would throw on his testimony is lost.

[205] In the SCSL case of *Brima* , the Trial Chamber held that '[i]t is well settled in the practice of international tribunals that hearsay evidence is admissible' (*Brima* Decision on Joint Defence Evidence to Exclude All Evidence from Witness TF1–277 Pursuant to Rule 89(C) and/or Rule 95 (24 May 2005), para 12. See further Boas, 'Creating Laws of Evidence', 48–58.

[206] *Galić* Decision on Interlocutory Appeal Concerning Rule 92*bis*(C) (7 Jun 2002), para 27. See section 21.7 for the admissibility of official reports.

[207] European Convention on Human Rights, Art 6(3)(d); International Covenant on Civil and Political Rights, Art 14(4)(e), upon which ICTY and ICTR Statutes, Arts 21 and 20 are based. As the European Court of Human Rights pointed out, *inter alia*, in *Kostovski v The Netherlands* (1989) 12 EHRR 434, para 41, '[i]n principle all the evidence has to be produced in the presence of the accused at a public hearing with a view to cross-examination, although statements obtained at a pre-trial stage could be used as evidence, provided the rights of the defence were respected'.

[208] *Aleksovski* Appeals Decision on Admissibility (16 Feb 1999).

Statute, Article 20(4)(e) ICTR Statute, and Article 17(4)(e) SCSL Statute, the Chambers have given a wide interpretation to this right, in that it applies to 'the witness testifying before the Trial Chamber and not to the initial declarant whose statement has been transmitted to this Trial Chamber by the witness'.[209] Cross-examination is the only tool available to the defence to test the reliability and credibility of the actual witness. The admission of hearsay evidence gravely undermines the tool of cross-examination.

The issue of hearsay arose for the first time in the *Tadić* case.[210] There the Trial Chamber held that there was no 'blanket prohibition on the admission of hearsay evidence',[211] but that its admission depends on its relevance and probative value, focusing on its reliability.[212] Many subsequent cases followed this example.[213] In the *Kordić* and *Čerkez* case approximately 40 transcripts from other trials were admitted. Only those which repeated testimonies that were already heard were excluded, due to lack of relevance. The Chamber also determined that the witnesses should be called where the transcripts addressed the guilt of the accused directly.[214] In the *Aleksovski* case[215] the Trial Chamber did not accept that the admission of a transcript from another case violated the fundamental right of the accused to confrontation and cross-examination guaranteed by the ICTY Statute.[216] However, the Trial Chamber added that 'this ruling will not preclude the application by the Defence to cross-examine the witnesses on the ground that there are significant relevant matters not covered by cross-examination in [the] *Blaškić* [case] which ought to be raised in this case'.[217] The ICTR and SCSL adopted a similar approach; the Chambers have the discretion to admit hearsay evidence, even where the source cannot be examined and is not corroborated by direct evidence.[218] As an SCSL Trial Chamber held, '[t]he probative value of hearsay evidence is something to be considered by the Trial Chamber at the end of the trial when weighing and evaluating the evidence as a whole, in light of the context and nature of the evidence itself, including the credibility and reliability of the relevant witness'.[219]

---

[209] *Blaškić* Hearsay Decision (21 Jan 1998), para 29.
[210] *Tadić* Decision on Hearsay (5 Aug 1996).
[211] Ibid, para 7.
[212] Ibid, para 19.
[213] See *Aleksovski* Appeals Decision on Admissibility (16 Feb 1999).
[214] *Kordić and Čerkez* Decision on the Tulica Report (29 Jul 1999).
[215] *Aleksovski* Appeals Decision on Admissibility (16 Feb 1999).
[216] Ibid, para 25.
[217] Ibid, para 28.
[218] *ICTR Prosecutor v Rwamakuba*, Trial Chamber Judgement (20 Sep 2006), para 34. See further, *Musema* Trial Judgment, para 51, where the Trial Chamber noted that 'hearsay evidence is not inadmissible *per se*, even when it cannot be examined at its source or when it is not corroborated by direct evidence. Rather, the Chamber has considered such hearsay evidence with caution in accordance with Rule 89'; see also *ICTR Prosecutor v Ntahobali et al*, Decision on Ntahobali's Motion to Rule Inadmissible the Evidence of Prosecution Witness 'TN' (1 Jul 2002), para 21, where the Trial Chamber held that 'hearsay evidence is permissible at the Chamber's discretion'. See also *Norman* Fofana-Appeal Against Decision Refusing Bail (11 Mar 2005), para 22.
[219] *Norman* Decision, ibid, para 15.

The process of admitting hearsay evidence is similar to the process of admitting other forms of evidence. The core elements are relevance, probative value and reliability.[220] In evaluating the relevance, probative value and reliability of the hearsay evidence:

the Trial Chamber will hear both the circumstances under which the evidence arose as well as the content of the statement. The Trial Chamber may be guided by, but not bound to, hearsay exceptions generally recognised by some national legal systems, as well as the truthfulness, voluntariness, and trustworthiness of the evidence, as appropriate.

In bench trials before the ad hoc tribunals this is the most efficient and fair method to determine the admissibility of out-of-court statements.[221] In sum, from the case law it appears that hearsay evidence is admitted as a rule, even where a statement constitutes multiple hearsay. This fact on its own gravely undermines the right to cross-examination, which is inherent to a fair trial. This disadvantage to the defence can be partly compensated if judges take it sufficiently into account when weighing the evidence.[222]

At the ICC hearsay evidence is similarly admissible. Challenges to hearsay evidence may affect its probative value, but not its admissibility.[223] For the purpose of the confirmation hearing, even anonymous hearsay is admissible. As was held by the Pre-Trial Chamber in *Lubanga*:

[T]here is nothing in the Statute or the Rules which expressly provides that the evidence which can be considered hearsay from anonymous sources is inadmissible per se. In addition, the Appeals Chamber has accepted that, for the purpose of the confirmation hearing, it is possible to use items of evidence which may contain anonymous hearsay, such as redacted versions of witness statements.[224]

Summaries of anonymous witness statements are also admissible for the purpose of the confirmation hearing, provided that the Pre-trial Chamber takes sufficient steps to ensure that such summaries 'are used in a manner that is not prejudicial to or inconsistent with the rights of the accused and with a fair and impartial trial'.[225]

---

[220] *Naletilić & Martinović* Appeal Judgement (3 May 2006), paras 217 and 516; *Milošević* Decision on Testimony of Defence Witness Dragan Jasovic (15 Apr 2005) 4; *Milutinović* Decision Denying Prosecution's Second Motion for Admission of Evidence Pursuant to Rule 92*bis* (13 Sep 2006), para. 5; *Prlić* Decision on Appeals Against Decision Admitting Transcript of Jadranko Prlić's Questioning into Evidence, para 52.

[221] *Tadić* Decision on Hearsay, para 19.

[222] In light of their task to ensure that the trial is fair Chambers are required to do so. See *Aleksovski* Decision on Prosecutor's Appeal on Admissibility of Evidence (16 Feb 1999), para. 15, and; *Semanza* Decision on the Defence Motion For Exclusion of Evidence on the Basis of Violations of the Rules of Evidence, Res Gestae, Hearsay and Violations of the Statute and Rules of the Tribunal, (23 Aug 2000). See also *Milošević* Decision on Testimony of Defence Witness Dragan Jasovic (15 Apr 2005) 5, where the Trial Chamber held that hearsay evidence may be admitted if sufficient indicia of reliability are established; *Galić* Decision on Interlocutory Appeal Concerning Rule 92*bis*(C) (7 Jun 2002), para 27.

[223] *Lubanga* Confirmation Decision, para 103; *Katanga* Confirmation Decision, paras 118–120. 137.

[224] *Lubanga*, ibid, para 101; reiterated in *Katanga*, ibid, para 118, which also relied on ECHR jurisprudence, particularly *Kostovski v The Netherlands*, discussed above, para 44.

[225] *Lubanga* Appeals Chamber Judgment of the Appeal of Mr Thomas Lubanga Dyilo against the decision of Pre-Trial Chamber I entitled First Decision on the Prosecution Requests and Amended Requests for Redactions under Rule 81 (14 Dec 2006), para 2.

21.7   The Investigator's Report

In civil law systems it is common for police investigators to file a dossier containing the results of their investigations. This may include witness statements, scientific reports, psychoanalysis reports and others. It is often considered unnecessary to call for testimony the witnesses whose statements are duly reported in the dossier. Judges rely on the accuracy of the police investigator's report.[226] This approach gravely undermines the right to cross-examine and is, in specific circumstances, severely criticised by the European Court of Human Rights.[227] The prosecution in the ad hoc tribunals has attempted to pursue this controversial practice which is encountered in some civil law countries, such as Belgium, France and the Netherlands.

In the ICTY *Kordić and Čerkez* case[228] the prosecutor proposed to submit into evidence[229] a dossier of evidence relating to the attack on Tulica that took place in June 1993. The dossier itself contained seven categories of documents:

(i)   five maps relevant to the presentation;
(ii) one video containing footage relevant to the presentation;
(iii) eight witness statements;
(iv) four court transcripts;
(v)   exhumation documents, including on-site reports, photographs and death certificates;
(vi) photographs, a schematic diagram and a map relating to destruction of property;
(vii) 13 photographic 'stills' taken from the video footage.

The prosecutor suggested calling the investigator for cross-examination by the defence in respect of the materials in his report, including the statements of persons who were not to be called as witnesses.[230] The defence objected on the basis that the inclusion of the Tulica report would amount to a violation of the fundamental right of the accused to 'examine, or have examined, the witnesses against him' (Article 21(4)(e) of the ICTY Statute). The defence underlined the fact that the report contained second, or third-hand hearsay evidence.[231] While confirming that relevant hearsay evidence may be admitted under r 89(C),[232] the Tribunal determined that not all categories of the proposed evidence should be held admissible. The report itself was not admitted into evidence as the investigator could not be qualified as a factual

---

[226] In France great importance is attached to a '*process-verbal*', the contents of which, in relation to 'contraventions' (ie, misdemeanours) are held to be true unless the contrary is proven (Code de Procédure Pénale, Art 537). As a result, the burden of proof is shifted. In relation to crimes the judges are able to assess the weight of the information contained in such '*procès-verbal*' in accordance with their inner conviction (Code de Procédure Pénale, Art 430); West *et al*, 221–22. In the Dutch system, an accused can be convicted on the contents of a '*process-verbal*' only (Wetboek van Strafvordering, Art 344(2)), which is an exception to the rule that evidence needs to be corroborated (Wetboek van Strafvordering, Arts 341(4) and 342(3)).

[227] In particular, the European Court of Human Rights has condemned this approach where witnesses are not called to testify without taking proper action to safeguard the right 'to examine or have examined witnesses against him' (Art 6(3)(d) ECHR). See, eg *Van Mechelen*, discussed above, at 691; *Visser v The Netherlands*, Judgment of 14 February 2002.

[228] *Kordić and Čerkez* Decision on the Tulica Report (29 Jul 1999).

[229] Ibid, para 7.

[230] Ibid, para 8.

[231] Ibid, para 9.

[232] Ibid, para 19.

witness, nor as an expert witness. He gathered materials long after the events took place and was thus not in a position to say anything more than what materials were actually contained in the dossier.[233] Instead, the Tribunal looked at the materials independently, rather than the report as a whole. As for the witness statements (iii), the Tribunal held that 'this is not an appropriate case for the exercise of the discretion under that provision [r 89(C)], as it would amount to the wholesale admission of hearsay untested by cross-examination, namely the attack on Tulica and would be of no probative value'.[234] As for the transcripts (iv), the Trial Chamber held that there was no justification for admitting the transcript of a witness testimony given earlier in the same trial. The inclusion of this testimony would therefore be 'unnecessarily repetitious'.[235] The transcripts of three other witnesses were found admissible, as these had been cross examined in the *Blaškić* case and were considered as sharing a common interest with the defence in the case in question. The defence was given the right to cross-examine the witnesses on matters which were not raised in the *Blaškić* case.[236] The Trial Chamber admitted into evidence the exhumation documents (v), consisting of an on-site report carried out by an Investigating Judge for the Sarajevo Cantonal Court, photograph documentation concerning exhumation autopsy and identification and death certificates. With regard to the on-site report the Trial Chamber, however, held that '[a]ny assumptions or conclusions which are expressed in this material will be disregarded by the Trial Chamber and will not form part of the record of evidence which it will consider in determining the innocence or guilt of the accused'.[237] Thus, the Chamber refused to admit a dossier as a whole without examining the materials independently.[238]

In the ICTY *Milošević* case the Trial Chamber refused to admit into evidence a summary of various written statements put together by a prosecution investigator, because the investigator's conclusions constituted hearsay evidence of little or no probative value and would not assist the Trial Chamber in performing its task of assessing the weight of the written statements whereupon the investigator drew his conclusions. That assessment did not require expertise beyond that which was within any capacity of a tribunal of fact; and the investigator's summary would not, in the eye of the public, appear to be an independent evaluation of the evidence. The investigator was further not allowed to testify as per the witness statements because they were not admissible pursuant to r 92*bis*; and the infringement of the right to cross-examine the accusers would not be remedied by allowing the defence to cross-examine the prosecution investigator.[239] The Appeals Chamber confirmed the Trial Chamber's decision.[240]

In the ICTR case of *Bizimungu et al* the Trial Chamber considered a prosecution application for the admission under r 89(C) of a report on anti-Tutsi propaganda

---

[233] Ibid, para 20.
[234] Ibid, para 23.
[235] Ibid, para 26.
[236] Ibid, para 28.
[237] Ibid, para 36
[238] Boas, 'Creating Laws of Evidence', 68–72.
[239] *Milošević*, English transcripts of 20 Feb 2002, 672–73 and of 30 May 2002, 5931–33, 5936, 5940–44.
[240] *Milošević* Decision on Admissibility of Prosecution Investigator's Evidence (30 Sep 2002), paras 17 and 21–24.

prepared by a Rwandese working for the prosecution. The Trial Chamber rejected the application due to incomplete disclosure of the sources upon which the report relied. This incomplete disclosure clearly undermined the right of the defence to effective cross-examination and the Chamber's ability to assess the authenticity, reliability, and probative value of the report and the credibility of the sources upon which it relied. However, the Trial Chamber conceived that reports based on the opinion of a consultant or investigator may be admissible provided that the report is based on the witness's own observation.[241]

In the ICTY case of *Martić* the Prosecutor was authorised to call an intelligence analyst. However, the Chamber attributed no weight to his views and conclusions.[242] There is as yet no ICC jurisprudence on the admissibility of this type of evidence.

21.8   Expert Evidence

At common law a witness cannot make a value judgment or express an opinion. The reason for this prohibition against value judgments or opinions is justified because the fact-finder is to draw his own conclusions on the facts brought before him; the witness should not replace this function of the fact-finder.[243] Exceptionally, experts are entitled to give their opinion within the limits of their expertise. If a person qualifies as an expert on the basis of his professional qualifications or expertise, which requires special skills and knowledge, and the expert's opinion is likely to be outside the experience and knowledge of a judge or jury, the opinion may be admitted into evidence.[244] If judges or jury members are capable of forming their own conclusions on the facts without the assistance of an expert opinion such opinion is irrelevant and therefore not admissible into evidence.

An important rule is the 'ultimate issue rule': the expert cannot testify as to the guilt of the alleged perpetrator.[245] Another important rule is that an expert cannot express the opinion of another expert or assistant-expert (primary facts). He is, however, permitted to rely on the opinions of other experts in forming his own

---

[241] *Bizimungu* Oral Decision (8 Oct 2004) 29–31.

[242] *Martić* Trial Chamber Judgement (12 Jun 2007), para 35.

[243] *R v Robb* (1991) 93 Cr App R 161; Allen, *Practical Guide to Evidence*, 307–16.

[244] In *R v Silver Lock* [1894] 2 QB 766, handwriting was considered to be an expertise on the basis that it required special skills and knowledge. See also *R v Turner* [1975] QB 834, *per* Lawton LJ, and *R v Robb*, ibid.

[245] See however the English case *R v Stockwell* (1993) 97 Cr App R 260, where it was found acceptable for an expert witness to give his opinion on an ultimate issue, such as identification, provided the judge directed the jury that they were not bound to accept the opinion. See also US Federal Rules of Evidence, r 704(a), which states: 'Except as provided in subdivision (b), testimony in the form of opinion or inference otherwise admissible is not objectionable because it embraces an ultimate issue to be decided by the trier of fact'. Rule 704(b) provides that when an accused's mental state or condition is in issue (such as premeditation in homicide, lack of predisposition in entrapment, or the true affirmative defence of insanity), an expert witness may not testify that the defendant did or did not have the mental state or condition constituting an element of the crime charged or of the defence.

opinion (expert's facts). It is very difficult not to rely to some extent on hearsay evidence, as one's expertise is normally based on someone else's expertise.[246]

In civil law systems generally there is little that binds the court in relation to expert opinion evidence. It is entirely within the discretion of the court to determine who can be qualified as an expert and on what basis. In practice, civil law courts tend to accept expert evidence without much scrutiny. This is so given that experts are mostly court appointed and, therefore, presumed neutral. The reliability of expert evidence has, therefore, rarely been questioned in civil law systems.[247] There are fewer limits regarding the subject matters which experts may address and there is no equivalence to the ultimate issue rule of common law.[248]

In principle, the ad hoc tribunals follow the common law approach. Testimony qualifies as expert testimony where it is 'intended to enlighten the judges on specific issues of a technical nature, requiring special knowledge in a specific field'.[249] The evidence given by the expert needs to be relevant and useful for the Chamber's deliberation.[250]

The party calling an expert must demonstrate the qualifications of the person as an expert, as well as the relevance and probative value of his testimony.[251] If the evidence relates to legal issues, rather than issues of a technical nature, it will not be admitted unless such legal issues fall outside the knowledge and expertise of professional judges, for instance, where they fall under domestic law.[252] In any other situations

---

[246] Under US Federal Rules on Evidence, rr 703 and 705, an expert may give a direct opinion upon facts and data, including technically inadmissible reports, provided the reports or other data are 'of a type reasonably relied upon by experts in the particular field in forming opinions or inferences upon the subject'. See *McCormick on Evidence*, 28–29.

[247] See, however, *Mantovanelli v France* (1997) 24 EHRR 32, where the European Court found that an expert opinion must be accompanied by some information concerning the methodology used in reaching its conclusion.

[248] PTC van Kampen, *Expert Evidence Compared: Rules and Practices in the Dutch and American Criminal Justice System* (Antwerp, Intersentia, 1998) 113–114, citing *Vogt v Germany* (1996) 21 EHRR 205, where a legal conclusion on ultimate issue in an expert report was accepted without any reasonable basis.

[249] *Akayesu* Decision on a Defence Motion for the appearance of an Accused as an Expert Witness (9 Mar 1998); reiterated in *Nahimana* Decision on the Expert Witnesses for the Defence (24 Jan 2003), para 2. In the case of *Prosecutor v Delić*, Decision on Paul Cornish's Status as an Expert, (20 Mar 2008), para. 12, a proposed military expert did not qualify as an expert because he lacked specialised knowledge of the Bosnian conflict, particularly central Bosnia. Similarly, in *Popović* Second Decision Regarding the Evidence of General Rupert Smith (11 Oct 2007) 4, a British general did not qualify as an expert in respect of the function and operation of the General Staff of the Bosnian Serb Army. He was, however, allowed to testify as a factual witness as per his personal observations with members of that army.

[250] *Nahimana* Decision on the Expert Witnesses for the Defence (24 Jan 2003), paras 6 and 11; *Bizimungu* Decision on Casimir Bizimungu's Urgent Motion for the Exclusion of the Report and Testimony of Deo Sebahire Mbonyinkebe (2 Sep 2005), para 12; *Nyiramasuhuko* Oral Decision on the Qualification of Mr Edmond Babin as Defence Expert Witness (13 Apr 2005), para 5; *Karemera* Order Relating to Defence Witness Bernard Lugan (5 May 2008), para 7; *Milošević* Decision on Admission of Expert Report of Robert Donia (15 Feb 2007), para 10; *ICTY Prosecutor v Stanišić and Simatović*, Decision on Prosecution's Submission of the Expert Report of Nina Tromp and Christian Nielsen Pursuant to Rule 94*bis* (18 Mar 2008), para 11; *Milošević* Decision on Admissibility of Expert Report of Vasilije Krestić (7 Dec 2005), para 6.

[251] *Bizimungu* Oral Decision on Qualification of Prosecution Witness Jean Rubaduka (24 Mar 2005).

[252] For instance, in *ICTY Prosecutor v Boškovski and Tarčulovski*, Decision on Prosecution's 94*bis* Notice re Expert Witness Slagjana Taseva (8 Feb 2008), a former employee of the Ministry of Interior of

legal expertise does not assist the professional judges who are well capable of drawing their own conclusions on legal matters.[253] In the *Military I* case, the ICTR Trial Chamber held that:

> ... [i]t is widely accepted and the parties in this case do not dispute that the role of an expert is to provide opinions or inferences to assist the finders of fact in understanding factual issues. In addition, there is no dispute that before being permitted to submit opinion testimony, the Chamber must find that the expert is competent in her proposed field or fields of expertise. The expert must possess some specialised knowledge acquired through education, experience, or training in a field that may assist the fact finders to understand the evidence or to assess a fact at issue.[254]

An expert witness is only permitted to give testimony which falls within the scope of his expertise.[255] It has also been held that expert witnesses cannot, in principle, testify as per the acts and conduct of the accused.[256] Most Chambers have admitted expert reports and testimony only to the extent that they addressed general matters, not where they speculate on the behaviour of the accused. The Chamber is the only competent body to make determinations on the ultimate issues of fact and law in each case.[257] Thus, in general, the tribunals respect the 'ultimate issue' rule of common law. The SCSL has been very explicit about upholding the ultimate issue

---

FYROM, who was also a Professor of criminal law, was allowed to provide expert opinion on the regulations and laws governing criminal investigations in FYROM. See also *Stakić* Appeal Judgement (22 Mar 2006), para 164.

[253] *Sesay* Decision on Admissibility of Certain Parts of Expert Report of Johan Hederstedt (29 Jul 2008), paras 23–24; *Nahimana* Decision on the Expert Witnesses for the Defence (24 Jan 2003), paras 16 and 22; *Nahimana* Decision to Reconsider the Trial Chamber's Decision of 24 January 2003 on the Defence Expert Witnesses (25 Feb 2003), para 4; *Stakić* Appeal Judgment, para 164; *Popović* Decision on the Admissibility of the Expert Report and Proposed Expert Testimony of Professor Schabas (1 Jul 2008). However, in the *Nahimana* Appeal Judgment, para 71, an expert was permitted to draw the legal conclusion that widespread attacks against the Tutsi population across Rwanda began after the plane crash on 6 April 1994.

[254] *Bagosora* Oral Decisions on Defence Objections and Motions to Exclude the Testimony and Report of the Prosecution's proposed Expert Witness, Dr Alison Des Forges, or to Postpone her Testimony at Trial (4 Sep 2002), para 5; see also *Bagosora* Decision on Motion for Exclusion of Expert Witness Statement of Filip Reyntjens (28 Sep 2004), para 8; *Nahimana* Oral Decision (20 May 2002) 122–26; *Martic* Decision on Prosecution's Motions for Admission of Transcripts Pursuant to Rule 92*bis* and of Expert Reports Pursuant to Rule 94*bis* (13 Jan 2006), para 22; *Bizimungu* Oral Decision on Qualification of Prosecution Expert Sebahire Deo Mbonyikebe (2 May 2005); *Nyiramasuhuko* Oral Decision on the Qualification of Mr. Edmond Babin as Defence Expert Witness, para 5.

[255] *Bizimungu* Decision on the Admissibility of the Expert Testimony of Dr. Binaifer Norwojee (8 Jul 2005), para 11.

[256] *Nahimana* Appeal Judgment, para 212; *Karemera* Decision on Joseph Nzirorera's Motion to Limit the Scope of Testimony of Expert Witnesses Alison Des Forges and Andre Guichaoua (2 Aug 2007), para 3; also see the SCSL cases *Norman* Decision on Prosecution Request for Leave to Call Additional Witnesses and for Orders for Protective Measures (21 Jun 2005) 4; *Taylor* Decision on Defence Application to Exclude the Evidence of Proposed Prosecution Witness Corinne Dufka or, in the alternative, to limit its scope and on urgent Prosecution request for decision (19 Jun 2008), para 21.

[257] *Semanza* Appeal Judgement (20 May 2005), para 304; *Bizimungu* Decision, ibid, para 12; *Bizimungu* Decision on Casimir Bizimungu's Urgent Motion for the Exclusion of the Report and Testimony of Deo Sebahire Mbonyinkebe, para 13; *ICTY Prosecutor v Kovačević*, Official Transcript (6 Jul 1998), at 71; *Kordić and Čerkez*, Official Transcript (28 Jan 2000) at 13, 268–306; *Milošević* Decision on Admission of Expert Report of Robert Donia, para 11; *Martić* Trial Judgement (12 Jun 2007), para 29, fn 35; *Milošević* Decision on Defence Expert Witnesses (21 Aug 2007), para 10; *Stanišić & Simatović* Decision on Prosecution's Submission of the Expert Report of Nina Tromp and Christian Nielsen Pursuant to Rule 94*bis*, para 12.

rule, stating in one case: 'we strongly opine that the said passages of the Report amount to a massive invasion of the fact-finding domain and exclusive prerogative of the Trial Chamber'.[258] Similarly, the ICTR Chamber in *Karemera et al* rejected expert evidence going to matters within the domain of the judges' determination of the facts and law. It held:

> The Trial Chamber, however, recalls the established jurisprudence of this Tribunal proscribing expert evidence from usurping the function of the Trial Chamber by offering opinions that are determinative of the guilt or innocence of the Accused or by adverting to the acts, conduct and mental state of the Accused. Admitting the evidence of Des Forges, as suggested by the Prosecution, would amount to usurping the functions of the Chamber in determining the guilt or not of the accused.[259]

On similar grounds the testimony of a Human Rights Watch researcher was limited to her investigations of sexual crimes in Rwanda, based on her interviews and investigations in the field. The judges rejected the legal conclusions she had drawn from those interviews.[260]

The ultimate issue rule has, however, not always been strictly applied. In a number of cases expert reports and testimony were admitted in full notwithstanding that portions thereof directly dealt with legal conclusions or the culpability of the accused.[261] For instance, in the *Military I* case, the Trial Chamber held:

> With respect to the sceptre raised by the defence that Dr DesForges should not be permitted to opine upon the ultimate issue, lest the parties forget, this matter is being tried by a panel of seasoned Judges who will not permit the opinion of an expert to usurp their exclusive domain as fact finders. Rules disallowing an expert to provide opinions and inferences on the ultimate issue are ordinarily directed at protecting against lay jurors from substituting the opinion of the expert for their independent assessment of the facts. There is no such danger here.[262]

Moreover, Trial Chambers have different levels of tolerance to the use of hearsay evidence and anonymous sources in expert testimony. In most situations, an expert does not have first-hand knowledge of the events he describes, in particular where it concerns an expertise in human rights violations, or other socio-political or historical matters.[263]

---

[258] *Sesay* Decision on Admissibility of Certain Parts of Expert Report of Johan Hederstedt (29 Jul 2008), paras 23–24, 39; *Taylor* Decision on Defence Application to Exclude the Evidence of Proposed Prosecution Witness Corinne Dufka, para 22.

[259] *Karemera* Decision on Prosecution Motion for Reconsideration on Prospective Experts Guichaoua, Nowrojee, and Des Forges, or for Certification (16 Nov 2007), para 21.

[260] *Bagosora*, Transcript (12 Jul 2004) 72–73; *Bizimungu* Decision on the Admissibility of the Expert Testimony of Dr Nowrojee, para 12.

[261] *ICTY Prosecutor v Boškovski and Tarčulovski*, Decision on Motion to Exclude the Prosecution's Proposed Evidence of Expert Bezruchenko and his Report (17 May 2007), para 14; *Nyiramasuhuko* Decision on Ntahobali and Nyiramasuhuko's Extremely Urgent Motions to Limit the Extent and Nature of the Report and Testimony of Filip Reyntjens (18 Sep 2007); *Semanza* Appeal Judgment, para 304; *Nahimana* Appeal Judgment, para 71.

[262] *Bagosora* Oral Decisions on Objections to Exclude Testimony (4 Sep 2002)13, 305–07.

[263] *Popović* Decision on Joint Defence Interlocutory Appeal Concerning the Status of Richard Butler as an Expert Witness (30 Jan 2008), para 2.

In the *Kovačević* case[264] the defence made an objection to the admission of a prosecution exhibit on the ground that it contained multiple hearsay and otherwise inadmissible evidence.[265] The document constituted a report of an expert, namely a judge, who summarised, analysed and collated information from 400 witnesses. The defence argued that it was denied the fundamental right to cross-examination and the right to confront witnesses, as the judge, the only witness available for cross-examination, was not a direct witness herself. The defence made the observation that '[t]hey cannot merely summarise evidence and introduce it under the guise of being an expert'.[266] The defence further argued:

> We're not talking about simply hearsay that an expert may use to fortify their expert opinion. We're talking about being denied the right to cross-examine a paper witness.[267]

May J responded:

> It is our view that the witness should be treated as an expert in this sense, an expert who has made a study of material and is therefore qualified to give evidence about it. The position being analogous to that of the historian. We take entirely the point made by the defence, that they cannot cross-examine the 400 witnesses on whose statements this evidence will be based. We understand that. But in this Tribunal we admit all types of evidence. The hearsay rule does not apply, but the issue of how much weight is given to this evidence is very much a matter for the Tribunal. And, in that connection, we shall, of course, bear in mind that it is hearsay. And, as I said earlier, sometimes hearsay upon hearsay. With those considerations in mind, we shall admit the report. But, I should make it quite plain, there is no question of this defendant being convicted on any count on the basis of this evidence. And we shall require other evidence before we consider taking any such course.[268]

In the above case, it is highly questionable why the judge in question qualified as an expert. The only apparent skill this judge had in relation to the case was the collection and analysis of materials, which is of a similar nature as the work of the prosecution. Indeed, there is little difference between a dossier submitted by an investigator or the report of a judge who has no particular expertise as a historian, sociologist, psychologist or other and whose report is based on information gathered from witnesses.[269] This was also recognised by an SCSL Trial Chamber, which took a different position in respect of a similar type of witness:

> It is clear on the evidence that Ms. Dufka has, over a period of time, collected and documented testimonies of various victims and witnesses, in essentially the same manner as that of an Investigator working with the Office of the Prosecutor. The commentary provided alongside does not, as the Prosecutor submits, establish 'clear patterns identifiable only by

---

[264] *Kovačević*, Official Transcript (6 Jul 1998).
[265] Ibid, 69–71.
[266] Ibid, 71.
[267] Ibid, 74.
[268] Ibid, 75.
[269] See *Nyiramasuhuko* Oral Decision on the Qualification of Mr Edmond Babin as Defence Expert Witness (13 Apr 2005), para 6, where the testimony of a police officer who had examined crime scenes, made sketches, photographs and videos did not qualify as expert testimony. The police officer was, however, allowed to testify as a factual witness. See also section 21.7, where it has already been demonstrated that reports of investigators employed by the prosecution do not qualify as expert reports.

an expert' and does not constitute specialist knowledge beyond the capability of the court to understand. Accordingly, the Trial Chamber finds that Ms. Dufka cannot properly be characterised as an expert.[270]

In the *Kordić and Čerkez* case the defence raised an objection to the expertise of a professor, the author of a book on ethnic cleansing in 1995.[271] The prosecution argued that the controversy surrounding his expertise should not be a ground for exclusion, but should rather be addressed during cross-examination.[272] May J raised concerns as regards the ultimate issue rule, as well as the relevance of the allegations.[273] The prosecutor responded that the document included conclusions:

> ... which are the principal matters that are outside the experience of the Chamber and upon which expertise is vital and helpful. And in his survey of and marshalling of the material and then, applying his analysis to reach the conclusions that precede the final conclusions, he is doing the work of an expert and not expressing final conclusions.[274]

The prosecutor moreover argued that:

> He gathers together the material with expertise that is not available to us. This is a recognised and respected area of expertise to which he's devoted some part of his life, entirely neutrally gathering materials that aren't available to us in their broad range and knowing where to look, and that marks him out and it gives him a particular insight and a particular value.[275]

Counsel for the defence objected, arguing that the professor was neither neutral nor an expert and had no expertise other than what the tribunal already had.[276] He stated about the professor:

> He has instead looked at a variety of newspaper documents, things supplied to him by the Tribunal from witnesses, some of whom have appeared and some of whom have not, and he has made his conclusion ... [H]e has made his conclusion having decided the credibility and reliability of witness statements, reports in news journals, accepted some and rejected others ... Cigar's report contains not only news articles but a number of, 'open sources which have been analysed with due regard to their reliability' ... Judge Cigar has decided who is reliable and who isn't, taking that entirely from your hands, and presents to you his analysis of the shadow case which I suggest.[277]

After the Trial Chamber deliberated on the matter, May J held:

> Much of the complaint made by the defence about this witness is a matter which is susceptible to cross-examination and is a question of weight. However, they raise a fundamental point, which is that what this witness effectively is doing is to provide evidence or provide opinion, more accurately, upon the very matters upon which this Trial Chamber is going to have to rule, and that, as they correctly point out, invades the right, power, and

---

[270] *Taylor* Decision on Defence Application to Exclude the Evidence of Proposed Prosecution Witness Corinne Dufka, para 13.
[271] *Kordić and Čerkez*, Official Transcript (28 Jan 2000).
[272] Ibid, 13, 267–68.
[273] Ibid, 13, 269–71.
[274] Ibid, 13, 271–72.
[275] Ibid, 13, 275.
[276] Ibid, 13, 289.
[277] Ibid, 13, 292–93.

duty of the Trial Chamber to rule upon this issue ... It is littered, if I may say, with examples of conclusions, drawing inferences, drawing conclusions, which it is the duty of this Trial Chamber to consider and to draw if appropriate or to reject. It's correctly pointed out that the witness hasn't heard the evidence. We have, and we have to decide the case. It's not a matter for him to decide ... We also don't think, and this is a matter where Rule 89(C) comes into play, that his evidence is going to assist us very much. 89(C) says we may admit any relevant material which it deems to have probative value. Because it's dealing with the matters which we have to deal with ultimately, drawing the conclusions and inferences which we have to draw, we think that it does not assist and is, therefore, not of probative value ... Accordingly, we shall exclude the evidence.[278]

Particularly at the ICTR, many historians and human rights researchers have been allowed to testify in respect of contextual matters, including the socio-economic and political situation leading up to the 1994 massacres; the reasons for the genocide and human rights abuses in 1994; the role of the media in Rwandan society, the role of the military in 1994 Rwanda and the civil defence structure.[279] Scholars have raised concerns about the use of social scientists and human rights researchers as experts in criminal trials, given the impossibility of forming certain opinions in this field, such that are required and expected from an expert witness.[280] In addition, their testimony, which is not of a technical nature frequently touches upon issues that are closely intertwined with the ultimate issues for the judges to determine.[281] Their opinions are generally formulated upon the narratives of others. Often, they are based on 'second, third, and even fourth hand testimony of victims and witnesses'.[282] This may be acceptable within the context of research into human rights abuses and should therefore not be read as criticism of their work. However, in a court of law, this raises difficulties given that the credibility of the witnesses whose stories are being told cannot be tested in cross-examination.

Objections have been raised in relation to non-disclosure of the identity of persons or sources that form the basis of the expert opinion. In one such case the Trial Chamber stated that there was no danger of a deprivation of the right to know the expert's sources, as the defence teams had ample opportunity to ask questions relating to the sources during cross-examination.[283] Yet, the use of anonymous sources may lead to unfairness against the accused. This is particularly so given that in their reports experts often reproduce hearsay evidence from other sources, which means that they themselves have not even tested these sources. It is true that the Defence can ask expert witnesses how they selected their sources and in what manner they assessed the truthfulness of their sources, as well as other questions on their

---

[278] Ibid, 13, 305–07.

[279] *Bagosora* Decision on Motion for Exclusion of Expert Witness Statement of Filip Reyntjens (28 Sep 2004), para 8.

[280] L Rosen, 'The Anthropologist as Expert Witness' (1977) 79 *American Anthropologist: New Series* 555.

[281] See, for instance, the testimony of Professor Reyntjens, given in the ICTR trial of Bagosora. *Bagosora*, Transcripts (22 Sep 2004) 4–9 (Reyntjens oral testimony).

[282] KL Fabian, 'Proof and Consequences: An Analysis of the Tadić & Akayesu Trials' (2000) 49 *DePaul Law Review* 981, citing MP Scharf, *Balkan Justice: The Story behind the First International War Crimes Trials since Nuremberg* (Durham, Carolina Academic Press, 1997) 128.

[283] *Bagosora* Oral Decisions on Objections to Exclude Testimony (4 Sep 2002), para 11.

methodology. The Defence and the Chamber are nonetheless deprived of an opportunity to assess the demeanour and credibility of the sources and the reliability of their stories. In addition, given that the identities of the sources are unknown the Defence is also hampered in conducting investigations into their credibility. The effectiveness of the cross-examination of the expert is, therefore, clearly undermined.[284]

For these reasons non-disclosure of the sources of the information on which the expert opinion is based may affect the reliability of the expert report or testimony to such an extent that it be largely discounted at the end of the day. However, as long as the expert opinion is not exclusively based on unidentified sources, this is a matter of weight, not of admissibility.[285]

The ICC regulations on expert evidence differ significantly from those of the ad hoc tribunals. The ICC Statute and Rules of Procedure and Evidence do not address the issue of expert evidence. However, pursuant to Regulation 44 of the Regulations of the Court, the Registrar shall create and maintain a list of experts in relation to whom there is 'an appropriate indication of expertise in the relevant field'. The Chamber may direct the joint instruction of an expert by the participants (Reg 44(2)); or may *proprio motu* instruct an expert (Reg 44(4)). A participant may apply to the Chamber for leave to instruct a further expert in addition to an expert jointly instructed if there is dispute about an issue of expertise (Reg 44(3). Regulation 44(5) grants the Chamber broad powers to control the engagement of experts. This Regulation provides:

> The Chamber may issue any order as to the subject of an expert report, the number of experts to be instructed, the mode of their instruction, the manner in which their evidence is to be presented and the time limits for the preparation and notification of their request.

This ICC Regulation is clearly influenced by civil law. This may have been a reaction to the use of partisan expert witnesses called by the parties at the ad hoc criminal tribunals. It is, however, questionable whether judicially appointed or instructed experts are going to be more neutral. Some scholars have expressed the view that judicial experts enjoy a 'false air of neutrality'.[286] Yet, as in civil law jurisdictions, ICC judicially appointed experts will most likely enjoy a greater presumption of reliability than experts called by one of the parties. It is, however, to be expected that the ICC will face similar difficulties as the ad hoc tribunals in terms of reliance on anonymous hearsay. The fact that neither the Chamber nor the Defence is in a position to test the evidence on the basis of which the expert opinion has been formed will not be resolved by appointing a court expert. There is presently insufficient jurisprudence on the issue to draw any final conclusions here.

---

[284] Fabian, 'Proof and Consequences', at 981.

[285] *Bizimungu* Decision on Defence Motion for Exclusion of Portions of Testimony of Expert Witness Dr. Alison Des Forges (2 Sep 2005), paras 5, 17 & 25; *Bagilishema* Trial Judgment (7 Jun 2001), para 139.

[286] L Rosen, 'The Anthropologist as Expert Witness' (1977) 79 *American Anthropologist, New Series* 570.

21.9   Character Evidence

A rule of common law provides that evidence which merely tends to prove the bad character of the accused or his previous misconduct is excluded because such evidence is highly prejudicial while irrelevant to the accused's guilt in the matter at issue.[287] An exception applies where the probative value of the evidence outweighs its prejudicial effect.[288] This is the case where the facts shown by the evidence are strikingly similar to the facts alleged by the prosecutor. Another exception applies where the accused produces evidence of his 'good' character, which may be rebutted by the prosecutor by bringing evidence of his 'bad' character. A final exception applies where the evidence does not tend to demonstrate the accused's guilt, but rather his motive, intent, plan or similar issues.[289] Civil law jurisdictions are unfamiliar with such a rule. Since the assessment of evidence is in the hands of professional judges, who are responsible for the factual and legal findings, they have access to the accused's prior criminal record. The purpose of this access is not to rely on it for any determination of guilt, but to determine the appropriate sentence if the accused is found guilty.[290]

The ad hoc tribunals have not incorporated an exclusionary rule in relation to character evidence. To the contrary, r 93 specifically allows for the admission of evidence of a consistent pattern of conduct relevant to serious violations of international humanitarian law. The term 'consistent pattern of conduct' seems to be broader than the common law term 'striking similarities'. Under certain conditions this Rule allows the admission of evidence that relates to events outside the temporal jurisdiction of the tribunals or the scope of the indictment if the evidence constitutes 'similar fact evidence' that demonstrates a consistent pattern of conduct.[291] The tribunal judges have qualified such evidence as circumstantial evidence, but apply this

---

[287] See eg *Makin v AG for New South Wales* [1894] AC 57, where the Privy Council held that the prosecution is not competent 'to adduce evidence tending to show that the accused has been guilty of criminal acts other than those covered by the indictment for the purpose of leading to the conclusion that the person is likely from his criminal conduct or character to have committed the offence for which he is being tried' (*per* Lord Herschell, at 65); see also US Federal and Revised Uniform Rules of Evidence, r 404(a) which provides that subject to a number of exceptions, '[e]vidence of a person's character or, a trait of his character is not admissible for the purpose of proving that he acted in conformity therewith on a particular occasion'.

[288] See *DPP v P* [1991] 2 AC 447, in which the Court of Appeal held it was not appropriate to single out a striking similarity as an essential feature of every case involving the admission of evidence of one victim on a charge relating to another victim. The principle was whether the probative force of the evidence was sufficiently great to make it just to admit the evidence, notwithstanding its prejudicial effect in showing the defendant's guilt of another crime (*per* Lord Mackay).

[289] See Federal and Revised Uniform Rules of Evidence, r 404(b) which provides: 'Evidence of other crimes, wrongs, or acts is not admissible to prove the character of a person in order to show that he acted in conformity therewith. It may, however, be admissible for other purposes, such as proof of motive, opportunity, intent, preparation, plan, knowledge, identity or absence of mistake or accident'. Rule 405(a), furthermore, allows opinion testimony as well as reputation testimony to prove character whenever any form of character evidence is appropriate. In addition, when character is 'in issue', it may also be proved by testimony about specific acts.

[290] M Damaška, 'Evidentiary Barriers to Conviction and Two Models of Criminal Procedure: A Comparative Study' (1972–73) 121 *University of Pennsylvania Law Review* 518–519.

[291] *ICTR Prosecutor v Ndlindliyimana et al*, Decision on Nzuwonemeye's Motion to Exclude Parts of Witness AOG's Testimony (30 Mar 2006), para 22.

Rule with caution.[292] The following factors must be considered in determining whether the evidence qualifies as 'similar fact evidence' and as such admissible under r 93:

1. proximity in time with the similar acts;
2. extent to which the other acts are similar in detail to the charged conduct;
3. number of occurrences of the similar acts;
4. any distinctive feature(s) unifying the incidents;
5. intervening events; and
6. any other factor which would tend to support or rebut the underlying unity of the similar acts.[293]

Similar fact evidence can further be used to undermine the credibility of the accused as a witness.[294] It may even be taken into account in relation to the guilt or innocence of the accused if relevant to prove identity or to disprove innocent associations,[295] to prove 'a pattern, design or systematic course of conduct by the accused where his explanation on the basis of coincidence would be an affront to common sense',[296] or where 'it bears on the questions as to whether the conduct alleged … was deliberate or accidental, and whether it is likely that a person of good character would have acted in the way alleged'.[297] Where evidence fails to pass the test of relevance, probative value and reliability under r 89(C), its prejudice outweighs its probative value or its admission is not otherwise in the interests of justice and as a result must be excluded.[298] Whether the admission of evidence under r 93 is in the interests of justice is based on a case-to-case determination, considering, in particular, its impact on the fairness of the proceedings.[299]

Evidence of past crimes, introduced merely to blacken the character of the accused and to demonstrate that the accused is 'capable of committing the offence, is inclined to commit the offence, or on some prior occasion actually did have the intent to

---

[292] *Krnojelac* Trial Judgment (15 Mar 2002), para 4, reads as follows: 'Evidence of a consistent pattern of conduct relevant to serious violations of international humanitarian law under the Statute was admitted pursuant to r 93(A) in the interests of justice. Such evidence is similar to circumstantial evidence. A circumstantial case consists of evidence of a number of different circumstances which, taken in combination, point to the existence of a particular fact upon which the guilt of the accused person depends because they would usually exist in combination only because a particular fact did exist. Such a conclusion must be established beyond a reasonable doubt. It is not sufficient that it is a reasonable conclusion available from that evidence. It must be the only reasonable conclusion available. If there is another conclusion which is also reasonably open from that evidence, and which is consistent with the non-existence of that fact, the conclusion cannot be drawn'.

[293] *Bagosora* Decision on Admissibility of Proposed Testimony of Witness DBY (18 Sep 2003), para 38.

[294] *Tadić* Appeals Judgment on Allegations of Contempt (31 Jan 2000), para 128.

[295] *Bagosora* Decision on Admissibility of Proposed Testimony of Witness DBY, paras 9–14; *Simba* Decision on the Defence Motion for Preclusion of Prosecution Evidence (31 Aug 2004), para 3; *Nahimana* Decision on Interlocutory Appeal, Separate Opinion of Judge Shahabuddeen (5 Sep 2000), para 20.

[296] Shahabuddeen Opinion, ibid, para 20.

[297] Ibid; *Tadić* Appeals Judgment on Allegations of Contempt, para 130.

[298] *Bagosora* Decision on Admissibility of Proposed Testimony of Witness DBY, paras 9–14; *Simba* Decision on the Defence Motion for Preclusion of Prosecution Evidence, para 3; *Nahimana* Separate Opinion of Judge Shahabuddeen, para 20. These arguments have further been confirmed by the Appeals Chamber in *Bagosora* Decision on Prosecutor's Interlocutory Appeals regarding Exclusion of Evidence (19 Dec 2003), para 13.

[299] See *Krnojelac* Trial Judgment, para 4; *Bagosora* Decision, ibid, para 13.

commit the criminal offence', is inadmissible under r 93.[300] This is so because such evidence is prejudicial in a manner that compels exclusion, outweighing its probative value, because it 'so severely blacken[s] the reputation of the accused as to make acquittal virtually impossible, even though the direct evidence of the commission of the offence is weak'.[301] Although often acknowledged that professional judges may be less susceptible to distraction or prejudice by the admission of irrelevant or prejudicial evidence than juries, 'dealing with evidence of past conduct may be unduly distracting and time consuming, leading to an unfocused trial that undermines the truth-finding function'.[302]

At the ICC there is no equivalent to r 93. Whether evidence that does not directly bear on the charges is admissible depends on the relevance such evidence has in relation to the charges. If such information bears on similar crimes it may not be fair to the accused to admit it, given the prejudicial effect of this information upon the fact-finders while adding no value to the case at hand. In one case before the ICC the issue arose in respect of information about similar attacks not charged. The Presiding Judge held that it is appropriate and necessary to put the relevant events in a context to better understand the possible responsibilities of the various individuals concerned and the conditions under which a plan may have possibly been carried out. Therefore, questions of a general nature about other attacks were allowed. However, the Presiding Judge stressed that such questions cannot be too specific so as to attribute responsibility to the accused for events which are not charged.[303]

21.10   Exclusion of Improperly Obtained Evidence

A rule excluding improperly obtained evidence exists in practically all legal systems, civil and common law alike. Civil law systems tend to focus on procedural matters, meaning that evidence will be excluded if obtained in violation of procedural fairness irrespective of its relevance.[304] Common law systems focus more on issues of reliability: if the prejudicial effect exceeds probative value the evidence will not be

---

[300] *ICTY Prosecutor v Kupreškić*, Decision on Evidence of Good Character of the Accused and the Defence of *Tu Quoque* (17 Feb 1999), para 31; *Bagosora* Decision on Admissibility of Proposed Testimony of Witness DBY, para 12; *Nahimana* Decision on the Interlocutory Appeals, Separate Opinion of Judge Shahabuddeen, para 20.

[301] *Bagosora* Decision, ibid, paras 12 and 17.

[302] *Bagosora* Decision, ibid, paras 12 and 28.

[303] *Katanga*, Transcripts (9 Feb 2010) 53; Transcripts (10 Feb 2010) 7–15, 32–34.

[304] This ground of exclusion has been adopted in most civil law systems under influence of the ECHR. In respect of France, see eg G Stefani, G Levasseur and B Bouloc, *Procédure Pénale*, 1867, 18th edn, (Paris, Dalloz, 2001) 222–24. The German system incorporated a number of '*Beweisverbote*' (prohibitions of evidence, non-admissibility of evidence) in paras 52–55 and 136(a) of the 1987/2001 Strafprozess Ordnung (Code of Criminal Procedure). See *Procédure Pénale d'Europe*, ibid, at 105. The Dutch system created a discretion for judges to exclude evidence if principles of fair administration of justice have been violated, depending on the gravity of the violation and the consequences thereof, in accordance with Art 359(a) of the Wet van Strafvordering (Code of Criminal Procedure).

admitted. To a more limited degree, evidence, the admission of which would affect fairness, may also be excluded at common law.[305]

The ICTY, ICTR, SCSL have included an exclusionary rule, r 95, in their Rules of Procedure and Evidence pursuant to which evidence must be excluded if obtained irregularly where this has had an adverse impact on its reliability or the integrity of the proceedings.[306] The drafters of the ICC have equally incorporated a similar provision in its Statute.[307] The Rule has been described as the 'residual exclusionary provision', and; as 'a summary of the provisions in the Rules which enable exclusion of evidence'.[308] The scope of r 95 of the ICTY, ICTR, and SCSL Rules is wide. In the *Delalić* case an ICTY Chamber recognised the importance of the source of the evidence for the determination of its reliability and held that for 'evidence to be reliable, it must be … obtained under circumstances which cast no doubt on its nature and character'.[309]

Another element of r 95 is the integrity of the proceedings, which includes respect for the fair trial rights embodied in the statutes, failure of which could lead to the exclusion of the evidence.[310] On the basis of r 95 certain pieces of evidence, such as

---

[305] See *Sang* [1980] AC 402, where Lord Diplock, at 437, held that judges have no discretion 'to refuse to admit relevant admissible evidence on the ground that it was obtained by improper or unfair means. The Court is not concerned with how it was obtained'. Even though s 78 of the Police and Criminal Evidence Act 1984 (PACE) incorporates the judicial discretion to exclude evidence if improperly obtained, *Chalkley* [1998] 2 Cr App R 79, *per* Lord Auld, 105–06, confirms the common law position set out in *Sang*. This approach may, however, have become invalidated in light of the incorporation of the ECHR through the adoption of the Human Rights Act 1998. In Canada, the position is similar. See *R v Wray* [1971] SCR 272 and *R v Harrer* [1995] 3 SCR 562. However, the Canadian Charter provides for an exclusionary remedy (Art 24(2)) if the manner with which the evidence was obtained is in violation of the Charter, in which case its admission would bring the administration of justice into disrepute. The US has shown considerable concern with the fairness in which evidence is obtained, even where the reliability of the evidence is not directly affected. This appears, *inter alia*, from *State v Brown* (1988) 543A 2d 750, 763 and *USA v Leon* (1984) 468 US 897. See also Federal and Revised Uniform Evidence Rules, r 403, which codifies the common law power of the judge to exclude relevant evidence, 'if its probative value is substantially outweighed by the danger of unfair prejudice, confusion of the issues, or misleading the jury or by considerations of undue delay, waste of time, or needless presentation of cumulative evidence'.

[306] Rule 95 ICTY and ICTR Rules provides: 'No evidence shall be admissible if obtained by methods which cast substantial doubt on its reliability or if its admission is antithetical to, and would seriously damage, the integrity of the proceedings'. SCSL Rule 95 reads differently. It provides: 'No evidence shall be admitted if its admission would bring the administration of justice into serious disrepute'. This Rule has, nonetheless, been interpreted similarly to ICTY and ICTR Rule 95. See, for instance, *Sesay* Decision on Defence Motion to Request the Trial Chamber to Rule that the Prosecution Moulding of Evidence is Impermissible (1 Aug, 2006), para 17, where the Chamber held that 'it is absolutely clear that no evidence shall be admissible if obtained by methods which could subsequently cast a substantial doubt on the evaluation of its reliability or if its admission could seriously damage the integrity of the proceedings'.

[307] Art 69(7) of the ICC Statute provides that:
'Evidence obtained by means of a violation of this Statute or internationally recognized human rights shall not be admissible if:
(a) The violation casts substantial doubt on the reliability of the evidence; or
(b) The admission of the evidence would be antithetical to and would seriously damage the integrity of the proceedings'.

[308] *Delalić* Decision on Zdravko Mucic's Motion for the Exclusion of Evidence (2 Sep 1997) [*Delalić* Decision on Exclusion of Evidence], paras 43–44.

[309] Ibid, para 41. See also *Haraqija & Morina* Decision on Morina and Haraqija Second Request for a Declaration of Inadmissibility and Exclusion of Evidence (Amended Public Redacted Version) (27 Nov 2008), para 19.

[310] *Delalić* Decision on Exclusion of Evidence, paras 43–45.

those obtained in an armed search,[311] in the course of irregular investigation procedures,[312] or by a breach of the Rules of Procedure and Evidence, may be found inadmissible.[313] Irregularities in the procedure may suffice to exclude the evidence obtained therein even where the quality of evidence is unaffected.[314] For instance, late or incomplete disclosure of evidence may prejudice the accused to such an extent that exclusion would be an appropriate remedy, notwithstanding that the quality of the evidence is not necessarily undermined.[315] As an ICTY Chamber held, 'if there is illegality and such illegality would be antithetical to and seriously damage the integrity of the proceedings if the evidence fruit of that illegality is admitted; then it has the duty not to admit that evidence'.[316]

Chambers assess whether any of the legal provisions of the Rules and Statute of their own tribunal have been violated. If such a violation occurred they may find a breach of r 95 even where this was undertaken in compliance with domestic law in the country where the evidence was obtained.[317] The reverse also holds true: where the collection of evidence was unlawful under domestic law, such evidence may nonetheless be admissible, provided that the integrity of the proceedings has not been seriously damaged.[318]

Not all irregularities lead to exclusion, particularly where the evidence is relevant, probative and reliable.[319] It appears that in recent years Chambers are less inclined to exclude irregularly obtained evidence unless the Defence clearly indicates that the

---

[311] *Kordić and Čerkez* Decision Stating Reasons for Trial Chamber's Ruling of 1 June 1999 Rejecting Defence Motion to Suppress Evidence (25 Jun 1999) 3–5.

[312] *Delalić* Decision on the Motion for the Exclusion of Evidence and Restitution of Evidence by the Accused Zejnil Delalić (25 Sep 1997), para 45; *Delalić* Trial Judgment (16 Nov 1998), para 65.

[313] *Delalić* Decision on the Tendering of Prosecution Exhibits 104–08 (9 Feb 1998), para 20; *Delalić* Trial Judgment, para 64; *Akayesu* Trial Judgment, para 95.

[314] See, however, the *Karemera* Decision on the Prosecutor's Motion for Admission of Certain Exhibits into Evidence (25 Jan 2008), para 16, where the Chamber held that a document seized at the time of the arrest of the accused, considered to be illegal, will not be excluded unless the Defence can demonstrate that the document was not reliable or that the admission of the document would seriously damage the integrity of the proceedings.

[315] *Brima* Decision on Joint Defence Motion on Disclosure of all Original Witness Statements, Interview Notes, and Investigator's Notes Pursuant to Rule 66 and/or 68 (4 May 2005), para 16; *Sesay* Decision on Defence Motion to Request the Trial Chamber to Rule that the Prosecution Moulding of Evidence is Impermissible (1 Aug 2006), para 11.

[316] *Brđanin* Decision on the Defence Objection to Intercept Evidence (3 Oct 2003), para 57.

[317] *Delalić* Decision on Zdravko Mucic's Motion for the Exclusion of Evidence (2 Sep 1997). This concerned a breach of the right to counsel. Although this restriction to the right of representation while being questioned by Austrian police and prosecution investigators during a criminal investigation was in accordance with Austrian law and was allowed under Art 6(3) of the ECHR, the Trial Chamber nevertheless considered it to be 'inconsistent with the unfettered right to counsel in Art 18(3) [of the Statute] and sub-Rule 42(A)(i) [of the Rules]'. On that ground, it excluded the statements made by the accused to the Austrian police as evidence under r 95.

[318] *Haraqija & Morina* Decision on Morina and Haraqija Second Request for a Declaration of Inadmissibility and Exclusion of Evidence (Amended Public Redacted Version), paras 25–26; *Brđanin* Decision on the Defence Objection to Intercept Evidence, para 61; *ICTR Prosecutor v Renzaho*, Decision on Exclusion of Testimony and Admission of Exhibit (20 Mar 2007), para 16. See, however, *Bagosora* Decision on Motion to Harmonise and Amend Witness Protection Orders (1 Jun 2005), para 15, where it was held that a violation of national law might be a consideration in determining whether evidence should be excluded under Rule 95, particularly where it has been 'obtained by methods which cast substantial doubt on its reliability or if its admission is antithetical to, and would seriously damage, the integrity of the proceedings'.

[319] See *Haraqija & Morina* Decision, ibid, paras 14 and 19, where it was held that, '[. . .] it is obvious that the drafters of the Rules specifically chose not to set out a rule providing for the automatic exclusion

irregularity has affected its reliability or the integrity of the proceedings. In a number of recent cases it has been held that evidence obtained unlawfully 'is not, *a priori*, inadmissible, but rather that the manner and surrounding circumstances in which evidence is obtained, as well as its reliability and effect on the integrity of the proceedings, will determine its admissibility. […] [I]t would be utterly inappropriate to exclude relevant evidence due to procedural considerations, as long as the fairness of the trial is guaranteed'.[320]

Where the fundamental rights of the accused are at stake the correct balance must be made between those rights and 'the essential interests of the international community in the prosecution of persons charged with serious violations of international humanitarian law'.[321] In line with the proportionality principle any restriction on a fundamental right 'must be in [the] service of a sufficiently important objective and must impair the right no more than is necessary to accomplish the objective'.[322]

The rights set out in Article 21 of the ICTY Statute, Article 20 of the ICTR Statute and Article 17 SCSL Statute are pivotal and of paramount importance. Exclusion of evidence even where its reliability is not in dispute is a likely consequence of a grave breach of one of these rights. In the ICTR case of *Zigiranyirazo* the Appeals Chamber excluded testimony of a key witness heard in the physical absence of the accused who was connected to his trial through a video-link. In excluding this testimony the Appeals Chamber emphasised that the right to be present, the right to counsel, the right to remain silent, the right to confront witnesses against oneself and the right to a speedy trial are 'indispensible cornerstones of justice'.[323] The Appeals Chamber considered that the Trial Chamber had not sufficiently explored alternative measures. Accordingly, the restrictions imposed on the fair trial rights of the accused were considered 'unwarranted and excessive in the circumstances and thus fail the test of proportionality'.[324] Given the importance and length of the testimony heard in the physical absence of the accused, apparent harm was done to him. On the ground that prejudice 'can only be presumed, as any attempt to prove or disprove actual prejudice from the record in an ongoing trial before any factual findings have been made would be purely speculative', the Appeals Chamber concluded that allowing the testimony to remain on the record 'would seriously damage the integrity of the proceedings. In such circumstances, Rule 95 of the Rules plainly requires the exclusion of such testimony'.[325]

---

of evidence illegally or unlawfully obtained and opted instead to leave the matter of admissibility of evidence irrespective of its provenance to be dealt with under and in accordance with Rules 89 and 95 […]'.

[320] *Brđanin* Decision on the Defence Objection to Intercept Evidence, paras 55, 63; *Haraqija & Morina* Decision, ibid, para 15; also see *Karemera* Decision on the Prosecutor's Motion for Admission of Certain Exhibits Into Evidence (25 Jan 2008), para 11.

[321] *Brđanin* Decision, ibid, para 62; also see *Karemera* Decision on the Prosecution Motion for Admission into Evidence of Post-Arrest Interviews with Joseph Nzirorera and Mathieu Ngirumpatse (2 Nov 2007), para 4.

[322] *Milošević* Decision on Interlocutory Appeal of the Trial Chamber's Decision on the Assignment of Defence Counsel (1 Nov 2004), para 17; *Zigiranyirazo* Decision on Interlocutory Appeal (30 Oct 2006), para 14.

[323] *Zigiranyirazo* Decision, ibid, para. 8; *Milošević* Decision, ibid, paras 11, 13.

[324] *Zigiranyirazo*, ibid, para 22.

[325] Ibid, para 24.

Particular care needs to be taken in respect of admissions made by the accused. To admit evidence of the accused's statement under r 95, the prosecution needs to prove 'convincingly and beyond reasonable doubt" that the statement was made voluntarily.[326] In the SCSL case of *Sesay* it was, however, held that if the Defence challenges the integrity of the prosecution in obtaining statements it must establish a *prima facie* case of 'foul play, either deliberate or negligent, by the Prosecution in order to justify an inquiry by the Chamber into the said process'.[327]

In accordance with Rules 42, 43 and 63, a suspect or an accused may be interviewed by the prosecution on a voluntary basis only. Voluntariness may be doubted where a suspect or accused has been impermissibly induced into subjecting himself to an interview.[328] During an interview the suspect or accused is entitled to remain silent, not answer any or some of the questions and to be represented by counsel. The right to be represented by counsel during an interview must be effective, which requires active involvement rather than mere presence.[329]

These principles must be fully respected, failure of which may lead to exclusion of the interview.[330] Failure to inform the accused of his rights may also lead to the exclusion of the interview as evidence against him.[331] However, where a statement is taken after the suspect or accused was properly advised of his rights and voluntarily waived them, such interview can be used to impeach the accused during his or her

---

[326] *Delalić* Decision on Zdravko Mucic's Motion For the Exclusion of Evidence, (2 Sept 1997), para 42; *Sesay* Written Reasons – Decision on the Admissibility of Certain Prior Statements of the Accused Given to the Prosecution (30 Jun 2008), para 52.

[327] *Sesay* Decision on Defence Motion to Request the Trial Chamber to Rule that the Prosecution Moulding of Evidence is Impermissible (1 Aug 2006), paras 16–18.

[328] See *Halilović* Decision on Interlocutory Appeal Concerning Admission of Record of Interview of the Accused from the Bar Table (19 Aug 2005), paras 36–42, 44–45, 54, 61–63, where the Appeals Chamber held that the prosecution's indication that the accused's 'full cooperation could have a positive influence on the Prosecution's position in respect to a potential application for provisional release' amounted to an impermissible inducement in circumstances where: the accused faced serious charges under the prospect of a potentially long sentence; a long and complex trial; a lengthy pre-trial detention at a considerable distance from his family and friends, and; an off-the-record discussion concerning the accused's request for clarification of agreements allegedly made with the Prosecutor which promised the withdrawal of the indictment in case of cooperation'. See also *Sesay*, Written Reasons – Decision on the Admissibility of Certain Prior Statements of the Accused Given to the Prosecution, paras 49–51, 68.

[329] *Blagoević* Decision on Prosecution's Motion for Clarification of Oral Decision Regarding Admissibility Of Accused's Statement (18 Sep 2003); *Halilović* Decision, ibid, paras 61–62.

[330] *Prlić* Decision on the Admission into Evidence of Slobodan Praljak's Evidence in the Case of Naletilić and Martinović (5 Sep 2007), paras 14 and 15; *Prlić* Decision on the Request for Admission of the Statement of Jadranko Prlić, para 12; *Kvočka* Appeals Chamber Judgment (25 Feb 2005), para 128; *Halilović* Decision, ibid, paras 14, 15; *Milutinović* Decision on Prosecution Motion to Admit Documentary Evidence (10 Oct 2006), paras 43 and 44; *Popović* Decision on Appeals Against Decision Admitting Material Related to Borovčanin's Questioning, para 32; *Sesay* Written Reasons – Decision on the Admissibility of Certain Prior Statements of the Accused Given to the Prosecution, para 38.

[331] See *Prlić* Decision on Prosecution Motion for the Admission into Evidence of the Testimony of Milivoj Petkovic given in Other Cases before the Tribunal (17 Oct 2007), para 15, where the Trial Chamber held that 'in order to be able to determine whether a witness has voluntarily waived the right to remain silent if there is a risk of self-incrimination, it is not sufficient to establish that the witness gave evidence voluntarily, without duress. The witness would have to know of the existence of this right and the consequences deriving from waiving it'.

testimony and, if the requirements of r 89(C) are met, admitted as evidence.[332] If, on the other hand, the waiver of the right to be represented by counsel was not voluntary, explicit, unequivocal and informed such interview may be excluded under r 95. This is so given that particularly during preliminary questioning this right is considered to be fundamental in order to ensure that the other rights of the suspect or accused are being respected.[333] The prosecution must establish the voluntariness of the interview and of the waiver of the right to representation 'convincingly and beyond reasonable doubt'.[334] In order to meet this burden the prosecution must establish that the suspect or accused was informed of his right to 'the *prompt* assistance of counsel, prior to and during *any* questioning. *Any implication that the right is conditional, or that the presence of counsel may be delayed until after the questioning, renders any waiver defective* ... Once the detainee has been fully apprised of his right to the assistance of counsel, he is in a position to voluntarily waive the right' [emphasis added].[335]

The exclusion as evidence of a statement taken from the suspect or accused in violation of his rights to voluntariness and legal representation does not necessarily prevent it from being used to impeach the accused if he decides to take the stand, provided it is sufficiently reliable.[336]

At the ICC, a provision similar to r 95 has been incorporated in the Statute. Article 69(7) provides:

Evidence obtained by means of a violation of this Statute or internationally recognized human rights shall not be admissible if:

(a) The violation casts substantial doubt on the reliability of the evidence; or
(b) The admission of the evidence would be antithetical to and would seriously damage the integrity of the proceedings.

Until now, few applications under this provision have been made, but it appears that the considerations thereto are similar to those under r 95 of the ad hoc tribunals. In *Lubanga*, evidence was obtained in the course of an unlawful search and seizure operation in DRC in the residence of a third party. This operation was conducted by the local prosecutor's office in the presence of an ICC investigator. It was held that this unlawful operation led to a breach of privacy, which is an internationally recognised human right, notwithstanding that it concerned the right to privacy of a third person.[337] Evidence obtained in this operation fell, therefore, within the ambit of Article 69(7). However, not all evidence obtained irregularly pursuant to Article 69(7) will be excluded because it does not necessarily follow that its reliability is

---

[332] *Nyiramasuhuko* Decision on Kanyabashi's Oral Motion to Cross-Examine Ntahobali Using Ntahobali's Statements to Prosecution Investigators in July 1997 (15 May 2006), para 80.

[333] *Bagosora* Decision on the Prosecutor's Motion for the Admission of Certain Materials Under Rule 89(C) (14 Oct 2004), para 21. See also *Zigiranyirazo* Decision on the Voir Dire Hearing of the Accused's Curriculum Vitae (29 Nov 2006), para 13; *Karemera* Decision on the Prosecution Motion for Admission into Evidence of Post-Arrest Interviews with Joseph Nzirorera and Mathieu Ngirumpatse (2 Nov 2007), paras 25, 32.

[334] *Delalić* Decision on Zdravko Mucic's Motion For the Exclusion of Evidence (2 Sep 1997), para 42; *Bagosora* Decision, ibid, paras 16–18.

[335] *Bagosora* Decision, ibid paras 17–18.

[336] *Mrkšić* Decision Concerning the Use of Statements Given by the Accused (9 Oct 2006).

[337] *Lubanga* Decision on the Admission of Material from the 'Bar Table' (24 Jun 2009), para 37.

affected, or that the integrity of the proceedings may be seriously damaged.[338] The Pre-Trial Chamber declined to exclude the evidence because its reliability was not affected.[339] Similarly, the Trial Chamber held that the evidence obtained in violation of an internationally recognised human right did not require exclusion under Article 69(7)(a) or (b).[340] In order to determine whether the proceedings have been seriously damaged the Chamber must balance a number of factors, including respect for the sovereignty of States, the rights of the person, the protection of victims and witnesses and the effective punishment of serious crimes.[341] In this particular case, the Chamber held that the proceedings were not seriously damaged, given that: a) the violation was not of a particularly grave nature; b) it was conducted against a third person, and; c) it was solely conducted under the responsibility of the local prosecutors in the mere presence of an ICC investigator.[342] As for its reliability, the Chamber took a document-by-document approach and held that some pieces of evidence were to be excluded under Article 69(7)(a), whilst others were not.[343]

In the case of *Katanga*, the Defence objected to the admission of a hearing transcript documenting the accused in the DRC on the ground that the interrogation contained in this transcript was conducted in the absence of legal representation.[344] For the purpose of the confirmation hearing, the Pre-Trial Chamber dismissed the objection on the grounds that the DRC has 'taken the approach that the presence of defence counsel at preliminary stages of proceedings is not mandatory, an approach which, to date, has not been found inconsistent with the requirements of a fair trial'.[345] Moreover, the Pre-Trial Chamber held that 'it has not been shown that this particular procedure amounted to a violation of internationally recognised human rights'. It thereby referred to jurisprudence of the European Court of Human Rights holding that '[. . .] although Article 6 will normally require that the accused be allowed to benefit from the assistance of a lawyer already at the initial stages of police interrogation, this right, which is not explicitly set out in the Convention, may be subject to restriction for good cause. The question, in each case, is whether the restriction, in the light of the entirety of the proceedings, has deprived the accused of a fair hearing'.[346] The Pre-Trial Chamber, therefore, declined to exclude the document pursuant to Article 69(7).[347] The same issue is still pending before the ICC Trial Chamber.[348]

---

[338] Ibid, para 41.
[339] *Lubanga* Confirmation Decision, para 85.
[340] *Lubanga* 'Bar Table' Admission Decision, para 48.
[341] Ibid, para 42.
[342] Ibid, para 47.
[343] Ibid, para 49.
[344] *Katanga & Ngudjol*, Defence Written Submissions on Fact and Law pursuant to Rule 121(9) (24 Jun 2008), paras 15–30.
[345] *Katanga* Confirmation Decision, para 97.
[346] *Murray v UK* (1995) 19 EHRR 193, para 63. See also *Magee v UK* (2001) 31 EHRR 35, para 41; *Brennan v UK* (2002) 34 EHRR 507 para 45; *Yurttas v Turkey*, Judgment (27 May 2004), Application No 25143/94 and 27098/95, para 73; *Ocalan v Turkey* (2003) 37 EHRR 10, para 140 – confirmed by the Grand Chamber in its Judgment of 12 May 2005 (2005) 41 EHRR 985, para 131; *Salduz v Turkey* (2008) 49 EHRR 19, para 22. Cited in *Katanga & Ngudjolo* Decision on the Confirmation of Charges, para 94.
[347] Katanga & Ngudjolo Confirmation of Charges Decision, para 98–99.
[348] *Katanga and Ngudjolo* Defence Objections to Admissibility in Principal and in Substance (23 Oct 2009).

21.11   Determination of Weight of Evidence

21.11.1   General Principles

Trial Chambers need to accord appropriate weight, if any, to evidence which has been admitted pursuant to r 89(C). As is apparent from earlier discussions the bar by which evidence is to be admitted is a low one. The mere admission of evidence during trial 'has no bearing on the weight which the Chamber subsequently attaches to it'.[349] The Tribunals have adopted a liberal system of proof, which means that legal provisions do not set out minimum requirements for a conviction, or directives to be followed in deliberating on the issue of guilt. In principle, the judges are entirely free to determine what weight, if any, to attach to the evidence admitted in each case. The only two exceptions to this judicial liberty in evaluating the evidence lie in r 90(B) of the ICTY and SCSL Rules and r 90(C) of the ICTR Rules, requiring corroboration of witnesses who did not take the oath, and in r 96 ICTY, ICTR, SCSL Rules, imposing that no corroboration shall be required in cases of sexual violence.

The only other legal obligation judges have is to issue a reasoned verdict pursuant to Articles 22(2) of the ICTY Statute, 21(2) of the ICTR Statute, 18 of the SCSL Statute and r 88(C) of the Rules, failure of which constitutes a ground of appeal. Accordingly, judges must justify their acceptance or rejection of the available evidence.[350] There is, however, no guiding principle on the extent to which they have to provide reasons as to their assessment of the credibility and reliability of witness testimony. The reliability and credibility of witness testimony has to be determined on a case-by-case basis.[351] They are not required to provide reasoning for each step in the process of weighing and assessing the evidence.[352] In addition, the Appeals Chamber has stated that although the evidence produced may not have been referred to by a Trial Chamber, based on the particular circumstances of a given case, it may nevertheless be reasonable to assume that the Trial Chamber had taken it into account.[353]

As a result of this statutory obligation upon judges to deliver a reasoned judgment, lengthy considerations have been included on the assessment of the evidence. Consequently, a number of guiding principles have evolved in the jurisprudence, some of which, such as the rules of corroboration in specific circumstances, have attained binding force. The leading principle nonetheless remains that evidence must be assessed in the overall circumstances and in its overall context. A tribunal of fact must never look at the evidence of each witness separately as if it existed in a hermetically sealed compartment; it is the accumulation of all the evidence in the case which must be considered. The evidence of one witness, when considered in isolation,

---

[349] *Limaj* Trial Judgment, para 12.
[350] ICTY Rules, r 98*ter* (C). In the *Furundzija* Appeal Judgment (21 Jul 2000), para 69, the ICTY relied on ECHR jurisprudence, stating that the right to a reasoned opinion is an aspect of the fair trial requirement embodied in Arts 20 and 21 of the Statute.
[351] *Ruiz Torija v Spain* (1994) 19 EHRR 553, para 29, cited in *Furundzija* Judgment, ibid, para 69.
[352] *Delalić* Appeal Judgment (20 Feb 2001), paras 481, 498; *Musema* Appeal Judgment, para 20; *Akayesu* Appeal Judgment, para 306.
[353] *Musema* Appeal Judgment, para 19; *Akayesu* Appeal Judgment, para 306.

may appear at first to be of poor quality, but may gain strength from other evidence in the case. The converse also holds true.[354]

One unfortunate consequence of this reasoning is that a person could be convicted on the basis of evidence that taken independently lacks relevance, probative value and reliability, but due to the existence of other evidence supporting a finding of guilt the evidence then becomes sufficiently reliable to secure a conviction. Chambers may also consider the weight of evidence individually. In the *Akayesu* case the Chamber held that the evidence, whether testimony or documentary, has to be assessed individually on its probative value 'according to its credibility and relevance to the allegations at issue'.[355] The Chamber thereby relies on the evidence produced by the parties. In addition, it may consider and rely on 'indisputable facts and on other elements relevant to the case, such as constitutive documents pertaining to the establishment and jurisdiction of the Tribunal, even if these were not specifically tendered in evidence by the parties during trial'.[356]

On occasions defendants have complained that the Chambers have not established sufficiently clear criteria in order to assess the weight of evidence.[357] In response the Appeals Chamber pointed out that 'it is neither possible nor proper to draw up an exhaustive list of criteria for the assessment of evidence, given the specific circumstances of each case and the duty of the judge to rule on each case in an impartial and independent manner'.[358] In this regard the ICTY Trial Chamber in *Strugar* held that:

> the general background circumstances to material events, and the actual course of material events, at times has offered valuable assistance in the task of determining where the truth lies in a body of conflicting and inconsistent oral and documentary evidence about a particular issue.... As will be seen, the Chamber has accepted some evidence notwithstanding the presence of contradicting or inconsistent evidence. At times, the Chamber rejected evidence despite the presence of other consistent evidence. At times, the Chamber has been persuaded it should accept only part of the evidence of a witness, while rejecting other parts. Where this has occurred it has been done in light of the other evidence on the issue and only after very careful scrutiny indeed of the witness and the evidence.[359]

In essence, the evidence needs to be 'reasonable' and 'reliable'.[360] Reliability has to be assessed in the context of the facts of each particular case and requires a consideration of the circumstances under which the evidence arose, its content, whether and how it is corroborated, as well as its truthfulness, voluntariness and trustworthiness.[361]

In compliance with the presumption of innocence as set out in Article 21(3) of the ICTY Statute, Art 20(3) of the ICTR Statute and Art 17(3) of the SCSL Statute, the

---

[354] *Tadić* Judgment on Allegations of Contempt, para 92.
[355] *Akayesu* Trial Judgment, para 131.
[356] Ibid.
[357] See, *inter alia, Kayishema and Ruzindana* Appeal Judgment, paras 307–11.
[358] Ibid, para 319.
[359] *ICTY Prosecutor v Strugar*, Trial Chamber Judgment (31 Jan 2005), para 7. See also *Brima* Trial Judgement, para 110 and *Sesay* Trial Judgement, para 489.
[360] *Kayishema and Ruzindana* Appeal Judgment, paras 320 and 322.
[361] *Tadić* Decision on Defence Motion on Hearsay, para 19; *Kajelijeli* Decision on Motion to Limit the Admissibility of Evidence (2 Jun 2001).

burden of proof beyond reasonable doubt lies with the prosecutor.[362] If the prosecutor does not succeed in discharging this burden in respect of every element of a crime and form of liability the judges must acquit the accused by virtue of r 87 of the ICTY, ICTR and SCSL Rules.[363] The accused is thereby entitled to the benefit of the doubt in accordance with the principle of *in dubio pro reo*.[364] Consequently, 'the evidence of the witnesses upon which the prosecution relied should be accepted as establishing beyond reasonable doubt the facts alleged, notwithstanding the evidence given by the accused and the witnesses upon which the Defence relied'.[365] Also, where more than one inference is reasonably open from a set of facts, 'the Chamber has been careful to consider whether an inference reasonably open on those facts was inconsistent with the guilt of the accused. If so, the onus and the standard of proof require that an acquittal be entered in respect of that count'.[366]

21.11.2 Corroboration

The Rules of Procedure and Evidence prescribe one situation where corroboration of the evidence is required and another in which it is not. As aforementioned, corroboration is required where a child who is 'sufficiently mature to be able to report the facts of which the child had knowledge and understands the duty to tell the truth' testifies without taking an oath pursuant to r 90(B) of the ICTY and SCSL Rules and r 90(C) of the ICTR Rules. In cases of sexual assault r 96 of the ICTY/ICTR/SCSL Rules make it explicit that no corroboration of the victim's testimony shall be required. Other than this the relevant instruments are silent on corroboration. Case law has, however, established that corroboration does not constitute a *sine qua non* requirement. In this respect the ad hoc tribunals differ from a number of civil law

---

[362] This principle has been confirmed by case law. See *Delalić,* Trial Chamber Judgment (16 Nov 1998), paras 599, 601, where the Chamber held that the onus of proof on the prosecutor was a general principle of law. See also *Kayishema and Ruzindana,* Trial Chamber Judgment (21 May 1999), para 84. There is a shift of burden where the defence 'makes an allegation, or when the allegation made by the Prosecutor is not an essential element of the charges of the indictment'. See *Delalić* Trial Judgment, para 602. In such situations the defence is required to prove its allegations on the balance of probabilities, ibid, para 603. See also *Krnojelac* Trial Judgment, para 3; *Kunarac, Kovac and Vukovic* Trial Judgment (22 Feb 2001), para 559; *SCSL Prosecutor v Sesay et al,* Trial Judgement (2 Mar 2009), para 475.

[363] ICTY Rule 87(A), which is similar to r 87(A) of the ICTR and SCSL Rules, provides: 'When both parties have completed their presentations of the case, the Presiding Judge shall declare the hearing closed, and the Trial Chamber shall deliberate in private. A finding of guilt may be reached only when a majority of the Trial Chamber is satisfied that guilt has been proved beyond reasonable doubt'. See *Tadić* Appeals Judgment on Allegations of Contempt against Prior Counsel, Milan Vujin, para 131; *Limaj* Trial Judgment, para 10.

[364] *Delalić* Trial Judgment, paras 601, 603; *Krnojelac* Trial Judgment, paras 5, 560; *Blagoević and Jokić* Trial Judgment, paras 18, 21; *Halilović* Trial Judgment, paras 12 and 15. See *Limaj* Trial Judgment, para 10; *Strugar* Trial Judgment, para 5, stating that if there is any inference reasonably open from the evidence inconsistent with the guilt of the accused the accused must be acquitted.

[365] *Akayesu* Trial Judgment, para 136. See also *Limaj* Trial Judgment, para 22.

[366] *Limaj* Trial Judgement, para 10; *Brđanin* Trial Judgement, para. 35; *Krnojelac* Trial Judgement, para 67; *Martić* Trial Judgement, para 24.

jurisdictions.[367] As regards the application of the civil law principle *unus testis, nullus testis* (one witness is no witness), which postulates that corroboration of evidence is required before any weight can be attached to it, the chambers of the ad hoc tribunals have denied the applicability of this principle, as follows: 'The Chamber can rule on the basis of a single testimony provided such testimony is, in its opinion, relevant and credible'.[368]

However, although corroboration is not required as a guarantee of the credibility of particular evidence, the Chambers are 'nevertheless aware of the importance of corroboration'.[369] Corroboration has been deemed necessary in specific circumstances, for instance, where internal inconsistencies and contradictions with other evidence demonstrated a poor, selective or tainted recollection of events.[370] Where the evidence is not in fact corroborated the Chambers scrutinise the evidence against the accused 'with great care before accepting it as sufficient to make a finding of guilt against the accused'.[371] The Trial Chamber may in such situations decide not to rely on the evidence at all.[372] Alternatively, 'the corroboration of testimonies, even by many witnesses, does not establish the credibility of those testimonies'.[373]

Furthermore, certain categories of evidence require corroboration in order for the judges to rely upon them for a finding of guilt. One such category is untested evidence directly implicating the accused. In this regard, the Appeals Chamber has incorporated the principles developed by the ECHR and held that 'all the evidence must normally be produced at a public hearing, in the presence of the accused, with a view to adversarial argument. There are exceptions to this principle, but they must not infringe the rights of the defence'.[374] A conviction cannot be based 'solely, or in a decisive manner', on untested evidence.[375] Accordingly, as was held by the Appeals Chamber, 'evidence which has not been cross-examined and goes to the acts and conduct of the accused or is pivotal to the Prosecution's case will require corroboration if used to establish a conviction'.[376] This approach is supported by the case law

---

[367] See, for instance, Arts 341(2) and 342(3) CCP of the Dutch Criminal Code of Procedure pursuant to which the testimony of a witness or the admissions from the accused must be corroborated. See further JF Nijboer, *De Waarde van het Bewijs* (Gouda Quint, 1996) 43.

[368] *Akayesu* Trial Judgment, para 135; *Rutaganda* Trial Judgment, para 18; *Musema* Trial Judgment, para 43; *Semanza* Appeals Judgment, para 153; *Gacumbitsi* Appeals Judgment, para 72; *Tadić* Trial Judgement, paras 535, 539; *Krnojelac* Trial Judgement, para 71; *SCSL Prosecutor v Brima et al*, Trial Judgement (20 Jun 2007), para 98.

[369] *Kayishema and Ruzindana* Trial Judgment, para 80; *Musema* Trial Judgment, paras 42 and 75: '[a]ny evidence which is supported by other evidence logically possesses a greater probative value than evidence which stands alone, unless both pieces of evidence are not credible'.

[370] *Fofana* Trial Judgement, para 283.

[371] *Krnojelac* Trial Judgment, para 8; *Brima* Trial Judgement, para 109; *Fofana* Trial Judgement, para 265.

[372] Ibid, para 71; *Brđanin* Trial Judgment, para 27.

[373] *Musema* Trial Judgment, para 46; *Tadić* Judgment on Allegation on Contempt Against Prior Counsel Milan Vujin, para 92.

[374] *Prlić* Appeals Decision on Transcripts of Jadranko Prlić, para 52.

[375] Ibid, para 53; reliance on *AM v Italy*, App No 37019/97, para 25; *Saïdi v France* (1994) 17 EHRR 251, paras 43–44; *Unterpertinger v Austria*, paras 31–33; *Lucà v Italy* (2001) 36 EHRR 807, paras 39–45. See also *Prosecutor v Haraqija & Morina* Appeals Chamber Judgment (23 Jul 2009), para 61.

[376] *Martić* Decision on Appeal Against the Trial Chamber Decision on the Evidence of Witness Milan Babić, para 20; *Martić* Trial Judgment, para 27; *Haraqija & Morina* Judgement on Allegations of Contempt (17 Dec 2008), para 23; *Milutinović* Decision on Prosecution Motion for Admission of Evidence Pursuant to Rule 92*quater* (16 Feb 2007), para 13; *Haradinaj* Decision on Prosecution's Motion for

of the ECHR, which allows the admissibility of untested evidence even where it goes to the acts and conduct of the accused, provided that 'a conviction is based solely or to a decisive degree on depositions that had been made by a person whom the accused has had no opportunity to examine or to have examined, whether during the investigation or at the trial, the rights of the defence are restricted to an extent that is incompatible with the guarantees provided by Article 6'.[377] Thus, statements admitted under r 92*quater* or r 92*quinquies* can only be relied upon if sufficiently corroborated. In the case of *Haraqija and Morina* the Chamber held that

> [i]n order for a piece of evidence to be able to corroborate untested evidence, it must not only induce a strong belief of truthfulness of the latter, ie enhance its probative value, but must also be obtained in an independent manner. Rejecting a technical approach to this issue, the Trial Chamber holds that corroborating evidence may include pieces of evidence that, although originating from the same source, arose under different circumstances, at different times and for different purposes. Such evidence would indeed meet the requirement of 'sufficient corroboration', which is aimed at preventing an encroachment on the rights of the accused.[378]

The Appeals Chamber affirmed that a conviction cannot rest decisively on untested evidence. It found that '[w]hether untested evidence is sufficiently corroborated is necessarily a fact specific inquiry and varies from case to case'.[379] In this particular case, the Appeals Chamber was not satisfied that the untested evidence from the co-accused was sufficiently corroborated, given that all other available evidence was also untested, consisting of double or triple hearsay. The Appeals Chamber, therefore, overturned the conviction of one of the accused.[380]

Another category of evidence that would be aided by corroboration is evidence given by a co-perpetrator. Co-perpetrators are frequently considered to be of diminished credibility, given that their answers are not trustworthy because they may seek to put the blame on the accused to avoid self-incrimination. Their evidence should, therefore, be treated with suspicion even where the co-perpetrator came to testify as a *viva voce* witness in the case and, as such, was subjected to the test of cross-examination. In most cases, although not a strict requirement, such evidence is only relied upon if corroborated.[381] For instance, in *Halilović*, the ICTY Chamber held as follows:

Admission of Evidence Pursuant to Rule 92*quater* and 13th Motion for Trial-Related Protective Measures (7 Sep 2007), para 12; *Prlić* Decision on the Prosecution Motion for Admission of a Written Statement Pursuant to Rule 92*quater* of the Rules (Hasan Rizvic), paras 22–23; *Prlić* Appeals Decision on Transcripts of Jadranko Prlić, para 53; *Blagoević* Trial Judgement, para 26; *Halilović* Trial Judgement, para 19.

[377] *Luca v Italy*, para 40; relied on in *Martić* Decision on Appeal Against the Trial Chamber Decision on the Evidence of Witness Milan Babic, para 20; *Haraqija* Contempt Judgment, para 24.

[378] *Haraqija* Contempt Judgment, para 41.

[379] *Haraqija & Morina* Appeals Judgment (23 Jul 2009), para 62.

[380] Ibid, paras 64–69.

[381] See *Cyangugu* Trial Judgement (25 Feb 2004), paras 92, 95, 108, 113, 118, 131, 135, 141, 174, 176, 216, 321, 403, 438, 484, 540, 587, where the Trial Chamber required corroboration of such testimony. In *Limaj* Trial Judgement, para 29, the Trial Chamber was extremely cautious of witnesses who were motivated by avoiding self-incrimination and considered one witness, who was clearly motivated as such, to be of diminished credibility. See also *Sesay* Trial Judgement, paras 497–498.

In evaluating the evidence given *viva voce* the Trial Chamber has given due regard, among other things, to the individual circumstances of the witness, including the witness' possible involvement in the events and the risk of self-incrimination, his relationship with the Accused and possible contamination between witnesses' testimonies. The Trial Chamber has considered the internal consistency of each witness' testimony and other features of their evidence, as well as whether corroborating evidence exists in the Trial record.... In light of the factors mentioned above, in particular the risk of self -incrimination and the possible contamination between witnesses' testimonies, the Trial Chamber is not fully satisfied that the evidence it has heard from certain witnesses was entirely reliable. The Trial Chamber has therefore treated their testimony with caution and has relied on it only if corroborated by other evidence.[382]

The inherent reliability is particularly undermined where evidence is given in an interview with the prosecution by a co-perpetrator who is jointly tried with the accused but does not himself testify. Due to the lack of oath and the test of cross-examination and demeanour such evidence must be treated with caution and, at a minimum, be corroborated.[383]

In respect of the ICC, in confirming the charges the Pre-Trial Chamber pronounced itself on the requirement of corroboration, holding that such was not required under the ICC rules in order to prove any crime. However, in certain circumstances, for instance where the evidence is given by children or anonymous witnesses, lack of corroboration may diminish the weight of the evidence.[384]

21.11.3   Documentary Evidence

As highlighted in the *Brđanin and Talić* case the standard of proof for admission of documents is lower than the standard which is applied when assessing the weight of the evidence.[385] In order to accord appropriate weight to a document, its authenticity and its source or authorship need to be considered.[386] The admission into evidence of a document does not have any bearing on the determination as to the authenticity or trustworthiness of the document. These are matters of weight to be assessed by the

---

[382] *Halilović* Trial Judgement, para 17; *Martić* Trial Judgement, para 25.

[383] *Prlić* Appeals Decision on Transcripts of Jadranko Prlić, paras 26, 38, 62; *Milošević* Decision on Admissibility of Prosecution Investigator's Evidence (30 Sep 2002), para 18; *Blagoević and Jokić* Decision on Prosecution's Motion for Clarification of Oral Decision Regarding Admissibility of Accused's Statement, (18 Sep 2003), paras 24, 26, 28, 33; *Limaj* Decision on the Prosecution's Motions to Admit Prior Statements as Substantive Evidence (25 April 2005), para 27; *Popović* Decision on the Admissibility of the Borovčanin Interview and the Amendment of the Rule 65*Ter* Exhibit List, para 65; and Judge Kimberly Prost's conclusion in his Partial Dissenting Opinion.

[384] *Katanga* Confirmation Decision, paras 150–151 and 156–160, relying on the *Lubanga* Confirmation Decision, para 120, fn 28.

[385] *Brđanin and Talić* Admission of Evidence Order, para 18.

[386] *Brđanin and Talić* Order on the Standards governing the admission of evidence (15 Feb 2002), paras 18 and 19, referring to the *Delalić* Decision on the Motion of the Prosecution for the Admissibility of Evidence (19 Mar 1998), para 20.

Trial Chamber at a later stage.[387] The absence of a signature or a stamp does not necessarily mean that a document lacks authenticity.[388] In order to determine the authenticity of a document, its form, contents and purported use, as well as the position of the parties on the matter, are crucial.[389] Although not a requirement for admission,[390] documents that were authenticated by a witness will generally be given more probative value than documents that were not introduced by a witness.[391]

As regards the form of documentary evidence the tribunals consider elements such as the originality of the copy, whether it is registered or enrolled with an institutional authority, if it is signed, sealed, certified or stamped, whether it is officially authorised by an authority or organisation and whether it is duly executed.[392] Regarding the content of a document the Chamber will consider all circumstances of the case, 'including its relation to oral testimony given before the Chamber pertaining to the content of the document'.[393] These factors are not conclusive. In addition, it should be noted that '[a]s a general rule, it is insufficient to rely on any one factor alone as proof or disproof of the authenticity of the document. Authenticity must be established through reference to all relevant factors'.[394]

Documents should not be considered in isolation. The Trial Chamber must review all the evidence and be satisfied that the prosecution proved beyond reasonable doubt their authenticity, reliability and completeness.[395] The Trial Chamber cannot, *a priori*, accept that the contents of the documents submitted are true, accurate and a complete portrayal of the facts.[396] The reliability, relevance and probative value of the documents in the overall context of the evidence must be established before any significant weight can be accorded to them. The Trial Chamber must rely on the best evidence available in the determination of the innocence or guilt of the accused.[397]

It has further been made clear that the reliability and credibility of the source may have an impact on the reliability and credibility of the document in question.[398] Where the source is the party which relies on the document this fact alone does not necessarily render the document unreliable.[399] Evidence aiming to support a defence of alibi is normally more reliable where its source is not the accused.[400]

---

[387] *Bizimungu* Decision on Bicamumpaka's Request for Certification to Appeal a Decision on 6 October 2004 on Bicamumpaka's Motion Opposing the Admissibility of Testimony of Witnesses GFA, GKB, and GAP (17 Nov 2004), para 14; *Limaj* Trial Judgment, para 12. See *Sesay* Trial Judgement, para 514.

[388] *Brđanin and Talić* Order, ibid, para 20; *Blagoević* Trial Judgement, para 29; *Halilović* Trial Judgement, para 21.

[389] *Musema* Trial Judgment, para 66.

[390] Save for at the SCSL, see section 21.5.

[391] *ICTY Prosecutor v Hadžihasanović & Kubura*, Decision on the Admissibility of Documents of the Defence of Enver Hadžihasanović, (22 Jun 2005), paras 33–35; *Orić* Trial Judgement (30 Jun 2006), para 29.

[392] *Musema* Trial Judgment, para 67.

[393] Ibid, para 70.

[394] Ibid, para 72.

[395] *Brđanin* Trial Judgment, para 32.

[396] Guidelines Standards Governing the Admission of Evidence, (23 Apr 2003), para 4; *Blagoević* Trial Judgement, para 29; *Halilović* Trial Judgement, para 21.

[397] Guidelines Standards Governing the Admission of Evidence, para 8.

[398] *Musema* Trial Judgment, para 63.

[399] Ibid, para 61.

[400] Ibid, para 63. On appeal Musema complained about this reasoning. It was held on his behalf that 'since all persons are entitled to equal treatment before the Tribunal, documents produced by him cannot be accorded a lesser status than documents produced by others' (*Musema* Appeal Judgment, para 40). The

In the ICC context the reliability of documentary evidence affects its weight more than its admissibility. The Pre-Trial Chamber held that this approach was most consistent with r 63(2) pursuant to which a Chamber is authorised to 'assess freely all evidence submitted in order to determine its relevance and admissibility in accordance with Article 69'.[401] The determination of the probative value of documentary evidence and its reliability is undertaken on a case-by-case basis. Inconsistencies in documentary or other evidence do not render it inadmissible for the purpose of the confirmation hearing. Instead, the Chamber will determine the weight of inconsistent evidence by looking at the evidence as a whole and consider its reliability and credibility.[402]

21.11.4   Hearsay Evidence

Whilst Trial Chambers tend to admit hearsay evidence in many situations they are generally more cautious in assessing the weight of hearsay evidence. On the one hand, hearsay evidence is treated as 'indirect evidence with the understanding that such evidence is as much evidence as direct evidence'.[403] On the other hand, Chambers are inclined to treat it with caution.[404] Indeed, the Appeals Chamber in *Milošević* confirmed that 'although it depends upon infinitely variable circumstances of the particular case, the weight or probative value to be afforded to hearsay evidence will usually be less than that given to the testimony of a witness who has given it under a form of oath and who has been cross-examined'.[405] The reason for this caution is that the reliability of the hearsay evidence 'may be affected by a potential compounding of errors of perception and memory'.[406]

Trial Chamber disagreed, but stated that 'it is correct to state that the sole fact that evidence is proffered by the accused is no reason to find it, *ipso facto*, less reliable', para 50.

[401]   *Katanga* Confirmation Decision, para 78.

[402]   Ibid, para 116.

[403]   *Brđanin* Trial Judgment, para 20.

[404]   *Rutaganda* Trial Judgment, para 18; *Sesay* Trial Judgement, para 495.

[405]   *Milošević* Decision on Admissibility of Prosecution Investigator's Evidence (30 Sep 2002), para 18; see also *Kordić and Čerkez* Appeal Judgment (17 Dec 2004), para 787; *Tadić* Separate Opinion of Judge Stephen on the Prosecutor's Motion Requesting Protective Measures for Victims and Witnesses (10 Aug 1995) 2–3; *Simba* Trial Judgment (13 Dec 2005), para 209; *Naletilić* Trial Judgement, para 11; *Brima* Trial Judgement, para 100; SCSL *Prosecutor v Fofana*, Decision on Appeal Against 'Decision on Prosecution's Motion for Judicial Notice and Admission of Evidence', Separate Opinion of Justice Robertson (16 May 2005), para 6.

[406]   *Kamuhanda* Decision on Kamuhanda's Motion to Admit Evidence Pursuant to Rule 89 of the Rules of Procedure and Evidence (10 Feb 2003), para 10; *Simić* Trial Judgment, para 23; *Naletilić* Trial Judgment, para 11 and *Krnojelac* Trial Judgment, para 70; *Fofana* Trial Judgement, para 264; *Sesay* Trial Judgement, para 495.

Particular emphasis has been placed on the reliability of hearsay evidence.[407] In order to test its reliability 'the content of the evidence and the circumstances under which it arose',[408] as well as its voluntariness, truthfulness and trustworthiness are factors to be considered.[409]

As a matter of law it is permissible to base a conviction on circumstantial or hearsay evidence.[410] However, caution is warranted in such circumstances. There may be good reason to consider whether hearsay evidence is supported by other credible and reliable evidence in support of a finding of guilt. In *Muvunyi*, the Appeals Chamber found that the Trial Chamber had not acted reasonably and with the requisite degree of caution when it relied on hearsay evidence from two witnesses to establish the systematic killing of Tutsi lecturers and students, notwithstanding their lack of detail in respect of those killings.[411]

Most Trial Chambers are reluctant to rely on uncorroborated hearsay evidence even if it is otherwise reliable and credible. One ICTY Trial Chamber has affirmed that hearsay evidence has no weight unless substantiated by other evidence and is moreover shown to be reliable.[412] In another context, the same Trial Chamber held: 'It will be important, however, to evaluate with care the reliability of any hearsay evidence which has been admitted before reliance is placed on it for the purpose of establishing guilt'.[413] The Appeals Chamber has confirmed that this is of paramount importance.[414] An ICTR Trial Chamber held that hearsay evidence, standing alone, has limited probative value and that '[t]he reliability of the testimony and its probative value are likely to depend primarily on corroborative or contradictory evidence to be presented later by the Defence or Prosecution'.[415] It has further regularly been held that hearsay evidence is not inadmissible *per se*, but is treated with caution,[416] 'taking into account that [its] source [has] neither been tested in cross-examination nor been the subject of an oath or solemn declaration'.[417]

Double hearsay raises greater concerns of reliability because the truthfulness of that information depends not only on the credibility of the witness and the accuracy of his observation, but also on the credibility and reliability of the declarant.[418]

---

[407] *Naletilić* Appeal Judgement, para 217.

[408] *Aleksovski* Decision on the Prosecutor's Appeal on Admissibility of Evidence (16 Feb 1999), para 15; *Limaj* Decision on the Prosecution's Motion to Admit Prior Statements as Substantive Evidence (25 Apr 2005), para 17.

[409] Aleksovski Decision, ibid, para 15; *Blagoević and Jokić* Trial Judgment, para 21; *Halilović* Trial Judgement, para 15; *Martić* Trial Judgment, para 24; *Brđanin* Trial Judgement, para 28; *Sesay* Trial Judgement, para 495.

[410] *Muvunyi* Appeal Judgement (29 Aug 2008), para 70; *Haraqija & Morina* Appeal Judgment, para 62; *Fofana and Kondewa*, CDF Appeal Judgement (28 May 2008), para 199.

[411] *Muvunyi* Appeal Judgement, para 70.

[412] *Limaj* Oral Ruling of 18 November 2004, 447–49.

[413] *Limaj* Decision on the Prosecution's Motions to Admit Prior Statements as Substantive Evidence (25 Apr 2005), para 27.

[414] *Prlić* Appeals Judgment, para 51; also *Aleksovski* Decision on Prosecutor's Appeal on Admissibility of Evidence (16 Feb 1999), para 25; *Popović* Decision on Appeals Against Decision Admitting Material Related to Borovčanin's Questioning (14 Dec 2007), para 50.

[415] *Bagosora* Decision on Admissibility of Evidence of Witness DP, para 8.

[416] *Nahimana* Trial Judgment, para 97.

[417] *Brima* Trial Judgement, para 100; also see *Krnojelac* Trial Judgment, para 70.

[418] *Ntakirutimana* Appeal Judgment, para 211. See also *Aleksovski* Decision on Prosecutor's Appeal on Admission of Evidence (16 Feb 1999), para 15; *Blaškić* Decision on the Standing Objection of the Defence to the Admission of Hearsay with no Inquiry as to its Reliability, para 12.

At the ICC it has been held that the fact that evidence is not based on direct observation but on hearsay may affect the probative value of that evidence, albeit not its admissibility for the purpose of the confirmation.[419] If the source is known the probative value of hearsay evidence is evaluated on a case-by-case basis, considering factors such as 'the consistency of the information itself and its consistency with the evidence as a whole, the reliability of the source and the possibility for the Defence to challenge the source'.[420] If the source of the hearsay evidence is unknown its probative value is further affected and must be considered in light of other evidence admitted for the purpose of the confirmation hearing.[421] Given the difficulties in ascertaining the truthfulness and authenticity of anonymous hearsay evidence, this type of evidence may, in general, only be used to corroborate other evidence.[422] The Pre-Trial Chamber has further indicated that it would exercise caution in relying on such evidence in order to affirm or reject any of the prosecution's assertions.[423]

As for the weight of summaries of anonymous witness statements the Appeals Chamber has determined that due consideration must be given to the diminished ability of the Defence to challenge the evidence because it has not received the full set of statements, the identities of the makers of the statements or other information which could authenticate them.[424] Following this Appeals Chamber's directive the Pre-Trial Chamber has held that hearsay evidence has a lower probative value if the Defence is not aware of the witness's identity and is not given the full witness statement.[425] It recognised that summaries have a lesser probative value than unredacted parts of redacted statements, interview notes or transcripts, but held that 'the difference in probative value between a summary and the unredacted parts of heavily redacted statements, interview notes or interview transcripts is minimal'.[426] Given the difficulties in assessing the probative value of anonymous summary evidence the lack of corroboration could affect the probative value of such summary.[427]

21.11.5 *Viva Voce* Testimony

In order to determine the credibility of *viva voce* witnesses the Trial Chamber must consider 'their demeanour, conduct and character', as well as 'the probability, consistency and other features of their evidence, including the corroboration which

---

[419] *Lubanga* Confirmation Decision, para 103; *Katanga* Confirmation Decision, para 137.

[420] *Katanga* Confirmation Decision, para 141.

[421] *Lubanga* Confirmation Decision, para 103; *Katanga* Confirmation Decision, paras 118–120.

[422] *Lubanga* Confirmation Decision, para 106; *Katanga* Confirmation Decision, paras 138, 140.

[423] *Katanga* Confirmation Decision, para 139.

[424] *Lubanga* Appeals Chamber Judgment of the Appeal of Mr Thomas Lubanga Dyilo against the Decision of Pre-Trial Chamber I entitled First Decision on the Prosecution Requests and Amended Requests for Redactions under Rule 81 (14 Dec 2006), para. 51.

[425] *Katanga* Confirmation Decision, para 159.

[426] *Katanga & Ngudjolo*, Corrigendum to the Decision on Evidentiary Scope of the Confirmation Hearing, Preventive Relocation and Disclosure under Article 67(2) of the Statute and Rule 77 of the Rules (25 Apr 2008), para 89.

[427] *Katanga* Confirmation Decision, para 160.

may be forthcoming from other evidence and circumstances of the case', as well as 'the knowledge of the facts upon which they give evidence, their disinterestedness, integrity [and] veracity'.[428]

The Appeals Chamber has confirmed the Trial Chamber's practice of considering 'inconsistencies in the light of its evaluation of the overall credibility of each particular witness'.[429] Trial Chambers further assess the credibility of witnesses 'on the basis of the circumstances surrounding the testimony as a whole, and in light of the testimony of the earlier witnesses',[430] as well as the exhibits admitted.[431] Factors undermining the credibility of a witness, such as an incentive to lie or a particular bias against the accused, must be considered. An SCSL Chamber has ruled that 'a witness with a self-interest to serve may seek to inculpate others and exculpate himself, but it does not follow that such a witness is incapable of telling the truth'.[432] The mere suggestion that a witness might be implicated in the commission of crimes is insufficient for the Trial Chamber to discard that witness's testimony.

Moreover, being from a different ethnic group or a victim, on its own, does not render a witness unreliable, but may, in particular circumstances, be a ground for doubting the reliability of such a witness in light of 'his individual testimony, and such concerns as the Defence may substantiate either in cross-examination or through its own evidence-in-chief'.[433] In *Limaj*, a number of former KLA members who testified for the prosecution against their former KLA fellows:

> left the Chamber with a distinct impression that it was materially influenced by a strong sense of association with the KLA in general, and one or more of the Accused in particular. It appeared that overriding loyalties had a bearing upon the willingness of some witnesses to speak the truth in court about some issues. It is not disputed that notions of honour and other group values have a particular relevance to the cultural background of witnesses with Albanian roots in Kosovo.[434]

Discrepancies between in-court testimony and earlier accounts or between the testimonies of different witnesses on the same events in relation to matters peripheral to the charges in the indictment in general weaken the credibility of the witness in question.[435] However, particularly where it concerns victim witnesses, minor discrepancies are to be expected in light of the time lapse between the events and the witness's testimony and the impact of trauma, none of which generally discredit the witness.[436] In this regard the ICTR Chamber in *Kayishema and Ruzindana* held:

---

[428] *Brđanin* Trial Judgment, para 25. See also *Akayesu* Appeal Judgment, para 128. *Blagoević* Trial Judgement, para 23; *Brima* Trial Judgement, para 108; *Fofana* Trial Judgement, para 256; *Sesay* Trial Judgement, para 486.

[429] *Akayesu* Appeal Judgment, para 136.

[430] *Simić* Trial Judgment, para 26.

[431] *Ntagerura* Appeal Judgment, paras 172–74.

[432] *Brima* Trial Judgement, para. 125.

[433] *Tadić* Trial Judgement, para 541.

[434] *Limaj* Trial Judgement, para 13.

[435] *Simić* Trial Judgment, para 22; *Krnojelac* Trial Judgment, para 69; *Blagoević* Trial Judgement, para 23.

[436] *Krnojelac* Trial Judgement, para 69; *Kunarac* Trial Judgement, para 564; *Vasiljević* Trial Judgement, para 21; *Brđanin* Trial Judgement, paras 25–26; *Strugar* Trial Judgement, para 8; *Fofana* Trial Judgement, para 262; *Sesay* Trial Judgement, paras 489–491.

The Chamber is aware of the impact of trauma on the testimony of witnesses. However, the testimonies cannot be simply disregarded because they describe traumatic and horrific realities. Some inconsistencies and imprecision in the testimonies are expected and were carefully considered in light of the circumstances faced by the witnesses.[437]

In the ICTR *Akayesu* case the Chamber worked on the basis of the assumption that all the witnesses suffered from post-traumatic or extreme stress disorders and '[i]nconsistencies or imprecisions in the testimonies, accordingly, have been assessed in the light of this assumption, personal background and the atrocities they have experienced or have been subjected to'.[438] Moreover, 'there is no recognised rule of evidence that traumatic circumstances necessarily render a witness's evidence unreliable. It must be demonstrated *in concreto* why "the traumatic context" renders a given witness unreliable'.[439]

Thus, Trial Chambers at the international criminal tribunals generally excuse witnesses who narrate 'repetitive, continuous or traumatic' events in court in front of the accused for the purpose of filling memory gaps regarding exact dates or time and/or to recollect the sequence of these events.[440] Some Chambers have, however, been more cautious in relying on traumatised witnesses. For instance, in the ICTY case of *Limaj*, in evaluating the reliability of the testimonies given by traumatised witnesses, the Trial Chamber took into consideration 'that any observation they made at the time may have been affected by stress and fear; this has called for particular scrutiny on the part of the Chamber'.[441] The Trial Chamber further took account of the possibility that cultural factors of loyalty and honour – the witnesses being so inter-connected – may have affected the reliability of the evidence given by traumatised witnesses.[442]

Whether or not a witness was honest in giving evidence is not the decisive factor in assessing the reliability of his testimony. Where a witness is considered credible the Trial Chamber must still make a determination on the reliability of his testimony. The objective reliability of the evidence constitutes the primary basis for accepting the evidence.[443] This is a case-by-case evaluation taking all above circumstances into consideration.

---

[437] *Kayishema and Ruzindana* Trial Judgment, para 75, where the Trial Chamber also stated that '[t]he possible traumatism of these witnesses caused by their painful experience of violence during the conflict in Rwanda is a matter of particular concern to the Chamber. The recounting of traumatic experience is likely to evoke memories of the fear and the pain once inflicted on the witness and thereby affect his or her ability fully or adequately to recount the sequence of events in a judicial context. The Chamber has considered the testimony of those witnesses in this light'; see *Akayesu* Trial Judgment, para 142; *Rutaganda* Trial Judgment, para 22. See also *Naletilić* Trial Judgement, para 10.

[438] *Akayesu* Trial Judgment, para 143.

[439] *Kunarac* Appeal Judgment, para 12; *Furundžija* Appeal Judgment, para 109, holding that '[t]here is no reason why a person with [post-traumatic stress disorder] cannot be a perfectly reliable witness'.

[440] *Kunarac* Appeal Judgment, para 267.

[441] *Limaj* Trial Judgment, para 15.

[442] Ibid.

[443] *Delalić [Čelebići]* Appeal Judgment, paras 491 and 506.

21.11.6   Prior Statements

A distinction should be drawn between: (1) witness statements and other non-judicial testimonies; (2) testimonies before the tribunal, and; (3) statements before other judicial bodies.[444] As regards discrepancies between witnesses' written statements and their oral statements in court the Trial Chamber held that the written statements of witnesses are not evidence *per se*, but may be so admitted, in part or in whole, to undermine a witness's credentials.[445] The Chamber will compare written statements with oral testimony and consider any discrepancies between the two. In so doing the Chamber will take account of the significant lapses of time between the events, written and oral statements,[446] language and translation problems and whether or not the witness had read the written statement.[447] It has further been recognised that 'it lies in the nature of criminal proceedings that a witness may be asked different questions at trial than in prior interviews and that he may remember additional details when specifically asked in court'.[448] Thus, a lot depends on the 'conditions under which the prior statement was provided, as well as on other factors relevant to, or indicia of, the prior statement's reliability or credibility, or both'.[449] Given the fact that the written statements were not made under solemn declaration and not taken by judicial officers 'the probative value attached to [them] is, in the Chamber's view, considerably less than direct sworn testimony before the Chamber, the truth of which has been subjected to the test of cross-examination'.[450]

The Trial Chamber in *Limaj* was faced with prior inconsistent statements of witnesses who had completely reversed their stories and declared themselves hostile to the prosecution. The Trial Chamber accepted that as a matter of principle, prior inconsistent statements may possibly have some positive probative force, at least if they corroborate other apparently credible evidence adduced from other witnesses during trial. In the proceedings at hand the Chamber was not persuaded that the prior inconsistent statements of two witnesses could be safely relied upon 'as the sole or principal basis for proof of a material fact. In the case of these two witnesses, this is especially so because each witness, in oral evidence, disavowed, in very material respects, what previously had been stated in the interview'.[451]

Trial Chambers will consider the prior statement in so far as the inconsistencies between the prior statement and the oral testimony 'raise doubt in relation to the particular piece of evidence in question or, where such inconsistencies are found to be

---

[444]   *Musema* Trial Judgment, para 83.

[445]   *Kayishema and Ruzindana* Trial Judgment, para 77.

[446]   Ibid, para 77; *Akayesu* Trial Judgment, para 140, where the Chamber held that memory over time naturally degenerates.

[447]   *Akayesu* Appeal Judgment, para 133; *Akayesu* Trial Judgment, para 137; *Rutaganda* Trial Judgment, para 19; *Musema* Trial Judgment, para 85.

[448]   *Limaj* Trial Judgment, para 13; *Naletilić* Trial Judgement, para 10; *Vasiljević* Trial Judgment, para 21; *Fofana* Trial Judgement, para 263; *Sesay* Trial Judgement, para 489–491; *Norman* Decision on Disclosure of Witness Statements, para 25.

[449]   *Musema* Trial Judgment, para 83.

[450]   *Akayesu* Trial Judgment, para 137; *Musema* Trial Judgment, para 86; *Naletilić* Trial Judgement, para. 12

[451]   *Limaj* Trial Judgment, para 14.

material to the witnesses' evidence as a whole'.[452] The Trial Chamber will listen to the explanation of the witnesses[453] for the inconsistencies that may occur and will, in light of all circumstances of the case determine whether this explanation removes the doubt. In order to remove the doubt, the explanation needs to be one of substance; an explanation of mere procedure does not suffice.[454] The Trial Chamber in the ICTR case of *Kayishema and Ruzindana* also held that a doubt can be removed with the corroboration of other evidence, even though corroboration is not necessary.[455]

Possible inconsistency between two testimonies by the same witness, both given under solemn declaration, affect the credibility and reliability of the later testimony.[456] The Chamber only assesses the credibility and reliability in the later test, as the earlier one has been assessed by another Chamber.[457] In assessing the probative value of statements made before other judicial bodies, the Chamber relies on general principles, 'taking into account the circumstances and conditions in which the documents were produced'.[458] However, 'judicial testimonies (and other testimonies made under oath or solemn declaration) tend, as a general rule, to demonstrate greater reliability than non-judicial testimonies'.[459]

21.11.7   Expert Evidence

The Trial Chamber will rely on expert evidence to the extent that the subject matter is within the expertise of the expert. Expert evidence must moreover be reliable. In weighing expert testimony the Trial Chamber will take into consideration the basis upon which the expert formed an opinion, and the expert's explanation thereto, corroboration with other evidence and the extent to which the accused has had the opportunity to test the accuracy of the information given by the expert.[460] The competence of the experts, the methodologies used and the credibility of their findings constitute important considerations in evaluating expert evidence.[461] Any alleged bias of the expert witness and his relationship to the accused are also matters

---

[452]   *Kayishema and Ruzindana* Trial Judgment, para 77.

[453]   *Musema* Trial Judgment, para 88.

[454]   An explanation commonly given is that the interviewer did not correctly transcribe what the witness said. In the absence of evidence supporting that allegation, such explanation does not normally remove the doubt raised. *Kayishema and Ruzindana* Trial Judgment, para 78. An explanation relating to the contents of the interview may, however, suffice to remove the doubt, ibid, para 79; *ICTR Prosecutor v Bagilishema*, Trial Chamber Judgment (7 Jun 2001), para 24, where it was held that issues such as traumas, lapse of time, language problems and others, may provide an adequate explanation for inconsistencies. However, where the inconsistencies cannot be so explained to the satisfaction of the Chamber the reliability of witness testimony may be questioned.

[455]   *Kayishema and Ruzindana* Trial Judgment, para 80.

[456]   *Musema* Trial Judgment, para 89.

[457]   Ibid, para 90.

[458]   Ibid, para 92.

[459]   Ibid, para 94.

[460]   *Bizimungu* Decision on Defence Motion for Exclusion of Portions of Testimony of Expert Witness Dr Alison Des Forges (2 Sep 2005), para 21; *Fofana* Trial Judgement, para 269.

[461]   *Blagoević and Jokić* Trial Judgment, para 27; *Vasiljević* Trial Judgement, para 20; *Martić* Trial Judgement, para 29; *Brima* Trial Judgement, para 150.

that may be weighed in assessing his or her credibility.[462] An expert who is more experienced than another is not necessarily accorded more weight.[463]

An expert's refusal to disclose his or her sources may be a factor undermining the weight of the relevant testimony, depending on the other sources the expert has used in forming his or her opinion.[464] In *Semanza*, the ICTR Chamber discounted expert evidence founded on 'unidentified sources', was hearsay and 'lacked sufficient details to be reliable'.[465] However, the Appeals Chamber in the same case in relation to another expert held that 'willingness to disclose particular resources and contacts if asked about specific matters' was sufficient.[466]

Expert evidence may complement, but not replace, oral testimony. A finding of guilt cannot be made exclusively on expert testimony.[467]

21.12 Free System of Proof

In conclusion, the evidentiary principles adopted and applied in the international criminal tribunals have developed in a manner allowing a wide judicial discretion in freely determining, on a case-to-case basis, whether evidence should be admitted and, if so, what weight should be attached to it. The general trend is to admit evidence and leave matters of probative value, relevance and reliability to be decided at the deliberation stage when its weight is being determined. The preference for admission rather than exclusion of any type of evidence has significantly strengthened over the years, in particular at the ICTY and SCSL. While initially certain types of evidence, such as written statements going to proof of the acts and conduct of the accused, were impermissible, such restrictions on admissibility have now been removed.

In other words, the international criminal tribunals have developed a free system of proof, similar to that in civil law jurisdictions.[468] As pointed out in the *Tadić* case: 'In the civil law system, the judge is responsible for determining the evidence that may be

---

[462] *Milošević* Decision on Admissibility of Expert Report of Vasilije Krestić (7 Dec 2005), para 5.

[463] *Kunarac* Appeal Judgment, para 21.

[464] *Bizimungu* Decision on Expert Witness Dr Alison Des Forges, paras 17 and 25; *Karemera* Decision on Joseph Nzirorera's Motion to Limit the Scope of Testimony of Expert Witnesses Alison Des Forges and Andre Guichaoua, paras 5, 17, 25.

[465] *Semanza* Trial Judgment, para 279.

[466] *Semanza* Appeal Judgement, para 305.

[467] *Nahimana* Appeal Judgment, para 509.

[468] In the French system this principle is referred to as *'le principe de la liberté des preuves'*, meaning that apart from the cases where the law provides otherwise, offences may be proven by any means of evidence and it is for the judge to decide according to his 'intime conviction' (ie inner conviction) (Art 427, Code de Procedure Pénale). Stefani *et al*, at 108, paras 131, 132, 117–18, para 150. The same principle of 'intime conviction' is found in Belgian law (Code d'Instruction Criminelle, Art 342). In Germany, the system of proof is one of *'Freibeweis'* (ie free proof), which means that judges are free in assessing the weight of evidence. They are nonetheless bound by means of proof incorporated in statutory law. See M Delmas-Marty, *Procédure Pénale d'Europe* (Paris, Dalloz, 1995) 65, 103, 105–06. The Dutch system of proof is similar to its German counterpart. The judges are free to assess the evidence on the basis of their *'rechterlijke overtuiging'* (judicial conviction), but have to base their judgment on those means of proof that are enumerated in the statutory law, in Wetboek van Strafrechtsvordering (Code of Criminal Procedure), Art 339(1).

presented during trial, guided primarily by its relevance and its revelation of truth'.[469] Common law systems, on the other hand, are familiar with exclusionary rules, such as rules that exclude irrelevant evidence in general[470] and more specifically hearsay evidence, similar fact or character evidence, opinion evidence, evidence protected by public immunity interest, evidence protected by legal privilege and improperly obtained evidence, in particular confessions that are made under pressure.

Thus, the ICTY and SCSL systems, once systems clearly influenced by principles of common law, have gradually shifted towards a system that is akin to civil law. This is perhaps not surprising or disconcerting, given that the international criminal tribunals share with civil law jurisdictions the fact that trials are conducted by professional judges who have to issue a reasoned decision at the end of the day. Professional judges are presumed to be able to base their findings on credible and reliable evidence only and avoid being misguided by irrelevant or unreliable evidence. In this regard, it has been noted that by virtue of their education and experience professional judges 'are able to ponder independently without prejudice to each and every case which will be brought before them'.[471]

However, with the increase in the admission of paper testimony instead of *viva voce* testimony and other types of hearsay, the ability of the judges to properly assess the evidence has significantly decreased. This is problematic, particularly in light of the fact that, unlike civil law jurisdictions, there is no investigative judge or other neutral officer who can take out-of-court evidence and assess the credibility of the witnesses. In the international criminal tribunals the judges can only rely on the prosecution for this exercise, but the latter has vested interests in the case.

Fortunately, the judges share this concern and have introduced new requirements for substantial corroboration of untested out-of-court evidence. It is, however, questionable whether this is a sufficient remedy for both the Defence and the Chamber to test and properly assess the evidence. It may be more appropriate to exclude such evidence, as is more frequent at the ICTR.

There are substantial grounds for arguing that judges should apply the test of admissibility pursuant to r 89(C) more rigorously and to exclude more evidence than they are ready to do now. There is no use in overwhelming the judges with massive amounts of paper evidence, much of which is not reliable or relevant. This may have the effect of distracting the judges from their important task to assess the guilt of the accused and to ascertain the truth. As has been pointed out by Judge Peter Murphy, former defence counsel before the ICTY, '[t]he indiscriminate admission of any and all material claimed to be evidence, far from being the only means of promoting a successful search for the truth, tends to bury the genuinely probative evidence in a

---

[469]   *Tadić* Decision on Hearsay, para 13.

[470]   See, eg, r 402 of the US Federal Rules of Evidence applied, which provides: 'All relevant evidence is admissible, except as otherwise provided ... evidence which is not relevant is not admissible'.

[471]   *Brima* Decision on the Prosecution Motion for Concurrent Hearing of Evidence Common to Cases SCSL-2004–15-PT and SCSL-2004–16-PT (11 May 2004), para 38; *Gbao* Order on the Urgent Request for Direction on the Time to Respond and/or an Extension of Time for the Filling of a Response to the Prosecution Motions (15 May 2003) 2; *Delalić* Decision on the Motion of the Prosecution for the Admissibility of Evidence (19 Jan 1998), para 20; and *Ntakirutimana* Decision on the Prosecutor's Motion to Join the Indictments (22 Feb 2001), para 26.

vast accumulation of evidential debris, resulting in long and inefficient trials, and frustrating rather than facilitating the task of judges trying to establish the truth'.[472]

---

[472] Murphy, 'Excluding Justice or Facilitating Justice?' 2, 3, where he expresses a similar view that 'far from furthering the search for truth through free proof, they actually frustrate their objective by making trials longer, more complex, and less efficient, and by tending to bury the truly important evidence in the midst of an enormous accumulation of evidential debris'. At 25–27 he cites Sir James Fitzjames Stephen who says, *inter alia*: 'No judge can possibly be expected, by the mere light of nature, to know how to set limits to the inquiries in which he is engaged, yet if he does not, an incalculable waste of time and energy, and a great weakening of the authority of his court, is sure to follow'.

22

The Status of Victims in International Criminal Law and Criminal Proceedings

22.1 The Legal Protection of Victims in International Law

There is considerable debate in international legal discourse whether every human rights violation corresponds to an automatic remedy for the victim. If this is not so, it follows that victims must provide proof of a substantive right to a remedy and *locus standi* in respect of each and every violation.[1] This seems to be a minority position, however, given that the general trend, particularly as this is expressly enshrined in the Basic Principles and Guidelines on the Right to a Remedy and Reparation for Victims of Gross Violations of International Human Rights Law and Serious Violations of International Humanitarian Law,[2] points to the opposite direction. The right to an effective and non-derogable remedy is amply recognised in all the global human rights instruments, namely Article 8 of the Universal Declaration of Human Rights, Article 2(3) of the International Covenant on Civil and Political Rights (ICCPR) and Article 14(1)[3] of the UN Convention against Torture. These, alongside regional human rights treaties, provide either for an individual entitlement to an effective remedy, or oblige States parties to ensure their availability to victims of crimes. The right to an effective remedy does not encompass merely a procedural right to seek redress, but includes a positive obligation to provide substantive

---

[1] This was claimed for example by the German Supreme Court in respect of the *Distomo Massacre case*, BGH – III ZR 245/98 (26 Jun 2003). The suit for reparations against Germany was initially brought about by survivors and relatives of the Distomo victims before Greek courts. See *Prefecture of Voiotia v Federal Republic of Germany, Areios Pagos (*Hellenic Court of Cassation*)* Case No.11/2000, Judgment (4 May 2000), (2001) 95 *American Journal of International Law* 198–204. See also C Tomuschat, *Human Rights: Between Idealism and Realism,* 2nd ed, (Oxford, Oxford University Press, 2008) 367ff, who argues against the existence of a right to reparation with regard to violations of humanitarian law.

[2] UN General Assembly Resolution 60/147, 16 Dec 2006 and Resolution 2005/30, UN Doc E/2005/23 (22 Apr 2005) UN Human Rights Commission on the same set of Principles. This was preceded twenty years earlier by the *Declaration of Basic Principles of Justice for Victims of Crime and Abuse of Power* (hereinafter Victims Declaration) GA Res 40/34 (29 Nov 1985). The 1985 Declaration remains the more authoritative of the two and has been cited as such by all ICC Chambers. See *ICC Prosecutor v Lubanga*, Decision on the Appeal of Victims to Participate in the Proceedings, (15 Dec 2008), para 48.

[3] UN Human Rights Committee, General Comment 29, States of Emergency (Article 4), UN Doc. CCPR/C/21/Rev.1/Add.11 (31 Aug 2001) para.14. The Committee stressed the non-derogable nature of this entitlement.

reparation.[4] The trend towards an automatic individual entitlement in respect of violations of human rights and humanitarian law seems to be shared also by the ICJ, as expressed in its Advisory Opinion in the *Palestinian Wall* case.[5] The right to a remedy is a feature found only in contemporary international instruments. It is absent, for example, in humanitarian law treaties adopted prior to the 1990s, despite the existence of provisions such as Article 3 of the 1907 Hague Convention IV and Article 91 of Protocol I of 1977, which require parties to pay compensation for violation of the laws and customs of war. These were addressed to States and were not meant to produce direct effect before national courts. Nonetheless, it is fair to argue that these treaties should be construed in accordance with contemporary developments, which necessitates reading a right to effective remedy therein. This evolutionary interpretation was recognised by the Report of the International Commission of Inquiry on Darfur (ICID), which emphasised that although the aforementioned treaty provisions were not originally intended to grant individual compensation rights, they had become implicit by reason of the significance of human rights, the corollary of their violation being a remedy for the victim. The Commission suggested that this entitlement was part of customary international law and proposed to the Security Council to set up a compensation commission.[6]

The existence of a right to a remedy in most cases does little to alleviate the suffering of victims and their families. More often than not their plights before legal arenas and national authorities are assumed by third parties, particularly NGOs, and their voice is on many occasions substituted by other agendas, irrespective if their ultimate objectives are generally laudable.[7] In this manner the suffering of victims is 'hijacked' with a view to pursuing so-called lawfare, although in the vast majority of cases such accusations are ill-placed. The concept of lawfare is typically employed in the legal and political literature to denote the communication of international law by non-State actors to the international community about the abusive behaviour of particular States.[8] The absence of the victims themselves in judicial and other international proceedings was recognised as problematic. It thus became readily apparent that victims should partake directly in all those judicial and investigative processes that gave rise to the infliction of crimes against them, particularly since an entitlement of a similar nature is recognised in all criminal justice systems. This has certainly been achieved through victim participation in truth and reconciliation commissions and more recently as civil parties before the ICC and the Extraordinary Chambers of the Courts of Cambodia (ECCC), both of which will be explored more fully later in this chapter. Of course, the process whereby natural persons possess legal standing and the right to participate actively as victims in international criminal

---

[4] Human Rights Committee, General Comment No. 31 [80] Nature of the General Legal Obligation Imposed on States Parties to the Covenant, UN Doc CCPR/C/21/Rev.1/Add.13 (26 May 2004), paras.15, 16.

[5] *Legal Consequences of the Construction of a Wall in the Occupied Palestinian Territory*, ICJ Advisory Opinion (9 Jul 2004), (2004) ICJ Reports 136, paras.149–160.

[6] Report of ICID (25 Jan 2005), UN Doc E/CN.4/2005/3 (11 Feb 2005), paras 591ff.

[7] M Mutua, *Human Rights: A Political and Cultural Critique* (Philadelphia, University of Pennsylvania Press, 2002) 27–39.

[8] T Yin, 'Boumediene and Lawfare' (2009) 43 *University of Richmond Law Review* 865; for a more thorough analysis of the concept see chapter 1.10.

proceedings is not straightforward. Such a status is determined on the basis of the victims' international legal personality. While it is true that a number of international instruments grant them certain rights it is not self-evident that they also endow them with international legal personality to enforce them before international *fora*. If this were not so then the victims of crimes falling within the jurisdiction of international criminal tribunals would possess an automatic right of participation and remedy. This is certainly not the case. The right of active participation is context-specific and exists only where it is specifically provided, in which case victims may be said to possess a degree of international legal personality.

The incorporation of a compensatory element in the granting of judicial participation rights to victims of human rights violations should not deflect the reader from other benefits accruing to the victim in his or her personal capacity; particularly, the psychological restoration of a sense of justice, empowerment over the perpetrators, setting out a historical record of the truth and others. These considerations were wholly absent from post WW II international criminal proceedings. They started to become relevant only gradually following the establishment of the ICTY and ICTR where the plight of gender victims was addressed through specific mechanisms. The rationale behind international legislative initiatives addressing victim participation combines both compensatory and non-compensatory elements. Thus, the Basic Principles recognise five basic forms of reparation: restitution, compensation, rehabilitation, satisfaction and guarantees of non-repetition. A yet more contemporary application of these principles has given rise to two additional distinct rights for victims of crime, which are relevant to our discussion; the right to physical protection, which is guaranteed by States as well as international criminal tribunals,[9] and the right to participation in criminal proceedings.

22.2   The Physical Protection of Victims of International Crimes

Prior to the recent proliferation of victim participation provisions in the statutes of international criminal tribunals, the recognition of victim rights in international law was mostly absent. This was largely, but not exclusively, due to the fact that the victims of human rights violations were already endowed with sufficient legal personality by which to pursue their civil claims before judicial and quasi-judicial human rights institutions, such as the European Court of Human Rights, or the Human Rights Committee and others. The limitation inherent in these mechanisms is that the victim cannot seek redress against perpetrators of crimes that are not agents or instrumentalities of the State. Moreover, victims are unable to pursue claims against perpetrators that do not share their nationality, or where the crime in question takes place outside the jurisdictional ambit of the relevant human rights

---

[9]   See for example, Art 68 (3) ICC Statute; ICTY Statute, Arts 15, 20, 22; ICTR Statute, Arts 14, 19, 21; Sierra Leone Special Court Statute, Arts 15(4), 16(4), 19(3).

convention.[10] Moreover, inter-State suits involving extensive human rights violations implicate reparations only between the States themselves, but more recently the African Commission on Human and Peoples Rights (ACHPR) has pointed out that reparation must necessarily trickle down to the victims.[11] To make things even worse, member States have been largely able to rely on the sovereign immunity of third States in order to deny particular victims from suing them for failing to provide adequate civil remedies.[12] As a result, public interest groups made use of tort legislation, particularly in the USA, in order to seek damages from persons accused of violating the rights of aliens abroad.[13] This was a particularly significant development because US courts did not afford any immunity from jurisdiction in respect of damages claims falling under the Aliens Tort Act. In all other respects, although victims of crimes committed by persons other than State agents were protected under the general terms of international human rights instruments, via the obligation of signatories to adopt and enforce adequate domestic criminal laws and civil remedies, they possessed no additional entitlements in international law on account of their victim status; apart from that of refugee under the 1951 Convention Relating to the Status of Refugees.[14]

What is at stake here is the position of the victim in international law in terms of physical, as opposed to legal, protection. This may be framed under the more general question as to whether States are under a duty to provide physical protection to the victims of international human rights violations. Traces of this duty are found scattered in various treaties that are largely unrelated to human rights. For example, victims of slavery on the high seas are to be released from their captors by foreign vessels that come across such ships. This duty comes with the logically corresponding obligation to remove said freed slaves to relative safety.[15] The same is true in respect of the 2000 Smuggling Protocol,[16] but more importantly the victims of trafficking are entitled to extensive rights under the 2000 Trafficking Protocol, under which the apprehending State no longer has the right to simply return them to their country of

---

[10] See *Banković and Others v Belgium and 16 Other Contracting States*, 11 BHRC 435, para 80, in which the E Ct HR held that acts taking place on Yugoslav territory by ECHR member States did not fall within the jurisdictional space of the Court. See also *Al-Skeini and Others v Secretary for the Defence* [2007] UKHL 26, in which the House of Lords denied jurisdiction in respect of claims arising from the activities of British troops in Iraq, save in respect of one of the victims who at the time was held in a detention centre effectively controlled by the British forces in Basra, Iraq. As for the others killed in Basra, the Court held that the UK armed forces did not exercise effective control of the area, such as to bring it within the juridical space of the European Convention on Human Rights.

[11] Democratic *Republic of Congo v Burundi Rwanda and Uganda* [DRC War case], Communication 227/98. 20th Activity Report Annex IV (ACHRP).

[12] See *Al-Adsani v UK*, Judgment (21 Nov 2001), 34 EHRR (2002), 11, paras 55–66, in which the European Court of Human Rights ruled, by a majority of one vote only, that the rule of immunity effectively trumps the right of access to justice as this emanates from the right to a fair trial.

[13] Aliens Tort Claims Act, 28 U.S.C. § 1350. Tort claims by victims of terrorist-related offences have also been brought under the Anti-Terrorism and Effective Death Penalty Act (AEPDA) 1996, 28 USC §§ 1603(b) and 1605(a)(7). See *Alejandre v Republic of Cuba* (1997) 996 F Supp 1239; *Flatow v Islamic Republic of Iran* (1998), 999 F Supp 1.

[14] 189 UNTS 150, Art 1(A)(2).

[15] See Art 99 of the 1982 UN Convention on the Law of the Sea (UNCLOS), (1982) 21 ILM 1261, which postulates that slaves are *ipso facto* free upon the seizure of a slave vessel.

[16] 2000 Protocol against the Smuggling of Migrants by Land, Sea and Air, Supplementing the UN Convention against Transnational Organised Crime, (2001) 40 ILM 335, Arts 9(1)(a) and 16.

origin.[17] More specifically, member States are under an obligation to protect and assist victims of trafficking irrespective of any consent as to their predicament that may have been secured by fraud, deception, abuse of power, vulnerability, or through other forms of exploitation.[18] Said victims are to be granted information on relevant court and administrative proceedings,[19] as well as 'assistance to enable their views and concerns to be presented and considered at appropriate stages of criminal proceedings against offenders, in a manner not prejudicial to the rights of the defence'.[20] Moreover, member States are under an obligation to ensure that their legislation effectively allows victims the possibility of obtaining compensation for damage suffered.[21] The incorporation of civil participation in criminal proceedings is hardly an innovation credited to recent international tribunals, but is the result of minimal, albeit sustained practice.

The aforementioned Trafficking Protocols, furthermore, devote significant space to the obligation of parties in respect of the physical security of victims.[22] To a very large degree, physical protection and avoidance of automatic or abusive refoulement is the first step towards the pursuit of civil action before a neutral forum. Although these duties as to the physical protection of the victims of human rights abuses have become far more entrenched in the last decade, they are generally enforced through the determination of NGOs. The attitude of most countries, even developed ones, is to view unsympathetically at times the plight of trafficked persons, those driven abroad by fear of persecution or the calamities of war. The physical protection of victims of international crimes is not a general duty incumbent on States, except insofar as this is expressly provided in an international treaty; it is, therefore, subject-specific. The definition of victims from one convention to another varies drastically, as is the case for example with the range of persons granted particular protection under the 1949 Geneva Conventions, although they are not strictly identified as victims.[23] The only general definition is that encountered in paragraph 8 of the 2006 Basic Principles.[24] Moreover, practice suggests a distinction between

---

[17] 2000 Protocol to Prevent, Suppress and Punish Trafficking in Persons, Especially Women and Children, Supplementing the UN Convention against Transnational Organised Crime, (2001) 40 ILM 335, Arts 7(1) and 6.

[18] Ibid, Arts 2 and 3(b). A similar victim-oriented approach is evident in the context of the 1961 Single Convention on Narcotic Drugs and the 1971 Convention on Psychotropic Substances, Arts 36(1)(b) and 22(1)(b) respectively of which, provide that parties must provide alternatives to conviction to abusers of drugs. Their victim status is therefore only indirectly recognised.

[19] 2000 Smuggling Protocol, Art 6(2)(a).

[20] Ibid, Art 6(20(b).

[21] Ibid, Art 6(6).

[22] Ibid, Arts 6(3)–(5) and 8.

[23] Convention for the Amelioration of the Condition of the Wounded and Sick in Armed Forces in the Field (No. I), 75 UNTS 31; Convention for the Amelioration of the Condition of the Wounded, Sick, and Ship-wrecked Members of Armed Forces at Sea (No. II), 75 UNTS 85; Convention Relative to the Treatment of Prisoners of War (No. III), 75 UNTS 135; Convention Relative to the Protection of Civilian Persons in Time of War (No. IV), 75 UNTS 287. In fact, Protocol I Additional to the 1949 Geneva Conventions and Relating to the Protection of Victims of International Armed Conflicts of 1977, 1125 UNTS 3, not only renders protected persons victims under its title, but extends this characterisation to protected persons under the 1949 Conventions through its Art 1(3).

[24] Principle 8 of the Basic Principles reads as follows: 'For purposes of the present document, victims are persons who individually or collectively suffered harm, including physical or mental injury, emotional suffering, economic loss or substantial impairment of their fundamental rights, through acts or omissions that constitute gross violations of international human rights law, or serious violations of international

direct and indirect victims (eg family members) and between individual and collective victims. Collective victimhood presupposes the existence of formal or informal groups that are targeted because of particular characteristics.[25] Violations against such collectivities most typically involve genocide or crimes against humanity. Finally, with the exception of the slavery provision in UNCLOS and the Smuggling and Trafficking Protocols, one can hardly contend that a customary rule exists with regard to a duty to provide physical assistance to foreign victims of international crimes, other than by granting refugee status or the protection dictated under international humanitarian law.[26] A far-fetched argument may also be made to the effect that the recently formulated Responsibility to Protect (R2P) doctrine is aimed at the physical protection of victims to war crimes, crimes against humanity and genocide.[27]

22.2.1 'Victims' of No Crimes at All!

Legal definitions are only as good as the objectives they purport to fulfil; otherwise, they may severely limit the range of persons entitled to protection. International law, as we have already discussed, links victimhood with a recognised human rights violation, albeit it does not grant the victim in each case a civil remedy. Persons may in fact suffer a similar fate without strictly speaking having been victims of human rights violations. By way of illustration, seafarers risk being stranded in a foreign harbour without any money or means of sustenance where their vessel of employment is impounded, seized, or the ship-owner becomes bankrupt. It is only recently that the seafarer's right to repatriation has found its way in a legally binding instrument, the 2006 ILO Maritime Labour Convention, albeit it is still sparsely ratified.[28] Under the current state of affairs, ship-owners can only be contractually bound to repatriate their seafarers and in practice the International Transport Workers' Federation (ITF) has set up a trust fund to finance this very purpose in respect of its stranded members. In many countries failure to repatriate a seafarer is either not viewed as a labour right in the domestic legal order, or as otherwise not

humanitarian law. Where appropriate, and in accordance with domestic law, the term "victim" also includes the immediate family or dependants of the direct victim and persons who have suffered harm in intervening to assist victims in distress or to prevent victimization'.

[25] See for example *Case of the Saramaka People v Suriname*, Preliminary Objections, Merits, Reparations and Costs, Int-Am Ct HR Decision (28 Nov 2007), Series C No 172.

[26] There is an argument that such a rule actually exists in Islamic law, at least in theory. See Hadith No. 753, Vol. 7, which refers to an obligation to offer help to the oppressed, as narrated by M bin Suwald, *Sahih Al Bukhari*, volume 3, book 43, number 625, Khan, MM. (trans.); Translation of Sahih Bukhari, available at: <http://www.usc.edu/dept/MSA/fundamentals/hadithSunnahh/bukhari>. References to oppressed people are replete in the Qur'an, such as 3:195, 7:137, 4:97, and 22:39. This obligation is also expressed through contemporary *fatwas*, such as that issued by Sheikh Hamid Al-Ali *et al* on Isma's Stance on Refugees (1 Jan 2006), which stipulated that 'Islam exhorts people to defend the oppressed, advocate the rights of the weak and rush to the rescue of people whose life is jeopardized'. K Zaat, 'The Protection of Forced Migrants in Islamic Law' (UNHCR, 2007) 10.

[27] See paras 138–39 of the 2005 UN World Summit Outcome, UN Doc A/60/L.1 (15 Sep 2005) and the subsequent endorsement of these paragraphs by SC Res 1674 (28 Apr 2006).

[28] Standard A2.1(4)(h)(i); Regulation 2.5.

susceptible to enforcement as a matter of international law. In this manner, a universally recognised entitlement does not exist, and any failure to repatriate seafarers is not deemed a violation of rights.[29] In the legal sense, therefore, these people are not victims.

Since the end of WW II numerous compensation schemes have arisen. Some of these were specifically designed to compensate victims of human rights violations, particularly in relation to international armed conflicts. Therein, the compensation was offered by the defeated Stated either voluntarily or by means of an agreement with the winning parties, which was usually the case.[30] Compensation funds may also be established by means of a Security Council resolution.[31] Equally, some States attempt to restore domestic historic injustices against a minority or indigenous group by instituting a compensatory process for their families.[32] International compensation trusts are by their very nature intended to disburse funds to particular classes of beneficiaries since the States parties setting them up will have already agreed on the existence of the relevant violation, whether committed by themselves (as is usually the case) or others. Thus, it is deemed that it is not open to the tribunal to deny the perpetration of the violation or the existence of claimants; its authority is simply to determine eligibility.[33] The objects of such trust funds, ie the class of beneficiaries for whose benefit their assets are intended, possess little or no freedom to forego their rights as these are reflected in the fund's terms of agreement. What this means is that although eligible beneficiaries may choose to exclude themselves from the process of disbursement, essentially by refusing to lodge a claim, the signing of the trust agreement itself generally entails the extinction of other individual claims in the future in respect of the same subject matter. The purpose of these compensation trusts is therefore akin to final settlement accords, but it is doubtful whether a claim arising out of an unlawful act of a State can always be extinguished in this manner, particularly where a beneficiary deems the compensation and the manner in which it is given inappropriate.

Typically the courts of the nationality of the beneficiaries will play a definitive role in the assessment of the validity of any settlement agreements reached by the various actors.[34] This process ensures that the rights enshrined in the relevant instruments,

---

[29] See PJ Bauer, 'The Maritime Labour Convention: An Adequate Guarantee of Seafarer Rights, or an Impediment to True Reforms?' (2008) 8 *Chicago Journal of International Law* 643.

[30] See Agreement of 17 Jul 2000 Concerning the Foundation 'Remembrance, Responsibility and the Future', (2000) 39 ILM 1298. The purpose of this agreement was to set up a compensation scheme in respect of persons used as slave labour by the government of Nazi Germany. The incumbent German government subsequently promulgated a law that implemented the agreement. Law on the Creation of a Foundation 'Remembrance, Responsibility and Future', 2 Aug 2000 (Federal Law Gazette I 1263), as amended by the Law of 21 Dec 2006 (Federal Law Gazette I 3343). Victims and their families may submit individual petitions to the Board of the Fund.

[31] See SC Res 692 (20 May 1991) in respect of the Compensation Fund for Iraq.

[32] Other purely domestic compensation funds include the US$ 1.25 billion trust fund set up to pay reparations to surviving Japanese-American internees during WW II. This was made possible through the adoption of the 1988 Civil Liberties Act, 50 App U.S.C.A § 1989b.

[33] *Chagos Islanders v Attorney-General & HM BIOT Commissioner* [2003] EWHC QB 2222, para 80. See S Allen, 'Looking Beyond the Bancoult Cases: International Law and the Prospect of Resettling the Chagos Islands' (2007) 7 *Human Rights Law Review* 441.

[34] The Claims Resolution Tribunal for Dormant Accounts (CRT-I) and its successor (CRT-II) resolved many thousands of claims related to dormant accounts of Holocaust victims held by Swiss banks. In 1999, a class action lawsuit against two Swiss banks was settled on the basis of a so-called Global Settlement

whether the more general treaty provisions or the specific injunctions in the implementing domestic laws, will be observed. This is exceptional, given that in the few instances where beneficiaries are recognised in the context of international trust funds they are not granted this range of protective measures.

The aforementioned compensation schemes concern human rights violations that have been duly recognised by the relevant parties as such. In many cases, however, an awarding State may choose to offer compensation to persons that have suffered a particular harm, without recognising them as victims or the harm as entailing a violation of rights. Thus, whereas these persons may be viewed as victims of harm (an event), they are not victims of an unlawful act or a human rights violation. The nature of the compensation, therefore, is of a goodwill character and the accompanying agreement usually stipulates that the class of beneficiaries waive any future claims before the courts of the compensating State. A typical example is the Compact of Free Association entered into between the USA and the Marshall Islands.[35] This Agreement provided for the award of compensation by the US, with an initial contribution of US$150 million, to the peoples of the Marshall Island atolls in respect of the effects related to the US nuclear testing in the area between 1946 and 1958. A subsequent Agreement between the parties for the Implementation of Section 177 of the Compact of Free Association was entered, which specifically set up a Fund in Article I. Parts of the Fund's dividends are to be distributed to the four affected atolls by means of distribution, placement in trust, or otherwise invested in a manner decided by the peoples of the atolls through their local distribution authorities.[36] Section II(6)(c) also envisaged the funding of a claims tribunal with jurisdiction over individual or class actions arising from the US nuclear tests in the islands. Equally, the British government set up a trust fund to compensate the Ilois people in respect of their removal from the Chagos Archipelago, which was not, however, determined to be an unlawful act. For this purpose it entered into an Agreement with Mauritius on 7 July 1982, which made available £4 million for the settlement of all claims with the Ilois people.[37] It is evident that the aforementioned compensation mechanisms fall outside the ambit of victimhood, at least as this is described in international law. Yet, from a factual point of view the persons harmed are no less victims than others that are formally so prescribed. Besides the receipt of compensation, these 'non-victims' are not entitled to the emerging right of civil participation in international criminal proceedings, assuming that the perpetrators were ever to be tried before an international tribunal. This right is described in detail in the following sections.

Agreement that was approved by a US court in 2000. Equally, a Plan of Allocation and Distribution that was proposed by the victims' representatives required court approval in order to trigger the distribution of US$ 800 million out of the US$ 1.25 billion Settlement Fund. See H Das, 'The Concept of Mass Claims and the Specificity of Mass Claims Resolution' in International Bureau of the Permanent Court of Arbitration (ed), *Redressing Injustices through Mass Claims Processes: Innovative Responses to Unique Challenges* (Oxford, Oxford University Press, 2006) 1, at 4.

[35] 48 USC § 1901.
[36] Art II(2)–(5), ibid.
[37] *Ilois Trust Fund v Permal*, 91 ILR 333.

22.3   Forms of Reparation

Reparation is broader than the term compensation, which is pecuniary in character; instead, some forms of reparation aim at satisfying solely the victim's sense of justice and dignity and as a result are devoid of a monetary element. The basic form of non-pecuniary reparation involves so-called satisfaction,[38] which, *inter alia*, encompasses within its ambit demands for cessation of violations, acknowledgment or declaration of the facts or of liability,[39] offer of apology by the perpetrator or the State and the imposition of sanctions on the wrongdoers.[40]

In terms of compensatory measures, these generally include compensation proper, restitution and rehabilitation. The three are reflected in Article 75(1) of the ICC Statute, but are indicative of the measures the ICC can take. Restitution requires the reversal of the harm inflicted on the victim and as a result it may be achieved in a number of ways depending on the particular harm and whether this is in fact reversible. An order for release from prison or detention in respect of persons detained in violation of international law is an obvious candidate, although its application is generally confined among international human rights bodies.[41] Rehabilitation concerns the provision of medical and psychological care to the victim as well as legal and social services.[42] The Inter-American Court of Human Rights has construed this form of reparation to be an obligation on incumbent States as a matter of priority.[43] The Statute of the Special Tribunal for Lebanon provides authority to its chambers to identify victims that have suffered harm as a result of the commission of crimes by an accused convicted by the Tribunal, but is not itself empowered to offer compensation.[44] Rather, based on a decision by the Special Tribunal and pursuant to the relevant national legislation, 'a victim or persons claiming through the victim, whether or not such victim had been identified as such by the Tribunal . . . may bring an action in a national court or other competent body to obtain compensation'.[45]

A more recent principle of indirect compensation has come about through so-called asset recovery and asset sharing which concerns the status of illicit funds or objects in the hands of a particular country following the arrest or prosecution of the culprit. Article 14(2) of the 2000 Transnational Organised Crime Convention requires

---

[38]   See 2005 Basic Principles, para 22.

[39]   The IA Ct HR has developed a distinct mechanism by which it orders States to apologise. See *Cantoral-Benavides v Peru*, Int-Am Ct HR Judgment on Reparations and Costs (3 Dec 2001), Series C No 88, para 81

[40]   In *Hachette Filipacchi Associés v France*, Judgment (14 Jun 2007) the Eur Ct HR held that the right to freedom of the press to impart information under Art 10 of the ECHR may be restricted in situations where the publication in question is not in the public interest, particularly if this also causes unnecessary grief to the victims and their families. In the case at hand, a leading magazine had published the motionless body of an assassinated prefect, which caused much distress to his family.

[41]   See *Assanidze v Georgia*, [2004] 39 EHRR 653, paras.202, 203; see 2005 Basic Principles, para 19. This states that restitution includes, moreover, as appropriate: restoration of liberty, enjoyment of human rights, identity, family life and citizenship, return to one's place of residence, restoration of employment and return of property.

[42]   2005 Basic Principles, para 21.

[43]   See *Barrios Altos v Peru*, Judgment on Reparation and Costs (30 Nov 2001), Series C No 87, para 40.

[44]   Art 25(1), Lebanon Special Tribunal Statute.

[45]   Ibid, Art 25(3).

requested States to 'give priority consideration to returning the confiscated proceeds of crime or property to the requesting State Party so that it can give compensation to the victims of the crime or return such proceeds of crime or property to their legitimate owners'. The 2003 Corruption Convention dedicates an entire chapter to asset recovery (chapter V), which in most part involves inter-State requests for freezing and returning illicit assets, the effects of which may thereafter trickle down to the beneficial owners. Article 57(3)(c) of the Convention, however, provides a residual, yet direct, right of compensation to victims of corruption and the legitimate owners of the seized assets through the asset sharing mechanism. The asset recovery mechanism may turn out to be a potent tool, besides individual compensation requests, in cases where corrupt dictators have siphoned entire fortunes abroad. In this manner, the recovery of such assets concerns the survival and welfare of the requesting State and is a matter relating to the exercise of the internal dimension of self-determination.

Finally, although compensation is the penultimate form of pecuniary reparation it should not be thought that it constitutes the prime pursuit of victims and their families around the world. Even when it is sought it is combined with its non-pecuniary counterparts. In its simplest form it consists of material and non-material (moral) damage, as this is assessed by the relevant court.[46] These are certainly recognised as falling within the ambit of Article 75 of the ICC Statute. On the contrary, so-called punitive damages, developed in Anglo-American jurisprudence are outside the scope of this provision and of all existing international tribunals. The object of such damages is to 'punish' the perpetrator for the violation and to deter possible repetition. However, a court may, without expressly awarding punitive damages, assess the individual circumstance of the violation on the victim and come to the conclusion that a more substantial compensation is warranted.

22.4   Victim Participation in International Criminal Proceedings

The participation of the victim in the criminal justice process is certainly not confined to recent developments before the International Criminal Court (ICC) and the ECCC. These are merely its most recent manifestations in the realm of international criminal justice. Four types of participation may be discerned as a matter of domestic criminal law and practice. Firstly, in civil law jurisdictions the victims may become civil parties to the criminal trial by subsuming their civil claim with that of the prosecutor. This generally means that they have as much right to the evidentiary process as the other parties, but only where this is relevant to their particular civil claim.[47] Secondly, the victims in some jurisdictions may assume the role of auxiliary prosecutor, but only in respect of specific offences. In this manner, the victims may

---

[46] The IA Ct HR has come up with an additional category, the so-called 'loss of enjoyment of life', which is not popular at all among States and other international tribunals. See *Loayza Tamayo v Peru* Int-Am Ct HR Judgment on Reparation and Costs (27 Nov 1998), Series C, No.42, para 151.

[47] See WT Pizzi, 'Crime Victims in German Courtrooms: A Comparative Perspective on American Problems' (1996) 32 *Stanford Journal of International Law* 37.

resume or activate a criminal suit where the prosecutor has usually decided to withdraw and at the same time pursue their civil claims. Thirdly, the victims may be allowed by the court to submit or read impact statements following the determination as to the guilt of the accused, with a view to determining sentencing.[48] The fourth mode of victim participation and which is mostly forgotten by commentators concerns the Islamic law practice of *diya* (compensation, but essentially so-called blood-money) and *qisās* (a claim for retaliatory punishment at the instigation of the victim and his or her family).[49] Unlike the other three forms of participation, the Islamic models actually entitle the victims to not only dictate the terms of the civil claim, but also to satisfy their sense of revenge. Finally, in situations where following a period of intense turmoil a truth commission is set up alongside a domestic or international criminal tribunal, the victims may be given the opportunity of direct representation in the organs of the truth commission. This is the case with East Timor's Commission for Reception, Truth and Reconciliation, some members of which may be nominated from a variety of human rights and victims groups, such as the Association of ex-Political Prisoners and the Association of Families of Disappeared Persons.[50]

22.4.1 The ICC

The right of victims to participate in international criminal proceedings is largely premised on the corresponding general principle of law of the same nature. The question of whether this should be further incorporated in the Statutes of international criminal tribunals is dependent on a variety of financial, political, practical and strategic considerations. Such rights are absent in the context of the ICTY and the ICTR, despite the plethora of protective measures granted to victims and witnesses.[51] Against this backdrop the drafters and lobbyists of the ICC Statute argued vehemently in favour not only of compensatory mechanisms, but also of

---

[48] BN McGonigle, 'Two for the Price of One: Attempts by the Extraordinary Chambers in the Courts of Cambodia to Combine Retributive and Restorative Justice Principles' (2009) 22 *Leiden Journal of International Law* 127, 137–38. This is also the case in respect of crimes that are indictable solely through a private right of action, unless the victim makes a formal request to the authorities. See Art 18, Saudi Law of Criminal Procedure [General Provisions], Royal Decree No M/39 (16 Oct 2001).

[49] The general concept of blood money predates Islam and was practiced extensively in the Arabian Peninsula well before the advent of Prophet Mohammed. In most Muslim criminal justice systems the legislation in *diya* and *qisās* is preceded by a detailed annex specifying the worth of each human organ or limb in terms of retaliation. See Oman Royal Decree No 118/2008 (7 Nov 2008), which provides for such an annex.

[50] UNTAET/REG/2001/10 (13 July 2001), s 4.3(a).

[51] Victims arising out of offences within the jurisdiction of the ICTY and ICTR may bring a civil action before a national court in order to obtain compensation, in accordance with Rule 106 of the ICTY's Rules of Procedure and Evidence. Generally, the role of otherwise victims is restricted to that of witness. The Presidents of the ICTY and ICTR proposed an amendment to their statutes that would allow for the granting of compensation in cases of miscarriage of justice and human rights violations. UN Doc S/2000/925 (6 Oct 2000) and S/2000/904 (26 Sep 2000). Exceptionally, in *ICTR Prosecutor v Rwamakuba*, Trial Chamber Judgment (20 Sep 2006), para 220, the tribunal held that the accused could file an application for an available remedy for the delay in assigning him counsel which caused a delay in his initial appearance and violated his fundamental rights. The Trial Chamber proceeded to award the accused

wider participation rights for victims in all phases of the proceedings. These efforts culminated in Article 68(3), which is central to this discussion and which reads as follows:

> When the personal interests of victims are affected, the Court shall permit their views and concerns to be presented and considered at stages of the proceedings determined to be appropriate by the Court and in a manner which is not prejudicial to or inconsistent with the rights of the accused and a fair and impartial trial.

This provision provided the impetus for similar clauses in the statutes of other hybrid tribunals, particularly Article 12.3 of UNTAET Regulation No 2000/30 (25 September 2000) in the Transitional Rules of Criminal Procedure of East Timor,[52] Articles 80–82 of the Provisional Criminal Procedure Code of Kosovo and Article 17 of the Statute of the Special Tribunal for Lebanon.[53] There are no major differences between these provisions, save for the fact that those in the Kosovo Code of Procedure are far more detailed than its other counterparts.

It is clear from the wording of Article 68(3) of the ICC Statute that the rights afforded to victims are not unlimited and moreover a particular cause of action must be demonstrated. The ICC chambers have strenuously showed their preference for a systematic over a casuistic approach to victim participation rights.[54] The Court has banished any doubt as to the legality of Article 68(3) by declaring that it is predicated on the internationally recognised rights to truth[55] and justice,[56] which are distinct from one another. It pointed to the fact that the incorporation of these rights in the Statute were consistent with available empirical data indicating that victims generally wish to participate in proceedings in order to 'have a declaration of the truth',[57] but also on grounds of maximum case management, given that the active participation of victims is central for clarity and the identification of factual gaps.[58] Such participation must nonetheless satisfy certain criteria. For one thing, a person qualifies as a victim if he or she has suffered some harm as a result of a crime falling with the jurisdiction of the Court in accordance with Rule 85(a) of the Court's Rules of Procedure and Evidence.[59] The term 'harm' has been found to mean any injury, loss or damage that is consistent with the legal meaning associated with these words.[60] A

---

compensation for moral injury caused and in a later Decision of 31 Jan 2007 moreover ordered the Registrar to offer an apology and to use its good offices to resettle the accused and his family.

[52] Available at: <http://www.un.org/peace/etimor/untaetR/reg200030.pdf>.

[53] Established pursuant to SC Res 1664 (29 Mar 2006) following an Agreement between Lebanon and the UN, as subsequently endorsed by SC Res 1757 (30 May 2007), to which the Statute is annexed.

[54] *ICC Prosecutor v Katanga et al*, Decision on Set of Procedural Rights Attached to the Procedural Status of Victims at the Pre-Trial Stage of the Case, (13 May 2008), paras 46ff.

[55] Ibid, para 32, which the Chamber traced to Arts 32–33 of the 1977 Protocol Additional to the Geneva Conventions of 12 August 1949, and Relating to the Protection of Victims of International Armed Conflicts [Protocol I], 1125 UNTS 3. This principle was reinforced by a string of cases relating to enforced disappearances, particularly in Latin America. See, for example, *Almohacid-Arellano et al v Chile*, Inter-American Court of Human Rights Judgment (26 Sep 2006), Ser C, No 154, paras 148ff.

[56] *Katanga* Decision, paras 37ff, for which the Court noted that it is distinct from the right to reparation.

[57] Ibid, para 31.

[58] Ibid, para 34.

[59] Rule 85(b) provides for the possibility of legal persons as victims.

[60] *ICC Prosecutor v Lubanga*, Judgment on the Appeals of the Prosecutor and the Defence against Trial Chamber's I Decision on Victim's Participation of 18 January 2008 (11 Jul 2008), para 31.

particular harm may be both personal and collective in nature, but this eventuality does not extinguish the personal right itself in favour of the collective.[61]

While it is clear that the participation of victims in the criminal proceedings produces a wide range of benefits, if unchecked it also has the potential to jeopardise the accused's right to a fair trial. It is crucial therefore to decipher when 'the victims' personal interests are affected', in accordance with the opening sentence of Article 68(3) of the Statute. Such a determination should be conducted in relation to the various stages of the proceedings taken a as a whole, rather than in relation to each specific procedural activity or individual piece of evidence.[62] Article 68(3) was not in fact intended to pre-determine the victims' procedural rights, but leaves their determination open to the Court's discretion, in accordance with Rules 91 and 92.[63]

What is the exact content of these rights? It is self-evident that they must be consistent with the pertinent general principles of law, whereby civil participants lack investigative powers – although they can certainly request any appropriate investigative steps – but are entitled to the investigation file at the close of proceedings and can generally propose any evidence, including calling witnesses as well as discuss the evidence, particularly through examination of witnesses.[64] That these are principles common to the vast majority of nations without any dispute is confirmed by the fact that they have never been challenged before any human rights tribunal as violating fair trial guarantees. The Court has held therefore that the granting of investigative powers to victims would run contrary to the aims of the ICC Statute. Equally, victims' rights of access to evidence can never exceed the corresponding access rights of the defence, thus eliminating disclosure rights. Consequently, victims cannot introduce additional information at the confirmation hearing.[65] The Court identified the following sets of procedural rights pertinent to victims: a) access, prior to and during the confirmation hearing, to the record of a case held by the Registry, including to the evidence filed by the Prosecutor and the Defence. This does not include access to *ex parte* decisions and filings; b) rights to make submissions on all issues relating to the admissibility and probative value of evidence which is relied upon at the confirmation hearing, as well as rights to examine such evidence during the same procedure; c) examination of witnesses; d) right to attend all public and closed session hearings, save for those that are *ex parte* in nature, and; e) the right to participate through oral motions.[66]

A recurring theme in the judicial work of the ICC chambers has been the issue of victim representation. While it is settled that rights are enjoyed also by persons other than the individual that suffered the direct harm (eg relatives), the position of who may legally represent under-age victims is unclear. This is particularly acute in the context of the current case law of the ICC because many of the charges relate to the forceful conscription of children, who have been victimised as a result. Given that

---

[61] Ibid, paras 35ff. Rule 85 does not have the effect of restricting the participation of victims solely to the crimes charged. Ibid, paras 41,53ff. The victim must, however, clearly demonstrate a link between the harm suffered and the crimes charged, ibid, paras 64ff.

[62] *Katanga* Decision on Procedural Rights, para 45(i).

[63] Ibid, paras 53ff.

[64] Ibid, paras 62–65.

[65] Ibid, paras 83, 88, 112 and 114.

[66] Ibid, paras 127ff.

many of them, while still minors at the time of proceedings, had not been reunited with their families or were disjointed and unsettled required an amplification of legal representation so as to provide some consistency with their predicament. The Court thus decided that under such circumstances that school principals satisfied the criteria of representation and that if particular representatives were deemed unsuitable the Court would make an appropriate decision on a case-by-case basis.[67]

It should be pointed out that not everyone agrees that victim participation in international criminal trials is in their best interests. This conclusion is based on the assumption that they are not likely to derive any benefit and that their participation places costs on other groups of victims.[68] This seems to be a minority view,[69] but it is not without some merit and it should not be lightly assumed that victim participation automatically guarantees the two goals identified by the ICC; ie setting the historical record straight and filling gaps in the facts. In fact, when these are elevated to goals that are simultaneous with the strict pursuits of criminal justice within the same institution their attainment may detract from the primary purpose of criminal tribunals. Some NGOs moreover criticise the ICC victim participation regime for engaging in typolatry and thus failing to effectively appreciate the victims' particular exigencies. By way of illustration they point to excessive form filling, the necessity to prove indigence to qualify for legal assistance – when it is well known that the particular victims are extremely impoverished – and disregard for the role of local intermediaries that help sensitise and assist victims with participation and reparation applications.[70]

22.4.2 The Extraordinary Chambers in the Courts of Cambodia (ECCC)

Just like the ICC process, victims have a right of participation in the ECCC proceedings.[71] However, this right is radically different in two respects from its ICC counterpart. On the one hand, it is not expressly mentioned in its founding instrument, the ECCC Statute,[72] while on the other hand, contrary to the ICC model, civil parties enjoy the same status as everybody else with 'active rights to participate… in

---

[67] *Lubanga* Decision on the Application of Victims to Participate in the Proceedings, paras 68ff.

[68] CP Trumbull, 'The Victims or Victim Participation in International Criminal Proceedings' (2008) 29 *Michigan Journal of International Law* 779.

[69] See C Stahn *et al*, 'Participation of Victims in Pre-Trial Proceedings of the ICC' (2006) 4 *Journal of International Criminal Justice* 219; M Dembour, E Haslam, 'Silencing Hearing? Victim-Witnesses at War Crimes Trials' (2004) 15 *European Journal of International Law* 151.

[70] Redress Trust, 'Victims' Central Role in Fulfilling the ICC's Mandate' (26 Nov 2009).

[71] For the purposes of the ECCC, anyone who has suffered from physical, psychological, or material harm as a direct consequence of the crimes committed in Cambodia by the Democratic Kampuchea regime between 17 Apr 1975 and 6 Jan 1979. ECCC Internal Rules, R.23 (2)(a).

[72] The UN Agreement's only reference to victims is found in Art 23, which states that 'the co-investigating judges, the co-prosecutors and the Extraordinary Chambers shall provide for the protection of victims and witnesses. Such protection measures shall include, but shall not be limited to, the conduct of *in camera* proceedings and the protection of the identity of a victim or witness'.

all criminal proceedings... starting from the investigative stage'.[73] This is clearly far wider than the ICC Statute, where victims must lodge an application before every hearing in order to convince the Court that their participation is appropriate. As to the normative origin of the right, Article 36 of the ECCC Statute simply proclaims that victims may institute appeals against decisions of the Chambers, thus implying that victims may become parties to the proceedings.[74] It is equally evident that civil proceedings for compensation are excluded from the wording of Article 38, according to which penalties 'shall be limited to imprisonment'.[75] The turning point for the granting of full participation rights to victims occurred as a result of the exercise of delegated authority. On 13 June 2007, the ECCC's Judicial Committee on the Rules of Procedure ('ECCC Rules Committee') issued Internal Rules ('2007 Internal Rules'), following extensive and confidential deliberations that conferred victims of crimes extensive participatory rights. The Committee justified this radical law-making exercise on the fact that the concept already existed in Cambodian law, albeit in the ECCC context it would be of a collective and non-financial nature. Under the 2007 Internal Rules a civil party enjoys the same rights as all other participants, such as the Prosecution and the Defence. This includes the right, among others, to: a) choose legal representation; b) specifically request investigation of crimes. In fact, victims can submit complaints to the co-Prosecutors, who must consider the victims' interests when considering whether to initiate an investigation or a prosecution; c) question witnesses and the accused; d) request the Chambers to take such measures that safeguard their safety and privacy during the proceedings; e) have access to documentation held by the Chambers, and; f) request collective and moral reparations.[76] This range of rights does not entitle civil parties to make submissions or recommendations concerning sentencing, including legal submissions on or the evaluation of facts or factors relevant only to sentencing.[77] Equally, civil parties are not permitted to question the character of the accused or of witnesses, but this restriction solely applies in relation to sentencing.[78] Overall, although it is true that the civil party's role is to support the prosecution,[79] their objectives are wholly different and any overlap should not be exaggerated.

This type of extensive victim participation is not without its problems. During the trial of Ieng Sary a victim activist used the court proceedings to enhance a particular agenda and insisted on directly addressing the defendant and his lawyer and thus interrupted significantly the flow of proceedings. The victim was asked to address the defendant through her lawyer, so she subsequently dismissed her lawyer. It thus became clear to the Chambers that victim participation could very well prove

---

[73] ECCC Pre-Trial Chamber Decision on Civil Party Participation in Provisional Detention Appeals, 20 Mar 2008, paras 36, 38.

[74] ECCC Statute, Art 36.

[75] This is hardly consistent with the right of civil party action as prescribed in Art 2 of the Cambodian Code of Criminal Procedure.

[76] ECCC Internal Rules, R.32; see ECCC Internal Rules, rules 74 and 105.

[77] *ECCC Prosecutor v Kaing* (Duch), Trial Chamber Decision on Civil Party Co-Lawyers' Joint Request for a Ruling on the Standing of Civil Party Lawyers to Make Submissions on Sentencing and Directions concerning the Questioning of the Accused, Experts and Witnesses Testifying on Character (9 Oct 2009), para 40.

[78] Ibid, paras 47–48.

[79] ECCC Internal Rules, R.23(1).

destructive if it was left unchecked. As a result and relying on Internal Rule 77(10), which provides that in pre-trial appeals 'the Co-Prosecutors and the lawyers for the parties may present brief observations', it was held that only the lawyers of the civil parties could address the Court, the witnesses and defendants, regardless if said civil parties are themselves lawyers.[80] A more recent amendment to the Internal Rules solidified this position.[81] Subsequently, on 5 September 2008, the ECCC Rules Committee amended the Internal Rules with a view to better regulating civil party involvement in court. The new amendments require victims who wish to partake in the process as civil parties to apply at least 10 days ahead of an initial hearing.[82] Moreover, ECCC judges were given the power to compel civil parties coalescing into a single group, where appropriate, and to be represented by common counsel.[83]

---

[80] *ECCC Prosecutor v Sari,* Written Version of Oral Decision of 1 Jul 2008 on the Civil Party's Request to Address the Court in Person (3 Jul 2008), para 3.

[81] ECCC Internal Rules, Rule 24(7)(i) [introduced on 6 March 2009]. The amended Rules state that it does not apply where a Civil Party is being interviewed, and does not prevent a Civil Party from answering questions put to him or her by the Chamber.

[82] ECCC Internal Rules, Rule 24(3).

[83] ECCC Internal Rules, Rule 24(8)(a)(b).

Index